APPLIED CORPORATE FINANCE

A USER'S MANUAL

SECOND EDITION

ASWATH DAMODARAN

STERN SCHOOL OF BUSINESS
NEW YORK UNIVERSITY
www.damodaran.com

 JOHN WILEY & SONS, INC.

ASSOCIATE PUBLISHER: Judith R. Joseph
PROJECT EDITOR: Cindy Rhoads
EDITORIAL ASSISTANT: Brigeth Rivera
SENIOR PRODUCTION EDITOR: Valerie A. Vargas
MARKETING MANAGER: Heather King
SENIOR DESIGNER: Karin Kincheloe
MEDIA EDITOR: Allison Morris
COVER PHOTO: © Michael Pole/Corbis Images
PRODUCTION SERVICES: mb editorial services

This book was set in 10/12 Times Ten Roman by Interactive Composition Corporation and printed and bound by Malloy Incorporated. The cover was printed by Phoenix Color.

This book is printed on acid-free paper. ∞

To order books or for customer service please, call 1-800-CALL WILEY (225-5945).

Library of Congress Cataloging in Publication Data:

Damodaran, Aswath.
 Applied corporate finance : a user's manual / Aswath Damodaran.—2nd ed.
  p. cm.
 Online instructional resources supplement the text.
 Includes bibliographical references and index.
 ISBN 0-471-66093-0 (pbk.)
  1. Corporations—Finance. I. Title.

 HG4011.D26 2005
 658.15—dc22

             2004065918

Printed in the United States of America

10 9 8 7 6 5 4 3 2 1

DEDICATION

*To Michele, whose task is both more difficult
and more important than mine, and to
Ryan, Brendan, Kendra, and Kiran,
who contribute to making it so.*

About the Author

Aswath Damodaran is Professor of Finance at the Stern School of Business at New York University and teaches the corporate finance and equity valuation courses in the MBA program. He received his MBA and PhD from the University of California at Los Angeles. His research interests lie in valuation, portfolio management, and applied corporate finance. He has published articles in the *Journal of Financial and Quantitative Analysis,* the *Journal of Finance,* the *Journal of Financial Economics,* and the *Review of Financial Studies*.

He has written three books on equity valuation (*Damodaran on Valuation, Investment Valuation,* and *The Dark Side of Valuation*) and two on corporate finance (*Corporate Finance: Theory and Practice* and *Applied Corporate Finance: A User's Manual*). He has coedited a book on investment management with Peter Bernstein (*Investment Management*) and has a book on investment philosophies (*Investment Philosophies*). His newest book, titled *Investment Fables,* was released in 2004.

Professor Damodaran was a visiting lecturer at the University of California, Berkeley, from 1984 to 1986, where he received the Earl Cheit Outstanding Teaching Award in 1985. He has been at New York University since 1986, received the Stern School of Business Excellence in Teaching Award (awarded by the graduating class) in 1988, 1991, 1992, 1999, and 2001 and was the youngest winner of the university-wide Distinguished Teaching Award in 1990. He was profiled in *Business Week* magazine as one of the top twelve business school professors in the United States in 1994.

PREFACE

Let me begin this preface with a confession of a few of my own biases. First, I believe that theory and the models that flow from it should provide the tools to understand, analyze, and solve problems. The test of a model or theory, then, should not be based on its elegance but on its usefulness in problem solving. Second, there is little in corporate financial theory that is new and revolutionary. The core principles of corporate finance are common sense and have changed little over time. That should not be surprising. Corporate finance is only a few decades old, and people have been running businesses for thousands of years; it would be exceedingly presumptuous of us to believe that they were in the dark until corporate finance theorists came along and told them what to do. To be fair, it is true that corporate financial theory has made advances in taking commonsense principles and providing structure, but these advances have been primarily on the details. The story line in corporate finance has remained remarkably consistent over time.

Talking about story lines allows me to set the first theme of this book. This book tells a story, which essentially summarizes the corporate finance view of the world. It classifies all decisions made by any business into three groups—decisions on where to invest the resources or funds that the business has raised, either internally or externally (the investment decision), decisions on where and how to raise funds to finance these investments (the financing decision), and decisions on how much and in what form to return funds back to the owners (the dividend decision). As I see it, the first principles of corporate finance can be summarized in Figure 1, which also lays out a site map for the book. Every section of this book relates to some part of this picture, and each chapter is introduced with it, with emphasis on that portion that will be analyzed in that chapter. (Note the chapter numbers below each section.) Put another way, there are no sections of this book that are not traceable to this framework.

As you look at the chapter outline for the book, you are probably wondering where the chapters on present value, option pricing, and bond pricing are, as well as the chapters on short-term financial management, working capital, and international finance. The first set of chapters, which I would classify as "tools" chapters, are now contained in the appendices, and I relegated them there not because I think that they are unimportant but because I want the focus to stay on the story line. It is important that we understand the concept of time value of money, but only in the context of measuring returns on investments better and valuing business. Option pricing theory is elegant and provides impressive insights, but only in the context of looking at options embedded in projects and financing instruments like convertible bonds.

The second set of chapters I excluded for a very different reason. As I see it, the basic principles of whether and how much you should invest in inventory, or

Figure 1   Corporate Finance: First Principles

MAXIMIZE THE VALUE
OF THE BUSINESS (FIRM)
Chapter 1, 12

The Investment Decision

Invest in assets that earn a return greater that the minimum acceptable hurdle rate

The Financing Decision

Find the right kind of debt for your firm and the right mix of debt and equity to fund your operations

The Dividend Decision

If you cannot find investments that make your minimum acceptable rate, return the cash to owners of your business

The **hurdle rate** should reflect the *riskiness* of the investment and the *mix of debt and equity* used to fund it
Chapter 3, 4

The **return** should reflect the *magnitude* and the *timing* of the *cash flows* as well as *all side effects*

Chapter 5, 6

The **optimal mix** of debt and equity *maximizes firm value*
Chapter 7, 8

The **right kind** of debt *matches the tenor of your assets*
Chapter 9

How much cash you can return depends on current and potential *investment opportunities*

Chapter 10

How you choose to return cash to the owners will depend on whether they *prefer dividends or buybacks*
Chapter 11

The principles are universal

Big Firms
U.S. Firms
Foreign Firms
Private Firms
Public Firms

how generous your credit terms should be, are no different than the basic principles that would apply if you were building a plant or buying equipment or opening a new store. Put another way, there is no logical basis for the differentiation between investments in the latter (which in most corporate finance books is covered in the capital budgeting chapters) and the former (which are considered in the working capital chapters). You should invest in either if and only if the returns from the investment exceed the hurdle rate from the investment; the fact that the one is short-term and the other is long-term is irrelevant. The same thing can be said about international finance. Should the investment or financing principles be different just because a company is considering an investment in Thailand and the cash flows are in Thai baht instead of in the United States, where the cash flows are in dollars? I do not believe so and, in my view, separating the decisions only leaves readers with that impression. Finally, most corporate finance books that have chapters on small firm management and private firm management use them to illustrate the differences between these firms and the more conventional large publicly traded firms used in the other chapters. Although such differences exist, the commonalities between different types of firms vastly overwhelm the differences, providing a testimonial to the internal consistency of corporate finance. In summary, the second theme of this book is the emphasis on the *universality of corporate financial principles* across different firms, in different markets, and across different types of decisions.

Apply
Apply
Apply

Disney
Deutsche Bank
Aracruz Celulose
Bookscape

The way I have tried to bring this universality to life is by using four firms through the book to illustrate each concept; they include a large, publicly traded U.S. corporation (Disney); a small, emerging market company (Aracruz Celulose, a Brazilian paper and pulp company); a financial service firm (Deutsche Bank); and a small private business (Bookscape, an independent New York City bookstore). Although the notion of using real companies to illustrate theory is neither novel nor revolutionary, there are, two key differences in the way they are used in this book. First, these companies are analyzed on every aspect of corporate finance introduced here, rather than just selectively in some chapters. Consequently, the reader can see for him- or herself the similarities and the differences in the way investment, financing, and dividend principles are applied to four very different firms. Second, I do not consider this to be a book where applications are used to illustrate theory but a book where the theory is presented as a companion to the illustrations. In fact, reverting back to my earlier analogy of theory providing the tools for understanding problems, this is a book where the problem solving takes center stage and the tools stay in the background.

Reading through the theory and the applications can be instructive and even interesting, but there is no substitute for actually trying things out to bring home both the strengths and weaknesses of corporate finance. There are several ways I have made this book a tool for active learning. One is to introduce *concept questions* at regular intervals that invite responses from the reader. As an example, consider the following illustration from Chapter 7.

7.2 The Effects of Diversification on Venture Capitalist

You are comparing the required returns of two venture capitalists who are interested in investing in the same software firm. One has all of his capital invested in only software firms, whereas the other has invested her capital in small companies in a variety of businesses. Which of these two will have the higher required rate of return?

☐ The venture capitalist who is invested only in software companies

☐ The venture capitalist who is invested in a variety of businesses

☐ Cannot answer without more information

Active
Learning

Concept
Questions

Live Case
Studies

This question is designed to check on a concept introduced in an earlier chapter on risk and return on the difference between risk that can be eliminated by holding a diversified portfolio and risk that cannot and then connecting it to the question of how a business seeking funds from a venture capitalist might be affected by this perception of risk. The answer to this question in turn will expose the reader to more questions about whether venture capital in the future will be provided by diversified funds and what a specialized venture capitalist (who invests in one sector alone) might need to do to survive in such an environment. This will allow readers to see what, for me at least, is one of the most exciting aspects of corporate finance—its capacity to provide a framework that can be used to make sense of the events that occur around us every day and make reasonable forecasts about future directions.

The second active experience in this book is found in the Live Case Studies at the end of each chapter. These case studies essentially take the concepts introduced in the chapter and provide a framework for applying them to any company the reader chooses. Guidelines on where to get the information to answer the questions are also provided.

Although corporate finance provides an internally consistent and straightforward template for the analysis of any firm, information is clearly the lubricant that allows us to do the analysis. There are three steps in the information process—acquiring the information, filtering what is useful from what is not, and keeping the information updated. Accepting the limitations of the printed page on all of these aspects, I have put the power of online information to use in several ways.

1. The case studies that require the information are accompanied by links to Web sites that carry this information.

2. The data sets that are difficult to get from the Internet or are specific to this book, such as the updated versions of the tables, are available on my own Web site (www.damodaran.com) and are integrated into the book. As an example, the table that contains the dividend yields and payout ratios by industry sectors for the most recent quarter is referenced in Chapter 9 as follows:

There is a data set online that summarizes dividend yields and payout ratios for U.S. companies, categorized by sector.

You can get to this table by going to the Web site for the book and checking for data sets under Chapter 9.

3. The spreadsheets used to analyze the firms in the book are also available on my Web site and are referenced in the book. For instance, the spreadsheet used to estimate the optimal debt ratio for Disney in Chapter 8 is referenced as follows:

This spreadsheet allows you to compute the optimal debt ratio firm value for any firm, using the same information used for Disney. It has updated interest coverage ratios and spreads built in (**capstru.xls**)

As with the data set listing, you can get this spreadsheet by going to the Web site for the book and checking under spreadsheets under Chapter 8. Since every illustration in this book is accompanied by a spreadsheet, you will find that there are small rounding differences in all of the illustrations. Please refer to the spreadsheet for the precise calculations.

As I set out to write this book, I had two objectives in mind. One was to write a book that not only reflects the way I teach corporate finance in a classroom but, more important, conveys the fascination and enjoyment I get out of the subject matter. The second was to write a book for practitioners that students would find useful, rather than the other way around. I do not know whether I have fully accomplished either objective, but I do know I had an immense amount of fun trying. I hope you do, too!

ACKNOWLEDGMENTS

I would like to acknowledge the hundreds of students who have patiently sat through my lectures, corrected my numerous errors, and provided invaluable suggestions on ways to present this material better. Their enthusiasm and energy provided the fuel for this book.

CONTENTS

CHAPTER 1

THE FOUNDATIONS

It's all corporate finance.
MY UNBIASED VIEW OF THE WORLD

Every decision made in a business has financial implications, and any decision that involves the use of money is a corporate financial decision. Defined broadly, everything that a business does fits under the rubric of corporate finance. It is, in fact, unfortunate that we even call the subject corporate finance, because it suggests to many observers a focus on how large corporations make financial decisions and seems to exclude small and private businesses from its purview. A more appropriate title for this book would be *Business Finance,* because the basic principles remain the same, whether one looks at large, publicly traded firms or small, privately run businesses. All businesses have to invest their resources wisely, find the right kind and mix of financing to fund these investments, and return cash to the owners if there are not enough good investments.

In this chapter, we will lay the foundation for the rest of the book by listing the three fundamental principles that underlie corporate finance—the investment, financing, and dividend principles—and the objective of firm value maximization that is at the heart of corporate financial theory.

THE FIRM: STRUCTURAL SET-UP

In the chapters that follow, we will use *firm* generically to refer to any business, large or small, manufacturing or service, private or public. Thus, a corner grocery store and Microsoft are both firms.

The firm's investments are generically termed *assets*. Although assets are often categorized by accountants into fixed assets, which are long-lived, and current assets, which are short-term, we prefer a different categorization. The assets that the firm has already invested in are called *assets in place,* whereas those assets that the firm is expected to invest in the future are called *growth assets*. Though it may seem strange that a firm can get value from investments it has not made yet, high-growth firms get the bulk of their value from these yet-to-be-made investments.

To finance these assets, the firm can raise money from two sources. It can raise funds from investors or financial institutions by promising investors a fixed claim (interest payments) on the cash flows generated by the assets, with a limited or no role in the day-to-day running of the business. We categorize this type of financing to be *debt*. Alternatively, it can offer a residual claim on the cash flows (i.e., investors can get what is left over after the interest payments have been made) and a much greater role in the operation of the business. We call this *equity*. Note that these definitions are general enough to cover both private firms, where debt may take the form of bank loans and equity is the owner's own money, as well as publicly traded companies, where the firm may issue bonds (to raise debt) and common stock (to raise equity).

Thus, at this stage, we can lay out the financial balance sheet of a firm as follows:

We will return this framework repeatedly through this book.

FIRST PRINCIPLES

Every discipline has first principles that govern and guide everything that gets done within it. All of corporate finance is built on three principles, which we will call, rather unimaginatively, the investment principle, the financing principle, and the dividend principle. The investment principle determines where businesses invest their resources, the financing principle governs the mix of funding used to fund these investments, and the dividend principle answers the question of how much earnings should be reinvested back into the business and how much returned to the owners of the business. These core corporate finance principles can be stated as follows:

- **The Investment Principle** Invest in assets and projects that *yield a return greater than the minimum acceptable hurdle rate*. The hurdle rate should be *higher for riskier projects* and should reflect the *financing mix* used—owners' funds (equity) or borrowed money (debt). Returns on projects should be measured based on *cash flows* generated and the *timing* of these cash flows; they should also consider both *positive and negative side effects* of these projects.

- *The Financing Principle*   Choose a *financing mix (debt and equity)* that maximizes the value of the investments made and *match the financing to nature of the assets* being financed.
- *The Dividend Principle*   If there are not enough investments that earn the hurdle rate, *return the cash* to the owners of the business. In the case of a publicly traded firm, the *form of the return*—dividends or stock buybacks—will depend on what stockholders prefer.

When making investment, financing and dividend decisions, corporate finance is single-minded about the ultimate objective, which is assumed to be maximizing the value of the business. These first principles provide the basis from which we will extract the numerous models and theories that comprise modern corporate finance, but they are also commonsense principles. It is incredible conceit on our part to assume that until corporate finance was developed as a coherent discipline starting just a few decades ago, people who ran businesses made decisions randomly with no principles to govern their thinking. Good businesspeople through the ages have always recognized the importance of these first principles and adhered to them, albeit in intuitive ways. In fact, one of the ironies of recent times is that many managers at large and presumably sophisticated firms with access to the latest corporate finance technology have lost sight of these basic principles.

The Objective of the Firm
No discipline can develop cohesively over time without a unifying objective. The growth of corporate financial theory can be traced to its choice of a single objective and the development of models built around this objective. The objective in conventional corporate financial theory when making decisions is to maximize the value of the business or firm. Consequently, any decision (investment, financial, or dividend) that increases the value of a business is considered a good one, whereas one that reduces firm value is considered a poor one. Although the choice of a singular objective has provided corporate finance with a unifying theme and internal consistency, it comes at a cost. To the degree that one buys into this objective, much of what corporate financial theory suggests makes sense. To the degree that this objective is flawed, however, it can be argued that the theory built on it is flawed as well. Many of the disagreements between corporate financial theorists and others (academics as well as practitioners) can be traced to fundamentally different views about the correct objective for a business. For instance, there are some critics of corporate finance who argue that firms should have multiple objectives where a variety of interests (stockholders, labor, customers) are met, and there are others who would have firms focus on what they view as simpler and more direct objectives, such as market share or profitability.

Given the significance of this objective for both the development and the applicability of corporate financial theory, it is important that we examine it much more carefully and address some of the very real concerns and criticisms it has garnered: It assumes that what stockholders do in their own self-interest is also in the best interests of the firm, it is sometimes dependent on the existence of efficient markets, and it is often blind to the social costs associated with value maximization. In the next chapter, we consider these and other issues and compare firm value maximization to alternative objectives.

The Investment Principle

Firms have scarce resources that must be allocated among competing needs. The first and foremost function of corporate financial theory is to provide a framework for firms to make this decision wisely. Accordingly, we define *investment decisions* to include not only those that create revenues and profits (such as introducing a new product line or expanding into a new market) but also those that save money (such as building a new and more efficient distribution system). Furthermore, we argue that decisions about how much and what inventory to maintain and whether and how much credit to grant to customers that are traditionally categorized as working capital decisions, are ultimately investment decisions as well. At the other end of the spectrum, broad strategic decisions regarding which markets to enter and the acquisitions of other companies can also be considered investment decisions.

Corporate finance attempts to measure the return on a proposed investment decision and compare it to a minimum acceptable **hurdle rate** to decide whether the project is acceptable. The hurdle rate has to be set higher for riskier projects and has to reflect the financing mix used, that is, the owner's funds (equity) or borrowed money (debt). In Chapter 3, we begin this process by defining risk and developing a procedure for measuring risk. In Chapter 4, we go about converting this risk measure into a hurdle rate, that is, a minimum acceptable rate of return, both for entire businesses and for individual investments.

Hurdle Rate: A minimum acceptable rate of return for investing resources in a project.

Having established the hurdle rate, we turn our attention to measuring the returns on an investment. In Chapter 5 we evaluate three alternative ways of measuring returns—conventional accounting earnings, cash flows, and time-weighted cash flows (where we consider both how large the cash flows are and when they are anticipated to come in). In Chapter 6 we consider some of the potential side costs that might not be captured in any of these measures, including costs that may be created for existing investments by taking a new investment, and side benefits, such as options to enter new markets and to expand product lines that may be embedded in new investments, and synergies, especially when the new investment is the acquisition of another firm.

The Financing Principle

Every business, no matter how large and complex, is ultimately funded with a mix of borrowed money (debt) and owner's funds (equity). With a publicly traded firm, debt may take the form of bonds and equity is usually common stock. In a private business, debt is more likely to be bank loans and an owner's savings represent equity. Though we consider the existing mix of debt and equity and its implications for the minimum acceptable hurdle rate as part of the investment principle, we throw open the question of whether the existing mix is the right one in the financing principle section. There might be regulatory and other real-world constraints on the financing mix that a business can use, but there is ample room for flexibility within these constraints. We begin this section in Chapter 7, by looking at the range of choices that exist for both private businesses and publicly traded firms between debt and equity. We then turn to the question of whether the existing mix of financing used by a business is optimal, given the objective function of maximizing firm value. Although the trade-off between the benefits and costs of borrowing are established in qualitative terms first, we also look at two quantitative approaches to arriving at the optimal mix in Chapter 8. In the first approach, we examine the specific conditions under which the optimal financing mix is the one that minimizes the minimum acceptable hurdle rate. In the second approach, we look at the effects on firm value of changing the financing mix.

When the optimal financing mix is different from the existing one, we map out the best ways of getting from where we are (the current mix) to where we would like to be (the optimal) in Chapter 9, keeping in mind the investment opportunities that the firm has and the need for timely responses, either because the firm is a takeover target or under threat of bankruptcy. Having outlined the optimal financing mix, we turn our attention to the type of financing a business should use, such as whether it should be long-term or short-term, whether the payments on the financing should be fixed or variable, and if variable, what it should be a function of. Using a basic proposition that a firm will minimize its risk from financing and maximize its capacity to use borrowed funds if it can match up the cash flows on the debt to the cash flows on the assets being financed, we design the perfect financing instrument for a firm. We then add additional considerations relating to taxes and external monitors (equity research analysts and ratings agencies) and arrive at strong conclusions about the design of the financing.

The Dividend Principle

Most businesses would undoubtedly like to have unlimited investment opportunities that yield returns exceeding their hurdle rates, but all businesses grow and mature. As a consequence, every business that thrives reaches a stage in its life when the cash flows generated by existing investments is greater than the funds needed to take on good investments. At that point, this business has to figure out ways to return the excess cash to owners. In private businesses, this may just involve the owner withdrawing a portion of his or her funds from the business. In a publicly traded corporation, this will involve either paying dividends or buying back stock. In Chapter 10, we introduce the basic trade-off that determines whether cash should be left in a business or taken out of it. For stockholders in publicly traded firms, we note that this decision is fundamentally one of whether they trust the managers of the firms with their cash, and much of this trust is based on how well these managers have invested funds in the past. In Chapter 11, we consider the options available to a firm to return cash to its owners—dividends, stock buybacks, and spin-offs—and investigate how to pick between these options.

CORPORATE FINANCIAL DECISIONS, FIRM VALUE, AND EQUITY VALUE

If the objective function in corporate finance is to maximize firm value, it follows that firm value must be linked to the three corporate finance decisions outlined—investment, financing, and dividend decisions. The link between these decisions and firm value can be made by recognizing that *the value of a firm is the present value of its expected cash flows, discounted back at a rate that reflects both the riskiness of the projects of the firm and the financing mix used to finance them.* Investors form expectations about future cash flows based on observed current cash flows and expected future growth, which in turn depend on the quality of the firm's projects (its investment decisions) and the amount reinvested back into the business (its dividend decisions). The financing decisions affect the value of a firm through both the discount rate and potentially through the expected cash flows.

This neat formulation of value is put to the test by the interactions among the investment, financing, and dividend decisions and the conflicts of interest that arise between stockholders and lenders to the firm, on one hand, and stockholders and managers, on the other. We introduce the basic models available to value a firm and its equity in Chapter 12, and relate them back to management decisions on investment, financial, and dividend policy. In the process, we examine the determinants of value and how firms can increase their value.

A REAL-WORLD FOCUS

The proliferation of news and information on real-world businesses making decisions every day suggests that we do not need to use hypothetical examples to illustrate the principles of corporate finance. We will use four businesses through this book to make our points about corporate financial policy:

1. ***Disney Corporation*** Disney Corporation is a publicly traded firm with wide holdings in entertainment and media. Most people around the world recognize the Mickey Mouse logo and have heard about or visited a Disney theme park or seen some or all of the Disney animated classic movies, but it is a much more diversified corporation than most people realize. Disney's holdings include real estate (in the form of time shares and rental properties in Florida and South Carolina), television (ABC and ESPN), publications, movie studios (Miramax, Touchstone, and Disney) and consumer products. Disney will help illustrate the decisions that large multibusiness and multinational corporations have to make as they are faced with the conventional corporate financial decisions—Where do we invest? How do we finance these investments? How much do we return to our stockholders?

2. ***Bookscape Books*** This company is a privately owned independent bookstore in New York City, one of the few left after the invasion of the bookstore chains, such as Barnes and Noble and Borders. We will take Bookscape Books through the corporate financial decision-making process to illustrate some of the issues that come up when looking at small businesses with private owners.

3. *Aracruz Celulose* Aracruz Celulose is a Brazilian firm that produces eucalyptus pulp and operates its own pulp mills, electrochemical plants, and port terminals. Although it markets its products around the world for manufacturing high-grade paper, we use it to illustrate some of the questions that have to be dealt with when analyzing a company in an environment where inflation is high and volatile and the economy itself is in transition.

4. *Deutsche Bank* Deutsche Bank is the leading commercial bank in Germany and is also a leading player in investment banking with its acquisition of Morgan Grenfell, the U.K. investment bank, and Banker's Trust in the United States. We will use Deutsche Bank to illustrate some of the issues that come up when a financial service firm has to make investment, financing and dividend decisions.

A RESOURCE GUIDE

To make the learning in this book as interactive and current as possible, we employ a variety of devices.

- This icon indicates that spreadsheet programs can be used to do some of the analysis that will be presented. For instance, there are spreadsheets that calculate the optimal financing mix for a firm as well as valuation spreadsheets.

- This symbol marks the second supporting device: updated data on some of the inputs that we need and use in our analysis that is available on the Web site for this book. Thus, when we estimate the risk parameters for firms, we will draw attention to the data set that is maintained on the Web site that reports average risk parameters by industry.

- At regular intervals, we will also ask readers to answer questions relating to a topic. These questions, which will generally be framed using real-world examples, will help emphasize the key points made in a chapter and will be marked with this icon.

- Finally, we will introduce a series of boxes titled "In Practice," which will look at issues that are likely to come up in practice and ways of addressing these issues.

SOME FUNDAMENTAL PROPOSITIONS ABOUT CORPORATE FINANCE

There are several fundamental arguments we will make repeatedly throughout this book.

1. *Corporate finance has an internal consistency* that flows from its choice of maximizing firm value as the only objective function and its dependence on a few bedrock principles: Risk has to be rewarded, cash flows matter more than accounting income, markets are not easily fooled, and every decision a firm makes has an effect on its value.

2. ***Corporate finance must be viewed as an integrated whole,*** rather than a collection of decisions. Investment decisions generally affect financing decisions and vice versa; financing decisions often influence dividend decisions and vice versa. Although there are circumstances under which these decisions may be independent of each other, this is seldom the case in practice. Accordingly, it is unlikely that firms that deal with their problems on a piecemeal basis will ever resolve these problems. For instance, a firm that takes poor investments may soon find itself with a dividend problem (with insufficient funds to pay dividends) and a financing problem (because the drop in earnings may make it difficult for them to meet interest expenses).

3. ***Corporate finance matters to everybody***   There is a corporate financial aspect to almost every decision made by a business; though not everyone will find a use for all the components of corporate finance, everyone will find a use for at least some *part* of it. Marketing managers, corporate strategists, human resource managers, and information technology managers all make corporate finance decisions every day and often don't realize it. An understanding of corporate finance will help them make better decisions.

4. ***Corporate finance is fun***   This may seem to be the tallest claim of all. After all, most people associate corporate finance with numbers, accounting statements, and hardheaded analyses. Although corporate finance is quantitative in its focus, there is a significant component of creative thinking involved in coming up with solutions to the financial problems businesses do encounter. It is no coincidence that financial markets remain breeding grounds for innovation and change.

5. ***The best way to learn corporate finance is by applying its models and theories to real-world problems***   Although the theory that has been developed over the past few decades is impressive, the ultimate test of any theory is application. As we show in this book, much (if not all) of the theory can be applied to real companies and not just to abstract examples, though we have to compromise and make assumptions in the process.

CONCLUSION

This chapter establishes the first principles that govern corporate finance. The investment principle specifies that businesses invest only in projects that yield a return that exceeds the hurdle rate. The financing principle suggests that the right financing mix for a firm is one that maximizes the value of the investments made. The dividend principle requires that cash generated in excess of good project needs be returned to the owners. These principles are the core for what follows in this book.

CHAPTER 2

THE OBJECTIVE IN DECISION MAKING

If you do not know where you are going, it does not matter how you get there.

ANONYMOUS

Corporate finance's greatest strength (and greatest weakness) is its focus on value maximization. By maintaining that focus, corporate finance preserves internal consistency and coherence and develops powerful models and theory about the right way to make investment, financing, and dividend decisions. It can be argued, however, that all of these conclusions are conditional on the acceptance of value maximization as the only objective in decision making.

In this chapter, we consider why we focus so strongly on value maximization and why, in practice, the focus shifts to stock price maximization. We also look at the assumptions needed for stock price maximization to be the right objective, what can go wrong with firms that focus on it, and at least partial fixes to some of these problems. We will argue strongly that even though stock price maximization is a flawed objective, it offers far more promise than alternative objectives because it is self-correcting.

CHOOSING THE RIGHT OBJECTIVE

Let's start with a description of what an objective is and the purpose it serves in developing theory. An objective specifies what a decision maker is trying to accomplish and by so doing provides measures that can be used to choose between alternatives. In most firms, the managers of the firm, rather than the owners, make the decisions about where to invest or how to raise funds for an investment. Thus, if stock price maximization is the objective, a manager choosing between two alternatives will choose the one that increases stock price more. In most cases, the objective is stated in terms of maximizing some function or variable, such as profits or growth, or minimizing some function or variable, such as risk or costs.

So why do we need an objective, and if we do need one, why can't we have several? Let's start with the first question. If an objective is not chosen, there is no systematic way to make the decisions that every business will be confronted with at some point in time. For instance, without an objective, how can Disney's managers decide whether the investment in a new theme park is a good one? There would be a menu of approaches for picking projects, ranging from reasonable ones like maximizing return on investment to obscure ones like maximizing the size of the firm, and no statements could be made about their relative value. Consequently, three managers looking at the same project may come to three separate conclusions.

If we choose multiple objectives, we are faced with a different problem. A theory developed around multiple objectives of equal weight will create quandaries when it comes to making decisions. For example, assume that a firm chooses as its objectives maximizing market share and maximizing current earnings. If a project increases market share and current earnings, the firm will face no problems, but what if the project under analysis increases market share while reducing current earnings? The firm should not invest in the project if the current earnings objective is considered, but it should invest in it based on the market share objective. If objectives are prioritized, we are faced with the same stark choices as in the choice of a single objective. Should the top priority be the maximization of current earnings or should it be maximizing market share? Because there is no gain, therefore, from having multiple objectives, and developing theory becomes much more difficult, we argue that there should be only one objective.

There are a number of different objectives that a firm can choose between when it comes to decision making. How will we know whether the objective that we have chosen is the right objective? A good objective should have the following characteristics.

a. It is *clear and unambiguous*. An ambiguous objective will lead to decision rules that vary from case to case and from decision maker to decision maker. Consider, for instance, a firm that specifies its objective to be increasing growth in the long term. This is an ambiguous objective because it does not answer at least two questions. The first is growth in what variable: Is it in revenue, operating earnings, net income, or earnings per share? The second is in the definition of the long term: Is it three years, five years, or a longer period?

b. It comes with a *clear and timely measure* that can be used to evaluate the success or failure of decisions. Objectives that sound good but don't come with a measurement mechanism are likely to fail. For instance, consider a retail firm that defines its objective as maximizing customer satisfaction. How exactly is customer satisfaction defined, and how is it to be measured? If no good mechanism exists for measuring how satisfied customers are with their purchases, not only will managers be unable to make decisions based on this objective but stockholders will also have no way of holding them accountable for any decisions they do make.

c. It *does not create costs for other entities or groups* that erase firm-specific benefits and leave society worse off overall. As an example, assume that a tobacco company defines its objective to be revenue growth. Managers of this firm would then be inclined to increase advertising to teenagers because it will increase sales. Doing so may create significant costs for society that overwhelm any benefits arising from the objective. Some may disagree with the inclusion of social costs and benefits and argue that a business only has a responsibility to its stockholders, not to society. This strikes us as shortsighted because the people who own and operate businesses are part of society.

THE CLASSICAL OBJECTIVE

There is general agreement, at least among corporate finance theorists that the objective when making decisions in a business is to maximize value. There is some disagreement on whether the objective is to maximize the value of the stockholder's stake in the business or the value of the entire business (firm), which besides stockholders includes the other financial claim holders (debt holders, preferred stockholders, etc.). Furthermore, even among those who argue for stockholder wealth maximization, there is a question about whether this translates into maximizing the stock price. As we will see in this chapter, these objectives vary in terms of the assumptions needed to justify them. The least restrictive of the three objectives, in terms of assumptions needed, is to maximize the firm value, and the most restrictive is to maximize the stock price.

Multiple Stakeholders and Conflicts of Interest

In the modern corporation, stockholders hire managers to run the firm for them; these managers then borrow from banks and bondholders to finance the firm's operations. Investors in financial markets respond to information about the firm revealed to them by the managers, and firms have to operate in the context of a larger society. By focusing on maximizing stock price, corporate finance exposes itself to several risks. Each of these stakeholders has different objectives, and there is the distinct possibility that there will be conflicts of interests among them. What is good for managers may not necessarily be good for stockholders; what is good for stockholders may not be in the best interests of bondholders; and what is beneficial to a firm may create large costs for society.

These conflicts of interests are exacerbated further when we bring in two additional stakeholders in the firm. First, the employees of the firm may have little or no interest in stockholder wealth maximization and may have a much larger stake in improving wages, benefits, and job security. In some cases, these interests may be in direct conflict with stockholder wealth maximization. Second, the customers of the business will probably prefer that products and services be priced lower to maximize their utility, but again this may conflict with what stockholders would prefer.

Potential Side Costs of Value Maximization

As we noted at the beginning of this section, the objective in corporate finance can be stated broadly as maximizing the value of the entire business, more narrowly as maximizing the value of the equity stake in the business, or even more narrowly as maximizing the stock price for a publicly traded firm. The potential side costs increase as the objective is narrowed.

If the objective when making decisions is to maximize firm value, there is a possibility that what is good for the firm may not be good for society. In other words, decisions that are good for the firm, insofar as they increase value, may create social costs. If these costs are large, we can see society paying a high price for value maximization, and the objective will have to be modified to allow for these costs. To be fair, however, this is a problem that is likely to persist in any system of private enterprise and is not peculiar to value maximization. The objective of value maximization may also face obstacles when there is separation of ownership and management, as there is in most large public corporations. When managers act as agents for the owners (stockholders), there is the potential for a conflict of interest between stockholder and managerial interests, which in turn can lead to decisions that make managers better off at the expense of stockholders.

When the objective is stated in terms of stockholder wealth, the conflicting interests of stockholders and bondholders have to be reconciled. Because stockholders are the decision makers and bondholders are often not completely protected from the side effects of these decisions, one way of maximizing stockholder wealth is to take actions that expropriate wealth from the bondholders, even though such actions may reduce the wealth of the firm.

Finally, when the objective is narrowed further to one of maximizing stock price, inefficiencies in the financial markets may lead to misallocation of resources and bad decisions. For instance, if stock prices do not reflect the long-term consequences of decisions, but respond, as some critics say, to short-term earnings effects, a decision that increases stockholder wealth (which reflects long-term earnings potential) may reduce the stock price. Conversely, a decision that reduces stockholder wealth but increases earnings in the near term may increase the stock price.

Why Corporate Finance Focuses on Stock Price Maximization

Much of corporate financial theory is centered on stock price maximization as the sole objective when making decisions. This may seem surprising given the potential side costs just discussed, but there are three reasons for the focus on stock price maximization in traditional corporate finance.

- Stock prices are the *most observable* of all measures that can be used to judge the performance of a publicly traded firm. Unlike earnings or sales, which are updated once every quarter or once every year, stock prices are updated constantly to reflect new information coming out about the firm. Thus, managers receive instantaneous feedback from investors on every action that they take. A good illustration is the response of markets to a firm announcing that it plans to acquire another firm. Although managers consistently paint a rosy picture of every acquisition that they plan, the stock price of the acquiring firm drops at the time of the announcement of the deal in roughly half of all acquisitions, suggesting that markets are much more skeptical about managerial claims.

- If investors are rational and markets are efficient, stock prices will reflect the long-term effects of decisions made by the firm. Unlike accounting measures, such as earnings, or sales measures, such as market share, which look at the effects on current operations of decisions made by a firm, the value of a stock is a function of the long-term health and prospects of the firm. In a rational market, the stock price is an attempt on the part of investors to measure this value. Even if they err in their estimates, it can be argued that an erroneous estimate of long-term value is better than a precise estimate of current earnings.

- Finally, choosing stock price maximization as an objective allows us to make categorical statements about the best way to pick projects and finance them and to test these statements with empirical observation.

2.1 WHICH OF THE FOLLOWING ASSUMPTIONS DO YOU NEED TO MAKE FOR STOCK PRICE MAXIMIZATION TO BE THE ONLY OBJECTIVE IN DECISION MAKING?

☐ Managers act in the best interests of stockholders.

☐ Lenders to the firm are fully protected from expropriation.

☐ Financial markets are efficient.

☐ There are no social costs.

☐ All of the above

☐ None of the above

IN PRACTICE: WHAT IS THE OBJECTIVE IN DECISION MAKING IN A PRIVATE FIRM OR A NON-PROFIT ORGANIZATION?

The objective of maximizing stock prices is a relevant objective only for firms that are publicly traded. How, then, can corporate finance principles be adapted for private firms? For firms that are not publicly traded, the objective in decision-making is the maximization of firm value. The investment, financing, and dividend principles we will develop in the chapters to come apply for both publicly traded firms, which focus on stock prices, and private businesses, which maximize firm value. Because firm value is not observable and has to be estimated, what private businesses will lack is the feedback—sometimes unwelcome—that publicly traded firms get from financial markets when they make major decisions.

It is, however, much more difficult to adapt corporate finance principles to a not-for-profit organization, because its objective is often to deliver a service in the most efficient way possible, rather than make profits. For instance, the objective of a hospital may be stated as delivering quality health care at the least cost. The problem, though, is that someone has to define the acceptable level of care, and the conflict between cost and quality will underlie all decisions made by the hospital. ∎

MAXIMIZE STOCK PRICES: THE BEST-CASE SCENARIO

If corporate financial theory is based on the objective of maximizing stock prices, it is worth asking when it is reasonable to ask managers to focus on this objective to the exclusion of all others. There is a scenario in which managers can concentrate on maximizing stock prices to the exclusion of all other considerations and not worry about side costs. For this scenario to unfold, the following assumptions have to hold.

1. *The managers of the firm put aside their own interests and focus on maximizing stockholder wealth* This might occur either because they are terrified of the power stockholders have to replace them (through the annual meeting or via the board of directors) or because they own enough stock in the firm that maximizing stockholder wealth becomes their objective as well.

2. *The lenders to the firm are fully protected from expropriation by stockholders* This can occur for one of two reasons. The first is a reputation effect, that is, that stockholders will not take any actions that hurt lenders now if they feel that doing so might hurt them when they try to borrow money in the future. The second is that lenders might be able to protect themselves fully by writing covenants proscribing the firm from taking any actions that hurt them.

3. *The managers of the firm do not attempt to mislead or lie* to financial markets about the firm's future prospects, and there is sufficient information for markets to make judgments about the effects of actions on long-term cash flows and value. Markets are assumed to be *reasoned and rational* in their assessments of these actions and the consequent effects on value.

4. *There are no social costs or social benefits* All costs created by the firm in its pursuit of maximizing stockholder wealth can be traced and charged to the firm.

With these assumptions, there are no side costs to stock price maximization. Consequently, managers can concentrate on maximizing stock prices. In the process, stockholder wealth and firm value will be maximized, and society will be made better off. The assumptions needed for the classical objective are summarized in pictorial form in Figure 2.1.

Figure 2.1   Stock Price Maximization: The Costless Scenario

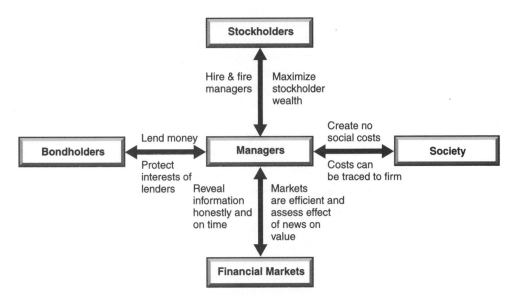

MAXIMIZE STOCK PRICES: REAL-WORLD CONFLICTS OF INTEREST

Even a casual perusal of the assumptions needed for stock price maximization to be the only objective when making decisions suggests that there are potential short-comings in each one. Managers might not always make decisions that are in the best interests of stockholders, stockholders do sometimes take actions that hurt lenders, information delivered to markets is often erroneous and sometimes misleading, and there are social costs that cannot be captured in the financial statements of the company. In the section that follows, we consider some of the ways real-world problems might trigger a breakdown in the stock price maximization objective.

Stockholders and Managers

In classical corporate financial theory, stockholders are assumed to have the power to discipline and replace managers who do not maximize their wealth. The two mechanisms that exist for this power to be exercised are the annual meeting, wherein stockholders gather to evaluate management performance, and the board of directors, whose fiduciary duty it is to ensure that managers serve stockholders' interests. Although the legal backing for this assumption may be reasonable, the practical power of these institutions to enforce stockholder control is debatable. In this section, we will begin by looking at the limits on stockholder power and then examine the consequences for managerial decisions.

The Annual Meeting

Every publicly traded firm has an annual meeting of its stockholders, during which stockholders can both voice their views on management and vote on changes to the corporate charter. Most stockholders, however, do not go to the annual meetings, partly because they do not feel that they can make a difference and partly because it would not make financial sense for them to do so.[1] It is true that investors can exercise their power with proxies,[2] but incumbent management starts off with a clear advantage.[3] Many stockholders do not bother to fill out their proxies; among those who do, voting for incumbent management is often the default option. For institutional stockholders with significant holdings in a large number of securities, the easiest option, when dissatisfied with incumbent management, is to "vote with their feet," which is to sell their stock and move on. An activist posture on the part of these stockholders would go a long way toward making managers more responsive to their interests, and there are trends toward more activism, which will be documented later in this chapter.

The Board of Directors

The board of directors is the body that oversees the management of a publicly traded firm. As elected representatives of the stockholders, the directors are obligated to ensure that managers are looking out for stockholder interests. They can change the top management of the firm and have a substantial influence on how it is run. On major decisions, such as acquisitions of other firms, managers have to get the approval of the board before acting.

The capacity of the board of directors to discipline management and keep them responsive to stockholders is diluted by a number of factors.

1. Many individuals who serve as directors do not spend much time on their fiduciary duties, partly because of other commitments and partly because many of them serve on the boards of several corporations. Korn-Ferry,[4] an executive recruiter, publishes a periodical survey of directorial compensation, and time spent by directors on their work illustrates this very clearly. In their 1992 survey, they reported that the average director spent 92 hours a year on board meetings and preparation in 1992, down from 108 in 1988, and was paid $32,352, up from $19,544 in 1988.[5] Although their 1998 survey did not measure the hours directors spent on their duties, it does mention that their average compensation had climbed to $37,924. As a result of scandals associated with lack of board

---

[1] An investor who owns 100 shares of stock in, say, Coca-Cola will very quickly wipe out any potential returns he makes on his investment if he or she flies to Atlanta every year for the annual meeting.

[2] A *proxy* enables stockholders to vote in absentia on boards of directors and on resolutions that will be coming to a vote at the meeting. It does not allow them to ask open-ended questions of management.

[3] This advantage is magnified if the corporate charter allows incumbent management to vote proxies that were never sent back to the firm. This is the equivalent of having an election in which the incumbent gets the votes of anybody who does not show up at the ballot box.

[4] Korn-Ferry surveys the boards of large corporations and provides insight into their composition.

[5] This understates the truc benefits received by the average director in a firm, because it does not count benefits and perquisites—insurance and pension benefits being the largest component. Hewitt Associates, an executive search firm, reports that 67 percent of 100 firms that they surveyed offer retirement plans for their directors.

oversight at companies like Enron and Worldcom, directors have come under more pressure to take their jobs seriously. The Korn-Ferry survey in 2002 noted an increase in hours worked by the average director to 183 hours a year and a corresponding surge in compensation.

2. Even those directors who spend time trying to understand the internal workings of a firm are stymied by their lack of expertise on many issues, especially relating to accounting rules and tender offers, and rely instead on outside experts.

3. In some firms, a significant percentage of the directors work for the firm, can be categorized as insiders and are unlikely to challenge the chief executive officer (CEO). Even when directors are outsiders, they are not independent, insofar as the company's CEO often has a major say in who serves on the board. Korn-Ferry's annual survey of boards also found in 1988 that 74 percent of the 426 companies it surveyed relied on recommendations by the CEO to come up with new directors, whereas only 16 percent used a search firm. In its 1998 survey, Korn-Ferry found a shift toward more independence on this issue, with almost three-quarters of firms reporting the existence of a nominating committee that is at least nominally independent of the CEO. The 2002 survey confirmed a continuation of this shift.

4. The CEOs of other companies are the favored choice for directors, leading to a potential conflict of interest, where CEOs sit on each other's boards.

5. Most directors hold only small or token stakes in the equity of their corporations, making it difficult for them to empathize with the plight of shareholders when stock prices go down. In a study in the late 1990s, Institutional Shareholder Services, a consultant, found that 27 directors at 275 of the largest corporations in the United States owned *no* shares at all, and about 5 percent of all directors owned fewer than five shares.

The net effect of these factors is that the board of directors often fails at its assigned role, which is to protect the interests of stockholders. The CEO sets the agenda, chairs the meeting, and controls the flow of information, and the search for consensus generally overwhelms any attempts at confrontation. Although there is an impetus toward reform, it has to be noted that these revolts were sparked not by board members but by large institutional investors.

The failure of the board of directors to protect stockholders can be illustrated with numerous examples from the United States, but this should not blind us to a more troubling fact. Stockholders exercise more power over management in the United States than in any other financial market. If the annual meeting and the board of directors are, for the most part, ineffective in the United States at exercising control over management, they are even more powerless in Europe and Asia as institutions that protect stockholders.

The Consequences of Stockholder Powerlessness

If the two institutions of corporate governance—annual meetings and the board of directors—fail to keep management responsive to stockholders, as argued in the previous section, we cannot expect managers to maximize stockholder wealth, especially when their interests conflict with those of stockholders. Consider the following examples.

1. *Fighting Hostile Acquisitions*

   When a firm is the target of a hostile takeover, managers are sometimes faced with an uncomfortable choice. Allowing the hostile acquisition to go through will allow stockholders to reap substantial financial gains but may result in the managers losing their jobs. Not surprisingly, managers often act to protect their own interests at the expense of stockholders:

   - The managers of some firms that were targeted by acquirers (raiders) for hostile takeovers in the 1980s were able to avoid being acquired by buying out the acquirer's existing stake, generally at a price much greater than the price paid by the acquirer and by using stockholder cash. This process, called **greenmail,** usually causes stock prices to drop, but it does protect the jobs of incumbent managers. The irony of using money that belongs to stockholders to protect them against receiving a higher price on the stock they own seems to be lost on the perpetrators of greenmail.

   - Another widely used antitakeover device is a **golden parachute,** a provision in an employment contract that allows for the payment of a lump-sum or cash flows over a period, if the manager covered by the contract loses his or her job in a takeover. Although there are economists who have justified the payment of golden parachutes as a way of reducing the conflict between stockholders and managers, it is still unseemly that managers should need large side payments to do what they are hired to do—maximize stockholder wealth.

   - Firms sometimes create **poison pills,** which are triggered by hostile takeovers. The objective is to make it difficult and costly to acquire control. A flipover right offers a simple example. In a flipover right, existing stockholders get the right to buy shares in the firm at a price well above the current stock price. As long as the existing management runs the firm; this right is not worth very much. If a hostile acquirer takes over the firm, though, stockholders are given the right to buy additional shares at a price much lower than the current stock price. The acquirer, having weighed in this additional cost, may very well decide against the acquisition.

   Greenmail, golden parachutes, and poison pills generally do not require stockholder approval and are usually adopted by compliant boards of directors. In all three cases, it can be argued, managerial interests are being served at the expenses of stockholder interests.

Greenmail: The purchase by the target company of a potential hostile acquirer's stake in a business at a premium over the price paid for that stake.

Golden Parachute: A contractual clause in a management contract that allows the manager to be paid a specified sum of money in the event control of the firm changes, usually in the context of a hostile takeover.

Poison Pill: A security or a provision that is triggered by the hostile acquisition of the firm, resulting in a large cost to the acquirer.

2. *Antitakeover Amendments*

Antitakeover amendments have the same objective as greenmail and poison pills, which is dissuading hostile takeovers, but differ on one very important count. They require the assent of stockholders to be instituted. There are several types of antitakeover amendments, all designed with the objective of reducing the likelihood of a hostile takeover. Consider, for instance, a *super-majority amendment;* to take over a firm that adopts this amendment, an acquirer has to acquire more than the 51 percent that would normally be required to gain control. Antitakeover amendments do increase the bargaining power of managers when negotiating with acquirers and could work to the benefit of stockholders,[6] but only if managers act in the best interests of stockholders.

2.2   ANTITAKEOVER AMENDMENTS AND MANAGEMENT TRUST

If as a stockholder in a company, you were asked to vote on an amendment to the corporate charter that would restrict hostile takeovers of your company and give your management more power, in which of the following types of companies would you be most likely to vote yes to the amendment?

☐ Companies where the managers promise to use this power to extract a higher price for you from hostile bidders.

☐ Companies that have done badly (in earnings and stock price performance) in the past few years.

☐ Companies that have done well (in earnings and stock price performance) in the past few years.

☐ I would never vote for such an amendment.

3. *Paying Too Much on Acquisitions*

There are many ways in which managers can make their stockholders worse off—by investing in bad projects, by borrowing too much or too little, and by adopting defensive mechanisms against potentially value-increasing takeovers. The quickest and perhaps the most decisive way to impoverish stockholders is to overpay on a takeover, because the amounts paid on takeovers tend to dwarf those involved in the other decisions. Of course, the managers of the firms doing the acquiring will argue that they never overpay on takeovers,[7] and that the high premiums paid in acquisitions can be justified using any number of reasons— there is **synergy,** there are strategic considerations, the target firm is undervalued and badly managed, and so on. The stockholders in acquiring firms do not seem

---

[6] As an example, when AT&T tried to acquire NCR in 1991, NCR had a super-majority antitakeover amendment. NCR's managers used this requirement to force AT&T to pay a much higher price for NCR shares than their initial offer.

[7] One explanation given for the phenomenon of overpaying on takeovers is that it is managerial hubris that drives the process.

to share the enthusiasm for mergers and acquisitions that their managers have, because the stock prices of bidding firms decline on the takeover announcements a significant proportion of the time.[8]

Synergy: The additional value created by bringing together two entities and pooling their strengths. In the context of a merger, synergy is the difference between the value of the merged firm and sum of the values of the firms operating independently.

These illustrations are not meant to make the case that managers are venal and selfish, which would be an unfair charge, but are manifestations of a much more fundamental problem; when there is conflict of interest between stockholders and managers, stockholder wealth maximization is likely to take second place to management objectives.

 This data set has the breakdown of CEO compensation for many U.S. firms for the most recent year.

ILLUSTRATION 2.1   Assessing Disney's Board of Directors

Over the past decade or so, Disney has emerged as a case study of weak corporate governance, where a powerful CEO, Michael Eisner, has been given free rein by a captive board of directors. We will look at Disney's board of directors in 1997, when *Fortune* magazine ranked it as having the worst board of the Fortune 500 companies and again in 2002, when it made the list of the five most improved boards.

At the end of 1996, Disney had 16 members on its board and the members are listed in Table 2.1, categorized by whether they work or worked for Disney (insiders) or not (outsiders).

Note that eight of the sixteen members on the board are or were Disney employees and that Eisner, in addition to being CEO, chaired the board. Of the eight outsiders, at least six had potential conflicts of interests because of their ties with either Disney or Eisner. The potential conflicts are listed in italics in Table 2.1. Given the composition of this board, it should come as no surprise that it failed to assert its power against incumbent management.[9]

In 1997, CALPERS, the California Public Employees Retirement System, suggested a series of checks to see if a board was likely to be effective in acting as a counterweight to a powerful CEO, including:

- Are a majority of the directors outside directors?

---

[8]See G. A. Jarrell, J. A. Brickley, and J. M. Netter, 1988, "The Market for Corporate Control: The Empirical Evidence since 1980," *Journal of Economic Perspectives*, 2, 49–68. In an extensive study of returns to bidder firms, these authors note that excess returns on these firms' stocks around the announcement of takeovers have declined from an average of 4.95 percent in the 1960s to 2 percent in the 1970s to –1 percent in the 1980s. Studies of mergers also generally conclude that the stock prices of bidding firms decline in more than half of all acquisitions.

[9]One case that cost Disney dearly was when Eisner prevailed on the board to hire Michael Ovitz, a noted Hollywood agent, with a generous compensation. A few years later, Ovitz left the company after falling out with Eisner, creating a multimillion-dollar liability for Disney. A 2003 lawsuit against Disney's board members contended that they failed in their fiduciary duty by not checking the terms of the compensation agreement before assenting to the hiring.

Table 2.1 DISNEY'S BOARD OF DIRECTORS 1996	
Insiders	**Outsiders**
Michael D. Eisner: CEO	Reveta F. Bowers: Head of school for the Center for Early Education, *where Mr. Eisner's children attended class*
Roy E. Disney: Head of animation department	
Sanford M. Litvack: Chief of corporate operations	
Richard A. Nunis: Chairman of Walt Disney Attractions	Ignacio E. Lozano, Jr.: Chairman of Lozano Enterprises, publisher of *La Opinion* newspaper in Los Angeles
*Raymond L. Watson: Disney chairman in 1983 and 1984	George J. Mitchell: Washington, D.C. attorney, former U.S. senator. *Disney paid Mr. Mitchell $50,000 for his consulting on international business matters in 1996. His Washington law firm was paid an additional $122,764*
*E. Cardon Walker: Disney chairman and chief executive, 1980–83	
*Gary L. Wilson: Disney chief financial officer, 1985–89	
*Thomas S. Murphy: Former chairman and chief executive of Capital Cities/ABC Inc.	Stanley P. Gold: President and chief executive of Shamrock Holdings, Inc., which *manages about $1 billion in investments for the Disney family*
	The Rev. Leo J. O'Donovan: President of Georgetown University, where one of Mr. Eisner's children attended college. *Mr. Eisner sat on the Georgetown board and has contributed more than $1 million to the school*
	Irwin E. Russell: Beverly Hills, Calif., attorney *whose clients include Mr. Eisner*
	Sidney Poitier: Actor
	Robert A. M. Stern: New York architect *who has designed numerous Disney projects.* He received $168,278 for those services in fiscal year 1996

*Former officials of Disney

- Is the chairman of the board independent of the company (and not the CEO of the company)?
- Are the compensation and audit committees composed entirely of outsiders?

When CALPERS put the companies in the Standard & Poor's (S&P) 500 through these tests in 1997, Disney was the only company that failed all the tests, with insiders on every one of the key committees.

Disney came under pressure from stockholders to modify its corporate governance practices between 1997 and 2002 and did make some changes to its board. Table 2.2 lists the board members at the end of 2002.

Note that many of the board members with conflicts of interests from 1996 continue to serve on the board. On a positive note, the number of insiders on the board has dropped from eight to six, but the board size remains at sixteen. In summary, although the board itself may be marginally more independent in 2002 than it was in 1997, it is still far from ideal in its composition.[10]

---

[10]As a postscript, it should be noted Stanley Gold and Roy Disney resigned from the board in early 2004, complaining about its lack of independence from Eisner.

	Table 2.2 DISNEY'S BOARD OF DIRECTORS 2002
Board Members	**Occupation**
Reveta Bowers	Head of school for the Center for Early Education
John Bryson	CEO and Chairman of Con Edison
Roy Disney	Head of Disney Animation
Michael Eisner	CEO of Disney
Judith Estrin	CEO of Packet Design (an Internet company)
Stanley Gold	CEO of Shamrock Holdings
Robert Iger	Chief operating officer, Disney
Monica Lozano	Chief operations officer, *La Opinion* (Spanish-language newspaper)
George Mitchell	Chairman of law firm (Verner, Liipfert, et al.)
Thomas S. Murphy	Former CEO, Capital Cities ABC
Leo O'Donovan	Professor of Theology, Georgetown University
Sidney Poitier	Actor, writer, and director
Robert A. M. Stern	Senior partner of Robert A. M. Stern Architects of New York
Andrea L. Van de Kamp	Chairman of Sotheby's West Coast
Raymond L. Watson	Chairman of Irvine Company (a real estate corporation)
Gary L. Wilson	Chairman of the board, Northwest Airlines

ILLUSTRATION **2.2   Corporate Governance at Aracruz: Voting and Nonvoting Shares**

Aracruz Celulose, like most Brazilian companies, had multiple classes of shares at the end of 2002. The common shares had all of the voting rights and were held by incumbent management, lenders to the company, and the Brazilian government. Outside investors held the nonvoting shares, which were called preferred shares,[11] and had no say in the election of the board of directors. At the end of 2002, Aracruz was managed by a board of seven directors, composed primarily of representatives of those who own the common (voting) shares, and an executive board, composed of three managers of the company.

Without analyzing the composition of the board of Aracruz, it is quite clear that there is the potential for a conflict of interest between voting shareholders who are fully represented on the board and preferred stockholders who are not. Although Brazilian law provides some protection for the latter, preferred stockholders have no power to change the existing management of the company and have little influence over major decisions that can affect their value.[12]

---

[11]This can create some confusion for investors in the United States, where preferred stock is stock with a fixed dividend and resembles bonds more than conventional common stock.

[12]This was brought home when Ambev, a large Brazilian beverage company, was acquired by Interbrand, a Belgian corporation. The deal enriched the common stock holders, but the preferred stock holders received little in terms of a premium and were largely bystanders.

ILLUSTRATION 2.3   Corporate Governance at Deutsche Bank: Cross-Holdings

Deutsche Bank follows the German tradition and legal requirement of having two boards. The board of managing directors, composed primarily of incumbent managers, develops the company's strategy, reviews it with the supervisory board, and ensures its implementation. The supervisory board appoints and recalls the members of the board of managing directors and, in cooperation with that board, arranges for long-term successor planning. It also advises the board of managing directors on the management of business and supervises it in its achievement of long-term goals.

A look at the supervisory board of directors at Deutsche Bank provides some insight into the differences between the U.S. and German corporate governance systems. The supervisory board at Deutsche Bank consists of twenty members, but eight are representatives of the employees. The remaining twelve are elected by shareholders, but employees clearly have a much bigger say in how companies are run in Germany and can sometimes exercise veto power over company decisions. Deutsche Bank's corporate governance structure is also muddied by cross-holdings. Deutsche Bank is the largest stockholder in Daimler Chrysler, the German automobile company, and Allianz, the German insurance company, is the largest stockholder in Deutsche Bank.

IN PRACTICE: Is There a Payoff to Better Corporate Governance?

Academics and activist investors are understandably enthused by moves toward giving stockholders more power over managers, but a practical question that is often not answered is what the payoff to better corporate governance is. Are companies where stockholders have more power over managers managed better and run more efficiently? If so, are they more valuable? Although no individual study can answer these significant questions, there are a number of different strands of research that offer some insight:

- In the most comprehensive study of the effect of corporate governance on value, a governance index was created for each of 1500 firms based on 24 distinct corporate governance provisions.[13] Buying stocks that had the strongest investor protections while simultaneously selling shares with the weakest protections generated an annual excess return of 8.5 percent. Every one-point increase in the index toward fewer investor protections decreased market value by 8.9 percent in 1999, and firms that scored high in investor protections also had higher profits, higher sales growth, and made fewer acquisitions. These findings are echoed in studies on firms in Korea and Germany.[14]

---

[13]P. A. Gompers, J. L. Ishii, and A. Metrick, 2003, "Corporate Governance and Equity Prices," *Quarterly Journal of Economics,* 118, 107–155. The data for the governance index were obtained from the Investor Responsibility Research Center, which tracks the corporate charter provisions for hundreds of firms.

[14]For Korea: B. S. Black, H. Jang, and W. Kim, 2003, *Does Corporate Governance Affect Firm Value? Evidence from Korea,* Stanford Law School Working Paper. For Germany: W. Drobetz, 2003, *Corporate Governance: Legal Fiction or Economic Reality?,* Working Paper, University of Basel.

- Actions that restrict hostile takeovers generally reduce stockholder power by taking away one of the most potent weapons available against indifferent management. In 1990, Pennsylvania considered passing a state law that would have protected incumbent managers against hostile takeovers by allowing them to override stockholder interests if other stakeholders were adversely impacted. In the months between the time the law was first proposed and the time it was passed, the stock prices of Pennsylvania companies declined by 6.90 percent.[15]

- There seems to be little evidence of a link between the composition of the board of directors and firm value. In other words, there is little to indicate that companies with boards that have fewer insiders trade at higher prices than companies with insider-dominated boards.[16]

- Although this is anecdotal evidence, the wave of corporate scandals—Enron, Worldcom, and Tyco—in the United States in 2000 and 2001 indicate a significant cost to having a compliant board. A common theme that emerged at problem companies was an ineffective board that failed to ask tough questions of an imperial CEO. ■

Stockholders and Bondholders

In a world where what is good for stockholders in a firm is also good for its bondholders (lenders), the latter might not have to worry about protecting themselves from expropriation. In the real world, however, there is a risk that bondholders who do not protect themselves may be taken advantage of in a variety of ways—by stockholders borrowing more money, paying more dividends, or undercutting the security of the assets on which the loans were based.

The Source of the Conflict

The source of the conflict of interest between stockholders and bondholders lies in the differences in the nature of the cash flow claims of the two groups. Bondholders generally have first claim on cash flows but receive fixed interest payments, assuming that the firm makes enough income to meet its debt obligations. Equity investors have a claim on the cash flows that are left over but have the option in publicly traded firms of declaring bankruptcy if the firm has insufficient cash flows to meet its financial obligations. Bondholders do not get to participate on the upside if projects succeed, but they bear a significant portion of the cost if projects fail. As a consequence, bondholders tend to view the risk in investments much more negatively than stockholders. There are many issues on which stockholders and bondholders are likely to disagree.

Some Examples of the Conflict

Existing bondholders can be made worse off by increases in borrowing, especially if these increases are large and affect the default risk of the firm, and these

---

[15]J. M. Karpoff, and P. H. Malatesta, 1990, "The Wealth Effects of Second-Generation State Takeover Legislation," *Journal of Financial Economics,* 25, 291–322.

[16]Sanjai Bhagat, and Bernard Black, 1999, "The Uncertain Relationship between Board Composition and Firm Performance," *Business Lawyer,* 54, 921–963.

bondholders are unprotected. The stockholders' wealth increases concurrently. This effect is dramatically illustrated in the case of acquisitions funded primarily with debt, where the debt ratio increases and the bond rating drops significantly. The prices of existing bonds fall to reflect the higher default risk.[17]

Dividend policy is another issue on which a conflict of interest may arise between stockholders and bondholders. The effect of higher dividends on stock prices can be debated in theory, with differences of opinion on whether it should increase or decrease prices, but the empirical evidence is clear. Increases in dividends, on average, lead to higher stock prices, whereas decreases in dividends lead to lower stock prices. Bond prices, on the other hand, react negatively to dividend increases and positively to dividend cuts. The reason is simple. Dividend payments reduce the cash available to a firm, thus making debt more risky.

The Consequences of Stockholder–Bondholder Conflicts

As these two illustrations make clear, stockholders and bondholders have different objectives and some decisions can transfer wealth from one group (usually bondholders) to the other (usually stockholders). Focusing on maximizing stockholder wealth may result in stockholders taking perverse actions that harm the overall firm but increase their wealth at the expense of bondholders.

It is possible that we are making too much of the expropriation possibility, for a couple of reasons. Bondholders are aware of the potential of stockholders to take actions that are inimical to their interests and generally protect themselves, either by writing in **covenants** or restrictions on what stockholders can do, or by taking an equity interest in the firm. Furthermore, the need to return to the bond markets to raise further funds in the future will keep many firms honest, because the gains from any one-time wealth transfer are likely to by outweighed by the reputation loss associated with such actions. These issues will be considered in more detail later in this book.

Bond Covenants: Covenants are restrictions built into contractual agreements. The most common reference in corporate finance to covenants is in bond agreements, and they represent restrictions placed by lenders on investment, financing, and dividend decisions made by the firm.

The Firm and Financial Markets

There is an advantage to maintaining an objective that focuses on stockholder or firm wealth rather than stock prices or the market value of the firm, because it does not require any assumptions about the efficiency or otherwise of financial markets. The downside, however, is that stockholder or firm wealth is not easily measurable, making it difficult to establish clear standards for success and failure. It is true that there are valuation models, some of which we will examine in this book, that attempt to measure equity and firm value, but they are based on a large number of

---

[17]In the leveraged buyout of Nabisco, existing bonds dropped in price 19 percent on the day of the acquisition, even as stock prices zoomed up.

essentially subjective inputs on which people may disagree. Because an essential characteristic of a good objective is that it comes with a clear and unambiguous measurement mechanism, the advantages of shifting to an objective that focuses on market prices is obvious. The measure of success or failure is there for all to see. Successful managers raise their firms' stock prices; unsuccessful managers reduce theirs.

To the extent that financial markets are efficient and use the information that is available to make measured and unbiased estimates of future cash flows and risk, market prices will reflect true value. In such markets, both the measurers and the measured will accept the market price as the appropriate mechanism for judging success and failure.

There are two potential barriers to this. The first is that information is the lubricant that enables markets to be efficient. To the extent that this information is hidden, delayed, or misleading, market prices will deviate from true value, even in an otherwise efficient market. The second problem is that there are many, both in academia and in practice, who argue that markets are not efficient, even when information is freely available. In both cases, decisions that maximize stock prices may not be consistent with long-term value maximization.

2.3   THE CREDIBILITY OF FIRMS IN CONVEYING INFORMATION

Do you think that the information revealed by companies about themselves is usually

☐   timely and honest?

☐   biased?

☐   fraudulent?

The Information Problem

Market prices are based on **information,** both **public** and **private.** In the world of classical theory, information about companies is revealed promptly and truthfully to financial markets. In the real world, there are a few impediments to this process. The first is that information is sometimes suppressed or delayed by firms, especially when it contains bad news. Although there is significant anecdotal evidence of this occurrence, the most direct evidence that firms do this comes from studies of earnings and dividend announcements. A study of earnings announcements noted that those announcements that had the worst news tended to be delayed the longest, relative to the expected announcement date.[18] In a similar vein, a study of earnings and dividend announcements by day of the week for firms on the New York Stock Exchange between 1982 and 1986 found that the announcements made on Friday, especially after the close of trading, contained more bad news than announcements made on any other day of the week.[19] This suggests that managers try to release bad news when markets are least active or closed because they fear that markets will overreact.

---

[18]S. H. Penman, 1987, "The Distribution of Earnings News over Time and Seasonalities in Aggregate Stock Returns," *Journal of Financial Economics,* 18(2), 199–228.

[19]A. Damodaran, 1989, "The Weekend Effect in Information Releases: A Study of Earnings and Dividend Announcements," *Review of Financial Studies,* 2(4), 607–623.

The second problem is more serious. In their zeal to keep investors happy and raise market prices, some firms release intentionally misleading information about current conditions and future prospects to financial markets. These misrepresentations can cause stock prices to deviate significantly from value. Consider the example of Bre-X, a Canadian gold mining company that claimed to have found one of the largest gold reserves in the world in Indonesia in the early 1990s. The stock was heavily touted by equity research analysts in the United States and Canada, but the entire claim was fraudulent. When the fraud came to light in 1997, the stock price tumbled, and analysts professed to be shocked that they had been misled by the firm. The more recent cases of Enron, Worldcom, and Parmalat suggest that this problem is not restricted to smaller, less followed companies and can persist even with strict accounting standards and auditing oversight.

The implications of such fraudulent behavior for corporate finance can be profound because managers are often evaluated on the basis of stock price performance. Thus Bre-X managers with options or bonus plans tied to the stock price probably did very well before the fraud came to light. Repeated violations of investor trust by companies can also lead to a loss of faith in equity markets and a decline in stock prices for all firms.

Public and Private Information: Public information refers to any information that is available to the investing public, whereas private information is restricted to only insiders or a few investors in the firm.

2.4 REPUTATION AND MARKET ACCESS

Which of the following types of firms is more likely to mislead markets? Explain.

- ☐ Companies that access markets infrequently to raise funds for operations—they raise funds internally.
- ☐ Companies that access markets frequently to raise funds for operations.
- ☐ Explain.

The Market Problem
The fear that managers have of markets overreacting or not assimilating information well into prices may be justified. Even if information flowed freely and with no distortion to financial markets, there is no guarantee that what emerges as the market price will be an unbiased estimate of true value. In fact, many would argue that the fault lies deeper and that investors are much too irrational and unreliable to come up with a good estimate of the true value. Some of the criticisms that have been mounted against financial markets are legitimate, some are overblown, and some are simply wrong, but we will consider all of them.

1. *Financial markets do not always reasonably and rationally assess the effects of new information on prices* Critics using this argument note that markets can be volatile, reacting to no news at all in some cases; in any case, the volatility in market prices is usually much greater than the volatility in any of the underlying fundamentals. The argument that financial markets are much too volatile, given the

underlying fundamentals, has some empirical support.[20] As for the irrationality of markets, the frequency with which you see bubbles in markets from the tulip bulb mania of the 1600s in Holland to the dot-com debacle of the late 1990s seems to be proof enough that emotions sometime get ahead of reason in markets.

2. ***Financial markets sometimes over react to information***   Analysts with this point of view point to firms that report earnings that are much higher or much lower than expected and argue that stock prices jump too much on good news and drop too much on bad news. The evidence on this proposition is mixed, though, because there are other cases where markets seem to underreact to news about firms. Overall, the only conclusion that all these studies agree on is that markets make mistakes in assessing the effect of news on value.

3. ***There are cases where insiders move markets to their benefit and often at the expense of outside investors***   This is especially true with illiquid stocks and is exacerbated in markets where trading is infrequent. Even with widely held and traded stocks, insiders sometimes use their superior access to information to get ahead of other investors.[21]

Notwithstanding these limitations, we cannot take away from the central contribution of financial markets. They assimilate and aggregate a remarkable amount of information on current conditions and future prospects into one measure—the price. No competing measure comes close to providing as timely or as comprehensive a measure of a firm's standing. The value of having market prices is best illustrated when working with a private firm as opposed to a public firm. Although managers of the latter may resent the second-guessing of analysts and investors, there is a great deal of value to knowing how investors perceive the actions that the firm takes.

2.5   ARE MARKETS SHORT-TERM?

Focusing on market prices will lead companies toward short-term decisions at the expense of long-term value.

☐   I agree with the statement.

☐   I do not agree with this statement.

Allowing managers to make decisions without having to worry about the effect on market prices will lead to better long-term decisions.

☐   I agree with this statement.

☐   I do not agree with this statement.

ILLUSTRATION 2.4   **Interaction with Financial Markets: A Case Study with Disney**

The complex interaction between firms and financial markets is best illustrated by examining what happens around earnings announcements. Consider, for instance,

---

[20]R. J. Shiller, 2000, *Irrational Exuberance,* Princeton: Princeton University Press.

[21]This is true even in the presence of strong insider trading laws, as is the case in the United States. Studies that look at insider trades registered with the Securities and Exchange Commission (SEC) seem to indicate that insider buying and selling does precede stock prices going up and down, respectively. The advantage is small, though.

Disney's earnings report for the last quarter of 2002, which was released to financial markets on February 1, 2003. The report contained the news that net income at the company dropped 42 percent from the prior year's level. The stock price increased by about 2 percent on the announcement of this bad news, because the reported earnings per share of 17 cents per share was higher than the 16 cents per share expected by analysts.

There are several interesting points that are worth making here. The first relates to the role that analysts play in setting expectations. In early 2003, for example, there were seventeen analysts working at brokerage houses and investment banks who provided estimates of earnings per share for Disney.[22] The lowest of the estimates was 13 cents per share, the highest was 20 cents per share, and the average (also called consensus) estimate was 16 cents per share. The second relates to the power of expectations. Any news that a company reports has to be measured relative to market expectations before it can be categorized as good or bad news. Thus, a report of a drop in earnings (as was the case with Disney in this example) can be good news because earnings did not drop as much as expected. Conversely, Disney reported an increase of 12 percent in earnings for the last quarter of 2003 (reported in February 2004) and saw its stock price decline slightly on the news because the increase was smaller than expected.

IN PRACTICE: Are Markets Short-Term?

There are many who believe that stock price maximization leads to a short-term focus for managers. The reasoning goes as follows: Stock prices are determined by traders, short-term investors, and analysts, all of whom hold the stock for short periods or spend their time trying to forecast next quarter's earnings. Managers who concentrate on creating long-term value rather than short-term results will be penalized by markets. Most of the empirical evidence that exists suggests that markets are much more long-term than they are given credit for.

1. There are hundreds of firms, especially small and start-up firms, that do not have any current earnings and cash flows and do not expect to have any in the near future but are still able to raise substantial amounts of money on the basis of expectations of success in the future. If markets were in fact as short-term as critics suggest, these firms should be unable to raise funds in the first place.

2. If the evidence suggests anything, it is that markets do not value current earnings and cash flows enough and value future earnings and cash flows too much. Studies indicate that stocks with low price-earnings ratios and high current earnings, have generally been underpriced relative to stocks with high price-earnings ratios.

3. The market response to research and development (R&D) and investment expenditure is not uniformly negative, as the "short-term" critics would lead you

_____

[22]These analysts are called sell-side analysts because their research is then offered to portfolio managers and other clients. The analysts who work for mutual funds are called buy-side analysts and toil in relative obscurity because their recommendations are for internal consumption at the mutual funds and are not publicized.

to believe. Instead, the response is tempered, with stock prices, on average, rising on the announcement of R&D and capital expenditures.

Do some investors and analysts focus on short-term earnings and not on long-term value? Of course. In our view, financial managers cater far too much to these investors and skew their decisions to meet their approval, fleeting though it might be. ■

The Firm and Society

Most management decisions have social consequences, and the question of how best to deal with these consequences is not easily answered. An objective of maximizing firm or stockholder wealth implicitly assumes that the social side costs are either trivial enough that they can be ignored or that they can be priced and charged to the firm. In many cases, neither of these assumptions is justifiable.

There are some cases in which the social costs are considerable but cannot be traced to the firm. In these cases, the decision makers, though aware of the costs, may choose to ignore the costs and maximize firm wealth. The ethical and moral dilemmas of forcing managers to choose between their survival (which may require stockholder wealth maximization) and the broader interests of society can be debated, but there is no simple solution that can be offered in this book.

In the cases where substantial social costs exist, and firms are aware of these costs, ethicists might argue that wealth maximization has to be sublimated to the broader interests of society, but what about those cases where firms create substantial social costs without being aware of these costs? John Manville Corporation, for instance, in the 1950s and 1960s produced asbestos with the intention of making a profit and was unaware of the potential of the product to cause cancer and other illnesses. Thirty years later, the lawsuits from those afflicted with asbestos-related disease have driven the company to bankruptcy.

To be fair, conflicts between the interests of the firm and the interests of society are not restricted to the objective of maximizing stockholder wealth. They may be endemic to a system of private enterprise, and there will never be a solution to satisfy the purists who would like to see a complete congruence between the social and firm interests.

2.6 CAN LAWS MAKE COMPANIES GOOD CITIZENS?

It has often been argued that social costs occur because governments do not have adequate laws on the books to punish companies that create social costs. The follow-up is that passing such laws will eliminate social costs.

☐ I agree with the statement.

☐ I do not agree with this statement.

ILLUSTRATION 2.5 **Assessing Social Costs**

The ubiquity of social costs is made clear when we look at three companies we are analyzing—Disney, Aracruz, and Deutsche Bank. These companies, in spite of their many differences, have social costs to consider.

- Disney was built and continues to market itself as the ultimate family-oriented company. When its only businesses were theme parks and animated movies, it faced relatively few conflicts. With its expansion into the movie business and TV broadcasting, Disney has exposed itself to new problems. To provide an illustration, the Southern Baptist Convention voted in 1997 to boycott Disney theme parks and movies in response to the airing of *Ellen,* a show on the ABC network, starring Ellen DeGeneres as a gay bookstore owner. It is because of this fear of a backlash that Disney maintains separate movie studios—Touchstone/Miramax for grown-up movies and Disney Studios for animated movies.

- Aracruz is at the center of the controversy about the deforestation of the rain forests in South America. In the later 1990s, Aracruz was accused by environmental groups of replacing old-growth forests in Brazil with eucalyptus plantations and displacing native and indigenous peoples from these areas.[23]

- Deutsche Bank has been challenged for its role as banker for the Nazis during the Holocaust. Its acquisition of Bankers Trust in 2000 was almost derailed by accusations that it had helped fund the construction of the concentration camp at Auschwitz during World War II. Both Deutsche Bank and Dresdner Bank were sued by survivors of the Holocaust for profiting from gold and other assets stolen from concentration camp victims during World War II.[24]

For all three companies, these accusations are serious not only because they damage their reputations but because they can also create serious economic costs. All three aggressively defended themselves against the charges and spent a substantial number of pages in their annual reports detailing what they do to be good corporate citizens.

IN PRACTICE: STAKEHOLDER WEALTH MAXIMIZATION AND BALANCED SCORECARDS

Some theorists have suggested that the best way to consider the interests of all of the different stakeholders in a modern corporation is to replace stockholder wealth maximization with a broader objective of stakeholder wealth maximization, where stakeholders include employees and society. Although it sounds wonderful as a concept, we believe that it is not a worthwhile alternative for the following reasons.

- When you have multiple stakeholders, with very different objectives, you will inevitably have to choose among them. For instance, laying off employees at a firm that is overstaffed will make stockholders and bondholders better off while creating costs to society. Stakeholder wealth maximization provides little direction on the proper way to balance these competing interests.

- Adding to the problem is the fact that not all of the costs and benefits to some stakeholders can be quantified. This is especially true of social costs and benefits, leaving the assessment to analysts who have their own biases.

---

[23]In the 1990s, the Tupinikim and Guarani Indians launched an international campaign against Aracruz in the state of Espirito Santo to recover and expand their traditional territories.

[24]A 1946 investigation by the U.S. military recommended that Deutsche Bank be liquidated and its top officials be tried as war criminals.

Figure 2.2 Stock Price Maximization in the Real World

- Most important, stakeholder wealth maximization makes managers accountable to no one by making them accountable to everyone. Managers can essentially go before each stakeholder and justify their failures by arguing that other stakeholder interests were being considered.

It may still be useful for firms to go beyond the proverbial bottom line, and a balanced scorecard attempts to do just that. As devised by Robert Kaplan, a Harvard strategy professor, balanced scorecards try to go beyond financial measures and look at customer satisfaction and internal business processes.[25] ∎

The Real World: A Pictorial Representation
We have spent the last few pages chronicling the problems in the real world with each of the linkages—managers and stockholders, stockholders and bondholders, firms and financial markets, and firms and society. Figure 2.2 summarizes the problems with each linkage in a pictorial representation.

ALTERNATIVES TO STOCK PRICE MAXIMIZATION

There are obvious problems associated with each of the linkages underlying wealth maximization. Stockholders often have little power over managers, and managers consequently put their interests above those of stockholders. Lenders who do not protect their interests often end up paying a price when decisions made by firms transfer wealth to stockholders. Information delivered to financial markets is often

---

[25]Robert S. Kaplan and David P. Norton, 1996, *The Balanced Scorecard: Translating Strategy into Action,* Cambridge: Harvard Business School Press.

erroneous, misleading, or delayed, and there are significant differences between price and market value. Finally, firms that maximize wealth may do so while creating large costs for society.

Given these problems, there are alternative courses of action that we can follow. One is to find a different system for keeping errant management in check. The second is to find an alternative objective for the firm. In this section, we will consider these alternatives.

A Different System for Disciplining Management (Corporate Governance)

In the system we have described thus far, stockholders bear the burden of replacing incompetent management; we can call this a market-based corporate governance system, where investors in financial markets govern how corporations are run. There are some who believe that this is too much of a responsibility to put on investors, who, as they see it, often operate with poor information and have short time horizons. Michael Porter, a leading thinker on corporate strategy, has argued that firms in the United States are hamstrung by the fact that investors are short-term and demand quick returns. He contrasts them with Japanese firms, which he argues can afford to adopt strategies that make sense in the long run, even though they might not maximize profits in the short term. He suggests that investors should form long-term relationships with firms and work with them to devise long-term strategies.[26] His view of the world is not unique and is shared by many corporate executives, even in the United States.

These executives argue that there are alternatives to the market-based corporate governance systems, where stockholders act to discipline and replace errant managers and stock prices measure their success. In the German and Japanese systems of corporate governance,[27] firms own stakes in other firms and often make decisions in the best interests of the industrial group they belong to rather than in their own interests. In these systems, the argument goes, firms will keep an eye on each other, rather than ceding power to the stockholders. In addition to being undemocratic— the stockholders are, after all, the owners of the firm—these systems suggests a profound suspicion of how stockholders might use the power if they get it and is heavily skewed toward maintaining the power of incumbent managers.

Although this approach may protect the system against the waste that is a by-product of stockholder activism and inefficient markets, it has its own disadvantages. Industrial groups are inherently more conservative than investors in allocating resources and thus are much less likely to finance high-risk and venture capital investments by upstarts who do not belong to the group. The other problem is that entire groups can be dragged down by the bad decisions of individual

---

[26]There is some movement toward relationship investing in the United States, where funds such as Allied Partners (run by Dillon Read), Corporate Partners (run by Lazard Freres), and Lens (run by activist Robert Monks) have attempted to create long-term relationships with the managers of firms.

[27]There are subtle differences between the Japanese and the German systems. The Japanese industrial groups, called *keiretsus,* are based primarily on cross-holdings of companies and evolved from family-owned businesses. The German industrial groups revolve around leading commercial banks, like Deutsche Bank or Dresdner Bank, with the bank holding substantial stakes in a number of industrial concerns.

firms.[28] In fact, the troubles that Japanese firms have had dealing with poor investments in the 1990s suggests to us that these alternative corporate governance systems, though efficient at dealing with individual firms that are poorly run, have a more difficult time adapting to and dealing with problems that are widespread. These problems, consequently, tend to fester and grow over time. For instance, while financial markets pushed corporate banks in the United States to confront their poor real estate loans in the late 1980s, Japanese banks spent much of the 1990s denying the existence of such loans on their books.[29]

Is there a way we can measure the effectiveness of alternative corporate governance systems? One suggestion is that corporate governance systems be measured on three dimensions—the capacity to restrict management's ability to obtain private benefits from control, to provide easy access to financial markets for firms that want capital, and the ease with which inefficient management is replaced. It can be argued that a market-based corporate governance system does a better job than alternative systems on all three counts.[30]

Choosing an Alternative Objective

Given its limitations, the easy answer would be to cast aside stock price maximization as an objective. The tough part is replacing it with another objective. It is not that there are no alternatives, but that the alternatives come with their own sets of problems and it is not at all obvious that there is a benefit to switching. This is especially true when the alternative objective is evaluated on the three criteria used to evaluate the wealth maximization objective: Is the objective clear and unambiguous? Does it come with a timely measure that can be used to evaluate success and failure? Does it create side costs that exceed the overall benefits? Let us consider three commonly offered alternatives to stock price maximization.

1. *Maximize Market Share*

   In the 1980s, Japanese firms inundated global markets with their products and focused their attention on increasing market share. Their apparent success at converting this market share to profits led other firms, including some in the United States, to also target market share as an objective. In concrete terms, this meant that investments that increased market share more were viewed more favorably than investments that increased them less. Proponents of this objective note that market share is observable and measurable like market price and does not require any of the assumptions about efficient financial markets that are needed to justify the stock price maximization objective.

---

[28]Many Korean industrial groups (called *chaebols*), which were patterned after the Japanese keiretsu, were pushed to the verge of bankruptcy in 1990s because one or two errant firms in the group made bad real estate loans or borrowed too much.

[29]S. N. Kaplan, 1997, "Corporate Governance and Corporate Performance, A Comparison of Germany, Japan and the United States," *Journal of Applied Corporate Finance,* 9(4), 86–93. He compares the U.S., German, and Japanese corporate governance systems. He finds that the U.S. system provides better incentives for firms performing well and that it is easier for companies in the United States to return cash to the stockholders.

[30]J. R. Macey, 1998, "Measuring the Effectiveness of Different Corporate Governance Systems: Towards a More Scientific Approach," *Journal of Applied Corporate Finance,* 10(4), 16–25.

Underlying the market share maximization objective is the belief (often un- stated) that higher market share will mean more pricing power and higher prof- its in the long run. If this is in fact true, maximizing market share is entirely con- sistent with the objective of maximizing firm value. However, if higher market share does not yield higher pricing power, and the increase in market share is accompanied by lower or even negative earnings, firms that concentrate on in- creasing market share can be worse off as a consequence. In fact, many of the same Japanese firms that were used by corporate strategists as their examples for why the focus on market share was a good one discovered the harsh down- side of this focus in the 1990s.

2. *Profit Maximization Objectives*

There are objectives that focus on profitability rather than value. The rationale for them is that profits can be measured more easily than value, and that higher profits translate into higher value in the long run. There are at least two prob- lems with these objectives. First, the emphasis on current profitability may result in short-term decisions that maximize profits now at the expense of long- term profits and value. Second, the notion that profits can be measured more precisely than value may be incorrect, given the leeway that accountants have to shift profits across periods.

In its more sophisticated forms, profit maximization is restated in terms of ac- counting returns (such as return on equity or capital) rather than dollar profits or even as excess returns (over a cost of capital). Although these variants may remove some of the problems associated with focusing on dollar profits next pe- riod, the problems with accounting measurements carry over into them as well.

3. *Size/Revenue Objectives*

There are a whole set of objectives that have little to do with stockholder wealth but focus instead on the size of the firm. In the 1970s, for instance, firms like Gulf & Western and ITT, with strong CEOs at their helms, were built up through acquisitions into giant conglomerates. There seemed to be no strategic imperative to these acquisitions, other than the desire on the part of the CEOs to increase the sizes of their corporate empires. Empire building may no longer be in vogue, but there have been cases where corporations have made decisions that increase their size and perceived power at the expense of stockholder wealth and profitability.

MAXIMIZE STOCK PRICES: SALVAGING A FLAWED OBJECTIVE

The alternatives to stock price maximization—a corporate governance system build around self-governance or choosing a different objective like maximizing market share—have their own limitations. In this section, we consider the case for salvaging stock price maximization as an objective but consider ways we can reduce some of the problems highlighted in the earlier section. In particular, we consider ways we can reduce the conflicts of interest between stockholders, bondholders, and man- agers and the potential for market failures. We also present an argument for stock price maximization based on the market's capacity to correct systematic mistakes quickly and effectively.

Conflict Resolution: Reducing Agency Problems

If the conflicts between stockholders, managers, and bondholders lie at the heart of the problems with stock price maximization, reducing these conflicts should make it a more palatable objective. In this section, we examine the linkages between stockholders and managers, stockholders and bondholders, firms and financial markets, and firms and society and look at how best we can reduce the side costs to maximizing stock prices.

Stockholders and Managers

There are clearly conflicts of interests between stockholders and managers, and the traditional mechanisms for stockholder control—annual meetings and boards of directors—often fail at their role of discipline management. This does not mean, however, that the chasm between the two groups is too wide to be bridged, either by closing the gap between their interests or by increasing stockholder power over managers.

Making Managers Think More Like Stockholders

As long as managers have interests that are distinct and different from the interests of the stockholders they serve, there is potential for conflict. One way to reduce this conflict is to provide managers with an equity stake in the firms they manage, either by providing them with stock or **warrants** on the stock. If this is done, the benefits that accrue to management from higher stock prices may provide an inducement to maximize stock prices.

There is a downside to doing this, which is that although it reduces the conflict of interest between stockholders and managers, it may exacerbate the other conflicts of interest highlighted in the prior section. It may increase the potential for expropriation of wealth from bondholders and the probability that misleading information will be conveyed to financial markets.

There is a final distinction that we need to make between stock-based compensation and warrant-based compensation. As we will see in the coming chapters, options can sometimes become more valuable as businesses become more risky. Consequently, managers who have substantial option holdings and little in common stock may be tempted to take on far more risk than would be desired by other shareholders in the firm.

Warrants: A security issued by a company that provides the holder with the right to buy a share of stock in the company at a fixed price during the life of the warrant.

2.7 STOCKHOLDER INTERESTS, MANAGERIAL INTERESTS, AND MANAGEMENT BUYOUTS

In a management buyout, the managers of the firm buy out the existing stockholders and make the company a private firm. Is this a way of reducing the conflict of interests between stockholders and managers? Explain.

☐ Yes

☐ No

More Effective Boards of Directors

In the past few years, there have been encouraging trends both in the composition and the behavior of boards, making them more effective advocates for stockholders. Korn-Ferry's survey of boards of directors at 900 large U.S. corporations in 1998 revealed the following.

- ***Boards have become smaller over time***   The median size of a board of directors has decreased from a range of between sixteen and twenty in the 1970s to between nine and eleven in 1998. The smaller boards are less unwieldy and more effective than larger boards.

- ***There are fewer insiders on boards***   In contrast to the six or more insiders that many boards had in the 1970s, only two directors in most boards in 1998 were insiders.

- ***Directors are increasingly compensated with stock and options in the company, instead of cash***   In 1973, only 4 percent of directors received compensation in the form of stock or options, whereas 78 percent did so in 1998. This stock compensation makes it more likely that directors will think like stockholders.

- ***More directors are identified and selected by a nominating committee rather than being chosen by the CEO of the firm***   In 1998, 75 percent of boards had nominating committees; the comparable statistic in 1973 was 2 percent.

Is there a payoff to a more active board? MacAvoy and Millstein (1998) present evidence that companies with more activist boards, where activism was measured based on indicators of board behavior, earned much higher returns on their capital than firms that had less active boards.[31]

Increasing Stockholder Power

There are many ways in which stockholder power over management can be increased. The first is to provide stockholders with better and more updated information, so that they can make informed judgments on how well the management is doing. The second is to have a large stockholder become part of incumbent management and have a direct role in decisions that the firm makes. The third is to have more "activist" institutional stockholders, who play a larger role in issues such as the composition of the board of directors, the question of whether to pass antitakeover amendments, and overall management policy. In recent years, some institutional investors have used their considerable power to pressure managers into becoming more responsive to their needs. Among the most aggressive of these investors has been CALPERS, one of the largest institutional investors in the country. Unfortunately, the largest institutional investors—mutual funds and pension fund companies—have remained largely apathetic.

It is also critical that institutional constraints on stockholders exercising their power be reduced. All common shares should have the same voting rights, state restrictions on takeovers have to be eliminated, and shareholder voting should be

---

[31]See P. W. MacAvoy, and I. M. Millstein, 1998, "The Active Board of Directors and its Effect on the Performance of Large Publicly Traded Companies," *Columbia Law Review*, 98, 1283–1322.

simplified. The legal system should come down hard on managers (and boards of directors) who fail to do their fiduciary duty. Ultimately, though, stockholders have to awaken to the reality that the responsibility for monitoring management falls to them. Like voters in a democracy, shareholders get the managers they deserve.

IN PRACTICE: THE LEGAL REMEDY

Can we legislate good corporate governance? Whether we can or not, legislators often try to fix what they see as significant corporate governance problems by passing laws. This is especially true in the aftermath of scandals, where stockholders, bondholders, and society bear the cost of managerial incompetence. As an example, after the accounting scandals in the United States in 2001 and 2002, the Sarbanes-Oxley Act was passed with the explicit intent of preventing future Enrons and Worldcoms. The act was far-reaching in its coverage, but large parts of it related to the composition of corporate boards and the responsibilities of boards. Without going into the provisions of the law, the objective was to create more transparency in the way boards were created, increase the independence of the directors from the CEO, and increase legal responsibilities of directors for managerial actions. Sarbanes-Oxley also substantially increased the information disclosure requirements for firms.

The other legal remedy that stockholders have is to sue the managers when they feel that they have been misled about future prospects. In recent years, class action lawsuits against companies whose stock prices have plummeted have multiplied, and plaintiffs have won large awards in some of these suits.

Although the right to sue when wronged may seem fundamental, legal remedies are likely to be both imperfect and very expensive ways of bringing about better corporate governance. In fact, the cost of complying with Sarbanes-Oxley has been substantial, and the only group that consistently is enriched by lawsuits is trial lawyers. ∎

2.8   INSIDE STOCKHOLDERS VERSUS OUTSIDE STOCKHOLDERS

There are companies like Microsoft where a large stockholder (Bill Gates) is the CEO and hence an insider. Is it possible that what is in Bill Gates's best interests as an "inside" stockholder may not be in the interests of a stockholder on the outside?

☐   Yes. Their interests may deviate.

☐   No. Their interests will not deviate.

If yes, provide an example of an action that may benefit the inside stockholder but not the outside stockholder.

The Threat of a Takeover

The perceived excesses of many takeovers in the 1980s drew attention to the damage created to employees and society by some of them. In movies and books, the raiders who were involved in these takeovers were portrayed as barbarians, while the firms being taken over were viewed as hapless victims. Although this may have been accurate in some cases, the reality was that most companies that were taken over deserved it. One analysis found that target firms in hostile takeovers in 1985 and 1986 were generally much less profitable than their competitors, had provided subpar returns to their stockholders, and had managers with significantly lower holdings of the equity. In short, badly managed firms were much more likely to become targets of hostile takeover bids.[32]

An implication of this finding is that takeovers operate as a disciplinary mechanism, keeping managers in check, by introducing a cost to bad management. Often, the very threat of a takeover is sufficient to make firms restructure their assets and become more responsive to stockholder concerns. It is not surprising, therefore, that legal attempts to regulate and restrict takeovers have had negative consequences for stock prices.

2.9 HOSTILE ACQUISITIONS: WHOM DO THEY HURT?

Given the information presented in this chapter, which of the following groups is the most likely to be protected by a law banning hostile takeovers?

☐ Stockholders of target companies

☐ Managers and employees of well-run target companies

☐ Managers and employees of badly run target companies

☐ Society

ILLUSTRATION 2.6 Restive Stockholders and Responsive Managers: The Disney Case
In 1997, Disney was widely perceived as having an imperial CEO in Michael Eisner and a captive board of directors. After a series of missteps including the hiring and firing of Michael Ovitz and bloated pay packages, Disney stockholders were restive, but there were no signs of an impending revolt at that time. As Disney's stock price slid between 1997 and 2000, though, this changed as more institutional investors made clear their displeasure with the state of corporate governance at the company. As talk of hostile takeovers and proxy fights filled the air, Disney was forced to respond. In its 2002 annual report, Disney listed the following corporate governance changes:

- Required at least two executive sessions of the board, without the CEO or other members of management present, each year.

- Created the position of management presiding director and appointed Senator George Mitchell to lead those executive sessions and assist in setting the work agenda of the board.

- Adopted a new and more rigorous definition of director independence.

- Required that a substantial majority of the board be made up of directors meeting the new independence standards.

- Provided for a reduction in committee size and the rotation of committee and chairmanship assignments among independent directors.

---

[32]A. Bhide, 1989, "The Causes and Consequences of Hostile Takeovers," *Journal of Applied Corporate Finance*, 2, 36–59.

- Added new provisions for management succession planning and evaluations of both management and board performance.

- Provided for enhanced continuing education and training for board members.

What changed between 1997 and 2002? Although we can point to an overall shift in the market toward stronger corporate governance, the biggest factor was poor stock price performance. The truth is that stockholders are often willing to overlook poor corporate governance and dictatorial CEOs if stock prices are going up but are less tolerant when stock prices decrease.

Toward the end of 2003, Roy Disney and Stanley Gold resigned from Disney's board of directors, complaining both about the failures of Eisner and about his autocratic style.[33] When the board of directors announced early in 2004 that Eisner would receive a $6.25 million bonus for his performance in 2003, some institutional investors voiced their opposition. Soon after, Comcast announced a hostile acquisition bid for Disney. At Disney's annual meeting in February 2004, Disney and Gold raised concerns about Eisner's management style and the still-captive board of directors; 43 percent of the stockholders voted against Eisner as director at the meeting. In a sense, the stars were lining up for the perfect corporate governance storm at Disney, with Eisner in the eye of the storm. Soon after the meeting, Disney announced that Eisner would step down as chairman of the board even though he would continue as CEO until his term expired in 2006.

IN PRACTICE: PROXY FIGHTS

In the section on annual meetings, we pointed out that many investors who are unable to come to annual meetings also fail to return their proxies, thus implicitly giving incumbent managers their votes. In a proxy fight, activist investors who want to challenge incumbent managers approach individual stockholders in the company and solicit their proxies, which they then can use in votes against the management slate.

In one very public and expensive proxy fight in 2002, David Hewlett, who was sitting on the board of Hewlett Packard (HP) at the time, tried to stop HP from buying Compaq by soliciting proxies from HP stockholders. After eight months of acrimony, HP finally won the fight with the bare minimum 51 percent of the votes. How did Hewlett come so close to stopping the deal? One advantage he had was that the Hewlett and Packard families owned a combined 18 percent of the total number of shares outstanding. The other was that Hewlett's position on the board and his access to internal information gave him a great deal of credibility when it came to fighting for the votes of institutional investors. The fact that he failed, even with these advantages, shows how difficult it is to win at a proxy fight. Even a failed proxy fight, though, often has the salutary effect of awakening incumbent managers to the need to at least consider what shareholders want. ■

---

[33]You can read Roy Disney's letter of resignation on the Web site for this book.

Stockholders and Bondholders

The conflict of interests between stockholders and bondholders can lead to actions that transfer wealth to the former from the latter. There are ways bondholders can obtain at least partial protection against some of these actions.

The Effect of Covenants

The most direct way for bondholders to protect themselves is to write in covenants in their bond agreements specifically prohibiting or restricting actions that may make them worse off. Many bond (and bank loan) agreements have covenants that do the following.

1. ***Restrict the firm's investment policy***   Investing in riskier businesses than anticipated can lead to a transfer of wealth from bondholders to stockholders. Some bond agreements put restrictions on where firms can invest and how much risk they can take on in their new investments, specifically to provide bondholders with the power to veto actions that are not in their best interests.

2. ***Restrict dividend policy***   In general, increases in dividends increase stock prices while decreasing bond prices because they reduce the cash available to the firm to meet debt payments. Many bond agreements restrict dividend policy by tying dividend payments to earnings.

3. ***Restrict additional leverage***   Some bond agreements require firms to get the consent of existing lenders before borrowing more money. This is done to protect the interests of existing secured bondholders.

Although covenants can be effective at protecting bondholders against some abuses, they do come with a price tag. In particular, firms may find themselves having to turn down profitable investments because of bondholder-imposed constraints and having to pay (indirectly through higher interest rates) for the legal and monitoring costs associated with the constraints.

Taking an Equity Stake

Because the primary reason for the conflict of interests between stockholders and bondholders lies in the nature of their claims, another way that bondholders can reduce the conflict of interest is by owning an equity stake in the firm. This can take the form of buying equity in the firm at the same time as they lend money to it, or it can be accomplished by making bonds convertible into stock at the option of the bondholders. In either case, bondholders who feel that equity investors are enriching themselves at the lenders' expense can become stockholders and share in the spoils.

Bond Innovations

In the aftermath of several bond market debacles in the late 1980s, bondholders became increasingly creative in protecting themselves with new types of bonds. Although we will consider these innovations in more detail later in this book, consider the example of puttable bonds. Unlike a conventional bond, where you are constrained to hold the bond to maturity, the holders of a puttable bond can put the bond back to the issuing company and get the face value of the bond if the company violates the conditions of the bond. For instance, a sudden increase in borrowing by the company or a drop in its bond rating can trigger this action.

Firms and Financial Markets

The information that firms convey to financial markets is often erroneous and sometimes misleading. The market price that emerges from financial markets can be wrong, partly because of inefficiencies in markets and partly because of the errors in the information. There are no easy or quick-fix solutions to these problems. In the long run, however, there are actions that will improve information quality and reduce deviations between price and value.

Improving the Quality of Information

Although regulatory bodies like the SEC can require firms to reveal more information and penalize those that provide misleading and fraudulent information, the quality of information cannot be improved with information disclosure laws alone. In particular, firms will always have a vested interest in when and what information they reveal to markets. To provide balance, therefore, an active external market for information has to exist where analysts who are not hired and fired by the firms that they follow collect and disseminate information. These analysts are just as likely to make mistakes as the firm, but they presumably should have a greater incentive to unearth bad news about the firm and disseminate that information to their clients. For this system to work, analysts have to be given free rein to search for good as well as bad news and make positive or negative judgments about a firm.

Making Markets More Efficient

Just as better information cannot be legislated into existence, markets cannot be made more efficient by edict. In fact, there is widespread disagreement on what is required to make markets more efficient. At the minimum, these are necessary (though not sufficient) conditions for more efficient markets:

a. Trading should be both inexpensive and easy. The higher transactions costs are, and the more difficult it is to execute a trade, the more likely it is that markets will be inefficient.

b. There should be free and wide access to information about firms.

c. Investors should be allowed to benefit when they pick the right stocks to invest in and to pay the price when they make mistakes.

Restrictions imposed on trading, although well intentioned, often lead to market inefficiencies. For instance, restricting short sales, where investors who don't own a stock can borrow and sell it if they feel it is overpriced, may seem like good public policy, but it can create a scenario in which negative information about stocks cannot be reflected adequately in prices.

Firms and Society

There will always be social costs associated with actions taken by firms, operating in their own best interests. The basic conundrum is as follows: Social costs cannot be ignored in making decisions, but they are also too nebulous to be factored explicitly into analyses. One solution is for firms to maximize firm or stockholder value, subject to a good citizen constraint, where attempts are made to minimize or alleviate social costs, even though the firm may not be under any legal obligation to do so. The problem with this approach, of course, is that the definition of a good citizen is likely to vary from firm to firm and from manager to manager.

Ultimately, the most effective way to make companies more socially responsible is to make it in their best economic interests to behave well. This can occur in two ways. First, firms that are construed as socially irresponsible could lose customers and profits. This was the galvanizing factor behind a number of specialty retailers in the United States disavowing the use of sweatshops and underage labor in other countries in making their products. Second, investors might avoid buying stock in these companies. As an example, many U.S. college and state pension plans have started reducing or eliminating their holding of tobacco stocks to reflect their concerns about the health effects of tobacco. In fact, investors now have access to "ethical mutual funds," which invest only in companies that meet a social consciousness threshold. Figure 2.3 summarizes the ways in which we can reduce potential side costs from stock price maximization.

Figure 2.3   Maximize Stock Prices but Minimize Side Costs

IN PRACTICE: CAN YOU ADD VALUE WHILE DOING GOOD?

Does doing social good hurt or help firms? On one side of this argument stand those who believe that firms that expend considerable resources to generate social good are misguided and are doing their stockholders a disservice. On the other side are those who believe that socially conscious firms are rewarded by consumers (with higher sales) and by investors (with higher values). The evidence is mixed and will undoubtedly disappoint both sides.

- Studies indicate that the returns earned by stockholders in socially conscious firms are no different than the returns earned by stockholders in the rest of the market. Studies of ethical mutual funds find that they neither lag nor lead other mutual funds.

- There is clearly a substantial economic cost borne by companies that are viewed by society as beyond the pale when it comes to creating social costs. Tobacco firms, for instance, have seen stock prices slide as investors avoid their shares and profits are hurt by legal costs.

- When firms are profitable and doing well, stockholders are usually willing to give managers the flexibility to use company money to do social good. Few investors in Microsoft begrudged its 1998 decision to give free computers to public libraries around the country. In firms that are doing badly, stockholders tend to be much more resistant to spending company money in mending society's ills.

Summarizing this evidence, we can draw some conclusions. First, a firm's foremost obligation is to stay financially healthy and increase value; firms that are losing money cannot afford to be charitable. Second, firms that create large social costs pay a high price in the long run. Finally, managers should not keep stockholders in the dark about the cost of meeting social obligations; after all, it is the stockholders' money that is being used for the purpose. ■

An Argument for Stockholder Wealth Maximization

Let us start off by conceding that all of the alternatives—choosing a different corporate governance system, picking an alternative objective and maximizing stock price with constraints—have limitations and lead to problems. The questions then become how each alternative deals with mistakes and how quickly errors get corrected. This is where stock price maximization does better than the alternatives. It is the only one of the three that is self-correcting, in the sense that excesses by any stakeholder attract responses in three waves.

1. *Market reaction*   The first and most immediate reaction comes from financial markets. Consider again the turmoil created when we have well-publicized failures like Enron. Not only did the market punish Enron (by knocking its stock and bond prices down) but it punished other companies that it perceived as being exposed to the same problems as Enron—weak corporate governance and opaque financial statements—by discounting their values as well.

2. *Group activism*   Following on the heels of the market reaction to any excess is outrage on the part of those who feel that they have been victimized by it. In

response to management excesses in the 1980s, we saw an increase in the number of activist investors and hostile acquisitions, reminding managers that there are limits to their power. In the aftermath of well-publicized scandals in the late 1980s where loopholes in lending agreements were exploited by firms, banks and bondholders began playing more active roles in management.

3. *Market innovations*   Markets often come up with innovative solutions to problems. In response to the corporate governance scandals in 2002 and 2003, Institutional Shareholder Services began scoring corporate boards on independence and effectiveness and offering these scores to investors. After the accounting scandals of the same period, the demand for forensic accounting, where accountants go over financial statements looking for clues of accounting malfeasance, increased dramatically. The bond market debacles of the 1980s gave birth to dozens of innovative bonds designed to protect bondholders. Even in the area of social costs, there are markets that have developed to quantify the cost.

Note that we have not mentioned another common reaction to scandal, which is legislation. Although the motives for passing new laws to prevent future excesses may be pure, laws are blunt instruments that are often ineffective for three reasons. First, they are almost never timely. It takes far more time for legislation to be put together than for markets to react, and the outrage has often subsided before the laws becomes effective. Second, laws written to prevent past mistakes often prove ineffective at preventing future mistakes, as circumstances change. Third, laws often have unintended consequences, whereby in the process of correcting one distortion, they create new ones.

A POSTSCRIPT: THE LIMITS OF CORPORATE FINANCE

Corporate finance has come in for more than its fair share of criticism in the past decade or so. There are many who argue that the failures of corporate America can be traced to its dependence on stock price maximization. Some of the criticism is justified and based on the limitations of a single-minded pursuit of stockholder wealth. Some of it, however, is based on a misunderstanding of what corporate finance is about.

Economics was once branded the gospel of Mammon, because of its emphasis on wealth. The descendants of those critics have labeled corporate finance as unethical, because of its emphasis on the bottom line and market prices. In restructuring and liquidations, it is true that value maximization for stockholders may mean that other stakeholders, such as customers and employees, lose out. In most cases, however, decisions that increase market value also make customers and employees better off. Furthermore, if the firm is really in trouble, either because it is being undersold by competitors or because its products are technologically obsolete, the choice is not between liquidation and survival but between a speedy resolution, which is what corporate financial theory would recommend, and a slow death, while the firm declines over time and costs society considerably more in the process.

The conflict between wealth maximization for the firm and social welfare is the genesis for the attention paid to ethics in business schools. There will never be an objective set of decision rules that perfectly factor in societal concerns, simply because many of these concerns are difficult to quantify and are subjective. Thus, corporate financial theory, in some sense, assumes that decision makers will not make decisions that create large social costs. This assumption that decision makers are for the most part ethical and will not create unreasonable costs for society or for other stakeholders is unstated but underlies corporate financial theory. When it is violated, it exposes corporate financial theory to ethical and moral criticism, though the criticism may be better directed at the violators.

2.10   WHAT DO YOU THINK THE OBJECTIVE OF THE FIRM SHOULD BE?

Having heard the pros and cons of the different objectives, the following statement best describes where I stand in terms of the right objective for decision making in a business.

☐ Maximize stock price or stockholder wealth, with no constraints

☐ Maximize stock price or stockholder wealth, with constraints on being a good social citizen

☐ Maximize profits or profitability

☐ Maximize market share

☐ Maximize revenues

☐ Maximize social good

☐ None of the above

CONCLUSION

Although the objective in corporate finance is to maximize firm value, in practice we often adopt the narrower objective of maximizing a firm's stock price. As a measurable and unambiguous measure of a firm's success, stock price offers a clear target for managers in the course of their decision-making.

Stock price maximization as the only objective can be problematic when the different players in the firm—stockholders, managers, lenders, and society—all have different interests and work at cross-purposes. These differences, which result in agency costs, can result in managers who put their interests over those of the stockholders who hired them, stockholders who try to take advantage of lenders, firms that try to mislead financial markets, and decisions that create large costs for society. In the presence of these agency problems, there are many who argue for an alternative to stock price maximization. Although this path is alluring, each of the alternatives, including using a different system of corporate governance or a different objective, comes with its own set of limitations.

Given the limitations of the alternatives, stock price maximization is the best of a set of imperfect choices for two reasons. First, we can reduce the agency problems between the different groups substantially by trying to align the interests of stockholders, managers, and lenders (using both rewards and punishment) and by punishing firms that lie to financial markets or create large social costs. Second, stock price maximization as an objective is self-correcting. In other words, excesses by any one of the groups (whether it be managers or stockholders) lead to reactions by the other groups that reduce the likelihood of the behavior being repeated in future periods.

I. CORPORATE GOVERNANCE ANALYSIS

Objective: To analyze the corporate governance structure of the firm and assess where the power in the firm lies—with incumbent management or with stockholders in the firm?

Key Questions

- Is this a company where there is a separation between management and owner-ship? If so, how responsive is management to stockholders?
- Is there a potential conflict between stockholders and lenders to the firm? If so, how is it managed?
- How does this firm interact with financial markets? How do markets get infor-mation about the firm?
- How does this firm view its social obligations and manage its image in society?

Framework for Analysis

1. *The Chief Executive Officer*

- Who is the CEO of the company? How long has he or she been CEO?
- If it is a "family-run" company, is the CEO part of the family? If not, what career path did the CEO take to get to the top? (Did he or she come from within the organization or from outside?)
- How much did the CEO make last year? What form did the compensation take (salary, bonus, and option components)?
- How much stock and options in the company does the CEO own?

2. *The Board of Directors*

- Who is on the board of directors of the company? How long have they served as directors?
- How many of the directors are inside directors?
- How many of the directors have other connections to the firm (as suppliers, clients, customers, etc.)?
- How many of the directors are CEOs of other companies?
- Do any of the directors have large stockholdings or represent those who do?

3. *Bondholder Concerns*

- Does the firm have any publicly traded debt?

- Are there are bond covenants (that you can uncover) that have been imposed on the firm as part of the borrowing?
- Do any of the bonds issued by the firm come with special protections against stockholder expropriation?

4. *Financial Market Concerns*

- How many analysts follow the firm?
- How much trading volume is there on this stock?

5. *Societal Constraints*

- What does the firm say about its social responsibilities?
- Does the firm have a particularly good or bad reputation as a corporate citizen?
- If it does, how has it earned this reputation?
- If the firm has been a recent target of social criticism, how has it responded?

Information Sources

For firms that are incorporated in the United States, information on the CEO and the board of directors is primarily in the filings made by the firm with the SEC. In particular, the 14-DEF will list the directors in the firm, their relationship with the firm, and details on compensation for both directors and top managers. You can also get information on trading done by insiders from the SEC filings. For firms that are not listed in the United States, this information is much more difficult to obtain. However, the absence of readily accessible information on directors and top management is revealing about the power that resides with incumbent managers.

Information on a firm's relationships with bondholders usually resides in the firm's bond agreements and loan covenants. Although this information may not always be available to the public, the presence of constraints shows up indirectly in the firm's bond ratings and when the firm issues new bonds.

The list of analysts following a firm can be obtained from publications, such as the *Nelson Directory of Securities Research*. For larger and more heavily followed firms, the archives of financial publications (the *Financial Times, Wall Street Journal, Forbes, Barron's*) can be useful sources of information.

Finally, the reputation of a firm as a corporate citizen is the toughest area to obtain clear information on, because it is only the outliers (the worst and the best corporate citizens) that make the news. The proliferation of socially responsible mutual funds, however, does give us a window on those firms that pass the tests (arbitrary though they sometimes are) imposed by these funds for a firm to be viewed as socially responsible.

 Online sources of information: Check the information at **www.stern.nyu.edu/~adamodar/cfin2E/project/data.htm**.

PROBLEMS AND QUESTIONS

1. There is a conflict of interest between stockholders and managers. In theory, stockholders are expected to exercise control over managers through the annual meeting or the board of directors. In practice, why might these disciplinary mechanisms not work?

2. Stockholders can transfer wealth from bondholders through a variety of actions. How would the following actions by stockholders transfer wealth from bondholders?
   a. An increase in dividends
   b. A leveraged buyout
   c. Acquiring a risky business

   How would bondholders protect themselves against these actions?

3. Stock prices are much too volatile for financial markets to be efficient. Comment.

4. Maximizing stock prices does not make sense because investors focus on short-term results and not on the long-term consequences. Comment.

5. There are some corporate strategists who have suggested that firms focus on maximizing market share rather than market prices. When might this strategy work, and when might it fail?

6. Antitakeover amendments can be in the best interests of stockholders. Under what conditions is this likely to be true?

7. Companies outside the United States often have two classes of stock outstanding. One class of shares is voting and is held by the incumbent managers of the firm. The other class is nonvoting and represents the bulk of traded shares. What are the consequences for corporate governance?

8. In recent years, top managers have been given large packages of options, giving them the right to buy stock in the firm at a fixed price. Will these compensation schemes make managers more responsive to stockholders? Why or why not? Are lenders to the firm affected by these compensation schemes?

9. *Reader's Digest* has voting and nonvoting shares. About 70 percent of the voting shares are held by charitable institutions, which are headed by the CEO of *Reader's Digest*. Assume that you are a large holder of the nonvoting shares. Would you be concerned about this set-up? What are some of the actions you might push the firm to take to protect your interests?

10. In Germany, large banks are often large lenders and large equity investors in the same firm. For instance, Deutsche Bank is the largest stockholder in Daimler Chrysler, as well as its largest lender. What are some of the potential conflicts that you see in these dual holdings?

11. It is often argued that managers, when asked to maximize stock price, have to choose between being socially responsible and carrying out their fiduciary duty. Do you agree? Can you provide an example where social responsibility and firm value maximization go hand in hand?

12. Assume that you are advising a Turkish firm on corporate financial questions, and that you do not believe that the Turkish stock market is efficient. Would you recommend stock price maximization as the objective? If not, what would you recommend?

13. It has been argued by some that convertible bonds (i.e., bonds that are convertible into stock at the option of the bondholders) provide one form of protection against expropriation by stockholders. On what is this argument based?

14. Societies attempt to keep private interests in line by legislating against behavior that might create social costs (such as polluting the water). If the legislation is comprehensive enough, does the problem of social costs cease to exist? Why or why not?

15. One of the arguments made for having legislation restricting hostile takeovers is that unscrupulous speculators may take over well-run firms and destroy them for personal gain. Allowing for the possibility that this could happen, do you think that this is sensible? If so, why? If not, why not?

CHAPTER 3

THE BASICS OF RISK

Risk, in traditional terms, is viewed as a negative and something to be avoided. Webster's dictionary, for instance, defines risk as "exposing to danger or hazard." The Chinese symbols for risk, reproduced here, give a much better description of risk.

The first symbol is the symbol for danger, and the second is the symbol for opportunity, making risk a mix of danger and opportunity. It illustrates very clearly the trade-off that every investor and business has to make—between the higher rewards

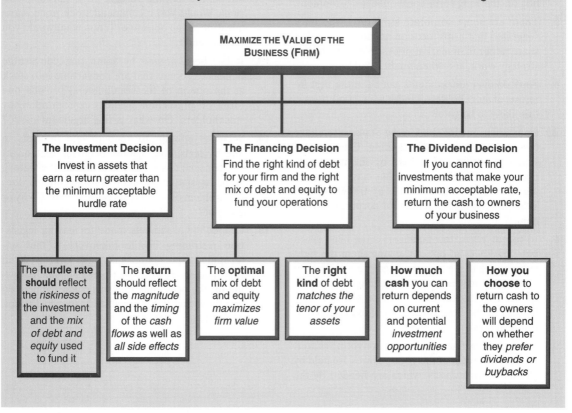

that potentially come with new opportunities and the higher risk that has to be borne as a consequence of the danger. The key test in finance is to ensure that when an investor is exposed to risk, he or she is appropriately rewarded for taking this risk.

In this chapter, we will lay the foundations for analyzing risk in corporate finance and present alternative models for measuring risk and converting these risk measures into acceptable hurdle rates.

MOTIVATION AND PERSPECTIVE IN ANALYZING RISK

Why do we need a model that measures risk and estimates expected return? A good model for risk and return provides us with tools to measure the risk in any investment and uses that measure to come up with the appropriate expected return on that investment; this expected return provides the hurdle rate in project analysis.

What makes the measurement of risk and expected return so challenging is that it can vary depending on whose perspective we adopt. When analyzing Disney's risk, for instance, we can measure it from the viewpoint of Disney's managers. Alternatively, we can argue that Disney's equity is owned by its stockholders and that it is their perspective on risk that should matter. Disney's stockholders, many of whom hold the stock as one investment in a larger portfolio, might perceive the risk in Disney very differently from Disney's managers, who might have the bulk of their capital, human and financial, invested in the firm. In this chapter, we will argue that risk in an equity investment has to be perceived through the eyes of investors in the firm. Because firms like Disney have thousands of investors, often with very different perspectives, we will go further. We will assert that risk has to be measured from the perspective of not just any investor in the stock, but of the *marginal investor,* defined to be the investor most likely to be trading on the stock at any given point in time. The objective in corporate finance is the maximization of firm value and stock price. If we want to stay true to this objective, we have to consider the viewpoint of those who set the stock prices, and they are the marginal investors.

Finally, the risk in a company can be viewed very differently by investors in its stock (equity investors) and by lenders to the firm (bondholders and bankers). Equity investors who benefit from upside as well as downside tend to take a much more sanguine view of risk than lenders who have limited upside but potentially high downside. We will consider how to measure equity risk in the first part of the chapter and risk from the perspective of lenders in the latter half of the chapter.

We will be presenting a number of different risk and return models in this chapter. To evaluate the relative strengths of these models, it is worth reviewing the characteristics of a good risk and return model.

1. It should come up with a measure of risk that applies to all assets and not just to a few.
2. It should clearly delineate what types of risk are rewarded and what are not and provide a rationale for the delineation.

3. It should come up with standardized risk measures. In other words, an investor presented with a risk measure for an individual asset should be able to draw conclusions about whether the asset is above-average or below-average risk.

4. It should translate the measure of risk into a rate of return that the investor should demand as compensation for bearing the risk.

5. It should work well not only at explaining past returns but also in predicting future expected returns.

EQUITY RISK AND EXPECTED RETURNS

To understand how risk is viewed in corporate finance, we present the analysis in three steps. First, we will define risk in terms of the distribution of actual returns around an expected return. Second, we will differentiate between risk that is specific to an investment or a few investments and risk that affects a much wider cross-section of investments. We will argue that when the marginal investor is well diversified, it is only the latter risk, called market risk, which will be rewarded. Third, we will look at alternative models for measuring this market risk and the expected returns that go with it.

I. Measuring Risk

Investors who buy an asset expect to make a return over the time horizon that they will hold the asset. The actual return that they make over this holding period may by very different from the expected return, and this is where the risk comes in. Consider an investor with a one-year time horizon buying a one-year Treasury bill (or any other default-free one-year bond) with a 5 percent expected return. At the end of the one-year holding period, the actual return that this investor would have on this investment will always be 5 percent, which is equal to the expected return. The return distribution for this investment is shown in Figure 3.1.

Figure 3.1   Returns on Risk-Free Investment

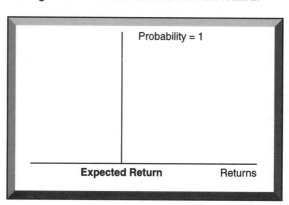

Figure 3.2 Probability Distribution for Risky Investments

This is a riskless investment, at least in nominal terms.[1]

To provide a contrast, consider an investor who invests in Disney. This investor, having done her research, may conclude that she can make an expected return of 30 percent on Disney over her one-year holding period. The actual return over this period will almost certainly not be equal to 30 percent; it might be much greater or much lower. The distribution of returns on this investment is illustrated in Figure 3.2.

In addition to the expected return, an investor now has to consider the following. First, the spread of the actual returns around the expected return is captured by the **variance** or *standard deviation* of the distribution; the greater the deviation of the actual returns from expected returns, the greater the variance. Second, the bias toward positive or negative returns is captured by the *skewness* of the distribution. The distribution in Figure 3.2 is positively skewed, because there is a greater likelihood of large positive returns than large negative returns. Third, the shape of the tails of the distribution is measured by the *kurtosis* of the distribution; fatter tails lead to higher kurtosis. In investment terms, this captures the tendency of the price of this investment to jump in either direction.

Variance in Returns: This is a measure of the squared difference between the actual returns and the expected returns on an investment.

In the special case of the normal distribution, returns are symmetric and investors do not have to worry about skewness and kurtosis, because there is no skewness and a normal distribution is defined to have a kurtosis of zero. In that case, it can be argued that investments can be measured on only two dimensions: (1) the "expected return" on the investment comprises the reward, and (2) the variance in anticipated

---

[1]Inflation takes a bite out of the nominal returns. To the extent that inflation is unpredictable, the real return can be uncertain even when the nominal return is not. In the example, for instance, an inflation rate of 3 percent will leave the investor with a real return on 2 percent, but an inflation rate of 6 percent will result in a real return of −1 percent.

Figure 3.3 Return Distribution Comparisons

returns makes up the risk on the investment. Figure 3.3 illustrates the return distributions on two investments with symmetric returns.

In this scenario, an investor faced with a choice between two investments with the same standard deviation but different expected returns will always pick the one with the higher expected return.

In the more general case, where distributions are neither symmetric nor normal, it is still conceivable (though unlikely) that investors still choose between investments on the basis of only the expected return and the variance, if they possess utility functions that allow them to do so.[2] It is far more likely, however, that they prefer positively skewed distributions to negatively skewed ones and distributions with a lower likelihood of jumps (lower kurtosis) over those with a higher likelihood of jumps (higher kurtosis). In this world, investors will trade off the good (higher expected returns and more positive skewness) against the bad (higher variance and kurtosis) in making investments. Among the risk and return models that we will be examining, one (the capital asset pricing model or the CAPM) explicitly requires that choices be made only in terms of expected returns and variances. Although it does ignore the skewness and kurtosis, it is not clear how much of a factor these additional moments of the distribution are in determining expected returns.

We should note that the return moments that we run into in practice are almost always estimated using past returns rather than future returns. The assumption we are making when we use historical variances is that past return distributions are good indicators of future return distributions. When this assumption is violated, as is the case when the asset's characteristics have changed significantly over time, the historical estimates may not be good measures of risk.

---

[2]A utility function is a way of summarizing investor preferences into a generic term called utility on the basis of some choice variables. In this case, for instance, investor utility or satisfaction is stated as a function of wealth. By doing so, we effectively can answer such questions as: Will an investor be twice as happy if he or she has twice as much wealth? Does each marginal increase in wealth lead to less additional utility than the prior marginal increase? In one specific form of this function, the quadratic utility function, the entire utility of an investor can be compressed into the expected wealth measure and the standard deviation in that wealth, which provides a justification for the use of a framework in which only the expected return (mean) and its standard deviation (variance) matter.

Figure 3.4   Returns on Disney Stock, 1999–2003

3.1   Do You Live in a Mean-Variance World?

Assume that you had to pick between two investments. They have the same expected return of 15 percent and the same standard deviation of 25 percent; however, investment A offers a very small possibility that you could quadruple your money, whereas investment B's highest possible payoff is a 60 percent return. Would you

☐   be indifferent between the two investments, because they have the same expected return and standard deviation?

☐   prefer investment A, because of the possibility of a high payoff?

☐   prefer investment B, because it is safer?

ILLUSTRATION **3.1   Calculation of Standard Deviation Using Historical Returns: Disney**
We collected the data on the returns we would have made on a monthly basis for every month from January 1999 to December 2003 on an investment in Disney stock. The monthly returns are graphed in Figure 3.4.

The average monthly return on Disney over the fifty-nine months was −0.07 percent. The standard deviation in monthly returns was 9.33 percent, and the variance in returns was 86.96 percent.[3] To convert monthly values to

---

[3]The variance is percent squared. In other words, if you stated the standard deviation of 9.33 percent in decimal terms, it would be 0.0933 but the variance of 89.96 percent would be 0.008996 in decimal terms.

annualized ones:

$$\text{Annualized Standard Deviation} = 9.33\% \times \sqrt{12} = 32.31\%$$

$$\text{Annualized Variance} = 86.96\% \times 12 = 1043.55\%$$

Without making comparisons to the standard deviations in stock returns of other companies, we cannot really draw any conclusions about the relative risk of Disney stock by just looking at its standard deviation.

There is a data set on the Web that summarizes standard deviations and variances of stocks in various sectors in the United States.

3.2 UPSIDE AND DOWNSIDE RISK

You are looking at the historical standard deviations over the past five years on two investments. Both have standard deviations of 35 percent in returns during the period, but one had an average return of −10 percent during the period, whereas the other had an average return of +40 percent during the period. Would you view them as equally risky?

☐ Yes

☐ No

Why do we not differentiate between upside risk and downside risk in finance?

IN PRACTICE: ESTIMATING ONLY DOWNSIDE RISK

The variance of a return distribution measures the deviation of actual returns from the expected return. In estimating the variance, we consider not only actual returns that fall below the average return (downside risk) but also those that lie above it (upside risk). As investors, we generally consider only the downside as risk. There is an alternative measure called the semi-variance that considers only downside risk. To estimate the semi-variance, we calculate the deviations of actual returns from the average return only if the actual return is less than the expected return; we ignore actual returns that are higher than the average return.

$$\text{Semi-Variance} = \sum_{t=1}^{t=n} \frac{(R_t - \text{Average Return})^2}{n}$$

where n = number of periods where actual return < average return.

With a normal distribution, the semi-variance will generate a value identical to the variance, but for any nonsymmetric distribution, the semi-variance will yield different values than the variance. In general, a stock that generates small positive returns in most periods, but very large negative returns in a few periods will have a semi-variance that is much higher than the variance. ■

II. Rewarded and Unrewarded Risk

Risk, as we defined it in the previous section, arises from the deviation of actual returns from expected returns. This deviation, however, can occur for any number of reasons, and these reasons can be classified into two categories—those that are specific to the investment being considered (called firm-specific risks) and those that apply across most or all investments (market risks).

The Components of Risk

When a firm makes an investment in a new asset or a project, the return on that investment can be affected by several variables, most of which are not under the direct control of the firm. Some of the risk comes directly from the investment, a portion from competition, some from shifts in the industry, some from changes in exchange rates, and some from macroeconomic factors. A portion of this risk, however, will be eliminated by the firm itself over the course of multiple investments and another portion by investors as they hold diversified portfolios.

The first source of risk is **project-specific;** an individual project may have higher or lower cash flows than expected, either because the firm misestimated the cash flows for that project or because of factors specific to that project. When firms take a large number of similar projects, it can be argued that much of this risk should be diversified away in the normal course of business. For instance, Disney, while considering making a new movie, exposes itself to estimation error—it may under- or overestimate the cost and time of making the movie, and may also err in its estimates of revenues from both theatrical release and the sale of merchandise. Because Disney releases several movies a year, it can be argued that some or much of this risk should be diversifiable across movies produced during the course of the year.[4]

Project Risk: Risk that affects only the project under consideration and may arise from factors specific to the project or estimation error.

The second source of risk is **competitive risk,** whereby the earnings and cash flows on a project are affected (positively or negatively) by the actions of competitors. A good project analysis will build in the expected reactions of competitors into estimates of profit margins and growth, but the actual actions taken by competitors may differ from these expectations. In most cases, this component of risk will affect more than one project and is therefore more difficult to diversify away in the normal course of business by the firm. Disney, for instance, in its analysis of revenues from its consumer product division, may err in its assessments of the strength and strategies of competitors like Toys 'R Us and Wal-Mart. Although Disney cannot diversify away its competitive risk, stockholders in Disney can, if they are willing to hold stock in the competitors.[5]

---

[4]To provide an illustration, Disney released *Treasure Planet,* an animated movie, in 2002, which cost $140 million to make and resulted in a $98 million write-off. A few months later, *Finding Nemo,* an animated Pixar/Disney movie, made hundreds of millions of dollars and became one of the biggest hits of 2003.

[5]Firms could conceivably diversify away competitive risk by acquiring their existing competitors. Doing so would expose them to attacks under antitrust laws, however, and would not eliminate the risk from as yet unannounced competitors.

Competitive Risk: The unanticipated effect on the cash flows in a project of competitor actions—these effects can be positive or negative.

The third source of risk is **industry-specific risk**—those factors that impact the earnings and cash flows of a specific industry. There are three sources of industry-specific risk. The first is *technology risk,* which reflects the effects of technologies that change or evolve in ways different from those expected when a project was originally analyzed. The second source is *legal risk,* which reflects the effect of changing laws and regulations. The third is *commodity risk,* which reflects the effects of price changes in commodities and services that are used or produced disproportionately by a specific industry. Disney, for instance, in assessing the prospects of its broadcasting division (Disney cable and ABC) is likely to be exposed to all three risks: to technology risk, as the lines between TV entertainment and the Internet are increasingly blurred by companies like Microsoft; to legal risk, as the laws governing broadcasting change; and to commodity risk, as the costs of making new TV programs change over time. A firm cannot diversify away its industry-specific risk without diversifying across industries, either with new projects or through acquisitions. Stockholders in the firm should be able to diversify away industry-specific risk by holding portfolios of stocks from different industries.

Industry-Specific Risk: Unanticipated effects on project cash flows of industry-wide shifts in technology or changes in laws or in the price of a commodity.

The fourth source of risk is **international risk.** A firm faces this type of risk when it generates revenues or has costs outside its domestic market. In such cases, the earnings and cash flows will be affected by unexpected exchange rate movements or by political developments. Disney, for instance, was clearly exposed to this risk with its 33 percent stake in Euro Disney, the theme park it developed outside Paris. Changes in the Euro/dollar exchange rate can have positive or negative implications for Disney's earnings from this investment. Some of this risk may be diversified away by the firm in the normal course of business by investing in projects in different countries whose currencies may not all move in the same direction. Citigroup and McDonalds, for instance, operate in many different countries and are much less exposed to international risk than was Wal-Mart in 1994, when its foreign operations were restricted primarily to Mexico. Companies can also reduce their exposure to the exchange rate component of this risk by borrowing in the local currency to fund projects; for instance, by borrowing money in pesos to invest in Mexico. Investors should be able to reduce their exposure to international risk by diversifying globally.

International Risk: This is the additional uncertainty created in cash flows of projects by unanticipated changes in exchange rates and by political risk in foreign markets.

The final source of risk is **market risk:** macroeconomic factors that affect essentially all companies and all projects to varying degrees. For example, changes in interest rates will affect the value of projects already taken and those yet to be taken both directly, through the discount rates, and indirectly, through the cash flows. Other factors that affect all investments include the term structure (the difference between short- and long-term rates), the risk preferences of investors (as investors become more risk-averse, more risky investments will lose value), inflation, and economic growth. Although expected values of all these variables enter into project analysis, unexpected changes in these variables will affect the values of these investments. Neither investors nor firms can diversify away this risk because all risky investments bear some exposure to this risk.

Market Risk: Market risk refers to the unanticipated changes in project cash flows created by changes in interest rates, inflation rates, and the economy that affect all firms, though to differing degrees.

3.3 RISK IS IN THE EYES OF THE BEHOLDER

A privately owned firm will generally end up with a higher discount rate for a project than would an otherwise similar publicly traded firm with diversified investors.

☐ True

☐ False

Does this provide a rationale for why a private firm may be acquired by a publicly traded firm?

Why Diversification Reduces or Eliminates Firm-Specific Risk

Why do we distinguish between the different types of risk? Risk that affects one or a few firms, which we categorized as firm-specific risk, can be reduced or even eliminated by investors as they hold more diversified portfolios due to two reasons.

- The first is that each investment in a **diversified** portfolio is a much smaller percentage of that portfolio. Thus, any risk that increases or reduces the value of only that investment or a small group of investments will have only a small impact on the overall portfolio.

Diversification: This is the process of holding many investments in a portfolio, either across the same asset class (e.g., stocks) or across asset classes (real estate, bonds).

- The second is that the effects of firm-specific actions on the prices of individual assets in a portfolio can be either positive or negative for each asset for any period. Thus, in large portfolios, it can be reasonably argued that this risk will average out to be zero and thus not impact the overall value of the portfolio.

In contrast, risk that affects most or all assets in the market will continue to persist even in large and diversified portfolios. For instance, other things being equal,

Figure 3.5 A Breakdown of Risk

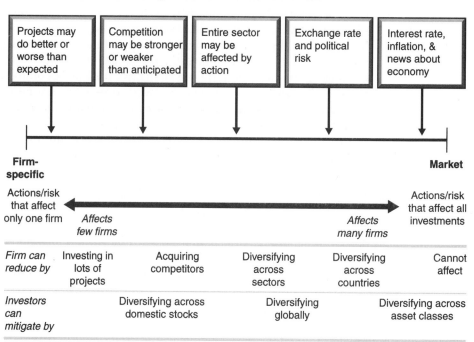

an increase in interest rates will lower the values of most assets in a portfolio. Figure 3.5 summarizes the different components of risk and the actions that can be taken by the firm and its investors to reduce or eliminate this risk.

Although the intuition for diversification reducing risk is simple, the benefits of diversification can also be shown statistically. In the last section, we introduced standard deviation as the measure of risk in an investment and calculated the standard deviation for an individual stock (Disney). When you combine two investments that do not move together in a portfolio, the standard deviation of that portfolio can be lower than the standard deviation of the individual stocks in the portfolio. To see how the magic of diversification works, consider a portfolio of two assets. Asset A has an expected return of μ_A and a variance in returns of σ_A^2, whereas asset B has an expected return of μ_B and a variance in returns of σ_B^2. The correlation in returns between the two assets, which measures how the assets move together, is ρ_{AB}.[6] The expected returns and variance of a two-asset portfolio can be written as a function of these inputs and the proportion of the portfolio going to each asset.

$$\mu_{\text{portfolio}} = w_A\mu_A + (1 - w_A)\mu_B$$
$$\sigma_{\text{portfolio}}^2 = w_A^2\, \sigma^{2A} + (1 - w_A)^2\, \sigma_B^2 + 2w_A(1 - w_A)\rho_{AB}\sigma_A\sigma_B$$

---

[6]The correlation is a number between -1 and $+1$. If the correlation is -1, the two stocks move in lockstep but in opposite directions. If the correlation is $+1$, the two stocks move together in sync.

where w_A = proportion of the portfolio in asset A. The last term in the variance formulation is sometimes written in terms of the covariance in returns between the two assets, which is

$$\sigma_{AB} = \rho_{AB}\sigma_A\sigma_B$$

The savings that accrue from diversification are a function of the correlation coefficient. Other things being equal, the higher the correlation in returns between the two assets, the smaller the potential benefits from diversification. The following example illustrates the savings from diversification.

ILLUSTRATION 3.2 **Variance of a Portfolio: Disney and Aracruz**
In the previous illustration, we computed the average return and standard deviation of returns on Disney stock between January 1999 and December 2003. Aracruz is a Brazilian stock, but it has been listed and traded in the U.S. market over the same period.[7] Using the same sixty months of data on Aracruz, we computed the average return and standard deviation on its returns:

	Disney	**Aracruz ADR**
Average monthly return	−0.07%	2.57%
Standard deviation in monthly returns	9.33%	12.62%

Over the period (1999–2003), Aracruz was a much more attractive investment than Disney but it was also much more volatile. We computed the correlation between the two stocks over the 60-month period to be 0.2665. Consider now a portfolio that is invested 90 percent in Disney and 10 percent in Aracruz ADR. The variance and the standard deviation of the portfolio can be computed as follows:

$$
\begin{aligned}
\text{Variance of portfolio} &= w_{Dis}^2\sigma_{Dis}^2 + (w_{Ara})^2\sigma_{Ara}^2 + 2w_{Dis}w_{Ara}\rho_{Dis,Ara}\sigma_{Dis}\sigma_{Ara} \\
&= (0.9)^2(0.0933)^2 + (0.1)^2(0.1262)^2 \\
&\quad + 2(0.9)(0.1)(0.2665)(0.0933)(0.1262) \\
&= 0.007767
\end{aligned}
$$

$$\text{Standard deviation of portfolio} = \sqrt{0.007767} = 0.0881 \text{ or } 8.81\%$$

The portfolio is less risky than either of the two stocks that go into it. In Figure 3.6, we graph the standard deviation in the portfolio as a function of the proportion of the portfolio invested in Disney stock.

---

[7]Like most foreign stocks, Aracruz has a listing for depository receipts or ADRs on the U.S. exchanges. Effectively, a bank buys shares of Aracruz in Brazil and issues dollar-denominated shares in the United States to interested investors. Aracruz's ADR price tracks the price of the local listing while reflecting exchange rate changes.

Figure 3.6   Standard Deviation of Portfolio

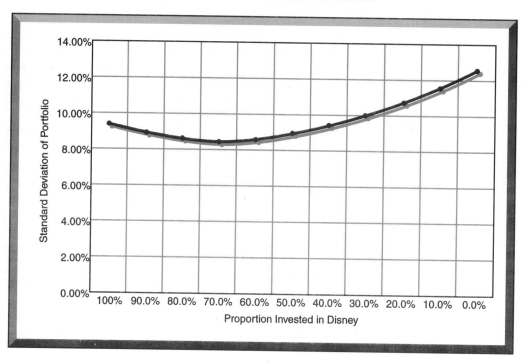

As the proportion of the portfolio invested in Aracruz shifts toward 100 percent, the standard deviation of the portfolio converges on the standard deviation of Aracruz.

The diversification benefits in this case can be traced to the correlation coefficient which is only 0.2665. As that correlation coefficient rises toward one, the diversification benefits will disappear.

Identifying the Marginal Investor

The marginal investor in a firm is the investor who is most likely to be trading at the margin and therefore has the most influence on the pricing of its equity. In some cases, this will be a large institutional investor, but institutional investors themselves can differ in several ways. The institution may be a taxable mutual fund or a tax-exempt pension fund, may be domestically or internationally diversified, and may vary on investment philosophy (value versus growth). In some cases, the marginal investors will be individuals; here again there can be wide differences depending on how diversified these individuals are and what their investment objectives may be. In still other cases, the marginal investors may be insiders in the firm who own a significant portion of the equity of the firm and are involved in the management of the firm.

Although it is difficult to identify the marginal investor in a firm, we would begin by breaking down the percent of the firm's stock held by individuals, institutions, and insiders in the firm. This information, which is available widely for U.S. stocks, can then be analyzed to yield the following conclusions:

- If the firm has relatively small institutional holdings but substantial holdings by wealthy individual investors, the marginal investor is *an individual investor with a significant equity holding* in the firm. In this case, we have to consider how diversified that individual investor's portfolio is to assess project risk. If the individual investor is not diversified, this firm may have to be treated like a private firm, and the cost of equity has to include a premium for all risk, rather than just nondiversifiable risk. If on the other hand, the individual investor is a wealthy individual with significant stakes in a large number of firms, a large portion of the risk may be diversifiable.

- If the firm has small institutional holdings and small insider holdings, its stock is held by large numbers of *individual investors with small equity holdings*. In this case, the marginal investor is an individual investor with a portfolio that may be only partially diversified. For instance, phone and utility stocks in the United States at least until recently had holdings dispersed among thousands of individual investors, who held the stocks for their high dividends. This preference for dividends meant, however, that these investors diversified across only those sectors where firms paid high dividends.

- If the firm has significant institutional holdings and small insider holdings, the marginal investor is almost always a *diversified, institutional investor*. In fact, we can learn more about what kind of institutional investor holds stock by examining the top fifteen or twenty largest stockholders in the firms and then categorizing them by tax status (mutual funds versus pension funds), investment objective (growth or value), and globalization (domestic versus international).

- If the firm has significant institutional holdings and large insider holdings, the choice for marginal investor becomes a little more complicated. Often, in these scenarios, the large insider is the founder or original owner for the firm, and often, this investor continues to be involved in the top management of the firm. Microsoft and Dell are good examples, with Bill Gates and Michael Dell being the largest stockholders in their firms. In most cases, however, the insider owner seldom trades the stock, and his or her wealth is determined by the level of the stock price, which is determined by institutional investors trading the stock. We would argue that the institutional investor is the marginal investor in these firms as well, though *the leading stockholder will influence corporate policy strongly, potentially leading to a clash between inside and outside stockholders*.

Thus, by examining the percent of stock held by different groups, and the largest investors in a firm, we should have a sense of who the marginal investor in the firm is and how best to assess and measure risk in corporate financial analysis.

ILLUSTRATION 3.3 Identifying the Marginal Investor

Who are the marginal investors in Disney, Aracruz, and Deutsche Bank? We begin to answer this question by examining whether insiders own a significant

Table 3.1 INVESTORS IN DISNEY, ARACRUZ, AND DEUTSCHE BANK

	Disney	Deutsche Bank	Aracruz (Nonvoting)
Mutual funds	31%	16%	29%
Other institutional investors	42%	58%	26%
Individuals	27%	26%	45%

Source: Value Line, Morningstar.

Table 3.2 LARGEST STOCKHOLDERS IN DISNEY, ARACRUZ, AND DEUTSCHE BANK

Disney	Deutsche Bank	Aracruz (Preferred)
Barclays Global (3.40%)	Allianz (4.81%)	Safra (10.74%)
State Street (3.10%)	La Caixa (3.85%)	BNDES (6.34%)
Fidelity (3.01%)	Capital Research (1.35%)	Scudder Kemper (1.03%)
Citigroup (3.00%)	Fidelity (0.50%)	BNP Paribas (0.56%)
Southeastern Asset (2.36%)	Frankfurt Trust (0.43%)	Barclays Global (0.29%)
State Farm Mutual (2.06%)	Aviva (0.37%)	Vanguard Group (0.18%)
Vanguard Group (1.93%)	Daxex (0.31%)	Banco Itau (0.12%)
JP Morgan Chase (1.83%)	Unifonds (0.29%)	Van Eck Associates (0.12%)
Mellon Bank (1.64%)	Fidelity (0.28%)	Pactual (0.11%)
Lord Abbet & Co (1.58%)	UBS Funds (0.21%)	Banco Bradesco (0.07%)

Source: Bloomberg.

portion of the equity in the firm and are involved in its top management. Although no such investors exist at Disney and Deutsche Bank, the voting shares in Aracruz are closely held by its incumbent managers. In Table 3.1, we examine the proportion of stock held in each of the firms by individuals and institutions, with the institutional holding broken down further into mutual fund and other institutional holdings.

All three companies are widely held by institutional investors. To break down the institutional investment, we examined the ten largest investors in each firm at the end of 2003 in Table 3.2, with the percent of the firm's stock held by each (in parentheses).

The ten largest investors in Disney are all institutional investors, suggesting that we are on safe ground when assuming that the marginal investor in Disney is likely to be both institutional and diversified. The largest single investor in Deutsche Bank is Allianz, a German insurance giant, reflecting again the cross-holding corporate governance structure favored by German corporations. However, the investors below Allianz on the table are all institutional investors, and about half of them are non-German. Here again, we can safely assume that the marginal investor is institutional and broadly diversified across at least European equities rather than just German stocks. The common shares in Aracruz, where the voting rights reside, are held by a handful of controlling stockholders, but trading in this stock is light.[8] The two largest holders of nonvoting common shares (which are called preferred shares in Brazil) in Aracruz, Safra and BNDES, are also holders of voting common stock and do not trade on their substantial holdings. The remaining shares are held largely by institutional investors, and many of them are from outside Brazil. Although there is a clear danger here that the company will be run for the benefit of the voting shareholders, the price of the voting stock is closely linked to the price of the preferred shares. Self-interest alone should induce the voting shareholders to consider the investors in the preferred shares as the marginal investors in the company.

Why Is the Marginal Investor Assumed to Be Diversified?
We can easily argue that investors can reduce their exposure to risk, but risk and return models in finance go further. They argue that the marginal investor, who sets prices for investments, is well diversified; thus, the only risk that will be priced is the risk as perceived by that investor. The justification that is offered is simple. The risk in an investment will always be perceived to be higher for an undiversified investor than for a diversified one, because the latter does not consider any firm-specific risk whereas the former does. If both investors have the same perceptions about future earnings and cash flows on an asset, the diversified investor will be willing to pay a higher price for that asset because of his or her risk perceptions. Consequently, the asset will end up being held by diversified investors over time.

Although this argument is powerful for stocks and other assets, which are liquid and traded in small units, it is less convincing for investments that are large and illiquid. Real estate in most countries is still held by investors who are undiversified and have the bulk of their wealth tied up in these investments. The benefits of diversification are strong enough, however, that securities, such as real estate investment trusts and mortgage-backed bonds, were created to allow investors to invest in real estate and stay diversified at the same time.

Note that diversification does not require investors to give up their pursuit of higher returns. Investors can be diversified and try to beat the market at the same time. For instance, investors who believe that they can do better than the market by buying stocks trading at low price-earnings (PE) ratios can still diversify by holding low PE stocks in a number of different sectors at the same time.

3.4   MANAGEMENT QUALITY AND RISK

A well-managed firm is less risky than a firm that is badly managed.
☐   True
☐   False

IN PRACTICE: WHO SHOULD DIVERSIFY? THE FIRM OR INVESTORS?

As noted in the last section, the exposure to each type of risk can be mitigated by either the firm or by investors in the firm. The question of who should do it can be

---

[8]Three stockholders, VCP, Safra, and Grupo Lorentzen, hold 28 percent each of the voting shares.

answered by comparing the costs faced by each. As a general rule, a firm should embark on actions that reduce risk only if it is cheaper for it to do so than it is for its investors. With a publicly traded firm, it will usually be much cheaper for investors to diversify away risk than it is for the firm. Consider, for instance, risk that affects an entire sector. A firm can reduce its exposure to this risk by either acquiring other firms, paying large premiums over the market price, or by investing large amounts in businesses where it does not have any expertise. Investors in the firm, on the other hand, can accomplish the same by expanding their portfolios to include stocks in other sectors or even more simply by holding diversified mutual funds. Because the cost of diversifying for investors is very low, firms should try to diversify away risk only if the cost is minimal or if the risk reduction is a side benefit from an action with a different objective. One example would be project risk. Because Disney is in the business of making movies, the risk reduction that comes from making lots of movies is essentially costless.

The choice is more complicated for private businesses. The owners of these businesses often have the bulk of their wealth invested in these businesses, and they can either try to take money out of the firms and invest it elsewhere or they can diversify their businesses. In fact, many family businesses in Latin America and Asia became conglomerates as they expanded, partly because they wanted to spread their risks. ■

III. Measuring Market Risk

Although most risk and return models in use in corporate finance agree on the first two step of this process—that is, that risk comes from the distribution of actual returns around the expected return and should be measured from the perspective of a marginal investor who is well diversified—they part ways on how to measure the nondiversifiable or market risk. In this section, we will provide a sense of how each of the basic models—the capital asset pricing model (CAPM), the arbitrage pricing model (APM), the multifactor model, and a risk proxy model—approaches the issue of measuring market risk.

A. The Capital Asset Pricing Model

The risk and return model that has been in use the longest and is still the standard in most real-world analyses is the CAPM. Although it has come in for its fair share of criticism over the years, it provides a useful starting point for our discussion of risk and return models.

1. Assumptions

Diversification has its attractions in terms of reducing the exposure of investors to firm specific risk, but most investors limit their diversification to holding relatively few assets. Even large mutual funds are reluctant to hold more than a few dozen stocks, and many of them hold as few as ten to twenty stocks. There are two reasons for this reluctance. The first is that the marginal benefits of diversification become smaller as the portfolio gets more diversified—the twenty-first asset added will generally provide a much smaller reduction in firm-specific risk than the fifth asset added and may not cover the marginal costs of diversification, which include transaction and monitoring costs. The second is that many investors (and funds) believe that they can find undervalued assets and thus choose not to hold those assets they believe to be correctly or overvalued.

The CAPM assumes that there are no transaction costs, all assets are traded, and investments are infinitely divisible (i.e., you can buy any fraction of a unit of the asset). It also assumes that there is no private information and that investors therefore cannot find under- or overvalued assets in the market. By making these assumptions, it eliminates the factors that cause investors to stop diversifying. With these assumptions in place, the logical end limit of diversification is to hold every traded risky asset (stocks, bonds, and real assets included) in your portfolio, in proportion to their market value.[9] This portfolio of every traded risky asset in the marketplace is called the *market portfolio.*

2. Implications for Investors

If every investor in the market holds the same market portfolio, how exactly do investors reflect their risk aversion in their investments? In the CAPM, investors adjust for their risk preferences in their allocation decisions, where they decide how much to invest in an asset with guaranteed returns—a **riskless asset**—and how much in risky assets (market portfolio). Investors who are risk-averse might choose to put much or even all of their wealth in the riskless asset. Investors who want to take more risk will invest the bulk or even all of their wealth in the market portfolio. Those investors who invest all their wealth in the market portfolio and still want to take on more risk would do so by borrowing at the riskless rate and investing in the same market portfolio as everyone else.

These results are predicated on two additional assumptions. First, there exists a riskless asset. Second, investors can lend and borrow at this riskless rate to arrive at their optimal allocations. There are variations of the CAPM that allow these assumptions to be relaxed and still arrive at conclusions that are consistent with the general model.

Riskless Asset: An asset where the actual return is always equal to the expected return.

3.5 EFFICIENT RISK TAKING

In the CAPM, the most efficient way to take a lot of risk is to
- ☐ buy a well-balanced portfolio of the riskiest stocks in the market.
- ☐ buy risky stocks that are also undervalued.
- ☐ borrow money and buy a well diversified portfolio.

---

[9]If investments are not held in proportion to their market value, investors are still losing some diversification benefits. Because there is no gain from overweighting some sectors and underweighting others in a market where the odds are random of finding undervalued and overvalued assets, investors will not do so.

3. Measuring the Market Risk of an Individual Asset

The risk of any asset to an investor is the risk added by that asset to the investor's overall portfolio. In the CAPM world, where all investors hold the market portfolio, the risk of an individual asset to an investor will be the risk that this asset adds on to the market portfolio. Intuitively, assets that move more with the market portfolio will tend to be riskier than assets that move less, because the movements that are un-related to the market portfolio will average out. Statistically, this added risk is mea-sured by the *covariance* of the asset with the market portfolio.

The covariance is a nonstandardized measure of market risk; knowing that the covariance of Disney with the market portfolio is 55 percent does not provide a clue as to whether Disney is riskier or safer than the average asset. We therefore standardize the risk measure by dividing the covariance of each asset with the market portfolio by the variance of the market portfolio. This yields the beta of the asset:

$$\text{Beta of an asset } i = \frac{\text{Covariance of asset } i \text{ with Market Portfolio}}{\text{Variance of the Market Portfolio}}$$

Because the covariance of the market portfolio with itself is its variance, the beta of the market portfolio, and by extension, the average asset in it is one. Assets that are riskier than average (using this measure of risk) will have betas that exceed one and assets that are safer than average will have betas that are lower than one. The risk-less asset will have a beta of zero.

4. Getting Expected Returns

The fact that every investor holds some combination of the riskless asset and the market portfolio leads to the next conclusion, which is that the expected return on an asset is linearly related to the **beta** of the asset. In particular, the expected return on an asset can be written as a function of the risk-free rate and the beta of that asset;

$$\text{Expected return on asset } i = R_f + \beta_i [E(R_m) - R_f]$$
$$= \text{Risk-free rate} + \text{Beta of asset } i*(\text{Risk premium on market portfolio})$$

where $E(R_m)$ = expected return on market portfolio.

To use the CAPM, we need three inputs. We will look at the estimation process in more detail in the next chapter, but each of these inputs is estimated as follows.

- The riskless asset is defined to be an asset for which the investor knows the expected return with certainty for the time horizon of the analysis. Consequently, the riskless rate used will vary depending on whether the time period for the expected return is one year, five years, or ten years.

- The risk premium is the premium demanded by investors for investing in the market portfolio, which includes all risky assets in the market, instead of invest-ing in a riskless asset. Thus, it does not relate to any individual risky asset but to risky assets as a class.

- The beta, which we defined to be the covariance of the asset divided by the market portfolio, is the only asset-specific input in this equation. In other words, the only reason two investments have different expected returns in the CAPM is because they have different betas.

In summary, in the CAPM, all of the market risk is captured in one beta, measured relative to a market portfolio, which at least in theory should include all traded assets in the market, held in proportion to their market value.

Beta: The beta of any investment in the CAPM is a standardized measure of the risk that it adds to the market portfolio.

3.6 WHAT DO NEGATIVE BETAS MEAN?

In the CAPM, there are assets that can have betas less than zero. When this occurs, which of the following statements describes your investment?

☐ This investment will have an expected return less than the riskless rate.

☐ This investment insures your "diversified portfolio" against some type of market risk.

☐ Holding this asset makes sense only if you are well diversified.

☐ All of the above.

IN PRACTICE: INDEX FUNDS AND MARKET PORTFOLIOS

Many critics of the CAPM seize on its conclusion that all investors in the market will hold the market portfolio, which includes all assets in proportion to their market value, as evidence that it is an unrealistic model. But is it? It is true that not all assets in the world are traded and that there are transaction costs. It is also true that investors sometimes trade on inside information and often hold undiversified portfolios. However, we can create portfolios that closely resemble the market portfolio using index funds. An index fund replicates an index by buying all of the stocks in the index in the same proportions that they form of the index. The earliest and still the largest one is the Vanguard 500 Index fund, which replicates the S&P 500 index. Today, we have access to index funds that replicate smaller companies in the United States, European stocks, Latin American markets, and Asian equities as well as bond and commodity markets. An investor can create a portfolio composed of a mix of index funds—the weights on each fund should be based on market values of the underlying market—which resembles the market portfolio; the only asset class that is usually difficult to replicate is real estate. ■

B. The Arbitrage Pricing Model

The restrictive assumptions in the CAPM and its dependence on the market portfolio have for long been viewed with skepticism by both academics and practitioners. In the late 1970s, an alternative and more general model for measuring risk, called the **arbitrage** pricing model (APM), was developed.[10]

---

[10]Stephen A. Ross, 1976, "The Arbitrage Theory of Capital Asset Pricing," *Journal of Economic Theory,* 13(3), 341–360.

Arbitrage: An investment that is riskless but delivers a return greater than the risk-less rate.

1. Assumptions

The APM is built on the simple premise that two investments with the same exposure to risk should be priced to earn the same expected returns. An alternative way of saying this is that if two portfolios have the same exposure to risk but offer different expected returns, investors will buy the portfolio that has the higher expected returns and sell the one with lower expected returns, until the expected returns converge.

Like the CAPM, the APM begins by breaking risk down into two components. The first is firm-specific and covers information that affects primarily the firm. The second is the market risk that affects all investment; this would include unanticipated changes in a number of economic variables, including gross national product, inflation, and interest rates. Incorporating this into the return model

$$R = E(R) + m + \epsilon$$

where m is the market-wide component of unanticipated risk and ϵ is the firm-specific component. The actual return (R) will differ from the expected return $[E(R)]$ as a consequence.

2. The Sources of Market-Wide Risk

Both the CAPM and the APM make a distinction between firm-specific and market-wide risk, but they part ways when it comes to measuring the market risk. The CAPM assumes that all of the market risk is captured in the market portfolio, whereas the APM allows for multiple sources of market-wide risk and measures the sensitivity of an investment to each source with a factor beta. In general, the market component of unanticipated returns can be decomposed into economic factors:

$$R = E(R) + m + \epsilon = E(R) + (\beta_1 F_1 + \beta_2 F_2 + \ldots + \beta_n F_n) + \epsilon$$

where β_j = sensitivity of investment to unanticipated changes in factor j and F_j = unanticipated changes in factor j.

3. The Effects of Diversification

The benefits of diversification have been discussed extensively in our treatment of the CAPM. The primary point of that discussion was that diversification of investments into portfolios eliminate firm-specific risk. The APM makes the same point and concludes that the return on a portfolio will not have a firm-specific component of unanticipated returns. The return on a portfolio can then be written as the sum of two weighted averages—that of the anticipated returns in the portfolio and that of the factor betas.

$$R_p = (w_1 E(R)_1 + w_2 E(R)_2 + \ldots + w_n E(R)_n) + (w_1 \beta_{1,1} + w_2 \beta_{1,2} + \ldots + w_n \beta_{1,n})F_1 \\ + (w_1 \beta_{2,1} + w_2 \beta_{2,2} + \ldots + w_n \beta_{2,n})F_2 \ldots$$

where w_j = portfolio weight on asset j; $E(R)_j$ = expected return on asset j; and $\beta_{i,j}$ = beta on factor i for asset j. Note that the firm-specific component of returns (ϵ) in the individual firm equation disappears in the portfolio as a result of diversification.

4. Expected Returns and Betas

The fact that the beta of a portfolio is the weighted average of the betas of the assets in the portfolio, in conjunction with the absence of arbitrage, leads to the conclusion that expected returns should be linearly related to betas. To see why, assume that there is only one factor and that there are three portfolios. Portfolio A has a beta of 2.0, and an expected return on 20 percent; portfolio B has a beta of 1.0 and an expected return of 12 percent; and portfolio C has a beta of 1.5 and an expected return on 15 percent. Note that the investor can put half of his or her wealth in portfolio A and half in portfolio B and end up with a portfolio with a beta of 1.5 and an expected return of 16 percent. Consequently no investor will choose to hold portfolio C until the prices of assets in that portfolio drop and the expected return increases to 16 percent. Alternatively, an investor can buy the combination of portfolio A and B, with an expected return of 16 percent, and sell portfolio C with an expected return of 15 percent and make a pure profit of 1 percent without taking any risk and investing any money. To prevent this arbitrage from occurring, the expected returns on every portfolio should be a linear function of the beta. This argument can be extended to multiple factors with the same results. Therefore, the expected return on an asset can be written as

$$E(R) = R_f + \beta_1[E(R_1) - R_f] + \beta_2[E(R_2) - R_f] \ldots + \beta_n[E(R_n) - R_f]$$

where R_f = expected return on a zero-beta portfolio, $E(R_j)$ = expected return on a portfolio with a factor beta of one for factor j and zero for all other factors. The terms in the brackets can be considered risk premiums for each of the factors in the model.

Note that the CAPM can be considered a special case of the APM, in which there is only one economic factor driving market-wide returns and the market portfolio is the factor.

$$E(R) = R_f + \beta_m[E(R_m) - R_f]$$

5. The APM in Practice

The APM requires estimates of each of the factor betas and factor risk premiums in addition to the riskless rate. In practice, these are usually estimated using historical data on stocks and a statistical technique called factor analysis. Intuitively, a factor analysis examines the historical data looking for common patterns that affect broad groups of stocks (rather than just one sector or a few stocks). It provides two output measures:

1. It specifies the *number of common factors* that affected stocks during the historical time period for which the data was available.

2. It measures the *beta of each investment* relative to each of the common factors, and provides an estimate of the actual risk premium earned by each factor.

The factor analysis does not, however, identify the factors in economic terms.

In summary, in the APM the market or nondiversifiable risk in an investment is measured relative to multiple unspecified macroeconomic factors, with the sensitivity of the investment relative to each factor being measured by a factor beta. The number of factors, the factor betas, and factor risk premiums can all be estimated using a factor analysis.

C. Multifactor Models for Risk and Return

The APM's failure to identify specifically the factors in the model may be a strength from a statistical standpoint but is a clear weakness from an intuitive standpoint. The solution seems simple: Replace the unidentified statistical factors with specified economic factors, and the resultant model should be intuitive while still retaining much of the strength of the APM. That is precisely what multifactor models do.

Deriving a Multifactor Model

Multifactor models generally are not based on extensive economic rationale but are determined by the data. Once the number of factors has been identified in the APM, the behavior of the factors over time can be extracted from the data. These factor time series can then be compared to the time series of macroeconomic variables to see if any of the variables are correlated over time with the identified factors.

For instance, a study from the 1980s suggested that the following macroeconomic variables were highly correlated with the factors that come out of factor analysis: industrial production, changes in the default spread of corporate bonds over the riskless rate, shifts in the term structure, **unanticipated inflation,** and changes in the real rate of return.[11] These variables can then be correlated with returns to come up with a model of expected returns with firm-specific betas calculated relative to each variable. The equation for expected returns will take the following form:

$$E(R) = R_f + \beta_{GNP}[E(R_{GNP}) - R_f] + \beta_i[E(R_i) - R_f] \ldots + \beta_\delta[E(R_\delta) - R_f]$$

where β_{GNP} = beta relative to changes in industrial production; $E(R_{GNP})$ = expected return on a portfolio with a beta of one on the industrial production factor, and zero on all other factors; β_i = beta relative to changes in inflation; $E(R_i)$ = expected return on a portfolio with a beta of one on the inflation factor, and zero on all other factors and so on.

The costs of going from the APM to a macroeconomic multifactor model can be traced directly to the errors that can be made in identifying the factors. The economic factors in the model can change over time, as will the risk premium associated with each one. For instance, oil price changes were a significant economic factor driving expected returns in the 1970s but are not as significant in other time periods. Using the wrong factor(s) or missing a significant factor in a multifactor model can lead to inferior estimates of cost of equity.

In summary, multifactor models, like the APM, assume that market risk can be captured best using multiple macroeconomic factors and estimating betas relative to each. Unlike the APM, multifactor models do attempt to identify the macroeconomic factors that drive market risk.

Unanticipated Inflation: This is the difference between actual inflation and expected inflation.

---

[11] N. Chen, R. Roll, and S. A. Ross, 1986, "Economic Forces and the Stock Market," *Journal of Business,* 59, 383–404.

D. Proxy Models

All of the models described so far begin by thinking about market risk in economic terms and then developing models that might best explain it. All of them, however, extract risk parameters by looking at historical data. There is a final class of risk and return models that start with past returns on individual stocks and then work backward by trying to explain differences in returns across long time periods using observable characteristics of the firms earning these returns. In other words, these models try to find common characteristics shared by firms that have historically earned higher returns and identify these characteristics as proxies for market risk.

Fama and French, in a highly influential study of the CAPM in the early 1990s, note that actual returns over long time periods have been highly correlated with price/book value ratios and market capitalization.[12] In particular, they note that firms with small market capitalization and low price-to-book ratios earned higher returns than other stocks between 1963 and 1990. They suggest that these measures and similar ones developed from the data be used as proxies for risk and that the regression coefficients be used to estimate expected returns for investments. They report the following regression for monthly returns on stocks on the New York Stock Exchange (NYSE), using data from 1963 to 1990.

$$R_t = 1.77\% - 0.11 \ln(MV) + 0.35 \ln(BV/MV)$$

where MV = market value of equity and BV = book value of equity. The values for **market value of equity and book-price** ratios for individual firms, when plugged into this regression, should yield expected monthly returns. For instance, a firm with a market value of $100 million and a book to market ratio of 0.5 would have an expected monthly return of 1.02 percent.

$$R_t = 1.77\% - 0.11 \ln(100) + 0.35 \ln(0.5) = 1.02\%$$

As data on individual firms have become richer and more easily accessible in recent years, these proxy models have expanded to include additional variables. In particular, researchers have found that price momentum (the rate of increase in the stock price over recent months) also seems to help explain returns; stocks with high price momentum tend to have higher returns in following periods.

In summary, proxy models measure market risk using firm characteristics as proxies for market risk, rather than the macroeconomic variables used by conventional multifactor models.[13] The firm characteristics are identified by looking at differences in returns across investments over very long time periods and correlating them with identifiable characteristics of these investments.

---

[12]E. F. Fama and K. R. French, 1992, "The Cross-Section of Expected Returns," *Journal of Finance,* 47, 427–466.

[13]Adding to the confusion, researchers in recent years have taken to describing proxy models also as multifactor models.

Book-to-Market Ratio: The ratio of the book value of equity to the market value of equity.

A Comparative Analysis of Risk and Return Models

All the risk and return models developed in this chapter have common ingredients. They all assume that only market-wide risk is rewarded, and they derive the expected return as a function of measures of this risk. Figure 3.7 presents a comparison of the different models.

The CAPM makes the most assumptions but arrives at the simplest model, with only one risk factor requiring estimation. The APM makes fewer assumptions but arrives at a more complicated model, at least in terms of the parameters that

Figure 3.7   Competing Models for Risk and Return in Finance

Step 1: Defining Risk

The risk in an investment can be measured by the variance in actual returns around an expressed return

| Riskless Investment | Low-Risk Investment | High-Risk Investment |
| E(R) | E(R) | E(R) |

Step 2: Differentiating between Rewarded and Unrewarded Risk

Risk that is specific to investment (firm-specific)
Can be diversified away in a portfolio
1. Each investment is a small proportion of portfolio
2. Risk averages out across investments in portfolio

Risk that affects all investments (market risk)
Cannot be diversified away since most assets are affected by it.

The marginal investor is assumed to hold a diversified portfolio. Thus, only market risk will be rewarded and priced.

Step 3: Measuring Market Risk

The CAPM	The APM	Multifactor Models	Proxy Models
If there is 1. no private information 2. no transaction cost The optimal diversified portfolio includes every traded asset. Everyone will hold this market portfolio. Market risk = Risk added by any investment to the market portfolio	If there are no arbitrage opportunities, then the market risk of any asset must be captured by betas relative to factors that affect all investments. Market risk = Risk exposures of any asset to market factors	Since market risk affects most or all investments, it must come from macro-economic factors. Market risk = Risk exposures of any asset to macro economic factors	In an efficient market, differences in returns across long periods must be due to market risk differences. Looking for variables correlated with returns should then give us proxies for this risk. Market risk = captured by the proxy variable(s)
Beta of asset relative to market portfolio (from a regression)	Betas of asset relative to unspecified market factors (from a factor analysis)	Betas of assets relative to specified macroeconomic factors (from a regression)	Equation relating returns to proxy variables (from a regression)

require estimation. In general, the CAPM has the advantage of being a simpler model to estimate and to use, but it will under perform the richer multifactor models when the company is sensitive to economic factors not well represented in the market index. For instance, oil companies, which derive most of their risk from oil price movements, tend to have low CAPM betas. Using a multifactor model, in which one of the factors may be capturing oil and other commodity price movements, will yield a better estimate of risk and higher cost of equity for these firms.[14]

The biggest intuitive block in using the APM is its failure to identify specifically the factors driving expected returns. Although this may preserve the flexibility of the model and reduce statistical problems in testing, it does make it difficult to understand what the beta coefficients for a firm mean and how they will change as the firm changes (or restructures).

Does the CAPM work? Is beta a good proxy for risk, and is it correlated with expected returns? The answers to these questions have been debated widely in the past two decades. The first tests of the model suggested that betas and returns were positively related, though other measures of risk (such as stock return variance) continued to explain differences in actual returns. This discrepancy was attributed to limitations in the testing techniques. In 1977, Roll, in a seminal critique of the model's tests, suggested that because the market portfolio (which should include every traded asset of the market) could never be observed, the CAPM could never be tested, and all tests of the CAPM were therefore joint tests of both the model and the market portfolio used in the tests. In other words, all that any test of the CAPM could show was that the model worked (or did not) given the proxy used for the market portfolio.[15] He argued that in any empirical test that claimed to reject the CAPM, the rejection could be of the proxy used for the market portfolio rather than of the model itself. Roll noted that there was no way to ever prove that the CAPM worked and thus no empirical basis for using the model.

The study by Fama and French, quoted earlier, examined the relationship between the betas of stocks and annual returns between 1963 and 1990 and concluded that there was little relationship between the two. They noted that market capitalization and book-to-market value explained differences in returns across firms much better than did beta and were better proxies for risk. These results have been contested on two fronts. First, Amihud, Christensen, and Mendelson, using the same data, performed different statistical tests, and showed that betas did in fact explain returns during the time period.[16] Second, Chan and Lakonishok look at a much longer time series of returns from 1926 to 1991 and found that the positive relationship between

---

[14]J. F. Weston and T. E. Copeland, 1992, *Managerial Finance,* Dryden Press. They used both approaches to estimate the cost of equity for oil companies in 1989 and came up with 14.4 percent with the CAPM and 19.1 percent using the APM.

[15]R. Roll, 1977, "A Critique of the Asset Pricing Theory's Tests: Part I: On Past and Potential Testability of Theory," *Journal of Financial Economics,* 4, 129–176.

[16]Y. Amihud, B. Christensen, and H. Mendelson, 1992, *Further Evidence on the Risk-Return Relationship,* Working Paper, New York University.

Figure 3.8　Returns and Betas: Ten Worst Months between 1926 and 1991

Source: Chan and Lakonishok.

betas and returns broke down only in the period after 1982.[17] They attribute this breakdown to indexing, which they argue led the larger capitalization, lower-beta stocks in the S&P 500 to outperform smaller cap, higher-beta stocks. They also find that betas are a useful guide to risk in extreme market conditions, with the riskiest firms (the 10 percent with highest betas) performing far worse than the market as a whole, in the ten worst months for the market between 1926 and 1991 (see Figure 3.8).

Although the initial tests of the APM and the multifactor models suggested that they might provide more promise in terms of explaining differences in returns, a distinction has to be drawn between the use of these models to explain differences in past returns and their use to get expected returns for the future. The competitors to the CAPM clearly do a much better job at explaining past returns because they do not constrain themselves to one factor, as the CAPM does. This extension to multiple factors does become more of a problem when we try to estimate expected returns for the future, because the betas and premiums of each of these factors have to be estimated. Because the factor premiums and betas are themselves volatile, the estimation error may wipe out the benefits that could be gained by moving from the CAPM to more complex models. The regression models that were offered as an alternative are even more exposed to this problem, because the variables that work best as proxies for market risk in one period (such as market capitalization) may not be the ones that work in the next period. This may explain why multifactor models have been accepted more widely in evaluating portfolio performance evaluation than in corporate finance; the former is focused on past returns, whereas the latter is concerned with future expected returns.

---

[17]L. K. Chan and J. Lakonishok, 1993, "Are the Reports of Beta's Death Premature?" *Journal of Portfolio Management,* 19, 51–62.

Ultimately, the survival of the CAPM as the default model for risk in real-world application is a testament to both its intuitive appeal and the failure of more complex models to deliver significant improvement in terms of expected returns. We would argue that a judicious use of the CAPM, without an overreliance on historical data, in conjunction with the accumulated evidence presented by those who have developed the alternatives to the CAPM,[18] is still the most effective way of dealing with risk in modern corporate finance.

IN PRACTICE: IMPLIED COSTS OF EQUITY AND CAPITAL

The controversy surrounding the assumptions made by each of the risk and return models outlined herein and the errors associated with the estimates from each has led some analysts to use an alternate approach for companies that are publicly traded. With these companies, the market price represents the market's best estimate of the value of the company today. If you assume that the market is right and you are willing to make assumptions about expected growth in the future, you can back out a cost of equity from the current market price. For example, assume that a stock is trading at $50 and that dividends next year are expected to be $2.50. Furthermore, assume that dividends will grow 4 percent a year in perpetuity. The cost of equity implied in the stock price can be estimated as follows.

Stock price = $50 = Expected dividends next year/(Cost of equity − Expected growth rate)

$$\$50 = 2.50/(r - 0.04)$$

Solving for r, r = 9%. This approach can be extended to the entire firm to compute the cost of capital.

Though this approach has the obvious benefit of being model-free, it has its limitations. In particular, the cost of equity will be a function of our estimates of growth and cash flows. If we use overly optimistic estimates of expected growth and cash flows, we will underestimate the cost of equity. It is also built on the presumption that the market price is right. ∎

THE RISK IN BORROWING: DEFAULT RISK AND THE COST OF DEBT

When an investor lends to an individual or a firm, there is the possibility that the borrower may default on interest and principal payments. This possibility of default is called default risk. Generally speaking, borrowers with higher default risk should pay higher interest rates on their borrowing than those with lower default risk. This section examines the measurement of default risk and its relationship to interest rates on borrowing.

In contrast to the general risk and return models for equity, which evaluate the effects of market risk on expected returns, models of default risk measure the consequences

---

[18]Barra, a leading beta estimation service, adjusts betas to reflect differences in fundamentals across firms (such as size and dividend yields). It is drawing on the regression studies that have found these to be good proxies for market risk.

of firm-specific default risk on promised returns. Although diversification can be used to explain why firm-specific risk will not be priced into expected returns for equities, the same rationale cannot be applied to bonds where investors have limited upside potential and much greater downside potential from firm-specific events. To see what we mean by limited upside potential, consider investing in a bond issued by a company. The coupons are fixed at the time of the issue, and these coupons represent the promised cash flow on the bond. The best-case scenario for you as an investor is that you receive the promised cash flows; you are not entitled to more than these cash flows, even if the company is wildly successful. All other scenarios contain only bad news, though in varying degrees, with the delivered cash flows being less than what was promised. Consequently, the expected return on a corporate bond is likely to reflect the firm-specific default risk of the firm issuing the bond.

The Determinants of Default Risk

The default risk of a firm is a function of its capacity to generate cash flows from operations and its financial obligations—including interest and principal payments.[19] It is also a function of how liquid a firm's assets are because firms with more liquid assets should have an easier time liquidating them in a crisis to meet debt obligations. Consequently, the following propositions relate to default risk.

- Firms that *generate high cash flows* relative to their financial obligations, have lower default risk than firms that generate low cash flows relative to obligations. Thus, firms with current investments that generate high cash flows will have lower default risk than will firms that are dependent on future growth opportunities.

- The *more stable the cash flows,* the lower is the default risk in the firm. Firms that operate in predictable and stable businesses will have lower default risk than will otherwise similar firms that operate in cyclical and/or volatile businesses, for the same level of indebtedness.

- The *more liquid a firm's assets,* for any given level of operating cash flows and financial obligations, the less default risk in the firm.

For as long as there have been borrowers, lenders have had to assess default risk. Historically, assessments of default risk have been based on financial ratios to measure the cash flow coverage (i.e., the magnitude of cash flows relative to obligations) and control for industry effects, to capture the variability in cash flows and the liquidity of assets across industries.

Default Risk and Interest Rates

When banks did much of the lending to firms, it made sense for them to expend the resources to make their own assessments of default risk, and they still do for most lenders. The advent of the corporate bond market created a demand for third-party assessments of default risk on the part of bondholders. This demand came from the need for economies of scale, because few individual bondholders had the resources

---

[19]"Financial obligation" refers to any payment that the firm has legally obligated itself to make, such as interest and principal payments. It does not include discretionary cash flows, such as dividend payments or new capital expenditures, which can be deferred or delayed, without legal consequences, though there may be economic consequences.

to make the assessment themselves. In the United States, this led to the growth of ratings agencies like Standard & Poor's (S&P) and Moody's, which made judgments of the default risk of corporations, using a mix of private and public information, converted these judgments into measures of default risk (bond ratings), and made these ratings public. Investors buying corporate bonds could therefore use the bond ratings as a shorthand measure of default risk.

The Ratings Process

The process of rating a bond starts when a company requests a rating from the ratings agency. This request is usually precipitated by a desire on the part of the company to issue bonds. Although ratings are not a legal prerequisite for bond issues, it is unlikely that investors in the bond market will be willing to buy bonds issued by a company that is not well known and has shown itself to be unwilling to put itself through the rigor of a bond rating process. It is not surprising, therefore, that the largest number of rated companies are in the United States, which has the most active corporate bond market, and that there are relatively few rated companies in Europe, where bank lending remains the norm for all but the largest companies.

The ratings agency then collects information from both publicly available sources, such as financial statements, and the company itself, and makes a decision on the rating. If it disagrees with the rating, the company is given the opportunity to present additional information. This process is presented schematically for one ratings agency, S&P, in Figure 3.9.

The ratings assigned by these agencies are letter ratings. A rating of AAA from S&P and Aaa from Moody's represents the highest rating granted to firms that are viewed as having the lowest default risk. As the default risk increases, the ratings decrease toward D for firms in default (S&P). Table 3.3 provides a description of the bond ratings assigned by the two agencies.

IN PRACTICE: INVESTMENT GRADE AND JUNK BONDS

Ratings can range from AAA (safest) to D (in default), but a rating at or above BBB by S&P (Baa for Moody's) is categorized as investment grade, reflecting the view of the ratings agency that there is relatively little default risk in investing in bonds issued by these firms. Bonds rated below BBB are generally categorized as junk bonds or high-yield bonds. Though it is an arbitrary dividing line, it is an important one for two reasons. First, many investment portfolios are restricted from investing in bonds below investment grade. Thus, the market for investment-grade bonds tends to be wider and deeper than that for bonds below that grade. Second, firms that are not rated investment grade have a tougher time when they try to raise new funding, and they also pay much higher issuance costs when they do. In fact, until the early 1980s, firms below investment grade often could not issue new bonds.[20] The perception that they are exposed to default risk also creates a host of other costs, including tighter supplier credit and tighter debt covenants. ∎

---

[20]In the early 1980s, Michael Milken and Drexel Burnham created the junk bond market, allowing for original issuance of junk bonds. They did this primarily to facilitate hostile takeovers by the acquirers of the era.

Figure 3.9 The Ratings Process

Determinants of Bond Ratings

The bond ratings assigned by agencies are primarily based on publicly available information, though private information conveyed by the firm to the rating agency does play a role. The rating that is assigned to a company's bonds will depend in large part on financial ratios that measure the capacity of the company to meet debt payments and generate stable and predictable cash flows. A multitude of financial ratios exist, but Table 3.4 summarizes some of the key ratios used to measure default risk.

Table 3.3 INDEX OF BOND RATINGS

S&P		Moody's	
AAA	The highest debt rating assigned. The borrower's capacity to repay debt is extremely strong.	Aaa	Judged to be of the best quality with a small degree of risk.
AA	Capacity to repay is strong and differs from the highest quality only by a small amount.	Aa	High quality but rated lower than Aaa because margin of protection may not be as large or because there may be other elements of long-term risk.
A	Has strong capacity to repay; borrower is susceptible to adverse effects of changes in circumstances and economic conditions.	A	Bonds possess favorable investment attributes but may be susceptible to risk in the future.
BBB	Has adequate capacity to repay, but adverse economic conditions or circumstances are more likely to lead to risk.	Baa	Neither highly protected nor poorly secured; adequate payment capacity.
BB, B, CCC, CC	Regarded as predominantly speculative, BB being the least speculative and CC the most.	Ba	Judged to have some speculative risk.
		B	Generally lacking characteristics of a desirable investment; probability of payment small.
D	In default or with payments in arrears.	Caa	Poor standing and perhaps in default.
		Ca	Very speculative; often in default.
		C	Highly speculative; in default.

Table 3.4 FINANCIAL RATIOS USED TO MEASURE DEFAULT RISK

Ratio	Description
Pretax interest coverage	= (pretax income from continuing operations + interest expense)/ gross interest expense
EBITDA interest coverage	= EBITDA/gross interest expense
Funds from operations/total debt (%)	= (net income from continuing operations + depreciation)/total debt
Free operating cash flow/total debt (%)	= (funds from operations – capital expenditures – change in working capital)/total debt
Pretax return on permanent capital (%)	= (pretax income from continuing operations + interest expense)/(average of beginning of the year and end of the year of long- and short-term debt, minority interest, and shareholders equity)
Operating income/sales (%)	= (sales – COGS – selling expenses – administrative expenses – R&D expenses)/sales
Long-term debt/capital (%)	= long-term debt/(long-term debt + equity)
Total debt/capitalization (%)	= total debt/(total debt + equity)

Table 3.5   FINANCIAL RATIOS BY BOND RATING: 1998–2000

	AAA	AA	A	BBB	BB	B	CCC
EBIT interest coverage (x)	17.5	10.8	6.8	3.9	2.3	1.0	0.2
EBITDA interest coverage (x)	21.8	14.6	9.6	6.1	3.8	2.0	1.4
Funds flow/total debt (%)	105.8	55.8	46.1	30.5	19.2	9.4	5.8
Free operating cash flow/total debt (%)	55.4	24.6	15.6	6.6	1.9	−4.5	−14.0
Return on capital (%)	28.2	22.9	19.9	14.0	11.7	7.2	0.5
Operating income/sales (%)	29.2	21.3	18.3	15.3	15.4	11.2	13.6
Long-term debt/capital (%)	15.2	26.4	32.5	41.0	55.8	70.7	80.3
Total debt/capital (%)	26.9	35.6	40.1	47.4	61.3	74.6	89.4
Number of firms	10	34	150	234	276	240	23

Source: S&P.

There is a strong relationship between the bond rating a company receives and its performance on these financial ratios. Table 3.5 provides a summary of the median ratios from 1998 to 2000 for different S&P ratings classes for manufacturing firms.

Note that the pretax interest coverage ratio and the EBITDA interest coverage ratio are stated in terms of times interest earned, whereas the rest of the ratios are stated in percentage terms.

Not surprisingly, firms that generate income and cash flows significantly higher than debt payments are profitable, have low debt ratios, and are more likely to be highly rated than are firms that do not have these characteristics. There will be individual firms whose ratings are not consistent with their financial ratios, however, because the ratings agency does bring subjective judgments into the final mix. Thus, a firm that performs poorly on financial ratios but is expected to improve its performance dramatically over the next period may receive a higher rating than that justified by its current financials. For most firms, however, the financial ratios should provide a reasonable basis for guessing at the bond rating.

There is a data set online that summarizes key financial ratios by bond rating class for the United States in the most recent period for which the data is available.

Bond Ratings and Interest Rates

The interest rate on a corporate bond should be a function of its default risk. If the rating is a good measure of the default risk, higher-rated bonds should be priced to yield lower interest rates than would lower rated bonds. The difference between the interest rate on a bond with default risk and a default-free government bond is called the default spread. This default spread will vary by maturity of the bond and can also change from period to period, depending on economic conditions. Table 3.6 summarizes default spreads in early 2004 for ten-year bonds in each ratings class (using S&P ratings) and the market interest rates on these bonds, based on a Treasury bond rate of 4 percent.

Table 3.6 provides default spreads at a point in time, but default spreads not only vary across time but can vary for bonds with the same rating but different maturities. From observation, the default spread for corporate bonds of a given ratings class

Table 3.6 DEFAULT SPREADS FOR RATINGS CLASSES: JANUARY 2004

Rating	Default Spread	Interest Rate on Bond
AAA	0.30%	4.30%
AA	0.50%	4.50%
A+	0.70%	4.70%
A	0.85%	4.85%
A–	1.00%	5.00%
BBB	1.50%	5.50%
BB	2.50%	6.50%
B+	3.25%	7.25%
B	4.00%	8.00%
B–	6.00%	10.00%
CCC	8.00%	12.00%
CC	10.00%	14.00%
C	12.00%	16.00%
D	20.00%	24.00%

Source: bondsonline.com.

seems to vary with the maturity of the bond. In Figure 3.10 we present the default spreads estimated for an AAA, BBB and CCC rated bond for maturities ranging from one to ten years in January 2004.

For the AAA and BBB ratings, the default spread widens for the longer maturities. For the B-rated bonds, the spreads widen as we go from one- to three-year maturities but narrow after that. Why might this be? It is entirely possible that this reflects where we are in the economic cycle. In early 2004, there were many cyclical firms in trouble because of the recession of the prior two years. If these firms survive in the short term (say, three years), improving earnings will reduce default risk in future years.

The default spreads presented in Table 3.6, after a good year for the stock markets and signs of an economic pickup, were significantly lower than the default spreads a year earlier. This phenomenon is not new. Historically, default spreads for every ratings class have increased during recessions and decreased during economic booms. The practical implication of this phenomenon is that default spreads for bonds have to be reestimated at regular intervals, especially if the economy shifts from low to high growth or vice versa.

A final point worth making here is that everything that has been said about the relationship between interest rates and bond ratings could be said more generally about interest rates and default risk. The existence of ratings is a convenience that makes the assessment of default risk a little easier for us when analyzing companies. In its absence, we would still have to assess default risk on our own and come up with estimates of the default spread we would charge if we were lending to a firm.

Figure 3.10 Default Spreads by Maturity; January 2004

Source: bondsonline.com.

 There is a data set on the Web that summarizes default spreads by bond rating class for the most recent period.

IN PRACTICE: RATINGS CHANGES AND INTEREST RATES

The rating assigned to a company can change at the discretion of the ratings agency. The adjustment is usually triggered by a change in a firm's operating health, a new security issue by the firm, or new borrowing. Other things remaining the same, ratings will drop if the operating performance deteriorates or if the firm borrows substantially more, and will improve if the firm reports higher earnings or raises new equity. In either case, though, the ratings agency is reacting to news that the rest of the market also receives. In fact, ratings agencies deliberate before making ratings changes, often putting a firm on a credit watch list before changing its ratings. Because markets can react instantaneously, it should come as no surprise that bond prices often decline before a ratings drop and increase before a ratings upgrade. In fact, studies indicate that much of the bond price reaction to deteriorating credit quality precedes a ratings drop.

This does not mean that there is no information in a ratings change. When ratings are changed, the market still reacts, but the reactions tend to be small. The biggest service provided by ratings agencies may be in providing a measure of default risk that is comparable across hundreds of rated firms, thus allowing bond investors a simple way of categorizing their potential investments. ■

CONCLUSION

Risk, as we define it in finance, is measured based on deviations of actual returns on an investment from its expected returns. There are two types of risk. The first, which we call equity risk, arises in investments where there are no promised cash flows, but there are expected cash flows. The second, default risk, arises on investments with promised cash flows.

On investments with equity risk, the risk is best measured by looking at the variance of actual returns around the expected returns, with greater variance indicating greater risk. This risk can be broken down into risk that affects one or a few investments, which we call firm-specific risk, and risk that affects many investments, which we refer to as market risk. When investors diversify, they can reduce their exposure to firm-specific risk. By assuming that the investors who trade at the margin are well diversified, we conclude that the risk we should be looking at with equity investments is the market risk. The different models of equity risk introduced in this chapter share this objective of measuring market risk, but they differ in how they do it. In the capital asset pricing model, exposure to market risk is measured by a market beta, which estimates how much risk an individual investment will add to a portfolio that includes all traded assets. The arbitrage pricing model and the multifactor model allow for multiple sources of market risk and estimate betas for an investment relative to each source. Regression or proxy models for risk look for firm characteristics, such as size, that have been correlated with high returns in the past and use these to measure market risk. In all these models, the risk measures are used to estimate the expected return on an equity investment. This expected return can be considered the cost of equity for a company.

On investments with default risk, risk is measured by the likelihood that the promised cash flows might not be delivered. Investments with higher default risk should have higher interest rates, and the premium that we demand over a riskless rate is the default premium. For most U.S. companies, default risk is measured by rating agencies in the form of a company rating; these ratings largely determine the interest rates at which these firms can borrow. Even in the absence of ratings, interest rates will include a default premium that reflects the lenders' assessments of default risk. These default risk-adjusted interest rates represent the cost of borrowing or debt for a business.

LIVE CASE STUDY

II. STOCKHOLDER ANALYSIS

Objective: To find out who the average and marginal investors in the company are. This is relevant because risk and return models in finance assume that the marginal investor is well diversified.

Key
Questions

- Who is the average investor in this stock? (Individual investor or pension fund, taxable or tax-exempt, small or large, domestic or foreign)
- Who is the marginal investor in this stock?

Framework for
Analysis

1. *Who holds stock in this company?*
   - How many stockholders does the company have?
   - What percent of the stock is held by institutional investors?
   - Does the company have listings in foreign markets? (If you can, estimate the percent of the stock held by non-domestic investors)

2. *Insider Holdings*
   - Who are the insiders in this company? (Besides the managers and directors, anyone with more than 5 percent is treated as an insider)
   - What role do the insiders play in running the company?
   - What percent of the stock is held by insiders in the company?
   - What percent of the stock is held by employees overall? (Include the holdings by employee pension plans)
   - Have insiders been buying or selling stock in this company in the most recent year?

Getting
Information on
Stockholder
Composition

Information about insider and institutional ownership of firms is widely available since both groups have to file with the SEC. These SEC filings are used to develop rankings of the largest holders of stock in firms. Insider activity (buying and selling) is also recorded by the SEC, though the information is not available until a few weeks after the filing.

Online sources of information: See
http://www.stern.nyu.edu/~adamodar/cfin2E/project/data.htm.

PROBLEMS AND QUESTIONS

(In the problems below, you can use a risk premium of 5.5 percent and a tax rate of 40 percent if none is specified.)

1. The following table lists the stock prices for Microsoft from 1989 to 1998. The company did not pay any dividends during the period

Year	Price
1989	$1.20
1990	$2.09
1991	$4.64
1992	$5.34
1993	$5.05
1994	$7.64
1995	$10.97
1996	$20.66
1997	$32.31
1998	$69.34

a. Estimate the average annual return you would have made on your investment.
b. Estimate the standard deviation and variance in annual returns.
c. If you were investing in Microsoft today, would you expect the historical standard deviations and variances to continue to hold? Why or why not?

2. Unicom is a regulated utility serving northern Illinois. The following table lists the stock prices and dividends on Unicom from 1989 to 1998.

Year	Price	Dividends
1989	$36.10	$3.00
1990	$33.60	$3.00
1991	$37.80	$3.00
1992	$30.90	$2.30
1993	$26.80	$1.60
1994	$24.80	$1.60
1995	$31.60	$1.60
1996	$28.50	$1.60
1997	$24.25	$1.60
1998	$35.60	$1.60

a. Estimate the average annual return you would have made on your investment.

b. Estimate the standard deviation and variance in annual returns.
c. If you were investing in Unicom today, would you expect the historical standard deviations and variances to continue to hold? Why or why not?

3. The following table summarizes the annual returns you would have made on two companies—Scientific Atlanta, a satellite and data equipment manufacturer, and AT&T, the telecommunications giant, from 1989 to 1998.

Year	Scientific Atlanta	AT&T
1989	80.95%	58.26%
1990	−47.37%	−33.79%
1991	31%	29.88%
1992	132.44%	30.35%
1993	32.02%	2.94%
1994	25.37%	−4.29%
1995	−28.57%	28.86%
1996	0.00%	−6.36%
1997	11.67%	48.64%
1998	36.19%	23.55%

a. Estimate the average and standard deviation in annual returns in each company.
b. Estimate the covariance and correlation in returns between the two companies.
c. Estimate the variance of a portfolio composed, in equal parts, of the two investments.

4. You are in a world where there are only two assets, gold and stocks. You are interested in investing your money in one, the other, or both assets. Consequently you collect the following data on the returns on the two assets over the last six years.

	Gold	Stock Market
Average return	8%	20%
Standard deviation	25%	22%
Correlation	−0.4	

a. If you were constrained to pick just one, which one would you choose?

b. You chose to invest only (or mainly?) in stocks, but a friend argues that this is wrong. He says that you are ignoring the big payoffs that you can get on gold. How would you go about alleviating his concern?

c. How would a portfolio composed of equal proportions in gold and stocks do in terms of mean and variance?

d. You now learn that GPEC (a cartel of gold-producing countries) is going to vary the amount of gold it produces with stock prices in the United States. (GPEC will produce less gold when stock markets are up and more when it is down.) What effect will this have on your portfolios? Explain.

5. You are interested in creating a portfolio of two stocks—Coca-Cola and Texas Utilities. Over the last decade, an investment in Coca-Cola stock would have earned an average annual return of 25 percent, with a standard deviation in returns of 36 percent. An investment in Texas Utilities stock would have earned an average annual return of 12 percent with a standard deviation of 22 percent. The correlation in returns across the two stocks is 0.28.

a. Assuming that the average and standard deviation, estimated using past returns, will continue to hold in the future, estimate the average returns and standard deviation of a portfolio composed 60 percent of Coca-Cola and 40 percent of Texas Utilities stock.

b. Estimate the minimum variance portfolio.

c. Now assume that Coca-Cola's international diversification will reduce the correlation to 0.20, while increasing Coca-Cola's standard deviation in returns to 45 percent. Assuming all of the other numbers remain unchanged, answer **a** and **b.**

6. Assume that you have half your money invested in Times Mirror, a media company, and the other half invested in Unilever, a consumer product giant. The expected returns and standard deviations on the two investments are summarized below.

	Times Mirror	Unilever
Expected return	14%	18%
Standard deviation	25%	40%

Estimate the variance of the portfolio as a function of the correlation coefficient (Start with −1 and increase the correlation to +1 in 0.2 increments).

7. You have been asked to analyze the standard deviation of a portfolio composed of the following three assets.

Investment	Expected Return	Standard Deviation
Sony Corporation	11%	23%
Tesoro Petroleum	9%	27%
Storage Technology	16%	50%

You have also been provided with the correlations across these three investments:

	Sony	Tesoro	Storage Tech
Sony	1.00	−0.15	0.20
Tesoro	−0.15	1.00	−0.25
Storage Tech	0.20	−0.25	1.00

Estimate the variance of a portfolio, equally weighted across all three assets.

8. You have been asked to estimate a minimum variance portfolio across a universe of 1,250 assets.

a. How many expected returns and variances would you need to compute?

b. How many covariances would you need to compute to obtain minimum variance portfolios?

9. Assume that the average variance of return for an individual security is 50 and that the average covariance is 10. What is the expected variance of a portfolio of 5, 10, 20, 50, and 100 securities? How many securities need to be held before the risk of a portfolio is only 10 percent more than the minimum?

10. Assume you have all your wealth ($1 million) invested in the Vanguard 500 index fund, and you expect to earn an annual return of 12 percent with a standard deviation in returns of 25 percent. Because you have become more risk-averse, you decide to shift $200,000 from the Vanguard fund to Treasury bills. The T bill rate is

5 percent. Estimate the expected return and standard deviation of your new portfolio.

11. Every investor in the CAPM owns a combination of the market portfolio and a riskless asset. Assume that the standard deviation of the market portfolio is 30 percent and the expected return on the portfolio is 15 percent. What proportion of the following investor's wealth would you suggest investing in the market portfolio and what proportion in the riskless asset? (The riskless asset has an expected return of 5 percent.)
   a. An investor who desires a portfolio with no standard deviation
   b. An investor who desires a portfolio with a standard deviation of 15 percent
   c. An investor who desires a portfolio with a standard deviation of 30 percent
   d. An investor who desires a portfolio with a standard deviation of 45 percent
   e. An investor who desires a portfolio with an expected return of 12 percent

12. The following table lists returns on the market portfolio and on Scientific Atlanta, each year from 1989 to 1998.

Year	Scientific Atlanta	Market Portfolio
1989	80.95%	31.49%
1990	−47.37%	−3.17%
1991	31%	30.57%
1992	132.44%	7.58%
1993	32.02%	10.36%
1994	25.37%	2.55%
1995	−28.57%	37.57%
1996	0.00%	22.68%
1997	11.67%	33.10%
1998	36.19%	28.32%

   a. Estimate the covariance in returns between Scientific Atlanta and the market portfolio.
   b. Estimate the variances in returns on both investments.
   c. Estimate the beta for Scientific Atlanta.

13. United Airlines has a beta of 1.50. The standard deviation in the market portfolio is 22 percent, and United Airlines has a standard deviation of 60 percent.
   a. Estimate the correlation between United Airlines and the market portfolio.
   b. What proportion of United Airlines' risk is market risk?

14. You are using the APM to estimate the expected return on Bethlehem Steel and have derived the following estimates for the factor betas and risk premiums.

Factor	Beta	Risk Premiums
1	1.2	2.5%
2	0.6	1.5%
3	1.5	1.0%
4	2.2	0.8%
5	0.5	1.2%

   a. Which risk factor is Bethlehem Steel most exposed to? Is there any way, within the APM, to identify the risk factor?
   b. If the risk-free rate is 5 percent, estimate the expected return on Bethlehem Steel.
   c. Now assume that the beta in the CAPM for Bethlehem Steel is 1.1 and the risk premium for the market portfolio is 5 percent. Estimate the expected return using the CAPM.
   d. Why are the expected returns different using the two models?

15. You are using the multifactor model to estimate the expected return on Emerson Electric and have derived the following estimates for the factor betas and risk premiums.

Macro-economic Factor	Measure	Beta	Risk Premiums $(R_{factor} - R_f)$
Level of interest rates	T bond rate	0.5	1.8%
Term structure	T bond rate − T bill rate	1.4	0.6%
Inflation rate	CPI	1.2	1.5%
Economic growth	GNP Growth rate	1.8	4.2%

With a riskless rate of 6 percent, estimate the expected return on Emerson Electric.

16. The following equation is reproduced from the study by Fama and French of returns between 1963 and 1990.

$$R_t = 1.77 - 0.11 \ln(MV) + 0.35 \ln(BV/MV)$$

where *MV* is the market value of equity in hundreds of millions of dollar and *BV* is the book value of equity in hundreds of millions of dollars. The return is a monthly return.

a. Estimate the expected annual return on Lucent Technologies. The market value of equity is $240 billion, and the book value of equity is $73.5 billion.

b. Lucent Technologies has a beta of 1.55. If the riskless rate is 6 percent, and the risk premium for the market portfolio is 5.5 percent, estimate the expected return.

c. Why are the expected returns different under the two approaches?

CHAPTER 4

RISK MEASUREMENT AND HURDLE RATES IN PRACTICE

In the last chapter, we presented the argument that the expected return on an equity investment should be a function of the market or nondiversifiable risk embedded in that investment. Here we turn our attention to how best to estimate the parameters of market risk in each of the models described in the previous chapter—the capital asset pricing model, the arbitrage pricing model, and the multifactor model. We will present three alternative approaches for measuring the market risk in an investment: the first is to use historical data on market prices for the firm considering the project,

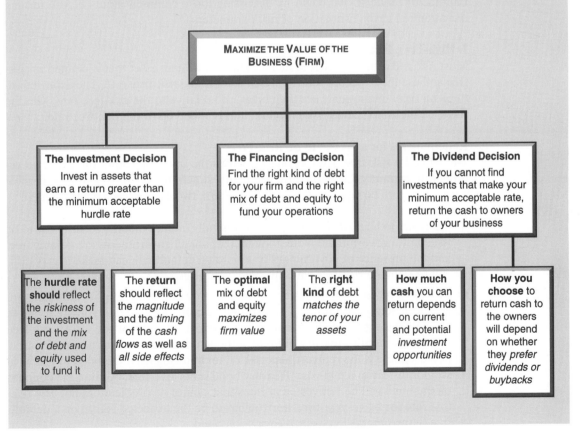

MAXIMIZE THE VALUE OF THE BUSINESS (FIRM)

The Investment Decision
Invest in assets that earn a return greater than the minimum acceptable hurdle rate

The Financing Decision
Find the right kind of debt for your firm and the right mix of debt and equity to fund your operations

The Dividend Decision
If you cannot find investments that make your minimum acceptable rate, return the cash to owners of your business

The **hurdle rate should** reflect the *riskiness* of the investment and the *mix of debt and equity* used to fund it

The **return** should reflect the *magnitude* and the *timing* of the *cash flows* as well as *all side effects*

The **optimal** mix of debt and equity *maximizes firm value*

The **right kind** of debt *matches the tenor of your assets*

How much cash you can return depends on current and potential *investment opportunities*

How you choose to return cash to the owners will depend on whether they *prefer dividends or buybacks*

the second is to use the market risk parameters estimated for other firms that are in the same business as the project being analyzed, and the third is to use accounting earnings or revenues to estimate the parameters.

In addition to estimating market risk, we will also discuss how best to estimate a riskless rate and a risk premium (in the CAPM) or risk premiums (in the APM and multifactor models) to convert the risk measures into expected returns. We will present a similar argument for converting default risk into a cost of debt and then bring the discussion to fruition by combining both the cost of equity and debt to estimate a cost of capital, which will become the minimum acceptable hurdle rate for an investment.

COST OF EQUITY

The *cost of equity* is the rate of return that investors require to invest in the equity of a firm. All of the risk and return models described in the previous chapter need a risk-free rate and a risk premium (in the CAPM) or premiums (in the APM and multifactor models). We begin by discussing those common inputs before turning our attention to the estimation of risk parameters.

I. Risk-Free Rate

Most risk and return models in finance start off with an asset that is defined as risk-free and use the expected return on that asset as the risk-free rate. The expected returns on risky investments are then measured relative to the risk-free rate, with the risk creating an expected risk premium that is added on to the risk-free rate.

Requirements for an Asset to be Risk-Free

We defined a risk-free asset as one for which the investor knows the expected returns with certainty. Consequently, for an investment to be risk-free, that is, to have an actual return be equal to the expected return, two conditions have to be met:

- There has to be *no default risk,* which generally implies that the security has to be issued by a government. Note, though, that not all governments are default-free, and the presence of government or sovereign default risk can make it very difficult to estimate risk-free rates in some currencies.

- There can be *no uncertainty about reinvestment rates,* which implies that there are no intermediate cash flows. To illustrate this point, assume that you are trying to estimate the expected return over a five-year period and that you want a risk-free rate. A six-month Treasury bill rate, although default-free, will not be risk-free, because there is the reinvestment risk of not knowing what the bill rate will be in six months. Even a five-year Treasury bond is not risk-free, because the coupons on the bond will be reinvested at rates that cannot be predicted today. The risk-free rate for a five-year time horizon has to be the expected return on a default-free (government) five-year zero coupon bond.

This clearly has painful implications for anyone doing corporate financial analysis, where expected returns often have to be estimated for multiple years. A purist's view of risk-free rates would then require different risk-free rates for each period and different expected returns. As a practical compromise, however, it is worth noting that the present value effect of using risk-free rates that vary from year to year tends to be small for most well-behaved term structures.[1] In these cases, we could use a duration matching strategy, where the duration of the default-free security used as the risk-free asset is matched up to the duration of the cash flows in the analysis.[2] If, however, there are very large differences in either direction between short-term and long-term rates, it does pay to use year-specific risk-free rates in computing expected returns.

Cash Flows and Risk-Free Rates: The Consistency Principle
The risk-free rate used to come up with expected returns should be measured consistently with how the cash flows are measured. If the cash flows are nominal, the risk-free rate should be in the same currency in which the cash flows are estimated. This also implies that it is not where a project or firm is located that determines the choice of a risk-free rate, but the currency in which the cash flows on the project or firm are estimated. Thus, Disney can analyze a proposed project in Mexico in dollars, using a dollar discount rate, or in pesos, using a peso discount rate. For the former, it would use the U.S. Treasury bond rate as the risk-free rate, but the latter would require a peso risk-free rate.

Under conditions of high and unstable inflation, valuation is often done in real terms. Effectively, this means that cash flows are estimated using real growth rates and without allowing for the growth that comes from price inflation. To be consistent, the discount rates used in these cases have to be real discount rates. To get a real expected rate of return, we need to start with a real risk-free rate. Although government bills and bonds offer returns that are risk-free in nominal terms, they are not risk-free in real terms, because inflation can be volatile. The standard approach of subtracting an expected inflation rate from the nominal interest rate to arrive at a real risk-free rate provides at best only an estimate of the real risk-free rate. Until recently, there were few traded default-free securities that could be used to estimate real risk-free rates; but the introduction of inflation-indexed Treasuries (called TIPs) has filled this void. An inflation-indexed Treasury security does not offer a guaranteed nominal return to buyers, but instead provides a guaranteed real return. In early 2004, for example, the inflation indexed U.S. ten-year Treasury bond rate was only 1.6 percent, much lower than the nominal ten-year bond rate of 4 percent.

---

[1]By "well-behaved term structures," we would include a normal upwardly sloping yield curve, where long term rates are at most 2–3 percent higher than short-term rates.

[2]In investment analysis, where we look at projects, these durations are usually between three and ten years. In valuation, the durations tend to be much longer because firms are assumed to have infinite lives. The duration in these cases is often well in excess of ten years and increases with the expected growth potential of the firm.

4.1 WHAT IS THE RIGHT RISK-FREE RATE?

The correct risk-free rate to use in the CAPM
- ☐ is the short-term government security rate.
- ☐ is the long-term government security rate.
- ☐ can be either, depending on whether the prediction is short-term or long-term.

IN PRACTICE: WHAT IF THERE IS NO DEFAULT-FREE RATE?

Our discussion to this point has been predicated on the assumption that governments do not default, at least on local currency borrowing. There are many emerging market economies where this assumption might not be viewed as reasonable. Governments in these markets are perceived as capable of defaulting even on local currency borrowing. When this is coupled with the fact that many governments do not borrow long-term in the local currency, there are scenarios in which obtaining a risk-free rate in that currency, especially for the long term, becomes difficult. In these cases, there are compromises that give us reasonable estimates of the risk-free rate.

- Look at the largest and safest firms in that market and use the rate that they pay on their long-term borrowings in the local currency as a base. Given that these firms still have default risk in spite of their size and stability, you would use a rate that is marginally lower than the corporate borrowing rate.[3]

- If there are long-term dollar-denominated forward contracts on the currency, you can use interest rate parity and the Treasury bond rate to arrive at an estimate of the local borrowing rate.[4]

- If the government does borrow long term in the local currency, you could adjust the government borrowing rate by the estimated default spread on the bond to arrive at a riskless local currency rate. The default spread on the government bond can be estimated using the local currency ratings that are available for many countries.[5] For instance, assume that the Brazilian government bond rate (in nominal Brazilian reals [BR]) is 14 percent and that the local currency rating assigned to the Brazilian government is BB+. If the default spread for bonds rated BB+ is 5 percent, the riskless BR rate would be 9 percent.

$$\text{Riskless BR Rate} = \text{Brazil Government Bond Rate} - \text{Default Spread}$$
$$= 14\% - 5\% = 9\%$$
■

---

[3]Reducing the corporate borrowing rate by 1 percent (which is the typical default spread on highly rated corporate bonds in the United States) to get a riskless rate yields reasonable estimates.

[4]For instance, if the current spot rate is 38.10 Thai baht per U.S. dollar, the ten-year forward rate is 61.36 baht per dollar, and the current ten-year U.S. Treasury bond rate is 5 percent, the ten-year Thai risk-free rate (in nominal baht) can be estimated as follows: $61.36 = (38.1)(1 + \text{Interest Rate}_{\text{Thai baht}})/(1 + 0.05)^{10}$. Solving for the Thai interest rate yields a ten-year risk free rate of 10.12 percent.

[5]Ratings agencies generally assign different ratings for local currency borrowings and dollar borrowings, with higher ratings for the former and lower ratings for the latter.

II. Risk Premium

The risk premium(s) is clearly a significant input in all of the asset pricing models. In the following section, we will begin by examining the fundamental determinants of risk premiums and then look at practical approaches to estimating these premiums.

What Is the Risk Premium Supposed to Measure?

The risk premium in the CAPM measures the extra return that would be demanded by investors for shifting their money from a riskless investment to the market portfolio of risky investments, on average. It should be a function of two variables:

1. ***Risk Aversion of Investors***   As investors become more risk-averse, they should demand a larger premium for shifting from the riskless asset. Although some of this risk aversion may be inherent, some of it is also a function of economic prosperity (when the economy is doing well, investors tend to be much more willing to take risk) and recent experiences in the market (risk premiums tend to surge after large market drops).

2. ***Riskiness of the Average Risk Investment***   As the riskiness of the average risk investment increases, so should the premium. This will depend on what firms are actually traded in the market, their economic fundamentals, and how involved they are in managing risk.

Because each investor in a market is likely to have a different assessment of an acceptable equity risk premium, the premium will be a weighted average of these individual premiums, where the weights will be based on the wealth the investor brings to the market. Put more directly, what Warren Buffett, with his substantial wealth, thinks is an acceptable premium will be weighted in far more into market prices than what you or I might think about the same measure.

In the APM and the multifactor models, the risk premiums used for individual factors are similar wealth-weighted averages of the premiums that individual investors would demand for each factor separately.

4.2   WHAT IS YOUR RISK PREMIUM?

Assume that stocks are the only risky assets and that you are offered two investment options:
- A riskless investment (say, a government security), on which you can make 4 percent
- A mutual fund of all stocks, on which the returns are uncertain

How much of an expected return would you demand to shift your money from the riskless asset to the mutual fund?

☐ Less than 4 percent
☐ Between 4 and 6 percent
☐ Between 6 and 8 percent
☐ Between 8 and 10 percent
☐ Between 10 and 12 percent
☐ More than 12 percent

Your answer to this question should provide you with a measure of your risk premium. (For instance, if your answer is 6 percent, your premium is 2 percent.)

Estimating Risk Premiums

There are three ways of estimating the risk premium in the CAPM: Large investors can be surveyed about their expectations for the future, the actual premiums earned over a past period can be obtained from historical data, and the implied premium can be extracted from current market data. The premium can be estimated only from historical data in the APM and the multifactor models.

1. Survey Premiums

Because the premium is a weighted average of the premiums demanded by individual investors, one approach to estimating this premium is to survey investors about their expectations for the future. It is clearly impractical to survey all investors; therefore, most surveys focus on portfolio managers who carry the most weight in the process. Morningstar regularly surveys individual investors about the return they expect to earn investing in stocks. Merrill Lynch does the same with equity portfolio managers and reports the results on its Web site. Although numbers do emerge from these surveys, very few practitioners actually use these survey premiums. There are three reasons for this reticence:

- There are no constraints on reasonability; individual money managers could provide expected returns that are lower than the risk-free rate, for instance.
- Survey premiums are extremely volatile; the survey premiums can change dramatically, largely as a function of recent market movements.
- Survey premiums tend to be short-term; even the longest surveys do not go beyond one year.

4.3   DO RISK PREMIUMS CHANGE?

In the previous question, you were asked how much of a premium you would demand for investing in a portfolio of stocks as opposed to a riskless asset. Assume that the market dropped by 20 percent last week, and you were asked the same question today. Would your premium be

- ☐   higher?
- ☐   lower?
- ☐   unchanged?

2. Historical Premiums

The most common approach to estimating the risk premium(s) used in financial asset pricing models is to base it on historical data. In the APM and multifactor models, the premiums are based on historical data on asset prices over very long time periods, which are used to extract factor-specific risk premiums. In the CAPM, the premium is defined as the difference between average returns on stocks and average returns on risk-free securities over an extended period of history.

Basics   In most cases, this approach is composed of the following steps. It begins by defining a time period for the estimation, which can range to as far back as 1871 for U.S. data. It then requires the calculation of the average returns on a stock index and average returns on a riskless security over the period. Finally, the difference between the average returns on stocks and the riskless return is defined as the risk premium looking forward. In doing this, we implicitly assume that

1. The risk aversion of investors has not changed in a systematic way across time. (The risk aversion may change from year to year, but it reverts back to historical averages.)
2. The average riskiness of the "risky" portfolio (stock index) has not changed in a systematic way across time.

Estimation Issues   Users of risk and return models may have developed a consensus that the historical premium is in fact the best estimate of the risk premium looking forward, but there are surprisingly large differences in the actual premiums used in practice. For instance, the risk premium estimated in the U.S. markets by different investment banks, consultants, and corporations range from 2 percent at the lower end to 12 percent at the upper end. Given that they almost all use the same database of historical returns, provided by Ibbotson Associates,[6] summarizing data from 1926, these differences may seem surprising. There are, however, three reasons for the divergence in risk premiums.

- *Time Period Used*   Although there are some who use all of the Ibbotson data, which goes back to 1926, there are many using data over shorter time periods, such as fifty, twenty, or even ten years to come up with historical risk premiums. The rationale presented by those who use shorter periods is that the risk aversion of the average investor is likely to change over time and using a shorter and more recent time period provides a more updated estimate. This has to be offset against a cost associated with using shorter time periods, which is the greater estimation error in the risk premium estimate. In fact, given the annual standard deviation in stock prices between 1928 and 2003 of 20 percent,[7] the standard error associated with the risk premium estimate can be estimated as follows for different estimation periods in Table 4.1.[8]

   Note that to get reasonable standard errors, we need very long time periods of historical returns. Conversely, the standard errors from ten- and twenty-year estimates are likely to be almost as large or larger than the actual risk premiums estimated. This cost of using shorter time periods seems, in our view, to overwhelm any advantages associated with getting a more updated premium.

---

[6]See "Stocks, Bonds, Bills, and Inflation," an annual publication that reports on the annual returns on stocks, Treasury bonds and bills, and inflation rates from 1926 to the present. Available online at www.ibbotson.com.

[7]For the historical data on stock returns, bond returns, and bill returns, check under Updated Data at www.damodaran.com.

[8]These estimates of the standard error are probably understated because they are based on the assumption that annual returns are uncorrelated over time. There is substantial empirical evidence that returns are correlated over time, which would make this standard error estimate much larger.

Table 4.1   STANDARD ERRORS IN RISK PREMIUM ESTIMATES

Estimation Period	Standard Error of Risk Premium Estimate
5 years	$20/\sqrt{5} = 8.94\%$
10 years	$20/\sqrt{10} = 6.32\%$
25 years	$20/\sqrt{25} = 4.00\%$
50 years	$20/\sqrt{50} = 2.83\%$

- ***Choice of Risk-Free Security***   The Ibbotson database reports returns on both Treasury bills and bonds and the risk premium for stocks can be estimated relative to each. Given that short-term rates have been lower than long-term rates in the United States for most of the past seven decades, the risk premium is larger when estimated relative to shorter-term government securities (such as Treasury bills). The risk-free rate chosen in computing the premium has to be consistent with the risk-free rate used to compute expected returns. For the most part, in corporate finance and valuation, the risk-free rate will be a long-term government bond rate and not a short-term rate. Thus the risk premium used should be the premium earned by stocks over Treasury bonds.

- ***Arithmetic and Geometric Averages***   The final sticking point when it comes to estimating historical premiums relates to how the average returns on stocks and Treasury bonds and bills are computed. The arithmetic average return measures the mean of the series of annual returns, whereas the geometric average looks at the compounded return.[9] Conventional wisdom argues for the use of the arithmetic average. In fact, if annual returns are uncorrelated over time and our objective was to estimate the risk premium for the next year, the arithmetic average is the best unbiased estimate of the premium. In reality, however, there are strong arguments that can be made for the use of geometric averages. First, empirical studies seem to indicate that returns on stocks are negatively correlated over time.[10] Consequently, the arithmetic average return is likely to overstate the premium. Second, although asset pricing models may be single-period models, the use of these models to get expected returns over long periods (such as five or ten years) suggests that the analysis is more likely to be over multiple years than for just the next year. In this context, the argument for geometric average premiums becomes even stronger.

In summary, the risk premium estimates vary across users because of differences in time periods used, the choice of Treasury bills or bonds as the risk-free rate, and

---

[9]The compounded return is computed by taking the value of the investment at the start of the period (Value_0) and the value at the end (Value_N) and then computing the following: Geometric Average $= (\text{Value}_N/\text{Value}_0)^{1/N} - 1$.

[10]In other words, good years are more likely to be followed by poor years and vice versa. The evidence on negative serial correlation in stock returns over time is extensive and can be found in E. F. Fama and K. R. French, 1988, "Permanent and Temporary Components of Stock Prices," *Journal of Political Economy,* 96, 246–273. Although they find that the one-year correlations are low, the five-year serial correlations are strongly negative for all size classes.

Table 4.2 HISTORICAL RISK PREMIUMS (%) FOR THE UNITED STATES, 1928–2003

	Stocks–Treasury Bills		Stocks–Treasury Bonds	
	Arithmetic	Geometric	Arithmetic	Geometric
1928–2003	7.92%	5.99%	6.54%	4.82%
1962–2003	6.09%	4.85%	4.70%	3.82%
1992–2003	8.43%	6.68%	4.87%	3.57%

the use of arithmetic as opposed to geometric averages. The effect of these choices is summarized in Table 4.2, which uses returns from 1928 to 2003.[11]

Note that the premiums can range from 3.57 percent to 8.43 percent, depending on the choices made. In fact, these differences are exacerbated by the fact that many risk premiums that are in use today were estimated using historical data from three, four, or even ten years ago. If we follow the propositions about picking a long-term geometric average premium over the long-term Treasury bond rate, the historical risk premium that makes the most sense is 4.82 percent.

Historical Premiums in Other Markets   Although historical data on stock returns is easily available and accessible in the United States, it is much more difficult to get for foreign markets. The most detailed look at these returns estimated the returns you would have earned on fourteen equity markets between 1900 and 2001 and compared these returns with those you would have earned investing in bonds.[12] Figure 4.1 presents the risk premiums—that is, the additional returns—earned by investing in equity over short-term and long-term government bonds over that period in each of the sixteen markets.

Although equity returns were higher than what you would have earned investing in government bonds or bills in each of the countries examined, there are wide differences across countries. If you had invested in Spain, for instance, you would have earned only 3 percent over government bills and 2 percent over government bonds on an annual basis by investing in equities. In France, in contrast, the corresponding numbers would have been 7.1 percent and 4.6 percent. When looking at forty- or fifty-year periods, therefore, it is entirely possible that equity returns can lag behind bond or bill returns, at least in some equity markets. In other words, the notion that stocks always win in the long run is not only dangerous but does not make sense. If stocks always beat riskless investments in the long run, they should be riskless to an investor with a long time horizon.

There is a data set on the Web that has yearly data on Treasury bill rates, Treasury bond rates, and returns and stock returns going back to 1928.

---

[11]The raw data on Treasury bill rates, Treasury bond rates, and stock returns was obtained from the Federal Reserve data archives maintained by the Fed in St. Louis.

[12]E. Dimson, P. March, and M. Staunton, 2002, *Triumph of the Optimists,* Princeton, NJ: Princeton University Press.

Figure 4.1 Equity Risk Premiums by Country

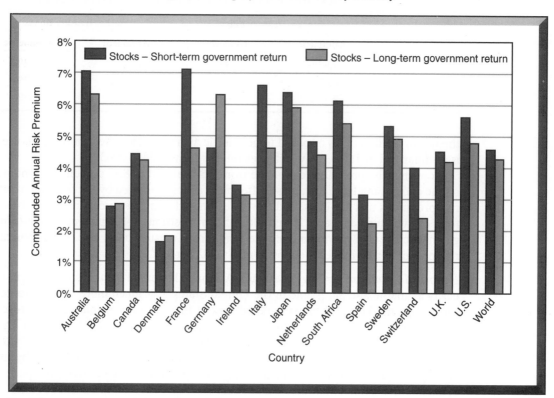

The differences in compounded annual returns between stocks and short-term governments/long-term governments is reported for each country. Data from Dimson et al. (2002).

A Modified Historical Risk Premium In many emerging markets, there is very little historical data, and what does exist is too volatile to yield a meaningful estimate of the risk premium. To estimate the risk premium in these countries, let us start with the basic proposition that the risk premium in any equity market can be written as

$$\text{Equity Risk Premium} = \text{Base Premium for Mature Equity Market} + \text{Country Premium}$$

The country premium could reflect the extra risk in a specific market. This boils down in our estimation to answering two questions:

- What should the base premium for a mature equity market be?
- How do we estimate the additional risk premium for individual countries?

To answer the first question, we will make the argument that the U.S. equity market is mature and that there is sufficient historical data to make a reasonable estimate of the risk premium. In fact, reverting back to our discussion of historical premiums in the U.S. market, we will use the geometric average premium earned by stocks over Treasury bonds of 4.82 percent between 1928 and 2003 as a mature market premium. We chose the long time period to reduce the standard error in our estimate, the Treasury bond to be consistent with our choice of a risk-free rate, and geometric averages to reflect our desire for a risk premium that we can use for longer-term expected returns. There are three approaches that we can use to estimate the country risk premium.

1. *Country Bond Default Spreads*   There are several measures of country risk, and one of the simplest and most easily accessible is the rating assigned to a country's debt by a ratings agency (S&P, Moody's, and IBCA all rate countries). These sovereign ratings measure default risk (rather than equity risk), but they are affected by many of the factors that drive equity risk—the stability of a country's currency, its budget and trade balances, and its political stability, for instance.[13] The other advantage of ratings is that they come with default spreads over the U.S. Treasury bond. For instance, Brazil was rated B2 in early 2004 by Moody's and the ten-year Brazilian C-bond, which is a dollar-denominated bond issued by the government, was priced to yield 10.01 percent, 6.01 percent more than the interest rate (4 percent) on a ten-year Treasury bond at the same time.[14] Analysts who use default spreads as measures of country risk typically add them on to both the cost of equity and debt of every company traded in that country. For instance, the cost of equity for a Brazilian company, estimated in U.S. dollars, will be 6.01 percent higher than the cost of equity of an otherwise similar U.S. company. If we assume that the risk premium for the United States and other mature equity markets is 4.82 percent, the cost of equity for a Brazilian company with a beta of 1.2 can be estimated as follows (with a U.S. Treasury bond rate of 4 percent).

$$\text{Cost of Equity} = \text{Risk-Free Rate} + \text{Beta} \times (\text{U.S. Risk Premium})$$
$$+ \text{Country Bond Default Spread}$$
$$= 4\% + 1.2(4.82\%) + 6.01\% = 15.79\%$$

In some cases, analysts add the default spread to the U.S. risk premium and multiply it by the beta. This increases the cost of equity for high-beta companies and lowers them for low-beta firms.

2. *Relative Standard Deviation*   There are some analysts who believe that the equity risk premiums of markets should reflect the differences in equity risk, as measured by the volatilities of these markets. A conventional measure of equity risk is the standard deviation in stock prices; higher standard deviations are

---

[13]The process by which country ratings are obtained is explained on the S&P Web site at www.ratings. standardpoor.com/criteria/index.htm.

[14]These yields were as of January 2004. Although this is a market rate and reflects current expectations, country bond spreads are extremely volatile and can shift significantly from day to day. To counter this volatility, the default spread can be normalized by averaging the spread over time or by using the average default spread for all countries with the same rating as Brazil in early 2004.

generally associated with more risk. If you scale the standard deviation of one market against another, you obtain a measure of relative risk.

$$\text{Relative Standard Deviation}_{\text{Country X}} = \frac{\text{Standard Deviation}_{\text{Country X}}}{\text{Standard Deviation}_{\text{U.S.}}}$$

This relative standard deviation when multiplied by the premium used for U.S. stocks should yield a measure of the total risk premium for any market.

$$\text{Equity Risk Premium}_{\text{Country X}} = \text{Risk Premium}_{\text{U.S.}} \times \text{Relative Standard Deviation}_{\text{Country X}}$$

Assume for the moment that you are using a mature market premium for the United States of 4.82 percent and the annual standard deviation of U.S. stocks is 20 percent. The annualized standard deviation in the Brazilian equity index is 36 percent,[15] yielding a total risk premium for Brazil:

$$\text{Equity Risk Premium}_{\text{Brazil}} = 4.82\% \times \frac{36\%}{20\%} = 8.68\%$$

The country risk premium can be isolated as follows:

$$\text{Country Risk Premium}_{\text{Brazil}} = 8.68\% - 4.82\% = 3.86\%$$

Although this approach has intuitive appeal, there are problems with using standard deviations computed in markets with widely different market structures and liquidity. There are very risky emerging markets that have low standard deviations for their equity markets because the markets are illiquid. This approach will understate the equity risk premiums in those markets.

3. *Default Spreads + Relative Standard Deviations*   The country default spreads that come with country ratings provide an important first step, but still only measure the premium for default risk. Intuitively, we would expect the country equity risk premium to be larger than the country default risk spread because equities are riskier than bonds. To address the issue of how much higher, we look at the volatility of the equity market in a country relative to the volatility of the country bond used to estimate the default spread. This yields the following estimate for the country equity risk premium.

$$\text{Country Risk Premium} = \text{Country Default Spread} \times \left(\frac{\sigma_{\text{Equity}}}{\sigma_{\text{Country Bond}}} \right)$$

To illustrate, consider the case of Brazil. As noted earlier, the dollar-denominated bonds issued by the Brazilian government trade with a default spread of 6.01 percent over the U.S. Treasury bond rate. The annualized standard deviation in the Brazilian equity index over the previous year is 36.0 percent, whereas the

---

[15]Both the U.S. and Brazilian standard deviations were computed using weekly returns for two years from the beginning of 2002 to the end of 2003. You could use daily standard deviations to make the same judgments, but they tend to have much more estimation error in them.

annualized standard deviation in the Brazilian C-bond is 28.2 percent.[16] The resulting additional country equity risk premium for Brazil is as follows:

$$\text{Brazil's Country Risk Premium} = 6.01\% \left(\frac{36.0\%}{28.2\%} \right) = 7.67\%$$

Note that this country risk premium will increase if the country default spread widens or if the relative volatility of the equity market increases. It is also *in addition* to the equity risk premium for a mature market. Thus the total equity risk premium for a Brazilian company using the approach and a 4.82 percent premium for the United States would be 12.49 percent.

Why should equity risk premiums have any relationship to country bond default spreads? A simple explanation is that an investor who can make 11 percent on a dollar-denominated Brazilian government bond would not settle for an expected return of 10.5 percent (in dollar terms) on Brazilian equity. This approach and the previous one both use the standard deviation in equity of a market to make a judgment about country risk premium, but they measure it relative to different bases. This approach uses the country bond as a base, whereas the previous one uses the standard deviation in the U.S. market. This approach assumes that investors are more likely to choose between Brazilian government bonds and Brazilian equity, whereas the previous approach assumes that the choice is across equity markets.

The three approaches to estimating country risk premiums will generally give different estimates, with the bond default spread and relative equity standard deviation approaches yielding lower country risk premiums than the melded approach that uses both the country bond default spread and the equity and bond market standard deviations. In the case of Brazil, for instance, the country risk premiums range from 3.86 percent using the relative equity standard deviation approach to 6.01 percent for the country bond approach to a high of 7.67 percent using the melded approach. We believe that the larger country risk premiums that emerge from the last approach are the most realistic for the immediate future, but country risk premiums may decline over time. Just as companies mature and become less risky over time, countries can mature and become less risky as well.

 IN PRACTICE: SHOULD THERE BE A COUNTRY RISK PREMIUM?

Is there more risk in investing in a Malaysian or Brazilian stock than there is in investing in the United States? The answer, to most, seems to be obviously affirmative. That, however, does not answer the question of whether there should be an additional risk premium charged when investing in those markets. Note that the only risk relevant for the purpose of estimating a cost of equity is market risk or risk that

---

[16]The standard deviation in C-bond returns was computed using weekly returns over two years as well. Because these returns are in dollars and the returns on the Brazilian equity index are in reals, there is an inconsistency here. We did estimate the standard deviation on the Brazilian equity index in dollars, but it made little difference to the overall calculation because the dollar standard deviation was close to 36 percent.

cannot be diversified away. The key question then becomes whether the risk in an emerging market is diversifiable or nondiversifiable risk. If, in fact, the additional risk of investing in Malaysia or Brazil can be diversified away, then there should be no additional risk premium charged. If it cannot, then it makes sense to think about estimating a country risk premium.

For purposes of analyzing country risk, we look at the marginal investor—the investor most likely to be trading on the equity. If that marginal investor is globally diversified, there is at least the potential for global diversification. If the marginal investor does not have a global portfolio, the likelihood of diversifying away country risk declines substantially. Even if the marginal investor is globally diversified, there is a second test that has to be met for country risk to not matter. All or much of country risk should be country-specific. In other words, there should be low correlation across markets. Only then will the risk be diversifiable in a globally diversified portfolio. If, on the other hand, stock markets across countries move together, country risk has a market risk component, is not diversifiable, and should command a premium. Whether returns across countries are positively correlated is an empirical question. Studies from the 1970s and 1980s suggested that the correlation was low, and this was an impetus for global diversification. Partly because of the success of that sales pitch and partly because economies around the world have become increasingly intertwined over the past decade or so, more recent studies indicate that the correlation across markets has risen. This is borne out by the speed at which troubles in one market, say, Russia, can spread to a market with which it has little or no obvious relationship, say, Brazil.

So where do we stand? We believe that although the barriers to trading across markets have dropped, investors still have a home bias in their portfolios and that markets remain partially segmented. Globally diversified investors are playing an increasing role in the pricing of equities around the world, but the resulting increase in correlation across markets has resulted in a portion of country risk becoming non-diversifiable or market risk. ■

 There is a data set on the Web that contains the updated ratings for countries and the risk premiums associated with each.

3. Implied Equity Premiums

There is an alternative to estimating risk premiums that does not require historical data or adjustments for country risk but does assume that the overall stock market is correctly priced. Consider, for instance, a very simple valuation model for stocks.

$$\text{Value} = \frac{\text{Expected Dividends Next Period}}{(\text{Required Return on Equity} - \text{Expected Growth Rate in Dividends})}$$

This is essentially the present value of dividends growing at a constant rate. Three of the four variables in this model can be obtained easily—the current level of the market (i.e., value), the expected dividends next period, and the expected growth rate in earnings and dividends in the long term. The only unknown is then the required return on equity; when we solve for it, we get an implied expected return on stocks. Subtracting out the risk-free rate will yield an implied equity risk premium.

Table 4.3 Expected Cash Flows on S&P 500	
Year	**Cash Flow on Index**
1	34.26
2	37.52
3	41.08
4	44.98
5	49.26
6	51.35

Note: Cash flow in the first year = 2.81% of 1111.91 (1.095).

To illustrate, assume that the current level of the S&P 500 Index is 900, the expected dividend yield on the index for the next period is 2 percent, and the expected growth rate in earnings and dividends in the long run is 7 percent. Solving for the required return on equity yields the following:

$$900 = \frac{900(0.02)}{r - 0.07}$$

Solving for r,

$$r - 0.07 = 0.02 \qquad r = 0.09 = 9\%$$

If the current risk-free rate is 6 percent, this will yield a risk premium of 3 percent.

This approach can be generalized to allow for high growth for a period and extended to cover cash flow-based rather than dividend-based models. To illustrate this, consider the S&P 500 Index on January 1, 2004. The index was at 1,111.91 and the dividend and buyback yield on the index in 2003 was roughly 2.81 percent.[17] In addition, the consensus estimate of growth in earnings for companies in the index was approximately 9.5 percent for the next five years,[18] and the ten-year Treasury bond rate on that day was 4.25 percent. Because a growth rate of 9.5 percent cannot be sustained forever, we employ a two-stage valuation model, where we allow dividends to grow at 9.5 percent for five years and then lower the growth rate to the Treasury bond rate of 4.25 percent after the five-year period.[19] Table 4.3 summarizes the expected cash flows for the next five years of high growth and the first year of stable growth thereafter.

If we assume that these are reasonable estimates of the cash flows and that the index is correctly priced, then

$$\text{Index Level} = 1{,}111.91 = \frac{34.26}{(1+r)} + \frac{37.52}{(1+r)^2} + \frac{41.08}{(1+r)^3} + \frac{44.98}{(1+r)^4}$$

$$+ \frac{49.26}{(1+r)^5} + \frac{49.26(1.0425)}{(r-0.0425)(1+r)^5}$$

---

[17]Stock buybacks during the year were added to the dividends to obtain a consolidated yield.

[18]We used the average of the analyst estimates for individual firms (bottom-up). Alternatively, we could have used the top-down estimate for the S&P 500 earnings.

[19]The Treasury bond rate is the sum of expected inflation and the expected real rate. If we assume that real growth is equal to the real interest rate, the long-term stable growth rate should be equal to the Treasury bond rate.

Note that the last term of the equation is the terminal value of the index, based on the stable growth rate of 4.25 percent, discounted back to the present. Solving for r in this equation yields the required return on equity of 7.94 percent. Subtracting out the Treasury bond rate of 4.25 percent yields an implied equity premium of 3.69 percent.

The advantage of this approach is that it is market-driven and forward-looking and does not require any historical data. Thus it can be used to estimate implied equity premiums in any market. However, it is bounded by whether the model used for the valuation is the right one and the availability and reliability of the inputs to that model. For instance, the equity risk premium for the Brazilian market in January 2004 was estimated from the following inputs. The index (Bovespa) was at 21,050 and the current dividend yield on the index was 4 percent. Earnings in companies in the index are expected to grow 14 percent (in U.S. dollar terms) over the next five years and 4.5 percent thereafter. These inputs yield a required return on equity of 10.70 percent, which when compared to the Treasury bond rate of 4 percent on that day results in an implied equity premium of 6.70 percent. For simplicity, we have used nominal dollar expected growth rates and Treasury bond rates,[20] but this analysis could have been done entirely in the local currency.

The implied equity premiums change over time much more than historical risk premiums. In fact, the contrast between these premiums and the historical premiums is best illustrated by graphing the implied premiums in the S&P 500 going back to 1960 in Figure 4.2.

In terms of mechanics, we used analyst estimates of growth rates in earnings and dividends as our projected growth rates and a two-stage dividend discount model (similar to the one we used to compute the implied premium in the last section). Looking at these numbers, we would draw the following conclusions.

- The implied equity premium has seldom been as high as the historical risk premium. Even in 1978, when the implied equity premium peaked, the estimate of 6.50 percent is well below what many practitioners use as the risk premium in their risk and return models. In fact, the average implied equity risk premium has been about 4 percent over the past forty years.

- The implied equity premium did increase during the 1970s as inflation increased. This does have interesting implications for risk premium estimation. Instead of assuming that the risk premium is a constant and is unaffected by the level of inflation and interest rates, which is what we do with historical risk premiums, it may be more realistic to change the risk premium as expected inflation and interest rates change.

 There is a data set on the Web that shows the inputs used to calculate the premium in each year for the U.S. market.

---

[20]The input that is most difficult to estimate for emerging markets is a long-term expected growth rate. For Brazilian stocks, we used the average consensus estimate of growth in earnings for the largest Brazilian companies that have listed ADRs. This estimate may be biased as a consequence.

Figure 4.2   Implied Premium for U.S. Equity Market

Source: Damodaran Online.

 This spreadsheet allows you to estimate the implied equity premium in a market (**implprem.xls**).

4.4 IMPLIED AND HISTORICAL PREMIUMS

Assume that the implied premium in the market is 3 percent and that you are using a historical premium of 7.5 percent. If you valued stocks using this historical premium, you are likely to find

☐ more undervalued stocks than overvalued ones.

☐ more overvalued stocks than undervalued ones.

☐ about as many undervalued as overvalued stocks.

III. Risk Parameters

The final set of inputs we need to put risk and return models into practice are the risk parameters for individual assets and projects. In the CAPM, the beta of the asset has to be estimated relative to the market portfolio. In the APM and multifactor model, the betas of the asset relative to each factor have to be measured. There are three approaches available for estimating these parameters; one is to use historical data on market prices for individual assets; the second is to estimate the betas from fundamentals; and the third is to use accounting data. We use all three approaches in this section.

A. Historical Market Betas

This is the conventional approach for estimating betas used by most services and analysts. For firms that have been publicly traded for a length of time, it is relatively straightforward to estimate returns that an investor would have made investing in its equity in intervals (such as a week or a month) over that period. These returns can then be related to returns on a equity market index to get a beta in the CAPM, or to multiple macroeconomic factors to get betas in the multifactor models, or put through a factor analysis to yield betas for the APM.

Standard Procedures for Estimating CAPM Parameters, Betas and Alphas
The standard procedure for estimating betas is to regress stock returns (R_j) against market returns (R_m)

$$R_j = a + bR_m$$

where a = intercept from the regression and b = slope of the regression = covariance $(R_j, R_m)/\sigma_m^2$.[21]

The *slope* of the regression corresponds to the beta of the stock and measures the riskiness of the stock.

The *intercept* of the regression provides a simple measure of performance during the period of the regression, relative to the CAPM.

$$R_j = R_f + \beta(R_m - R_f)$$
$$\quad = R_f(1 - \beta) + \beta R_m \qquad \text{Capital Asset Pricing Model}$$
$$R_j = a + bR_m \qquad \text{Regression Equation}$$

Thus, a comparison of the intercept (a) to $R_f (1 - \beta)$ should provide a measure of the stock's performance, at least relative to the CAPM.[22]

If $a > R_f(1 - \beta)$ Stock did better than expected during regression period
$a = R_f(1 - \beta)$ Stock did as well as expected during regression period
$a < R_f(1 - \beta)$ Stock did worse than expected during regression period

The difference between a and $R_f(1 - \beta)$ is called **Jensen's alpha** and provides a measure of whether the asset in question under- or outperformed the market, after adjusting for risk, during the period of the regression.

The third statistic that emerges from the regression is the **R squared** (R^2) of the regression. Although the statistical explanation of the R^2 is that it provides a measure of the goodness of fit of the regression, the financial rationale for the R^2 is that it provides an estimate of the proportion of the risk (variance) of a firm that can be attributed to market risk; the balance $(1 - R^2)$ can then be attributed to firm-specific risk.

---

[21] Appendix 1 provides a brief overview of ordinary least squares regressions.

[22] The regression can be run using returns in excess of the risk-free rate for both the stock and the market. In that case, the intercept of the regression should be zero if the actual returns equal the expected returns from the CAPM, greater than zero if the stock does better than expected, and less than zero if it does worse than expected.

The final statistic worth noting is the *standard error of the beta estimate*. The slope of the regression, like any statistical estimate, is estimated with error, and the standard error reveals the magnitude of the error. The standard error can also be used to arrive at confidence intervals for the "true" beta value from the slope estimate.

Jensen's Alpha: This is the difference between the actual return on an asset and the return you would have expected it to make during a past period, given what the market did, and the asset's beta.

R Squared (R^2): The R squared measures the proportion of the variability of a dependent variable that is explained by an independent variable or variables in a regression.

Estimation Issues

There are three decisions the analyst must make in setting up the regression described. The first concerns the *length of the estimation period*. The trade-off is simple: A longer estimation period provides more data, but the firm itself might have changed in its risk characteristics over the time period. Disney and Deutsche Bank have changed substantially in terms of both business mix and financial leverage over the past few years, and any regression that we run using historical data will be affected by these changes.

The second estimation issue relates to the *return interval*. Returns on stocks are available on annual, monthly, weekly, daily, and even intraday bases. Using daily or intraday returns will increase the number of observations in the regression, but it exposes the estimation process to a significant bias in beta estimates related to nontrading.[23] For instance, the betas estimated for small firms, which are more likely to suffer from nontrading, are biased downward when daily returns are used. Using weekly or monthly returns can reduce the nontrading bias significantly.[24]

The third estimation issue relates to the choice of a *market index* to be used in the regression. The standard practice used by most beta estimation services is to estimate the betas of a company relative to an index of the market in which its stock trades. Thus the betas of German stocks are estimated relative to the Frankfurt DAX, British stocks relative to the FTSE, Japanese stocks relative to the Nikkei, and U.S. stocks relative to the S&P 500. This practice may yield an estimate that is a reasonable measure of risk for the parochial or purely domestic investor, but it may not be the best approach for an international or cross-border investor, who would be better served with a beta estimated relative to an international index.

---

[23]The nontrading bias arises because the returns in nontrading periods is zero (even though the market may have moved up or down significantly in those periods). Using these nontrading period returns in the regression will reduce the correlation between stock returns and market returns and the beta of the stock.

[24]The bias can also be reduced using statistical techniques.

ILLUSTRATION **4.1** **Estimating CAPM Risk Parameters for Disney**

In assessing risk parameters for Disney, the returns on the stock and the market index are computed as follows,

1. The returns to a stockholder in Disney are computed month by month from January 1999 to December 2003. These returns include both dividends and price appreciation and are defined as follows:

$$\text{Stock Return}_{\text{Disney},j} = (\text{Price}_{\text{Disney},j} - \text{Price}_{\text{Disney},j-1} + \text{Dividends}_{\text{Disney},j})/\text{Price}_{\text{Disney},j-1}$$

where Stock Return$_{\text{Disney},j}$ = returns to a stockholder in Disney in month j;

Price$_{\text{Disney},j}$ = price of Disney stock at the end of month j; and

Dividends$_{\text{Disney},j}$ = dividends on Disney stock in month j.

Dividends are added to the returns of the month in which the stock went ex-dividend.[25] If there was a stock split during the month,[26] the returns have to take into account the split factor, because stock prices will be affected.[27]

2. The returns on the S&P 500 are computed for each month of the same time period, using the level of the index at the end of each month, and the monthly dividend yield on stocks in the index.

$$\text{Market Return}_{\text{S\&P 500},j} = (\text{Index}_j - \text{Index}_{j-1} + \text{Dividends}_t)/\text{Index}_{j-1}$$

where Index$_j$ is the level of the index at the end of month j and Dividend$_j$ is the dividends paid on the index in month j. Although the S&P 500 and the NYSE Composite are the most widely used indices for U.S. stocks, they are at best imperfect proxies for the market portfolio in the CAPM, which is supposed to include all traded assets.

Figure 4.3 graphs monthly returns on Disney against returns on the S&P 500 index from January 1999 to December 2003.

The regression statistics for Disney are as follows:[28]

a. *Slope of the Regression = 1.01* This is Disney's beta, based on returns from 1999 to 2003. Using a different time period for the regression or different return intervals (weekly or daily) for the same period can result in a different beta.

---

[25]The ex-dividend day is the day by which the stock has to be bought for an investor to be entitled to the dividends on the stock. On the ex-dividend day, the stock trades without the dividend.

[26]A split changes the number of shares outstanding in a company without affecting any of its fundamentals. Thus, in a three-for-two split, there will be 50 percent more shares outstanding after the split. Because the overall value of equity has not changed, the stock price will drop by an equivalent amount $(1 - 100/150 = 33.33\%)$.

[27]Although there were no stock splits in the time period of the regression, Disney did have a three-for-one stock split in July 1998. The stock price dropped significantly, and if not factored in will result in very negative returns in that month. Splits can be accounted for as follows:

$$\text{Return}_{\text{Disney},j} = (\text{Factor}_j \times \text{Price}_{\text{Disney},j} - \text{Price}_{\text{Disney},j-1} + \text{Factor} \times \text{Dividends}_j)/\text{Price}_{\text{Disney},j-1}$$

The factor would be set to 3 for July 1998 and the ending price would be multiplied by 3, as would the dividends per share, if they were paid after the split.

[28]The regression statistics are computed in the conventional way. Appendix 1 explains the process in more detail.

Figure 4.3   Disney versus S&P 500: 1999–2003

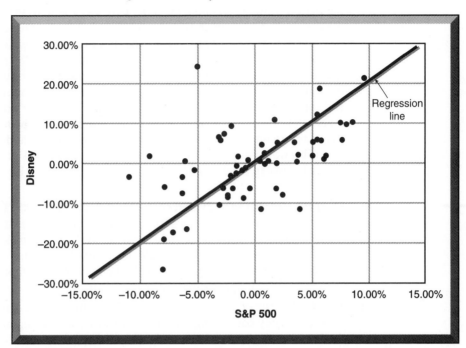

Source: Bloomberg.

b. ***Intercept of the Regression = 0.0467 percent***   This is a measure of Disney's performance, but only when it is compared with $R_f (1 - \beta)$.[29] The monthly risk-free rate (because the returns used in the regression are monthly returns) between 1999 and 2003 averaged 0.313 percent, resulting in the following estimate for the performance:

$$R_f (1 - \beta) = 0.313\% (1 - 1.01) = -0.0032\%$$

$$\text{Intercept} - R_f (1 - \beta) = 0.0467\% - (-0.0032\%) = 0.05\%$$

This analysis suggests that Disney's stock performed 0.05 percent better than expected, when expectations are based on the CAPM, on a monthly basis between January 1999 and December 2003. This results in an annualized excess return of approximately 0.60 percent.

$$\text{Annualized Excess Return} = (1 + \text{Monthly Excess Return})^{12} - 1$$
$$= (1 + 0.0005)^{12} - 1 = +0.0060 \text{ or } 0.60\%$$

---

[29]In practice, the intercept of the regression is often called the alpha and compared to zero. Thus a positive intercept is viewed as a sign that the stock did better than expected and a negative intercept as a sign that the stock did worse than expected. In truth, this can be done only if the regression is run in terms of excess returns, that is, returns over and above the risk-free rate in each month for both the stock and the market index.

By this measure of performance, Disney did slightly better than expected during the period of the regression, given its beta and the market's performance over the period. Note, however, that this does not imply that Disney would be a good investment looking forward. It also does not provide a breakdown of how much of this excess return can be attributed to industry-wide effects and how much is specific to the firm. To make that breakdown, the excess returns would have to be computed over the same period for other firms in the entertainment industry and compared with Disney's excess return. The difference would be then attributable to firm-specific actions. In this case, for instance, the average annualized excess return on other entertainment firms between 1999 and 2003 was 1.33 percent. This would imply that Disney stock underperformed its peer group by 0.73 percent between 1999 and 2003, after adjusting for risk. (Firm-specific Jensen's alpha = 0.60% − 1.33% = −0.73%)

c. **R^2 of the Regression = 29 percent**   This statistic suggests that 29 percent of the risk (variance) in Disney comes from market sources (interest rate risk, inflation risk, etc.) and that the balance of 71 percent of the risk comes from firm-specific components. The latter risk should be diversifiable, and is therefore unrewarded. Disney's R^2 is higher than the median R^2 of companies listed on the NYSE, which was approximately 21 percent in 2003.

d. **Standard Error of Beta Estimate = 0.20**   This statistic implies that the true beta for Disney could range from 0.81 to 1.21 (subtracting or adding one standard error to the beta estimate of 1.01) with 67 percent confidence and from 0.61 to 1.41 (subtracting or adding two standard errors to the beta estimate of 1.01) with 95 percent confidence. These ranges may seem large, but they are not unusual for most U.S. companies. This suggests that we should consider regression estimates of betas with caution.

4.5   THE RELEVANCE OF R^2 TO AN INVESTOR

Assume that, having done the regression analysis, both Disney and Amgen, a biotechnology company, have betas of 1.01. Disney, however, has an R^2 of 31 percent, while Amgen has an R^2 of only 15 percent. If you had to pick between these investments, which one would you choose?

☐ Disney, because it's higher R^2 suggests that it is less risky

☐ Amgen, because it's lower R^2 suggests a greater potential for high returns

☐ I would be indifferent, because they both have the same beta

Would your answer be any different if you were running a well-diversified fund?

IN PRACTICE: USING A SERVICE BETA

Most analysts who use betas obtain them from an estimation service; Merrill Lynch, Barra, Value Line, S&P, Morningstar, and Bloomberg are some of the well-known services. All begin with regression betas and make what they feel are necessary changes to make them better estimates for the future. Although most of these services do not reveal the internal details of this estimation, Bloomberg is an honorable exception. The following is the beta calculation page from Bloomberg for Disney, using the same period as our regression (January 1999 to December 2003).

Source: Bloomberg.

Although the time period is identical to the one used in our earlier regression, there are subtle differences between this regression and the earlier one in Figure 4.1. First, Bloomberg uses price appreciation in the stock and the market index in estimating betas and ignores dividends.[30] This does not make much of a difference for a Disney, but it could make a difference for a company that either pays no dividends or pays significantly higher dividends than the market. Second, Bloomberg also computes what they call an adjusted beta, which is estimated as follows:

$$\text{Adjusted Beta} = \text{Raw Beta}(0.67) + 1(0.33)$$

These weights do not vary across stocks, and this process pushes all estimated betas toward one. Most services employ similar procedures to adjust betas toward one. In doing so, they are drawing on empirical evidence that suggests that the betas for most companies over time tend to move toward the average beta, which is one. This may be explained by the fact that firms get more diversified in their product mix and client base as they get larger.

Generally, betas reported by different services for the same firm can be very different because they use different time periods (some use two years and others five years), different return intervals (daily, weekly, or monthly), different market indices, and different post-regression adjustments. Although these beta differences may be troubling, the beta estimates delivered by each of these services comes with a standard error, and it is very likely that all of the betas reported for a firm fall within the range of the standard errors from the regressions. ∎

---

[30]This is why the intercept in the Bloomberg graph (-0.03%) is slightly different from the intercept estimated earlier in the chapter (0.05%). The beta and R^2 are identical.

Figure 4.4 Estimating Aracruz's Beta: Choice of Indices

Source: Bloomberg.

ILLUSTRATION **4.2 Estimating Historical Betas for Aracruz and Deutsche Bank**
Aracruz is a Brazilian company, and we can regress returns on the stock against a Brazilian index, the Bovespa, to obtain risk parameters. The stock also had an ADR listed on the U.S. exchanges, and we can regress returns on the ADR against a U.S. index to obtain parameters. Figure 4.4 presents both graphs for the January 1999–December 2003 time period.

How different are the risk parameters that emerge from the two regressions? Aracruz has a beta of 1.00 when the ADR is regressed against the S&P 500, and a beta of only 0.22 when the local listing is regressed against the Bovespa.[31] Each regression has its own problems. The Bovespa is a narrow index dominated by a few liquid stocks and does not represent the broad spectrum of Brazilian equities. Although the S&P 500 is a broader index, the returns on the ADR have little relevance to a large number of non-U.S. investors who bought the local listing.

Deutsche Bank does not have an ADR listed in the United States, but we can regress return against a multitude of indices. Table 4.4 presents comparisons of the results of the regressions of returns on Deutsche Bank against three indices—a German equity index (DAX), an index of large European companies (FTSE Euro 300), and a global equity index (Morgan Stanley Capital Index, MSCI).

Here again, the risk parameters estimated for Deutsche Bank are a function of the index used in the regression. The standard error is lowest (and the R^2 is highest) for the regression against the DAX; this is not surprising because Deutsche Bank is

---

[31]The biggest source of the difference is one month (January 1999). In that month, Aracruz had a return of 133 percent in the São Paulo exchange, whereas the ADR dropped by 9.67 percent in the same month. The disparity in returns can be attributed to a steep devaluation in the Brazilian real in that month.

Table 4.4	DEUTSCHE BANK RISK PARAMETERS: INDEX EFFECT		
	DAX	**FTSE Euro 300**	**MSCI**
Intercept	1.24%	1.54%	1.37%
Beta	1.05	1.52	1.23
Standard error of beta	0.11	0.19	0.25
R^2	62%	52%	30%

a large component of the DAX. The standard error gets larger and the R^2 gets lower as the index is broadened to initially include other European stocks and then expanded to global stocks.

IN PRACTICE: WHICH INDEX SHOULD WE USE TO ESTIMATE BETAS?

In most cases, analysts are faced with a mind-boggling array of choices among indices when it comes to estimating betas; there are more than 20 broad equity indices ranging from the Dow 30 to the Wilshire 5000 in the United States alone. One common practice is to use the index that is most suited for the investor who is looking at the stock. Thus, if the analysis is being done for a U.S. investor, the S&P 500 is used. This is generally not appropriate. By this rationale, an investor who owns only two stocks should use an index composed of only those stocks to estimate betas.

The right index to use in analysis should be determined by the holdings of the marginal investor in the company being analyzed. Consider Aracruz and Deutsche Bank in the earlier illustration. If the marginal investors in these companies are investors who hold only domestic stocks—just Brazilian stocks in the case of Aracruz or German stocks in the case of Deutsche—we can use the regressions against the local indices. If the marginal investor is a global investor, a more relevant measure of risk will emerge by using the global index. Over time, you would expect global investors to displace local investors as the marginal investors, because they will perceive far less of the risk as market risk and thus pay a higher price for the same security. Thus, one of the ironies of this notion of risk is that Aracruz will be less risky to an overseas investor who has a global portfolio than to a Brazilian investor with all of his or her wealth in Brazilian assets. ■

Standard Procedures for Estimating Risk Parameters in the APM
and Multifactor Model
Like the CAPM, the APM defines risk to be nondiversifiable risk, but unlike the CAPM, the APM allows for multiple economic factors in measuring this risk. Although the process of estimation of risk parameters is different for the APM, many of the issues raised relating to the determinants of risk in the CAPM continue to have relevance for the APM.

The parameters of the APM are estimated from a **factor analysis** on historical stock returns, which yields the number of common economic factors determining these returns, the risk premium for each factor, and the factor-specific betas for each firm.

Once the factor-specific betas are estimated for each firm, and the factor premiums are measured, the APM can be used to estimated expected returns on a stock.

$$\text{Cost of Equity} = R_f + \sum_{j=1}^{j=k} \beta_j(E[R_j] - R_f)$$

where R_f = risk-free rate, β_j = beta specific to factor j, $E(R_j) - R_f$ = risk premium per unit of factor j risk, and k = number of factors. In a multifactor model, the betas are estimated relative to the specified factors, using historical returns data for each firm.

 Factor Analysis: This is a statistical technique in which past data is analyzed with the intent of extracting common factors that might have affected the data.

B. Fundamental Betas

The beta for a firm may be estimated from a regression, but it is determined by fundamental decisions that the firm has made on what business to be in, how to run that business, and the degree to which the firm uses debt. In this section, we will examine an alternative way of estimating betas, where we are less reliant on historical data and more cognizant of the intuitive underpinnings of betas.

Determinants of Betas

The beta of a firm is determined by three variables: (1) the type of business or businesses the firm is in, (2) the degree of operating leverage in the firm, and (3) the firm's financial leverage. Much of the discussion in this section will be couched in terms of CAPM betas, but the same analysis can be applied to the betas estimated in the APM and the multifactor model as well.

Type of Business Because betas measure the risk of a firm relative to a market index, the more sensitive a business is to market conditions, the higher its beta. Thus, other things remaining equal, **cyclical firms** can be expected to have higher betas than noncyclical firms. For instance, companies involved in housing and automobiles, two sectors of the economy that are very sensitive to economic conditions, will have higher betas than companies involved in food processing and tobacco, which are relatively insensitive to business cycles.

Building on this point, we would also argue that the degree to which a product's purchase is discretionary will affect the beta of the firm manufacturing the product. Thus, the betas of discount retailers, such as Wal-Mart, should be lower than the betas of high-end specialty retailers, such as Tiffany's or Gucci, because consumers can defer the purchase of the latter's products during bad economic times.

It is true that firms have only limited control over how discretionary a product or service is to their customers. There are firms, however, that have used this limited control to maximum effect to make their products less discretionary to buyers and by extension lowered their business risk. One approach is to make the product or service a much more integral and necessary part of everyday life, thus making its purchase more of a requirement. A second approach is to effectively use advertising and marketing to build brand loyalty. The objective in good advertising, as we see it, is to make discretionary products or services seem like necessities to the target audience. Thus corporate strategy, advertising, and marketing acumen can, at the margin, alter business risk and betas over time.

Cyclical Firm: A cyclical firm has revenues and operating income that tend to move strongly with the economy—up when the economy is doing well and down during recessions.

4.6 BETAS AND BUSINESS RISK

Polo Ralph Lauren, the upscale fashion designer, went public in 1997. Assume that you were asked to estimate its beta. Based on what you know about the firm's products, would you expect the beta to be

☐ greater than one?

☐ about one?

☐ less than one?

Why?

Degree of Operating Leverage   The degree of **operating leverage** is a function of the cost structure of a firm and is usually defined in terms of the relationship between fixed costs and total costs. A firm that has high operating leverage (i.e., high fixed costs relative to total costs) will also have higher variability in operating income than would a firm producing a similar product with low operating leverage.[32] Other things remaining equal, the higher variance in operating income will lead to a higher beta for the firm with high operating leverage.

Although operating leverage affects betas, it is difficult to measure the operating leverage of a firm, at least from the outside, because fixed and variable costs are often aggregated in income statements. It is possible to get an approximate measure of the operating leverage of a firm by looking at changes in operating income as a function of changes in sales.

Degree of Operating Leverage = % Change in Operating Profit/% Change in Sales

For firms with high operating leverage, operating income should change more than proportionately when sales change, increasing when sales increase and decreasing when sales decline.

Can firms change their operating leverage? Although some of a firm's cost structure is determined by the business it is in (an energy utility has to build costly power plants, and airlines have to lease expensive planes), firms in the United States have become increasingly inventive in lowering the fixed cost component in their total costs. Labor contracts that emphasize flexibility and allow the firm to make its labor costs more sensitive to its financial success; joint venture agreements, where the fixed costs are borne by someone else; and subcontracting of manufacturing, which reduces the need for expensive plant and equipment, are only some of the manifestations of this phenomenon. The arguments for such actions may be couched in terms of competitive advantages and cost flexibility, but they do reduce the operating leverage of the firm and its exposure to market risk.

---

[32]To see why, compare two firms with revenues of $100 million and operating income of $10 million but assume that the first firm's costs are all fixed, whereas only half of the second firm's costs are fixed. If revenues increase at both firms by $10 million, the first firm will report a doubling of operating income (from $10 to $20 million), whereas the second firm will report a rise of 55 percent in its operating income (because costs will rise by $4.5 million, 45 percent of the revenue increment).

Table 4.5 DEGREE OF OPERATING LEVERAGE: DISNEY

Year	Net Sales	Change in Sales	EBIT	Change in EBIT
1987	$2,877		$756	
1988	$3,438	19.50%	$848	12.17%
1989	$4,594	33.62%	$1,177	38.80%
1990	$5,844	27.21%	$1,368	16.23%
1991	$6,182	5.78%	$1,124	–17.84%
1992	$7,504	21.38%	$1,287	14.50%
1993	$8,529	13.66%	$1,560	21.21%
1994	$10,055	17.89%	$1,804	15.64%
1995	$12,112	20.46%	$2,262	25.39%
1996	$18,739	54.71%	$3,024	33.69%
1997	$22,473	19.93%	$3,945	30.46%
1998	$22,976	2.24%	$3,843	–2.59%
1999	$23,435	2.00%	$3,580	–6.84%
2000	$25,418	8.46%	$2,525	–29.47%
2001	$25,172	–0.97%	$2,832	12.16%
2002	$25,329	0.62%	$2,384	–15.82%
2003	$27,061	6.84%	$2,713	13.80%
1987–2003		15.83%		10.09%
1996–2003		11.73%		4.42%

Source: Compustat.

Operating Leverage: A measure of the proportion of the operating expenses of a company that are fixed costs.

ILLUSTRATION 4.3 Measuring Operating Leverage for Disney

In Table 4.5, we estimate the degree of operating leverage for Disney from 1987 to 2003 using earnings before interest and taxes (EBIT) as the measure of operating income.

The degree of operating leverage changes dramatically from year to year, because of year-to-year swings in operating income. Using the average changes in sales and operating income over the period, we can compute the operating leverage at Disney:

$$\text{Operating Leverage} = \% \text{ Change in EBIT} / \% \text{ Change in Sales}$$
$$= 10.09\% / 15.83\% = 0.64$$

There are two important observations that can be made about Disney over the period, though. First, the operating leverage for Disney is lower than the operating leverage for other entertainment firms, which we computed to be 1.12.[33] This would

---

[33]To compute this statistic, we looked at the aggregate revenues and operating income of entertainment companies each year from 1987 to 2003.

suggest that Disney has lower fixed costs than its competitors. Second, the acquisition of Capital Cities by Disney in 1996 may be affecting the operating leverage. Looking at the numbers since 1996, we get an even lower estimate of operating leverage:

$$\text{Operating Leverage}_{1996-03} = 4.42\%/11.73\% = 0.38$$

We would not read too much into these numbers because Disney has such a wide range of businesses. We would hypothesize that Disney's theme park business has higher fixed costs (and operating leverage) than its movie division.

4.7   SOCIAL POLICY AND OPERATING LEVERAGE

Assume that you are comparing a European automobile manufacturing firm with a U.S. automobile firm. European firms are generally much more constrained in terms of laying off employees, if they get into financial trouble. What implications does this have for betas, if they are estimated relative to a common index?

☐   The European firm will have much a higher beta than the U.S. firm.

☐   The European firm will have a similar beta to the U.S. firm.

☐   The European firm will have a much lower beta than the U.S. firm.

IN PRACTICE: SHOULD SMALL OR HIGH-GROWTH FIRMS HAVE HIGHER BETAS THAN LARGER AND MORE MATURE FIRMS?

Though the answer may seem obvious at first sight—that smaller, higher-growth firms are riskier than larger firms—it is not an easy question to answer. If the question were posed in terms of total risk, smaller and higher-growth firms will tend to be riskier simply because they have more volatile earnings streams (and their market prices reflect that). When it is framed in terms of betas or market risk, smaller and higher-growth firms should have higher betas only if the products and services they offer are more discretionary to their customers or if they have higher operating leverage. It is possible that smaller firms operate in niche markets and sell products that customers can delay or defer buying and that the absence of economies of scale lead to higher fixed costs for these firms. These firms should have higher betas than their larger counterparts. It is also possible that neither condition holds for a particular small firm. The answer will therefore depend on both the company in question and the industry in which it operates.

In practice, analysts often add what is called a small firm premium to the cost of equity for smaller firms. This small firm premium is usually estimated from historical data and is the difference between the average annual returns on small market cap stocks and the rest of the market—about 3 to 3.5 percent when we look at the 1926–2003 period. This practice can be dangerous for three reasons. The first is that the small firm premium has been volatile and disappeared for an extended period in the 1980s. The second is that the definition of a small market cap stock varies across time and that the historical small cap premium is largely attributable to the smallest (among the small cap) stocks. The third is that using a constant small stock premium adjustment removes any incentive that the analyst may have to examine the product characteristics and operating leverage of individual small market cap companies more closely. ∎

Degree of Financial Leverage   Other things remaining equal, an increase in financial leverage will increase the equity beta of a firm. Intuitively, we would expect the fixed interest payments on debt to increase earnings per share in good times and to push it down in bad times.[34] Higher leverage increases the variance in earnings per share and makes equity investment in the firm riskier. If all of the firm's risk is borne by the stockholders (i.e., the beta of debt is zero),[35] and debt creates a tax benefit to the firm, then

$$\beta_L = \beta_u(1 + [1 - t][D/E])$$

where β_L = levered beta for equity in the firm, β_u = unlevered beta of the firm (i.e., the beta of the firm without any debt), t = marginal tax rate for the firm, and D/E = debt/equity ratio. The marginal tax rate is the tax rate on the last dollar of income earned by the firm and generally will not be equal to the effective or average rates; it is used because interest expenses save taxes on the marginal income. Intuitively, we expect that as leverage increases (as measured by the debt to equity ratio), equity investors bear increasing amounts of market risk in the firm, leading to higher betas. The tax factor in the equation captures the benefit created by the tax deductibility of interest payments.

The unlevered beta of a firm is determined by the types of businesses in which it operates and its operating leverage. This unlevered beta is often also referred to as the *asset beta* because its value is determined by the assets (or businesses) owned by the firm. Thus, the equity beta of a company is determined both by the riskiness of the business it operates in as well as the amount of financial leverage risk it has taken on. Because financial leverage multiplies the underlying business risk, it stands to reason that firms that have high business risk should be reluctant to take on financial leverage. It also stands to reason that firms operating in relatively stable businesses should be much more willing to take on financial leverage. Utilities, for instance, have historically had high debt ratios but not high betas, mostly because their underlying businesses have been stable and fairly predictable.

Breaking risk down into business and financial leverage components also provides some insight into why companies have high betas because they can end up with high betas in one of two ways—they can operate in a risky business, or they can use very high financial leverage in a relatively stable business.

ILLUSTRATION 4.4   **Effects of Financial Leverage on Betas: Disney**
From the regression for the period 1999 to 2003, Disney had a beta of 1.01. To estimate the effects of financial leverage on Disney, we began by estimating the average debt/equity ratio between 1999 and 2003 using market values for debt and equity.

Average Market Debt/Equity Ratio between 1999 and 2003 = 27.5%

---

[34]Interest expenses always lower net income, but the fact that the firm uses debt instead of equity implies that the number of shares will also be lower. Thus, the benefit of debt shows up in earnings per share.

[35]If we ignore the tax effects, we can compute the levered beta as $\beta_L = \beta_u(1 + D/E)$. If debt has market risk (i.e., its beta is greater than zero), the original formula can be modified to take it into account. If the beta of debt is β_D, the beta of equity can be written as $\beta_L = \beta_u[1 + (1 - t)(D/E)] - \beta_D(1 - t)D/E$.

Table 4.6   FINANCIAL LEVERAGE AND BETAS

Debt to Capital	Debt/Equity Ratio	Beta	Effect of Leverage
0.00%	0.00%	0.86	0.00
10.00%	11.11%	0.92	0.06
20.00%	25.00%	1.00	0.14
30.00%	42.86%	1.09	0.23
40.00%	66.67%	1.22	0.36
50.00%	100.00%	1.40	0.54
60.00%	150.00%	1.67	0.81
70.00%	233.33%	2.12	1.26
80.00%	400.00%	3.02	2.16
90.00%	900.00%	5.72	4.86

The unlevered beta is estimated using a marginal corporate tax rate of 37.3%:[36]

$$\text{Unlevered Beta} = \text{Current Beta}/(1 + [1 - \text{Tax Rate}][\text{Average Debt/Equity}])$$
$$= 1.01/(1 + [1 - 0.373][0.275]) = 0.8615$$

The levered beta at different levels of debt can then be estimated:

$$\text{Levered Beta} = \text{Unlevered Beta} \times [1 + (1 - \text{Tax Rate})(\text{Debt/Equity})]$$

For instance, if Disney were to increase its debt equity ratio to 10 percent, its equity beta will be

$$\text{Levered Beta}(@10\% D/E) = 0.8615 \times (1 + [1 - 0.373][0.10]) = 0.9155$$

If the debt equity ratio were raised to 25 percent, the equity beta would be

$$\text{Levered Beta}(@25\% D/E) = 0.8615 \times [1 + (1 - 0.373)(0.25)] = 1.00$$

Table 4.6 summarizes the beta estimates for different levels of financial leverage ranging from 0 to 90 percent (debt as a percent of total capital).

As Disney's financial leverage increases, the beta increases concurrently.

This spreadsheet allows you to estimate the unlevered beta for a firm and compute the betas as a function of the leverage of the firm (**levbeta.xls**).

There is a data set on the Web that has marginal tax rates for different countries.

---

[36]The marginal corporate tax rate in the United States in 2003 was 35 percent. The marginal state and local tax rates, corrected for federal tax savings, is estimated by Disney in its annual report to be 2.3 percent. Disney did report some offsetting tax benefits that reduced their effective tax rate to 35 percent. We assumed that these offsetting tax benefits were temporary.

IN PRACTICE: Dueling Tax Rates

The marginal tax rate, which is the tax rate on marginal income (or the last dollar of income) is a key input not only for the levered beta calculation but also for the after-tax cost of debt, which we will be estimating later in this chapter. Estimating it can be problematic because firms seldom report it in their financials. Most firms report an effective tax rate on taxable income in their annual reports and filings with the SEC. This rate is computed by dividing the taxes paid by the net taxable income, reported in the financial statement. The effective tax rate can be different from the marginal tax rate for several reasons.

- If it is a small firm and the tax rate is higher for higher income brackets, the average tax rate across all income will be lower than the tax rate on the last dollar of income. For larger firms, where most of the income is at the highest tax bracket, this is less of an issue.

- Publicly traded firms, at least in the United States, often maintain two sets of books, one for tax purposes and one for reporting purposes. They generally use different accounting rules for the two and report lower income to tax authorities and higher income in their annual reports. Because taxes paid are based on the tax books, the effective tax rate will usually be lower than the marginal tax rate.

- Actions that defer or delay the payment of taxes can also cause deviations between marginal and effective tax rates. In the period when taxes are deferred, the effective tax rate will lag the marginal tax rate. In the period when the deferred taxes are paid, the effective tax rate can be much higher than the marginal tax rate.

The best source of the marginal tax is the tax code of the country where the firm earns its operating income. If there are state and local taxes, they should be incorporated into the marginal tax rate as well. For companies in multiple tax locales, the marginal tax rate used should be the average of the different marginal tax rates, weighted by operating income by locale. ∎

Bottom-Up Betas

Breaking down betas into their business, operating leverage, and financial leverage components provides an alternative way of estimating betas, whereby we do not need past prices on an individual firm or asset to estimate its beta.

To develop this alternative approach, we need to introduce an additional feature that betas possess that proves invaluable. The beta of two assets put together is a weighted average of the individual asset betas, with the weights based on market value. Consequently, the beta for a firm is a weighted average of the betas of all of different businesses it is in. Thus, the bottom-up beta for a firm, asset, or project can be estimated as follows.

1. Identify the business or businesses that make up the firm whose beta we are trying to estimate. Most firms provide a breakdown of their revenues and operating income by business in their annual reports and financial filings.

2. Estimate the average unlevered betas of other publicly traded firms that are primarily or only in each of these businesses. In making this estimate, we have to

consider the following estimation issues:

- *Comparable Firms*   In most businesses, there are at least a few comparable firms and in some businesses, there can be hundreds. Begin with a narrow definition of comparable firms, and widen it if the number of comparable firms is too small.

- *Beta Estimation*   Once a list of comparable firms has been put together, we need to estimate the betas of each of these firms. Optimally, the beta for each firm will be estimated against a common index. If that proves impractical, we can use betas estimated against different indices.

- *Unlever First or Last*   We can compute an unlevered beta for each firm in the comparable firm list, using the debt to equity ratio, and tax rate for that firm, or we can compute the average beta, debt to equity ratio, and tax rate for the sector and unlever using the averages. Given the standard errors of the individual regression betas, we would suggest the latter approach.

- *Averaging Approach*   The average beta across the comparable firms can be either a simple average or a weighted average, with the weights based on market capitalization. Statistically, the savings in standard error are larger if a simple averaging process is used.

- *Adjustment for Cash*   Investments in cash and marketable securities have betas close to zero. Consequently, the unlevered beta that we obtain for a business by looking at comparable firms may be affected by the cash holdings of these firms. To obtain an unlevered beta cleansed of cash:

$$\text{Unlevered Beta Corrected for Cash} = \frac{\text{Unlevered Beta}}{(1 - \text{Cash/Firm Value})}$$

3. To calculate the unlevered beta for the firm, we take a weighted average of the business unlevered betas, using the proportion of firm value derived from each business as the weights. These firm values will have to be estimated because divisions of a firm usually do not have market values available.[37] If these values cannot be estimated, we can use operating income or revenues as weights. We could also take into account the cash holdings of the firm by computing it as a percent of firm value and attaching a beta of zero if the cash is invested in riskless securities (like commercial paper or Treasury bills) or a higher beta if it is invested in riskier securities (like corporate bonds). This weighted average is called the bottom-up unlevered beta.

4. Calculate the current debt to equity ratio for the firm, using market values if available. Alternatively, use the target debt to equity ratio specified by the management of the firm or industry-typical debt equity ratios.

5. Estimate the levered beta for the firm (and each of its businesses) using the unlevered beta from Step 3 and the debt to equity ratio from Step 4.

Clearly, this process rests on being able to identify the unlevered betas of individual businesses.

---

[37]The exception is when you have tracking stocks with each division traded separately in financial markets.

There are three advantages associated with using bottom-up betas, and they are significant:

- We can estimate betas for firms that have no price history because all we need is an identification of the business or businesses they operate in. In other words, we can estimate bottom-up betas for initial public offerings, private businesses, and divisions of companies.

- Because the beta for the business is obtained by averaging across a large number of regression betas, it will be more precise than any individual firm's regression beta estimate. The standard error of the average beta estimate will be a function of the number of comparable firms used in Step 2 and can be approximated as follows:

$$\sigma_{\text{Average Beta}} = \frac{\text{Average } \sigma_{\text{Beta}}}{\sqrt{\text{Number of Firms}}}$$

Thus, the standard error of the average of the betas of 100 firms, each of which has a standard error of 0.25, will be only $0.025(0.25/\sqrt{100})$.

- The bottom-up beta can reflect recent and even forthcoming changes to a firm's business mix and financial leverage because we can change the mix of businesses and the weight on each business in making the beta estimate.

 There is a data set on the Web that has updated betas and unlevered betas by business sector in the United States.

ILLUSTRATION 4.5 Bottom-Up Beta for Disney

Disney is an entertainment firm with diverse holdings. In addition to its theme parks, it has significant investments in broadcasting and movies. To estimate Disney's beta, we broke their business into four major components:

1. **Studio entertainment,** which is the production and acquisition of motion pictures for distribution in theatrical, television, and home video markets as well as TV programming for network and syndication markets. Disney produces movies under five imprints: Walt Disney Pictures, Touchstone Pictures, Hollywood Pictures, Miramax, and Dimension.

2. **Media networks,** which includes the ABC television and radio networks and reflects the acquisition made in 1995. In addition, Disney has an extensive exposure in the cable market through the Disney channel, A&E, and ESPN, among others.

3. **Park resorts,** which include Walt Disney World (in Orlando, Florida) and Disneyland (in Anaheim, California), as well as royalty holdings in Tokyo Disneyland and Euro Disney. The hotels and villas at each of these theme parks are considered part of the parks because they derive their revenue almost exclusively from visitors to these parks.

4. **Consumer products,** which includes a grab bag of businesses including Disney's retail outlets, its licensing revenues, software, interactive products, and publishing.

Business	Comparable Firms	Number of Firms	Average Levered Beta	D/E	Unlevered Beta	Cash/Firm Value	Unlevered Beta Corrected for Cash

Table 4.7   ESTIMATING UNLEVERED BETAS FOR DISNEY'S BUSINESS AREAS

Business	Comparable Firms	Number of Firms	Average Levered Beta	D/E	Unlevered Beta	Cash/Firm Value	Unlevered Beta Corrected for Cash
Media networks	Radio and TV broadcasting companies	24	1.22	20.45%	1.08	0.75%	1.0850
Parks and resorts	Theme park and entertainment firms	9	1.58	120.76%	0.89	2.77%	0.9105
Studio entertainment	Movie companies	11	1.16	27.96%	1.98	14.08%	1.1435
Consumer products	Toy and apparel retailers; entertainment software	77	1.06	9.18%	1.00	12.08%	1.1353

This breakdown reflects Disney's reporting in its annual report. In reality, there are a number of smaller businesses that Disney is in that are embedded in these four businesses, including:

- *Cruise lines*   Disney operates two ships—*Disney Magic* and *Disney Wonder*—that operate out of Florida and visit Caribbean ports.
- *Internet operations*   Disney made extensive investments in the GO network and other online operations. Much of this investment was written off by 2002, but they still represent a potential source of future revenues.
- *Sports franchises*   Disney owns the National Hockey League franchise, the Mighty Ducks of Anaheim; in 2002 it sold its stake in the Anaheim Angels, a Major League Baseball team.

Without detailed information on the operations of these businesses, we will assume that they represent too small a portion of Disney's overall revenues to make a significant difference in the risk calculation. For the four businesses for which we have detailed information, we estimated the unlevered beta by looking at comparable firms in each business. Table 4.7 summarizes the comparables used and the unlevered beta for each of the businesses. (Tax rate of 35 percent was used.)

To obtain the beta for Disney, we have to estimate the weight that each business is of Disney as a company. The value for each of the divisions was estimated by applying the typical revenue multiple at which comparable firms trade to the revenue reported by Disney for that segment in 2003.[38] The unlevered beta for Disney as a company in 2003 is a value-weighted average of the betas of each of the different business areas. Table 4.8 summarizes this calculation.

---

[38]We first estimated the enterprise value for each firm by adding the market value of equity to the book value of debt and subtracting out cash. We divided the aggregate enterprise value by revenues for all of the comparable firms to obtain the EV/Sales multiples. We did not use the averages of these revenue multiples of the individual firms because a few outliers skewed the results. Disney has about $1.2 billion in cash, but that represents about 1.71 percent of firm value and will have a negligible impact on the beta. We have ignored it in computing the beta for Disney's equity.

Table 4.8 ESTIMATING DISNEY'S UNLEVERED BETA

Business	Revenues in 2003 (in Millions)	EV/Sales	Estimated Value (in Millions)	Firm Value Proportion	Unlevered Beta
Media networks	$10,941	3.41	$37,278.62	49.25%	1.0850
Parks and resorts	$6,412	2.37	$15,208.37	20.09%	0.9105
Studio entertainment	$7,364	2.63	$19,390.14	25.62%	1.1435
Consumer products	$2,344	1.63	$3,814.38	5.04%	1.1353
Disney	$27,061		$75,691.51	100.00%	1.0674

The equity beta can then be calculated using the current financial leverage for Disney as a firm. Combining the market value of equity of $55,101 million with an estimated market value of debt of $14,668 million,[39] we arrive at the levered (equity) beta for Disney:

$$\text{Equity Beta for Disney} = 1.0674[1 + (1 - 0.373)(14,668/55,101)] = 1.2456$$

This contrasts with the beta of 1.01 that we obtained from the regression and is, in our view, a much truer reflection of the risk in Disney.

IN PRACTICE: CAN'T FIND COMPARABLE FIRMS?

A problem faced by analysts using the bottom-up approach for some firms is a paucity of comparable firms, either because the company is unique in terms of the product it offers or because the bulk of the firms in the sector are private businesses. Rather than fall back on the regression approach, which is likely to yield a very wide range for the beta, we would suggest one of the following ways to expand the comparable firm sample.

- *Geographic expansion* When analyzing firms from smaller markets, such as Brazil or Greece, the number of comparable firms will be small if we restrict ourselves only to firms in the market. One way to increase sample size is to consider firms in the same business that are listed and traded in other markets—European markets for Greece and Latin American markets for Brazil. With commodity companies that trade in global markets, like paper and oil companies, we can consider a global sample.

- *Production chain* Another way to expand the sample is to look for firms that either provide supplies to the firm that you are analyzing or firms that feed off your firm. For instance, when analyzing book retailers, we can consider book publishers part of the sample because the fortunes of the two are entwined. It is unlikely that one of these groups can have a good year without the other partaking in the success.

- *Customer specialization* Using the same rationale, the betas of firms that derive the bulk of their revenues from a sector is best estimated using firms in the sector. Thus, the beta of a law firm that derives all of its revenues from investment banks can be estimated by looking at the betas of investment banks. ∎

---

[39]The details of this calculation will be explored later in this chapter.

Table 4.9   BETAS AND LEVERAGE OF PUBLICLY TRADED BOOK RETAILERS AND PUBLISHERS

Firm	Beta	Debt (in Millions)	Equity (in Millions)	Cash (in Millions)
Books-A-Million	0.532	$45	$45	$5
Borders Group	0.844	$182	$1,430	$269
Barnes & Noble	0.885	$300	$1,606	$268
Courier Corp.	0.815	$1	$285	$6
Info Holdings	0.883	$2	$371	$54
John Wiley & Sons	0.636	$235	$1,662	$33
Scholastic Corp.	0.744	$549	$1,063	$11
	0.7627	$1,314	$6,462	$645

ILLUSTRATION 4.6   **Bottom-Up Beta for Bookscape Books**

We cannot estimate a regression beta for Bookscape Books, the private firm, because it does not have a history of past prices. We can, however, estimate the beta for Bookscape Books using the bottom-up approach. Because we were able to find only three publicly traded book retailers in the United States, we expanded the sample to include book publishers. We list the betas of these firms as well as debt, cash, and equity values in Table 4.9.

Although the firms in this sample are very different in terms of market capitalization, the betas are consistently lower than one. To estimate the unlevered beta for the sector, we use the average beta across the firms in conjunction with the aggregate values of debt and market value of equity (with a marginal tax rate of 35 percent):

$$\text{Debt to Equity Ratio for Industry} = 1{,}314/6{,}462 = 20.33\%$$

$$\text{Unlevered Beta} = 0.7627/[1 + (1 - 0.35)(0.2033)] = 0.6737$$

To correct for cash, we use the aggregate cash balance across the firms:

$$\text{Unlevered Beta Corrected for Cash} = 0.6737/[1 - 645/(1{,}314 + 6{,}462)] = 0.7346$$

Because Bookscape has a negligible cash balance, the unlevered beta for book retailing of 0.7346 is also the unlevered beta for the firm.

Because the debt/equity ratios used in computing levered betas are market debt equity ratios, and the only debt equity ratio we can compute for Bookscape is a book value debt equity ratio, we have assumed that Bookscape is *close to the industry average* debt to equity ratio of 20.33 percent. Using a marginal tax rate of 40 percent (based on personal income tax rates) for Bookscape, we get a levered beta of 0.82.

$$\text{Levered Beta for Bookscape} = 0.7346[1 + (1 - 0.40)(0.2033)] = 0.82$$

ILLUSTRATION 4.7   **Bottom-Up Beta for Aracruz**

The bottom-up beta for Aracruz is difficult to estimate if we remain within its home market (Brazil) for two reasons. First, there are only three publicly traded firms within the market that are in the same line of business as Aracruz (i.e., paper and pulp production). Second, the betas for all Brazilian firms are unreliable because the index used to estimate these betas, the Bovespa, is a narrow one, dominated by a few large companies.

There are three groups of comparable firms that we can use in the bottom-up beta estimate:

- *Emerging market paper and pulp companies*   This is a much larger sample of firms. Although the individual firm betas may be skewed by the limitations of the local indices, the errors should average out over the sample.

- *U.S. paper and pulp companies*   The advantage gained is not just in terms of the number of firms but also in terms of reliable betas. The peril in this approach is that the risk in U.S. companies can be different from the risk in Brazilian firms because of regulatory differences.[40]

- *Global paper and pulp companies*   This is the largest group and includes a diverse group of companies in both emerging and developed markets. Because betas are measures of relative risk, we argue that barring significant differences in regulation and monopoly power across markets, it is reasonable to compare betas across markets.

	Number of Firms	Average Beta	D/E	Unlevered Beta	Cash/Value	Unlevered Beta Corrected for Cash
Emerging markets	111	0.6895	38.33%	0.5469	6.58%	0.585
U.S.	34	0.7927	83.57%	0.5137	2.09%	0.525
Global	288	0.6333	38.88%	0.5024	6.54%	0.538

The tax rates used were 32 percent for emerging market companies, 35 percent for U.S. companies, and 33 percent for global companies, based on averaging the marginal tax rates in each group. The unlevered beta of emerging market companies is slightly higher than the U.S. and global groupings. Although the average beta for U.S. companies is higher than the rest of the sample, the difference is entirely due to the higher debt to equity ratios of these companies. We will use an emerging market unlevered beta of 0.585 as the beta for the paper and pulp business in which Aracruz is involved.

We can estimate the unlevered beta for Aracruz in two steps. First, we consider the asset composition for Aracruz. In addition to being in the paper business, Aracruz has a cash balance of 1,018 million BR, which is roughly 7.07 percent of the firm value. Because this is much larger than the typical cash balances of the companies on our comparable firm list, and the beta of cash is zero, the unlevered beta for Aracruz can be estimated as follows:

$$\text{Unlevered Beta for Aracruz} = (0.9293)(0.585) + (0.0707)(0) = 0.5440$$

Aracruz had gross debt outstanding of 4,094 million BR in 2003 and a market value of equity of 9,189 million BR, leading to a debt/equity ratio of 44.59 percent.

---

[40]As a counterpoint, paper and pulp companies are commodity companies and are governed by the vagaries of the price of paper and pulp. In other words, there is a reasonable argument to be made that paper and pulp companies globally are governed by the same primary risk factors.

Allowing for a tax rate of 34 percent (the Brazilian marginal tax rate), the levered beta for Aracruz can then be estimated as follows:

$$\text{Levered Beta for Aracruz} = 0.5440[1 + (1 - 0.34)(0.4459)] = 0.7040$$

If we wanted a levered beta for just the paper business of Aracruz, we would use the unlevered beta for the paper and pulp business and the gross debt to equity ratio for the firm:

$$\text{Levered Beta for Paper Business} = 0.585[1 + (1 - 0.34)(0.4459)] = 0.7576$$

IN PRACTICE: GROSS DEBT OR NET DEBT

Many analysts in Europe and Latin America prefer to subtract the cash from the gross debt to arrive at a net debt figure. Although there is no conceptual problem with this approach, they should remain consistent. Consider the calculation of unlevered and levered betas in Illustration 4.7. First, the computation of unlevered beta for the emerging market paper and pulp companies would have been based on the net debt to equity ratio for firms in the sector rather than the debt to equity ratio:

$$\text{Net Debt/Equity} = (\text{Gross Debt} - \text{Cash})/\text{Equity} = 29.22\%$$

$$\begin{aligned}\text{Unlevered Beta} &= \text{Levered Beta}/[1 + (1 - \text{Tax Rate})(\text{Net D/E})] \\ &= 0.6895/[1 + (1 - 0.32)(-0.2922)] = 0.5751\end{aligned}$$

This unlevered beta is already corrected for cash, and no further adjustments are needed. To make the levered beta calculation for Aracruz, we would use the net debt to equity ratio for the company. The net debt is computed by subtracting Aracruz's cash balance of 1,018 million BR from its gross debt of 4,094 million BR yielding a net debt to equity ratio of 33.47 percent.

$$\begin{aligned}\text{Levered Beta for Aracruz} &= \text{Unlevered Beta}\,[1 + (1 - \text{Tax Rate})(\text{Net D/E})] \\ &= 0.5751[1 + (1 - 0.34)(0.3347)] = 0.7022\end{aligned}$$

Again, we can dispense with the adjustment for cash because the net debt to equity ratio captures the cash holdings.

Notice that the levered beta of 0.7040 computed for Aracruz in Illustration 4.7 does not exactly match the computation using the net debt to equity ratio. The reason lies in an implicit assumption that we make when we net cash against debt. We assume that both debt and cash are riskless and that the tax benefit from debt is exactly offset by the tax paid on interest earned on cash. It is generally not a good idea to net debt if the debt is very risky or if the interest rate earned on cash is substantially lower than the interest rate paid on debt.

With a net debt to equity ratio, there is one more potential complication. Any firm that has a cash balance that exceeds its debt will have negative net debt and using this negative net D/E ratio will yield an unlevered beta that exceeds the levered beta. Although this may trouble some, it makes sense because the unlevered beta reflects the beta of the business that the firm operates in. Firms that have vast cash balances that exceed their borrowing can have levered betas that are lower than the unlevered betas of the businesses they operate in. ∎

ILLUSTRATION **4.8** **Bottom-Up Beta for Deutsche Bank**

There are a few banks in Germany that can be viewed as competitors to Deutsche Bank, though none of them are as large as it is or have as large of a stake in investment banking. Because the rules and regulatory constraints governing banking in the United States are different from the rules governing banks in much of Europe, we will look at the betas of European banks with market capitalizations exceeding $5 billion to estimate the beta for the commercial banking arm of Deutsche Bank. To estimate the beta of Deutsche Bank's investment banking arm, we use the betas of investment banking firms in the United States. The results are presented below.

Comparable Firms	Number of Firms	Average Beta
Large commercial banks in Europe	58	0.7345
U.S. investment banks	9	1.5167

Note that we do not adjust for differences in financial leverage because regulatory constraints and the needs of the business keep the leverage of most commercial banks at similar levels.[41] The beta for Deutsche Bank as a firm can be estimated as a weighted average of these two betas. Using estimating market value weights of 69 percent for the commercial banking and 31 percent for the investment banking arms (based on the revenues that Deutsche Bank made from each in the most recent year), we arrive at a beta for Deutsche Bank's equity:[42]

$$\text{Deutsche Bank's Beta} = 0.7345(0.69) + 1.5167(0.31) = 0.9767$$

This beta will change over time as the weights on the businesses change.

Calculating Betas after a Major Restructuring

The bottom-up process of estimating betas provides a solution when firms go through a major restructuring, where they change both their business mix and leverage. In these cases, the regression betas are misleading because they do not fully reflect the effects of these changes. Disney's beta, estimated from the bottom-up approach, is likely to provide a more precise estimate than the beta from a regression, given Disney's changing business mix and its increase in financial leverage in recent years. In fact, a firm's beta can be estimated even before the restructuring becomes effective using this approach. In the illustration that follows, for instance, we estimate Disney's beta just before and after its acquisition of Capital Cities/ABC in 1995, allowing for the changes in both the business mix and the leverage.

ILLUSTRATION **4.9** **Beta of a Firm after an Acquisition: Disney/Capital Cities**

In 1995, Disney announced that it was acquiring Capital Cities, the owner of the ABC television and radio network, for approximately $120 per share, and that it

---

[41]Regulators often specify capital ratios, calculated in terms of book values of debt and equity that banks must meet to stay in business. Most banks stay close to these ratios, though some tend to be better capitalized than others.

[42]Deutsche Bank does not explicitly break down income into commercial banking and investment banking components. The firm reported 5,470 million Euros in trading revenues (investment banking) and 15,179 million Euros in net interest revenues and fiduciary commissions (commercial banking).

would finance the acquisition partly through the issue of $10 billion in debt. At the time of the acquisition, Disney had a market value of equity of $31.1 billion, debt outstanding of $3.186 billion, and a levered beta of 1.15. Capital Cities, based on the $120 offering price, had a market value of equity of $18.5 billion, debt outstanding of $615 million, and a levered beta of 0.95.

To evaluate the effects of the acquisition on Disney's beta, we do the analysis in two parts. First, we examine the effects of the merger on the business risk of the combined firm, by estimating the unlevered betas of the two companies, and calculating the combined firm's unlevered beta (using a tax rate of 36 percent for both firms).

$$\text{Disney's Unlevered Beta} = 1.15/[1 + (1 - 0.36) \times (3,186/31,100)] = 1.08$$

$$\text{Capital Cities Unlevered Beta} = 0.95/[1 + (1 - 0.36) \times (615/18,500)] = 0.93$$

The unlevered beta for the combined firm can be calculated as the weighted average of the two unlevered betas, with the weights being based on the *market values of the two firms*.[43]

$$\text{Value of Disney} = \$31,100 + \$3,186 = \$34,286 \text{ million}$$

$$\text{Value of Capital Cities} = \$18,500 + \$615 = \$19,115 \text{ million}$$

$$\text{Unlevered Beta for Combined Firm} = 1.08(34,286/53,401) + 0.93(19,115/53,401)$$
$$= 1.026$$

Then we examine the effects of the financing of the merger on the betas by calculating the debt/equity ratio for the combined firm after the acquisition. Because Disney is assuming the old debt of Capital Cities, we add that debt to Disney's existing debt and add the additional $10 billion in debt used to fund this acquisition:[44]

$$\text{Postacquisition Debt} = \text{Capital Cities Old Debt} + \text{Disney's Old Debt} + \text{New Debt}$$
$$= \$615 + \$3,186 + \$10,000 = \$13,801 \text{ million}$$

$$\text{Postacquisition Equity} = \text{Disney's Old Equity} + \text{New Equity Used for Acquisition}$$
$$= \$31,100 + \$8,500 = \$39,600 \text{ million}$$

where

$$\text{New Equity} = \text{Total Cost of Acquisition} - \text{New Debt Issued}$$
$$= \$18,500 - \$10,000 = \$8,500 \text{ million}$$

Notice that the equity in Capital Cities of $18,500 million disappears after the acquisition and is replaced with new debt of $10,000 million and new Disney equity of $8,500 million. The debt/equity ratio can then be computed as follows.

$$\text{D/E Ratio} = 13,801/39,600 = 34.82\%$$

---

[43]Unlevered betas should always be weighted based on firm values. With levered (equity) betas, the values of equity can be used as weights.

[44]If Disney had paid off Capital Cities' old debt instead of assuming it, we could have ignored it in the debt calculation. However, Disney would then have had to raise an extra $615 million in financing to fund this acquisition.

This debt/equity ratio in conjunction with the new unlevered beta for the combined firm yields a new beta of

$$\text{New Beta} = 1.026[1 + 0.64(0.3482)] = 1.25$$

Based on this computation, we would expect Disney's beta to increase from 1.15 to 1.25 after the acquisition of Capital Cities.

C. Accounting Betas

A third approach is to estimate the beta of a firm or its equity from accounting earnings rather than from traded prices. Thus, changes in earnings at a division or a firm, on a quarterly or annual basis, can be regressed against changes in earnings for the market, in the same periods, to arrive at an estimate of a "market beta" to use in the CAPM. The approach has some intuitive appeal, but it suffers from three potential pitfalls. First, accounting earnings tend to be smoothed out relative to the underlying value of the company, resulting in betas that are "biased down," especially for risky firms, or "biased up," for safer firms. In other words, betas are likely to be closer to one for all firms using accounting data. Second, accounting earnings can be influenced by nonoperating factors, such as changes in depreciation or inventory methods, and by allocations of corporate expenses at the division level. Finally, accounting earnings are measured, at most, once every quarter, and often only once every year, resulting in regressions with few observations and not much power.

ILLUSTRATION 4.10   Estimating Accounting Betas: Bookscape Books

Bookscape Books, even though it is a private business, has been in existence since 1980 and has accounting earnings going back to that year. Table 4.10 summarizes accounting earnings changes at Bookscape and for companies in the S&P 500 for each year since 1980.

Regressing the changes in profits at Bookscape against changes in profits for the S&P 500 yields the following:

Bookscape Earnings Change = 0.1003 + 0.7329 (S&P 500 Earnings Change)

Based on this regression, the beta for Bookscape is 0.73. In calculating this beta, we used net income to arrive at an equity beta. Using operating earnings for both the firm and the S&P 500 should yield the equivalent of an unlevered beta.

Technically, there is no reason why we cannot estimate accounting betas for Disney, Aracruz Cellulose, and Deutsche Bank. In fact, for Disney, we could get net income numbers every quarter, which increases the data we have in the regression. We could even estimate accounting betas by division, because the divisional income is reported. We do not attempt to estimate accounting betas for the following reasons:

1. To get a sufficient number of observations in our regression, we would need to go back in time at least ten years and perhaps more. The changes that many large companies undergo over time make this a hazardous exercise.

2. Publicly traded firms smooth out accounting earnings changes even more than private firms do. This will bias the beta estimates toward one.

 There is a data set on the Web that has earnings changes, by year, for the S&P 500 going back to 1960.

Table 4.10	EARNINGS FOR BOOKSCAPE VERSUS S&P 500	
Year	**S&P 500**	**Bookscape**
1980	3.01%	3.55%
1981	1.31%	4.05%
1982	−8.95%	−14.33%
1983	−3.84%	47.55%
1984	26.69%	65.00%
1985	−6.91%	5.05%
1986	−7.93%	8.50%
1987	11.10%	37.00%
1988	42.02%	45.17%
1989	5.52%	3.50%
1990	−9.58%	−10.50%
1991	−12.08%	−32.00%
1992	−5.12%	55.00%
1993	9.37%	31.00%
1994	36.45%	21.06%
1995	30.70%	11.55%
1996	1.20%	19.88%
1997	10.57%	16.55%
1998	−3.35%	7.10%
1999	18.13%	14.40%
2000	15.13%	10.50%
2001	−14.94%	−8.15%
2002	6.81%	4.05%
2003	14.63%	12.56%

Market, Fundamental, and Accounting Betas: Which One Do We Use?

For most publicly traded firms, betas can be estimated using accounting data, market data, or fundamentals. Because the betas will almost never be the same, the question then becomes one of choosing among them. We would almost never use accounting betas for all of the reasons already specified. We are almost as reluctant to use historical market betas for individual firms because of the standard errors in beta estimates, the failures of the local indices, and the inability of these regressions to reflect the effects of major changes in the business and financial risk at the firm. Fundamental betas, in our view, provide the best beta estimates because they not only are more precise (because of the averaging) but also allow us to reflect changes in business and financial mix. In summary, we will use the fundamental estimates of equity betas of 1.25 for Disney, 0.82 for Bookscape, 0.70 for Aracruz, and 0.98 for Deutsche Bank.

IV. Estimating the Cost of Equity

Having estimated the risk-free rate, the risk premium(s), and the beta(s), we can now estimate the expected return from investing in equity at any firm. In the CAPM,

Table 4.11   LEVERED BETA AND COST OF EQUITY: DISNEY

Business	Unlevered Beta	D/E Ratio	Levered Beta	Cost of Equity
Media networks	1.0850	26.62%	1.2661	10.10%
Parks and resorts	0.9105	26.62%	1.0625	9.12%
Studio entertainment	1.1435	26.62%	1.3344	10.43%
Consumer products	1.1353	26.62%	1.3248	10.39%
Disney	1.0674	26.62%	1.2456	10.00%

this expected return can be written as:

$$\text{Expected Return} = \text{Risk-Free Rate} + \text{Beta} \times \text{Expected Risk Premium}$$

where the risk-free rate would be the rate on a long-term government bond; the beta would be either the historical, fundamental, or accounting beta; and the risk premium would be either the historical premium or an implied premium.

In the APM and multifactor model, the expected return would be written as follows:

$$\text{Expected Return} = \text{Risk-Free Rate} + \sum_{j-1}^{j=n} \beta_j \times \text{Risk Premium}_j$$

where the risk-free rate is the long-term government bond rate; β_j is the beta relative to factor j, estimated using historical data or fundamentals; and Risk Premium$_j$ is the risk premium relative to factor j, estimated using historical data.

The expected return on an equity investment in a firm, given its risk, has key implications for both equity investors in the firm and the managers of the firm. For equity investors, it is the *rate they need to make* to be compensated for the risk that they have taken on investing in the equity of a firm. If after analyzing a stock, they conclude that they cannot make this return, they would not buy it; alternatively, if they decide they can make a higher return, they would make the investment. For managers in the firm, the return that investors need to make to break even on their equity investments becomes the return that they have to try to deliver to keep these investors from becoming restive and rebellious. Thus, it becomes the rate that they have to beat in terms of returns on their equity investments in individual projects. In other words, this is the *cost of equity* to the firm.

ILLUSTRATION 4.11   Estimating the Cost of Equity

In Illustration 4.5, we estimated a bottom-up levered beta for Disney and each of its divisions. Using the prevailing Treasury bond rate of 4 percent and the historical risk premium of 4.82 percent from Table 4.2, we estimate the cost of equity for Disney as a company and for each of its divisions, listed in Table 4.11.

Note that because none of the divisions carry their own debt, we have assumed that they are all funded using the same mix of debt and equity as Disney as a company.[45] The costs of equity vary across the remaining divisions, with studio entertainment having the highest beta and parks and resorts the lowest.[46]

---

[45]Disney provides no breakdown of debt by division. If it did, we could use division-specific debt to equity ratios.

[46]If we consider cash as a division, the cost of equity is the risk-free rate because cash is invested in commercial paper and Treasuries.

Table 4.12 COST OF EQUITY FOR DEUTSCHE BANK

Business	Beta	Cost of Equity	Weights
Commercial banking	0.7345	7.59%	69%
Investment banking	1.5167	11.36%	31%
Deutsche Bank		8.76%	

To estimate the cost of equity for Deutsche Bank, we will use the same risk premium (4.82 percent) that we have used for the United States because Deutsche's business is still primarily in mature markets in Europe and the United States. Using the ten-year German Euro bond rate of 4.05 percent as the Euro risk-free rate and Deutsche Bank's bottom-up beta of 0.98, the cost of equity for Deutsche Bank is shown in Table 4.12.[47]

Note that the cost of equity for investment banking is significantly higher than the cost of equity for commercial banking, reflecting the higher risks.

For Aracruz, we will add the country risk premium for Brazil of 7.67 percent, estimated earlier in the chapter, to the mature market premium, estimated from the United States, of 4.82 percent to arrive at a total risk premium of 12.49 percent. The cost of equity in U.S. dollars for Aracruz as a company can then be computed using the bottom-up beta estimated in Illustration 4.7:

$$\text{Cost of Equity} = \text{Risk-Free Rate in US\$} + \text{Beta} \times \text{Risk Premium}$$
$$= 4\% + 0.7040(12.49\%) = 12.79\%$$

As an emerging market company, Aracruz clearly faces a much higher cost of equity than its competitors in developed markets. We can also compute a cost of equity for Aracruz in real terms, by using a real risk-free rate in this calculation. Using the ten-year inflation-index U.S. treasury bond of 2 percent as the real risk-free rate, Aracruz's real cost of equity is:

$$\text{Cost of Equity} = 2\% + 0.7040(12.49\%) = 10.79\%$$

If we want to compute the cost of equity in nominal BR terms, the adjustment is more complicated and requires estimates of expected inflation rates in Brazil and the United States. If we assume that the expected inflation in BR is 8 percent and in U.S. dollars is 2 percent, the cost of equity in BR terms is:

Cost of Equity in BR
$$= (1 + \text{Cost of Equity in \$})[(1 + \text{Inflation Rate}_{\text{Brazil}})/(1 + \text{Inflation Rate}_{\text{U.S.}})] - 1$$
$$= (1.1279)[(1.08)/(1.02)] - 1 = 0.1943 \text{ or } 19.43\%$$

Note that these estimates of cost of equity are affected by the cash holdings of Aracruz. We can estimate the cost of equity for the paper and pulp business of

[47]There are about eight countries that issue ten-year Euro-denominated bonds. We used the German Euro bond rate as the risk-free rate, not because Deutsche Bank was a German company but because this rate was the lowest of the government bond rates. The Greek and Spanish ten-year Euro bond rates were about 0.20 percent higher, reflecting the perception of default risk in those countries. We would continue to use the German Euro bond rate to value Greek and Spanish companies in Euros.

Aracruz (independent of the cash holdings) by using the levered beta of 0.7576 for the business estimated in Illustration 4.7:

$$\text{Real Cost of Equity (Paper Business)} = 2.00\% + 0.7576(12.49\%) = 11.46\%$$

$$\text{US\$ Cost of Equity (Paper Business)} = 4.00\% + 0.7576(12.49\%) = 13.46\%$$

$$\text{Nominal BR Cost of Equity (Paper Business)} = 1.1346[(1.08)/(1.02)] - 1 = 20.13\%$$

Finally, for Bookscape, we will use the beta of 0.82 estimated from Illustration 4.6 in conjunction with the risk-free rate and risk premium for the United States:

$$\text{Cost of Equity} = 4\% + 0.82(4.82\%) = 7.97\%$$

This cost of equity may seem incongruously low for a small, privately held business, but it is legitimate if we assume that the only risk that matters is nondiversifiable risk.

IN PRACTICE: RISK, COST OF EQUITY, AND PRIVATE FIRMS

Implicit in the use of beta as a measure of risk is the assumption that the marginal investor in equity is a well-diversified investor. Although this is a defensible assumption when analyzing publicly traded firms, it becomes much more difficult to sustain for private firms. The owner of a private firm generally has the bulk of his or her wealth invested in the business. Consequently, he or she cares about the total risk in the business rather than just the market risk. Thus, for a business like Bookscape, the beta that we have estimated of 0.82 (leading to a cost of equity of 7.97 percent) will understate the risk perceived by the owner. There are three solutions to this problem:

1. Assume that the business is run with the near-term objective of sale to a large publicly traded firm. In such a case, it is reasonable to use the market beta and cost of equity that comes from it.

2. Add a premium to the cost of equity to reflect the higher risk created by the owner's inability to diversify. This may help explain the high returns that some venture capitalists demand on their equity investments in fledgling businesses.

3. Adjust the beta to reflect total risk rather than market risk. This adjustment is relatively simple, because the R^2 of the regression measures the proportion of the risk that is market risk. Dividing the market beta by the square root of the R^2 (which yields the correlation coefficient) yields a total beta. In the Bookscape example, the regressions for the comparable firms against the market index have an average R^2 of about 16 percent. The total beta for Bookscape can then be computed as follows:

$$\text{Total Beta} = (\text{Market Beta})/\sqrt{R^2} = 0.82/\sqrt{0.16} = 2.06$$

Using this total beta would yield a much higher and more realistic estimate of the cost of equity.

$$\text{Cost of Equity} = 4\% + 2.06\,(4.82\%) = 13.93\%$$

Thus, private businesses will generally have much higher costs of equity than their publicly traded counterparts, with diversified investors. Although many of them ultimately capitulate by selling to publicly traded competitors or going public, some firms choose to remain private and thrive. To do so, they have to diversify on their own (as many family-run businesses in Asia and Latin America did) or accept the lower value as a price paid for maintaining total control. ■

FROM COST OF EQUITY TO COST OF CAPITAL

Equity is undoubtedly an important and indispensable ingredient of the financing mix for every business, but it is only one ingredient. Most businesses finance some or much of their operations using debt or some hybrid of equity and debt. The costs of these sources of financing are generally very different from the cost of equity, and the minimum acceptable hurdle rate for a project will reflect their costs as well, in proportion to their use in the financing mix. Intuitively, the *cost of capital* is the weighted average of the costs of the different components of financing—including debt, equity, and hybrid securities—used by a firm to fund its investments.

4.8   INTEREST RATES AND THE RELATIVE COSTS OF DEBT AND EQUITY

It is often argued that debt becomes a more attractive mode of financing than equity as interest rates go down and a less attractive mode when interest rates go up. Is this true?

☐ Yes

☐ No

Why or why not?

The Costs of Nonequity Financing

To estimate the cost of the funding that a firm raises, we have to estimate the costs of all of the nonequity components. In this section, we consider the cost of debt first and then extend the analysis to consider hybrids, such as preferred stock and convertible bonds.

The Cost of Debt

The *cost of debt* measures the current cost to the firm of borrowing funds to finance projects. In general terms, it is determined by the following variables:

1. *The current level of interest rates*   As interest rates rise, the cost of debt for firms will also increase.

2. *The default risk of the company*   As the **default risk** of a firm increases, the cost of borrowing money will also increase.

3. *The tax advantage associated with debt*   Because interest is tax-deductible, the after-tax cost of debt is a function of the tax rate. The tax benefit that accrues from paying interest makes the after-tax cost of debt lower than the pretax cost. Furthermore, this benefit increases as the tax rate increases.

After-Tax Cost of Debt = Pretax Cost of Debt (1 − Marginal Tax Rate)

Default Risk: The risk that a firm will fail to make obligated debt payments, such as interest expenses or principal payments.

 4.9   Costs of Debt and Equity

Can the cost of equity ever be lower than the cost of debt for any firm at any stage in its life cycle?

☐   Yes

☐   No

Estimating the Default Risk and Default Spread of a Firm
The simplest scenario for estimating the cost of debt occurs when a firm has long-term bonds outstanding that are widely traded and have no special features, such as convertibility or first claim on assets, skewing interest rates. The market price of the bond, in conjunction with its coupon and maturity, can serve to compute a yield we use as the cost of debt. This approach works for firms that have dozens of outstanding bonds that are liquid and trade frequently.

Many firms have bonds outstanding that do not trade on a regular basis. Because these firms are usually rated, we can estimate their costs of debt by using their ratings and associated default spreads. Thus, Disney with a BBB+ rating can be expected to have a cost of debt approximately 1.25 percent higher than the Treasury bond rate because this is the spread typically paid by BBB+ firms.

Some companies choose not to get rated. Many smaller firms and most private businesses fall into this category. Ratings agencies have sprung up in many emerging markets, but there are still a number of markets in which companies are not rated on the basis of default risk. When there is no rating available to estimate the cost of debt, there are two alternatives:

- *Recent Borrowing History*   Many firms that are not rated still borrow money from banks and other financial institutions. By looking at the most recent borrowings made by a firm, we can get a sense of the default spreads being charged and use these spreads to come up with a cost of debt.

- *Estimate a Synthetic Rating and Default Spread*   An alternative is to play the role of a ratings agency and assign a rating to a firm based on its financial ratios; this rating is called a synthetic rating. To make this assessment, we begin with rated firms and examine the financial characteristics shared by firms within each ratings class. Consider a very simpler version, where the ratio of operating income to interest expense, the interest coverage ratio, is computed for each rated firm. In Table 4.13, we list the range of interest coverage ratios for small manufacturing firms in each S&P ratings class.[48] We also report the typical default spreads for bonds in each ratings class.[49]

---

[48]This table was developed in early 2000, by listing all rated firms with market capitalization lower than $2 billion and their interest coverage ratios, and then sorting firms based on their bond ratings. The ranges were adjusted to eliminate outliers and to prevent overlapping ranges.

[49]These default spreads are obtained from an online site, found at www.bondsonline.com. You can find default spreads for industrial and financial service firms; these spreads are for industrial firms.

Table 4.13   INTEREST COVERAGE RATIOS AND RATINGS

Interest Coverage Ratio	Rating	Typical Default Spread
>12.5	AAA	0.35%
9.50–12.50	AA	0.50%
7.50–9.50	A+	0.70%
6.00–7.50	A	0.85%
4.50–6.00	A–	1.00%
4.00–4.50	BBB	1.50%
3.50–4.00	BB+	2.00%
3.00–3.50	BB	2.50%
2.50–3.00	B+	3.25%
2.00–2.50	B	4.00%
1.50–2.00	B–	6.00%
1.25–1.50	CCC	8.00%
0.80–1.25	CC	10.00%
0.50–0.80	C	12.00%
<0.65	D	20.00%

Source: Compustat and Bondsonline.com.

Now consider a private firm with $10 million in earnings before interest and taxes and $3 million in interest expenses; it has an interest coverage ratio of 3.33. Based on this ratio, we would assess a synthetic rating of BB for the firm and attach a default spread of 3.50 percent to the risk-free rate to come up with a pretax cost of debt.

By basing the synthetic rating on the interest coverage ratio alone, we run the risk of missing the information that is available in the other financial ratios used by ratings agencies. The approach described can be extended to incorporate other ratios. The first step would be to develop a score based on multiple ratios. For instance, the Altman z-score, which is used as a proxy for default risk, is a function of five financial ratios, which are weighted to generate a z-score. The ratios used and their relative weights are usually based on past history on defaulted firms. The second step is to relate the level of the score to a bond rating, much as we did in Table 4.13 with interest coverage ratios. In making this extension, though, note that complexity comes at a cost. Credit or z-scores may, in fact, yield better estimates of synthetic ratings than those based only on interest coverage ratios, but changes in ratings arising from these scores are much more difficult to explain than those based on interest coverage ratios. That is the reason we prefer the flawed but more transparent ratings from interest coverage ratios.

Short-Term and Long-Term Debt
Most publicly traded firms have multiple borrowings—short-term and long-term bonds and bank debt with different terms and interest rates. Although there are some analysts who create separate categories for each type of debt and attach a different cost to each category, this approach is both tedious and dangerous. Using it, we can conclude that short-term debt is cheaper than long-term debt and that secured debt is cheaper than unsecured debt.

The solution is simple. Combine all debt—short- and long-term, bank debt and bonds—and attach the long-term cost of debt to it. In other words, add the default spread to the long-term risk-free rate and use that rate as the pretax cost of debt. Firms will undoubtedly complain, arguing that their effective cost of debt can be lowered by using short-term debt. This is technically true, largely because short-term rates tend to be lower than long-term rates in most developed markets, but it misses the point of computing the cost of debt and capital. If this is the hurdle rate we want our long-term investments to beat, we want the rate to reflect the cost of long-term borrowing and not short-term borrowing. After all, a firm that funds long-term projects with short-term debt will have to return to the market to roll over this debt.

Operating Leases and Other Fixed Commitments
The essential characteristic of debt is that it gives rise to a tax-deductible *obligation that firms have to meet in both good times and bad, and the failure to meet this obligation can result in bankruptcy or loss of equity control over the firm.* If we use this definition of debt, it is quite clear that what we see reported on the balance sheet as debt may not reflect the true borrowings of the firm. In particular, a firm that leases assets and categorizes them as operating leases owes substantially more than is reported in the financial statements.[50] After all, a firm that signs a lease commits to making the lease payment in future periods and risks the loss of assets if it fails to make the commitment.

For corporate financial analysis, we should treat all lease payments as financial expenses and convert future lease commitments into debt by discounting them back to the present, using the current pretax cost of borrowing for the firm as the discount rate. The resulting present value can be considered the debt value of operating leases and can be added on to the value of conventional debt to arrive at a total debt figure. To complete the adjustment, the operating income of the firm will also have to be restated:

Adjusted Operating Income
    = Stated Operating Income + Operating Lease Expense for the Current Year
        − Depreciation on Leased Asset

In fact, this process can be used to convert any set of financial commitments into debt.

Book and Market Interest Rates
When firms borrow money, they often do so at fixed rates. When they issue bonds to investors, this rate that is fixed at the time of the issue is called the coupon rate. The cost of debt is not the coupon rate on outstanding bonds, nor is it the rate at which

---

[50]In an operating lease, the lessor (or owner) transfers only the right to use the property to the lessee. At the end of the lease period, the lessee returns the property to the lessor. Because the lessee does not assume the risk of ownership, the lease expense is treated as an operating expense in the income statement, and the lease does not affect the balance sheet. In a capital lease, the lessee assumes some of the risks of ownership and enjoys some of the benefits. Consequently, the lease, when signed, is recognized both as an asset and as a liability (for the lease payments) on the balance sheet. The firm gets to claim depreciation each year on the asset and also deducts the interest expense component of the lease payment each year. In general, capital leases recognize expenses sooner than equivalent operating leases.

the company was able to borrow at in the past. Although these factors may help determine the interest cost the company will have to pay in the current year, they do not determine the pretax cost of debt in the cost of capital calculations. Thus, a company that has debt that it took on when interest rates were low cannot contend that it has a low cost of debt.

To see why, consider a firm that has $2 billion of debt on its books and assume that the interest expense on this debt is $80 million. The book interest rate on the debt is 4 percent. Assume also that the current risk-free rate is 6 percent. If we use the book interest rate of 4 percent in our cost of capital calculations, we require the projects we fund with the capital to earn more than 4 percent to be considered good investments. Because we can invest that money in Treasury bonds and earn 6 percent, without taking any risk, this is clearly not a high enough hurdle. To ensure that projects earn more than what we can make on alternative investments of equivalent risk today, the cost of debt has to be based on market interest rates today rather than book interest rates.

Assessing the Tax Advantage of Debt

Interest is tax-deductible, and the resulting tax savings reduce the cost of borrowing to firms. In assessing this tax advantage, we should keep the following things in mind.

- Interest expenses offset the marginal dollar of income and the tax advantage has to be therefore calculated using the marginal tax rate.

$$\text{After-Tax Cost of Debt} = \text{Pretax Cost of Debt} \, (1 - \text{Marginal Tax Rate})$$

- To obtain the tax advantages of borrowing, firms have to be profitable. In other words, there is no tax advantage from interest expenses to a firm that has operating losses. It is true that firms can carry losses forward and can offset them against profits in future periods. The most prudent assessment of the tax effects of debt will therefore provide for no tax advantages in the years of operating losses and will begin adjusting for tax benefits only in future years when the firm is expected to have operating profits.

$$\text{After-Tax Cost of Debt} = \text{Pretax Cost of Debt} \qquad \text{If Operating Income} < 0$$

$$\text{Pretax Cost of Debt} \, (1 - t) \qquad \text{If Operating Income} > 0$$

ILLUSTRATION 4.12 **Estimating the Costs of Debt**

Disney, Deutsche Bank, and Aracruz are all rated companies, and we will estimate their pretax costs of debt based on their ratings. To provide a contrast, we will also estimate synthetic ratings for Disney and Aracruz. For Bookscape, we will use the synthetic rating of BBB, estimated from the interest coverage ratio to assess the pretax cost of debt.

- ***Bond Ratings*** S&P, Moody's, and Fitch rate all three companies, but the ratings are consistent, and we will use the S&P ratings and the associated default spreads (from Table 3.4 in Chapter 3) to estimate the costs of debt in Table 4.14.

Table 4.14 COST OF DEBT

	S&P Rating	Risk-Free Rate	Default Spread	Cost of Debt	Tax Rate	After-Tax Cost of Debt
Disney	BBB+	4% ($)	1.25%	5.25%	37.3%	3.29%
Deutsche Bank[a]	AA−	4.05% (Eu)	1.00%	5.05%	38%	3.13%
Aracruz[51]	B+	4% ($)	3.25%	7.25%	34%	4.79%

[a]Default spread for financial service firms is higher.

The marginal tax rates of the United States (Disney), Brazil (Aracruz), and Germany (Deutsche Bank) are used to compute the after-tax cost of debt. We will assume that all of Disney's divisions have the same cost of debt and marginal tax rate as the parent company.

- **Synthetic Ratings** For Bookscape, there are no recent borrowings on the books, thus making the synthetic rating for the firm our only choice. In 2003, Bookscape had operating income of $2 million and interest expenses of $500,000. The resulting interest coverage ratio is 4, yielding a synthetic rating of BBB for the firm. Adding the default spread of 1.5 percent associated with that rating to the risk-free rate results in a pretax cost of debt of 5.50 percent. The after-tax cost of debt is computed using a 40 percent marginal tax rate:

$$\text{After-Tax Cost of Debt} = 5.5\%(1 - 0.40) = 3.30\%$$

IN PRACTICE: ACTUAL AND SYNTHETIC RATINGS

It is usually easy to estimate the cost of debt for firms that have bond ratings available for them. There are, however, a few potential problems that sometimes arise in practice.

- **Disagreement between ratings agencies** Although the ratings are consistent across agencies for many firms, there are a few firms over which the ratings agencies disagree, with one agency assigning a much higher or lower rating to the firm than the others.

- **Multiple bond ratings for same firm** Because ratings agencies rate bonds, rather than firms, the same firm can have many bond issues with different ratings depending on how the bond is structured and secured.

- **Lags or errors in the rating process** Ratings agencies make mistakes, and there is evidence that ratings changes occur after the bond market has already recognized the change in the default risk.

---

[51]With Aracruz, one troublesome aspect of the pretax cost of debt is that it is lower than the rate at which the Brazilian government can borrow. Although there are some cases where we would add the default spread of the country to that of the firm to get to a pretax cost of debt, Aracruz may be in a stronger position to borrow in U.S. dollars than the Brazilian government because it sells its products in a global market and gets paid in dollars. The default spread based purely on the rating is 4.25 percent, but we used a smaller default spread of 3.25 percent to reflect the firm's strong financial standing and large cash balance.

It is a good idea to estimate synthetic ratings even for firms that have actual ratings. If there is disagreement between ratings agencies or a firm has multiple bond ratings, the synthetic rating can operate as a tie-breaker. If there is a significant difference between actual and synthetic ratings, and there is no fundamental reason that can be pinpointed for the difference, the synthetic rating may be providing an early signal of a ratings agency mistake.

We computed the synthetic ratings for Disney and Aracruz using the interest coverage ratios:

Disney: Interest coverage ratio = 2,805/758 = 3.70   Synthetic rating = A–

Aracruz: Interest coverage ratio = 888/339 = 2.62   Synthetic rating = BBB

Although Disney's synthetic rating is close to its actual rating of BBB+, the synthetic rating for Aracruz is much higher than its rating of B+. The reason for the discrepancy lies in the fact that Aracruz has two ratings—one for its local currency borrowings of BBB– and one for its dollar borrowings of B+. We used the latter to estimate the cost of debt because almost all of Aracruz's debt is dollar debt. You can also consider the difference to be a reflection of the riskiness of Brazil as a country and the penalty that Aracruz pays for being a Brazilian company. In fact, we can quantify this difference by measuring the difference in interest rates (in U.S. dollar terms) of Aracruz with the synthetic and actual ratings:

Cost of Debt with Actual Rating of B+: 4% + 3.25% = 7.25%

Cost of Debt with Synthetic Rating of BBB: 4% + 1.50% = 5.50%

Country Default Penalty Attached to Aracruz Debt = 7.25% − 5.50% = 1.75% ■

Calculating the Cost of Preferred Stock

Preferred stock shares some of the characteristics of debt—the preferred dividend is prespecified at the time of the issue and is paid out before common dividend—and some of the characteristics of equity—the payments of preferred dividends are not tax-deductible. Since preferred stock is perpetual, the cost of preferred stock can be written as follows:

$$k_{ps} = \text{Preferred Dividend per Share/Market Price per Preferred Share}$$

This approach assumes that the dividend is constant in dollar terms forever and that the preferred stock has no special features (convertibility, callability, etc.). If such special features exist, they will have to be valued separately to come up with a good estimate of the cost of preferred stock. In terms of risk, preferred stock is safer than common equity but riskier than debt. Consequently, it should, on a pretax basis, command a higher cost than debt and a lower cost than equity.

ILLUSTRATION 4.13 **Calculating the Cost of Preferred Stock: Disney and Deutsche Bank** Both Disney and Deutsche Bank have preferred stock outstanding. The preferred dividend yields on the issues are computed in March 2004 in Table 4.15.

Table 4.15 COST OF PREFERRED STOCK			
Company	Preferred Stock Price	Annual Dividends/Share	Dividend Yield
Disney	$26.74	$1.75	1.75/26.74 = 6.54%
Deutsche Bank	103.75 Euros	6.60 Euros	6.6/103.75 = 6.36%

Notice that the cost of preferred stock for Disney is higher than its pretax cost of debt of 5.25 percent and is lower than its cost of equity of 10 percent. For Deutsche Bank as well, the cost of preferred stock is higher than its pretax cost of debt (5.05 percent) and is lower than its cost of equity of 8.76 percent. For both firms, the market value of preferred stock is so small relative to the market values of debt and equity that it makes almost no impact on the overall cost of capital.

4.10 WHY DO COMPANIES ISSUE PREFERRED STOCK?

Which of the following are good reasons for a company issuing preferred stock?
- ☐ Preferred stock is cheaper than equity.
- ☐ Preferred stock is treated as equity by the ratings agencies and regulators.
- ☐ Preferred stock is cheaper than debt.
- ☐ Other

Explain.

Calculating the Cost of Other Hybrid Securities

In general terms, *hybrid securities* share some of the characteristics of debt and some of the characteristics of equity. A good example is a convertible bond, which can be viewed as a combination of a straight bond (debt) and a conversion option (equity). Instead of trying to calculate the cost of these hybrid securities individually, they can be broken down into their debt and equity components and treated separately.

In general, it is not difficult to decompose a hybrid security that is publicly traded (and has a market price) into debt and equity components. In the case of a convertible bond, this can be accomplished in two ways:

- An option pricing model can be used to value the conversion option, and the remaining value of the bond can be attributed to debt.

- The convertible bond can be valued as if it were a straight bond, using the rate at which the firm can borrow in the market, given its default risk (pretax cost of debt) as the interest rate on the bond. The difference between the price of the convertible bond and the value of the straight bond can be viewed as the value of the conversion option.

If the convertible security is not traded, we have to value both the straight bond and the conversion options separately.

ILLUSTRATION 4.14 Breaking Down a Convertible Bond into Debt and Equity Components: Disney

In March 2004, Disney had **convertible** bonds outstanding with nineteen years left to maturity and a coupon rate of 2.125 percent trading at $1,064 a bond. Holders of this bond have the right to convert the bond into 33.9444 shares of stock any time over the bond's remaining life.[52] To break the convertible bond into straight bond and conversion option components, we will value the bond using Disney's pretax cost of debt of 5.25 percent:[53]

 Convertible Debt: Debt that can be converted into stock at a specified rate, called the conversion ratio.

Straight Bond Component
= Value of a 2.125% coupon bond due in 19 years with a market interest rate of 5.25%
= PV of $21.25 in coupons[54] each year for 19 years + PV of $1,000 at end of year 19

$$= 21.25\left[\frac{1 - (1.0525)^{-19}}{0.0525}\right] + \frac{1,000}{(1.0525)^{19}} = \$629.91$$

Conversion Option = Market Value of Convertible − Value of Straight Bond
= $1,064 − $629.91 = $434.09

The straight bond component of $629.91 is treated as debt, whereas the conversion option of $434.09 is treated as equity.

4.11 INCREASES IN STOCK PRICES AND CONVERTIBLE BONDS

As stock prices go up, which of the following is likely to happen to the convertible bond? (You can choose more than one.)

☐ The convertible bond will increase in value.

☐ The straight bond component of the convertible bond will decrease in value.

☐ The equity component of the convertible bond will increase as a percentage of the total value.

☐ The straight bond component of the convertible bond will increase as a percentage of the total value.

Explain.

Calculating the Weights of Debt and Equity Components

Once we have costs for each of the different components of financing, all we need are weights on each component to arrive at a cost of capital. In this section, we consider the choices for weighting, the argument for using market value weights, and whether the weights can change over time.

---

[52]At this conversion ratio, the price that investors would be paying for Disney shares would be $29.46, much higher than the stock price of $20.46 prevailing at the time of the analysis.

[53]This rate was based on a ten-year Treasury bond rate. If the five-year Treasury bond rate had been substantially different, we would have recomputed a pretax cost of debt by adding the default spread to the five-year rate.

[54]The coupons are assumed to be annual. With semiannual coupons, you would divide the coupon by two and apply a semiannual rate to calculate the present value.

Choices for Weighting

In computing weights for debt, equity, and preferred stock, we have two choices. We can take the accounting estimates of the value of each funding source from the balance sheet and compute book value weights. Alternatively, we can use or estimate market values for each component and compute weights based on relative market value. *As a general rule, the weights used in the cost of capital computation should be based on market values.* This is because the cost of capital is a forward-looking measure and captures the cost of raising new funds to finance projects. Because new debt and equity has to be raised in the market at prevailing prices, the market value weights are more relevant.

There are some analysts who continue to use book value weights and justify them using three arguments, none of which are convincing:

- *Book value is more reliable than market value because it is not as volatile*
  Although it is true that book value does not change as much as market value, this is more a reflection of weakness than strength, because the true value of the firm changes over time as new information comes out about the firm and the overall economy. We would argue that market value, with its volatility, is a much better reflection of true value than is book value.[55]

- *Using book value rather than market value is a more conservative approach to estimating debt ratios*   The book value of equity in most firms in developed markets is well below the value attached by the market, whereas the book value of debt is usually close to the market value of debt. Because the cost of equity is much higher than the cost of debt, the cost of capital calculated using book value ratios will be lower than those calculated using market value ratios, making them less conservative estimates, not more so.[56]

- *Because accounting returns are computed based on book value, consistency requires the use of book value in computing cost of capital*   Although it may seem consistent to use book values for both accounting return and cost of capital calculations, it does not make economic sense. The funds invested in these projects can be invested elsewhere, earning market rates, and the costs should therefore be computed at market rates and using market value weights.

Estimating Market Values

In a world where all funding was raised in financial markets and securities were continuously traded, the market values of debt and equity should be easy to get. In practice, there are some financing components with no market values available,

---

[55]There are some who argue that stock prices are much more volatile than the underlying true value. Even if this argument is justified (and it has not conclusively been shown to be so), the difference between market value and true value is likely to be much smaller than the difference between book value and true value.

[56]To illustrate this point, assume that the market value debt ratio is 10 percent, and the book value debt ratio is 30 percent, for a firm with a cost of equity of 15 percent and an after-tax cost of debt of 5 percent. The cost of capital can be calculated as follows:

$$\text{With Market Value Debt Ratios: } 15\%(0.9) + 5\%(0.1) = 14\%$$
$$\text{With Book Value Debt Ratios: } 15\%(0.7) + 5\%(0.3) = 12\%$$

even for large publicly traded firms, and none of the financing components are traded in private firms.

The Market Value of Equity

The market value of equity is generally the number of shares outstanding times the current stock price. Because it measures the cost of raising funds today, it is not good practice to use average stock prices over time or some other normalized version of the price.

- **Multiple classes of shares**   If there is more than one class of shares outstanding, the market values of all of these securities should be aggregated and treated as equity. Even if some of the classes of shares are not traded, market values have to be estimated for nontraded shares and added to the aggregate equity value.
- **Equity options**   If there are other equity claims in the firm—warrants and conversion options in other securities—these should also be valued and added on to the value of the equity in the firm. In the past decade, the use of options as management compensation has created complications, because the value of these options has to be estimated.

How do we estimate the value of equity for private businesses? We have two choices. One is to estimate the market value of equity by looking at the multiples of revenues and net income at which publicly traded firms trade. The other is to bypass the estimation process and use the market debt ratio of publicly traded firms as the debt ratio for private firms in the same business. This is the assumption we made for Bookscape, when we used the industry average debt to equity ratio for the book/publishing business as the debt to equity ratio for Bookscape to compute levered betas.

The Market Value of Debt

The market value of debt is usually more difficult to obtain directly because very few firms have all of their debt in the form of bonds outstanding, trading in the market. Many firms have nontraded debt, such as bank debt, which is specified in book value terms but not market value terms. To get around the problem, many analysts make the simplifying assumptions that the book value of debt is equal to its market value. Although this is not a bad assumption for mature companies in developed markets, it can be a mistake when interest rates and default spreads are volatile.

A simple way to convert book value debt into market value debt is to treat the entire debt on the books as a coupon bond, with a coupon set equal to the interest expenses on all of the debt and the maturity set equal to the face-value weighted average maturity of the debt, and to then value this coupon bond at the current cost of debt for the company. Thus, the market value of $1 billion in debt, with interest expenses of $60 million and a maturity of six years, when the current cost of debt is 7.5 percent can be estimated as follows:

$$\text{Estimated Market Value of Debt} = 60 \left[\frac{\left(1 - \dfrac{1}{(1.075)^6} \right)}{0.075} \right] + \frac{1,000}{(1.075)^6} = \$929.59$$

This is an approximation; a more accurate computation would require valuing each debt issue separately using this process. As a final point, we should add the present value of operating lease commitments to this market value of debt to arrive at an aggregate value for debt in computing the cost of capital.

IN PRACTICE: CAN FINANCING WEIGHTS CHANGE OVER TIME?

Using the current market values to obtain weights will yield a cost of capital for the current year. But can the weights attached to debt and equity and the resulting cost of capital change from year to year? Absolutely, and especially in the following scenarios:

- *Young firms* Young firms often are all equity-funded largely because they do not have the cash flows (or earnings) to sustain debt. As they become larger, increasing earnings and cash flow usually allow for more borrowing. When analyzing firms early in their life cycle, we should allow for the fact that the debt ratio of the firm will probably increase over time toward the industry average.

- *Target debt ratios and changing financing mix* Mature firms sometimes decide to change their financing strategies, pushing toward target debt ratios that are much higher or lower than current levels. When analyzing these firms, we should consider the expected changes as the firm moves from the current to the target debt ratio.

As a general rule, we should view the cost of capital as a year-specific number and change the inputs each year. Not only will the weights attached to debt and equity change over time, but so will the estimates of beta and the cost of debt. In fact, one of the advantages of using bottom-up betas is that the beta each year can be estimated as a function of the expected debt to equity ratio that year. ∎

ILLUSTRATION 4.15 Market Value and Book Value Debt Ratios: Disney and Aracruz
Disney has a number of debt issues on its books, with varying coupon rates and maturities. Table 4.16 summarizes Disney's outstanding debt.

The debt has a weighted average maturity of 11.53 years. To convert the book value of debt to market value, we use the current pretax cost of debt for Disney of

Table 4.16 DEBT AT DISNEY: SEPTEMBER 2003				
Debt	**Face Value**	**Stated Interest Rate**	**Maturity**	**Weighted Maturity**
Commercial paper	$0	2.00%	0.5	0.0000
Medium-term paper	$8,114	6.10%	15	9.2908
Senior convertibles	$1,323	2.13%	10	1.0099
Other US$-denominated debt	$597	4.80%	15	0.6836
Privately placed debt	$343	7.00%	4	0.1047
Euro medium-term debt	$1,519	3.30%	2	0.2319
Preferred stock	$485	7.40%	1	0.0370
Cap Cities debt	$191	9.30%	9	0.1312
Other	$528	3.00%	1	0.0403
Total	$13,100	5.60%		11.5295

5.25 percent as the discount rate, $13,100 as the book value of debt and the current year's interest expenses of $666 million as the coupon:

Estimated MV of Disney Debt

$$= 666 \left[\frac{\left(1 - \frac{1}{(1.0525)^{11.53}}\right)}{0.0525} \right] + \frac{13,100}{(1.0525)^{11.53}} = \$12,915 \text{ million}$$

To this amount, we add the present value of Disney's operating lease commitments. This present value is computed by discounting the lease commitment each year at the pretax cost of debt for Disney (5.25 percent):[57]

Year	Commitment (in Millions)	Present Value (in Millions)
1	$271.00	$257.48
2	$242.00	$218.46
3	$221.00	$189.55
4	$208.00	$169.50
5	$275.00	$212.92
6–9 (each year)	$258.25 (annual)	$704.93
Debt value of leases =		$1,752.85

Adding the debt value of operating leases to the market value of debt of $12,915 million yields a total market value for debt of $14,668 million at Disney.

Aracruz has debt with a book value of 3,946 million BR, interest expenses of 339 million BR in the current year, and an average maturity for the debt of 3.20 years. Because most of the debt is dollar debt, we used the nominal dollar pretax cost of debt for the firm of 7.25 percent (from Illustration 4.12).[58] The market value of Aracruz debt is:

$$\text{MV of Aracruz Debt} = 339 \left[\frac{\left(1 - \frac{1}{(1.0725)^{3.20}}\right)}{0.0725} \right] + \frac{3,946}{(1.0725)^{3.20}}$$

$$= 4,094 \text{ million BR}$$

There are no lease commitments reported in Aracruz's financial statements.[59]

In Table 4.17 we contrast the book values of debt and equity with the market values for Disney and Aracruz. The market value of equity is estimated using the current market price and the number of shares outstanding.

---

[57]Disney reports total commitments of $1,033 million beyond year six. Using the average commitment from years one through five as an indicator, we assumed that this total commitment would take the form of an annuity of $258.25 million a year for four years.

[58]If the debt had been predominantly nominal BR debt, we would have used a nominal BR cost of debt.

[59]Although many companies outside the United States do not provide details on lease commitments in future years, Aracruz publishes financial statements that use U.S. accounting standards for its ADR listing.

Table 4.17 BOOK VALUE VERSUS MARKET VALUE: DEBT RATIOS

	BV:Debt	BV:Equity	BV:D/(D+E)	MV:Debt	MV:Equity	MV:D/(D+E)
Disney	$13,100	$24,219	35.10%	$14,668	$55,101	21.02%
Aracruz	$3,946	$5,205	43.12%	$4,094	$9,189	30.82%

For Disney, the market value debt ratio of 21.02 percent is much lower than the book value debt ratio of 35.10 percent. For Aracruz, the market debt ratio is 30.82 percent, lower than the book debt ratio of 43.12 percent.

Estimating and Using the Cost of Capital

With the estimates of the costs of the individual components—debt, equity and preferred stock (if any)—and the market value weights of each of the components, the cost of capital can be computed. Thus if E, D, and PS are the market values of equity, debt, and preferred stock respectively, the cost of capital can be written as follows:

$$\text{Cost of Capital} = k_E[E/(D + E + PS)] + k_D[D/(D + E + PS)] + k_{PS}[PS/(D + E + PS)]$$

The cost of capital is a measure of the composite cost of raising money that a firm faces. It will generally be lower than the cost of equity, which is the cost of just equity funding.

It is a source of confusion to many analysts that both the cost of equity and the cost of capital are used as hurdle rates in investment analysis. The way to resolve this confusion is to recognize when it is appropriate to use each one.

- If we want to adopt the perspective of just the equity investors in a business or a project and measure the returns earned just by these investors on their investment, the cost of equity is the correct hurdle rate to use. In measuring the returns to equity investors then, we have to consider only the income or cash flows left over after all other claimholders needs (interest payments on debt and preferred dividends, for instance) have been met.

- If the returns that we are measuring are composite returns to all claimholders, based on earnings before payments to debt and preferred stockholders, the comparison should be to the cost of capital.

Although these principles are abstract, we will consider them in more detail in the next chapter when we look at examples of projects.

ILLUSTRATION 4.16 Estimating Cost of Capital

Culminating the analysis in this chapter, we first estimate the costs of capital for each of Disney's divisions. In making these estimates, we use the costs of equity that we obtained for the divisions in Illustration 4.11 and Disney's cost of debt from Illustration 4.12. We also assume that all of the divisions are funded with the same mix of

Table 4.18	COST OF CAPITAL FOR DISNEY'S DIVISIONS				
Business	**Cost of Equity**	**After-Tax Cost of Debt**	**E/(D+E)**	**D/(D+E)**	**Cost of Capital**
Media networks	10.10%	3.29%	78.98%	21.02%	8.67%
Parks and resorts	9.12%	3.29%	78.98%	21.02%	7.90%
Studio entertainment	10.43%	3.29%	78.98%	21.02%	8.93%
Consumer products	10.39%	3.29%	78.98%	21.02%	8.89%
Disney	10.00%	3.29%	78.98%	21.02%	8.59%

Table 4.19	COST OF CAPITAL FOR ARACRUZ: REAL AND U.S. DOLLAR				
	Levered Beta	**Cost of Equity**	**After-Tax Cost of Debt**	**D/(D+E)**	**Cost of Capital**
In real terms					
Paper and pulp	0.7576	11.46%	3.47%	30.82%	9.00%
Cash	0.0000	2.00%			2.00%
Aracruz	0.7040	10.79%	3.47%	30.82%	8.53%
In U.S. dollar terms					
Paper and pulp	0.7576	13.46%	4.79%	30.82%	10.79%
Cash	0.0000	4.00%			4.00%
Aracruz	0.7040	12.79%	4.79%	30.82%	10.33%

debt and equity as the parent company. Table 4.18 provides estimates of the costs of capital for the divisions.

The cost of capital for Disney as a company is 8.59 percent, but the costs of capitals vary across divisions with a low of 7.90 percent for the parks and resorts division to a high of 8.93 percent for studio entertainment.

To estimate the cost of capital in both real and nominal U.S. dollar terms for Aracruz, we use the cost of equity (from Illustration 4.11) and the after-tax cost of debt (from Illustration 4.12) and report the estimates in Table 4.19.

The nominal dollar costs of capital can be converted into nominal BR costs of capital using the differential inflation rates in the two countries, just as the cost of equity was earlier in the chapter.

When estimating the cost of equity for Bookscape, we assumed that the company would be funded using the same market debt to equity ratio as the book/publishing industry. Staying consistent, we will use the market debt to capital ratio to compute the cost of capital for the firm. We will also present two estimates of the cost of capital—one using the market beta and the other using the total beta.

	Beta	**Cost of Equity**	**After-Tax Cost of Equity**	**D/(D+E)**	**Cost of Capital**
Market beta	0.82	7.97%	3.30%	16.90%	7.18%
Total beta	2.06	13.93%	3.30%	16.90%	12.14%

The cost of capital estimated using the total beta is a more realistic estimate, given that this is a private company, and we will use it as the cost of capital for Bookscape in the coming chapters.

IN PRACTICE: EQUITY, DEBT, AND COST OF CAPITAL FOR BANKS

Note that we did not estimate a cost of capital for Deutsche Bank even though we have estimates of the costs of equity and debt for the firm. The reason is simple and goes to the heart of how firms view debt. For nonfinancial service firms, debt is a source of capital and is used to fund real projects—building a factory or making a movie. For banks, debt is raw material that is used to generate profits. Boiled down to its simplest elements, it is a bank's job to borrow money (debt) at a low rate and lend it out at a higher rate. It should come as no surprise that when banks (and their regulators) talk about capital, they mean equity capital.[60]

There is also a practical problem in computing the cost of capital for a bank. If we define debt as any fixed commitment where failure to meet the commitment can lead to loss of equity control, the deposits made by customers at bank branches would qualify and the debt ratio of a bank will very quickly converge on 100 percent. If we define it more narrowly, we still are faced with a problem of where to draw the line. A pragmatic compromise is to view only long-term bonds issued by a bank as debt, but it is an artificial one. Deutsche Bank, for instance, had long-term debt in December 2003 with a value of 82.0 billion Euros, common equity with a market value of 41.0 billion Euros and preferred stock with a market value of 4.1 billion Euros. Using the cost of equity of 8.76 percent (from Illustration 4.11), the after-tax cost of debt of 3.13 percent from Illustration 4.12 and the cost of preferred stock (6.36 percent) from Illustration 4.13:

$$\text{Cost of capital} = 3.13\%(82.0/127.1) + 8.76\%(41.0/127.1) + 6.36\%(4.1/127.1)$$
$$= 5.05\%$$

With Deutsche Bank, we will do almost all of our analyses using the cost of equity rather than the cost of capital. ∎

Conclusion

This chapter explains the process of estimating discount rates, by relating them to the risk and return models described in the previous chapter:

- The cost of equity can be estimated using risk and return models—the CAPM, where risk is measured relative to a single market factor; the APM, where the cost of equity is determined by the sensitivity to multiple unspecified economic factors; or a multifactor model, where sensitivity to macroeconomic variables is used to measure risk.

---

[60]All of the capital ratios that govern banks are stated in terms of book value of equity, though equity is defined broadly to include preferred stock.

- In all of these models, the key inputs are the risk-free rate, the risk premiums, and the beta (in the CAPM) or betas (in the APM). The last of these inputs is usually estimated using historical data on prices; in the case of private firms, they might have to be estimated using comparable publicly traded firms.
- Although the betas are estimated using historical data, they are determined by the fundamental decisions that a firm makes on its business mix, operating leverage, and financial leverage.

- The cost of capital is a weighted average of the costs of the different components of financing, with the weights based on the market values of each component. The cost of debt is the market rate at which the firm can borrow long term, adjusted for any tax advantages of borrowing. The cost of preferred stock, on the other hand, is the preferred dividend yield.
- The cost of capital is the minimum acceptable hurdle rate that will be used to determine whether to invest in a project.

LIVE CASE STUDY

RISK AND RETURN: ANALYSIS FOR THE FIRM

Objective: To develop a risk profile for your company, estimate its risk parameters, and use these parameters to estimate costs of equity and capital for the firm.

Key Questions

- What is the risk profile of your company? (How much overall risk is there in this firm? Where is this risk coming from [market, firm, industry or currency]? How is the risk profile changing?)
- What is the performance profile of an investment in this company? What return would you have earned investing in this company's stock? Would you have under- or outperformed the market? How much of the performance can be attributed to management?
- How risky is this company's equity? Why? What is its cost of equity?
- How risky is this company's debt? What is its cost of debt?
- What is this company's current cost of capital?

Framework for Analysis

1. ***Estimating Historical Risk Parameters (Top-Down Betas)***
Run a regression of returns on your firm's stock against returns on a market index, preferably using monthly data and five years of observations. (Or)

If you have access to Bloomberg, go into the beta calculation page and print the page (after setting return intervals to monthly and using five years of data).

- What is the intercept of the regression? What does it tell you about the performance of this company's stock during the period of the regression?
- What is the slope of the regression? What does it tell you about the risk of the stock? How precise is this estimate of risk? (Provide a range for the estimate.)
- What portion of this firm's risk can be attributed to market factors? What portion to firm-specific factors? Why is this important?
- How much of the risk for this firm is due to business factors? How much of it is due to financial leverage?

2. ***Comparing to Sector Betas (Bottom-Up Betas)***
- Break down your firm by business components and estimate a business beta for each component.
- Attach reasonable weights to each component and estimate a unlevered beta for the firm.
- Using the current leverage of the company, estimate a levered beta for each component.

3. *Choosing Between Betas*

- Which of the betas that you have estimated for the firm would you view as more reliable? Why?
- Using the beta that you have chosen, estimate the expected return on an equity investment in this company to a short-term investor and a long-term investor.
- As a manager in this firm, how would you use this expected return?

4. *Estimating Default Risk and Cost of Debt*

- If your company is rated,
  - What is the most recent rating for the firm?
  - What is the default spread and interest rate associated with this rating?
  - If your company has bonds outstanding, estimate the yield to maturity on a long-term bond. Why might this be different from the rate estimated from the bond rating?
  - What is the company's marginal tax rate?
- If your company is not rated,
  - Does it have any recent borrowings? If yes, what interest rate did the company pay on these borrowing?
  - Can you estimate a synthetic rating? If yes, what interest rate would correspond to this rating?

5. *Estimating Cost of Capital*

- What is the market value of equity? Estimate a market value for debt. (To do this you might have to collect information on the average maturity of the debt, the interest expenses in the most recent period and the book value of the debt.) What are the weights of debt and equity?
- What is the cost of capital for the firm?

Getting Information on Risk and Return

If you want to run a regression of stock returns against a market index to estimate a beta, you will need to estimate past returns for both the stock and index. Several services (including Bloomberg and S&P) provide access to the data. If you want a beta estimate for your firm, you can find it online or look it up in Value Line. If you want to estimate bottom-up betas, based on comparable firms, you will first have to identify the businesses that your firm operates in (which should be available in the firm's 10-K), find comparable firms in each business, and then estimate the average beta and debt to equity ratio for these firms.

You can find the rating for your company from the S&P and Moody publications that list all traded bonds and their ratings. Alternatively, you can estimate an interest coverage ratio and a synthetic rating.

Online Sources of Information:
See **www.stern.nyu.edu/~adamodar/cfin2E/project/data.htm**.

PROBLEMS AND QUESTIONS

(In the problems below, you can use a risk premium of 5.5 percent and a tax rate of 40 percent if none is specified.)

1. In December 1995, Boise Cascade's stock had a beta of 0.95. The Treasury bill rate at the time was 5.8 percent, and the Treasury bond rate was 6.4 percent. The firm had debt outstanding of $1.7 billion and a market value of equity of $1.5 billion; the corporate marginal tax rate was 36 percent.
   a. Estimate the expected return on the stock for a short-term investor in the company.
   b. Estimate the expected return on the stock for a long-term investor in the company.
   c. Estimate the cost of equity for the company.

2. As noted in problem 1, Boise Cascade had debt outstanding of $1.7 billion and a market value of equity of $1.5 billion; the corporate marginal tax rate was 36 percent.
   a. Assuming that the current beta of 0.95 for the stock is reasonable, estimate the unlevered beta for the company.
   b. How much of the risk in the company can be attributed to business risk and how much to financial leverage risk?

3. Biogen, a biotechnology firm, had a beta of 1.70 in 1995. It had no debt outstanding at the end of that year.
   a. Estimate the cost of equity for Biogen, if the Treasury bond rate is 6.4 percent.
   b. What effect will an increase in long-term bond rates to 7.5 percent have on Biogen's cost of equity?
   c. How much of Biogen's risk can be attributed to business risk?

4. Genting Berhad is a Malaysian conglomerate with holdings in plantations and tourist resorts. The beta estimated for the firm, relative to the Malaysian stock exchange, is 1.15, and the long-term government borrowing rate in Malaysia is 11.5 percent. (Malaysian risk premium is 12 percent.)
   a. Estimate the expected return on the stock.
   b. If you were an international investor, what concerns (if any) would you have about using the beta estimated relative to the Malaysian index? If you have concerns, how would you modify the beta?

5. You have just done a regression of monthly stock returns of HeavyTech, a manufacturer of heavy machinery, on monthly market returns over the past five years and come up with the following regression:

$$R_{\text{Heavy Tech}} = 0.5\% + 1.2\,R_M$$

The variance of the stock is 50 percent, and the variance of the market is 20 percent. The current Treasure bill rate is 3 percent. (It was 5 percent one year ago.) The stock is currently selling for $50, down $4 over the past year, and has paid a dividend of $2 during the past year and expects to pay a dividend of $2.50 over the next year. The NYSE composite has gone down 8 percent over the past year, with a dividend yield of 3 percent. HeavyTech has a tax rate of 40 percent.
   a. What is the expected return on HeavyTech over the next year?
   b. What would you expect HeavyTech's price to be one year from today?
   c. What would you have expected HeavyTech's stock returns to be over the past year?
   d. What were the actual returns on HeavyTech over the past year?
   e. HeavyTech has $100 million in equity and $5 million in debt. It plans to issue $50 million in new equity and retire $50 million in debt. Estimate the new beta.

6. Safecorp, which owns and operates grocery stores across the United States, currently has $50 million in debt and $100 million in equity outstanding. Its stock has a beta of 1.2. It is planning a leveraged buyout, where it will increase its debt/equity ratio to 8. If the tax rate is 40 percent, what will the beta of the equity in the firm be after the leveraged buyout?

7. Novell, which had a market value of equity of $2 billion and a beta of 1.50, announced that it was acquiring WordPerfect, which had a market value of equity of $1 billion and a beta of 1.30. Neither firm had any debt in its financial structure at the time of the acquisition, and the corporate tax rate was 40 percent.
   a. Estimate the beta for Novell after the acquisition, assuming that the entire acquisition was financed with equity.

b. Assume that Novell had to borrow the $1 billion to acquire WordPerfect. Estimate the beta after the acquisition.

8. You are analyzing the beta for Hewlett Packard and have broken down the company into four broad business groups, with market values and betas for each group.

Business Group	Market Value of Equity	Beta
Mainframes	$2.0 billion	1.10
Personal computers	2.0 billion	1.50
Software	1.0 billion	2.00
Printers	3.0 billion	1.00

HP had $1 billion in debt outstanding.

a. Estimate the beta for Hewlett Packard as a company. Is this beta going to be equal to the beta estimated by regressing past returns on their stock against a market index? Why or why not?

b. If the Treasury bond rate is 7.5 percent, estimate the cost of equity for Hewlett Packard. Estimate the cost of equity for each division. Which cost of equity would you use to value the printer division?

c. Assume that HP divests itself of the mainframe business and pays the cash out as a dividend. Estimate the beta for HP after the divestiture.

9. The following table summarizes the percentage changes in operating income, percentage changes in revenue, and betas for four pharmaceutical firms.

Firm	% Change in Revenue	% Change in Operating Income	Beta
PharmaCorp	27%	25%	1.00
SynerCorp	25%	32%	1.15
BioMed	23%	36%	1.30
Safemed	21%	40%	1.40

a. Calculate the degree of operating leverage for each of these firms.

b. Use the operating leverage to explain why these firms have different betas.

10. A prominent beta estimation service reports the beta of Comcast Corporation, a major cable TV operator, to be 1.45. The service claims to use weekly returns on the stock over the prior five years and the NYSE composite as the market index to estimate betas. You replicate the regression using weekly returns over the same period and arrive at a beta estimate of 1.60. How would you reconcile the two estimates?

11. Battle Mountain is a mining company that mines gold, silver, and copper in mines in South America, Africa, and Australia. The beta for the stock is estimated to be 0.30. Given the volatility in commodity prices, how would you explain the low beta?

12. You have collected returns on AnaDone, a large diversified manufacturing firm, and the NYSE index for five years:

Year	Returns (%) for AnaDone	Returns (%) for NYSE
1981	10%	5%
1982	5%	15%
1983	–5%	8%
1984	20%	12%
1985	–5%	–5%

a. Estimate the intercept (alpha) and slope (beta) of the regression.

b. If you bought stock in AnaDone today, how much would you expect to make as a return over the next year? (The six-month Treasury bill rate is 6 percent.)

c. Looking back over the past five years, how would you evaluate AnaDone's performance relative to the market?

d. Assume now that you are an undiversified investor and that you have all of your money invested in AnaDone. What would be a good measure of the risk that you are taking on? How much of this risk would you be able to eliminate if you *diversify?*

e. AnaDone is planning to sell off one of its divisions. The division under consideration has assets which comprise half of the book value of AnaDone and 20 percent of the market value. Its beta is twice the average beta for AnaDone (before divestment). What will the beta of AnaDone be after divesting this division?

13. You run a regression of monthly returns of Mapco, an oil- and gas-producing firm, on the S&P 500 Index and come up with the following output for the period 1991 to 1995.

Intercept of the regression = 0.06%

X-coefficient of the regression = 0.46

Standard error of X-coefficient = 0.20

$$R^2 = 5\%$$

There are 20 million shares outstanding, and the current market price is $2. The firm has $20 million in debt outstanding. (The firm has a tax rate of 36 percent.)

a. What would an investor in Mapco's stock require as a return, if the Treasury bond rate is 6 percent?

b. What proportion of this firm's risk is diversifiable?

c. Assume now that Mapco has three divisions of equal size (in market value terms). It plans to divest itself of one of the divisions for $20 million in cash and acquire another for $50 million. (It will borrow $30 million to complete this acquisition.) The division it is divesting is in a business line where the average unlevered beta is 0.20, and the division it is acquiring is in a business line where the average unlevered beta is 0.80. What will the beta of Mapco be after this acquisition?

14. You have just run a regression of monthly returns of American Airlines (AMR) against the S&P 500 over the past five years. You have misplaced some of the output and are trying to derive it from what you have.

a. You know the R^2 of the regression is 0.36, and that your stock has a variance of 67 percent. The market variance is 12 percent. What is the beta of AMR?

b. You also remember that AMR was not a very good investment during the period of the regression and that it did worse than expected (after adjusting for risk) by 0.39 percent a month for the five years of the regression. During this period, the average risk-free rate was 4.84 percent. What was the intercept on the regression?

c. You are comparing AMR to another firm that also has an R^2 of 48 percent. Will the

two firms have the same beta? If not, why not?

15. You have run a regression of *monthly* returns on Amgen, a large biotechnology firm, against *monthly* returns on the S&P 500 Index, and come up with the following output:

$$R_{stock} = 3.28\% + 1.65 R_{Market}$$

$$R^2 = 0.20$$

The current one-year Treasury bill rate is 4.8 percent and the current thirty-year bond rate is 6.4 percent. The firm has 265 million shares outstanding, selling for $30 per share.

a. What is the expected return on this stock over the next year?

b. Would your expected return estimate change if the purpose was to get a discount rate to analyze a thirty-year capital budgeting project?

c. An analyst has estimated correctly that the stock did 51.10 percent better than expected annually during the period of the regression. Can you estimate the annualized risk-free rate that she used for her estimate?

d. The firm has a debt/equity ratio of 3 percent and faces a tax rate of 40 percent. It is planning to issue $2 billion in new debt and acquire a new business for that amount, with the same risk level as the firm's existing business. What will the beta be after the acquisition?

16. You have just run a regression of monthly returns on MAD, a newspaper and magazine publisher, against returns on the S&P 500, and arrived at the following result:

$$R_{MAD} = -0.05\% + 1.20 R_{S\&P}$$

The regression has an R^2 of 22 percent. The current Treasure bill rate is 5.5 percent and the current Treasure bond rate is 6.5 percent. The risk-free rate during the period of the regression was 6 percent. Answer the following questions relating to the regression:

a. Based on the intercept, you can conclude that the stock did

i. 0.05 percent worse than expected on a monthly basis, during the regression.

ii. 0.05 percent better than expected on a monthly basis during the period of the regression.

iii. 1.25 percent better than expected on a monthly basis during the period of the regression.

iv. 1.25 percent worse than expected on a monthly basis during the period of the regression.

v. None of the above.

b. You now realize that MAD went through a major restructuring at the end of last month (which was the last month of your regression), and made the following changes:

- The firm sold off its magazine division, which had an unlevered beta of 0.6, for $20 million.
- It borrowed an additional $20 million, and bought back stock worth $40 million.

After the sale of the division and the share repurchase, MAD had $40 million in debt and $120 million in equity outstanding. If the firm's tax rate is 40 percent, reestimate the beta after these changes.

17. Time Warner, the entertainment conglomerate, has a beta of 1.61. Part of the reason for the high beta is the debt left over from the leveraged buyout of Time by Warner in 1989, which amounted to $10 billion in 1995. The market value of equity at Time Warner in 1995 was also $10 billion. The marginal tax rate was 40 percent.

a. Estimate the unlevered beta for Time Warner.

b. Estimate the effect of reducing the debt ratio by 10 percentage points each year for the next two years on the beta of the stock.

18. Chrysler, the automotive manufacturer, had a beta of 1.05 in 1995. It had $13 billion in debt outstanding in that year and 355 million shares trading at $50 per share. The firm had a cash balance of $8 billion at the end of 1995. The marginal tax rate was 36 percent.

a. Estimate the unlevered beta of the firm.

b. Estimate the effect of paying out a special dividend of $5 billion on this unlevered beta.

c. Estimate the beta for Chrysler after the special dividend.

19. You are trying to estimate the beta of a private firm that manufactures home appliances. You have managed to obtain betas for publicly traded firms that also manufacture home appliances.

Firm	Beta	Debt (in Millions)	MV of Equity (in Millions)
Black & Decker	1.40	$2,500	$3,000
Fedders	1.20	$5	$200
Maytag	1.20	$540	$2,250
National Presto	0.70	$8	$300
Whirlpool	1.50	$2,900	$4,000

The private firm has a debt equity ratio of 25 percent and faces a tax rate of 40 percent. The publicly traded firms all have marginal tax rates of 40 percent, as well.

a. Estimate the beta for the private firm.

b. What concerns, if any, would you have about using betas of comparable firms?

20. As the result of stockholder pressure, RJR Nabisco is considering spinning off its food division. You have been asked to estimate the beta for the division and decide to do so by obtaining the beta of comparable publicly traded firms. The average beta of comparable publicly traded firms is 0.95, and the average debt/equity ratio of these firms is 35 percent. The division is expected to have a debt ratio of 25 percent. The marginal corporate tax rate is 36 percent.

a. What is the beta for the division?

b. Would it make any difference if you knew that RJR Nabisco had a much higher fixed cost structure than the comparable firms used here?

21. Southwestern Bell, a phone company, is considering expanding its operations into the media business. The beta for the company at the end of 1995 was 0.90, and the debt/equity ratio was 1. The media business is expected to be 30 percent of the overall firm value in 1999, and the average beta of comparable firms is 1.20; the average debt/equity ratio for these firms is 50 percent. The marginal corporate tax rate is 36 percent.

a. Estimate the beta for Southwestern Bell in 1999, assuming that it maintains its current debt/equity ratio.

b. Estimate the beta for Southwestern Bell in 1999, assuming that it decides to finance its media operations with a debt/equity ratio of 50 percent.

22. The chief financial officer of Adobe Systems, a software manufacturing firm, has approached you for some advice regarding the beta of his company. He subscribes to a service that estimates Adobe System's beta each year, and he has noticed that the beta estimates have gone down every year since 1991—2.35 in 1991 to 1.40 in 1995. He would like the answers to the following questions.

    a. Is this decline in beta unusual for a growing firm?

    b. Why would the beta decline over time?

    c. Is the beta likely to keep decreasing over time?

23. You are analyzing Tiffany's, an upscale retailer, and find that the regression estimate of the firm's beta is 0.75; the standard error for the beta estimate is 0.50. You also note that the average unlevered beta of comparable specialty retailing firms is 1.15.

    a. If Tiffany's has a debt/equity ratio of 20 percent, estimate the beta for the company based on comparable firms. (The tax rate is 40 percent.)

    b. Estimate a range for the beta from the regression.

    c. Assume that Tiffany is rated BBB and that the default spread for BBB rated firms is 1 percent. If the T-bond rate is 6.5 percent, estimate the cost of capital for the firm.

CHAPTER 5

MEASURING RETURN ON INVESTMENTS

In Chapter 4, we developed a process for estimating costs of equity, debt, and capital and presented an argument that the cost of capital is the minimum acceptable hurdle rate when considering new investments. We also argued that an investment has to earn a return greater than this hurdle rate to create value for the owners of a business. In this chapter, we turn to the question of how best to measure the return on a project. In doing so, we will attempt to answer the following questions:

- What is a project? In particular, how general is the definition of an investment and what are the different types of investment decisions that firms have to make?
- In measuring the return on a project, should we look at the cash flows generated by the project or at the accounting earnings?

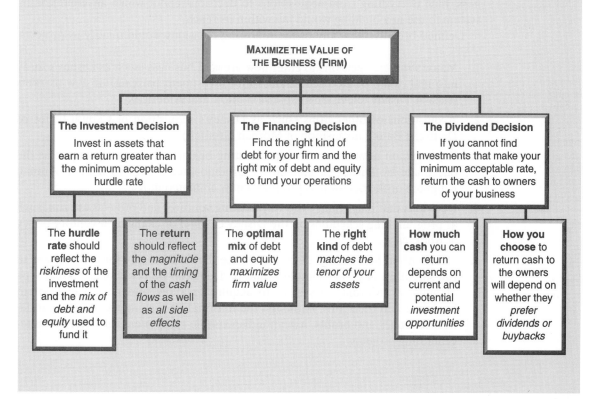

- If the returns on a project are unevenly spread over time, how do we consider (or should we not consider) differences in returns across time?

We will illustrate the basics of investment analysis using three hypothetical projects: an online book ordering service for Bookscape, a new theme park in Thailand for Disney, and a plant to manufacture linerboard for Aracruz Celulose.

WHAT IS A PROJECT?

Investment analysis concerns which projects a company should accept and which it should reject; accordingly, the question of what makes up a project is central to this and the following chapters. The conventional project analyzed in capital budgeting has three criteria: (1) a large up-front cost, (2) cash flows for a specific time period, and (3) a **salvage value** at the end, which captures the value of the assets of the project when the project ends. Although such projects undoubtedly form a significant proportion of investment decisions, especially for manufacturing firms, it would be a mistake to assume that investment analysis stops there. If a project is defined more broadly to include any decision that results in using the scarce resources of a business, then everything from acquisitions to decisions about which air conditioning system to use in a building would fall within its reach.

Defined broadly then, any of the following decisions would qualify as projects:

1. Major strategic decisions to enter new areas of business (such as Disney's foray into real estate or Deutsche Bank's into investment banking) or new markets (such as Disney television's expansion into Latin America).

2. Acquisitions of other firms (such as Disney's acquisition of Capital Cities or Deutsche Bank's acquisition of Morgan Grenfell).

3. Decisions on new ventures within existing businesses or markets, such as the one made by Disney to expand its Orlando theme park to include Animal Kingdom or the decision to produce a new animated movie.

4. Decisions that may change the way existing ventures and projects are run, such as programming schedules on the Disney channel or changing inventory policy at Bookscape.

5. Decisions on how best to deliver a service that is necessary for the business to run smoothly. A good example would be Deutsche Bank's choice of what type of financial information system to acquire to allow traders and investment bankers to do their jobs. Although the information system itself might not deliver revenues and profits, it is an indispensable component for other revenue-generating projects.

Figure 5.1 The Project Continuum

Prerequisite   Complementary   Independent   Mutually Exclusive

Investment decisions can be categorized on a number of different dimensions. The first relates to how the project affects other projects the firm is considering and analyzing. Some projects are independent of other projects, and thus can be analyzed separately, whereas other projects are **mutually exclusive**—that is, taking one project will mean rejecting other projects. At the other extreme, some projects are prerequisites for other projects down the road, and others are complementary. In general, projects can be categorized as falling somewhere on the continuum between prerequisites and mutually exclusive, as depicted in Figure 5.1.

The second dimension that can be used to classify a project is its ability to generate revenues or reduce costs. The decision rules that analyze revenue generating projects attempt to evaluate whether the earnings or cash flows from the projects justify the investment needed to implement them. When it comes to cost-reduction projects, the decision rules examine whether the reduction in costs justifies the up-front investment needed for the projects.

Salvage Value: The estimated liquidation value of the assets invested in a project at the end of the project life.

Mutually Exclusive Projects: A group of projects is said to be mutually exclusive when acceptance of one of the projects implies that the rest have to be rejected.

ILLUSTRATION 5.1 **Project Descriptions**
In this chapter and parts of the next, we will use three hypothetical projects to illustrate the basics of investment analysis.

- The first project we will look at is a proposal by Bookscape to add an *online book ordering and information service.* Although the impetus for this proposal comes from the success of online ventures like Amazon.com, Bookscape's service will be more focused on helping customers research books and find the ones they need rather than on price. Thus, if Bookscape decides to add this service, it will have to hire and train well-qualified individuals to answer customer queries, in addition to investing in the computer equipment and phone lines that the service will require. This project analysis will help illustrate some of the issues that come up when private businesses look at investments and also when businesses take on projects that have risk profiles different from their existing ones.

- The second project we will analyze is a *proposed theme park for Disney in Bangkok, Thailand*. Disneyworld Bangkok, which will be patterned on Disneyland Paris and Walt Disney World in Florida, will require a huge investment in infrastructure and take several years to complete. This project analysis will bring several issues to the forefront, including questions of how to deal with projects when the cash flows are in a foreign currency and what to do when projects have very long lives.

- The third project we will consider is a *plant in Brazil to manufacture linerboard* for Aracruz Celulose. Linerboard is a stiffened paper product that can be transformed into cardboard boxes. This investment is a more conventional one, with an initial investment, a fixed lifetime, and a salvage value at the end. We will, however, do the analysis for this project from an equity standpoint to illustrate the generality of investment analysis. In addition, in light of concerns about inflation, we will do the analysis entirely in real terms.

HURDLE RATES FOR FIRMS VERSUS HURDLE RATES FOR PROJECTS

In the previous chapter we developed a process for estimating the costs of equity and capital for firms. In this chapter, we will extend the discussion to hurdle rates in the context of new or individual investments.

Using the Firm's Hurdle Rate for Individual Projects

Can we use the costs of equity and capital that we have estimated for the firms for individual projects? In some cases we can, but only if all investments made by a firm are similar in terms of their risk exposure. As a firm's investments become more diverse, the firm may no longer be able to use its cost of equity and capital to evaluate these projects. Projects that are riskier have to be assessed using a higher cost of equity and capital than projects that are safer. In this chapter, we consider how to estimate project costs of equity and capital.

What would happen if a firm chose to use its cost of equity and capital to evaluate all projects? This firm would find itself overinvesting in risky projects and underinvesting in safe projects. Over time, the firm will become riskier, as its safer businesses find themselves unable to compete with riskier businesses.

Cost of Equity for Projects

In assessing the beta for a project, we will consider three possible scenarios. The first scenario is the one where all the projects considered by a firm are similar in their exposure to risk; this homogeneity makes risk assessment simple. The second scenario is one in which a firm is in multiple businesses with different exposures to risk, but projects within each business have the same risk exposure. The third scenario is the most complicated wherein each project considered by a firm has a different exposure to risk.

1. Single Business: Project Risk Similar within Business

When a firm operates in only one business and all projects within that business share the same risk profile, the firm can use its overall cost of equity as the cost of equity for the project. Because we estimated the cost of equity using a beta for the firm in Chapter 4, this would mean that we would use the same beta to estimate the cost of equity for each project that the firm analyzes. The advantage of this approach is that it does not require risk estimation prior to every project, providing managers with a fixed benchmark for their project investments. The approach is restricting, though, because it can be usefully applied only to companies that are in one line of business and take on homogeneous projects.

2. Multiple Businesses with Different Risk Profiles: Project Risk Similar within Each Business

When firms operate in more than one line of business, the risk profiles are likely to be different across different businesses. If we make the assumption that projects taken within each business have the same risk profile, we can estimate the cost of equity for each business separately and use that cost of equity for all projects within that business. Riskier businesses will have higher costs of equity than safer businesses, and projects taken by riskier businesses will have to cover these higher costs. Imposing the firm's cost of equity on all projects in all businesses will lead to overinvesting in risky businesses (because the cost of equity will be set too low) and underinvesting in safe businesses (because the cost of equity will be set too high).

How do we estimate the cost of equity for individual businesses? When the approach requires equity betas, we cannot fall back on the conventional regression approach (in the CAPM) or factor analysis (in the APM) because these approaches require past prices. Instead, we have to use one of the two approaches that we described in the last section as alternatives to regression betas—bottom-up betas based on other publicly traded firms in the same business, or accounting betas, estimated based on the accounting earnings for the division.

3. Projects with Different Risk Profiles

As a purist, you could argue that each project's risk profile is, in fact, unique and that it is inappropriate to use either the firm's cost of equity or divisional costs of equity to assess projects. Although this may be true, we have to consider the trade-off. Given that small differences in the cost of equity should not make a significant difference in our investment decisions, we have to consider whether the added benefits of analyzing each project individually exceed the costs of doing so.

When would it make sense to assess a project's risk individually? If a project is large in terms of investment needs relative to the firm assessing it and has a very different risk profile from other investments in the firm, it would make sense to assess the cost of equity for the project independently. The only practical way of estimating betas and costs of equity for individual projects is the bottom-up beta approach.

Cost of Debt for Projects

In the previous chapter, we noted that the cost of debt for a firm should reflect its default risk. With individual projects, the assessment of default risk becomes much more difficult, because projects seldom borrow on their own; most firms borrow money for all the projects that they undertake. There are three approaches to estimating the cost of debt for a project:

- One approach is based on the argument that because the borrowing is done by the firm rather than by individual projects, the cost of debt for a project should be the cost of debt for the firm considering the project. This approach makes the most sense when the projects being assessed are small relative to the firm taking them and thus have little or no appreciable effect on the firm's default risk.

- Look at the project's capacity to generate cash flows relative to its financing costs and estimate default risk and cost of debt for the project. You can also estimate this default risk by looking at other firms that take similar projects, and use the typical default risk and cost of debt for these firms. This approach generally makes sense when the project is large in terms of its capital needs relative to the firm and has different cash flow characteristics (both in terms of magnitude and volatility) from other investments taken by the firm.

- The third approach applies when a project actually borrows its own funds, with lenders having no recourse against the parent firm, in case the project defaults. This is unusual, but it can occur when investments have significant tangible assets of their own and the investment is large relative to the firm considering it. In this case, the cost of debt for the project can be assessed using its capacity to generate cash flows relative to its financing obligations. In the last chapter, we used the bond rating of a firm to come up with the cost of debt for the firm. Although projects may not be rated, we can still estimate a rating for a project based on financial ratios, and this can be used to estimate default risk and the cost of debt.

Financing Mix and Cost of Capital for Projects

To get from the costs of debt and equity to the cost of capital, we have to weight each by their relative proportions in financing. Again, the task is much easier at the firm level, where we use the current market values of debt and equity to arrive at these weights. We may borrow money to fund a project, but it is often not clear whether we are using the debt capacity of the project or the firm's debt capacity. The solution to this problem will again vary depending on the scenario we face.

- When we are estimating the financing weights for small projects that do not affect a firm's debt capacity, the financing weights should be those of the firm before the project.

- When assessing the financing weights of large projects, with risk profiles different from that of the firm, we have to be more cautious. Using the firm's financing mix to compute the cost of capital for these projects can be misleading, because the project being analyzed may be riskier than the firm as a whole and thus incapable of carrying the firm's debt ratio. In this case, we would argue for the use of the average debt ratio of the other firms in the business in assessing the cost of capital of the project.

- The financing weights for stand-alone projects that are large enough to issue their own debt should be based on the actual amounts borrowed by the projects. For firms with such projects, the financing weights can vary from project to projects, as will the cost of debt.

Table 5.1 COST OF DEBT AND DEBT RATIO: PROJECT ANALYSES		
Project Characteristics	**Cost of Debt**	**Debt Ratio**
Project is small and has cash flow characteristics similar to the firm	Firm's cost of debt	Firm's debt ratio
Project is large and has cash flow characteristics different from the firm	Cost of debt of comparable firms	Average debt ratio of comparable firms
Stand-alone project	Cost of debt for project (based on actual or synthetic ratings)	Debt ratio for project

In summary, the cost of debt and debt ratio for a project will reflect the size of the project relative to the firm, and its risk profile, again relative to the firm. Table 5.1 summarizes our analyses.

ILLUSTRATION 5.2   Estimating Hurdle Rates for Individual Projects

Using the principles of estimation that we just laid out, we can estimate the hurdles rates for the three projects that we are analyzing in this chapter.

- *Bookscape Online Information and Ordering Service*   Because the beta and cost of equity that we estimated for Bookscape as a company reflect its status as a book store, we will reestimate the beta for this online project by looking at publicly traded Internet retailers. The unlevered total beta of Internet retailers is 4.20,[1] and we assume that this project will be funded with the same mix of debt and equity (D/E = 20.33%) that Bookscape uses in the rest of the business. We will also assume that Bookscape's tax rate of 40 percent and pretax cost of debt of 5.5 percent apply to this project as well.

    Levered Beta for Online Service = 4.20[1 + (1 − 0.4)(0.2033)] = 4.712

    Cost of Equity for Online Service = 4% + 4.712(4.82%) = 26.71%

    Cost of Capital for Online Service = 26.71%(0.831) + 5.5%(1 − 0.4)(0.169)
    = 22.76%

- *Disneyworld Bangkok*   We did estimate a cost of equity of 9.12 percent for the Disney theme park business in the last chapter, using a bottom-up levered beta of 1.0625 for the business. The only concern we would have with using this cost of equity for this project is that it may not adequately reflect the additional risk associated with the theme park being in an emerging market. To counter this risk, we compute the cost of equity for the theme park using a risk premium that

---

[1]The unlevered market beta for internet retailers is 2.10, and the average correlation of these stocks with the market is 0.50. The unlevered total beta is therefore 2.10/0.5 = 4.20.

includes a country risk premium for Thailand:[2]

$$\text{Cost of Equity in US\$} = 4\% + 1.0625(4.82\% + 3.30\%) = 12.63\%$$

$$\text{Cost of Capital in US\$} = 12.63\%(0.7898) + 3.29\%(0.2102) = 10.66\%$$

Note that we have assumed that Disney will maintain its overall debt ratio of 21.02 percent and its current after-tax cost of debt in funding this project.

- *Aracruz Paper Plant* We estimated the cost of equity and capital for Aracruz's paper business in Chapter 4 in real, U.S. dollar, and nominal BR terms. We will use the real costs of equity and capital because our cash flows will be estimated in real terms as well:

$$\text{Real Cost of Equity for Paper Business} = 11.46\%$$

$$\text{Real Cost of Capital for Paper Business} = 9.00\%$$

IN PRACTICE: EXCHANGE RATE RISK, POLITICAL RISK, AND FOREIGN PROJECTS

When computing the cost of capital for the Disneyworld Bangkok project, we adjusted the cost of capital for the additional risk associated with investing in Thailand. Although it may seem obvious that a foreign investment will carry more risk for Disney than an investment in the United States, the question of whether discount rates should be adjusted for country risk is not an easy one to answer. It is true that a Thai investment will carry more risk for Disney than an investment in the United States, both because of exchange rate risk (the cash flows will be in Thai baht and not in U.S. dollars) and because of political risk (arising from Thailand's emerging market status). However, this risk should affect the discount rate only if it cannot be diversified away by the marginal investors in Disney.

To analyze whether the risk in Thailand is diversifiable to Disney, we went back to our assessment of the marginal investors in the company in Chapter 3, where we noted that they were primarily diversified institutional investors. Not only does exchange rate risk affect different companies in their portfolios very differently—some may be hurt by a strengthening dollar and others may be helped—but these investors can hedge exchange rate risk if they so desire. If the only source of risk in the project were exchange rate, we would be inclined to treat it as diversifiable risk and not adjust the cost of capital. The issue of political risk is more confounding. To the extent that political risk is not only more difficult to hedge but also more likely to carry a nondiversifiable component, especially when we are considering risky emerging markets, the cost of capital should be adjusted to reflect it.

---

[2]We use the same approach used to estimate the country risk premium for Brazil in Chapter 4. The rating for Thailand is Baa1, and the default spread for the country bond is 1.50 percent. Multiplying this by the relative volatility of 2.2 of the equity market in Thailand (standard deviation of equity/standard deviation of country bond) yields a country risk premium of 3.3 percent.

In short, whether we adjust the cost of capital for foreign projects will depend both on the firm that is considering the project and the country in which the project is located. If the marginal investors in the firm are diversified and the project is in a country with relatively little or no political risk, we would be inclined not to add a risk premium on to the cost of capital. If the marginal investors in the firm are diversified and the project is in a country with significant political risk, we would add a political risk premium to the cost of capital. If the marginal investors in the firm are not diversified, we would adjust the discount rate for both exchange rate and political risk. ■

MEASURING RETURNS: THE CHOICES

On all of the investment decisions just described, we have to choose between alternative approaches to measuring returns on the investment made. We will present our argument for return measurement in three steps. First, we will contrast accounting earnings and cash flows and argue that cash flows are much better measures of true return on an investment. Second, we will note the differences between total and incremental cash flows and present the case for using incremental cash flows in measuring returns. Finally, we will argue that cash flows that occur earlier in a project life should be weighted more than cash flows that occur later in a project life and that the return on an investment should be measured using time-weighted cash flows.

A. Accounting Earnings versus Cash Flows

The first and most basic choice we have to make when it comes to measuring returns is the one between the accounting measure of income on a project—measured in accounting statements, using accounting principles and standards—and the cash flow generated by a project, measured as the difference between the cash inflows in each period and the cash outflows.

Why Are Accounting Earnings Different from Cash Flows?

Accountants invest substantial time and resources in coming up with ways of measuring the income made by a project. In doing so, they subscribe to some generally accepted accounting principles. Generally accepted accounting principles require the recognition of revenues when the service for which the firm is getting paid has been performed in full or substantially and has received in return either cash or a receivable that is both observable and measurable. For expenses that are directly linked to the production of revenues (like labor and materials), expenses are recognized in the same period in which revenues are recognized. Any expenses that are not directly linked to the production of revenues are recognized in the period in which the firm consumes the services. Although the objective of distributing revenues and expenses fairly across time is worthy, the process of accrual accounting creates an accounting earnings number that can be very different from the cash flow generated by a project in any period. There are three significant factors that account for this difference.

1. Operating versus Capital Expenditure

Accountants draw a distinction between expenditures that yield benefits only in the immediate period or periods (such as labor and material for a manufacturing firm) and those that yield benefits over multiple periods (such as land, buildings, and long-lived equipment). The former are called *operating expenses* and are subtracted from revenues in computing the accounting income, whereas the latter are *capital expenditures* and are not subtracted from revenues in the period that they are made. Instead, the expenditure is spread over multiple periods and deducted as an expense in each period; these expenses are called depreciation (if the asset is a tangible asset like a building) or amortization (if the asset is an intangible asset, such as a patent or a trademark).

Although the capital expenditures made at the beginning of a project are often the largest part of investment, many projects require capital expenditures during their lifetime. These capital expenditures will reduce the cash available in each of these periods.

5.1 WHAT ARE RESEARCH AND DEVELOPMENT EXPENSES?

Research and development (R&D) expenses are generally considered to be operating expenses by accountants. Based on our categorization of capital and operating expenses, would you consider R&D expenses to be

☐ operating expenses.

☐ capital expenses.

☐ operating or capital expenses, depending on the type of research being done.

Why?

2. Noncash Charges

The distinction that accountants draw between operating and capital expenses leads to a number of accounting expenses, such as depreciation and amortization, which are not cash expenses. These noncash expenses, though depressing accounting income, do not reduce cash flows. In fact, they can have a significant positive impact on cash flows if they reduce the tax paid by the firm because some noncash charges reduce taxable income and the taxes paid by a business. The most important of such charges is depreciation, which, although reducing taxable and net income, does not cause a cash outflow. In effect, depreciation and amortization is added back to net income to arrive at the cash flows on a project.

For projects that generate large depreciation charges, a significant portion of the cash flows can be attributed to the tax benefits of depreciation, which can be written as follows

$$\text{Tax Benefit of Depreciation} = \text{Depreciation} \times \text{Marginal Tax Rate}$$

Although depreciation is similar to other tax-deductible expenses in terms of the tax benefit it generates, its impact is more positive because it does not generate a concurrent cash outflow.

Amortization is also a noncash charge, but the tax effects of amortization can vary depending on the nature of the amortization. Some amortization, such as the amortization of the price paid for a patent or a trademark, are tax-deductible and reduce both accounting income and taxes. Thus they provide tax benefits similar to depreciation. Other amortization, such as the amortization of the premium paid on an acquisition (called goodwill), reduces accounting income but not taxable income. This amortization does not provide a tax benefit.

Although there are a number of different depreciation methods used by firms, they can be classified broadly into two groups. The first is *straight line depreciation,* whereby equal amounts of depreciation are claimed each period for the life of the asset. The second group includes *accelerated depreciation methods,* such as double-declining balance depreciation, which result in more depreciation early in the asset life and less in the later years.

3. Accrual versus Cash Revenues and Expenses

The accrual system of accounting leads to revenues being recognized when the sale is made, rather than when the customer pays for the good or service. Consequently, accrual revenues may be very different from cash revenues for three reasons. First, some customers, who bought their goods and services in prior periods, may pay in this period; second, some customers who buy their goods and services in this period (and are therefore shown as part of revenues in this period) may defer payment until the future. Finally, some customers who buy goods and services may never pay (bad debts). In some cases, customers may even pay in advance for products or services that will not be delivered until future periods.

A similar argument can be made on the expense side. Accrual expenses, relating to payments to third parties, will be different from cash expenses, because of payments made for material and services acquired in prior periods and because some materials and services acquired in current periods will not be paid for until future periods. Accrual taxes will be different from cash taxes for exactly the same reasons.

When material is used to produce a product or deliver a service, there is an added consideration. Some of the material used may have been acquired in previous periods and was brought in as inventory into this period, and some of the material that is acquired in this period may be taken into the next period as inventory.

Accountants define net working capital as the difference between current assets (such as inventory and accounts receivable) and current liabilities (such as accounts payable and taxes payable). Differences between accrual earnings and cash earnings, in the absence of noncash charges, can be captured by changes in the net working capital. A decrease in noncash working capital will increase cash flows, whereas an increase will decrease cash flows.

IN PRACTICE: THE PAYOFF TO MANAGING WORKING CAPITAL

Firms that are more efficient in managing their working capital will see a direct payoff in terms of cash flows. Efficiency in working capital management implies that the firm has reduced its net working capital needs without adversely affecting its revenues and earnings. Broadly defined, there are four ways net working capital can be reduced:

1. Firms need to maintain an inventory of produced goods to meet customer demand, but minimizing this inventory while meeting these objectives can produce a lower net working capital. In fact, recent advances in technology that use information systems for just-in-time production have helped U.S. firms reduce their inventory needs significantly.

2. Firms that sell goods and services on credit can reduce their net working capital needs by inducing customers to pay their bills faster and by improving their collection procedures.

3. Firms can also look for suppliers who offer more generous credit terms because accounts payable can be used to finance inventory and accounts receivable.

4. Firms that need cash for operational reasons can reduce their net working capital by keeping this cash balance to its minimum. ■

From Accounting Earnings to Cash Flows

The three factors outlined can cause accounting earnings to deviate significantly from the cash flows. To get from after-tax operating earnings, which measures the earnings to the firm, to cash flows to the firm, we have to

- *Add back all noncash charges,* such as depreciation and amortization, to the operating earnings.
- *Subtract out* all cash outflows that represent *capital expenditures.*
- *Net out the effect of changes in noncash working capital,* that is, changes in accounts receivable, inventory, and accounts payable. If noncash working capital increased, the cash flows will be reduced by the change, whereas if it decreased, there is a cash inflow.

The first two adjustments change operating earnings to account for the distinction drawn by accountants between operating and capital expenditures, whereas the last adjustment converts accrual revenues and expenses into cash revenues and expenses.

Cash Flow to Firm = Earnings Before Interest and Taxes (1 − tax rate)
+ Depreciation & Amortization − Change in Noncash Working Capital
− Capital Expenditures

The cash flow to the firm is a predebt, after-tax cash flow that measures the cash generated by a project for all claim holders in the firm after reinvestment needs have been met.

To get from net income, which measures the earnings of equity investors in the firm, to cash flows to equity investors requires the additional step of considering the net cash flow created by repaying old debt and taking on new debt. The difference between new debt issues and debt repayments is called the net debt, and it has to be added back to arrive at cash flows to equity. In addition, other cash flows to nonequity claim holders in the firm, such as preferred dividends, have to be netted from cash flows.

$$\text{Cash Flow to Equity} = \text{Net Income} + \text{Depreciation \& Amortization}$$
$$- \text{ Change in Noncash Working Capital} - \text{Capital Expenditures}$$
$$+ \text{ (New Debt Issues} - \text{Debt Repayments)} - \text{Preferred Dividends}$$

The cash flow to equity measures the cash flows generated by a project for equity investors in the firm, after taxes, debt payments, and reinvestment needs.

5.2 EARNINGS AND CASH FLOWS

If the earnings for a firm are positive, the cash flows will also be positive.
☐ True
☐ False
Why or why not?

IN PRACTICE: MANAGING EARNINGS

Companies that have seen the effect on their stock prices of not meeting analyst expectations on earnings have learned over the past decade to manage their earnings. Accounting standards allow some leeway for firms to move earnings across periods by deferring revenues or expenses or choosing a different accounting method for recording expenses. Companies not only work at holding down expectations on the part of analysts following them but also use accounting flexibility to move earnings across time to beat expectations. It should come as no surprise that firms like Microsoft and Intel consistently beat analyst estimates of earnings.

The phenomenon of managing earnings has profound implications for a number of actions that firms may take, from how they sell their products and services to what kinds of projects they invest in to the firms they acquire and how they account for such investments. Although Microsoft and Intel have not been guilty of accounting manipulation and have worked strictly within the rules of the game, other companies that have tried to replicate their success have had to resort to far more questionable methods to report earnings that beat expectations. ■

The Case for Cash Flows

When earnings and cash flows are different, as they are for many projects, we must examine which one provides a more reliable measure of performance. Accounting earnings, especially at the equity level (net income), can be manipulated at least for individual periods, through the use of creative accounting techniques. A book titled *Accounting for Growth,* which garnered national headlines in the United Kingdom and cost the author, Terry Smith, his job as an analyst at UBS Phillips & Drew, examined twelve legal accounting techniques commonly used to mislead investors about the profitability of individual firms. To show how creative accounting techniques can increase reported profits, Smith highlighted such companies as

Maxwell Communications and Polly Peck, both of which eventually succumbed to bankruptcy.

The second reason for using cash flow is much more direct. No business that we know of accepts earnings as payment for goods and services delivered; all of them require cash. Thus, a project with positive earnings and negative cash flows will drain cash from the business undertaking it. Conversely, a project with negative earnings and positive cash flows might make the accounting bottom line look worse but will generate cash for the business undertaking it.

B. Total versus Incremental Cash Flows

The objective when analyzing a project is to answer the question: Will taking this project make the entire firm or business more valuable? Consequently, the cash flows we should look at in investment analysis are the cash flows the project creates for the firm or business considering it. We will call these incremental cash flows.

Differences between Incremental and Total Cash Flows

The total and the incremental cash flows on a project will generally be different for two reasons. First, some of the cash flows on an investment may have occurred already and therefore are unaffected by whether we take the investment or not. Such cash flows are called sunk costs and should be removed from the analysis. The second is that some of the projected cash flows on an investment will be generated by the firm, whether this investment is accepted or rejected. Allocations of fixed expenses, such as general and administrative costs, usually fall into this category. These cash flows are not incremental, and the analysis needs to be cleansed of their impact.

1. Sunk Costs

There are some expenses related to a project that are incurred before the project analysis is done. One example would be expenses associated with a test market done to assess the potential market for a product prior to conducting a full-blown investment analysis. Such expenses are called *sunk costs*. Because they will not be recovered if the project is rejected, sunk costs are not incremental and therefore should not be considered as part of the investment analysis. This contrasts with their treatment in accounting statements, which do not distinguish between expenses that have already been incurred and expenses that are still to be incurred.

One category of expenses that consistently falls into the sunk cost column in project analysis is R&D, which occurs well before a product is even considered for introduction. Firms that spend large amounts on R&D, such as Merck and Intel, have struggled to come to terms with the fact that the analysis of these expenses generally occur after the fact, when little can be done about them.

IN PRACTICE: WHO WILL PAY THE SUNK COSTS?

Although sunk costs should not be treated as part of investment analysis, a firm does need to cover its sunk costs over time or it will cease to exist. Consider, for example, a firm like McDonald's, which expends considerable resources in test marketing products before introducing them. Assume, on the ill-fated McLean Deluxe (a low-fat hamburger introduced in 1990), that the test market expenses amounted to $30 million and that the net present value of the project, analyzed after the test market, amounted to $20 million. The project should be taken. If this is the pattern for every project McDonald's takes on, however, it will collapse under the weight of its test marketing expenses. To be successful, the *cumulative* net present value of its successful projects will have to exceed the *cumulative* test marketing expenses on both its successful and unsuccessful projects. ■

2. Allocated Costs

An accounting device created to ensure that every part of a business bears its fair share of costs is *allocation,* whereby costs that are not directly traceable to revenues generated by individual products or divisions are allocated across these units, based on revenues, profits, or assets. Although the purpose of such allocations may be fairness, their effect on investment analyses have to be viewed in terms of whether they create incremental cash flows. An allocated cost that will exist with or without the project being analyzed does not belong in the investment analysis.

Any increase in administrative or staff costs that can be traced to the project is an incremental cost and belongs in the analysis. One way to estimate the incremental component of these costs is to break them down on the basis of whether they are fixed or variable and, if variable, what they are a function of. Thus, a portion of administrative costs may be related to revenue, and the revenue projections of a new project can be used to estimate the administrative costs to be assigned to it.

ILLUSTRATION 5.3   Dealing with Allocated Costs

Case 1   Assume that you are analyzing a retail firm with general and administrative (G&A) costs currently of $600,000 a year. The firm currently has five stores, and the G&A costs are allocated evenly across the stores; the allocation to each store is $120,000. The firm is considering opening a new store; with six stores, the allocation of G&A expenses to each store will be $100,000.

In this case, assigning a cost of $100,000 for G&A costs to the new store in the investment analysis would be a mistake, because it is not an incremental cost—the total G&A cost will be $600,000, whether the project is taken or not.

Case 2   In the previous analysis, assume that all the facts remain unchanged except for one. The total G&A costs are expected to increase from $600,000 to $660,000 as a consequence of the new store. Each store is still allocated an equal amount; the new store will be allocated one-sixth of the total costs, or $110,000.

In this case, the allocated cost of $110,000 should not be considered in the investment analysis for the new store. The *incremental* cost of $60,000 ($660,000 − $600,000), however, should be considered as part of the analysis.

IN PRACTICE: WHO WILL PAY FOR HEADQUARTERS?

As in the case of sunk costs, the right thing to do in project analysis (i.e., considering only direct incremental costs) may not add up to create a firm that is financially healthy. Thus, if a company like Disney does not require individual movies that it analyzes to cover the allocated costs of general administrative expenses of the movie division, it is difficult to see how these costs will be covered at the level of the firm.

In 2003, Disney's corporate shared costs amounted to $443 million. Assuming that these general administrative costs serve a purpose, which otherwise would have to be borne by each of Disney's business, and that there is a positive relationship between the magnitude of these costs and revenues, it seems reasonable to argue that the firm should estimate a fixed charge for these costs that every new investment has to cover, even though this cost may not occur immediately or as a direct consequence of the new investment. ∎

The Argument for Incremental Cash Flows

When analyzing investments it is easy to get tunnel vision and focus on the project or investment at hand, acting as if the objective of the exercise is to maximize the value of the individual investment. There is also the tendency, with perfect hindsight, to require projects to cover all costs that they have generated for the firm, even if such costs will not be recovered by rejecting the project. The objective in investment analysis is to maximize the value of the business or firm taking the investment. Consequently, it is the cash flows that an investment will add on in the future to the business, that is, the incremental cash flows, that we should focus on.

ILLUSTRATION 5.4   **Estimating Cash Flows for an Online Book Ordering Service: Bookscape**

As described in Illustration 5.1, Bookscape is considering investing in an online book ordering and information service, which will be staffed by two full-time employees. The following estimates relate to the costs of starting the service and the subsequent revenues from it.

1. The initial investment needed to start the service, including the installation of additional phone lines and computer equipment, will be $1 million. These investments are expected to have a life of four years, at the end of which they will have no salvage value. The investments will be depreciated straight line over the four-year life.

2. The revenues in the first year are expected to be $1.5 million, growing 20 percent in year two, and 10 percent in the two years following.

3. The salaries and other benefits for the employees are estimated to be $150,000 in year one, and grow 10 percent a year for the following three years.

4. The cost of the books is assumed to be 60 percent of the revenues in each of the four years.

5. The working capital, which includes the inventory of books needed for the service and the accounts receivable (associated with selling books on credit) is

Table 5.2   EXPECTED OPERATING INCOME ON BOOKSCAPE ONLINE

	1	2	3	4
Revenues	$1,500,000	$1,800,000	$1,980,000	$2,178,000
Operating expenses				
Labor	$150,000	$165,000	$181,500	$199,650
Materials	$900,000	$1,080,000	$1,188,000	$1,306,800
Depreciation	$250,000	$250,000	$250,000	$250,000
Operating income	*$200,000*	*$305,000*	*$360,500*	*$421,550*
Taxes	$80,000	$122,000	$144,200	$168,620
After-tax operating income	$120,000	$183,000	$216,300	$252,930

Table 5.3   FROM OPERATING INCOME TO AFTER-TAX CASH FLOWS

	0 (Now)	1	2	3	4
After-tax operating income		$120,000	$183,000	$216,300	$252,930
+ Depreciation		$250,000	$250,000	$250,000	$250,000
− Change in working capital	$150,000	$30,000	$18,000	$19,800	$0
+ Salvage value					$217,800
After-tax cash flows	−$1,150,000	$340,000	$415,000	$446,500	$720,730

expected to amount to 10 percent of the revenues; the investments in working capital have to be made at the beginning of each year. At the end of year four, the entire working capital is assumed to be salvaged.

6. The tax rate on income is expected to be 40 percent, which is also the marginal tax rate for Bookscape.

Based on this information, we estimate the operating income for Bookscape Online in Table 5.2.

To get from operating income to cash flows, we add back the depreciation charges and subtract out the working capital requirements (which are the changes in working capital from year to year). We also show the initial investment of $1 million as a cash outflow right now (year zero) and the salvage value of the entire working capital investment in year four (see Table 5.3).

Note that there is an initial investment in working capital, which is 10 percent of the first year's revenues, invested at the beginning of the year. Each subsequent year has a change in working capital that represents 10 percent of the revenue change from that year to the next. In year four, the cumulative investment in working capital over the four years ($217,800) is salvaged, resulting in a positive cash flow.[3]

---

[3]Salvaging working capital is essentially the equivalent of having a going-out-of-business sale, where all the inventory is sold at cost and all accounts receivable are collected.

5.3 THE EFFECTS OF WORKING CAPITAL

In the analysis, we assumed that Bookscape would have to maintain additional inventory for its online book service. If, instead, we had assumed that Bookscape could use its existing inventory (i.e., from its regular bookstore), the cash flows on this project will

☐ increase.

☐ decrease.

☐ remain unchanged.

Explain.

ILLUSTRATION 5.5   Estimating Incremental Cash Flows: Disney Theme Park

The theme parks to be built near Bangkok, modeled on Disneyland Paris, will include a Magic Kingdom to be constructed, beginning immediately, and becoming operational at the beginning of the second year, and a second theme park modeled on Epcot at Orlando to be constructed in the second and third year and becoming operational at the beginning of the fourth year. The following is the set of assumptions that underlie the investment analysis.

1. The cash flows will be estimated in nominal dollars, even though the actual cash flows will be in Thai baht.

2. The cost of constructing Magic Kingdom will be $3 billion, with $2 billion to be spent right now and $1 billion to be spent a year from now. Disney has already spent $0.5 billion researching the proposal and getting the necessary licenses for the park; none of this investment can be recovered if the park is not built.

3. The cost of constructing Epcot II will be $1.5 billion, with $1 billion spent at the end of the second year and $0.5 billion at the end of the third year.

4. The revenues at the two parks and the resort properties at the parks are based on projected attendance figures until the tenth year and an expected inflation rate of 2 percent (in U.S. dollars). Starting in year ten, the revenues are expected to grow at the inflation rate. Table 5.4 summarizes the revenue projections.

   Note that the revenues at the resort properties are set at 25 percent of the revenues at the theme parks.

5. The operating expenses are assumed to be 60 percent of the revenues at the parks and 75 percent of revenues at the resort properties.

6. The depreciation will be calculated as a percent of the remaining book value of the fixed assets at the end of each year. In addition, the parks will require capital maintenance investments each year, specified as a percent of the depreciation that year. Table 5.5 lists both these statistics by year.[4]

   The capital maintenance expenditures are low in the early years, when the parks are still new but increase as the parks age. After year ten, both depreciation and capital expenditures are assumed to grow at the inflation rate (2 percent).

---

[4]Capital maintenance expenditures are capital expenditures to replace fixed assets that break down or become obsolete. This is in addition to the regular maintenance expenses that will be necessary to keep the parks going, which are included in operating expenses.

Table 5.4 REVENUE PROJECTIONS: DISNEYWORLD BANGKOK

Year	Magic Kingdom	Epcot II	Resort Properties	Total
1	$0	$0	$0	$0
2	$1,000	$0	$250	$1,250
3	$1,400	$0	$350	$1,750
4	$1,700	$300	$500	$2,500
5	$2,000	$500	$625	$3,125
6	$2,200	$550	$688	$3,438
7	$2,420	$605	$756	$3,781
8	$2,662	$666	$832	$4,159
9	$2,928	$732	$915	$4,575
10	$2,987	$747	$933	$4,667
Beyond	Revenues grow 2% a year forever			

Table 5.5 DEPRECIATION AND CAPITAL MAINTENANCE PERCENTAGES

Year	Depreciation as % of Book Value	Capital Maintenance as % of Depreciation
1	0.00%	0.00%
2	12.70%	50.00%
3	11.21%	60.00%
4	9.77%	70.00%
5	8.29%	80.00%
6	8.31%	90.00%
7	8.34%	100.00%
8	8.38%	105.00%
9	8.42%	110.00%
10	8.42%	110.00%

7. Disney will also allocate corporate G&A costs to this project, based on revenues; the G&A allocation will be 15 percent of the revenues each year. It is worth noting that a recent analysis of these expenses found that only one-third of these expenses are variable (and a function of total revenue) and that two-thirds are fixed. After year ten, these expenses are also assumed to grow at the inflation rate of 2 percent.

8. Disney will have to maintain noncash working capital (primarily consisting of inventory at the theme parks and the resort properties, netted against accounts payable) of 5 percent of revenues, with the investments being made at the *end of each year*.

9. The income from the investment will be taxed at Disney's marginal tax rate of 37.6 percent.

The projected operating earnings at the theme parks, starting in the first year of operation (which is the second year) are summarized in Exhibit 5.1. Note that the project has no income or expenses until year two, when the first park becomes operational and that the project is expected to have an operating loss of $262 million in that year. We have assumed that the firm will have enough income in its other businesses to claim the tax benefits from these losses (37.3 percent of the loss) in the same year. If this had been a stand-alone project, we would have had to carry the losses forward into future years and reduce taxes in those years.

These operating earnings can be contrasted with the after-tax cash flows in Exhibit 5.2, with the projected capital expenditures shown as part of the cash flows. In estimating these cash flows, we have made the following adjustments:

- Added back the depreciation and amortization each year, because it is a noncash charge.

- Subtracted out the maintenance capital expenditures in addition to the primary capital expenditures because these are cash outflows.

- Added back the after-tax portion of the allocated G&A costs that are fixed and therefore not an incremental effect of the project.

After-Tax Fixed Allocated G&A
= (2/3)(Allocated G&A Expense)(1 − Tax Rate)

- Subtracted out the working capital requirements each year, which represent the change in working capital from the prior year. In this case, we have assumed that the working capital investments are made at the end of each year.

The investment of $3 billion in Disneyworld Bangkok Magic Kingdom is shown at time zero (as $2 billion) and in year one (as $1 billion). The investment of $0.5 billion that will not be recovered because it has already been spent is not considered because it is a sunk cost.

5.4 DIFFERENT DEPRECIATION METHODS FOR TAX PURPOSES AND FOR REPORTING

The depreciation that we used for the project is assumed to be the same for both tax and reporting purposes. Assume now that Disney uses more accelerated depreciation methods for tax purposes and straight-line depreciation for reporting purposes. In estimating cash flows, we should use the depreciation numbers from the

☐ tax books.

☐ reporting books.

Explain.

This spreadsheet allows you to estimate the cash flows to the firm on a project (**capbudg.xls**).

Exhibit 5.1 Estimated Operating Earnings at Disneyworld Bangkok (in Millions)

	Now (0)	1	2	3	4	5	6	7	8	9	10
Magic Kingdom	$0	$0	$1,000	$1,400	$1,700	$2,000	$2,200	$2,420	$2,662	$2,928	$2,987
Epcot II	$0	$0	$0	$0	$300	$500	$550	$605	$666	$732	$747
Resort and properties	$0	$0	$250	$350	$500	$625	$688	$756	$832	$915	$933
Total revenues			*$1,250*	*$1,750*	*$2,500*	*$3,125*	*$3,438*	*$3,781*	*$4,159*	*$4,575*	*$4,667*
Magic Kingdom: operating expenses	$0	$0	$600	$840	$1,020	$1,200	$1,320	$1,452	$1,597	$1,757	$1,792
Epcot II: operating expenses	$0	$0	$0	$0	$180	$300	$330	$363	$399	$439	$448
Resort and properties: operating expenses	$0	$0	$188	$263	$375	$469	$516	$567	$624	$686	$700
Depreciation and amortization	$0	$0	$537	$508	$430	$359	$357	$358	$361	$366	$369
Allocated G&A Costs	$0	$0	$188	$263	$375	$469	$516	$567	$624	$686	$700
Operating income	$0	$0	*–$262*	*–$123*	*$120*	*$329*	*$399*	*$474*	*$554*	*$641*	*$658*
Taxes	$0	$0	–$98	–$46	$45	$123	$149	$177	$206	$239	$245
Operating income after taxes			*–$165*	*–$77*	*$75*	*$206*	*$251*	*$297*	*$347*	*$402*	*$412*
Depreciation calculations											
Preproject investment	$500										
New investment: Magic Kingdom	$2,000	$1,000									
New investment: Epcot II	$0	$0	$1,000	$500	$0	$0	$0	$0	$0	$0	$0
Capital maintenance			$268	$305	$301	$287	$321	$358	$380	$403	$406
Depreciation as % of book value			12.5%	11%	9.5%	8%	8%	8%	8%	8%	8%
Depreciation	$0		$537	$508	$430	$359	$357	$358	$361	$366	$369
Book value of fixed assets[a]	$2,500	$3,500	$4,232	$4,529	$4,400	$4,328	$4,292	$4,292	$4,310	$4,347	$4,384

[a]Book value of fixed assets in year t = Book value of fixed assets in year $t-1$ + New Investment + Capital Maintenance − Depreciation.

Exhibit 5.2 OPERATING CASH FLOWS AT DISNEYWORLD BANGKOK (IN MILLIONS)

	Now (0)	1	2	3	4	5	6	7	8	9	10
Operating income after taxes			–$164	–$77	$75	$206	$250	$297	$347	$402	$412
+ Depreciation and amortization			$537	$508	$430	$359	$357	$358	$361	$366	$369
– Capital expenditures	$2,000	$1,000	$1,268	$805	$301	$287	$321	$358	$380	$403	$406
– Change in working capital	$0	$0	$63	$25	$38	$31	$16	$17	$19	$21	$5
+ Nonincremental allocated expense $(1 - t)$		$0	$78	$110	$157	$196	$216	$237	$261	$287	$293
Cash flow to firm	–$2,000	–$1,000	–$880	–$289	$324	$443	$486	$517	$571	$631	$663

ILLUSTRATION 5.6   Estimating Cash Flows to Equity for a New Plant: Aracruz

Aracruz Celulose is considering a plan to build a state-of-the-art plant to manufacture linerboard. The plant is expected to have a capacity of 750,000 tons and will have the following characteristics:

1. It will require an initial investment of 250 million BR. At the end of the fifth year, an additional investment of 50 million BR will be needed to update the plant.

2. Aracruz plans to borrow 100 million BR at a real interest rate of 5.25 percent, using a ten-year term loan (where the loan will be paid off in equal annual increments).

3. The plant will have a life of ten years. During that period, the depreciable portion of the plant (and the additional investment in year five), not including salvage value, will be depreciated using double declining balance depreciation, with a life of ten years.[5] At the end of the tenth year, the plant is expected to be sold for its salvage value of 75 million BR.

4. The plant will be partly in commission in a couple of months but will have a capacity of only 650,000 tons in the first year and 700,000 tons in the second year before getting to its full capacity of 750,000 tons in the third year.

5. The capacity utilization rate will be 90 percent for the first three years and rise to 95 percent after that.

---

[5] With double declining balance depreciation, we double the straight line rate (which would be 10 percent a year, in this case with a ten-year life) and apply that rate to the remaining depreciable book value. We apply this rate to the investment in year five as well. We switch to straight line depreciation in the sixth year because straight line depreciation yields a higher value (and depreciates down to salvage value).

6. The price per ton of linerboard is currently 400 BR and is expected to keep pace with inflation for the life of the plant.

7. The variable cost of production, primarily labor and material, is expected to be 55 percent of total revenues; there is a fixed cost of 50 million BR, which will grow at the inflation rate.

8. The working capital requirements are estimated to be 15 percent of total revenues, and the investments have to be made at the beginning of each year. At the end of the tenth year, it is anticipated that the entire working capital will be salvaged.

9. Aracruz's corporate tax rate of 34 percent will apply to this project as well.

Before we estimate the net income on this project, we have to consider the debt payments each year and break them down into interest and principal payments. Table 5.6 summarizes the results.

Note that although the total payment remains unchanged, the breakdown into interest and principal payments changes from year to year.

Exhibit 5.3 summarizes the net income from plant investment to Aracruz each year for the next ten years. Note that all of the projections are in real cash flows. Consequently, the price of paper (which grows at the same rate as inflation) is kept constant in real terms, as is any other item having this characteristic.

In Exhibit 5.4 we estimate the cash flows to equity from the plant to Aracruz. To arrive at these cash flows, we do the following:

- Subtract out the portion of the initial capital expenditures that comes from equity; of the initial investment of 250,000 BR, only 150,000 BR comes from equity. In year five, there is an additional investment of 50,000 BR.

- Add back depreciation and amortization, because they are noncash charges.

Table 5.6 DEBT PAYMENTS: ARACRUZ PAPER PLANT

Year	Beginning Debt	Interest Expense	Principal Repaid	Total Payment	Ending Debt
1	R$100,000	R$5,250	R$7,858	R$13,108	R$92,142
2	R$92,142	R$4,837	R$8,271	R$13,108	R$83,871
3	R$83,871	R$4,403	R$8,705	R$13,108	R$75,166
4	R$75,166	R$3,946	R$9,162	R$13,108	R$66,004
5	R$66,004	R$3,465	R$9,643	R$13,108	R$56,361
6	R$56,361	R$2,959	R$10,149	R$13,108	R$46,212
7	R$46,212	R$2,426	R$10,682	R$13,108	R$35,530
8	R$35,530	R$1,865	R$11,243	R$13,108	R$24,287
9	R$24,287	R$1,275	R$11,833	R$13,108	R$12,454
10	R$12,454	R$654	R$12,454	R$13,108	R$0

Exhibit 5.3 Estimated Net Income from Paper Plant Investment: Aracruz Celulose (in 1000s of Brazilian Real, Real Terms)

	1	2	3	4	5	6	7	8	9	10
Capacity (in 1000s)	650	700	750	750	750	750	750	750	750	750
Utilization rate (%)	90%	90%	90%	95%	95%	95%	95%	95%	95%	95%
Production	585	630	675	713	713	713	713	713	713	713
Price per ton	400	400	400	400	400	400	400	400	400	400
Revenues	234,000	252,000	270,000	285,000	285,000	285,000	285,000	285,000	285,000	285,000
Operating expenses	178,700	188,600	198,500	206,750	206,750	206,750	206,750	206,750	206,750	206,750
Depreciation	35,000	28,000	22,400	17,920	14,336	21,469	21,469	21,469	21,469	21,469
Operating income	20,300	35,400	49,100	60,330	63,914	56,781	56,781	56,781	56,781	56,781
– Interest Expense	5,250	4,837	4,403	3,946	3,465	2,959	2,426	1,865	1,275	654
Taxable income	15,050	30,563	44,697	56,384	60,449	53,822	54,355	54,916	55,506	56,127
– Taxes	5,117	10,391	15,197	19,170	20,553	18,300	18,481	18,671	18,872	19,083
Net income	9,933	20,171	29,500	37,213	39,896	35,523	35,874	36,244	36,634	37,044
Beg. book value	250,000	215,000	187,000	164,600	146,680	182,344	160,875	139,406	117,938	96,469
– Depreciation	35,000	28,000	22,400	17,920	14,336	21,469	21,469	21,469	21,469	21,469
End book value	215,000	187,000	164,600	146,680	182,344	160,875	139,406	117,938	96,469	75,000
DDB depreciation	$35,000	$28,000	$22,400	$17,920	$14,336	$21,469	$17,175	$12,881	$8,588	$4,294
Straight line (based on remaining life)	$17,500	$15,556	$14,000	$12,800	$11,947	$21,469	$21,469	$21,469	$21,469	$21,469

Exhibit 5.4 CASH FLOWS TO EQUITY FROM PAPER PLANT: ARACRUZ CELULOSE (IN 1000S OF BRAZILIAN REAL)

	Now	1	2	3	4	5	6	7	8	9	10
Net income		9,933	20,171	29,500	37,213	39,896	35,523	35,874	36,244	36,634	37,044
+ Depreciation & amortization		35,000	28,000	22,400	17,920	14,336	21,469	21,469	21,469	21,469	21,469
− Capital expenditures	250,000	0	0	0	0	50,000	0	0	0	0	0
+ New debt issues	100,000										
− Change in working capital	35,100	2,700	2,700	2,250	0	0	0	0	0	0	(42,750)
− Principal repayments		7,858	8,271	8,705	9,162	9,643	10,149	10,682	11,243	11,833	12,454
+ Salvage value											75,000
Cash flow to equity	(185,100)	34,375	37,201	40,945	45,971	(5,411)	46,842	46,661	46,470	46,270	163,809

- Subtract the changes in working capital; because investments in working capital are made at the beginning of each period, the initial investment in working capital of 35.1 million BR is made at time 0 and is 15 percent of revenues in year one. The changes in working capital in the years that follow are 15 percent of the changes in revenue in those years. At the end of year ten, the entire investment in working capital is recovered as salvage.

- Subtract the principal payments that are made to the bank in each period, because these are cash outflows to the equity investors.

- Add the salvage value of the plant in year ten to the total cash flows, because this is a cash inflow to equity investors.

The cash flows to equity measure the cash flows that equity investors at Aracruz can expect to receive from investing in the plant.

5.5 THE EFFECTS OF DEBT FINANCING ON CASH FLOWS TO EQUITY

In the analysis, we assumed an additional capital expenditure of 50 million BR in year five, financed entirely with funds from equity; the cash flow to equity in year five (from Exhibit 5.4) is −5,411 million BR. If, instead, we had assumed the 50 million BR had come from new borrowing, the cash flow to equity in year five will

☐ increase by 50 million BR.

☐ decrease by 50 million BR.

☐ remain unchanged.

Explain.

This spreadsheet allows you to estimate the cash flows to equity on a project (**capbudgeq.xls**).

IN PRACTICE: ESTIMATING EXPECTED REVENUES AND CASH FLOWS

How do we estimate a project's expected revenues and expenses? The key word in this question is *estimate*. No one, no matter what his or her skill at forecasting and degree of preparation, can forecast with certainty how a risky project will do. There are generally three ways in which we can make these forecasts:

a. ***Experience and History*** The process of estimating project revenues and expenses is simplest for firms that consider the same kind of projects repeatedly. These firms can use their experience from similar projects that are already in operation to estimate expected values for new projects. Disney, for instance, can use its experiences with its existing theme parks in making its estimates for Disneyworld Bangkok.

b. *Market Testing* If the project being assessed is different from the firm's existing business, we may need a preliminary assessment of the market before actually investing in the project. In a market survey, potential customers are asked about the product or service being considered to gauge the interest they would have in acquiring it. The results usually are qualitative and indicate whether the interest is strong or weak, allowing the firm to decide whether to use optimistic forecasts for revenues (if the interest is strong) or pessimistic forecasts (if the interest is weak). Companies that need more information will often test market the concept on smaller markets, before introducing it on a larger scale. Test marketing not only allows firms to test out the product or service directly but also yields far more detailed information about the potential size of the market.

c. *Scenario Analysis* There are cases in which a firm is considering introducing a product to a market it knows well, but there is considerable uncertainty introduced by external factors that the firm cannot control. In such cases, a firm may decide to consider different scenarios, and the revenues and expenses on the project under each scenario. Although the concept is simple, it has four critical components. The first is the determination of which factors the scenarios will be built around. The second component is determining the number of scenarios to analyze for each factor. Although more scenarios may be more realistic than fewer, it becomes more difficult to collect information and differentiate between the scenarios in terms of project revenues. The third component is the estimation of project revenues and expenses under each scenario. The final component is the assignment of probabilities to each scenario.

We have laid out three ways of estimating revenues and expenses for projects, but none of these approaches yields perfect estimates. Although some project risk may come from estimation error, a large portion of risk comes from real uncertainty about the future. Improving estimation techniques, using more market testing, and performing scenario analysis may reduce estimation error but cannot eliminate real uncertainty. This is why we incorporate a risk premium into the discount rate. ∎

C. Time-Weighted versus Nominal Cash Flows
Very few projects with long lifetimes generate earnings or cash flows evenly over their lives. In sectors with huge investments in infrastructure, such as telecommunications,

the earnings and cash flows might be negative for an extended period (say, ten to twenty years) before they turn positive. In other sectors, the cash flows peak early and then gradually decrease over time. Whatever the reason for the unevenness of cash flows, a basic question that has to be addressed when measuring returns is whether they should reflect the timing of the cash flows. We will argue that they should, with earlier cash flows being weighted more when computing returns than cash flows later in a project life.

Why Cash Flows across Time Are Not Comparable

There are three reasons why cash flows across time are not comparable, and a cash flow in the future is worth less than a similar cash flow today:

1. Individuals *prefer present consumption to future consumption.* People would have to be offered more in the future to give up present consumption—this is called the *real rate of return.* The greater the real rate of return, the greater the difference in value between a cash flow today and an equal cash flow in the future.

2. When there is *monetary inflation,* the value of currency decreases over time. The greater the inflation, the greater the difference in value between a cash flow today and an equal cash flow in the future.

3. Any *uncertainty (risk)* associated with the cash flow in the future reduces the value of the cash flow. The greater the uncertainty associated with the cash flow, the greater the difference between receiving the cash flow today and receiving an equal amount in the future.

The process by which future cash flows are adjusted to reflect these factors is called *discounting,* and the magnitude of these factors is reflected in the *discount rate.* Thus the present value of a cash flow (CF_t) at a point in time t in the future, when the discount rate is r, can be written as follows:

$$\text{Present Value of Cash Flow} = CF_t\left(\frac{1}{(1 + r)^t}\right)$$

Note that the second term in the brackets, $(1/[1 + r]^t)$, is called the discount factor and effectively weights the cash flow by when it occurs. The differences in weights across time will depend entirely on the level of the discount rate. Consequently, when discount rates are high, which could be due to high real rates, high inflation, and/or high uncertainty, returns that occur further in the future will be weighted less. Appendix 3 includes a more complete discussion of the mechanics of present value.

The Case for Time-Weighted Returns

If we accept the arguments that cash flows measure returns more accurately than earnings and that the incremental cash flows more precisely estimate returns than total cash flows, we should logically follow up by using discounted cash flows (i.e., time-weighted returns) rather than nominal cash flows for two reasons.

1. Nominal cash flows at different points in time are not comparable and cannot be aggregated to arrive at returns. Discounted cash flows, on the other hand, convert all cash flows on a project to today's terms and allow us to compute returns more consistently.

2. If the objective in investment analysis is to maximize the value of the business taking the investments, we should be weighting cash flows that occur early more than cash flows that occur later, because investors in the business will also do so.

5.6   TIME HORIZONS AND TIME WEIGHTING

Calculating present values for cash flows leads to a greater weighting for cash flows that occur sooner and a lower weighting for cash flows that occur later. Does it necessarily follow that using present value (as opposed to nominal value) makes managers more likely to take short-term projects over long-term projects?

☐   Yes

☐   No

Why or why not?

INVESTMENT DECISION RULES

Having estimated the accounting earnings, cash flows, and time-weighted cash flows on an investment, we are still faced with the crucial decision of whether we should take the investment. In this section, we will consider a series of investment decision rules and put them to the test.

What Is an Investment Decision Rule?

When faced with new investments and projects, firms have to decide whether to invest in them or not. We have been leading up to this decision over the last few chapters, but investment decision rules allow us to formalize the process and specify what conditions need to be met for a project to be acceptable. Although we will be looking at a variety of investment decision rules in this section, it is worth keeping in mind what characteristics we would like a good investment decision rule to have.

- First, a good investment decision rule has to maintain a fair balance between allowing a manager analyzing a project to bring in his or her *subjective assessments* into the decision and ensuring that different projects are judged *consistently*. Thus, an investment decision rule that is too mechanical (by not allowing for subjective inputs) or too malleable (where managers can bend the rule to match their biases) is not a good rule.

- Second, a good investment decision rule will allow the firm to further the stated objective in corporate finance, which is to *maximize the value of the firm*. Projects that are acceptable using the decision rule should increase the value of the firm accepting them, whereas projects that do not meet the requirements would destroy value if the firm invested in them.

- Third, a good investment decision rule should *work across a variety of investments*. Investments can be revenue-generating investments (such as Disney making a new movie) or they can be cost-saving investments (as would be the case if Aracruz adopted a new system to manage inventory). Some projects have large up-front costs (as is the case with the Disney theme park), whereas other projects may have costs spread out across time. A good investment rule will provide an answer on all of these different kinds of investments.

Does there have to be only one investment decision rule? Although many firms analyze projects using a number of different investment decision rules, one rule has to dominate. In other words, when the investment decision rules lead to different conclusions on whether the project should be accepted or rejected, one decision rule has to be the tie-breaker and can be viewed as the primary rule.

Accounting Income–Based Decision Rules

Many of the oldest and most established investment decision rules have been drawn from the accounting statements and, in particular, from accounting measures of income. Some of these rules are based on income to equity investors (i.e., net income), and others are based on operating income.

Return on Capital

The return on capital on a project measures the returns earned by the firm on its total investment in the project. Consequently, it is a return to all claimholders in the firm on their collective investment in a project. Defined generally,

$$\text{Return on Capital (Pretax)} = \frac{\text{Earnings Before Interest and Taxes}}{\text{Average Book Value of Capital Invested in Project}}$$

$$\text{Return on Capital (After-Tax)}$$
$$= \frac{\text{Earnings Before Interest and Taxes } (1 \; - \; \text{Tax Rate})}{\text{Average Book Value of Capital Invested in Project}}$$

To illustrate, consider a one-year project, with an initial investment of $1 million, and earnings before interest and taxes (EBIT) of $300,000. Assume that the project has a salvage value at the end of the year of $800,000, and that the tax rate is 40 percent. In terms of a timeline, the project has the following parameters:

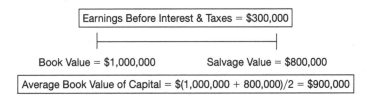

The pretax and after-tax returns on capital can be estimated as follows:

$$\text{Return on Capital (Pretax)} = \frac{\$300,000}{\$900,000} = 33.33\%$$

$$\text{Return on Capital (After-Tax)} = \frac{\$300,000(1 - 0.40)}{\$900,000} = 20\%$$

Although this calculation is rather straightforward for a one-year project, it becomes more involved for multiyear projects, where both the operating income and the book value of the investment change over time. In these cases, the return on capital can either be estimated each year and then averaged over time or the average operating income over the life of the project can be used in conjunction with the average investment during the period to estimate the average return on capital.

The after-tax return on capital on a project has to be compared to a hurdle rate that is defined consistently. The return on capital is estimated using the earnings before debt payments and the total capital invested in a project. Consequently, it can be viewed as return to the firm, rather than just to equity investors. Consequently, the cost of capital should be used as the hurdle rate.

If the After-Tax Return on Capital > Cost of Capital → Accept the Project

If the After-Tax Return on Capital < Cost of Capital → Reject the Project

For instance, if the company considering this project had a cost of capital of 10 percent, it would view the investment in the new project as a good one.

ILLUSTRATION 5.7   Estimating and Using Return on Capital in Decision Making: Disney and Bookscape
In Illustrations 5.4 and 5.5, we estimated the operating income from two projects—an investment by Bookscape in an online book ordering service and an investment in a theme park in Bangkok by Disney. We will estimate the return on capital on each of these investments using our earlier estimates of operating income. Table 5.7 summarizes the estimates of operating income and the book value of capital at Bookscape.

Table 5.7   **RETURN ON CAPITAL ON BOOKSCAPE ONLINE**

	1	2	3	4	Average
After-tax operating income	$120,000	$183,000	$216,300	$252,930	$193,058
BV of capital: beginning	$1,150,000	$930,000	$698,000	$467,800	
BV of capital: ending	$930,000	$698,000	$467,800	$0	
Average BV of capital	$1,040,000	$814,000	$582,900	$233,900	$667,700
Return on capital	11.54%	22.48%	37.11%	108.14%	28.91%

Table 5.8 Return on Capital for Disney Theme Park Investment (Income and Capital in Millions)

Year	After-Tax Operating Income	BV of Capital: Beginning	BV of Capital: Ending	Average BV of Capital	ROC
1	$0	$2,500	$3,500	$3,000	NA
2	−$165	$3,500	$4,294	$3,897	−4.22%
3	−$77	$4,294	$4,616	$4,455	−1.73%
4	$75	$4,616	$4,525	$4,570	1.65%
5	$206	$4,525	$4,484	$4,504	4.58%
6	$251	$4,484	$4,464	$4,474	5.60%
7	$297	$4,464	$4,481	$4,473	6.64%
8	$347	$4,481	$4,518	$4,500	7.72%
9	$402	$4,518	$4,576	$4,547	8.83%
10	$412	$4,576	$4,617	$4,596	8.97%

The book value of capital each year includes the investment in fixed assets and the noncash working capital. If we average the year-specific returns on capital, the average return on capital is 44.82 percent, but this number is pushed up by the extremely high return in year four. A better estimate of the return on capital is obtained by dividing the average after-tax operating income ($193,058) over the four years by the average capital invested ($667,700) over this time, which yields a return on capital of 28.91 percent. Because this exceeds the cost of capital that we estimated in Illustration 5.2 for this project of 22.76 percent, the return on capital approach would suggest that this is a good project.

In Table 5.8, we estimate operating income, book value of capital, and return on capital (ROC) for Disneyworld Bangkok. The operating income estimates are from Exhibit 5.1.

The book value of capital includes the investment in fixed assets (capital expenditures), net of depreciation, and the investment in working capital that year. The return on capital each year is computed based on the average book value of capital invested during the year. The average after-tax return on capital over the ten-year period is 4.23 percent. Here, the return on capital is lower than the cost of capital that we estimated in Illustration 5.2 to be 10.66 percent, and this suggests that Disney should not make this investment.

Return on Equity

The return on equity looks at the return to equity investors, using the accounting net income as a measure of this return. Again, defined generally,

$$\text{Return on Equity} = \frac{\text{Net Income}}{\text{Average Book Value of Equity Investment in Project}}$$

To illustrate, consider a four-year project with an initial equity investment of $800, and the following estimates of net income in each of the four years:

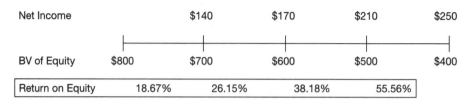

Net Income		$140	$170	$210	$250
BV of Equity	$800	$700	$600	$500	$400
Return on Equity	18.67%	26.15%	38.18%	55.56%	

Like the return on capital, the return on equity tends to increase over the life of the project, as the book value of equity in the project is depreciated.

Just as the appropriate comparison for the return on capital is the cost of capital, the appropriate comparison for the return on equity is the *cost of equity,* which is the rate of return equity investors demand.

If the Return on Equity > Cost of Equity → Accept the Project

If the Return on Equity < Cost of Equity → Reject the Project

The cost of equity should reflect the riskiness of the project being considered and the financial leverage taken on by the firm. When choosing between mutually exclusive projects of similar risk, the project with the higher return on equity will be viewed as the better project.

Illustration 5.8 Estimating Return on Equity: Aracruz Celulose

Consider again the analysis of the paper plant for Aracruz Celulose that we started in Illustration 5.6. Table 5.9 summarizes the book value of equity and the estimated net income (from Exhibit 5.3) for each of the next ten years in thousands of real BR.

To compute the book value of equity in each year, we first compute the book value of the fixed assets (plant and equipment), add to it the book value of the working capital in that year, and subtract out the outstanding debt. The return on equity (ROE) each year is obtained by dividing the net income in that year by the average book value of equity invested in the plant in that year. The increase in the return on equity over time occurs because the net income rises while the book value of equity decreases. The average real return on equity of 23.24 percent on the paper plant project is compared to the real cost of equity for this plant, which is 11.46 percent, suggesting that this is a good investment.

Assessing Accounting Return Approaches

How well do accounting returns measure up to the three criteria we listed for a good investment decision rule? In terms of maintaining balance between allowing managers to bring into the analysis their judgments about the project and ensuring consistency between analysis, the accounting returns approach falls short. It fails because it is significantly affected by accounting choices. For instance, changing from straight-line to accelerated depreciation affects both the earnings and the book

Table 5.9 Return on Equity: Aracruz Paper Plant

Year	Net Income	Beg. BV: Assets	Depreciation	Capital Exp.	Ending BV: Assets	BV of Working Capital	Debt	BV: Equity	Average BV: Equity	ROE
0		0	0	250,000	250,000	35,100	100,000	185,100		
1	9,933	250,000	35,000	0	215,000	37,800	92,142	160,658	172,879	5.75%
2	20,171	215,000	28,000	0	187,000	40,500	83,871	143,629	152,144	13.26%
3	29,500	187,000	22,400	0	164,600	42,750	75,166	132,184	137,906	21.39%
4	37,213	164,600	17,920	0	146,680	42,750	66,004	123,426	127,805	29.12%
5	39,896	146,680	14,336	50,000	182,344	42,750	56,361	168,733	146,079	27.31%
6	35,523	182,344	21,469	0	160,875	42,750	46,212	157,413	163,073	21.78%
7	35,874	160,875	21,469	0	139,406	42,750	35,530	146,626	152,020	23.60%
8	36,244	139,406	21,469	0	117,938	42,750	24,287	136,400	141,513	25.61%
9	36,634	117,938	21,469	0	96,469	42,750	12,454	126,764	131,582	27.84%
10	37,044	96,469	21,469	0	75,000	0	0	75,000	100,882	36.72%
Average										23.24%

value over time, thus altering returns. Unless these decisions are taken out of the hands of individual managers assessing projects, there will be no consistency in the way returns are measured on different projects.

Does investing in projects that earn accounting returns exceeding their hurdle rates lead to an increase in firm value? The value of a firm is the present value of expected cash flows on the firm over its lifetime. Because accounting returns are based on earnings rather than cash flows and ignore the time value of money, investing in projects that earn a return greater than the hurdle rates will not necessarily increase firm value. Conversely, some projects that are rejected because their accounting returns fall short of the hurdle rate may have increased firm value. This problem is compounded by the fact that the returns are based on the book value of investments, rather than the cash invested in the assets.

Finally, the accounting return works better for projects that have a large up-front investments and generate level income over time. For projects that do not require a significant initial investment, the returns on capital and equity have less meaning. For instance, a retail firm that leases store space for a new store will not have a significant initial investment and may have a very high return on capital as a consequence.

Note that all of the limitations of the accounting return measures are visible in the last two illustrations. First, the Disney example does not differentiate between money already spent and money still to be spent; rather, the sunk cost of $0.5 billion is shown in the initial investment of $3.5 billion. Second, in both the Bookscape and Aracruz analyses, as the book value of the assets decreases over time, largely as a consequence of depreciation, the operating income rises, leading to an increase in the return on capital. With the Disney analysis, there is one final and very important concern. The return on capital was estimated over ten years, but the project life is likely to be much longer. After all, Disney's existing theme parks in the United States are more than three decades old and generate substantial cash flows for the firm still. Extending the project life will push up the return on capital and may make this project viable.

Notwithstanding these concerns, accounting measures of return endure in investment analysis. Although this fact can be partly attributed to the unwillingness of financial managers to abandon familiar measures, it also reflects the simplicity and intuitive appeal of these measures. More important, as long as accounting measures of return are used by investors and equity research analysts to assess the overall performance of firms, these same measures of return will be used in project analysis.

 This spreadsheet allows you to estimate the average return on capital on a project (**capbudg.xls**).

Returns on Capital and Equity for Entire Firms
The discussion of returns on equity and capital has so far revolved around individual projects. It is possible, however, to calculate the return on equity or capital for an

entire firm, based on its current earnings and book value. The computation parallels the estimation for individual projects but uses the values for the entire firm:

$$\text{Return on Capital (ROC or ROIC)}$$

$$= \frac{\text{EBIT}(1 - t)}{(\text{Book Value of Debt} + \text{Book Value of Equity})}$$

$$\text{Return on Equity} = \frac{\text{Net Income}}{\text{Book Value of Equity}}$$

We use book value rather than market value because it represents the capital investment in existing investments. To preserve consistency, the book values used should reflect either the book values at the start of the period (over which the return in earned) or the average capital invested over the period. This return can be used as an approximate measure of the returns that the firm is making on its existing investments or assets, as long as the following assumptions hold:

1. The income used (operating or net) is income derived from existing projects and is not skewed by expenditures designed to provide future growth (such as R&D expenses) or one-time gains or losses.

2. More important, the book value of the assets used measures the actual investment that the firm has in these assets. Here again, stock buybacks, one-time charges and goodwill amortization can create serious distortions in the book value.[6]

3. The depreciation and other noncash charges that usually depress income are used to make capital expenditures that maintain the existing asset's income earning potential.

If these assumptions hold, the return on capital becomes a reasonable proxy for what the firm is making on its existing investments or projects, and the return on equity becomes a proxy for what the equity investors are making on their share of these investments.

With this reasoning, a firm that earns a return on capital that exceeds it cost of capital can be viewed as having, on average, good projects on its books. Conversely, a firm that earns a return on capital that is less than the cost of capital can be viewed as having, on average, bad projects on its books. From the equity standpoint, a firm that earns a return on equity that exceeds its cost of equity can be viewed as earning surplus returns for its stockholders, whereas a firm that does not accomplish this is taking on projects that destroy stockholder value.

---

[6]Stock buybacks and large write-offs will push down book capital and result in overstated accounting returns. Acquisitions that create large amounts of goodwill will push up book capital and result in understated returns on capital.

Table 5.10 RETURN ON CAPITAL AND COST OF CAPITAL COMPARISON

Company	EBIT $(1 - t)$ (Millions)	BV of Debt (Millions)	BV of Equity (Millions)	BV of Capital	Return on Capital	Cost of Capital	ROC – Cost of Capital
Disney	$1,701	$14,130	$23,879	$38,009	4.48%	8.59%	−4.12%
Aracruz	R$586	R$2,862	R$6385	R$9,248	6.34%	9.00%	−2.66%
Bookscape	$1.2	0	$4.5	$4.5	26.67%	12.14%	14.53%

ILLUSTRATION 5.9 **Evaluating Current Investments**

In Table 5.10, we summarize the current returns on capital and costs of capital for Disney, Aracruz, and Bookscape. The book values of debt and equity at the end of the previous financial year (2002) were added together to compute the book value of capital invested at the beginning of 2003, and the operating income for the most recent financial year (2003) is used to compute the return on capital.[7] Considering the issues associated with measuring debt and cost of capital for financial services firms, we have not computed the values for Deutsche Bank.

The marginal tax rates used in Chapter 4 are used here as well. Although this analysis suggests that only Bookscape is earning excess returns, the following factors should be considered:

1. The book value of capital is affected fairly dramatically by accounting decisions. In particular, Disney's capital invested increased by almost $20 billion from 1995 to 1996 as a result of the acquisition of Capital Cities and Disney's decision to use purchase accounting. If they had chosen pooling instead, they would have reported a much higher return on capital.

2. We have used the operating income from the most recent year, notwithstanding the volatility in the income. To smooth out the volatility, we can compute the average operating income over the past three years and use it in computing the return on capital; this approach generates a "normalized" return on capital of 4.36 percent for Disney and 3.40 percent for Aracruz. Both are still below the cost of capital.

3. We did not adjust the operating income or the book value of capital to include operating leases that were outstanding at the end of the prior year. If we had made the adjustment for Disney and Bookscape, the returns on capital would have changed to 4.42 percent and 12.68 percent respectively.

4. For Aracruz, we assume that because the book values are adjusted for inflation, the return on capital is a real return on capital and can be compared to the real cost of capital.[8]

---

[7]Some analysts use average capital invested over the year, obtained by averaging the book value of capital at the beginning and end of the year. By using the capital invested at the beginning of the year, we have assumed that capital invested during the course of year is unlikely to generate operating income during that year.

[8]Brazilian accounting standards allow for the adjustment of book value for inflation.

Table 5.11   Return on Equity and Cost of Equity Comparisons

Company	Net Income (Millions)	BV of Equity (Millions)	ROE	Cost of Equity	ROE − Cost of Equity
Disney	$1,267	$23,879	5.31%	10.00%	−4.70%
Aracruz	R$428	R$6,385	6.70%	10.79%	−4.09%
Bookscape	$1.320	$4.5	29.33%	13.93%	15.40%
Deutsche Bank	€1,365	€29,991	4.55%	8.76%	−4.21%

The analysis can also be done purely in equity terms. To do this, we would first compute the return on equity for each company by dividing the net income for the most recent year by the book value of equity at the beginning of the year and compare it to the cost of equity. Table 5.11 summarizes these results.

The conclusions are similar, with Bookscape earning excess returns, whereas the other companies all have returns that lag the cost of equity.

There is a data set on the Web that summarizes, by sector, returns on equity and capital as well as costs of equity and capital.

IN PRACTICE: Economic Value Added (EVA)

Economic value added is a value enhancement concept that has caught the attention both of firms interested in increasing their value and portfolio managers looking for good investments. EVA is a measure of dollar surplus value created by a firm or project and is measured by doing the following:

$$\text{Economic Value Added (EVA)}$$
$$= (\text{Return on Capital} - \text{Cost of Capital})\,(\text{Capital Invested})$$

The return on capital is measured using "adjusted" operating income, where the adjustments eliminate items that are unrelated to existing investments,[9] and the capital investment is based on the book value of capital but is designed to measure the capital invested in existing assets. Firms that have positive EVA are firms that are creating surplus value, and firms with negative EVA are destroying value.

Although EVA is usually calculated using total capital, it can be easily modified to be an equity measure:

$$\text{Equity EVA} = (\text{Return on Equity} - \text{Cost of Equity})$$
$$\times (\text{Equity Invested in Project or Firm})$$

Again, a firm that earns a positive equity EVA is creating value for its stockholders, and a firm with a negative equity EVA is destroying value for its stockholders.

---

[9]Stern Stewart, which is the primary proponent of the EVA approach, claims to make as many as 168 adjustments to operating income to arrive at the true return on capital.

The measures of excess returns that we computed in the tables in the last illustration can be easily modified to become measures of EVA:

Company	ROC – Cost of Capital	BV of Capital (in Millions)	EVA (in Millions)	ROE – Cost of Equity	BV of Equity (in Millions)	Equity EVA (in Millions)
Disney	−4.12%	$38,009	−$1,565	−4.70%	$23,879	−$1,122
Aracruz	−2.66%	R$9,248	−R$246	−4.09%	R$6,385	−R$261
Bookscape	14.53%	$4.5	$0.654	15.40%	4.5	$0.693
Deutsche Bank	NMF	NMF	NMF	−4.21%	€29,991	−€1,262

Note that EVA converts the percentage excess returns in these tables to absolute excess returns, but it is affected by the same issues of earnings and book value measurement. ■

5.7 STOCK BUYBACKS, RETURN ON CAPITAL, AND EVA

When companies buy back stock, they are allowed to reduce the book value of their equity by the market value of the stocks bought back. When the market value of equity is well in excess of book value of equity, buying back stock will generally

☐ increase the return on capital but not affect the EVA.

☐ increase the return on capital and increase the EVA.

☐ not affect the return on capital but increase the EVA.

☐ none of the above.

Why or why not?

There is a data set on the Web that summarizes, by sector, the economic value added and the equity economic value added in each.

Cash Flow–Based Decision Rules

Payback

The **payback** on a project is a measure of how quickly the cash flows generated by the project cover the initial investment. Consider a project that has the following cash flows:

The payback on this project is between two and three years and can be approximated, based on the cash flows to be 2.6 years.

As with the other measures, the payback can be estimated either for all investors in the project or just for the equity investors. To estimate the payback for the entire firm, the cash flows to the firm are added up until they cover the total initial investment. To estimate payback just for the equity investors, the cash flows to equity are cumulated until they cover the initial equity investment in the project.

■ **Payback:** The length of time it will take for nominal cash flows from the project to cover the initial investment.

Illustration 5.10   Estimating Payback for the Bookscape Online Service

This example estimates the payback from the viewpoint of the firm, using the Bookscape online service cash flows estimated in Illustration 5.4. Table 5.12 summarizes the annual cash flows and their cumulated value.

The initial investment of $1.15 million is covered sometime in the third year, leading to a payback of between two and three years. If we assume that cash flows occur uniformly over the course of the year:

$$\text{Payback for Project} = 2 + (\$395{,}000/\$446{,}500) = 2.88 \text{ years}$$

Table 5.12   PAYBACK FOR BOOKSCAPE ONLINE

Year	Cash Flow in Year	Cumulated Cash Flow
0	−$1,150,000	
1	$340,000	−$810,000
2	$415,000	−$395,000
3	$446,500	$51,500
4	$720,730	$772,230

Using Payback in Decision Making

Although it is uncommon for firms to make investment decisions based solely on the payback, surveys suggest that some businesses do in fact use payback as their primary decision mechanism. In those situations where payback is used as the primary criterion for accepting or rejecting projects, a maximum acceptable payback period is typically set. Projects that pay back their initial investment sooner than this maximum are accepted, and projects that do not are rejected.

Firms are much more likely to employ payback as a secondary investment decision rule and use it either as a constraint in decision making (e.g., accept projects that earn a return on capital of at least 15 percent, as long as the payback is less than ten years) or to choose between projects that score equally well on the primary decision rule (e.g., when two mutually exclusive projects have similar returns on equity, choose the one with the lower payback).

Biases, Limitations, and Caveats

The payback rule is a simple and intuitively appealing decision rule, but it does not use a significant proportion of the information that is available on a project.

Figure 5.2   Using Payback for Mutually Exclusive Projects

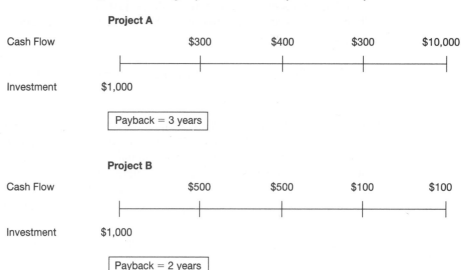

- By restricting itself to answering the question, "When will this project make back its initial investment?" it ignores what happens after the initial investment is recouped. This is a significant shortcoming when deciding between mutually exclusive projects. To provide a sense of the absurdities this can lead to, assume that you are picking between two mutually exclusive projects with the cash flows shown in Figure 5.2.

    On the basis of the payback alone, project B is preferable to project A because it has a shorter payback period. Most decision makers would pick project A as the better project, however, because of the high cash flows that result after the initial investment is paid back.

- The payback rule is designed to cover the conventional project that involves a large up-front investment followed by positive operating cash flows. It breaks down, however, when the investment is spread over time or when there is no initial investment.

- The payback rule uses nominal cash flows and counts cash flows in the early years the same as cash flows in the later years. Because money has time value, however, recouping the nominal initial investment does not make the business whole again, because that amount could have been invested elsewhere and earned a significant return.

Discounted Cash Flow Measures

Investment decision rules based on discounted cash flows not only replace accounting income with cash flows but explicitly factor in the time value of money. The two most widely used discounted cash flows rules are *net present value* and the *internal rate of return*.

Net Present Value (NPV)

The **net present value** of a project is the sum of the present values of each of the cash flows—positive as well as negative—that occurs over the life of the project. The general formulation of the NPV rule is as follows:

$$\text{NPV of Project} = \sum_{t=1}^{t=N} \frac{CF_t}{(1 + r)^t} - \text{Initial Investment}$$

where CF_t = cash flow in period t, r = discount rate, and N = life of the project.

Thus, the NPV of a project with the cash flows depicted in Figure 5.3 and a discount rate of 12 percent can be written as:

Figure 5.3 NPV of a Project

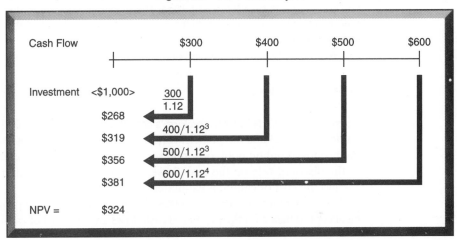

Once the NPV is computed, the decision rule is extremely simple because the hurdle rate is already factored in the present value.

If the NPV > 0   →   Accept the Project
If the NPV < 0   →   Reject the Project

Note that an NPV that is greater than zero implies that the project makes a return greater than the hurdle rate. Illustrations 5.11 and 5.12 illustrate the two approaches.

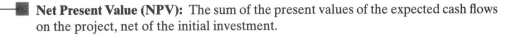 **Net Present Value (NPV):** The sum of the present values of the expected cash flows on the project, net of the initial investment.

 This spreadsheet allows you to estimate the NPV from cash flows to the firm on a project (**capbudg.xls**).

Year	Annual Cash Flow	Present Value of Cash Flow
0	$(1,150,000)	$(1,150,000)
1	$340,000	$276,969
2	$415,000	$275,392
3	$446,500	$241,366
4	$720,730	$317,380
NPV		$(38,893)

Table 5.13 CASH FLOW TO THE FIRM ON BOOKSCAPE ONLINE

5.8 THE SIGNIFICANCE OF A POSITIVE NPV

Assume that you have analyzed a $100 million project using a cost of capital of 15 percent and come up with an NPV of $1 million. The manager who has to decide on the project argues that this is too small an NPV for a project of this size and that this indicates a poor project. Is this true?

☐ Yes. The NPV is only 1 percent of the initial investment.

☐ No. A positive NPV indicates a good project.

Explain your answer.

ILLUSTRATION 5.11 NPV from the Firm's Standpoint: Bookscape Online

Table 5.13 calculates the present value of the cash flows to Bookscape as a firm from the proposed online book ordering service using the cost of capital of 22.76 percent as the discount rate on the cash flows. (The cash flows are estimated in Illustration 5.4 and the cost of capital is estimated in Illustration 5.2.)

This project has an NPV of –$38,893, suggesting that it is a project that should not be accepted based on the projected cash flows and the cost of capital of 22.76 percent.

ILLUSTRATION 5.12 NPV from the Firm's Standpoint: Disneyworld Bangkok

In estimating the cash flows to discount for Disney's theme park in Thailand, the first point to note when computing the NPV of the proposed theme park is the fact that it has a life far longer than the ten years shown in Exhibit 5.2. To bring in the cash flows that occur after year ten, when cash flows start growing at 2 percent, the inflation rate forever, we draw on a present value formula for a growing perpetuity (see Appendix 3):

$$\text{Present Value of Cash Flows after Year 10} = \text{Cash Flow in Year 11}/(\text{WACC} - g)$$
$$= \$663 \text{ million}/(0.1066 - 0.02)$$
$$= \$7,810 \text{ million}$$

The cost of capital of 10.66 percent is the cost of capital for one theme park that we estimated in Illustration 5.2. This present value is called the *terminal value* and occurs at the end of year ten.

Table 5.14 presents the NPV of the proposed park estimated using the cash flows in millions of U.S. dollars from Exhibit 5.2 and Disney's cost of capital, in dollar terms, of 10.66 percent.

	Table 5.14	NPV OF DISNEYWORLD BANGKOK	
Year	Annual Cash Flow (Millions)	Terminal Value (Millions)	Present Value (Millions)
0	−$2,000		−$2,000
1	−$1,000		−$904
2	−$880		−$718
3	−$289		−$213
4	$324		$216
5	$443		$267
6	$486		$265
7	$517		$254
8	$571		$254
9	$631		$254
10	$663	$7,810	$3,076
Net Present Value (NPV) =			$749

The NPV of this project is positive. This suggests that it is a good project that will earn $749 million in surplus value for Disney.

NPV and Currency Choices
When analyzing a project, the cash flows and discount rates can often be estimated in one of several currencies. For a project like the Disney theme park, the obvious choices are the project's local currency (Thai baht) and the company's home currency (U.S. dollars), but we can in fact use any currency to evaluate the project. When switching from one currency to another, we have to go through the following steps:

1. ***Estimate the expected exchange rate for each period of the analysis*** For some currencies (Euro, yen, or British pound), we can obtain estimates of expected exchange rates from the financial markets in the form of forward rates. For other currencies, we have to estimate the exchange rate, and the soundest way to do so is to use the expected inflation rates in the two currencies in question. For instance, we can estimate the expected baht/$ exchange rate in n years:

$$\text{Expected Rate } (Bt/\$)_n = Bt/\$ \text{ (Today)}$$
$$\times \left[\frac{(1 + \text{Expected Inflation}_{\text{Thailand}})}{(1 + \text{Expected Inflation}_{\text{U.S.}})} \right]^n$$

We are assuming that purchasing power ultimately drives exchange rates—this is called purchasing power parity.

2. ***Convert the expected cash flows from one currency to another in future periods, using these exchange rates*** Multiplying the expected cash flows in one currency by the expected exchange rate will accomplish this.

3. ***Convert the discount rate from one currency to another*** We cannot discount cash flows in one currency using discount rates estimated in another. To convert a discount rate from one currency to another, we will again use expected inflation rates in the two currencies. A dollar cost of capital can be converted into a Thai baht cost of capital as follows:

$$\text{Cost of Capital(Bt)} = (1 + \text{Cost of Capital [\$]})$$

$$\times \frac{(1 + \text{Exp Inflation}_{\text{Thailand}})}{(1 + \text{Exp Inflation}_{\text{U.S.}})} - 1$$

Compute the NPV by discounting the converted cash flows (from step 2) at the converted discount rate (from step 3). The NPV should be identical in both currencies but only because the expected inflation rates were used to estimate the exchange rates. If the forecasted exchange rates diverge from purchasing power parity, we can get different NPVs, but our currency views are then contaminating our project analysis.

ILLUSTRATION 5.13 NPV in Thai Baht: Disneyworld Bangkok

In Illustration 5.12, we computed the NPV for Disneyworld Bangkok in dollar terms to be $749 million. The entire analysis could have been done in Thai baht terms. To do this, the cash flows would have to be converted from dollars to Thai baht, and the discount rate would then have been a Thai baht discount rate. To estimate the expected exchange rate, we will assume that the expected inflation rate is 10 percent in Thailand and 2 percent in the United States and that the current exchange rate is 42.09 Bt per U.S. dollar. The projected exchange rate in one year will be:

$$\text{Expected Exchange Rate in Year 1} = 42.09 \text{ Bt} \times (1.10/1.02) = 45.39 \text{ Bt/\$}$$

Similar analyses will yield exchange rates for each of the next ten years.

The dollar cost of capital of 10.66 percent, estimated in Illustration 5.1, is converted to a baht cost of capital using the expected inflation rates:

$$\text{Cost of Capital (Bt)} = (1 + \text{Cost of Capital [\$]})$$

$$\times \frac{(1 + \text{Exp Inflation}_{\text{Thailand}})}{(1 + \text{Exp Inflation}_{\text{U.S.}})} - 1$$

$$= (1.1066)(1.10/1.02) - 1 = 19.34\%$$

Table 5.15 summarizes exchange rates, cash flows, and the present value for the proposed Disney theme parks, with the analysis done entirely in Thai baht.

Note that the NPV of 31,542 million Bt is exactly equal to the dollar NPV computed in Illustration 5.12, converted at the current exchange rate of 42.09 Bt per dollar.

$$\text{NPV in dollars} = \text{NPV in Bt/Current Exchange Rate}$$
$$= 31,542/42.09 = \$749 \text{ million}$$

Table 5.15 **Expected Cash Flows from Disney Theme Park in Thai Baht**

Year	Cash Flow (Millions $)	Bt/$	Cash Flow (Millions Bt)	Present Value (Millions Bt)
0	−2,000	42.09	−84,180	−84,180
1	−1,000	45.39	−45,391	−38,034
2	−880	48.95	−43,075	−30,243
3	−289	52.79	−15,262	−8,979
4	324	56.93	18,420	9,080
5	443	61.40	27,172	11,223
6	486	66.21	32,187	11,140
7	517	71.40	36,920	10,707
8	571	77.01	43,979	10,687
9	631	83.04	52,412	10,671
10	8,474	89.56	758,886	129,470
NPV of Disney Theme Park =				31,542

IN PRACTICE: Terminal Value, Salvage Value, and NPV

When estimating cash flows for an individual project, practicality constrains us to estimate cash flows for a finite period—three, five, or ten years, for instance. At the end of that finite period, we can make one of three assumptions.

- The most conservative one is that the project ceases to exist and its assets are worthless. In that case, the final year of operation will reflect only the operating cash flows from that year.
- We can assume that the project will end at the end of the analysis period and that the assets will be sold for salvage. Although we can try to estimate salvage value directly, a common assumption that is made is that salvage value is equal to the book value of the assets. For fixed assets, this will be the undepreciated portion of the initial investment, whereas for working capital, it will be the aggregate value of the investments made in working capital over the course of the project life.
- We can also assume that the project will not end at the end of the analysis period and try to estimate the value of the project on an ongoing basis—this is the terminal value. In the Disney theme park analysis, for instance, we assumed that the cash flows will continue forever and grow at the inflation rate each year. If that seems too optimistic, we can assume that the cash flows will continue with no growth for a finite period or even that they will drop by a constant rate each year.

The right approach to use will depend on the project being analyzed. For projects that are not expected to last for long periods, we can use either of the first two approaches; a zero salvage value should be used if the project assets are likely to become obsolete by the end of the project life (e.g., computer hardware), and salvage can be set to book value if the assets are likely to retain significant value (e.g., buildings).

For projects with long lives, the terminal value approach is likely to yield more reasonable results but with one caveat. The investment and maintenance assumptions made in the analysis should reflect its long life. In particular, capital maintenance expenditures will be much higher for projects with terminal value because the assets have to retain their earning power. For the Disney theme park, the capital maintenance expenditures climb over time and become larger than depreciation as we approach the terminal year. ■

5.9 CURRENCY CHOICES AND NPV

A company in a high-inflation economy has asked for your advice regarding which currency to use for investment analysis. The company believes that using the local currency to estimate the NPV will yield too low a value because domestic interest rates are very high and would push up the discount rate. Is this true?

☐ Yes. A higher discount rate will lead to lower NPV.

☐ No.

Explain your answer.

NPV: Firm versus Equity Analysis

In the previous analysis, the cash flows we discounted were prior to interest and principal payments, and the discount rate we used was the weighted average cost of capital. In NPV parlance, we were discounting cash flows to the entire firm (rather than just its equity investors) at a discount rate that reflected the costs to different claimholders in the firm to arrive at an NPV. There is an alternative. We could have discounted the cash flows left over after debt payments for equity investors at the cost of equity and arrived at an NPV to equity investors.

Will the two approaches yield the same NPV? As a general rule, they will, but only if the following assumptions hold:

- The debt is correctly priced and the market interest rate used to compute the cost of capital is the right one, given the default risk of the firm. If not, it is possible that equity investors can gain (if interest rates are set too low) or lose (if interest rates are set too high) to bondholders. This in turn can result in the NPV to equity being different from the NPV to the firm.

- The same assumptions are made about the financing mix used in both calculations. Note that the financing mix assumption affects the discount rate (cost of capital) in the firm approach and the cash flows (through the interest and principal payments) in the equity approach.

Given that the two approaches yield the same NPV, which one should we choose to use? Many practitioners prefer discounting cash flows to the firm at the cost of capital; it is easier to do because the cash flows are before debt payments and therefore we do not have to estimate interest and principal payments explicitly. Cash flows to equity are more intuitive, though, because most of us think of cash flows left over after interest and principal payments as residual cash flows.

Table 5.16   CASH FLOW TO EQUITY ON LINERBOARD PLANT (IN THOUSANDS)

Year	Cash Flow to Equity	PV of Cash Flow
0	(185,100 BR)	(185,100 BR)
1	34,375 BR	30,840 BR
2	37,201 BR	29,943 BR
3	40,945 BR	29,568 BR
4	45,971 BR	29,784 BR
5	(5,411 BR)	(3,145 BR)
6	46,842 BR	24,427 BR
7	46,661 BR	21,830 BR
8	46,470 BR	19,505 BR
9	46,270 BR	17,424 BR
10	163,809 BR	55,342 BR
NPV		70,418 BR

ILLUSTRATION **5.14   NPV from the Equity Investors' Standpoint: Paper Plant for Aracruz**
The NPV is computed from the equity investors' standpoint for the proposed linerboard plant for Aracruz using real cash flows to equity, estimated in Exhibit 5.4, and a real cost of equity of 11.46 percent. Table 5.16 summarizes the cash flows and the present values.

The net present value of 70.418 million BR suggests that this is a good project for Aracruz to take on.

The analysis was done entirely in real terms, but using nominal cash flows and discount rates would have had no impact on the NPV. The cash flows will be higher because of expected inflation, but the discount rate will increase by exactly the same magnitude, thus resulting in an identical NPV. The choice between nominal and real cash flows therefore boils down to one of convenience. When inflation rates are low, it is better to do the analysis in nominal terms because taxes are based on nominal income. When inflation rates are high and volatile, it is easier to do the analysis in real terms or in a different currency with a lower expected inflation rate.

5.10   EQUITY, DEBT, AND NPV

In the project just described, assume that Aracruz had used all equity to finance the project instead of its mix of debt and equity. Which of the following is likely to occur to the NPV?

☐   The NPV will go up because the cash flows to equity will be much higher; there will be no interest and principal payments to make each year.

☐   The NPV will go down because the initial equity investment in the project will much higher.

☐   The NPV will remain unchanged because the financing mix should not affect the NPV.

☐   The NPV might go up or down, depending on . . .

Explain your answer.

Properties of the NPV Rule
The NPV has several important properties that make it an attractive decision rule.

1. NPVs Are Additive   The NPVs of individual projects can be aggregated to arrive at a cumulative NPV for a business or a division. No other investment decision rule has this property. The property itself has a number of implications.

- The value of a firm can be written in terms of the present values of the cash flows of the projects it has already taken on as well as the expected NPVs of prospective future projects:

$$\text{Value of a Firm} = \sum \text{Present Value of Cash Flows on Projects in Place}$$

$$+ \sum \text{NPV of Cash Flows on Expected Future Projects}$$

  The first term in this equation captures the value of assets in place, whereas the second term measures the value of *expected future growth*. Note that the present value of projects in place is based on anticipated future cash flows on these projects.

- When a firm terminates an existing project that has a negative present value based on anticipated future cash flows, the value of the firm will increase by that amount. Similarly, when a firm invests in a new project with an expected negative NPV, the value of the firm will decrease by that amount.

- When a firm divests itself of an existing asset, the price received for that asset will affect the value of the firm. If the price received exceeds the present value of the anticipated cash flows on that project to the firm, the value of the firm will increase with the divestiture; otherwise, it will decrease.

- When a firm invests in a new project with a positive NPV, the value of the firm will be affected depending on whether the NPV meets expectations. For example, a firm like Microsoft is expected to take on high positive NPV projects, and this expectation is built into value. Even if the new projects taken on by Microsoft have positive NPV, there may be a drop in value if the NPV does not meet the high expectations of financial markets.

- When a firm makes an acquisition and pays a price that exceeds the present value of the expected cash flows from the firm being acquired, it is the equivalent of taking on a negative NPV project and will lead to a drop in value.

2. Intermediate Cash Flows Are Invested at the Hurdle Rate   Implicit in all present value calculations are assumptions about the rate at which intermediate cash flows get reinvested. The NPV rule assumes that intermediate cash flows on a projects—that is, cash flows that occur between the initiation and the end of the project—get reinvested at the **hurdle rate,** which is the cost of capital if the cash flows are to the firm and the cost of equity if the cash flows are to equity investors. Given that both the cost of equity and capital are based on the returns that can be made on alternative investments of equivalent risk, this assumption is reasonable.

3. NPV Calculations Allow for Expected Term Structure and Interest Rate Shifts   In all the examples throughout in this chapter, we have assumed that the discount rate remains unchanged over time. This is not always the case, however; the NPV can be computed using time-varying discount rates. The general formulation for the NPV rule is as follows:

$$\text{NPV of Project} = \sum_{t=1}^{t=N} \frac{CF_t}{\prod_{j=1}^{j=t}(1 + r_j)} - \text{Initial Investment}$$

where CF_t = cash flow in period t, r_t = one-period discount rate that applies to period t, and N = life of the project. The discount rates can change for three reasons:

- The level of interest rates may change over time, and the term structure may provide some insight on expected rates in the future.
- The risk characteristics of the project may be expected to change in a predictable way over time, resulting in changes in the discount rate.
- The financing mix on the project may change over time, resulting in changes in both the cost of equity and the cost of capital.

Hurdle Rate: The minimum acceptable rate of return that a firm will accept for taking a given project.

ILLUSTRATION 5.15   NPV Calculation with Time-Varying Discount Rates
Assume that you are analyzing a four-year project investing in computer software development. Furthermore, assume that the technological uncertainty associated with the software industry leads to higher discount rates in future years.

Cash Flow	$300	$400	$500	$600
Discount Rate	10%	11%	12%	13%
Investment	<$1,000>			

The present value of each of the cash flows can be computed as follows.

PV of Cash Flow in Year 1 = $300/1.10 = $272.72

PV of Cash Flow in Year 2 = $400/(1.10 × 1.11) = $327.60

PV of Cash Flow in Year 3 = $500/(1.10 × 1.11 × 1.12) = $365.63

PV of Cash Flow in Year 4 = $600/(1.10 × 1.11 × 1.12 × 1.13) = $388.27

NPV of Project = $272.72 + $327.60 + $365.63 + $388.27 − $1,000.00 = $354.23

5.11   CHANGING DISCOUNT RATES AND NPV

In the analysis just done, assume that you had been asked to use one discount rate for all of the cash flows. Is there a discount rate that would yield the same NPV as the one above?

☐   Yes

☐   No

If yes, how would you interpret this discount rate?

Biases, Limitations, and Caveats
In spite of its advantages and its linkage to the objective of value maximization, the NPV rule continues to have its detractors, who point out two limitations.

- The NPV is stated in absolute rather than relative terms and does not therefore factor in the scale of the projects. Thus, project A may have an NPV of $200, whereas project B has an NPV of $100, but project A may require an initial investment that is 10 or 100 times larger than project B. Proponents of the NPV rule argue that it is surplus value, over and above the hurdle rate, no matter what the investment.

- The NPV rule does not control for the life of the project. Consequently, when comparing mutually exclusive projects with different lifetimes, the NPV rule is biased toward longer-term projects.

Internal Rate of Return
The **internal rate of return (IRR)** is based on discounted cash flows. Unlike the NPV rule, however, it takes into account the project's scale. It is the discounted cash flow analog to the accounting rates of return. Again, in general terms, the IRR is that discount rate that makes the NPV of a project equal to zero. To illustrate, consider again the project described at the beginning of the NPV discussion.

Internal Rate of Return = 24.89%

At the internal rate of return, the NPV of this project is zero. The linkage between the NPV and the IRR is most obvious when the NPV is graphed as a function of the discount rate in a **net present value profile.** An NPV profile for the project described is illustrated in Figure 5.4.

The NPV profile provides several insights on the project's viability. First, the internal rate of return is clear from the graph—it is the point at which the profile crosses the *x*-axis. Second, it provides a measure of how sensitive the NPV—and, by extension, the project decision—is to changes in the discount rate. The slope of the NPV profile is a measure of the discount rate sensitivity of the project. Third, when mutually exclusive projects are being analyzed, graphing both NPV profiles together

Figure 5.4   NPV Profile

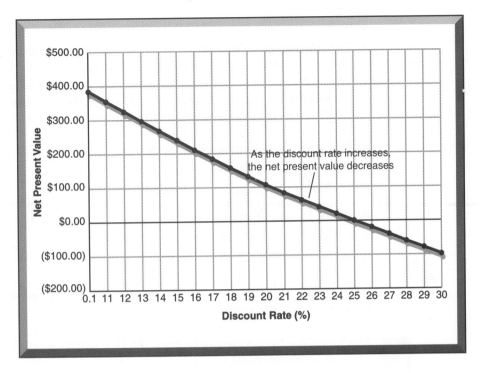

provides a measure of the break-even discount rate—the rate at which the decision maker will be indifferent between the two projects.

Internal Rate of Return (IRR): The rate of return earned by the project based on cash flows, allowing for the time value of money.

NPV Profile: This measures the sensitivity of the NPV to changes in the discount rate.

5.12   DISCOUNT RATES AND NPV

In the project just described, the NPV decreased as the discount rate was increased. Will this always be the case?

☐ Yes

☐ No

If no, when might the NPV go up as the discount rate is increased?

Using the IRR

One advantage of the IRR is that it can be computed even in cases where the hurdle rate is unknown. While this is true for the calculation of the IRR, it is *not true* when the decision maker has to use the IRR to decide whether to invest in a project. At that stage in the process, the IRR has to be compared to the hurdle rate—if the IRR is greater than the hurdle rate, the project is a good one; alternatively, the project should be rejected.

Like the NPV, the IRR can be computed in one of two ways:

- The IRR can be calculated based on the cash flows to the firm and the total investment in the project. This IRR has to be compared to the cost of capital.
- The IRR can be calculated based on the cash flows to equity and the equity investment in the project. If it is estimated with these cash flows, it has to be compared to the cost of equity, which should reflect the riskiness of the project.

A. IRR is computed on cash flows to the firm

If the IRR > Cost of Capital $\rightarrow$ Accept the Project

If the IRR < Cost of Capital $\rightarrow$ Reject the Project

B. IRR is computed on cash flows to equity

If the IRR > Cost of Equity $\rightarrow$ Accept the Project

If the IRR < Cost of Equity $\rightarrow$ Reject the Project

When choosing between projects of equivalent risk, the project with the higher IRR is viewed as the better project.

 This spreadsheet allows you to estimate the IRR based on cash flows to the firm on a project (**capbudgeq.xls**).

ILLUSTRATION 5.16   Estimating the IRR Based on Cash Flows to the Firm: Disneyworld Bangkok

The cash flows to the firm from Disneyworld Bangkok, are used to arrive at a NPV profile for the project in Figure 5.5.

The IRR in dollar terms on this project is 11.97 percent, which is *higher* than the cost of capital of 10.66 percent. These results are consistent with the findings from the NPV rule, which also recommended investing in the theme park.[10]

ILLUSTRATION 5.17   Estimating IRR Based on Cash Flows to Equity: Aracruz Celulose

The NPV profile depicted in Figure 5.6 is based on the equity investment and the cash flows to equity estimated for the paper plant for Aracruz.

The IRR (in real terms) on this project is 18.39 percent, which is *higher* than the real cost of equity of 11.46 percent. Again, these results are consistent with the findings from the NPV rule, which also recommended accepting this investment.

Biases, Limitations, and Caveats

The IRR is the most widely used discounted cash flow rule in investment analysis, but it does have some serious limitations.

---

[10]The terminal value of the project itself is a function of the discount rate used. That is why the IRR function in Excel will not yield the right answer. Instead, the NPV has to be recomputed at every discount rate and the IRR is the point at which the NPV = 0.

Figure 5.5   NPV Profile for Disney Theme Park

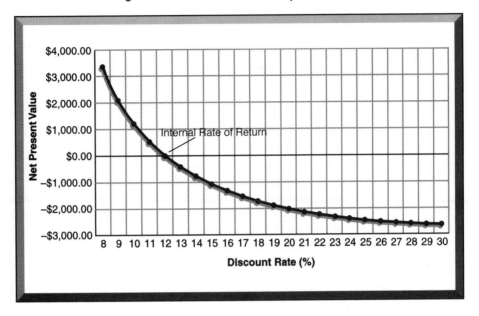

Figure 5.6   NPV Profile on Equity Investment in Paper Plant: Aracruz

Figure 5.7 Cash Flows on Investment

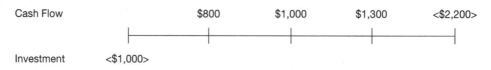

Cash Flow $800 $1,000 $1,300   <$2,200>

Investment   <$1,000>

- Because the IRR is a scaled measure, it tends to bias decision makers toward smaller projects, which are much more likely to yield high percentage returns, and away from larger ones.

- There are a number of scenarios in which the IRR cannot be computed or is not meaningful as a decision tool. The first is when there is no or only a very small initial investment and the investment is spread over time. In such cases, the IRR cannot be computed or, if computed, is likely to be meaningless. The second is when there is more than one internal rate of return for a project, and it is not clear which one the decision maker should use.

ILLUSTRATION **5.18** **Multiple IRR Projects**

Consider a project to manufacture and sell a consumer product, with a hurdle rate of 12 percent, that has a four-year life and cash flows over those four years. The project, which requires the licensing of a trademark, requires a large payment at the end of the fourth year. Figure 5.7 shows the cash flows.

The NPV profile for this project, shown in Figure 5.8, reflects the problems that arise with the IRR measure.

As you can see, this project has two IRRs: 6.60 percent and 36.55 percent. Because the hurdle rate falls between these two IRRs, the decision on whether to take the project will change depending on which IRR is used. To make the right decision in this case, the decision maker would have to look at the NPV profile. If, as in this case, the NPV is positive at the hurdle rate, the project should be accepted. If the NPV is negative at the hurdle rate, the project should be rejected.

IN PRACTICE: MULTIPLE IRRS: WHY THEY EXIST AND WHAT TO DO ABOUT THEM

The IRR can be viewed mathematically as a root to the present value equation for cash flows. In the conventional project, where there is an initial investment and positive cash flows thereafter, there is only one sign change in the cash flows, and one root—that is, there is a unique IRR. When there is more than one sign change in the cash flows, there will be more than one IRR.[11] In Figure 5.7, for example, the cash flow changes sign from negative to positive in year one, and from positive to negative in year four, leading to two IRRs.

---

[11]Although the number of IRRs will be equal to the number of sign changes, some IRRs may be so far out of the realm of the ordinary (e.g., 10,000 percent) that they may not create the kinds of problems described here.

Lest this be viewed as some strange artifact that is unlikely to happen in the real world, note that many long-term projects require substantial reinvestment at intermediate points in the project and that these reinvestments may cause the cash flows in those years to become negative. When this happens, the IRR approach will run into trouble.

There are a number of solutions suggested to the multiple IRR problems. One is to use the hurdle rate to bring the negative cash flows from intermediate periods back to the present. Another is to construct an NPV profile. In either case, it is much simpler to estimate and use the NPV. ■

Comparing NPV and IRR

The NPV and the IRR are viewed as competing investment decision rules, and they generally yield similar conclusions in most cases. The differences between the two rules are most visible when decision makers are choosing between mutually exclusive projects.

Differences in Scale

The NPV of a project is stated in dollar terms and does not factor in the scale of the project. The IRR, by contrast, is a percentage rate of return, which is standardized for the scale of the project. When choosing between mutually exclusive projects with very different scales, this can lead to different conclusions.

Figure 5.8 NPV Profile for Multiple IRR Project

Figure 5.9   NPV and IRR: Different Scale Projects

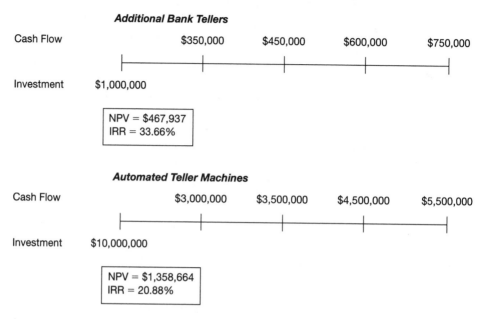

Additional Bank Tellers

Cash Flow $350,000 $450,000 $600,000 $750,000

Investment $1,000,000

NPV = $467,937
IRR = 33.66%

Automated Teller Machines

Cash Flow $3,000,000 $3,500,000 $4,500,000 $5,500,000

Investment $10,000,000

NPV = $1,358,664
IRR = 20.88%

ILLUSTRATION 5.19   NPV and IRR for Projects of Different Scale

Assume that you are a small bank and you are comparing two mutually exclusive projects. The first project, which is hire four extra tellers at the branches that you operate, requires an initial investment of $1 million and produces the cash flow revenues shown in Figure 5.9. The second project requires an investment of $10 million in an automated teller machine (ATM) and is likely to produce the much higher cash flows (shown in Figure 5.9) as well. The hurdle rate is 15 percent for both projects.

The two decision rules yield different results. The NPV rule suggests that project B is the better project, whereas the IRR rule leans toward project A. This is not surprising, given the differences in scale.

Which rule yields the better decision? The answer depends on the **capital rationing** constraints faced by the business making the decision. When there are no capital rationing constraints (i.e., the firm has the capacity to raise as much capital as it needs to take prospective projects), the NPV rule provides the right answer—project B should be picked over project A. If the firm has limited capital and has to apportion it across a number of good projects, however, then taking Project B may lead to the rejection of good projects later on. In those cases, the IRR rule may provide the better solution. The capital rationing question is dealt with in more detail in Chapter 6.

Capital Rationing: The scenario where the firm does not have sufficient funds—either on hand or in terms of access to markets—to take on all of the good projects it might have.

Figure 5.10   NPV and IRR: Reinvestment Assumption

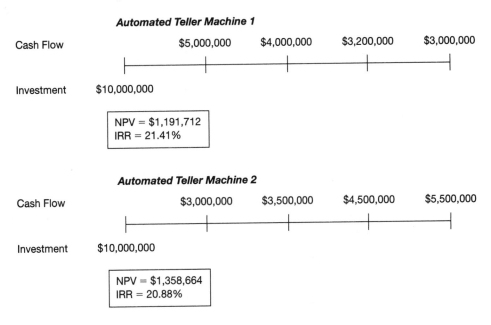

Differences in Reinvestment Rate Assumption

Although the differences between the NPV rule and the IRR rules due to scale are fairly obvious, there is a subtler and much more significant difference between them relating to the reinvestment of intermediate cash flows. As pointed out earlier, the NPV rule assumes that intermediate cash flows are reinvested at the hurdle rate, whereas the IRR rule assumes that intermediate cash flows are reinvested at the IRR. As a consequence, the two rules can yield different conclusions, even for projects with the same scale, as illustrated in Figure 5.10.

In this case, the NPV rule ranks the second investment higher, whereas the IRR rule ranks the first investment as the better project. The differences arise because the NPV rule assumes that intermediate cash flows get invested at the hurdle rate, which is 15 percent. The IRR rule assumes that intermediate cash flows get reinvested at the IRR of that project. Although both projects are affected by this assumption, it has a much greater effect for project A, which has higher cash flows earlier on. The reinvestment assumption is made clearer if the expected end balance is estimated under each rule.

$$\text{End Balance for ATM1 with IRR of } 21.41\% = \$10,000,000 \times 1.2141^4$$
$$= \$21,730,887$$

$$\text{End Balance for ATM2 with IRR of } 20.88\% = \$10,000,000 \times 1.2088^4$$
$$= \$21,353,673$$

To arrive at these end balances, however, the cash flows in years one, two, and three will have to be reinvested at the IRR. If they are reinvested at a lower rate, the end balance on these projects will be lower, and the actual return earned will be lower than the IRR even though the cash flows on the project came in as anticipated.

The reinvestment rate assumption made by the IRR rule creates more serious consequences the longer the term of the project and the higher the IRR, because it implicitly assumes that the firm has and will continue to have a fountain of projects yielding returns similar to that earned by the project under consideration.

IN PRACTICE: A SOLUTION TO THE REINVESTMENT RATE PROBLEM: THE MODIFIED INTERNAL RATE OF RETURN

One solution that has been suggested for the reinvestment rate assumption is to assume that intermediate cash flows get reinvested at the hurdle rate—the cost of equity if the cash flows are to equity investors and the cost of capital if they are to the firm—and to calculate the IRR from the initial investment and the terminal value. This approach yields what is called the **modified internal rate of return (MIRR),** as illustrated in Figure 5.11, for a four-year investment with a hurdle rate of 15 percent.

The MIRR is lower than the IRR because the intermediate cash flows are invested at the hurdle rate of 15 percent instead of the IRR of 24.89 percent.

There are many who believe that the MIRR is neither fish nor fowl, because it is a mix of the NPV rule and the IRR rule. From a practical standpoint, the MIRR becomes a weighted average of the return on an individual project and the hurdle rate the firm uses, with the weights on each depending on the magnitude and

Figure 5.11   IRR versus MIRR

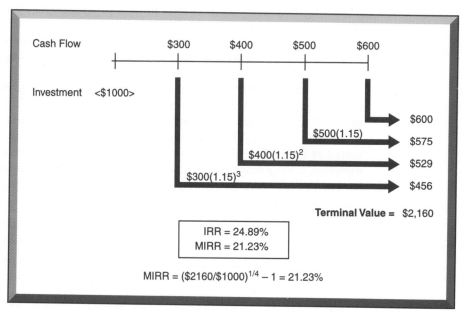

timing of the cash flows—the larger and earlier the cash flows on the project, the greater the weight attached to the hurdle rate. Furthermore, the MIRR approach will yield the same choices as the NPV approach for projects of the same scales and lives. ∎

Modified Internal Rate of Return (MIRR): The IRR computed on the assumption that intermediate cash flows are reinvested at the hurdle rate.

WHERE DO GOOD PROJECTS COME FROM?

In the process of analyzing new investments in the preceding chapters, we have contended that good projects have a positive NPV and earn an IRR greater than the hurdle rate. Although these criteria are certainly valid from a measurement standpoint, they do not address the deeper questions about good projects, including the economic conditions that make for a good project and why it is that some firms have a more ready supply of good projects than others.

Implicit in the definition of a good project is the existence of **excess returns** to the firm considering the project. In a competitive market for real investments, the existence of these excess returns should act as a magnet, attracting competitors to take on similar investments. In the process, the excess returns should dissipate over time; how quickly they dissipate will depend on the ease with which competition can enter the market and provide close substitutes and on the magnitude of any differential advantages that the firm with the good projects might possess. Consider an extreme scenario, whereby the firm with the good projects has no differential advantage in cost or product quality over its competitors, and new competitors can enter the market easily and at low cost to provide substitutes. In this case, the excess returns on these projects should disappear very quickly.

An integral basis for the existence of a good project is therefore the creation and maintenance of barriers to new or existing competitors taking on equivalent or similar projects. These barriers can take different forms, including

a. *Economies of Scale* Some projects might earn high returns only if they are done on a large scale, thus restricting competition from smaller companies. In such cases, large companies in this line of business may be able to continue to earn supernormal returns on their projects because smaller competitors will not be able to replicate them.

b. *Cost Advantages* A business might work at establishing a cost advantage over its competitors, either by being more efficient or by taking advantage of arrangements that its competitors cannot use. For example, in the late 1980s, Southwest Airlines was able to establish a cost advantage over its larger competitors, such as American Airlines and United, and the company exploited this cost advantage to earn much higher returns.

c. *Capital Requirements* Entry into some businesses might require such large investments that it discourages competitors from entering, even though projects in those businesses may earn above-market returns. For example, assume that Boeing is faced with a large number of high-return projects in the aerospace business. Although this scenario would normally attract competitors, the huge initial investment needed to enter this business would enable Boeing to continue to earn these high returns.

d. *Product Differentiation* Some businesses continue to earn excess returns by differentiating their products from those of their competitors, leading to either higher profit margins or higher sales. This differentiation can be created in a number of ways—through effective advertising and promotion (Coca-Cola), technical expertise (Sony), better service (Nordstrom), and responsiveness to customer needs.

e. *Access to Distribution Channels* Those firms that have much better access to the distribution channels for their products than their competitors are better able to earn excess returns. In some cases, the restricted access to outsiders is due to tradition or loyalty to existing competitors. In other cases, the firm may actually own the distribution channel, and competitors may not be able to develop their own distribution channels because the costs are prohibitive.

f. *Legal and Government Barriers* In some cases, a firm may be able to exploit investment opportunities without worrying about competition because of restrictions on competitors from product patents the firm may own or government restrictions on competitive entry.

Excess Returns: Returns that are greater than the returns that would normally be earned for an investment of equivalent risk.

Quality of Management and Project Quality

In the preceding section we examined some of the factors that determine the attractiveness of the projects a firm will face. Some factors, such as government restrictions on entry, may largely be out of the control of incumbent management, but there are other factors that can clearly be influenced by management.[12] Considering each of the factors already discussed, for instance, we would argue that a good management team can increase both the number of and the excess returns on available projects by

- *investing in projects that exploit any economies of scale that the firm may possess;* in addition, management can look for ways it can create economies of scale in the firm's existing operations.

- *establishing and nurturing cost advantages over its competitors;* some cost advantages may arise from labor negotiations, and others may result from long-term strategic decisions made by the firm.

---

[12]When government policy is influenced by lobbying by firms, it can be argued that even these factors may be affected by the management of a firm.

- *taking actions that increase the initial cost for new entrants into the business;* one of the primary reasons Microsoft was able to dominate the computer software market in the early 1990s was its ability to increase the investment needed to develop and market new business software programs.

- *nurturing markets in which the company's differential advantage is greatest, in terms of either cost of delivery or brand name value*   In some cases, this will involve expanding into foreign markets, as both Levi Strauss and McDonald's did in the 1980s to exploit their brand name recognition in those markets. In other cases, this may require concentrating on segments of an existing market, as The Gap did, when it opened its Old Navy stores to cater to more bargain-conscious consumers.

- *improving the firm's reputation for customer service and product delivery;* this will enable the firm to increase both profits and returns. One of the primary factors behind Chrysler's financial recovery in the 1980s was the company's ability to establish a reputation for producing good-quality cars and minivans.

- *developing distribution channels that are unique and cannot be easily accessed by competitors*   Avon, for instance, employed a large sales force to go door to door to reach consumers who could not be reached by other distribution channels.

- *obtaining patents on products or technologies that keep out the competition and earn high returns;* doing so may require large investments in R&D over time. It can be argued that success of pharmaceutical companies, small and large, can be traced to their capacity to patent blockbuster drugs.

Although the quality of management is typically related to the quality of projects a firm possesses, a good management team does not guarantee the existence of good projects. In fact, there is a rather large element of chance involved in the process; even the best-laid plans of the management team to create project opportunities may come to naught if circumstances conspire against them—a recession may upend a retailer, or an oil price shock may cause an airline to lose money.

The Role of Acquisitions

As firms mature and increase in size, they are often confronted with a quandary. Instead of being cash-poor and project-rich, they find that their existing projects generate far more in cash than they have available projects in which to invest. This can be attributed partly to size and partly to competition. As they face up to their new status as cash-rich companies, with limited investment opportunities, acquiring other firms with a ready supply of high-return projects looks like an attractive option, but there is a catch. If these firms are publicly traded, the market price already reflects the expected higher returns not only on existing projects but also on expected future projects. In terms of present value, the value of a firm can be written as

Value of Firm = Present Value of Cash Flows from Existing Projects
    + Net Present Value of Cash Flows from Expected Future Projects

Thus, firms that are earning excess returns on their existing projects and are expected to maintain this status in the future will sell at prices that reflects these expectations. Accordingly, even if the cash-rich firm pays a fair price to acquire one of these firms, it has to earn more than the expected excess returns to be able to claim any premium from the acquisition. To put this in perspective, assume that you are considering the acquisition of a firm that is earning 25 percent on its projects, when the cost of capital on these projects is 12 percent, and it is expected to maintain these high returns for the foreseeable future. A fair price attached to this acquisition will reflect this expectation. All this implies that an acquisition will earn excess returns for the acquirer if and only if one of the following conditions holds:

- The acquisition is done at a price below the fair price (i.e., the company is significantly undervalued).
- The acquisition is done at a price that reflects the expectation that the firm will earn 25 percent but the acquirer manages to earn an even higher return, say 30 percent, on future projects.
- The acquisition enables the firm to take on investments that it would not have taken on as an independent firm; the NPV of these additional projects will then be a bonus that is earned by the acquiring firm. This is the essence of synergy, and we will deal with how best to measure it in the next chapter.
- The acquisition lowers the cost of capital for the acquired company, leading to an increase in NPV, even though the returns may come in as expected.[13]

Overall, it is clear that internally generated projects have better odds of success than do acquisitions since we do not pay a premium for market expectations up front.

5.13   FIRM VALUE AND OVERPAYMENT ON ACQUISITIONS

Megatech Corporation, a large software firm with a market value for its equity of $100 million, announces that it will be acquiring FastMail Corporation, a smaller software firm, for $15 million. On the announcement, Megatech's stock price drops by 3 percent. Based on these facts, estimate the amount the market thinks Megatech should have paid for FastMail.

☐ $15 million
☐ $3 million
☐ $12 million

How does NPV additivity enter into your answer?

---

[13]This can be difficult to do, because the cost of capital reflects market risk (from equity) and default risk (from debt). An acquisition cannot reduce market risk, although it can reduce firm-specific risk. It is possible that the default risk of a target firm can decrease when it is acquired by a more stable, safer firm but the latter is then providing a subsidy to the former.

CONCLUSION

Investment analysis is arguably the most important part of corporate financial analysis. In this chapter we defined the scope of investment analysis and examined a range of investment analysis techniques, ranging from accounting rate of return measures, such as return of equity and return on capital, to discounted cash flow techniques, such as NPV and IRR. In general, it can be argued that:

- Any decision that requires the use of resources is an investment decision; thus, investment decisions cover everything from broad strategic decisions such as acquisitions at one extreme to narrower operating decisions such as how much inventory to carry at the other.
- There are two basic approaches to investment analysis; in the equity approach, the returns to equity investors from a project are measured against the cost of equity to decide on whether to take a project; in the firm approach, the returns to all investors in the firm are measured against the cost of capital to arrive at the same judgment.
- Accounting rate of return measures, such as return on equity or return on capital, generally work better for projects that have large initial investments, earnings that are roughly equal to the cash flows, and level earnings over time. For most projects, accounting returns will increase over time, as the book value of the assets is depreciated.
- Payback, which looks at how quickly a project returns its initial investment in nominal cash flow terms, is a useful secondary measure of project performance or a measure of risk, but it is not a very effective primary technique because it does not consider cash flows after the initial investment is recouped. Discounted cash flow methods provide the best measures of true returns on projects because they are based on cash flows and consider the time value of money.
- Among discounted cash flow methods, NPV provides an unscaled measure, whereas IRR provides a scaled measure of project performance. Both methods require the same information, and for the most part they provide the same conclusions when used to analyze independent projects. The IRR does tend to overstate the return on good projects because it assumes that intermediate cash flows get reinvested at the IRR. When analyzing mutually exclusive projects, the IRR is biased toward smaller projects and may be the more appropriate decision rule for firms that have capital constraints.

LIVE CASE STUDY

ESTIMATING EARNINGS AND CASH FLOWS (ONLY IF FEASIBLE)

Objective: To estimate earnings and cash flows on a typical project for the firm, to analyze a firm's existing investments, and identify differential advantages that explain excess returns on existing investments.

Key Questions

- Does your firm have a typical investment?
- If so, can you estimate the earnings and cash flows on a typical investment?
- What are the firm's competitive strengths and differential advantages, if any?
- Does this firm earn excess returns on its existing projects? If yes, can it maintain the competitive strengths that allowed it to earn these excess returns? If not, what can it do to start earning excess returns on its projects?
- Does the firm have poor investments? If so, what might be the reasons for the poor returns?

Framework for Analysis

1. *Typical Investment*
   - Does your firm take a few or several investments each year?
   - Do these investments have much in common?
   - If so, what do they have in common and what are the differences?

2. *Earnings and Cash Flows*
   - What is the typical life of an investment made by your firm?
   - What is the pattern of earnings on such an investment?
   - What is the pattern of cash flows on such an investment?
   - Based on the company's aggregate numbers, can you estimate the earnings and cash flows on a hypothetical investment?

3. *Analyzing Existing Investments*
   - What is the accounting return that the firm earns on its existing investments? How does this compare with the cost of equity and capital?
   - What was the firm's economic value added in the most recent financial year? How does it compare with the previous year?
   - What, if anything, do the accounting returns and economic value added tell you about the quality of the firm's existing investments?

4. *Assessing Competitive Strengths*

- Who are the primary competitors to this firm, and how does the firm compare to them in terms of both quantitative (size, profitability, risk) and qualitative measures (quality of management, service)?

- Does the firm have any special strength that no other firm in the sector possesses?

- Does the firm lag other firms in the sector on any of the measures?

5. *Evaluating Sustainability of Competitive Strengths*

- Are the firm's competitors catching up with the firm on its strengths?

- Are there new competitors either in the market or on the horizon who could compete with the firm on its strengths?

Getting Information on Projects

Firms do describe their investments, though not in significant detail, in their annual reports. The statement of cash flows will provide some breakdown, as will the footnotes to the financial statements.

Online Sources of Information:
See **www.stern.nyu.edu/~adamodar/cfin2E/project/data.htm**.

PROBLEMS AND QUESTIONS

(In the problems below, you can use a risk premium of 5.5 percent and a tax rate of 40 percent if none is specified.)

1. You have been given the following information on a project:
   - It has a five-year lifetime
   - The initial investment in the project will be $25 million, and the investment will be depreciated straight line, down to a salvage value of $10 million at the end of the fifth year.
   - The revenues are expected to be $20 million next year and to grow 10 percent a year after that for the remaining four years.
   - The cost of goods sold, excluding depreciation, is expected to be 50 percent of revenues.
   - The tax rate is 40 percent.

   a. Estimate the pretax return on capital, by year and on average, for the project.
   b. Estimate the after-tax return on capital, by year and on average, for the project.
   c. If the firm faced a cost of capital of 12 percent, should it take this project?

2. Now assume that the facts in Problem 1 remain unchanged except for the depreciation method, which is switched to an accelerated method with the following depreciation schedule:

Year	% of Depreciable Asset
1	40%
2	24%
3	14.4%
4	13.3%
5	13.3%

   Depreciable Asset = Initial Investment − Salvage Value

   a. Estimate the pretax return on capital, by year and on average, for the project.
   b. Estimate the after-tax return on capital, by year and on average, for the project.
   c. If the firm faced a cost of capital of 12 percent, should it take this project?

3. Consider again the project described in Problem 1 (assume that the depreciation reverts to a straight line). Assume that 40 percent of the initial investment for the project will be financed with debt, with an annual interest rate of 10 percent and a balloon payment of the principal at the end of the fifth year.

   a. Estimate the return on equity, by year and on average, for this project.
   b. If the cost of equity is 15 percent, should the firm take this project?

4. Answer true or false to the following statements:
   a. The return on equity for a project will always be higher than the return on capital on the same project.
   b. If the return on capital is less than the cost of equity, the project should be rejected.
   c. Projects with high financial leverage will have higher interest expenses and lower net income than projects with low financial leverage and thus end up with a lower return on equity.
   d. Increasing the depreciation on an asset will increase the estimated return on capital and equity on the project.
   e. The average return on equity on a project over its lifetime will increase if we switch from straight line to double declining balance depreciation.

5. Under what conditions will the return on equity on a project be equal to the IRR, estimated from cash flows to equity investors, on the same project?

6. You are provided with the projected income statements for a project:

Year	1	2	3	4
Revenues ($)	$10,000	$11,000	$12,000	$13,000
− Cost of goods sold ($)	$4,000	$4,400	$4,800	$5,200
− Depreciation	$4,000	$3,000	$2,000	$1,000
= EBIT	$2,000	$3,600	$5,200	$6,800

   - The tax rate is 40 percent.
   - The project required an initial investment of $15,000 and an additional investment of $2,000 at the end of year two.
   - The working capital is anticipated to be 10 percent of revenues, and the working capital

investment has to be made at the beginning of each period.

a. Estimate the free cash flow to the firm for each of the four years.

b. Estimate the payback period for investors in the firm.

c. Estimate the NPV to investors in the firm, if the cost of capital is 12 percent. Would you accept the project?

d. Estimate the IRR to investors in the firm. Would you accept the project?

7. Consider the project described in Problem 6. Assume that the firm plans to finance 40 percent of its net capital expenditure and working capital needs with debt.

a. Estimate the cash flow to equity for each of the four years.

b. Estimate the payback period for equity investors in the firm.

c. Estimate the NPV to equity investors if the cost of equity is 16 percent. Would you accept the project?

d. Estimate the IRR to equity investors in the firm. Would you accept the project?

8. You are provided with the following cash flows on a project:

Year	Cash Flow to Firm ($)
0	–10,000,000
1	$4,000,000
2	$5,000,000
3	$6,000,000

Plot the NPV profile for this project. What is the IRR? If this firm had a cost of capital of 10 percent and a cost of equity of 15 percent, would you accept this project?

9. You have estimated the following cash flows on a project:

Year	Cash Flow to Equity ($)
0	–$4,750,000
1	$4,000,000
2	$4,000,000
3	–$3,000,000

Plot the NPV profile for this project. What is the IRR? If the cost of equity is 16 percent, would you accept this project?

10. Estimate the MIRR for the project described in Problem 9. Does it change your decision on accepting this project?

11. You are analyzing two mutually exclusive projects with the following cash flows:

Year	A	B
0	–$4,000,000	–$4,000,000
1	$2,000,000	$1,000,000
2	$1,500,000	$1,500,000
3	$1,250,000	$1,700,000
4	$1,000,000	$2,400,000

a. Estimate the NPV of each project, assuming a cost of capital of 10 percent. Which is the better project?

b. Estimate the IRR for each project. Which is the better project?

c. What reinvestment rate assumptions are made by each of these rules? Can you show the effect on future cash flows of these assumptions?

d. What is the MIRR on each of these projects?

12. You have a project that does not require an initial investment but has its expenses spread over the life of the project. Can the IRR be estimated for this project? Why or why not?

13. Businesses with severe capital rationing constraints should use IRR more than NPV. Do you agree? Explain.

14. You have to pick between three mutually exclusive projects with the following cash flows to the firm:

Year	Project A	Project B	Project C
0	–$10,000	$5,000	–$15,000
1	$8,000	$5,000	$10,000
2	$7,000	–$8,000	$10,000

The cost of capital is 12 percent.

a. Which project would you pick using the NPV rule?

b. Which project would you pick using the IRR rule?

c. How would you explain the differences between the two rules? Which one would you rely on to make your choice?

15. You are analyzing an investment decision, in which you will have to make an initial investment of $10 million and you will be generating annual cash flows to the firm of $2 million every year, growing at 5 percent a year, forever.
  a. Estimate the NPV of this project, if the cost of capital is 10 percent.
  b. Estimate the IRR of this project.

16. You are analyzing a project with a thirty-year lifetime, with the following characteristics:
  - The project will require an initial investment of $20 million and additional investments of $5 million in year ten and $5 million in year twenty.
  - The project will generate earnings before interest and taxes of $3 million each year. (The tax rate is 40 percent.)
  - The depreciation will amount to $500,000 each year, and the salvage value of the equipment will be equal to the remaining book value at the end of year thirty.
  - The cost of capital is 12.5 percent.
  a. Estimate the NPV of this project.
  b. Estimate the IRR on this project. What might be some of the problems in estimating the IRR for this project?

17. You are trying to estimate the NPV of a three-year project, where the discount rate is expected to change over time.

Year	Cash Flow to Firm	Discount Rate
0	−$15,000	9.5%
1	$5,000	10.5%
2	$5,000	11.5%
3	$10,000	12.5%

  a. Estimate the NPV of this project. Would you take this project?
  b. Estimate the IRR of this project. How would you use the IRR to decide whether to take this project?

18. Barring the case of multiple IRRs, is it possible for the NPV of a project to be positive while the IRR is less than the hurdle rate? Explain.

19. You are helping a manufacturing firm decide whether it should invest in a new plant. The initial investment is expected to be $50 million, and the plant is expected to generate after-tax cash flows of $5 million a year for the next twenty years. There will be an additional investment of $20 million needed to upgrade the plant in ten years. If the discount rate is 10 percent,
  a. Estimate the NPV of the project.
  b. Prepare an NPV profile for this project.
  c. Estimate the IRR for this project. Is there any aspect of the cash flows that may prove to be a problem for calculating IRR?

20. You have been asked to analyze a project where the analyst has estimated the return on capital to be 37 percent over the ten-year lifetime of the project. The cost of capital is only 12 percent, but you have concerns about using the return on capital as an investment decision rule. Would it make a difference if you knew that the project was employing an accelerated depreciation method to compute depreciation? Why?

21. Accounting rates of return are based on accounting income and book value of investment, whereas internal rates of return are based on cash flows and take into account the time value of money. Under what conditions will the two approaches give you similar estimates?

CHAPTER 6

PROJECT INTERACTIONS, SIDE COSTS, AND SIDE BENEFITS

In much of our discussion so far, we have assessed projects independently of other projects that the firm already has or might have in the future. Disney, for instance, was able to look at Disneyworld Bangkok standing alone and analyze whether it was a good or bad investment. In reality, projects at most firms have interdependencies with and consequences for other projects. Disney may be able to increase both movie and merchandise revenues because of the new theme park in Thailand and may face higher advertising expenditures because of its Asian expansion.

In this chapter, we examine a number of scenarios in which the consideration of one project affects other projects. We start with the most extreme case, whereby investing in one project leads to the rejection of one or more other projects; this is the

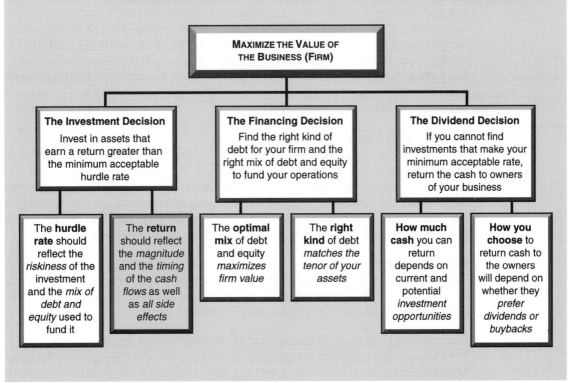

229

case when firms have to choose between mutually exclusive investments. We then consider a less extreme scenario, in which a firm with constraints on how much capital it can raise considers a new project. Accepting this project reduces the capital available for other projects that the firm considers later in the period and thus can affect their acceptance; this is the case of capital rationing.

Projects can create costs for existing investments by using shared resources or excess capacity, and we consider these side costs next. Projects sometimes generate benefits for other projects, and we analyze how to bring these benefits into the analysis. In the final part of the chapter, we introduce the notion that projects often have options embedded in them, and how ignoring these options can result in poor project decisions.

MUTUALLY EXCLUSIVE PROJECTS

Projects are mutually exclusive when only one of the set of projects can be accepted by a firm. Projects may be mutually exclusive for different reasons. They may each provide a way of getting a needed service, but any one of them is sufficient for the service, as is the case when the owner of a commercial building chooses among a number of different air conditioning or heating systems for the building. Alternatively, projects may provide alternative approaches to the future; a firm that has to choose between a "high-margin, low-volume" strategy and a "low-margin, high-volume" strategy for a product can choose only one of the two.

In choosing among mutually exclusive projects, we continue to use the same rules we developed for analyzing independent projects. The firm should choose the project that adds the most to its value. Although this concept is relatively straightforward when the projects are expected to generate cash flows for the same number of periods (have the same project life), as you will see, it can become more complicated when the projects have different lives.

Projects with Equal Lives

When comparing projects with the same lives, a business can make its decision in one of two ways. It can compute the net present value (NPV) of each project and choose the one with the highest positive NPV (if the projects generate revenue) or the one with the lowest negative NPV (if the projects create costs). Alternatively, it can compute the differential cash flow between two projects and base its decision on the NPV or the internal rate of return (IRR) of the differential cash flow.

Comparing NPVs

The simplest way of choosing among mutually exclusive projects with equal lives is to compute the NPVs of the projects and choose the one with the highest NPV. This decision rule is consistent with firm value maximization.

ILLUSTRATION 6.1   Mutually Exclusive Cost-Minimizing Projects with Equal Lives

Bookscape is choosing between alternative vendors who are offering phone systems. Both systems have five-year lives, and the appropriate cost of capital is 10 percent

Figure 6.1   Cash Flows on Phone Systems

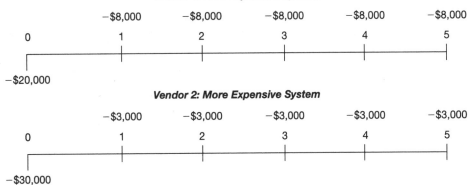

for both projects. Figure 6.1 summarizes the expected cash outflows on the two investments.

The more expensive system is also more efficient, resulting in lower annual costs. The NPVs of these two systems can be estimated as follows:

$$\text{NPV of Less Expensive System} = -\$20{,}000 - \$8{,}000\,\frac{\left[1-(1.10)^{-5}\right]}{0.10}$$

$$= -\$50{,}326$$

$$\text{NPV of More Expensive System} = -\$30{,}000 - \$3{,}000\,\frac{\left[1-(1.10)^{-5}\right]}{0.10}$$

$$= -\$41{,}372$$

The NPV of all costs is much lower with the second system, making it the better choice.

Differential Cash Flows

An alternative approach for choosing between two mutually exclusive projects is to compute the difference in cash flows each period between the two investments. Thus, if A and B are mutually exclusive projects with estimated cash flows over the same life time (n), the differential cash flows can be computed as shown in Figure 6.2.

In computing the differential cash flows, the project with the larger initial investment becomes the project against which the comparison is made. In practical terms, this means that Cash Flow $_{B-A}$ is computed if B has a higher initial investment than A, and Cash Flow$_{A-B}$ is computed if A has a higher initial investment than B. If we compare more than two projects, we still compare one pair at a time, and the less attractive project is dropped at each stage.

The differential cash flows can be used to compute the NPV, and the decision rule can be summarized as follows:

If $\text{NPV}_{B-A} > 0$ Project B is better than project A

If $\text{NPV}_{B-A} < 0$ Project A is better than project B

Figure 6.2   Estimating Differential Cash Flows

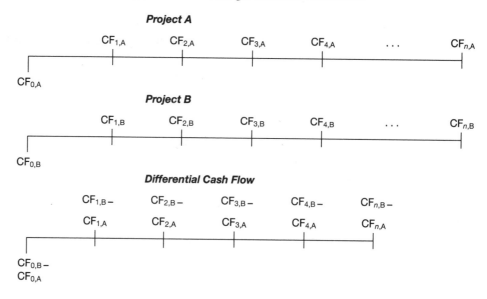

Notice two points about the differential NPV. The first is that it provides the same result as would have been obtained if the business had computed NPVs of the individual projects and then taken the difference between them.

$$NPV_{B-A} = NPV_B - NPV_A$$

The second is that this approach works only when the two projects being compared have the same risk level and discount rates, because only one discount rate can be used on the differential cash flows. By contrast, computing project-specific NPVs allows for the use of different discount rates on each project.

The differential cash flows can also be used to compute an IRR, which can guide us in selecting the better project.

If IRR_{B-A} > Hurdle Rate   Project B is better than project A

If IRR_{B-A} < Hurdle Rate   Project A is better than project B

Again, this approach works only if the projects are of equivalent risk.

6.1   Mutually Exclusive Projects with Different Risk Levels

When comparing mutually exclusive projects with different risk levels and discount rates, what discount rate should we use to discount the differential cash flows?

☐   The higher of the two discount rates

☐   The lower of the two discount rates

☐   An average of the two discount rates

☐   None of the above

Explain your answer.

Figure 6.3 Cash Flows on Phone Systems

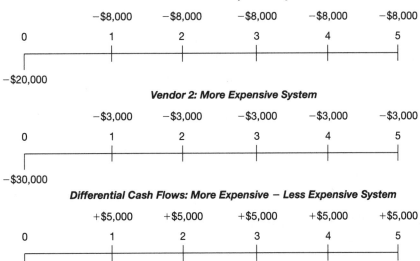

ILLUSTRATION **6.2** **Differential Cash Flows: NPV and IRR**

Consider again the phone systems analyzed in Illustration 6.1. The differential cash flows can be estimated as shown in Figure 6.3.

The more expensive system costs $10,000 more to install but saves Bookscape $5,000 a year. Using the 10 percent discount rate, we estimate the NPV of the differential cash flows as follows:

$$\text{NPV of Differential Cash Flows} = -\$10{,}000 + \$5{,}000 \frac{[1 - (1.10)^{-5}]}{0.10}$$

$$= +\$8{,}954$$

This NPV is equal to the difference between the NPVs of the individual projects, and it indicates that the system that costs more up front is also the better system from the viewpoint of NPV. The IRR of the differential cash flows is 41.04 percent, which is higher than the discount rate of 10 percent, once again suggesting that the more expensive system is the better one from a financial standpoint.

Projects with Different Lives

In many cases, firms have to choose among projects with different lives.[1] In doing so, they can no longer rely solely on the NPV. This is so because, as a nonscaled figure, the

---

[1]G. W. Emery, 1982, "Some Guidelines for Evaluating Capital Investment Alternatives with Unequal Lives," *Financial Management,* 11, 14–19.

Figure 6.4 Cash Flows on Projects with Unequal Lives

NPV is likely to be higher for longer-term projects; the NPV of a project with only two years of cash flows is likely to be lower than one with thirty years of cash flows.

Assume that you are choosing between a five-year and a ten-year project, with the cash flows shown in Figure 6.4. A discount rate of 12 percent applies for each.

The NPV of the first project is $442, whereas the NPV of the second project is $478. On the basis on NPV alone, the second project is better, but this analysis fails to factor in the additional NPV that could be made by the firm from years six to ten in the project with a five-year life.

In comparing a project with a shorter life to one with a longer life, the firm must consider that it will be able to invest again with the shorter-term project. Two conventional approaches—project replication and equivalent annuities—assume that when the current project ends, the firm will be able to invest in the same project or a very similar one.

Project Replication

One way of tackling the problem of different lives is to assume that projects can be replicated until they have the same lives. Thus, instead of comparing a five-year to a ten-year project, we can compute the NPV of investing in the five-year project twice and compare it to the NPV of the ten-year project. Figure 6.5 presents the resulting cash flows.

The NPV of investing in the five-year project twice is $693, whereas the net present value of the ten-year project remains at $478. These NPVs now can be compared because they correspond to two investment choices that have the same life.

This approach has limitations. On a practical level, it can become tedious to use when the number of projects increases and the lives do not fit neatly into multiples of each other. For example, an analyst using this approach to compare a seven-year, a nine-year, and a thirteen-year project would have to replicate these projects to 819 years to arrive at an equivalent life for all three. It is also difficult to argue that a firm's project choice will essentially remain unchanged over time, especially if the projects being compared are very attractive in terms of NPV.

Figure 6.5 Cash Flows on Projects with Unequal Lives: Replicated with Poorer Project

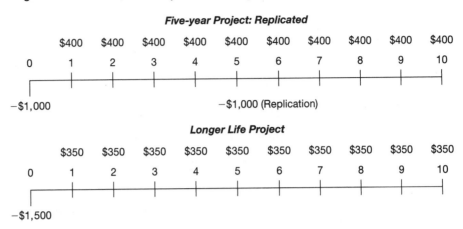

ILLUSTRATION 6.3 **Project Replication to Compare Projects with Different Lives**
Suppose you are deciding whether to buy a used car, which is inexpensive but does not give very good mileage, or a new car, which costs more but gets better mileage. The two options are listed in Table 6.1.

Assume that you drive 5,000 miles a year and that your cost of capital is 15 percent. This choice can be analyzed with replication.

Step 1: Replicate the projects until they have the same lifetime; in this case, that would mean buying used cars five consecutive times and new cars four consecutive times.

a. Buy a used car every four years for twenty years.

Maintenance costs: $1,500 every year for twenty years

Fuel costs: $1,000 every year for twenty years (5,000 miles at twenty cents a mile).

Table 6.1 **EXPECTED CASH FLOWS ON NEW VERSUS USED CAR**

	Used Car	New Car
Initial cost	$3,000	$8,000
Maintenance costs/year	$1,500	$1,000
Fuel costs/mile	$0.20	$0.05
Lifetime	4 years	5 years

b. Buy a new car every five years for twenty years

Year: 0   5   10   15   20

Investment: −8,000   −8,000   −8,000   −8,000

Maintenance costs: $1,000 every year for twenty years

Fuel costs: $250 every year for twenty years (5,000 miles at five cents a mile)

Step 2: Compute the NPV of each stream.

NPV of replicating used cars for 20 years = −22,225.61

NPV of replicating new cars for 20 years = −22,762.21

The NPV of the costs incurred by buying a used car every four years is less negative than the NPV of the costs incurred by buying a new car every five years, given that the cars will be driven 5,000 miles every year. As the mileage driven increases, however, the relative benefits of owning and driving the more efficient new car will also increase.

Equivalent Annuities

We can compare projects with different lives by converting their net present values into *equivalent annuities*. These equivalent annuities can be compared legitimately across projects with different lives. The NPV of any project can be converted into an annuity using the following calculation.

$$\text{Equivalent Annuity} = \text{Net Present Value} \times \frac{r}{\left[1 - (1 + r)^{-n}\right]}$$

where r = project discount rate and n = project lifetime. Note that the NPV of each project is converted into an annuity using that project's life and discount rate and that the second term in the equation is the annuity factor (see Appendix 3).[2] Thus, this approach is flexible enough to use on projects with different discount rates and lifetimes. Consider again the example of the five-year and ten-year projects from the previous section. The NPVs of these projects can be converted into annuities as follows:

$$\text{Equivalent Annuity for 5-Year Project} = \$442 \times \frac{0.12}{\left[1 - (1.12)^{-5}\right]} = \$122.62$$

$$\text{Equivalent Annuity for 10-Year Project} = \$478 \times \frac{0.12}{\left[1 - (1.12)^{-10}\right]}$$
$$= \$84.60$$

---

[2]This can be obtained just as easily using the present value functions in a financial calculator or a present value factor table.

The NPV of the five-year project is lower than the NPV of the ten-year project, but using equivalent annuities, the five-year project yields $37.98 more per year than the ten-year project.

Although this approach does not explicitly make an assumption of project replication, it does so implicitly. Consequently, it will always lead to the same decision rules as the replication method. The advantage is that the equivalent annuity method is less tedious and will continue to work even in the presence of projects with infinite lives.

 This spreadsheet allows you to compare projects with different lives, using the equivalent annuity approach (**eqann.xls**).

ILLUSTRATION 6.4   Equivalent Annuities to Choose between Projects with Different Lives
Consider again the choice between a new car and a used car described in Illustration 6.3. The equivalent annuities can be estimated for the two options as follows:

Step 1:   Compute the NPV of each project individually (without replication).

$$\text{NPV of Buying a Used Car} = -\$3,000 - \$2,500 \times \frac{[1 - (1.15)^{-4}]}{0.15}$$
$$= -\$10,137$$

$$\text{NPV of Buying a New Car} = -\$8,000 - \$1,250 \times \frac{[1 - (1.15)^{-5}]}{0.15}$$
$$= -\$12,190$$

Step 2:   Convert the NPVs into equivalent annuities.

$$\text{Equivalent Annuity of Buying a Used Car} = -\$10,137 \times \frac{0.15}{[1 - (1.15)^{-4}]}$$
$$= -\$3,551$$

$$\text{Equivalent Annuity of Buying a New Car} = -\$12,190 \times \frac{0.15}{[1 - (1.15)^{-5}]}$$
$$= -\$3,637$$

Based on the equivalent annuities of the two options, buying a used car is more economical than buying a new car.

Calculating Break-Even
When an investment that costs more initially but is more efficient and economical on an annual basis is compared with a less expensive and less efficient investment, the choice between the two will depend on how much the investments get used. For instance, in Illustration 6.4, the less expensive used car is the more economical choice if the mileage is less than 5,000 miles in a year. The more efficient new car

Figure 6.6 Equivalent Annual Costs as a Function of Miles Driven

will be the better choice if the car is driven more than 5,000 miles. The *break-even* is the number of miles at which the two alternatives provide the same equivalent annual cost, as is illustrated in Figure 6.6.

The break-even point occurs at roughly 5,500 miles; if there is a reasonable chance that the mileage driven will exceed this, the new car becomes the better option.

ILLUSTRATION 6.5 Using Equivalent Annuities as a General Approach for Multiple Projects

The equivalent annuity approach can be used to compare multiple projects with different lifetimes. For instance, assume that Disney is considering three storage alternatives for its consumer products division:

Alternative	Initial Investment	Annual Cost	Project Life
Build own storage system	$10 million	$0.5 million	Infinite
Rent storage system	$2 million	$1.5 million	12 years
Use third-party storage	—	$2.0 million	1 year

These projects have different lives; the equivalent annual costs have to be computed for the comparison. Because the cost of capital computed for the consumer products business in Chapter 4 is 8.89 percent, the equivalent annual costs can be computed as follows:[3]

Alternative	NPV of Costs	Equivalent Annual Cost
Build own storage system	$15.62 million	$1.39 million
Rent storage system	$12.80 million	$1.78 million
Use third-party storage	$1.84 million	$2.00 million

Based on the equivalent annual costs, Disney should build its own storage system, even though the initial costs are the highest for this option.

6.2   MUTUALLY EXCLUSIVE PROJECTS WITH DIFFERENT RISK LEVELS

Assume that the cost of the third-party storage option will increase 2.5 percent a year forever. What would the equivalent annuity for this option be?

☐ $2.05 million

☐ $2.50 million

☐ $2 million

☐ None of the above

Explain your answer.

Project Comparison Generalized

To compare projects with different lives, we can make specific assumptions about the types of projects that will be available when the shorter-term projects end. To illustrate this point, we can assume that the firm will have no positive NPV projects when its current projects end; this will lead to a decision rule whereby the NPVs of projects can be compared, even if they have different lives. Alternatively, we can make specific assumptions about the availability and the attractiveness of projects in the future, leading to cash flow estimates and present value computations. Going back to the five-year and ten-year projects considered earlier in the chapter (Figure 6.4), assume that future projects will not be as attractive as current projects. More specifically, assume that the annual cash flows on the second five-year project that will be taken when the first five-year project ends will be $320 instead of $400. The NPVs of these two investment streams can be computed as shown in Figure 6.7.

The NPV of the first project, replicated to have a life of ten years, is $529. This is still higher than the NPV of $478 of the longer-life project. The firm will still pick the shorter-life project, though the margin in terms of NPV has shrunk.

This problem is not avoided by using IRRs. When the IRR of a short-term project is compared to the IRR of a long-term project, there is an implicit assumption that future projects will continue to have similar IRRs.

---

[3]The cost of the first system is based on a perpetuity of $0.5 million a year. The NPV can be calculated as follows: NPV = 10 + 0.5/0.0889 = $15.62 million. To convert it back to an annuity, all you need to do is multiply the NPV by the discount rate: Equivalent Annuity = 15.62 × 0.0889 = $1.39 million.

Figure 6.7 Cash Flows on Projects with Unequal Lives: Replicated with Poorer Project

Five-year Project: Replicated

	$400	$400	$400	$400	$400	$320	$320	$320	$320	$320
0	1	2	3	4	5	6	7	8	9	10

−$1,000   −$1,000 (Replication)

Longer Life Project

	$350	$350	$350	$350	$350	$350	$350	$350	$350	$350
0	1	2	3	4	5	6	7	8	9	10

−$1,500

The Replacement Decision: A Special Case of Mutually Exclusive Projects

In a *replacement decision,* we evaluate the replacement of an existing investment with a new one, generally because the existing investment has aged and become less efficient. In a typical replacement decision,

- the replacement of old equipment with new equipment will require an initial cash outflow, because the money spent on the new equipment will exceed any proceeds obtained from the sale of the old equipment.
- there will be cash savings (inflows) during the life of the new investment as a consequence of either the lower operating costs arising from the newer equipment or the higher revenues flowing from the investment. These cash inflows will be augmented by the tax benefits accruing from the greater depreciation that will arise from the new investment.
- the salvage value at the end of the life of the new equipment will be the differential salvage value—that is, the excess of the salvage value on the new equipment over the salvage value that would have been obtained if the old equipment had been kept for the entire period and had not been replaced.

This approach has to be modified if the old equipment has a remaining life that is much shorter than the life of the new equipment replacing it.

This spreadsheet allows you to analyze a replacement decision (**replace.xls**).

ILLUSTRATION 6.6 **Analyzing a Replacement Decision**

Bookscape would like to replace an antiquated packaging system with a new one. The old system has a book value of $50,000 and a remaining life of ten years and could be sold for $15,000, net of capital gains taxes, right now. It would be replaced with a new machine that costs $150,000, has a depreciable life of ten years, and annual operating costs that are $40,000 lower than with the old machine. Assuming straight-line depreciation for both the old and the new systems, a 40 percent tax rate, and no salvage value on either machine in ten years, the replacement decision cash flows can be estimated as follows:

$$\text{Net Initial Investment in New Machine} = -\$150,000 + \$15,000$$
$$= -\$135,000$$

$$\text{Depreciation on the old system} = \$5,000$$

$$\text{Depreciation on the new system} = \$15,000$$

Annual Tax Savings from Additional Depreciation on New Machine
$$= (\text{Depreciation on Old Machine} - \text{Depreciation on New Machine})(\text{Tax Rate})$$
$$= (\$15,000 - \$5,000) \times 0.4 = \$4,000$$

$$\text{Annual After-Tax Savings in Operating Costs} = \$40,000(1 - 0.4) = \$24,000$$

The cost of capital for the company is 12.14 percent, resulting in an NPV from the replacement decision of

$$\text{NPV of Replacement Decision} = -\$135,000 + \$28,000 \times \frac{[1 - (1.1214)^{-10}]}{0.1214}$$
$$= \$22,303$$

This result would suggest that replacing the old packaging machine with a new one will increase the firm's value by \$22,303 and would be a wise move to make.

CAPITAL RATIONING

In evaluating capital investments, we have implicitly assumed that investing capital in a good project has no effect on subsequent projects that the firm may consider. Implicitly, we assume that firms with good investment prospects (with positive NPV) can raise capital from financial markets at a fair price, and without paying transaction costs. In reality, however, it is possible that the capital required to finance a project can cause managers to reject other good projects because the firm has limited access to capital. *Capital rationing* occurs when a firm is unable to invest in projects that earn returns greater than the hurdle rates.[4] Firms may face capital rationing constraints because they do not have either the capital on hand or the capacity and willingness to raise the capital needed to finance these projects. This implies that the firm does not have the capital to accept all the positive NPV projects available.

Reasons for Capital Rationing Constraints
In theory, there will be no capital rationing constraint as long as a firm can follow this series of steps in locating and financing investments:

1. The firm identifies an attractive investment opportunity.

2. The firm goes to financial markets with a description of the project to seek financing.

---

[4]For discussions of the effect of capital rationing on the investment decision, see J. H. Lorie and L. J. Savage, 1955, "Three Problems in Rationing Capital," *Journal of Business,* 28, 229–239; and H. M. Weingartner, 1977, "Capital Rationing: *n* Authors in Search of a Plot, *Journal of Finance,* 32, 1403–1432.

3. Financial markets believe the firm's description of the project.

4. The firm issues securities—that is, stocks and bonds—to raise the capital needed to finance the project at fair market prices. Implicit here is the assumption that markets are efficient and that expectations of future earnings and growth are built into these prices.

5. The cost associated with issuing these securities is minimal.

If this were the case for every firm, then every worthwhile project would be financed and no good project would ever be rejected for lack of funds; in other words, there would be no capital rationing constraint.

The sequence described depends on a several assumptions, some of which are clearly unrealistic, at least for some firms. Let's consider each step even more closely.

1. **Project Discovery** The implicit assumption that firms know when they have good projects on hand underestimates the uncertainty and the errors associated with project analysis. In very few cases can firms say with complete certainty that a prospective project will be a good one.

2. **Firm Announcements and Credibility** Financial markets tend to be skeptical about announcements made by firms, especially when such announcements contain good news about future projects. Because it is easy for any firm to announce that its future projects are good, regardless of whether this is true or not, financial markets often require more substantial proof of the viability of projects.

3. **Market Efficiency** If the securities issued by a firm are underpriced by markets, firms may be reluctant to issue stocks and bonds at these low prices to finance even good projects. In particular, the gains from investing in a project for existing stockholders may be overwhelmed by the loss from having to sell securities at or below their estimated true value. To illustrate, assume that a firm is considering a project that requires an initial investment of $100 million and has an NPV of $10 million. Also assume that the stock of this company, which management believes should be trading for $100 per share, is actually trading at $80 per share. If the company issues $100 million of new stock to take on the new project, its existing stockholders will gain their share of the NPV of $10 million, but they will lose $20 million ($100 million – $80 million) to new investors in the company. There is an interesting converse to this problem. When securities are overpriced, there may be a temptation to overinvest, because existing stockholders gain from the very process of issuing stock to new investors.

4. **Flotation Costs** These are costs associated with raising funds in financial markets, and they can be substantial. If these costs are larger than the NPV of the projects considered, it would not make sense to raise these funds and finance the projects.

Sources of Capital Rationing

What are the sources of capital rationing? Going through the process described in the last section in Table 6.2, we can see the possible reasons for capital rationing at each step.

Table 6.2   CAPITAL RATIONING: THEORY VERSUS PRACTICE

	In Theory	In Practice	Source of Rationing
1. Project discovery	A business uncovers a good investment opportunity.	A business believes, given the underlying uncertainty, that it has a good project.	Uncertainty about true value of projects may cause rationing.
2. Information	The business conveys information about the project to financial markets.	The business attempts to convey information to financial markets.	Difficulty in conveying information to markets may cause rationing.
3. Market response	Financial markets believe the firm; i.e., the information is conveyed credibly.	Financial markets may not believe the announcement.	The greater the credibility gap, the greater the rationing problem.
4. Market efficiency	The securities issued by the business (stocks and bonds) are fairly priced.	The securities issued by the business may not be correctly priced.	With underpriced securities, firms will be unwilling to raise funds for projects.
5. Flotation costs	There are no costs associated with raising funds for projects.	There are significant costs associated with raising funds for projects.	The greater the flotation costs, the larger will be the capital rationing problem.

Table 6.3   THE CAUSES OF CAPITAL RATIONING

Cause	# Firms	%
Debt limit imposed by outside agreement	10	10.7
Debt limit placed by management external to firm	3	3.2
Limit placed on borrowing by internal management	65	69.1
Restrictive policy imposed on retained earnings	2	2.1
Maintenance of target EPS or PE ratio	14	14.9

Source: Martin and Scott (1976).

The three primary sources of capital rationing constraints, therefore, are a firm's lack of credibility with financial markets, market underpricing of securities, and flotation costs.

Researchers have collected data on firms to determine whether they face capital rationing constraints and, if so, to identify the sources of such constraints. One such survey was conducted by Scott and Martin and is summarized in Table 6.3.[5]

---

[5]J. D. Martin and D. F. Scott, 1976, "Debt Capacity and the Capital Budgeting Decision," *Financial Management,* 5(2), 7–14.

This survey suggests that although some firms face capital rationing constraints as a result of external factors largely beyond their control, such as issuance costs and credibility problems, most firms face self-imposed constraints, such as restrictive policies to avoid overextending themselves by investing too much in any period. In some cases, managers are reluctant to issue additional equity because they fear that doing so will dilute the control they have over the company.

Looking at the sources of capital rationing, it seems clear that smaller firms with more limited access to capital markets are more likely to face capital rationing constraints than larger firms. Using similar reasoning, private businesses and emerging market companies are more likely to have limited capital than publicly traded and developed market companies.

Project Selection with Capital Rationing

Whatever the reason, many firms have capital rationing constraints, limiting the funds available for investment. Consequently, the investment analysis techniques developed in Chapter 5, such as NPV, may prove inadequate because they are based on the premise that all good projects will be accepted. In this section, we examine some of the measures to incorporate the capital rationing constraint into project evaluations.

IRR

As we noted in Chapter 5, one reason many firms continue to use IRRs rather than NPV in their investment decisions is because they perceive themselves to be subject to capital rationing. Because the IRR is a percentage measure of return, it measures the return to a dollar of invested capital and provides a way of directing capital to those investments where this return is highest. The limitations of the IRR approach were also examined in Chapter 5, especially with its reinvestment rate assumptions and the potential for multiple and misleading IRRs.

Profitability Index

The profitability index is the simplest method of including capital rationing in investment analysis. It is particularly useful for firms that have a constraint for the current period only and relatively few projects. A scaled version of the NPV, the profitability index is computed by dividing the NPV of the project by the initial investment in the project.[6]

$$\text{Profitability Index} = \text{NPV/Initial Investment}$$

The profitability index provides a rough measure of the NPV the firm gets for each dollar it invests. To use it in investment analysis, we first compute it for each investment the firm is considering, and then pick projects based on the profitability index, starting with the highest values and working down until we reach the capital constraint. When capital is limited and a firm cannot accept every positive NPV project,

---

[6]There is another version of the profitability index, whereby the present value of all cash inflows is divided by the present value of cash outflows. The resulting ranking will be the same as with the profitability index as defined in this chapter.

the profitability index identifies the highest cumulative NPV from the funds available for capital investment.

Although the profitability index is intuitively appealing, it has several limitations. First, it assumes that the capital rationing constraint applies to the current period only and does not include investment requirements in future periods. Thus, a firm may choose projects with a total initial investment that is less than the current period's capital constraint, but it may expose itself to capital rationing problems in future periods if these projects have outlays in those periods. A related problem is the classification of cash flows into an initial investment that occurs now and operating cash inflows that occur in future periods. If projects have investments spread over multiple periods and operating cash outflows, the profitability index may measure the project's contribution to value incorrectly. Finally, the profitability index does not guarantee that the total investment will add up to the capital rationing constraint. If it does not, we have to consider other combinations of projects, which may yield a higher NPV. Although this is feasible for firms with relatively few projects, it becomes increasing unwieldy as the number of projects increases.

ILLUSTRATION 6.7 Using the Profitability Index to Select Projects

Assume that Bookscape, as a private firm, has limited access to capital, and a capital budget of $100,000 in the current period. The projects available to the firm are listed in Table 6.4.

Note that all the projects have positive NPVs and would have been accepted by a firm not subject to a capital rationing constraint.

To choose among these projects, we compute the profitability index of each project in Table 6.5.

The profitability index of 0.40 for project A means that the project earns an NPV of forty cents for every dollar of initial investment. Based on the profitability index, we should accept projects B, C, and G. This combination of projects would exhaust the capital budget of $100,000 while maximizing the NPV of the projects accepted. This analysis also highlights the cost of the capital rationing constraint for this firm; the NPV of the projects rejected as a consequence of the constraint is $70 million.

Table 6.4 AVAILABLE PROJECTS		
Project	Initial Investment (in 1000s)	NPV (1000s)
A	$25	$10
B	40	20
C	5	5
D	100	25
E	50	15
F	70	20
G	35	20

Table 6.5 PROFITABILITY INDEX FOR PROJECTS

Project	Initial Investment (1000s)	NPV (1000s)	Profitability Index	Ranking
A	$25	$10	0.40	4
B	60	30	0.50	3
C	5	5	1.00	1
D	100	25	0.25	7
E	50	15	0.30	5
F	70	20	0.29	6
G	35	20	0.57	2

Building in Capital Rationing Constraints into Analysis

We recommend that firms separate the capital rationing constraint from traditional investment analysis so they can observe how much these constraints cost. In the simplest terms, the cost of a capital rationing constraint is the total NPV of the good projects that could not be taken for lack of funds. There are two reasons why this knowledge is useful. First, if the firm is faced with the opportunity to relax these constraints, knowing how much these constraints cost will be useful. For instance, the firm may be able to enter into a strategic partnership with a larger firm with excess funds and use the cash to take the good projects that would otherwise have been rejected, sharing the NPV of these projects. Second, if the capital rationing is self-imposed, managers in the firm are forced to confront the cost of the constraint. In some cases, the sheer magnitude of this cost may be sufficient for them to drop or relax the constraint.

6.3 MUTUALLY EXCLUSIVE PROJECTS WITH DIFFERENT RISK LEVELS

Assume in Illustration 6.7 that the initial investment required for project B was $40,000. Which of the following would be your best combination of projects given your capital rationing constraint of $100,000?

☐ B, C, and G
☐ A, B, C, and G
☐ A, B, and G
☐ Other

IN PRACTICE: USING A HIGHER HURDLE RATE

Many firms choose what seems to be a more convenient way of selecting projects, when they face capital rationing— they raise the hurdle rate to reflect the severity of the constraint. If the definition of capital rationing is that a firm cannot take all the positive NPV projects it faces, raising the hurdle rate sufficiently will ensure that the problem is resolved or at least hidden. For instance, assume that a firm has a true cost of capital of 12 percent,[7] a capital rationing constraint of $100 million, and

---

[7] By "true cost of capital," we mean a cost of capital that reflects the riskiness of the firm and its financing mix.

positive NPV projects requiring an initial investment of $250 million. At a higher cost of capital, fewer projects will have positive NPVs. At some cost of capital, say 18 percent, the positive NPV projects remaining will require an initial investment of $100 million or less.

There are problems that result from building the capital rationing constraint into the hurdle rate. First, once the adjustment has been made, the firm may fail to correct it for shifts in the severity of the constraint. Thus, a small firm may adjust its cost of capital from 12 percent to 18 percent to reflect a severe capital rationing constraint. As the firm gets larger, the constraint will generally become less restrictive, but the firm may not decrease its cost of capital accordingly. Second, increasing the discount rate will yield NPVs that do not convey the same information as those computed using the correct discount rates. The NPV of a project, estimated using the right hurdle rate, is the value added to the firm by investing in that project; the present value estimated using an adjusted discount rate cannot be read the same way. Finally, adjusting the hurdle rate penalizes all projects equally, whether or not they are capital-intensive. ■

SIDE COSTS FROM PROJECTS

In much of the project analyses that we have presented in this chapter, we have assumed that the resources needed for a project are newly acquired; this includes not only the building and the equipment but also the personnel needed to get the project going. For most businesses considering new projects, this is an unrealistic assumption, however, because many of the resources used on these projects are already part of the business and will just be transferred to the new project. When a business uses such resources, there is the potential for an **opportunity cost**—the cost created for the rest of the business as a consequence of this project. This opportunity cost can be a significant portion of the total investment needed on a project. Ignoring these costs because they are not explicit can lead to bad investments.

1. Opportunity Costs

The opportunity cost for a resource is simplest to estimate when there is a current alternative use for the resource, and we can estimate the cash flows lost by using the resource on the project. It becomes more complicated when the resource does not have a current use but does have potential future uses. In that case, we have to estimate the cash flows forgone on those future uses to estimate the opportunity costs.

Resource with a Current Alternative Use

The general framework for analyzing opportunity costs begins by asking whether there is any other use for the resource right now. In other words, if the project that is considering using the resource is not accepted, what are the uses to which the resource will be put and what cash flows will be generated as a result?

- The resource might be rented out, in which case the rental revenue lost is the opportunity cost of the resource. For example, if the project is considering the use of a vacant building already owned by the business, the potential revenue from renting out this building will be the opportunity cost.

• The resource could be sold, in which case the sales price, net of any tax liability and lost depreciation tax benefits, would be the opportunity cost for the resource.

• The resource might be used elsewhere in the firm, in which case the cost of replacing it is the opportunity cost. Thus, the transfer of experienced employees from established divisions to a new project creates a cost to these divisions, which has to be factored into the decision making.

Sometimes, decision makers have to decide whether the opportunity cost will be estimated based on the lost rental revenue, the foregone sales price or the cost of replacing the resource. When such a choice has to be made, it is the highest of the costs—that is, the best alternative forgone—that should be considered as an opportunity cost.

Opportunity Cost: The cost assigned to a project resource that is already owned by the firm. It is based on the next best alternative use.

6.4 SUNK COSTS AND OPPORTUNITY COSTS

A colleague argues that resources that a firm owns already should not be considered in investment analysis because the cost is a sunk cost. Do you agree?

☐ Yes

☐ No

How would you reconcile the competing arguments of sunk and opportunity costs?

ILLUSTRATION **6.8** Estimating the Opportunity Cost for a Resource with a Current Alternative Use

Working again with the Bookscape Online example, assume that the following additional information is provided:

• Although Bookscape Online will employ only two full-time employees, it is estimated that the additional business associated with online ordering and the administration of the service itself will add to the workload for the current general manager of the bookstore. As a consequence, the salary of the general manager will be increased from $100,000 to $120,000 next year; it is expected to grow 5 percent a year after that for the remaining three years of the online venture. After the online venture is ended in the fourth year, the manager's salary will revert back to its old levels.

• It is also estimated that Bookscape Online will utilize an office that is currently used to store financial records. The records will be moved to a bank vault, which will cost $1000 a year to rent.

The opportunity cost of the addition to the general manager's workload lies in the additional salary expenditure that will be incurred as a consequence. Taking the present value of the after-tax costs (using a 40 percent tax rate) over the next four years,

Table 6.6	PRESENT VALUE OF ADDITIONAL SALARY EXPENSES			
	1	**2**	**3**	**4**
Increase in salary	$20,000	$21,000	$22,050	$23,153
After-tax salary expense	$12,000	$12,600	$13,230	$13,892
Present value	$9,775	$8,361	$7,152	$6,117

using the cost of capital of 22.76 percent estimated in Illustration 5.2, yields the values in Table 6.6. The cumulative present value of the costs is $31,406.

Turning to the second resource—a storage space originally used for the financial records—if this project is taken, the opportunity cost is the cost of the bank vault.

$$\text{Additional Storage Expenses per Year} = \$1,000$$

$$\text{After-Tax Additional Storage Expenses per Year} = \$1,000(1 - 0.40) = \$600$$

$$\text{PV of After-Tax Storage Expenses for 4 Years} = \$600 \times \frac{[1 - (1.2276)^{-4}]}{0.2276}$$

$$= \$1,475.48$$

The opportunity costs estimated for the general manager's added workload ($31,406) and the storage space ($1,475) are in present value terms and can be added on to <$38,893> that we computed as the NPV of Bookscape Online in Illustration 5.11. The NPV becomes more negative.

$$\text{NPV with Opportunity Costs} = \text{NPV without Opportunity Costs}$$
$$+ \text{PV of Opportunity Costs}$$
$$= -\$38,893 - \$31,406 - \$1,475$$
$$= -\$71,774$$

The cash flows associated with the opportunity costs could alternatively have been reflected in the years in which they occur. Thus, the additional salary and storage expenses could have been added to the operating expenses of the store in each of the four years. As Table 6.7 indicates, this approach would yield the same NPV and would have clearly been the appropriate approach if the IRR were to be calculated.

Note that this NPV confirms our earlier finding—this project should not be taken.

Table 6.7	NPV WITH OPPORTUNITY COSTS: ALTERNATE APPROACH	
Year	**Cash Flow with Opportunity Costs**	**Present Value**
0	−$1,150,000	−$1,150,000
1	327,400	266,705
2	401,800	266,633
3	432,670	233,890
4	706,238	310,998
	NPV =	−$71,774

Opportunity Costs of Resources with No Current Alternative Use

In some cases, a resource being considered for use in a project will have no current alternative use, but the business will have to forgo alternative uses in the future. One example would be excess capacity on a machine or a computer. Most firms cannot lease or sell excess capacity, but using that capacity now for a new product may cause the businesses to run out of capacity much earlier than they would otherwise. There are two approaches that firms use to deal with excess capacity:

- They assume that excess capacity is free, because it is not being used currently and cannot be sold off or rented, in most cases.
- They allocate a portion of the book value of the plant or resource to the project. Thus, if the plant has a book value of $100 million and the new project uses 40 percent of it, $40 million will be allocated to the project.

We will argue that neither of these approaches considers the opportunity cost of using excess capacity because the opportunity cost usually comes from costs that the firm will face in the future as a consequence of using up excess capacity today. By using up excess capacity on a new project, the firm will run out of capacity sooner than if it did not take the project. When it does run out of capacity, it has to take one of two paths:

- New capacity will have to be bought or built, in which case the opportunity cost will be the higher cost in present value terms of doing this earlier rather than later.
- Production will have to be cut back on one of the product lines, leading to a loss in cash flows that would have been generated by the lost sales.

Again, this choice is not random, because the logical action to take is the one that leads to the lower cost, in present value terms, for the firm. Thus, if it is cheaper to lose sales rather than build new capacity, the opportunity cost for the project being considered should be based on the lost sales.

A general framework for pricing excess capacity for purposes of investment analysis asks three questions:

1. If the new project is not taken, when will the firm run out of capacity on the equipment or space that is being evaluated?
2. If the new project is taken, when will the firm run out of capacity on the equipment or space that is being evaluated? Presumably, with the new project using up some of the excess capacity, the firm will run out of capacity sooner than it would have otherwise.
3. What will the firm do when it does run out of capacity? The firm has two choices: It can cut back on production of the least profitable product line and make less profits than it would have without a capacity constraint. In this case, the opportunity cost is the present value of the cash flows lost as a consequence. It can buy or build new capacity, in which case the opportunity cost is the difference in present value between investing earlier rather than later.

2. Product Cannibalization

Product cannibalization refers to the phenomenon whereby a new product introduced by a firm competes with and reduces sales of the firm's existing products. On one level, it can be argued that this is a negative incremental effect of the new product, and the lost cash flows or profits from the existing products should be treated as costs in analyzing whether to introduce the product. Doing so introduces the possibility that the new product will be rejected, however. If this happens, and a competitor then exploits the opening to introduce a product that fills the niche that the new product would have and consequently erodes the sales of the firm's existing products, the worst of all scenarios is created—the firm loses sales to a competitor rather than to itself.

Thus, the decision on whether to build in the lost sales created by product cannibalization will depend on the potential for a competitor to introduce a close substitute to the new product being considered. Two extreme possibilities exist: The first is that close substitutes will be offered almost instantaneously by competitors; the second is that substitutes cannot be offered.

- If the business in which the firm operates is extremely competitive and there are no barriers to entry, it can be assumed that the product cannibalization will occur anyway, and the costs associated with it have no place in an incremental cash flow analysis. For example, in considering whether to introduce a new brand of cereal, a company like Kellogg's can reasonably ignore the expected product cannibalization that will occur because of the competitive nature of the cereal business and the ease with which Post or General Mills could introduce a close substitute. Similarly, it would not make sense for Compaq to consider the product cannibalization that will occur as a consequence of introducing an updated notebook computer because it can be reasonably assumed that a competitor, say, IBM or Dell, would create the lost sales anyway with their versions of the same product if Compaq does not introduce the product.

- If a competitor cannot introduce a substitute—because of legal restrictions such as patents, for example—the cash flows lost as a consequence of product cannibalization belong in the investment analysis at least for the period of the patent protection. For example, a pharmaceutical company that has the only patented drug available to treat ulcers may hold back on introducing a potentially better new ulcer drug because of fears of product cannibalization.[8]

In most cases, there will be some barriers to entry, ensuring that a competitor will either introduce an imperfect substitute, leading to much smaller erosion in existing product sales, or that a competitor will not introduce a substitute for some period of time, leading to a much later erosion in existing product sales. In this case, an intermediate solution whereby some of the product cannibalization costs are considered

---

[8]Even the patent system does not offer complete protection against competition. It is entirely possible that another pharmaceutical company may come into the market with its own ulcer drug and cause the lost sales anyway.

may be appropriate. Note that brand name loyalty is one potential barrier to entry. Firms with stronger brand loyalty should therefore factor into their investment analysis more of the cost of lost sales from existing products as a consequence of a new product introduction.

 Product Cannibalization: Sales generated by one product that come at the expense of other products manufactured by the same firm.

 6.5 PRODUCT CANNIBALIZATION AT DISNEY

In coming up with revenues on its proposed theme park in Thailand, Disney estimates that 15 percent of the revenues at the park will be generated from people who would have gone to Disneyland in California if the new park did not exist. When analyzing the project in Thailand, would you use

☐ the total revenues expected at the park?

☐ only 85 percent of the revenues, because 15 percent of the revenues would have come to Disney anyway?

☐ a compromise estimated at a point that lies between the first two numbers?

Explain.

PROJECT SYNERGY

When a project under consideration creates positive benefits (in the form of cash flows) for other projects that a firm may have, **project synergies** are created. For instance, assume that you are a clothing retailer considering whether to open an up-scale clothing store for children in the same shopping center where you already own a store that caters to an adult clientele. In addition to generating revenues and cash flows on its own, the children's store might increase the traffic to the adult store and increase profits there. That additional profit, and its ensuing cash flow, must be factored into the analysis of the new store.

Sometimes the project synergies are not with existing projects but with other projects being considered contemporaneously. In such cases, the best way to analyze the projects is jointly, because examining each separately will lead to a much lower NPV. Thus, a proposal to open a children's clothing store and an adult clothing store in the same shopping center will have to be treated as a joint investment analysis, and the NPV will have to be calculated for both stores together. A positive NPV would suggest opening both stores, whereas a negative NPV would indicate that neither should be opened.

 Project Synergy: The increase in cash flows that accrue to other projects, as a consequence of the project under consideration.

ILLUSTRATION 6.9 Cash Flow Synergies with Existing Projects

Assume that Bookscape is considering adding a café to its bookstore. The café, it is hoped, will make the bookstore a more attractive destination for would-be shoppers. The following information relates to the proposed café:

- The initial cost of remodeling a portion of the store to make it a café and of buying equipment is expected to be $150,000. This investment is expected to have a life of five years, during which period it will be depreciated using straight-line depreciation. None of the cost is expected to be recoverable at the end of the five years.
- The revenues in the first year are expected to be $60,000, growing at 10 percent a year for the next four years.
- There will be one employee, and the total cost for this employee in year one is expected to be $30,000 growing at 5 percent a year for the next four years.
- The cost of the material (food, drinks, etc.) needed to run the café is expected to be 40 percent of revenues in each of the five years.
- An inventory amounting to 5 percent of the revenues has to be maintained; investments in the inventory are made at the beginning of each year.
- The tax rate for Bookscape as a business is 40 percent.

Based on this information, the estimated cash flows on the café are shown in Table 6.8.

Note that the working capital is fully salvaged at the end of year five, resulting in a cash inflow of $4,392.

To compute the NPV, we will use Bookscape's cost of capital of 12.14 percent (from Chapter 4). In doing so, we recognize that this is the cost of capital for a bookstore and that this is an investment in a café. It is, however, a café whose good fortunes rest with how well the bookstore is doing and whose risk is therefore the risk

Table 6.8	ESTIMATING CASH FLOWS FROM OPENING BOOKSCAPE CAFÉ					
	Year 0	**1**	**2**	**3**	**4**	**5**
Investment	−$150,000					
Revenues		$60,000	$66,000	$72,600	$79,860	$87,846
Labor		$30,000	$31,500	$33,075	$34,729	$36,465
Materials		$24,000	$26,400	$29,040	$31,944	$35,138
Depreciation		$30,000	$30,000	$30,000	$30,000	$30,000
Operating income		−$24,000	−$21,900	−$19,515	−$16,813	−$13,758
Taxes		−$9,600	−$8,760	−$7,806	−$6,725	−$5,503
After-tax operating income		−$14,400	−$13,140	−$11,709	−$10,088	−$8,255
+ Depreciation		$30,000	$30,000	$30,000	$30,000	$30,000
−Δ Working capital	$3,000	$300	$330	$363	$399	−$4,392
Cash flow to firm	−$153,000	$15,300	$16,530	$17,928	$19,513	$26,138
PV at 12.14%	−$153,000	$13,644	$13,146	$12,714	$12,341	$14,742
Working capital		$3,000	$3,300	$3,630	$3,993	$4,392

Table 6.9 **INCREMENTAL CASH FLOWS FROM SYNERGY**

	Year 1	2	3	4	5
Increased revenues	$500,000	$550,000	$605,000	$665,500	$732,050
Operating margin (%)	10.00%	10.00%	10.00%	10.00%	10.00%
Operating income	$50,000	$55,000	$60,500	$66,550	$73,205
Operating income after taxes	$30,000	$33,000	$36,300	$39,930	$43,923
PV of cash flows at 12.14%	$26,753	$26,244	$25,744	$25,253	$24,772

associated with the bookstore. The present value of the cash inflows is less than the initial investment of $150,000, resulting in an NPV of −$86,413. This suggests that this is not a good investment based on the cash flows it would generate.

Note, however, that this analysis is based on looking at the café as a stand-alone entity and that one of the benefits of the café is that is that it might attract more customers to the store and get them to buy more books. For purposes of our analysis, assume that the café will increase revenues at the store by $500,000 in year one, growing at 10 percent a year for the following four years. In addition, assume that the pretax operating margin on these sales is 10 percent. The incremental cash flows from the synergy are shown in Table 6.9.

The present value of the incremental cash flows generated for the bookstore as a consequence of the café is $128,767. Incorporating this into the present value analysis yields the following:

$$\text{NPV of Cafe} = -\$86,413 + \$128,767 = \$42,354$$

By incorporating the cash flows from the synergy into the analysis, we can see that the café is a good investment for Bookscape.

6.6 SYNERGY BENEFITS

In the analysis, the cost of capital for both the café and the bookstore was identical at 12.14 percent. Assume that the cost of capital for the café had been 15 percent, whereas the cost of capital for the bookstore had stayed at 12.14 percent. Which discount rate would you use for estimating the present value of synergy benefits?

☐ 15 percent
☐ 12.14 percent
☐ An average of the two discount rates
☐ Could be 12.14 percent or 15 percent depending on . . .

Explain.

IN PRACTICE: THE VALUE OF SYNERGY: DISNEY'S ANIMATED MOVIES

Disney has a well-deserved reputation for finding synergy in its movie operations, especially its animated movies. Consider, for instance, some of the spin-offs from its recent movies:

1. Plastic action figures and stuffed toys are produced and sold at the time the movies are released, producing profits for Disney both from its own stores and from royalties from sales of the merchandise at other stores.

2. Joint promotions of the movies with fast-food chains, such as McDonald's and Burger King, where the chains give away movie merchandise with their kid's meals and reduce Disney's own advertising costs for the movie by promoting it.

3. With its acquisition of Capital Cities, Disney now has a broadcasting outlet for cartoons based on successful movies (*Aladdin, The Lion King, The Little Mermaid*), which generate production and advertising revenues for Disney.

4. Disney has also made successful Broadway musicals of its hit movies, *Beauty and the Beast* and *The Lion King,* and plans to use the theater that it now owns on Broadway to produce more such shows.

5. Disney's theme parks all over the world benefit indirectly as these movies attract more people to the parks.

6. Disney produces computer software and video games based on its animated movie characters.

7. Finally, Disney has been extremely successful in promoting the video and DVD releases of its movies as must-have items for video collections.

In fact, on its best-known classics, such as *Snow White,* Disney released the movie in theaters dozens of times between the original release in 1937 and the eventual video release in 1985, making substantial profits each time. More recently, the company has released its masterworks on DVD, with special features added and a premium price. ■

Synergy in Acquisitions

Synergy is often a motive in acquisitions, but it is used as a way of justifying huge premiums and is seldom analyzed objectively. The framework we developed for valuing synergy in projects can be applied to valuing synergy in acquisitions. The key to the existence of synergy is that the target firm controls a specialized resource that becomes more valuable when combined with the bidding firm's resources. The specialized resource will vary depending on the merger. Horizontal mergers occur when two firms in the same line of business merge. In that case, the synergy must come from some form of economies of scale, which reduce costs, or from increased market power, which increases profit margins and sales. Vertical integration occurs when a firm acquires a supplier of inputs into its production process or a distributor or retailer for the product it produces. The primary source of synergy in this case comes from more complete control of the chain of production. This benefit has to be weighed against the loss of efficiency from having a captive supplier who does not have any incentive to keep costs low and compete with other suppliers.

When a firm with strengths in one functional area acquires another firm with strengths in a different functional area (functional integration), synergy may be gained by exploiting the strengths in these areas. Thus, when a firm with a good distribution network acquires a firm with a promising product line, value is gained by combining these two strengths. The argument is that both firms will be better off after the merger.

Most reasonable observers agree that there is a potential for operating synergy, in one form or the other, in many takeovers. Some disagreement exists, however, over whether synergy can be valued and, if so, how much that value should be. One school of thought argues that synergy is too nebulous to be valued and that any systematic attempt to do so requires so many assumptions that it is pointless. We disagree. It is true that valuing synergy requires assumptions about future cash flows and growth, but the lack of precision in the process does not mean that an unbiased estimate of value cannot be made. Thus we maintain that synergy can be valued by answering two fundamental questions:

1. *What form is the synergy expected to take?* The benefits of synergy have to show up in one of the inputs into value, as higher revenues, a healthier operating margin, more investment opportunities, or higher growth in the future. To value synergy, we need to identify which of these inputs will most likely be affected and by how much.

2. *When can the synergy be expected to start affecting cash flows?* Even if there are good reasons for believing that synergy exists in a particular merger, it is unlikely that these benefits will accrue instantaneously after the merger is completed. It often takes time to integrate the operations of two firms, and the difficulty of doing so increases with the sizes of the firms. If we have to wait for the higher cash flows that arise as a result of synergy, the value of synergy decreases.

Once these questions are answered, the value of synergy can be estimated using an extension of investment analysis techniques. First, the firms involved in the merger are valued independently by discounting expected cash flows to each firm at the weighted average cost of capital for that firm. Second, the value of the combined firm, with no synergy, is obtained by adding the values obtained for each firm in the first step. Third, the effects of synergy are built into expected growth rates and cash flows, and the combined firm is revalued with synergy. The difference between the value of the combined firm with synergy and the value of the combined firm without synergy provides a value for synergy.

OPTIONS EMBEDDED IN PROJECTS

In Chapter 5, we examined the process for analyzing a project and deciding whether to accept the project. In particular, we noted that a project should be accepted only if the returns on the project exceed the hurdle rate; in the context of cash flows and discount rates, this translates into projects with positive NPVs. The limitation with traditional investment analysis, which analyzes projects on the basis of expected cash flows and discount rates, is that it fails to consider fully the myriad options that are usually associated with many projects.

In this section, we will begin by first describing what an option is and why they matter and then analyze three options that are embedded in many capital budgeting projects. The first is the option to delay a project, especially when the firm has exclusive rights to the project. The second is the option to expand a project to cover new products or markets some time in the future. The third is the option to abandon a project if the cash flows do not measure up to expectations. These are generically called **real options** since the underlying asset is a real asset (a project) rather than a financial asset. With each of these options, we will present both the intuitive implications of valuing them as options as well as the details of using option pricing models to value them. Appendix 4 contains more detail on these models.

Real Option: An option on a nontraded asset, such as an investment project or a gold mine.

Options: Description and Determinants of Value

An option derives its value from an underlying asset, and has a cash payoff that is contingent on what happens to the value of the underlying asset. There are two types of options. With a call option, you get the right to buy the underlying asset at a fixed price, called a strike price, whereas with put options, you get the right to sell the underlying asset at a fixed price. Because you have the right, as the holder of the option, to buy or sell the underlying asset and not an obligation, you will exercise an option only if it makes sense for you to do so. With a call option, that will occur when the value of the underlying asset is greater than your strike price, whereas with a put, it is when the value is lower.

As explained in Appendix 4, the value of an option ultimately rests on six variables—the value, volatility, and expected dividends of the underlying asset; the strike price and the life of the option; and the level of interest rates. Without delving into the minutiae of option pricing models, it is still worth noting the differences between valuing conventional assets or projects on the one hand and options on the other. The first is that conventional assets can be valued by discounting expected cash flows at a risk-adjusted discount rate, whereas options are valued at a premium over their exercise value. The premium can be attributed to the choice that the holder of the option makes as to when and whether to exercise. The second is that increasing risk and uncertainty reduce the value of conventional assets, but they increase the value of options. This is because the holders of options can never be forced to exercise an option, which protects them against downside risk but preserves upside potential.

Because of these two differences, this section is necessary. If an investment has options embedded in it, conventional NPV will miss the option premium and understate the value of the investment. In addition, the option portion of the investment may benefit as the investment becomes more risky, even as the rest of the investment becomes less valuable.

The Option to Delay a Project

Projects are typically analyzed based on their expected cash flows and discount rates at the time of the analysis; the NPV computed on that basis is a measure of its value and acceptability at that time. Expected cash flows and discount rates change over time, however, and so does the NPV. Thus, a project that has a negative NPV now may have a positive NPV in the future. In a competitive environment, in which individual firms have no special advantages over their competitors in taking projects, this may not seem significant. In an environment where a project can be taken by only one firm (because of legal restrictions or other barriers to entry to competitors), however, the changes in the project's value over time give it the characteristics of a call option.

Describing the Option to Delay

In the abstract, assume that a project requires an initial investment of X and that the present value of expected cash inflows computed right now is V. The NPV of this project is the difference between the two:

$$NPV = V - X$$

Now assume that the firm has exclusive rights to this project for the next *n* years, and that the present value of the cash inflows may change over that time because of changes in either the cash flows or the discount rate. Thus, the project may have a negative NPV right now, but it may still become a good project if the firm waits. Defining V as the present value of the cash flows, the firm's decision rule on this project can be summarized as follows:

If $V > X$ project has positive NPV
If $V < X$ project has negative NPV

This relationship can be presented in a payoff diagram of cash flows on this project, as shown in Figure 6.8, assuming that the firm holds out until the end of the period for which it has exclusive rights to the project.

Figure 6.8   The Option to Delay a Project

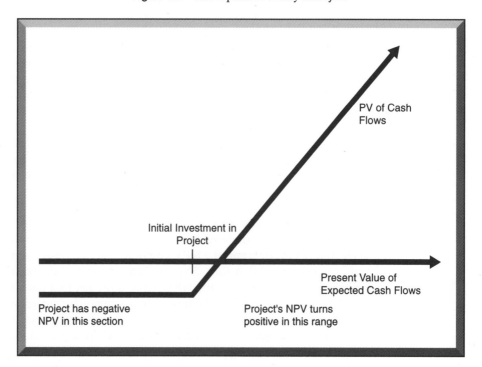

Note that this payoff diagram is that of a call option—the underlying asset is the project; the strike price of the option is the investment needed to take the project; and the life of the option is the period for which the firm has rights to the project. The present value of the cash flows on this project and the expected variance in this present value represent the value and variance of the underlying asset.

Valuing the Option to Delay

On the surface, the inputs needed to apply option pricing models to valuing the option to delay are the same as those needed for any application: the value of the underlying asset, the variance in the value, the time to expiration on the option, the strike price, the riskless rate, and the equivalent of the dividend yield. Actually estimating these inputs for valuing real options can be difficult, however.

Value of the Underlying Asset

In the case of product options, the underlying asset is the project itself. The current value of this asset is the present value of expected cash flows from initiating the project now, which can be obtained by doing a standard capital budgeting analysis. There is likely to be a substantial amount of estimation error in the cash flow estimates and the present value. Rather than being viewed as a problem, this uncertainty should be viewed as the reason why the project delay option has value. If the expected cash flows on the project were known with certainty and were not expected to change, there would be no need to adopt an option pricing framework, because there would be no value to the option.

Variance in the Value of the Asset

As noted in the previous section, there is likely to be considerable uncertainty associated with the cash flow estimates and the present value that measures the value of the asset now, partly because the potential market size for the product may be unknown and partly because technological shifts can change the cost structure and profitability of the product. The variance in the present value of cash flows from the project can be estimated in one of three ways. First, if similar projects have been introduced in the past, the variance in the cash flows from those projects can be used as an estimate. Second, probabilities can be assigned to various market scenarios, cash flows estimated under each scenario, and the variance estimated across present values. Finally, the average variance in firm value of publicly traded companies that are in the business that the project will be in can be used. Thus, the average variance in firm value of biotechnology companies can be used as the variance to price the option to delay a biotechnology project.

The value of the option is largely derived from the variance in cash flows—the higher the variance, the higher the value of the project delay option. Thus, the value of an option to invest in a project in a stable business will be less than the value of one in an environment in which technology, competition, and markets are all changing rapidly.

Exercise Price on Option

A project delay option is exercised when the firm owning the rights to the project decides to invest in it. The cost of making this investment is equivalent to the exercise price of the option. For simplicity, it is best to assume that this cost remains constant (in present value dollars) and that any uncertainty associated with the product is reflected in the present value of cash flows on the product.

Expiration of the Option and the Riskless Rate

The project delay option expires when the rights to the project lapse; investments made after the project rights expire are assumed to deliver an NPV of zero as competition drives returns down to the required rate. The riskless rate to use in pricing the option should be the rate that corresponds to the life of the option.

Dividend Yield

Once the NPV turns positive, there is a cost borne in delaying making an investment. Because the project rights expire after a fixed period, and excess profits (which are the source of positive present value) are assumed to disappear after that time as new competitors emerge, each year of delay translates into one less year of value-creating cash flows.[9] If the cash flows are evenly distributed over time, and the life of the option is n years, the cost of delay can be written as:

$$\text{Annual cost of delay} = \frac{1}{n}$$

Thus, if the project rights are for twenty years, the annual cost of delay works out to 5 percent a year.

There is a data set online that summarizes, by sector, the variances in firm value and equity value for companies in each sector in the United States.

6.7 COST OF DELAY AND EARLY EXERCISE

For typical listed options on financial assets, it is argued that early exercise is almost never optimal. Is this true for real options as well? Explain.

☐ Yes

☐ No

ILLUSTRATION 6.10 Valuing a Patent

Assume that a pharmaceutical company has been approached by an entrepreneur who has patented a new drug to treat ulcers. The entrepreneur has obtained FDA approval and has the patent rights for the next seventeen years. Although the drug shows promise, it is still very expensive to manufacture and has a relatively small market. Assume that the initial investment to produce the drug is $500 million and the present value of the cash flows from introducing the drug now is only $350 million. The technology and the market are volatile, and the annualized standard deviation in the present value, estimated from a simulation is 25 percent.[10]

Although the NPV of introducing the drug now is negative, the rights to this drug may still be valuable because of the variance in the present value of the cash flow. In

---

[9]A value-creating cash flow is one that adds to the NPV because it earns in excess of the required return for investments of equivalent risk.

[10]This simulation would yield an expected value for the project of $350 million and the standard deviation in that value of 25 percent.

other words, it is entirely possible that this drug may not only be viable but extremely profitable a year or two from now. To value this right, we first define the inputs to the option pricing model:

Value of the Underlying Asset (S)
= PV of Cash Flows from Project if Product Introduced Now
= $350 million

Strike Price (K) = Initial Investment Needed to Introduce the Product
= $500 million

Variance in Underlying Asset's Value = $(0.25)^2 = 0.0625$

Time to Expiration = Life of the Patent = 17 years

Cost of Delay (Dividend Yield in Option Model) = 1/Life of the Patent
= 1/17 = 5.88%

Assume that the seventeen-year riskless rate is 4 percent. The value of the option can be estimated as follows:

Call Value = $350 \exp^{(-0.0588)(17)}(0.4439) - 500 \exp^{(-0.04)(17)}(0.1206)$
= $26.60 million

Thus, this ulcer drug, which has a negative NPV if introduced now, is still valuable to its owner.

6.8 How Much Would You Pay for This Option?

Assume that you are negotiating for a pharmaceutical company that is trying to buy this patent. What would you pay?

☐ $26.60 million
☐ more than $26.60 million
☐ less than $26.60 million

Explain.

Intuitive Implications

Several interesting implications emerge from the analysis of the option to delay a project. First, a project may have a negative NPV based on expected cash flows today, but the rights to this project can still be valuable because of the option characteristics. Thus, although a negative NPV should encourage a firm to reject investing in an investment or technology, it should not lead it to conclude that the rights to it are worthless. Second, a project may have a positive NPV but still not be accepted right away because the firm may gain by waiting and accepting the project in a future period, for the same reasons that investors do not always exercise an option just because it is in the money. This is more likely to happen if the firm has the rights to the project for a long time and the variance in project inflows is high. To illustrate, assume that a firm has the patent rights to produce a new type of disk drive for computer systems and that building a new plant will yield a positive NPV right now. If the technology for manufacturing the disk drive is in flux, however, the firm may delay taking the project in the hopes that the improved technology will increase the expected cash flows and consequently the value of the project.

The Option to Expand a Project

In some cases, firms invest in projects because doing so allows them to either take on other investments or enter other markets in the future. In such cases, it can be argued that the initial projects yield expansion options for a firm, and that the firm should therefore be willing to pay a price for such options. It is easiest to understand this option if you consider the projects in sequence. The initial project is not an option and may very well have a negative NPV. However, investing in the initial project gives the firm the opportunity to make a second investment—expanding into a new market or introducing a new product—later in time. The firm can choose to exploit this opportunity or ignore it, but the choice that it has gives the second investment the characteristics of an option.

Describing the Option to Expand

To examine the option to expand using the same framework developed earlier, assume that the present value of the expected cash flows from expanding into the new market is V, and the total investment needed to enter this market is X. Furthermore, assume that the firm has a fixed time horizon, at the end of which it has to make the final decision on whether to take advantage of this expansion opportunity. Finally, assume that the firm cannot move forward on this opportunity if it does not take the initial project. This scenario implies the option payoffs shown in Figure 6.9.

Figure 6.9   The Option to Expand a Project

As you can see, at the expiration of the fixed time horizon, the firm will expand into the new market if the present value of the expected cash flows at that point in time exceeds the cost of expansion.

Valuing the Option to Expand
To understand how to estimate the value of the option to expand, let us begin by recognizing that there are two projects that usually drive this option. The first generally has a negative NPV and is recognized as a poor investment, even by the firm investing in it. The second project is the potential to expand that comes with the first project. The second project represents the underlying asset for the option. The inputs have to be defined accordingly.

- The present value of the cash flows that you would generate if you were to invest in the second project today (the expansion option) is the value of the underlying asset—S in the option pricing model.
- If there is substantial uncertainty about the expansion potential, the present value is likely to be volatile and change over time as circumstances change. The variance in this present value is what you would want to use to value the expansion option. Because projects are not traded, you have to either estimate this variance from simulations or use the variance in values of publicly traded firms in the business.
- The cost that you would incur up front if you invest in the expansion today is the equivalent of the strike price.
- The life of the option is fairly difficult to define because there is usually no externally imposed exercise period. When valuing the option to expand, the life of the option will be an internal constraint imposed by the firm on itself. For instance, a firm that invests on a small scale in China might impose a constraint that it either will expand within five years or pull out of the market. Why might it do so? There may be considerable costs associated with maintaining the small presence, or the firm may have scarce resources that have to be committed elsewhere.

As with other real options, there may be a cost to waiting once the expansion option becomes viable. That cost will take the form of cash flows that will be lost on the expansion project if it is not taken or a cost imposed on the firm until it makes its final decision. For instance, the firm may have to pay a fee every year until it makes its final decision.

ILLUSTRATION 6.11   Valuing an Option to Expand: Disney Entertainment
Assume that Disney is considering investing $100 million to create a Spanish version of the Disney Channel to serve the growing Mexican market. Assume also that a financial analysis of the cash flows from this investment suggests that the present value of the cash flows from this investment to Disney will be only $80 million. Thus, by itself, the new channel has a negative NPV of $20 million.

One factor that does have to be considered in this analysis is that if the market in Mexico turns out to be more lucrative than currently anticipated, Disney could expand its reach to all of Latin America with an additional investment of $150 million any time over the next ten years. Although the current expectation is that the cash flows from having a Disney channel in Latin America will have a present value of only $100 million, there is considerable uncertainty about both the potential for such an channel and the shape of the market itself, leading to significant variance in this estimate.

The value of the option to expand can now be estimated, by defining the inputs to the option pricing model as follows:

Value of the Underlying Asset (S) = PV of Cash Flows from Expansion to Latin America, if Done Now = $100 million

Strike Price (K) = Cost of Expansion into Latin America = $150 million

We estimate the standard deviation in the estimate of the project value by using the annualized standard deviation in firm value of publicly traded entertainment firms in the Latin American markets, which is approximately 30 percent.

Variance in Underlying Asset's Value = $0.30^2 = 0.09$

Time to Expiration = Period for which Expansion Option Applies = 10 years

Assume that the ten-year riskless rate is 4 percent. The value of the option can be estimated as follows:

Call Value = $100(0.6803) - 150 \exp^{(-0.04)(10)}(0.3156) = \$36.30$ million

In other words, even though this expansion opportunity has a negative NPV today of −$50 million, the option to take it is worth $36.30 million. Because this option is dependent on making the initial investment in the Spanish channel, this value can be added on to the NPV of −$20 million on the initial investment.

NPV of Disney Channel in Mexico = $80 million − $100 million
= −$20 million

Value of Option to Expand = $36.30 million

NPV of Project with Option to Expand = −$20 million + $36.3 million
= $16.3 million

Considered as a package, Disney should invest in the Mexican project because the option to expand into the Latin American market more than compensates for the negative NPV of the Mexican project.

Tests for Expansion Option to Have Value
Not all investments have options embedded in them, and not all options, even if they do exist, have value. To assess whether an investment creates valuable options that need to be analyzed and valued, we need to understand three key questions

1. *Is the first investment a prerequisite for the later investment/expansion? If not, how necessary is the first investment for the later investment/expansion?* Consider our earlier analysis of the value of a patent or the value of an undeveloped

oil reserve as options. A firm cannot generate patents without investing in research or paying another firm for the patents, and it cannot get rights to an undeveloped oil reserve without bidding on it at a government auction or buying it from another oil company. Clearly, the initial investment here (spending on R&D, bidding at the auction) is required for the firm to have the second investment. Now consider the Disney investment in a Spanish-language channel, without which presumably it cannot expand into the larger Latin American market. Unlike the patent and undeveloped reserves examples, the initial investment is not a prerequisite for the second, though management might view it as such. The connection gets even weaker, and the option value lower, when we look at one firm acquiring another to have the option to be able to enter a large market. Acquiring an Internet service provider to have a foothold in the online retailing market or buying a Chinese brewery to preserve the option to enter the Chinese beer market would be examples of less valuable options.

2. *Does the firm have an exclusive right to the later investment/expansion? If not, does the initial investment provide the firm with significant competitive advantages on subsequent investments?* The value of the option ultimately derives not from the cash flows generated by the second and subsequent investments but from the excess returns generated by these cash flows. The greater the potential for excess returns on the second investment, the greater the value of the expansion option. The potential for excess returns is closely tied to how much of a competitive advantage the first investment provides the firm when it takes subsequent investments. At one extreme, again, consider investing in R&D to acquire a patent. The patent gives the firm that owns it the exclusive rights to produce that product, and if the market potential is large, the right to the excess returns from the project. At the other extreme, the firm might get no competitive advantages on subsequent investments, in which case it is questionable whether there can be any excess returns on these investments. In reality, most investments will fall in the continuum between these two extremes, with greater competitive advantages being associated with higher excess returns and larger option values.

3. *How sustainable are the competitive advantages?* In a competitive marketplace, excess returns attract competitors, and competition drives out excess returns. The more sustainable the competitive advantages possessed by a firm, the greater the value of the options embedded in the initial investment. The sustainability of competitive advantages is a function of two forces. The first is the *nature of the competition;* other things remaining equal, competitive advantages fade much more quickly in sectors where there are aggressive competitors. The second is the *nature of the competitive advantage.* If the resource controlled by the firm is finite and scarce (as is the case with natural resource reserves and vacant land), the competitive advantage is likely to be sustainable for longer periods. Alternatively, if the competitive advantage comes from being the first mover in a market or from having technological expertise, it will come under assault far sooner. The most direct way of reflecting this competitive advantage in the value of the option is in its life; the life of the option can be set to the period of competitive advantage and only the excess returns earned over this period counts toward the value of the option.

Practical Considerations

The practical considerations associated with estimating the value of the option to expand are similar to those associated with valuing the option to delay. In most cases, firms with options to expand have no specific time horizon by which they have to make an expansion decision, making these open-ended options or at best options with arbitrary lives. Even in those cases where a life can be estimated for the option, neither the size nor the potential market for the product may be known, and estimating either can be problematic. To illustrate, consider the Disney expansion example. We adopted a period of ten years, at the end of which Disney has to decide one way or another on its future expansion in Latin America, but it is entirely possible that this time frame is not specified at the time of the first investment. Furthermore, we have assumed that both the cost and the present value of expansion are known initially. In reality, the firm may not have good estimates for either before starting its Mexican cable channel because it does not have much information on the underlying market.

Intuitive Implications

The option to expand is implicitly used by firms to rationalize taking investments that have negative NPV but provide significant opportunities to tap into new markets or sell new products. Although the option pricing approach adds rigor to this argument by estimating the value of this option, it also provides insight into those occasions when it is most valuable. In general, the option to expand is clearly more valuable for more volatile businesses with higher returns on projects (such as biotechnology or computer software) than in stable businesses with lower returns (such as housing, chemicals or automobiles).

It can also be argued that R&D provides one immediate application for this methodology. Investing in R&D is justified by noting that it provides the basis for new products for the future. In recent years, however, more firms have stopped accepting this explanation at face value as a rationale for spending more money on R&D and have started demanding better returns from their investments.

Firms that spend considerable amounts of money on R&D or test marketing are often stymied when they try to evaluate these expenses, because the payoffs are often in terms of future projects. At the same time, there is the very real possibility that after the money has been spent, the products or projects may turn out not to be viable; consequently, the expenditure is treated as a sunk cost. In fact, it can be argued that what emerges from R&D—patents or technological expertise—has the characteristics of a call option. If this is true, the amount spent on the R&D is the cost of the call option, and the patents that might emerge from the research provide the value for option.

Several logical implications emerge from this view of R&D. First, research expenditures should provide much higher value for firms that are in volatile technologies or businesses because the higher variance in product or project cash flows creates more valuable call options. It follows, then, that R&D at pharmaceutical firms should be redirected to areas where little is known and there is substantial uncertainty—gene therapy, for example—and away from areas where there is more stability. Second, the value of research and the optimal amount to be spent on research will change over time as businesses mature. The best example is the pharmaceutical industry—drug companies spent most of the 1980s investing substantial amounts in research and earning high returns on new products, as the health care business expanded. In the 1990s, however, as health care costs started leveling off and the business matured, many of these companies found that they were not getting the same payoffs on research and started cutting back.

6.9 R&D Expenditures and Option Pricing

If we perceive R&D expenses as the price of acquiring options (product patents), R&D expenditures will have most value if directed to

☐ areas where the technology is stable and the likelihood of success is high.

☐ areas where the technology is volatile, though the likelihood of success is low.

☐ Neither.

Explain.

IN PRACTICE: Are Strategic Considerations Really Options?

Many firms faced with projects that do not meet their financial benchmarks use the argument that these projects should be taken anyway because of strategic considerations. In other words, it is argued that these projects will accomplish other goals for the firm or allow the firm to enter into other markets. Although we are wary of how this argument is used to justify poor projects, there are cases where these strategic considerations are really referring to options embedded in projects—options to produce new products or expand into new markets.

Take the example of the Disney Channel expansion into Mexico and Latin America project. The project, based on conventional capital budgeting, has a negative NPV, but it should be taken nevertheless because it gives Disney the option to enter a potentially lucrative market. Disney might well use the strategic considerations argument to accept the project anyway.

The differences between using real options and the strategic considerations argument are the following:

1. Real options assigns value to only some of the strategic considerations that firms may have. For instance, the option to enter the Latin American market has value because of the variance in the estimates of the value of entering the market and the fact that Disney has to take the smaller project (the Mexican venture) first to get the option. However, strategic considerations that are not clearly defined and have little exclusivity, such as "corporate image" or "growth potential," may not have any value from an option pricing standpoint.

2. Option pricing attempts to put a dollar value on the strategic consideration. As a consequence, the existence of strategic considerations does not guarantee that the project will be taken. In the Disney example, the Mexican venture should not be taken if the value of the option to enter the Latin American market is less than $20 million. ■

The Option to Abandon a Project

The final option to consider here is the option to abandon a project when its cash flows do not measure up to expectations. Generally, the option to abandon a project later will make that project more attractive to investors now.

Describing the Option to Abandon

To illustrate the option to abandon, assume that you have invested in a project and that V is the remaining value on a project if you continue it to the end of its life. Now, assume that you can abandon the project today and that L is the liquidation or abandonment value for the same project. If the project has a life of n years, the value of continuing the project can be compared to the liquidation (abandonment) value—if it is higher, the project should be continued; if it is lower, the holder of the abandonment option could consider abandoning the project.

$$\text{Payoff from owning an abandonment option} = 0 \quad \text{if } V > L$$
$$= L \quad \text{if } V < L$$

These payoffs are graphed in Figure 6.10.

Unlike the prior two cases, the option to abandon takes on the characteristics of a put option.

Figure 6.10 The Option to Abandon a Project

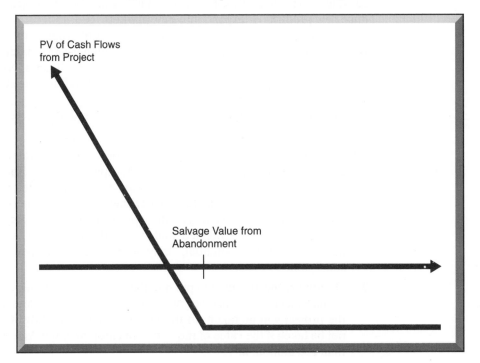

ILLUSTRATION 6.12   Valuing Disney's Option to Abandon: A Real Estate Investment

Assume that Disney is considering taking a twenty-five-year project that requires an initial investment of $250 million in a real estate partnership to develop time-share properties with a south Florida real estate developer and where the present value of expected cash flows is $254 million. Although the NPV of $4 million is small for a project of this size, assume that Disney has the option to abandon this project at any time in the next five years by selling its share back to the developer for $150 million. A simulation of the cash flows on this time-share investment yields a standard deviation in the present value of the cash flows from being in the partnership of 20 percent.

The value of the abandonment option can be estimated by determining the characteristics of the put option:

$$\text{Value of the Underlying Asset (S)} = \text{PV of Cash Flows from Project}$$
$$= \$254 \text{ million}$$

$$\text{Strike Price (K)} = \text{Salvage Value from Abandonment} = \$150 \text{ million}$$

$$\text{Variance in Underlying Asset's Value} = 0.20^2 = 0.04$$

$$\text{Time to Expiration} = \text{Abandonment Period} = 5 \text{ years}$$

$$\text{Dividend Yield} = 1/\text{Life of the Project}$$
$$= 1/25$$
$$= 0.04 \text{ (We are assuming that the project's present value}$$
$$\text{will drop by roughly } 1/n \text{ each year into the project)}$$

Assume that the five-year riskless rate is 4 percent. The value of the put option can be estimated as follows:

$$\text{Call Value} = 254 \exp^{(-0.04)(5)}(0.9194) - 150 \exp^{(-0.04)(5)}(0.8300) = \$89.27 \text{ million}$$

$$\text{Put Value} = \$89.27 - 254 \exp^{(-0.04)(5)} + 150 \exp^{(-0.04)(5)} = \$4.13 \text{ million}$$

The value of this abandonment option has to be added on to the NPV of the project of $4 million, yielding a total NPV with the abandonment option of $8.13 million.

6.10   ABANDONMENT VALUE AND PROJECT LIFE

Consider the project just described. Assume that three years into the project, the cash flows are coming in 20 percent below expectations. What will happen to the value of the option to abandon?

☐   It will increase.

☐   It will decrease.

☐   It may increase or decrease, depending on . . .

Explain.

Intuitive Implications

The fact that the option to abandon has value provides a rationale for firms to build the flexibility to scale back or terminate projects if they do not measure up to expectations. Firms can do this in a number of ways. The first and most direct way is to build in the option contractually with those parties that are involved in the project.

Thus, contracts with suppliers may be written on an annual basis, rather than for the long-term, and employees may be hired on a temporary basis rather than permanently. The physical plant used for a project may be leased on a short-term basis, rather than bought, and the financial investment may be made in stages rather than as an initial lump sum. Although there is a cost to building in this flexibility, the gains may be much larger, especially in volatile businesses. The option to abandon is particularly valuable for smaller companies investing in large projects, where the investment in the project represents a significant percentage of the firm's capital.

CONCLUSION

Projects often create side costs and benefits that are not captured in the initial estimates of cash flows used to estimate returns. In this chapter, we examined some of these indirect costs and benefits:

- Investing in one project may prevent a firm from taking alternative investments if these are mutually exclusive. If projects have equal lives and there are no capital rationing constraints, we can pick the investment with the higher NPV. If this is not the case, we have to find ways of controlling for differences in project lives (by computing an equivalent annuity) and for differences in scale (by computing profitability indices).
- Opportunity costs measure the costs of resources that the company already owns that might be used for a new project. Although the business might not spend new money acquiring these resources, there are consequences in terms of the cash flows that have to be reflected in the returns.
- Projects may also provide benefits for other projects for a firm. These benefits, which also take the form of cash flows, should be reflected in the returns.
- Projects may also create options that are valuable—options to expand into new markets and produce new products. When such options exist, conventional discounted cash flow models will tend to understate the value of investments.

In summary, the project returns have to reflect all of the side costs and benefits.

PROBLEMS AND QUESTIONS

(In the problems below, you can use a risk premium of 5.5 percent and a tax rate of 40 percent if none is specified.)

1. A small manufacturing firm, which has limited access to capital, has a capital rationing constraint of $150 million and is faced with the following investment projects (numbers in millions):

Project	Initial Investment	NPV
A	$25	$10
B	$30	$25
C	$40	$20
D	$10	$10
E	$15	$10
F	$60	$20
G	$20	$10
H	$25	$20
I	$35	$10
J	$15	$5

a. Which of these projects would you accept? Why?

b. What is the cost of the capital rationing constraint?

2. A closely held, publicly traded firm faces self-imposed capital rationing constraints of $100 million in this period and $75 million in the next period. It has to choose among the following projects (in millions):

INVESTMENT OUTLAY

Project	Current Period	Next Period	NPV
A	$20	$10	$20
B	$25	$15	$20
C	$30	$30	$15
D	$15	$15	$20
E	$40	$25	$30
F	$10	$10	$10
G	$20	$15	$20
H	$30	$25	$35
I	$35	$25	$25
J	$25	$15	$10

Set up the investment problem, assuming that fractions and multiples of projects cannot be taken.

3. You own a rental building in the city and are interested in replacing the heating system. You are faced with the following alternatives:

a. A solar heating system, which will cost $12,000 to install and $500 a year to run and will last forever (assume that your building will, too).

b. A gas heating system, which will cost $5,000 to install and $1,000 a year to run and will last twenty years.

c. An oil heating system, which will cost $3,500 to install and $1,200 a year to run and will last fifteen years.

If your opportunity cost is 10 percent, which of these three options is best for you?

4. You are trying to choose a new siding for your house. A salesman offers you two choices:

- Wood siding, which will last ten years and cost $5,000 to install and $1,000/year to maintain
- Aluminum siding, which will last forever, cost $15,000 to install, and will have a lower maintenance cost per year

If your discount rate is 10 percent, how low would your maintenance costs have to be for you to choose the aluminum siding?

5. You have just been approached by a magazine with an offer for renewing your subscription. You can renew for one year at $20, two years for $36, or three years at $45. Assuming that you have an opportunity cost of 20 percent and the cost of a subscription will not change over time, which of these three options should you choose?

6. You have been hired as a capital budgeting analyst by a sporting goods firm that manufactures athletic shoes and has captured 10 percent of the overall shoe market. (The total market is worth $100 million a year.) The fixed costs associated with manufacturing these shoes is $2 million a year, and variable costs are 40 percent of revenues. The company's tax rate is 40 percent. The firm believes that it can increase its market share to 20 percent by investing $10 million in a new distribution system (which can be depreciated over the system's life of 10 years to a salvage value of zero) and spending $1 million a year in additional advertising. The company proposes to continue to maintain working capital at 10 percent of annual revenues. The discount rate to be used for this project is 8 percent.

a. What is the initial investment for this project?

b. What is the annual operating cash flow from this project?

c. What is the NPV of this project?

d. How much would the firm's market share have to increase for you to be indifferent to taking or rejecting this project?

7. You are considering the possibility of replacing an existing machine that has a book value of $500,000, a remaining depreciable life of five years, and a salvage value today of $300,000. The replacement machine will cost $2 million and have a ten-year life. Assuming that you use straight-line depreciation and that neither machine will have any salvage value at the end of the next ten years, how much would you need to save each year to make the change (the tax rate is 40 percent)?

8. You are helping a bookstore decide whether it should open a coffee shop on the premises. The details of the investment are as follows:

- The coffee shop will cost $50,000 to open; it will have a five-year life and be depreciated straight line over the period to a salvage value of $10,000.

- The sales at the shop are expected to be $15,000 in the first year and grow 5 percent a year for the following four years.

- The operating expenses will be 50 percent of revenues.

- The tax rate is 40 percent.

- The coffee shop is expected to generate additional sales of $20,000 next year for the book shop, and the pretax operating margin is 40 percent. These sales will grow 10 percent a year for the following four years.

a. Estimate the net present value of the coffee shop without the additional book sales.

b. Estimate the present value of the cash flows accruing from the additional book sales.

c. Would you open the coffee shop?

9. The lining of a plating tank must be replaced every three years at the cost of approximately $2,000. A new lining material has been developed that is more resistant to the corrosive effects of the plating liquid and will cost approximately $4,000. If the required rate of return is 20 percent and annual property taxes and insurance amount to about 4 percent of the initial investment, how long must the new lining last to be more economical than the present one?

10. You are a small business owner considering two alternatives for your phone system.

	Plan A	Plan B
Initial cost	$50,000	$120,000
Annual maintenance cost	$9,000	$6,000
Salvage value	$10,000	$20,000
Life	20 years	40 years

The discount rate is 8 percent. Which alternative would you pick?

11. You have been asked to compare three alternative investments and make a recommendation.

- Project A has an initial investment of $5 million and after-tax cash flows of $2.5 million a year for the next five years.

- Project B has no initial investment, after-tax cash flows of $1 million a year for the next ten years, and a salvage value of $2 million (from working capital).

- Project C has an initial investment of $10 million, another investment of $5 million in ten years, and after-tax cash flows of $2.5 million a year forever.

The discount rate is 10 percent for all three projects. Which of the three projects would you pick? Why? (Ignore depreciation.)

12. You are the manager of a pharmaceutical company and are considering what type of laptop computers to buy for your salespeople to take with them on their calls.

- You can buy fairly inexpensive (and less powerful) older machines for about $2,000 each. These machines will be obsolete in three years and are expected to have an annual maintenance cost of $150.

- You can buy newer and more powerful laptops for about $4,000 each. These machines will last five years and are expected to have an annual maintenance cost of $50.

If your cost of capital is 12 percent, which option would you pick and why?

13. You are the supervisor of a town where the roads are in need of repair. You have a limited budget and are considering two options:

   • You can patch up the roads for $100,000, but you will have to repeat this expenditure every year to keep the roads in reasonable shape.

   • You can spend $400,000 to repave and repair the roads, in which case your annual expenditures on maintenance will drop.

If your discount rate is 10 percent, how much would the annual expenditures have to drop in the second option for you to consider it?

14. You are the manager of a specialty retailing firm that is considering two strategies for getting into the Malaysian retail market. Under the first strategy, the firm will make an initial investment of $10 million and can expect to capture about 5 percent of the overall market share. Under the second strategy, the firm will make a much larger commitment of $40 million for advertising and promotion and can expect to capture about 10 percent of the market share. If the overall size of the market is $200 million, the firm's cost of capital is 12 percent, and the typical life of a project in the firm is fifteen years, what would the after-tax operating margin have to be for the firm to consider the second strategy? (You can assume that the firm leases its stores and has no depreciation or capital expenditures.)

15. You work for a firm that has limited access to capital markets. As a consequence, it has only $20 million available for new investments this year. The firm does have a ready supply of good projects, and you have listed all the projects.

Project	Initial Investment (million)	NPV (million)	IRR (%)
I	$10	$3	21%
II	$5	$2.5	28%
III	$15	$4	19%
IV	$10	$4	24%
V	$5	$2	20%

a. Based on the profitability index, which of these projects would you take?

b. Based on the IRR, which of these projects would you take?

c. Why might the two approaches give you different answers?

16. You are the owner of a small hardware store, and you are considering opening a gardening store in a vacant area in the back of your present store. You estimate that it will cost you $50,000 to set up the new store, and that you will generate $10,000 in after-tax cash flows from the store for the life of the store (which is expected to be ten years). The one concern you have is that you have limited parking; by opening the gardening store you run the risk of not having enough parking for customers who shop at your hardware store. You estimate that the lost sales from such occurrences would amount to $3,000 a year, and that your after-tax operating margin on sales at the hardware store is 40 percent. If your discount rate is 14 percent, would you open the gardening store?

17. You are the manager of a grocery store, and you are considering offering baby-sitting services to your customers. You estimate that the licensing and set up costs will amount to $150,000 initially and that you will be spending about $60,000 annually to provide the service. As a result of the service, you expect sales at the store, which is $5 million currently, to increase by 20 percent; your after-tax operating margin is 10 percent. If your cost of capital is 12 percent, and you expect the store to remain open for ten years, would you offer the service?

18. You run a financial service firm where you replace your employee's computers every three years. You have 500 employees, and each computer costs $2,500 currently—the old computers can be sold for $500 each. The new computers are generally depreciated straight line over their three-year lives to a salvage value of $500. A computer-service firm offers to lease you the computers and replace them for you at no cost, if you will pay a leasing fee of $5 million a year (which is tax-deductible). If your tax rate is 40 percent, would you accept the offer?

19. You are examining the viability of a capital investment in which your firm is interested. The

project will require an initial investment of $500,000 and the projected revenues are $400,000 a year for five years. The projected cost-of-goods-sold is 40 percent of revenues and the tax rate is 40 percent. The initial investment is primarily in plant and equipment and can be depreciated straight line over five years (the salvage value is zero). The project makes use of other resources that your firm already owns:

- Two employees of the firm, each with a salary of $40,000 a year, who are currently employed by another division, will be transferred to this project. The other division has no alternative use for them, but they are covered by a union contract that will prevent them from being fired for three years (during which time they would be paid their current salary).
- The project will use excess capacity in the current packaging plant. Although this excess capacity has no alternative use now, it is estimated that the firm will have to invest $250,000 in a new packaging plant in year four as a consequence of this project using up excess capacity (instead of year eight as originally planned).
- The project will use a van currently owned by the firm. Although the van is not currently being used, it can be rented out for $3,000 a year for five years. The book value of the van is $10,000 and it is being depreciated straight line (with five years remaining for depreciation).
- The discount rate to be used for this project is 10 percent.

a. What (if any) is the opportunity cost associated with using the two employees from another division?

b. What (if any) is the opportunity cost associated with the use of excess capacity of the packaging plant?

c. What (if any) is the opportunity cost associated with the use of the van ?

d. What is the after-tax operating cash flow each year on this project?

e. What is the NPV of this project?

20. Your company is considering producing a new product. You have a production facility that is currently used to only 50 percent of capacity, and you plan to use some of the excess capacity for the new product. The production facility cost $50 million five years ago when it was built and is being depreciated straight line over twenty-five years (in real dollars, assume that this cost will stay constant over time). (See table below.)

The new product has a life of ten years, the tax rate is 40 percent, and the appropriate discount rate (real) is 10 percent.

a. If you take on this project, when would you run out of capacity?

b. When you run out of capacity, what would you lose if you chose to cut back production (in present value after-tax dollars)? (You have to decide which product you are going to cut back production on.)

c. What would the opportunity cost to be assigned to this new product be if you chose to build a new facility when you run out of capacity instead of cutting back on production?

21. You are an analyst for a sporting goods corporation that is considering a new project that will take advantage of excess capacity in an existing plant. The plant has a capacity to produce 50,000 tennis racquets, but only 25,000 are being produced currently though sales of the rackets are increasing 10 percent a year. You want to use some of the remaining capacity to manufacture 20,000 squash rackets each year for the next ten years (which will use up 40 percent of the total capacity), and this market is assumed to be stable (no growth). An average tennis racquet sells for $100 and costs $40 to make. The tax rate for the corporation is 40 percent, and the discount rate is 10 percent. Is there an opportunity cost involved? If so, how much is it?

Product Line	Capacity Used (%)	Growth Rate (%)/Year Currently	Revenues Currently ($ million)	Fixed Cost ($ million) /Year	Variable Cost ($ million) /Year
Old product	50	5	100	25	50
New product	30	10	80	20	44

CHAPTER 7

CAPITAL STRUCTURE: OVERVIEW OF THE FINANCING DECISION

In the past few chapters, we examined the investment principle and argued that projects that earn a return greater than the minimum acceptable hurdle rate are good projects. In coming up with the cost of capital, which we defined to be the minimum acceptable hurdle rate, however, we used the existing mix of debt and equity used by the firm.

In this chapter, we examine the choices that a firm has in terms of both debt and equity and how these choices change over a firm's life cycle. In particular, we look at how the choices change as a firm goes from being a small, private business to a large publicly traded corporation. We then evaluate the basic trade-off between using debt

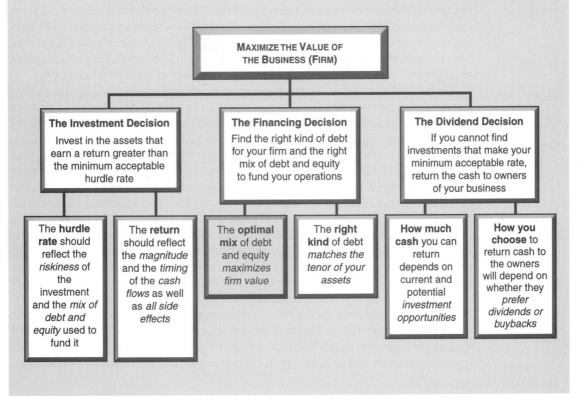

and equity by weighing the benefits of borrowing against its costs. We close the chapter by examining when the costs of borrowing exactly offset its benefits, which essentially makes debt irrelevant, and the implications for corporate finance.

THE CHOICES: TYPES OF FINANCING

There are only two ways in which any business can raise money—debt or equity. This may seem simplistic, given the array of choices firms have in terms of financing vehicles. We will begin this section with a discussion of the characteristics of debt and equity and then look at a range of financing vehicles available within each of these categories. We will then examine a range of securities that share some characteristics with debt and some with equity and are therefore called **hybrid securities.**

Hybrid Security: Any security that shares some of the characteristics of debt and some characteristics of equity.

The Continuum between Debt and Equity

Although the distinction between debt and equity is often made in terms of bonds and stocks, its roots lie in the nature of the cash flow claims of each type of financing. The first distinction is that a *debt claim* entitles the holder to a contractual set of cash flows (usually interest and principal payments), whereas an *equity claim* entitles the holder to any residual cash flows after meeting all other promised claims. This remains the fundamental difference, but other distinctions have arisen, partly as a result of the tax code and partly as a consequence of legal developments.

The second distinction, which is a logical outgrowth of the nature of cash flow claims (contractual versus residual), is that debt has a prior claim on both cash flows on a period-to-period basis (for interest and principal payments) and on the assets of the firm (in the case of liquidation). Third, the tax laws have generally treated interest expenses, which accrue to debt holders, very differently and often much more advantageously than dividends or other cash flows that accrue to equity. In the United States, for instance, interest expenses are tax-deductible to the entity paying them, and thus create tax savings, whereas dividend payments have to be made out of after-tax cash flows. Fourth, debt usually has a fixed maturity date, at which point the principal is due, whereas equity generally has an infinite life. Finally, equity investors, by virtue of their claim on the residual cash flows of the firm, are generally given the bulk of or all of the control of the management of the firm. Debt investors, on the other hand, play a much more passive role in management, exercising at most veto power over significant financial decisions.[1] These differences are summarized in Figure 7.1.

To summarize, debt is defined as any financing vehicle that is a contractual claim on the firm (and not a function of its operating performance), creates tax-deductible payments, has a fixed life, and has a priority claim on cash flows in both operating periods and in bankruptcy. Conversely, equity is defined as any financing

---

[1]Veto power is usually exercised through covenants or restrictions written into bond agreements.

Figure 7.1   Debt versus Equity

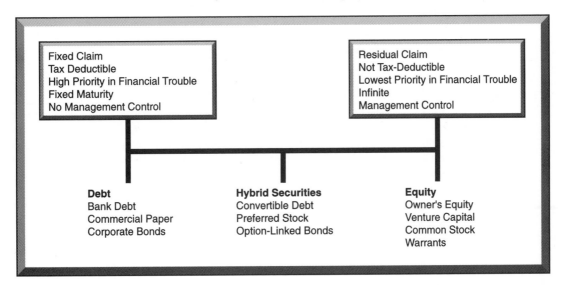

vehicle that is a residual claim on the firm, does not create a tax advantage from its payments, has an infinite life, does not have priority in bankruptcy, and provides management control to the owner. Any security that shares characteristics with both is a hybrid security.

IN PRACTICE: A Financing Checklist for Classifying Securities

Some new securities at first sight are difficult to categorize as either debt or equity. To check where on the spectrum between straight debt and straight equity these securities fall, answer the following questions:

1. *Are the payments on the securities contractual or residual?*
   - If contractual, it is closer to debt.
   - If residual, it is closer to equity.
2. *Are the payments tax-deductible?*
   - If yes, it is closer to debt.
   - If no, if is closer to equity.
3. *Do the cash flows on the security have a high priority or a low priority if the firm is in financial trouble?*
   - If it has high priority, it is closer to debt.
   - If it has low priority, it is closer to equity.
4. *Does the security have a fixed life?*
   - If yes, it is closer to debt.
   - If no, it is closer to equity.

5. *Does the owner of the security get a share of the control of management of the firm?*

- If no, it is closer to debt.
- If yes, if is closer to equity ■

7.1 IS THIS DEBT OR IS IT EQUITY?

You have been asked to classify a security as debt or equity and have been provided the following characteristics for the security: It requires fixed monthly payments that are tax-deductible and it has an infinite life. Its claims on the cash flows of the firm, during operation, and on the assets, if the firm goes bankrupt, come after all debt holders' claims (including unsecured debt) are met.

☐ It is debt.

☐ It is equity.

☐ It is a hybrid security.

A. EQUITY

Although most people think of equity in terms of common stock, the equity claim on a business can take a variety of forms, depending partly on whether the firm is privately owned or publicly traded and partly on the firm's growth and risk characteristics. Private firms have fewer choices available than do publicly traded firms, because they cannot issue securities to raise equity. Consequently, they have to depend either on the owner or a private entity, usually a venture capitalist, to bring in the equity needed to keep the business operating and expanding. Publicly traded firms have access to capital markets, giving them a wider array of choices.

Owner's Equity

Most businesses, including the most successful companies of our time, such as Microsoft and Wal-Mart, started off as small businesses with one or a few individuals providing the seed money and plowing back the earnings of the firm into the businesses. These funds, brought in by the owners of the company, are referred to as the *owner's equity* and provide the basis for the growth and eventual success of the business.

Venture Capital and Private Equity

As small businesses succeed and grow, they typically run into is a funding constraint, where the funds that they have access to are insufficient to cover their investment and growth needs. A **venture capitalist** or private equity investor provides equity financing to small and often risky businesses in return for a share of the ownership of the firm.

Generally speaking, the capacity to raise funds from alternative sources and/or to go public will increase with the size of the firm and decrease with the uncertainty about its future prospects. Thus, smaller and riskier businesses are more likely to seek venture capital and are also more likely to be asked to give up a greater share of the value of the firm when receiving the venture capital.

Venture Capital: Equity capital provided to a private firm by an investor(s) in exchange for a share of the ownership of the firm.

7.2 THE EFFECTS OF DIVERSIFICATION ON VENTURE CAPITALISTS

You are comparing the required returns of two venture capitalists who are interested in investing in the same software firm. One venture capitalist has all of his capital invested in only software firms, whereas the other has invested her capital in small companies in a variety of businesses. Which of these two will demand the higher required rate of return?

☐ The venture capitalist who is invested only in software companies.

☐ The venture capitalist who is invested in a variety of businesses.

☐ Cannot answer without more information.

If both venture capitalists had the same expected cash flow estimates for the business, which one would demand a larger share of the ownership for the same capital investment?

☐ The venture capitalist with the higher required rate of return.

☐ The venture capitalist with the lower required rate of return.

Common Stock

The conventional way for a publicly traded firm to raise equity is to issue common stock at a price the market is willing to pay. For a newly listed company, this price is estimated by an investment banker and is called the offering price. For an existing publicly traded company, the price at which additional equity is issued is usually based on the current market price. In some cases, the common stock issued by a company is uniform; that is, each share receives a proportional share of both the cash flows (such as dividends) and the voting rights. In other cases, different classes of common stock will provide different dividends and voting rights.

Common stock is a simple security, and it is relatively easy to understand and value. In fact, it can be argued that common stock makes feasible all other security choices for a publicly traded firm because a firm without equity cannot issue debt or hybrid securities. The accounting treatment of common stock follows well-established precedent and can be presented easily within the conventional format of financial statements.

Warrants

In recent years, firms have started looking at equity alternatives to common stock. One alternative used successfully by Japanese companies in the late 1980s involved **warrants,** where the holders received the right to buy shares in the company at a fixed price sometime in the future in return for paying for the warrants up front. Because their value is derived from the price of the underlying common stock, warrants have to be treated as another form of equity.

Why might a firm use warrants rather than common stock to raise equity? We can think of several reasons. First, warrants are priced based on the implied volatility assigned to the underlying stock; the greater the volatility, the greater the value. To the degree that the market overestimates how risky a firm is, the firm may gain by using warrants and option-like securities. Second, warrants by themselves create no financial obligations at the time of the issue. Consequently, issuing warrants is a good way for a high-growth firm to raise funds, especially when current cash flows are low or negative. Third, for financial officers who are sensitive to the dilution created by issuing common stock, warrants seem to provide the best of both worlds—they do not create any new additional shares currently while they raise equity investment funds for current use.

Warrant: A security issued by a company that provides the holder with the right to buy a share of stock in the company at a fixed price during the life of the warrant.

7.3 STOCK PRICE VARIANCE AND THE USE OF WARRANTS

Companies with high variance in their stock prices should use warrants more than companies with low variance in their stock prices, because warrant prices increase with variance.

☐ True

☐ False

Explain.

IN PRACTICE: VALUING WARRANTS

Warrants are long-term call options, but standard option pricing models are based on the assumption that exercising an option does not affect the value of the underlying asset. This may be true for listed options on stocks, but it is not true for warrants, because their exercise increases the number of shares outstanding and brings fresh cash into the firm, both of which will affect the stock price. The expected negative impact (dilution) of their exercise will make warrants less valuable than otherwise similar call options. There are two significant differences between the inputs we use to value conventional options (see Appendix 4 for more on option pricing models) and the inputs used to value a dilution-adjusted option.

Step 1: The stock price is adjusted for the expected dilution from warrant exercise.

$$\text{Dilution-Adjusted } S = (Sn_s + Wn_w)/(n_s + n_w)$$

where S = current value of the stock; n_s = number of shares outstanding; W = market value of warrants outstanding; and n_w = number of warrants outstanding. When the warrants are exercised, the number of shares outstanding will increase, reducing the stock price. The numerator reflects the market value of equity, including both stocks and warrants outstanding. Making this adjustment will lower the stock price used in the option pricing model and hence the value of the warrant.

Step 2: The variance used in the option pricing formula is the variance in the value of the equity in the company (i.e., the value of stocks plus warrants, not just the stocks). ■

Contingent Value Rights

Contingent value rights provide investors with the right to sell stocks for a fixed price and thus derive their value from the volatility of the stock and the desire on the part of investors to hedge their losses. *Put options,* which are traded on the option exchanges, give their holders a similar right to sell the underlying stock at a fixed price. There are two primary differences between contingent value rights and put options. First, the proceeds from the contingent value rights sales go to the firm, whereas those from the sale of listed put options go to private parties. Second, contingent value rights tend to be much more long-term than typical listed put options.

There are several reasons why a firm may choose to issue contingent value rights. The most obvious is that the firm believes it is significantly undervalued by the market. In such a scenario, the firm may offer contingent value rights to take advantage of its belief and to provide a signal to the market of the undervaluation. Contingent value rights are also useful if the market is overestimating volatility and the put price reflects this misestimated volatility. Finally, the presence of contingent value rights as insurance may attract new investors to the market for the common stock.

Contingent Value Rights: A contingent value right provides the holder with the right to sell a share of stock in the underlying company at a fixed price during the life of the right.

B. DEBT

The clear alternative to using equity, which is a residual claim, is to borrow money. Borrowing creates an obligation to make cash flow payments in operation and provides the lender with prior claims if the firm is in financial trouble.

Bank Debt

Historically, the primary source of borrowed money for all private firms and many publicly traded firms has been banks, with the interest rates on the debt based on the perceived risk of the borrower. Bank debt provides the borrower with several advantages. First, it can be used for borrowing relatively small amounts of money; in contrast, bond issues thrive on economies of scale, with larger issues having lower costs. Second, if the company is neither well known nor widely followed, bank debt provides a convenient mechanism to convey information to the lender that will help in both pricing and evaluating the loan; in other words, a borrower can provide internal information about projects and the firm to the lending bank. The presence of hundreds of investors in bond issues makes this both costly and not feasible if bonds are issued as the primary vehicle for debt. Finally, to issue bonds, firms have to submit to being rated by ratings agencies and provide sufficient information to make this rating Dealing with a rating agency might be much more difficult and costly for many firms, especially smaller firms, than dealing with a lending bank.

Besides being a source of both long-term and short-term borrowing for firms, banks also often offer them a flexible option to meet unanticipated or seasonal financing needs. This option is a *line of credit*, which the firm can draw on only if it needs financing. In most cases, a line of credit specifies an amount the firm can borrow and links the interest rate on the borrowing to a market rate, such as the prime rate or Treasury rates. The advantage of having a line of credit is that it provides the firm with access to the funds without having to pay interest costs if the funds remain unused. Thus, it is a useful type of financing for firms with volatile working capital needs. In many cases, however, the firm is required to maintain a compensating balance on which it earns either no interest or below-market rates. For instance, a firm that wants a $20 million line of credit from a bank might need to maintain a compensating balance of $2 million, on which it earns no interest. The opportunity cost of having this compensating balance must be weighed against the higher interest costs that will be incurred by taking on a more conventional loan to cover working capital needs.

Bonds

For larger, publicly traded firms, an alternative to bank debt is to issue bonds. Generally speaking, bond issues have several advantages for these firms. The first is that bonds often carry more favorable financing terms than equivalent bank debt, largely because risk is shared by a larger number of financial market investors. The second is that bond issues might provide a chance for the issuer to add on special features that could not be added on to bank debt. For instance, bonds can be convertible into common stock or be tied to commodity prices (commodity bonds). When issuing bonds, firms have to make a variety of choices, including the maturity of the borrowing (short-term or long-term), whether the bonds should have fixed interest payments or an interest rate tied to market rates (fixed and floating rates), the nature of the security offered to those buying the bonds (secured versus unsecured) and how the bonds will be repaid over time. In Chapter 9, we will examine how best to make these choices.

7.4 CORPORATE BONDS AND BANK DEBT

If a company can issue corporate bonds, it should not use bank debt.
- ☐ True
- ☐ False

Explain.

Leases

A firm often borrows money to finance the acquisition of an asset needed for its operations. An alternative approach that accomplishes the same goal is to lease the asset. In a lease, the firm commits to making fixed payments to the owner of the asset for the rights to use the asset. These fixed payments are either fully or partially tax-deductible, depending on how the lease is categorized for accounting purposes. Failure to make lease payments initially results in the loss of the leased asset but can also result in bankruptcy, though the claims of the lessors (owners of the leased assets) may sometimes be subordinated to the claims of other lenders to the firm.

A lease agreement is usually categorized as either an operating lease or a capital lease. For *operating leases,* the term of the lease agreement is shorter than the life of the asset, and the present value of lease payments is generally much lower than the actual price of the asset. At the end of the life of the lease, the asset reverts back to the lessor, who will either offer to sell it to the lessee or lease it to somebody else. The lessee usually has the right to cancel the lease and return the asset to the lessor. Thus, the ownership of the asset in an operating lease clearly resides with the lessor, with the lessee bearing little or no risk if the asset becomes obsolete. Operating leases cover the store spaces leased out by specialty retailing firms like The Gap and Ann Taylor, for instance.

A *capital lease* generally lasts for the life of the asset, with the present value of lease payments covering the price of the asset. A capital lease generally cannot be canceled, and the lease can be renewed at the end of its life at a reduced rate or the asset acquired by the lessee at a favorable price. In many cases, the lessor is not obligated to pay insurance and taxes on the asset, leaving these obligations up to the lessee; the lessee consequently reduces the lease payments, leading to what are called *net leases.* A capital lease places substantial risk on the shoulders of the lessee if the asset loses value or becomes obsolete. Although the differences between operating and financial leases are obvious, some lease arrangements do not fit neatly into one or another of these extremes; rather, they share some features of both types of leases. These leases are called *combination leases.*

7.5 DEBT MATURITY AND INTEREST RATES

Assume that long-term interest rates are much higher than short-term rates (a steeply upward-sloping yield curve) and that your investment banker advises you to issue short-term debt because it is cheaper than long-term debt. Is this statement true?

☐ Yes

☐ False

Why or why not?

IN PRACTICE: LEASING VERSUS BORROWING

If borrowing money to buy an asset and leasing the asset are both variations on debt, why might a firm choose one over the other? We can think of several factors that may sway firms in this choice:

1. *Service Reasons* In some cases, the lessor of an asset will bundle service agreements with the lease agreement and offer to provide the lessee with service support during the life of the lease. If this service is unique—either because of the lessor's reputation or because the lessor is also the manufacturer of the asset—and if the cost of obtaining this service separately is high, the firm may choose to lease rather than buy the asset. IBM, for instance, has traditionally leased computers to users, with an offer to service them when needed.

2. *Flexibility* Some lease agreements provide the lessee with the option to exchange the asset for a different or upgraded version during the life of the lease. This flexibility is particularly valuable when the firm is unsure of its needs and

when technology changes rapidly. Flexibility is also useful when the asset is required for a period much shorter than the life of the asset, because buying the asset and selling it again is expensive in terms of transaction time and cost.

3. *Tax Reasons* The classic reason provided for leasing is that different entities face different tax rates. An entity with a high tax rate buys an asset and leases it to one with no or a low tax rate. By doing so, the lessor obtains the tax benefits, which are greater because of its higher tax rate. The lessee, in turn, gets the use of the asset and also gains by sharing in some of the tax benefits.

In addition, if a lease qualifies as an operating lease, it essentially operates as off-balance-sheet debt and may make firms that use it look safer to a careless analyst. If firms consider leasing as an alternative to borrowing, the choice becomes primarily financial. Operating leases create lease obligations to the firm, and these obligations are tax-deductible. The present value of these after-tax lease obligations has to be weighed against the present value of the after-tax cash flows that would have been generated if the firm had borrowed the money and bought the asset instead. The after-tax cash flows from borrowing and buying the asset have to include not only the interest and principal payments on the debt but also the tax benefits accruing from depreciation from owning the asset and the expected value of the asset at the end of operations. ∎

C. Hybrid Securities

Summarizing our analysis thus far, equity represents a residual claim on the cash flows and assets of the firm and is generally associated with management control. Debt, on the other hand, represents a fixed claim on the cash flows and assets of the firm and is usually not associated with management control. There are a number of securities that do not fall neatly into either of these two categories; rather, they share some characteristics with equity and some with debt. These securities are called hybrid securities.

Convertible Debt

A **convertible bond** is a bond that can be converted into a predetermined number of shares, at the discretion of the bondholder. Although it generally does not pay to convert at the time of the bond issue, conversion becomes a more attractive option as stock prices increase. Firms generally add conversions options to bonds to lower the interest rate paid on the bonds.

In a typical convertible bond, the bondholder is given the option to convert the bond into a specified number of shares of stock. The *conversion ratio* measures the number of shares of stock for which each bond may be exchanged. Stated differently, the *market conversion value* is the current value of the shares for which the bonds can be exchanged. The *conversion premium* is the excess of the convertible bond value over the conversion value of the bond.

Thus, a convertible bond with a par value of $1,000, which is convertible into fifty shares of stock, has a conversion ratio of 50. The conversion ratio can also be used to compute a conversion price—the par value divided by the conversion ratio—yielding a conversion price of $20. If the current stock price is $25, the market conversion value is $1,250 (50 × $25). If the convertible bond is trading at $1,300, the conversion premium is $50.

IN PRACTICE: A Simple Approach to Decomposing Debt and Equity

The value of a convertible bond can be decomposed into straight debt and equity components using a simple approach. Because the price of a convertible bond is the sum of the straight debt and the conversion option components, the value of the straight bond component in conjunction with the market price of the convertible bond should be sufficient to estimate the conversion option component, which is also the equity component:

$$\text{Value of Conversion Option} = \text{Price of Convertible Bond} \\ - \text{Value of Straight Bond Component}$$

The value of the straight bond component can be estimated using the coupon payments on the convertible bond, the maturity of the bond, and the market interest rate the company would have to pay on a regular debt issue. This last input can be estimated directly if the company has standard bonds in the market place, or it can be based on the bond rating, if any, assigned to the company.

For instance, assume that you have a ten-year convertible bond, with a 5 percent coupon rate trading at $1,050, and that the company has a debt rating of BBB (with a market interest rate of 8 percent). The value of the bond and equity components can be estimated as follows:

$$\text{Bond Component} = \$50 \,(\text{PVA}, 10 \text{ years}, 8\%) + 1{,}000/1.08^{10} = \$799$$

$$\text{Equity Component} = \$1{,}050 - \$799 = \$251 \qquad \blacksquare$$

Convertible Bond: Debt that can be converted into equity at a rate that is specified as part of the debt agreement (conversion rate).

7.6 Convertible Debt and Yields

The yields on convertible bonds are much lower than the yields on straight bonds issued by a company. Therefore, convertible debt is cheaper than straight debt.

☐ True
☐ False
Why or why not?

Preferred Stock

Preferred stock is another security that shares some characteristics with debt and some with equity. Like debt, preferred stock creates a fixed dollar payment (dividend); if the firm does not have the cash to pay the dividend, it is accumulated and paid in a period when there are sufficient earnings. Like debt, preferred stock-holders do not have a share of control in the firm, and their voting privileges are strictly restricted to issues that might affect their claims on the firm's cash flows or assets. Like equity, payments to preferred stockholders are not tax-deductible and come out of after-tax cash flows. Also like equity, preferred stock does not have a maturity date when the face value is due. In terms of priority, in the case of bankruptcy, preferred stockholders have to wait until the debt holders' claims have been met before receiving any portion of the assets of the firm.

Although accountants and ratings agencies continue to treat preferred stock as equity, it can be argued that the fixed commitments that preferred stock create are like debt obligations and have to be dealt with likewise. The obligations created by preferred stock are generally less onerous than those created by debt, however, because they are generally cumulated, cannot cause default, and do not have priority over debt claims in the case of bankruptcy.

Unlike convertible debt, which can be decomposed into equity and debt components, preferred stock cannot really be treated as debt because preferred dividends are not tax-deductible and certainly cannot be viewed as the equivalent of equity because of the differences in cash flow claims and control. Consequently, preferred stock is treated as a third component of capital, in addition to debt and equity, for purposes of capital structure analysis and for estimating the cost of capital.

Preferred Stock: A hybrid security. Like debt, it has a promised payment (the preferred dividend) in each period. Like equity, its cash flows are not tax-deductible, and it has an infinite life.

7.7 PREFERRED STOCK AND EQUITY

Many ratings agencies and regulators treat preferred stock as equity in computing debt ratios, because it does not have a finite maturity and firms cannot be forced into bankruptcy if they fail to pay preferred dividends. Do you agree with this categorization?

☐ Yes

☐ No

Why or why not?

Option-Linked Bonds

In recent years, firms have recognized the value of combining options with straight bonds to create bonds that more closely match the firm's specific needs. We considered one with convertible bonds. Consider two other examples. In the first, commodity companies issued bonds linking the principal and even interest payments to the price of the commodity. Thus interest payments would rise if the price of the commodity increased and vice versa. The benefit for the company was that it tailored the cash flows on the bond to the cash flows of the firm and reduced the likelihood of default. These **commodity-linked bonds** can be viewed as a combination of a bond and a call option on the underlying commodity. In the second example, consider insurance companies that have recently issued bonds whereby the principal on the bond is reduced in the case of a specified catastrophe and remains unaffected in its absence. For instance, an insurance firm that has the bulk of its revenues coming from homeowners' insurance in California might attach a provision that reduces principal and/or interest in the case of a major earthquake. Again, the rationale is to provide the firm with some breathing room when it needs it the most—when a catastrophe creates huge cash outflows for the firm.

Commodity-Linked Bonds: Bonds where the interest and/or the principal payments are linked to the price of the commodity. In most cases, the payments will increase with the price of the commodity and decrease if it drops.

ILLUSTRATION 7.1   Financing Choices in 2003–2004: Disney and Aracruz

Table 7.1 summarizes the existing debt and preferred stock at Disney, broken down by maturity, currency, and whether the debt is fixed or floating rate.

Of the total debt and preferred stock of $13,100 million, 23.31 percent is floating rate and 11.60 percent is in a foreign currency (Euros). In addition, Disney did specify that $2,457 million in debt would come due in the next year, which is 18.76 percent of the total debt outstanding. In addition, as noted in Chapter 4, Disney has more than $2 billion in operating lease commitments with a present value of $1.75 billion.

Aracruz reported as $1,371.5 million in gross debt outstanding in December 2003 and provided the breakdown of the debt in Table 7.2. Of the total debt, 15.53 percent is in local currency and none of the debt was floating rate debt.

Table 7.1   **DEBT BREAKDOWN FOR DISNEY: SEPTEMBER 2003 (DATA IN $ MILLIONS)**

Type of Debt	2003 (Million)	Stated Interest Rate	Floating (Million)	Fixed (Million)	Matures In
Medium-term paper	$8,114	6.07%	$1,510	$6,604	2006–2022
Convertible senior notes	1,323	2.13%	0	1,323	2023
Other US$-denominated debt	597	5.74%	0	597	2004–2032
Privately placed debt	343	7%	343	0	2007
Euro medium-term debt (~$)	1,519	2.84%	1,099	420	2004–2007
Preferred stock	485	7.56%	102	383	2004
Capital Cities debt	191	9.08%	0	191	2021
Other	528	NA	0	528	2006
Total	13,100	5.16%	3,054	10,046	

Table 7.2   **DEBT OUTSTANDING (IN U.S. DOLLAR TERMS) AT ARACRUZ (IN MILLIONS)**

Debt Due In	Local Currency (BR Stated in $)	US$ (Millions)	Total	% of Debt Due in Year
2004	$43.2	$348.9	$392.1	28.59%
2005	$38.3	$85.0	$123.3	8.99%
2006	$38.4	$177.9	$216.3	15.77%
2007	$38.4	$228.5	$266.9	19.46%
2008	$36.5	$124.2	$160.7	11.72%
2009 and after	$18.2	$194	$212.2	15.47%
Total	$213	$1,158.5	$1371.5	

FINANCING CHOICES AND A FIRM'S LIFE CYCLE

We spent the last section looking at the different financing choices available to a firm. They all represent external financing, that is, funds raised from outside the firm. Many firms meet the bulk of their funding needs internally with cash flows from existing assets. In this section, we begin by presenting the distinction between internal and external financing and the factors that may affect how much firms draw on each source. We then turn our attention again to external financing. We consider how and why the financing choices may change as a firm goes through different stages of its life cycle, from start-up to expansion to high growth to stable growth and on to decline. We will follow up by looking at why some choices dominate in some stages and do not play a role in others.

Internal versus External Financing

Cash flows generated by the existing assets of a firm can be categorized as internal financing. Because these cash flows belong to the equity owners of the business, they are called *internal equity*. Cash flows raised outside the firm, whether from private sources or from financial markets, can be categorized as *external financing*. External financing can, of course, take the form of new debt, new equity, or hybrids.

A firm may prefer internal to external financing for several reasons. For private firms, external financing is typically difficult to raise, and even when it is available (from a venture capitalist, for instance) it is accompanied by a loss of control (the venture capitalist wants a share of control). For publicly traded firms, external financing may be easier to raise, but it is still expensive in terms of issuance costs (especially in the case of new equity). Internally generated cash flows, on the other hand, can be used to finance operations without incurring large transaction costs or losing control.

Despite these advantages, there are limits to the use of internal financing to fund projects. First, firms have to recognize that internal equity has the same cost as external equity, before the transaction cost differences are factored in. The cost of equity, computed using a risk and return model, such as the CAPM or APM, applies as much to internal as to external equity. Thus, Disney has a cost of equity of 10.00 percent for internal equity (or retained earnings) and external equity (new stock or equity option issues). This equivalence implies that a project financed with internal equity should pass the same test as a project financed with external equity; Disney has to earn a return on equity for investors that is greater than 10 percent on projects funded with either external equity or retained earnings. Second, internal equity is clearly limited to the cash flows generated by the firm for its stockholders. Even if the firm does not pay dividends, these cash flows may not be sufficient to finance the firm's projects. Depending entirely on internal equity can therefore result in project delays or the possible loss of these projects to competitors. Third, managers should not make the mistake of thinking that the stock price does not matter just because they use only internal equity for financing projects. In reality, stockholders in firms whose stock prices have dropped are much less likely to trust their managers to reinvest their cash flows for them than are stockholders in firms with rising stock prices.

Growth, Risk, and Financing

As firms grow and mature, their cash flows and risk exposure follow fairly predictable patterns. Cash flows become larger, relative to firm value, and risk approaches the average risk for all firms. The financing choices that a firm makes will reflect these changes. To understand these choices, let us consider five stages in a firm's life cycle:

1. *Start-Up* This represents the initial stage after a business has been formed. Generally, this business will be a private business, funded by owner's equity and perhaps bank debt. It will also be restricted in its funding choices, as it attempts to gain customers and get established.

2. *Expansion* Once a firm succeeds in attracting customers and establishing a presence in the market, its funding needs increase as it looks to expand. Because this firm is unlikely to be generating high cash flows internally at this stage and investment needs will be high, the owners will generally look to private equity or venture capital initially to fill the gap. Some firms in this position will make the transition to publicly traded firms and raise the funds they need by issuing common stock.

3. *High Growth* With the transition to a publicly traded firm, financing choices increase. Although the firm's revenues are growing rapidly, earnings are likely to lag behind revenues and internal cash flows will lag behind reinvestment needs. Generally, publicly traded firms at this stage will look to more equity issues, in the form of common stock, warrants, and other equity alternatives. If they are using debt, convertible debt is most likely to be used to raise capital.

4. *Mature Growth* As growth starts leveling off, firms will generally find two phenomena occurring. The earnings and cash flows will continue to increase rapidly, reflecting past investments, and the need to invest in new projects will decline. The net effect will be an increase in the proportion of funding needs covered by internal financing and a change in the type of external financing used. These firms will be more likely to use debt in the form of bank debt or corporate bonds to finance their investment needs.

5. *Decline* The last stage in this corporate life cycle is decline. Firms in this stage will find both revenues and earnings starting to decline as their businesses mature and new competitors overtake them. Existing investments are likely to continue to produce cash flows, albeit at a declining pace, and the firm has little need for new investments. Thus, internal financing is likely to exceed reinvestment needs. Firms are unlikely to be making fresh stock or bond issues but are more likely to be retiring existing debt and buying back stock. In a sense, the firm is gradually liquidating itself.

Figure 7.2 summarizes both the internal financing capabilities and external financing choices of firms at different stages in the growth life cycle.

Not all firms go through these five phases, and the choices are not the same for all of them. First, many firms never make it past the start-up stage in this process. Of the tens of thousands of businesses that are started each year by entrepreneurs,

Figure 7.2 Life Cycle Analysis of Financing

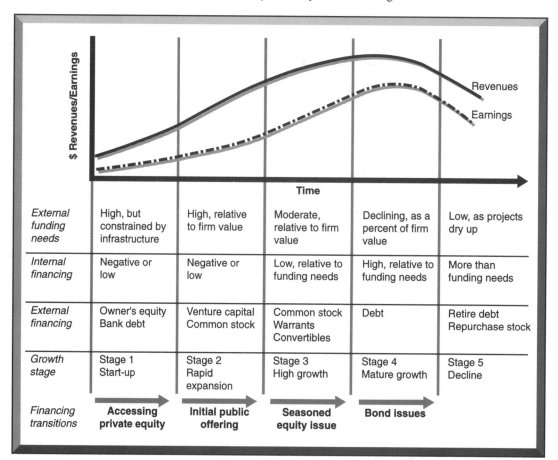

	High, but constrained by infrastructure	High, relative to firm value	Moderate, relative to firm value	Declining, as a percent of firm value	Low, as projects dry up
External funding needs	High, but constrained by infrastructure	High, relative to firm value	Moderate, relative to firm value	Declining, as a percent of firm value	Low, as projects dry up
Internal financing	Negative or low	Negative or low	Low, relative to funding needs	High, relative to funding needs	More than funding needs
External financing	Owner's equity Bank debt	Venture capital Common stock	Common stock Warrants Convertibles	Debt	Retire debt Repurchase stock
Growth stage	Stage 1 Start-up	Stage 2 Rapid expansion	Stage 3 High growth	Stage 4 Mature growth	Stage 5 Decline
Financing transitions	**Accessing private equity**	**Initial public offering**	**Seasoned equity issue**	**Bond issues**	

many fail to survive, and even those that survive often continue as small businesses with little expansion potential. Second, not all successful private firms become publicly traded corporations. Some firms, like Cargill and Koch Industries, remain private and manage to raise enough capital to continue growing at healthy rates over long periods. Third, there are firms like Microsoft that are in high growth and seem to have no need for external financing, because internal funds prove more than sufficient to finance this growth. There are high-growth firms that issue debt, and low-growth firms that raise equity capital. In short, there are numerous exceptions, but the life cycle framework still provides a useful device to explain why different kinds of firms do what they do and what causes them to deviate from the prescribed financing choices.

Note that while we look at a firm's choices in terms of debt and equity at different stages in the growth life cycle, there are two things we do not do in this analysis. First, we do not explain in any detail why firms at each stage in the growth life cycle pick the types of financing that they do. Second, we do not consider what kind of debt is best for a firm—short-term or long-term, dollar or foreign currency, fixed rate or floating rate. The reason is that this choice has more to do with the types of assets the firm owns and the nature of the cash flows from these assets than with where in its life cycle a firm is in. We will return to examine this issue in more detail in Chapter 9.

How Firms Have Actually Raised Funds

In the first part of this chapter, we noted the range of choices in terms of both debt and equity that are available to firms to raise funds. Before we look at which of these choices should be used, it is worth noting how firms have historically raised funds for operations. Firms have used debt, equity, and hybrids to raise funds, but their dependence on each source has varied across time. In the United States, for instance, firms collectively have raised external financing more through debt issues than equity issues, and have primarily raised equity funds internally from operations. Figure 7.3 illustrates the proportion of funds from new debt and equity issues, as well as from internal funds, for U.S. corporations between 1975 and 2001.

In every year, firms have relied more heavily on internal financing to meet capital needs than on external financing. Furthermore, when external financing is used, it is more likely to be new debt rather than new equity or preferred stock.

There are wide differences across firms in the United States in how much and what type of external financing is used. The evidence is largely consistent with the

Figure 7.3   External and Internal Financing at U.S. Firms (as Percent of Total Financing)

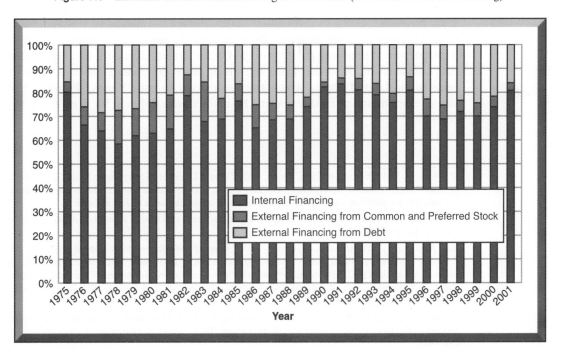

Source: Compustat.

conclusions that emerge from looking at a firm's place in the growth cycle in Figure 7.2. Fluck, Holtz-Eakin, and Rosen looked at several thousand firms that were incorporated in Wisconsin; most of these firms were small, private businesses.[2] The authors find that these firms depend almost entirely on internal financing, owner's equity, and bank debt to cover capital needs. The proportion of funds provided by internal financing increases as the firms became older and more established. A small proportion of private businesses manage to raise capital from venture capitalists and private equity investors. Many of these firms ultimately plan on going public, and the returns to the private equity investors come at the time of the public offering. Bradford and Smith looked at sixty computer-related firms prior to their initial public offerings (IPOs) and noted that forty-one of these firms had private equity infusions before the public offering.[3] The median number of private equity investors in these firms was between two and three, and the median proportion of the firm owned by these investors was 43.8 percent; an average of 3.2 years elapsed between the private equity investment and the IPO at these firms. Although this is a small sample of firms in one sector, it does suggest that private equity plays a substantial role in allowing firms to bridge the gap between private businesses and publicly traded firms.

When we compare the financing patterns of U.S. companies to companies in other countries, we find some evidence that U.S. companies are much more heavily dependent on debt than equity for external financing than their counterparts in other countries. Figure 7.4 summarizes new security issues in the G-7 countries between 1984 to 1991.[4]

Net equity in Figure 7.4 refers to the difference between new equity issues and stock buybacks. Firms in the United States, during the period of this comparison, bought back more stock than they issued, leading to negative net equity. In addition, a comparison of financing patterns in the United States, Germany, and Japan reveals that German and Japanese firms are much more dependent on bank debt than firms in the United States, which are much likely to issue bonds.[5] Figure 7.5 provides a comparison of bank loans and bonds as sources of debt for firms in the three countries.[6]

---

[2]Z. Fluck, D. Holtz-Eakin, and H. S. Rosen, 1998, "Where Does the Money Come From? The Financing of Small Entrepreneurial Enterprises," Working Paper, NYU Salomon Center. This is a unique data set because this information is usually either not collected or not available to researchers.

[3]T. Bradford and R. C. Smith, 1997, "Private Equity: Sources and Uses," *Journal of Applied Corporate Finance,* 10(1), 89–97.

[4]See Raghuram G. Rajan and L. Zingales, 1995, "What Do We Know about Capital Structure? Some Evidence from International Data," *Journal of Finance,* 50(5), 1421–1460. This is based on OECD data, summarized in the OECD publication "Financial Statements of Non-Financial Enterprises." The G-7 countries represent seven of the largest economies in the world. The leaders of these countries meet every year to discuss economic policy.

[5]A. Hackethal and R. H. Schmidt, 1999, "Financing Patterns: Measurement Concepts and Empirical Results," Working Paper, University of Frankfurt. They compare financing patterns in the three countries.

[6]The study looked at the new debt issues made by companies between 1990 and 1996 in each of the three countries.

Figure 7.4   Financing Patterns for G-7 Countries 1984–1991 (as Percent of Total)

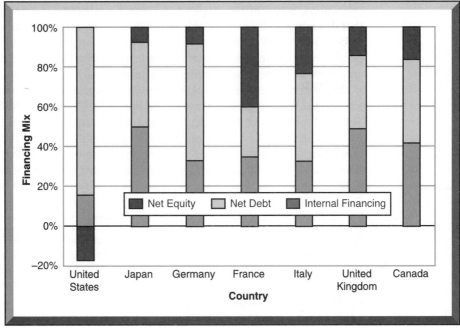

Source: OECD.

Figure 7.5   Bonds versus Bank Loans 1990–1996 (as Percent of New Debt)

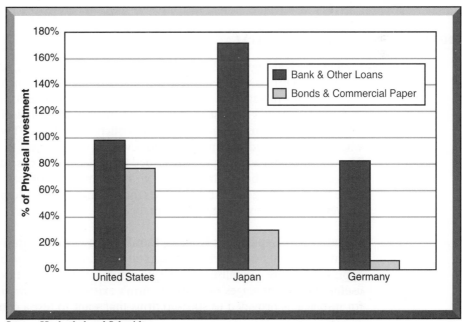

Source: Hackethal and Schmidt.

There is also some evidence that firms in some emerging markets, such as Brazil and India, use equity (internal and equity) much more than debt to finance their operations. Some of this dependence can be attributed to government regulation that discourages the use of debt, either directly by requiring the debt ratios of firms to be below specified limits or indirectly by limiting the deductibility of interest expenses for tax purposes. One of the explanations for the greater dependence of U.S. corporations on debt issues relies on where they are in their growth life cycle. Firms in the United States, in contrast to firms in emerging markets, are much more likely to be in the mature growth stage of the life cycle. Consequently, firms in the United States should be less dependent on external equity. Another factor is that firms in the United States have far more access to corporate bond markets than do firms in other markets. Firms in other markets, for instance, often have to raise new debt from banks, rather than bond markets. This may constrain them in the use of new debt.

7.8 CORPORATE BOND MARKETS AND THE USE OF DEBT

Companies in Europe and emerging markets have historically depended on bank debt to borrow and have had limited access to corporate bond markets. In recent years, their access to corporate bond markets, both domestically and internationally, has increased. As a result, which of the following would you expect to happen to debt ratios in these countries?

☐ Debt ratios should go up.

☐ Debt ratios should go down.

☐ Debt ratios should not change much.

There is a data set online that has aggregate internal and external financing for U.S. firms from 1975 to the present.

THE PROCESS OF RAISING CAPITAL

Looking back at Figure 7.2, we note four financing transitions, where the source of funding for a firm is changed by the introduction of a new financing choice. The first occurs when a private firm approaches a private equity investor or venture capitalist for new financing. The second occurs when a private firm decides to offer its equity to financial markets and become a publicly traded firm. The third takes place when a publicly traded firm decides to revisit equity markets to raise more equity. The fourth occurs when a publicly traded firms decides to raise debt from financial markets by issuing bonds. In this section, we examine the process of making each of these transitions. Because the processes for making seasoned equity and bond issues are very similar, we will consider them together.

Private Firm Expansion: Raising Funds from Private Equity

Private firms that need more equity capital than can be provided by their owners can approach venture capitalists and private equity investors. Venture capital can prove useful at different stages of a private firm's existence. *Seed-money venture capital,* for instance, is provided to start-up firms that want to test a concept or develop a new product, whereas *start-up venture capital* allows firms that have established products and concepts to develop and market them. Additional rounds of venture capital allow private firms that have more established products and markets to expand. There are five steps associated with how venture capital gets to be provided to firms and how venture capitalists ultimately profit from these investments.

1. ***Provoke Equity Investor's Interest***   The first step that a private firm wanting to raise private equity has to take is to get private equity investors interested in investing in it. There are a number of factors that help the private firm at this stage. One is the *type of business* that the private firm is in and how attractive this business is to private equity investors. The second factor is the track record of the top manager(s) of the firm. Top managers, who have a track record of converting private businesses into publicly traded firms, have an easier time raising private equity capital.

2. ***Valuation and Return Assessment***   Once private equity investors become interested in investing in a firm, the value of the private firm has to be assessed by looking at its prospects. This is usually done using the *venture capital method*, whereby the earnings of the private firm are forecast in a future year, when the company can be expected to go public. These earnings, in conjunction with a price-earnings multiple, estimated by looking at publicly traded firms in the same business, is used to assess the value of the firm at the time of the IPO; this is called the *exit or terminal value*.

   For instance, assume that Bookscape is expected to have an IPO in three years and that the net income in three years for the firm is expected to be $4 million. If the price-earnings ratio of publicly traded retail firms is 25, this would yield an estimated exit value of $100 million. This value is discounted back to the present at what venture capitalists call a *target rate of return,* which measures what venture capitalists believe is a justifiable return, given the risk to which they are exposed. This target rate of return is usually set at a much higher level than the traditional cost of equity for the firm.[7]

$$\text{Discounted Terminal Value} = \text{Estimated Exit Value}_n/(1 + \text{Target Return})^n$$

   Using the Bookscape example again, if the venture capitalist requires a target return of 30 percent on his or her investment, the discounted terminal value for Bookscape would be

$$\text{Discounted Terminal Value for Bookscape} = \$100 \text{ million}/1.30^3 = \$45.52 \text{ million}$$

3. ***Structuring the Deal***   In structuring the deal to bring private equity into the firm, the private equity investor and the firm have to negotiate two factors. First, the investor has to determine what proportion of the value of the firm he or she will demand in return for the private equity investment. The owners of the firm, on the other hand, have to determine how much of the firm they are willing to give up in return for the capital. In these assessments, the amount of new capital being brought into the firm has to be measured against the estimated firm value. In the

---

[7]For instance, the target rate of return for private equity investors is in excess of 30 percent.

Bookscape example, assuming that the venture capitalist is considering investing $12 million, he or she would want to own at least 26.36 percent of the firm.[8]

$$\text{Ownership Proportion} = \text{Capital Provided/Estimated Value}$$
$$= \$12/\$45.52 = 26.36\%$$

Second, the private equity investor will impose constraints on new investments and fresh financing on the managers of the firm in which the investment is being made. This is to ensure that the private equity investors are protected and that they have a say in how the firm is run.

4. ***Postdeal Management*** Once the private equity investment has been made in a firm, the investor will often take an active role in the management of the firm. Private equity investors and venture capitalists bring not only a wealth of management experience to the process but also contacts that can be used to raise more capital and get fresh business for the firm.

5. ***Exit*** Private equity investors and venture capitalists invest in private businesses because they are interested in earning a high return on these investments. How will these returns be manifested? There are three ways a private equity investor can profit from an investment in a business. The first and usually the most lucrative alternative is an IPO made by the private firm. Although venture capitalists do not usually liquidate their investments at the time of the IPO, they can sell at least a portion of their holdings once they are traded.[9] The second alternative is to sell the private business to another firm; the acquiring firm might have strategic or financial reasons for the acquisition. The third alternative is to withdraw cash flows from the firm and liquidate the firm over time. This strategy would not be appropriate for a high-growth firm, but it may make sense if investments made by the firm no longer earn excess returns.

From Private to Publicly Traded Firm: The IPO

A private firm is restricted in its access to external financing, both for debt and equity. In our earlier discussion of equity choices, we pointed out the hard bargain venture capitalists extract for investing equity in a private business. As firms become larger and their capital needs increase, some of them decide to become publicly traded and to raise capital by issuing shares of their equity to financial markets.

Staying Private versus Going Public

When a private firm becomes publicly traded, the primary benefit is increased access to financial markets and capital for projects. This access to new capital is a significant gain for high-growth businesses with large and lucrative investment opportunities. A secondary benefit is that the owners of the private firm are able to cash in on their

---

[8]Many private equity investors draw a distinction between premoney valuation, or the value of the company without the cash inflow from the private equity investor, and postmoney valuation, which is the value of the company with the cash influx from the private equity investors. They argue that their ownership of the firm should be based on the former (lower) value.

[9]B.S. Black and R. J. Gilson, 1998, "Venture Capital and the Structure of Capital Markets: Banks versus Stock Markets," *Journal of Financial Economics,* 47, 243–277. They argue that one of the reasons why venture capital is much more active in the United States than in Japan or Germany is because the option to go public is much more easily exercised in the United States.

success by attaching a market value to their holdings. These benefits have to be weighed against the potential costs of being publicly traded. The most significant of these costs is the loss of control that may ensue from being a publicly traded firm. As firms get larger and the owners are tempted to sell their holdings over time, the owner's share of the outstanding shares will generally decline. If the stockholders in the firm come to believe that the owner's association with the firm is hurting rather than helping it, they may decide to put pressure for the owner's removal.

Other costs associated with being a publicly traded firm are the information disclosure requirements and the legal requirements.[10] A private firm experiencing challenging market conditions (declining sales, higher costs) may be able to hide its problems from competitors, whereas a publicly traded firm has no choice but to reveal the information. Yet another cost is that the firm has to spend a significant portion of its time on investor relations, a process in which equity research analysts following the firm are cultivated and provided with information about the firm's prospects.[11]

Overall, the net trade-off to going public will generally be positive for firms with large growth opportunities and funding needs. It will be smaller for firms that have smaller growth opportunities, substantial internal cash flows, and owners who value the complete control they have over the firm.

Steps in an IPO

Assuming that the benefits outweigh the costs, there are five steps involved in an IPO.

Step 1:   *Choose an investment banker based on reputation and marketing skills.* In most IPOs, this investment banker underwrites the issue and guarantees a specified price for the stock. This investment banker then puts together a group of several banks (called a syndicate) to spread the risk of the offering and to increase marketing reach.[12]

Step 2:   *Assess the value of the company and set issue details.* This valuation is generally done by the lead investment bank, with substantial information provided by the issuing firm. The value is sometimes estimated using discounted cash flow models. More often, though, the value is estimated by using a multiple, like a price-earnings ratio, and by looking at the pricing of comparable firms that are already publicly traded. Whichever approach is used, the absence of substantial historical information, in conjunction with the fact that these are small companies with high growth prospects, makes the estimation of value an uncertain one at best. Once the value for the company has been estimated, the value per share is obtained by dividing by the number of

---

[10]The costs are twofold. One is the cost of producing and publicizing the information itself. The other is the loss of control over how much information is released and when to reveal it to others.

[11]"Cultivated" may sound like an odd word choice, but it is accurate. Buy recommendations from equity research analysts following the firm provoke investor interest and can have a significant impact on the stock price; sell recommendations, on the other, can cause the stock price to drop. This is especially true for small, lightly followed firms.

[12]In 2004, Google broke with precedent and decided to go public without an investment banking syndicate backing it. Using an auction process to set the stock price, it saved itself the normal costs associated with issuance fees. It remains to be seen whether Google is unique or the vanguard of a new trend.

shares, which is determined by the price range the issuer would like to have on the issue. If the equity in the firm is valued at $50 million, for example, the number of shares would be set at 5 million to get a target price range of $10, or at 1 million shares to get a target price range of $50 per share. The final step in this process is to set the offering price per share. Most investment banks set the offering price below the estimated value per share for two reasons. First, it reduces the bank's risk exposure. If the offering price is set too high and the investment bank is unable to sell all of the shares offered, it has to use its own funds to buy the shares at the offering price. Second, investors and investment banks view it as a good sign if the stock increases in price in the immediate aftermath of the issue. For the clients of the investment banker who get the shares at the offering price, there is an immediate payoff; for the issuing company, the ground has been prepared for future issues.

Step 3: *Gauge investor demand at the offering price.* In setting the offering price, investment bankers have the advantage of first checking investor demand. This process, which is called *building the book,* involves polling institutional investors prior to pricing an offering to gauge the extent of the demand for an issue. It is also at this stage in the process that the investment banker and issuing firm will present information to prospective investors in a series of presentations called *road shows*. In this process, if the demand seems very strong, the offering price will be increased; in contrast, if the demand seems weak, the offering price will be lowered. In some cases, a firm will withdraw an IPO at this stage if investors are not enthusiastic about it.[13]

Step 4: *Meet SEC filing requirements and issue a prospectus.* To make a public offering in the United States, a firm has to meet several requirements. First, it has to file a registration statement and prospectus with the SEC, providing information about its financial history, its forecasts for the future, and how it plans to use the funds it raises from the IPO. The prospectus provides information about the riskiness and prospects of the firm for prospective investors in its stock. The SEC reviews this information and either approves the registration or sends out a deficiency memorandum asking for more information. While the registration is being reviewed, the firm may not sell any securities, though it can issue a preliminary prospectus, called a *red herring,* for informational purposes only. Once the registration has been approved by the SEC, the firm can place a *tombstone advertisement* in newspapers and other publications listing the offering and syndicate banks.

Step 5: *Allocate stock to those who apply to buy it at offering price.* If the demand for the stock exceeds the supply (which will happen if the offering price is set too low), the firm will have to ration the stock. If the supply exceeds the demand, the investment banker will have to fulfill the underwriting guarantee and buy the remaining stock at the offering price.

---

[13]One study of IPOs between 1979 and 1982 found that 29 percent of firms terminated their IPOs at this stage in the process.

Figure 7.6   Issuance Costs by Size of Issue (as Percent of Proceeds)

Source: Ritter.

On the offering date—the first date the shares can be traded—the market price is determined by supply and demand. If the offering price has been set too high, as is sometimes the case, the investment bankers will have to discount the offering to sell it and make up the difference to the issuer because of the underwriting agreement. If the offering price is set too low, as is often the case, the traded price on the offering date will be much higher than the offering price, thus enriching those who were allocated shares in the IPO.

The Costs of Going Public

There are three costs associated with an IPO. First, the firm must consider the legal and administrative cost of making a new issue, including the cost of preparing registration statements and filing fees. Second, the firm should examine the underwriting commission—the gross spread between the offering price and what the firm receives per share, which goes to cover the underwriting, management, and selling fees on the issue. This commission can be substantial and decreases as the size of the issue increases. Figure 7.6 summarizes the average issuance and underwriting costs for issues of different sizes, reported by Ritter (1998).[14]

The third cost is any underpricing on the issue, which provides a windfall to the investors who get the stock at the offering price and sell it at the much higher market

---

[14]J. Ritter, 1998, "Initial Public Offerings," *Contemporary Finance Digest,* 2, 5–30.

Figure 7.7 Underpricing as Percent of Price, by Issue Size

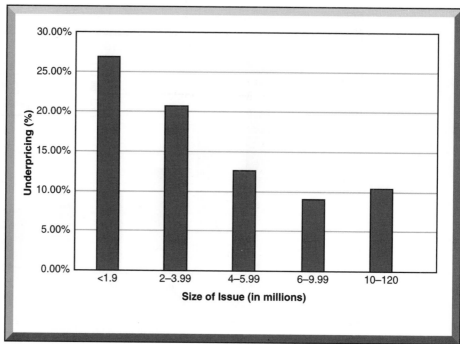

Source: Ibbotson, Sindelar, and Ritter.

price. Thus, for Netscape, whose offering price was $29 and whose stock opened at $50, the difference of $21 per share on the shares offered is an implicit cost from underpricing. Although precise estimates vary from year to year, the average IPO seems to be underpriced by 10 to 15 percent. Ibbotson, Sindelar, and Ritter, in a study of the determinants of underpricing, estimate its extent as a function of the size of the issue.[15] Figure 7.7 summarizes the underpricing as a percent of the price by size of issue.

Private firms tend to pick investment bankers based on reputation and expertise, rather than price. A good reputation provides the credibility and the comfort level needed for investors to buy the stock of the firm; expertise applies not only to the pricing of the issue and the process of going public but also to other financing decisions that might be made in the aftermath of a public issue. The investment banking agreement is then negotiated, rather than opened up for competition.

ILLUSTRATION 7.2 The IPO for United Parcel Service (UPS)

On July 21, 1999, UPS, the world's largest private package company, announced plans to sell its shares to the public. The company, which was wholly owned by its

---

[15]Roger G. Ibbotson, J. L. Sindelar, and J. R. Ritter, 1994, "The Market's Problems with the Pricing of Initial Public Offerings," *Journal of Applied Corporate Finance,* 7(1), 66–74.

managers and employees, announced that it was going public to raise capital to make acquisitions in the future. UPS reported revenues of $24.8 billion and net income of $1.7 billion in 1998 and at that time employed about 330,000 people.

UPS followed the initial announcement by filing a prospectus with the SEC on the same day, announcing its intention of creating two classes of shares. Class A shares, with ten votes per share, would be held by the existing owners of UPS, and class B shares, having one vote per share, would be offered to the public.

The firm chose Morgan Stanley as its lead investment banker, and Morgan Stanley put together a syndicate that included Goldman Sachs and Merrill Lynch as senior comanagers. Other comanagers included Credit Suisse, Salomon Smith Barney, and Warburg Dillon Read. On October 20, 1999, UPS filed a statement with the SEC (called an S-1 registration statement) announcing that it planned to issue 109.4 million shares (about 10 percent of the 1.1 billion outstanding shares) at a price range of $36 to $42,[16] and that the IPO would occur sometime in early November.

Based on the strong demand from institutional investors, gauged in the process of building the book, the investment banking syndicate increased the offering price to $50 per share on November 8, 1999, and set the offering date at November 10, 1999. At that time, it was the largest IPO ever by a U.S. company.

On November 10, 1999, the stock went public. The stock price jumped to $70.1325 from the offering price of $50. At the end of the trading day, UPS shares were trading at $67.25. Based on this price and the total number of shares outstanding, the market value of UPS was assessed at $80.9 billion.

7.9 THE COST OF UNDERPRICING

Assume that the market is correct in its assessment of UPS value and that the investment bankers underpriced the issue. How much did the underpricing cost the owners of UPS?

☐ About $22 billion

☐ About $50 billion

☐ About $2.2 billion

☐ None of the above

IN PRACTICE: THE UNDERPRICING OF IPOs

Investment bankers generally underprice IPOs and are fairly open about the fact that they do. This gives rise to two questions. First, why don't the offering firms express more outrage about the value left on the table by the underpricing? Second, can investors take advantage of the underpricing by subscribing to dozens of IPOs? There are answers to both questions.

It is true that an underpriced IPO results in less proceeds going to the issuing firm. However, the loss of wealth is a function of how much of the equity of the firm is offered in the initial offering. If, as in the UPS offering, only 10 percent of the

---

[16]The process by which this price range was set was not made public. We would assume that it was partially based on how the market was pricing two other publicly traded rivals—FedEx and Airborne Freight.

stock is being offered, we can see why many issuing firms go along with the under-pricing. The favorable publicity associated with a strong opening day of trading may act as promotion for subsequent offerings that the firm plans to make in future months or even years.

It is not easy constructing an investment strategy that takes advantage of IPO mispricing. If an investor applies for shares in a number of offerings, he or she is likely to get all the shares requested in the offerings that are overpriced and only a fraction of the shares requested in the offerings that are underpriced (where there will be rationing because of excess demand). The resulting portfolio will be over-weighted in overpriced public offerings and underweighted in the underpriced offerings, and the returns will not match up to those reported in IPO studies. ■

The Choices for a Publicly Traded Firm

Once a firm is publicly traded, it can raise new financing by issuing more common stock, equity options, or corporate bonds. Additional equity offerings made by firms that are already publicly traded are called seasoned equity issues. In making stock and bond offerings, a publicly traded firm has several choices. It can sell these secu-rities with underwritten general subscriptions, where stocks and bonds are offered to the public at an offering price guaranteed by the investment banker. It can also privately place both bonds and stocks with institutional investors or issue stocks and bonds directly to investors without any middlemen.

General Subscriptions

In a *general subscription,* the issue is open to any member of the general public to subscribe. In that sense, it is very similar to an IPO, though there are some basic differences:

- *Underwriting Agreement* The underwriting agreement of an IPO almost always involves a firm guarantee and is generally negotiated with the investment banker, whereas the underwriting agreements for seasoned issues take on a wider variety of forms. First, there is the potential for competitive bids to arise on seasoned issues, because investment bankers have the information to promise a fixed price.[17] There is evidence that competitive bids reduce the issuance costs, though firms continue to prefer negotiated offerings. Second, seasoned issues also offer a wider range of underwriting guarantees; some issues are backed up by a *best efforts guarantee,* which does not guarantee a fixed price; other issues come with *standby guarantees,* where the investment banker provides back-up support, in case the actual price falls below the offering price. The payoff from relaxing the guarantee comes as lower underwriting commissions.

- *Pricing of Issue* The issuer of an IPO has to estimate the value of the firm and then the per-share value before pricing the issue, whereas the pricing of a sea-soned issue starts with the current market price, simplifying the process. Often, the price of a seasoned issue will be set just below the current market price.

---

[17]The information takes two forms. The first are the filings that every publicly traded firm has to make with the SEC. The other, and more important, is the current stock price.

The overall evidence on the cost of public offerings indicates that it is still much more expensive to issue stock rather than bonds, and the cost of the issue decreases with the size of the issue.

Private Placements

An alternative to a general subscription is a *private placement,* in which securities are sold directly to one or a few investors. The terms for the securities are negotiated between the two parties. The primary advantage of private placements over general subscriptions is the lower cost, because there are fewer intermediaries and no need for underwriting guarantees or marketing. There are also substantial savings in time and administrative costs because the SEC registration requirements are bypassed. The other advantages are that the terms of the bond can be tailored to meet the specific needs of the buyer, and the firm can convey proprietary information (presumably positive) to the potential investors.

The primary disadvantage of private placements is that there are relatively few potential investors because large private placements may expose the investor to firm-specific risks. This is why private placements of corporate bonds are much more common than private placement of equity. In a typical private placement, the buyer tends to be a long-term institutional investor, such as a life insurance company or a pension fund. These investors tend to invest in these bonds and hold them until maturity. Private placements generally range from $25 million to $250 million in size and have more restrictions associated with them than typical corporate bond issues.

Rights Offerings

The third option available to seasoned issuers is a *rights offering*. In this case, instead of trying to sell new stock at the current market price to all investors, the existing investors in the firm are given the right to buy additional shares, in proportion to their current holdings, at a price much lower than the current market price.

A company that uses a rights offering generally issues one right for each outstanding common share, allowing each stockholder to use those rights to buy additional shares in the company at a *subscription price,* generally much lower than the market price. Rational stockholders will either exercise the right or sell it. Those investors who let a right expire without doing either will find that the market value of their remaining holding shrinks—the market price will almost certainly drop when the rights are exercised because the subscription price is set much lower than the market price. In general, the value of a right should be equal to the difference between the stock price with the rights attached—the *rights-on price*—and the stock price without the rights attached—the *ex-rights price*. The reasoning is simple. If this were not true, there would be opportunities for easy profits on the part of investors and the resulting price would not be stable. To illustrate, if the price of the right were greater than the difference between the rights-on price and the ex-rights price, every stockholder would be better off selling the right rather than exercising it. This, in turn, would push the price down toward the equilibrium price. If the price of the right were lower than the difference between the rights-on and the ex-rights price, there would be an equally frenzied rush to buy the right and exercise it, which in turn would push the price up toward the equilibrium price. The value of a right can be estimated using the following equation:

$$\text{Price of a Right} = (\text{Rights-On Price} - \text{Subscription Price})/(n + 1)$$

where n is the number of rights required for each new share.

Rights offerings are a much less expensive way of raising capital than public issues, for two reasons. First, the underwriting commissions are much lower, because a rights offering has little risk of not receiving subscriptions if the subscription price is set well below the market price. Second, the other transaction and administrative costs should also be lower because there is a far smaller need for marketing and distribution.

What is the drawback of making a rights issue? The primary reservation seems to be that it increases the number of shares outstanding far more than a general subscription at the existing stock price. To illustrate, a firm that makes a rights issue at $5 per share when the stock price is $10 will have to issue 10 million shares to raise $50 million. In contrast, the same firm would have had to issue only 5 million shares if the issue had been at the existing stock price of $10. Some financial managers argue that this dilutes the share holding and lowers the market price. Although this is true in a technical sense, the existing stockholders should not object because they are the only ones who receive the rights. In other words, the stock price will drop, but everyone will own proportionately more shares in the firm. In general, firms in the United States have been much more reluctant to use rights issues than European firms, in spite of the significant cost savings that could accrue from them. Part of this reluctance can be attributed to the fear of dilution.

ILLUSTRATION **7.3** Valuing a Rights Offering: Tech Temp

Tech Temp has 10 million shares outstanding trading at $25 per share. It needs to raise $25 million in new equity and decides to make a rights offering. Each stockholder is provided with one right for every share owned, and five rights can be used to buy an additional share in the company at $12.50 per share. The value of a right can be calculated as follows:

	Before Rights Exercised	**After Rights Exercised**
Number of shares	10 million	12 million
Value of equity	$250 million	$275 million
Price per share	$25.00	$22.92

The rights-on price is $25.00 per share, and the ex-rights price is $22.92, leading to a per-right value of $2.08. This can be confirmed by using the equation:

$$\text{Value per Right} = (\text{Rights-On Price} - \text{Subscription Price})/(n + 1)$$
$$= (\$25 - \$12.50)/(5 + 1) = \$12.50/6 = \$2.08$$

If the rights price were greater than this value, investors would want to sell their rights. Alternatively, if the rights could be acquired for less than $2.08, there would be an opportunity to gain by acquiring the rights at the lower price and exercising them.

This spreadsheet allows you to estimate the ex-rights price and the value per right in a rights issue (**rights.xls**).

7.10 RIGHTS ISSUES AND EXISTING STOCKHOLDERS

Assume that you own 1,000 shares in Tech Temp, trading at $25 a share, and that you receive the rights described in the last illustration. Assume also that due to an oversight, you neither exercise the right nor sell it. How much would you expect to lose as a result of the oversight?

☐ Nothing; you still own the shares

☐ $416

☐ $2,080

☐ $12,500

Shelf Registrations

Firms that want to raise external financing have to disclose information and file the required statements with the SEC before they can issue securities. This registration process is costly and time-consuming and is one reason why some firms rely on internal financing. In response to this criticism, the SEC simplified its rules and allowed firms more flexibility in external financing. Rule 415, which was issued in 1982, allows firms to make a *shelf registration,* in which they can file a single prospectus for a series of issues they expect to make over the next two years.

Besides making the process less cumbersome, shelf registration also gives firms more flexibility in terms of timing because stock and bond issues can be made when windows of opportunity open up. Thus, a firm might make a shelf registration for $200 million in bonds and make the bond issue later when interest rates are at a low point. This flexibility in timing also allows firms to open up the process to aggressive bidding from investment banks, reducing transaction costs substantially. Some firms make the issues themselves rather than use investment bankers because the process is simpler and faster.

Overall, the spreads on new issues, especially for bonds, have been under pressure since the passage of shelf registration. In spite of its benefits, however, shelf registration is more likely to be used by large firms making bond issues and less likely to be used by small firms making equity issues.

THE TRADE-OFF OF DEBT

Now that we have defined debt and considered how financing choices change as a function of where a firm is in its life cycle, we can tackle a fundamental question. Why use debt instead of equity? In this section, we will first examine the benefits of using debt instead of equity and then follow up by looking at the costs.

The Benefits of Debt

In the broadest terms, debt provides two differential benefits over equity. The first is the *tax benefit:* Interest payments on debt are tax-deductible, whereas cash flows on equity are not. The second is the *added discipline imposed on management* by having to make payments on debt. Both benefits can and should be quantified if firms want to make reasonable judgments on debt capacity.

1. Debt Has a Tax Advantage

The primary benefit of debt relative to equity is the tax advantage it confers on the borrower. In the United States, interest paid on debt is tax-deductible, whereas cash flows on equity (such as dividends) have to be paid out of after-tax cash flows. For the most part, this is true in other countries as well, though some countries try to provide partial protection against the **double taxation** of dividends by providing a tax credit to investors who receive the dividends for the corporate taxes paid (Britain) or by taxing retained earnings at a rate higher than dividends (Germany).

The tax benefits from debt can be presented in three ways. The first two measure the benefit in absolute terms, whereas the third measures it as a percentage cost.

- In the first approach, the dollar tax savings in any financial year created by interest expenses can be computed by multiplying the interest expenses by the marginal tax rate of the firm. Consider a firm that borrows B to finance it operations, on which it faces an interest rate of r percent, and assume that it faces a marginal tax rate of t on income. The annual tax savings from the interest tax deduction can be calculated as follows:

$$\text{Annual Interest Expense Arising from the Debt} = rB$$

$$\text{Annual Tax Savings Arising from the Interest Payment} = trB$$

- In the second approach, we can compute the present value of tax savings arising from interest payments over time. The present value of the annual tax savings can be computed by making three other assumptions. The first is that the debt is perpetual, which also means that the dollar savings are a perpetuity. The second is that the appropriate discount rate for this cash flow is the interest rate on the debt because it reflects the riskiness of the debt. The third is that the expected tax rate for the firm will remain unchanged over time and that the firm is in a tax-paying position. With these three assumptions, the present value of the savings can be computed as follows:

$$\text{Present Value of Tax Savings from Debt} = trB/r = tB$$
$$= \text{Marginal Tax Rate} \times \text{Debt}$$

Although the conventional view is to look at the tax savings as a perpetuity, the approach is general enough to be used to compute the tax savings over a shorter period (say, ten years). Thus, a firm that borrows $100 million at 8 percent for ten years and has a tax rate of 40 percent, can compute the present value of its tax savings as follows:

$$\begin{aligned}
\text{Present Value of Interest Tax Savings} \\
= \text{Annual Tax Savings (PV of Annuity)} \\
= (0.08 \times 0.4 \times \$100 \text{ million}) \text{ (PV of Annuity, 8\%, 10 years)} \\
= \$21.47 \text{ million}
\end{aligned}$$

When asked to analyze the effect of adding debt on value, some analysts use a shortcut and simply add the tax benefit from debt to the value of the firm with no debt:

Value of Levered Firm with Debt B = Value of Unlevered Firm + tB

The limitation of this approach is that it considers only the tax benefit from borrowing and none of the additional costs. It also yields the unrealistic conclusion that firm value always increases as you borrow more money.

- In the third approach, the tax benefit from debt is expressed in terms of the difference between the pretax and after-tax cost of debt. To illustrate, if r is the interest rate on debt, and t is the marginal tax rate, the after-tax cost of borrowing (k_d) can be written as follows:

After-Tax Cost of Debt (k_d) = $r(1 - t)$

This is the familiar formula used for calculating the cost of debt in the cost of capital calculation. In this formula, the after-tax cost of debt is a decreasing function of the tax rate. A firm with a tax rate of 40 percent, which borrows at 8 percent, has an after-tax cost of debt of 4.8 percent. Another firm with a tax rate of 70 percent, which borrows at 8 percent, has an after-tax cost of debt of 2.4 percent.

Other things remaining equal, the benefits of debt are much greater when tax rates are higher. Consequently, there are three predictions that can be made about debt ratios across companies and across time.

- The debt ratios of entities facing higher tax rates should be higher than the debt ratios of comparable entities facing lower tax rates. Other things remaining equal, you would expect German companies that face a 38.5 percent marginal corporate tax rate to borrow more money than Irish companies that face a 12.5 percent marginal corporate tax rate.
- If tax rates increase over time, we would expect debt ratios to go up over time as well, reflecting the higher tax benefits of debt.
- Companies with large net operating losses carried forward should get far less in tax benefits from debt than firms without these net operating losses.

Double Taxation: There is double taxation when the same income gets taxed twice, once at the entity level and once at the individual level. Thus, dividends, which are paid out of after-tax corporate profits, are double-taxed when individuals have to pay taxes on them as well.

There is a data set online that summarizes by sector the average effective tax rates of companies in each sector.

You have been asked to assess the after-tax cost of debt for a firm that has $2 billion in net operating losses to carry forward, and operating income of roughly $2 billion this year. If the company can borrow at 8 percent, and the marginal corporate tax rate is 40 percent, the after-tax cost of debt this year is

☐ 8 percent.

☐ 4.8 percent.

What would your after-tax cost of debt be next year?

2. Debt May Make Managers More Disciplined

In the 1980s, in the midst of the leveraged buyout boom, a group of practitioners and academics, led by Michael Jensen at Harvard, developed and expounded a new rationale for borrowing, based on improving firms' efficiency in the utilization of their free cash flows. **Free cash flows** represent cash flows made on operations over which managers have discretionary spending power—they may use them to take projects, pay them out to stockholders, or hold them as idle cash balances. The group argued that managers in firms that have substantial free cash flows and no or low debt have such a large cash cushion against mistakes that they have no incentive to be efficient in either project choice or project management. One way to introduce discipline into the process is to force these firms to borrow money, because borrowing creates the commitment to make interest and principal payments, increasing the risk of default on projects with substandard returns. It is this difference between the forgiving nature of the equity commitment and the inflexibility of the debt commitment that has led some to call equity a cushion and debt a sword.

The underlying assumptions in this argument are that there is a conflict of interest between managers and stockholders and that managers will not maximize shareholder wealth without a prod (debt). From our discussion in Chapter 2, it is clear that these assumptions are grounded in fact. Most large U.S. corporations employ managers who own only a very small portion of the outstanding stock in the firm; they receive most of their income as managers rather than stockholders. Furthermore, evidence indicates that managers at least sometimes put their interests ahead those of stockholders.

The argument that debt adds discipline to the process also provides an interesting insight into management perspectives on debt. Based purely on managerial incentives, the optimal level of debt may be much lower than that estimated based on shareholder wealth maximization. Left to themselves, why would managers want to burden themselves with debt, knowing full well that they will have to become more efficient and pay a larger price for their mistakes? The corollary to this argument is that the debt ratios of firms in countries in which stockholder power to influence or remove managers is minimal will be much lower than optimal because managers enjoy a more comfortable existence by carrying less debt than they can afford to. Conversely, as stockholders acquire power, they will push these firms to borrow more money and, in the process, increase their stock prices.

Do increases in debt lead to improved efficiency and higher returns on investments? The answer to this question should provide some insight into whether the argument for added discipline has some basis. A number of studies have attempted to answer this question, though most have done so indirectly.

- Firms that are acquired in hostile takeovers are generally characterized by poor performance in terms of both accounting profitability and stock returns. Bhide, for instance, noted that the return on equity of these firms is 2.2 percent below their peer group, whereas the stock returns are 4 percent below the peer group's returns.[18] Although this poor performance by itself does not constitute support for the free cash flow hypothesis, Palepu presented evidence that target firms in acquisitions carry less debt than similar firms that are not taken over.[19]

- There is evidence that increases in financial leverage are followed by improvements in operating efficiency, as measured by operating margins and returns on capital. Palepu presented evidence of modest improvements in operating efficiency at firms involved in leveraged buyouts.[20] Kaplan and Smith in separate studies also found that firms earn higher returns on capital following leveraged buyouts.[21] Denis and Denis presented more direct evidence on improvements in operating performance after **leveraged recapitalizations**.[22] In their study of twenty-nine firms that increased debt substantially, they report a median increase in the return on assets of 21.5 percent. Much of this gain seems to arise out of cutbacks in unproductive capital investments, because the median reduction in capital expenditures of these firms is 35.5 percent.

Of course, we must consider that the evidence presented is consistent with a number of different hypotheses. For instance, it is possible that the management itself changes at these firms and that the change of management rather than the additional debt leads to higher investment returns.

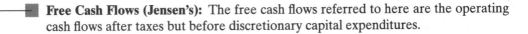

Free Cash Flows (Jensen's): The free cash flows referred to here are the operating cash flows after taxes but before discretionary capital expenditures.

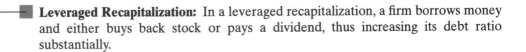

Leveraged Recapitalization: In a leveraged recapitalization, a firm borrows money and either buys back stock or pays a dividend, thus increasing its debt ratio substantially.

---

[18]A. Bhide, 1993, "Reversing Corporate Diversification," in *The New Corporate Finance: Where Theory Meets Practice,* ed. D. H. Chew Jr., New York: McGraw-Hill.

[19]K. G. Palepu, 1986, "Predicting Takeover Targets: A Methodological and Empirical Analysis," *Journal of Accounting and Economics,* 8(1), 3–35.

[20]K. G. Palepu, 1990, "Consequences of Leveraged Buyouts," *Journal of Financial Economics,* 26, 247–262.

[21]See S. N. Kaplan, 1989, "Campeau's Acquisition of Federated: Value Destroyed or Value Added?" *Journal of Financial Economics,* 25, 191–212; A. J. Smith, 1990, "Corporate Ownership Structure and Performance: The Case of Management Buyouts," *Journal of Financial Economics,* 27, 143–164.

[22]David J. Denis and D. K. Denis, 1993, "Leveraged Recaps in the Curbing of Corporate Overinvestment," *Journal of Applied Corporate Finance,* 6(1), 60–71.

7.12 DEBT AS A DISCIPLINING MECHANISM

Assume that you buy into the argument that debt adds discipline to management. Which of the following types of companies will most benefit from debt adding this discipline?

☐ Conservatively financed, privately owned businesses

☐ Conservatively financed, publicly traded companies with a wide and diverse stock holding

☐ Conservatively financed, publicly traded companies, with an activist and primarily institutional holding.

(By "conservatively financed," we mean primarily with equity.)

The Costs of Debt

As any borrower will attest, debt certainly has disadvantages. In particular, borrowing money can expose the firm to default and eventual liquidation, increase the agency problems arising from the conflict between the interests of equity investors and lenders, and reduce the flexibility of the firm to take actions now or in the future.

1. Debt Increases Expected Bankruptcy Costs

The primary concern when borrowing money is the increase in expected bankruptcy costs that typically follows. The expected bankruptcy cost can be written as a product of the probability of bankruptcy and the direct and indirect costs of bankruptcy.

The Probability of Bankruptcy

The probability of bankruptcy is the likelihood that a firm's cash flows will be insufficient to meet its promised debt obligations (interest or principal). Although such a failure does not automatically imply bankruptcy, it does trigger default, with all its negative consequences. Using this definition, the probability of bankruptcy should be a function of both the size of the operating cash flows of the firm—larger cash flows should reduce the likelihood of default—and the volatility in these cash flows—more volatile cash flows should result in a higher probability of bankruptcy. Accordingly, the probability of bankruptcy increases marginally for all firms as they borrow more money, irrespective of how large their cash flows might be, and the increase should be greater for firms in riskier businesses.

The Cost of Bankruptcy

The cost of going bankrupt is neither obvious nor easily quantified. It is true that bankruptcy is a disaster for all involved in the firm—lenders often get a fraction of what they are owed, and equity investors get nothing—but the overall cost of bankruptcy includes the indirect costs on operations of being perceived as having high default risk.

a. Direct Costs   The direct, or deadweight, cost of bankruptcy is that which is incurred in terms of cash outflows at the time of bankruptcy. These costs include the legal and administrative costs of a bankruptcy, as well as the present value effects of delays in paying out the cash flows. In a widely quoted study of railroad bankruptcies in the 1970s, Warner estimated the legal and administrative costs of eleven railroads to be on average 5.3 percent of the value of the assets at the time of the bankruptcy. He also estimated that it took, on average, thirteen years before the railroads were reorganized and released from the bankruptcy costs.[23] These costs, although certainly not negligible, are not overwhelming, especially in light of two additional factors. First, the direct cost as a percentage of the value of the assets decreases to 1.4 percent if the asset value is computed five years before the bankruptcy. Second, railroads in general are likely to have higher bankruptcy costs than other companies because of the nature of their assets (real estate and fixed equipment).

b. Indirect Costs   If the only costs of bankruptcy were the direct costs, the low leverage maintained by many firms would be puzzling. There are, however, much larger costs associated with taking on debt and increasing default risk, which arise prior to the bankruptcy, largely as a consequence of the perception that a firm is in financial trouble. The first is the perception on the part of the customers that the firm is in trouble. When this happens, customers may stop buying the product or service because of the fear that the company will go out of business. In 1980, for example, when car buyers believed that Chrysler was on the verge of bankruptcy, they chose instead to buy from Ford and GM, largely because they were concerned about receiving service and parts for their cars after their purchases. Similarly, in the late 1980s, when Continental Airlines found itself in financial trouble, business travelers switched to other airlines because they were unsure about whether they would be able to accumulate and use their frequent-flier miles on the airline. The second indirect cost is the stricter terms suppliers start demanding to protect themselves against the possibility of default, leading to an increase in working capital and a decrease in cash flows. The third cost is the difficulty the firm may experience trying to raise fresh capital for its projects—both debt and equity investors are reluctant to take the risk, leading to capital rationing constraints and the rejection of good projects.

Given this reasoning, the indirect costs of bankruptcy are likely to be higher for the following types of firms:[24]

- ***Firms that sell durable products with long lives that require replacement parts and service***   Thus, a personal computer manufacturer would have higher indirect costs associated with bankruptcy than would a grocery store.

- ***Firms that provide goods or services for which quality is an important attribute but is difficult to determine in advance***   Because the quality cannot be determined easily in advance, the reputation of the firm plays a significant role in whether the customer will buy the product in the first place. For instance, the perception that an airline is in financial trouble may scare away customers who worry that the planes belonging to the airline will not be maintained properly.

---

[23]J. N. Warner, 1977, "Bankruptcy Costs: Some Evidence," *Journal of Finance,* 32, 337–347.

[24]See A. Shapiro, 1989, *Modern Corporate Finance,* New York: Macmillan; S. Titman, 1984, "The Effect of Capital Structure on a Firm's Liquidation Decision," *Journal of Financial Economics,* 13, 1371–75.

- *Firms producing products whose value to customers depends on the services and complementary products supplied by independent companies*   Returning to the example of personal computers, a computer system is valuable only insofar as there is software available to run on it. If the firm manufacturing the computers is perceived to be in trouble, it is entirely possible that the independent suppliers that produce the software might stop providing it. Thus, if Apple Computers gets into financial trouble, many software manufacturers might stop producing software for its machines, leading to an erosion in its potential market.

- *Firms that sell products that require continuous service and support from the manufacturer*   A manufacturer of copying machines, for which constant service seems to be a necessary operating characteristic, would be affected more adversely by the perception of default risk than would a furniture manufacturer, for example.

Implications for Optimal Capital Structure

If the expected bankruptcy cost is indeed the product of the probability of bankruptcy and the direct and indirect bankruptcy cost, interesting and testable implications emerge for capital structure decisions.

- Firms operating in businesses with volatile earnings and cash flows should use debt less than otherwise similar firms with stable cash flows. For instance, regulated utilities in the United States have high leverage because the regulation and the monopolistic nature of their businesses result in stable earnings and cash flows. At the other extreme, toy manufacturing firms, such as Mattel, can have large shifts in income from one year to another, based on the commercial success or failure of a single toy.[25] These firms should use leverage far less in meeting their funding needs.

- If firms can structure their debt in such a way that the cash flows on the debt increase and decrease with their operating cash flows, they can afford to borrow more. This is because the probability of default is greatest when operating cash flows decrease and the concurrent reduction in debt cash flows makes the default risk lower. Commodity companies, whose operating cash flows increase and decrease with commodity prices, may be able to use more debt if the debt payments are linked to commodity prices. Similarly, a company whose operating cash flows increase as interest rates (and inflation) go up and decrease when interest rates go down may be able to use more debt if the debt has a floating rate feature.

- If an external entity provides protection against bankruptcy, by providing either insurance or bailouts, firms will tend to borrow more. To illustrate, the deposit insurance offered by the FSLIC and the FDIC enables savings and loans and banks to maintain higher leverage than they otherwise could. Although one can argue for this insurance on the grounds of preserving the integrity of the financial

---

[25]In years past, a single group of toys, such as the Teenage Mutant Ninja Turtles or the Power Rangers, could account for a substantial proportion of a major toy manufacturer's profits.

system, undercharging for the insurance will accentuate this tendency and induce high-risk firms to take on too much debt, letting taxpayers bear the cost. Similarly, governments that step in and regularly bail out firms on social grounds (e.g., to save jobs) will encourage all firms to overuse debt.

- Because the direct bankruptcy costs are higher, when the assets of the firm are not easily divisible and marketable, firms with assets that can be easily divided and sold should be able to borrow more than firms with assets that do not share these features. Thus, a firm, such as Weyerhaeuser, whose value comes from its real estate holdings should be able to borrow more money than a firm such as Coca-Cola, which derives a great deal of its value from its brand name (which is not easily separable or liquid).

- Firms that produce products that require long-term servicing and support generally should have lower leverage than firms whose products do not share this feature, as discussed before.

7.13   DEBT AND BANKRUPTCY

Rank the following companies on the magnitude of bankruptcy costs from most to least, taking into account both direct and indirect costs:

☐   A grocery store
☐   An airplane manufacturer
☐   A high-technology company

Explain.

There is a data set online that summarizes variances in operating earnings by sector.

2. Debt Creates Agency Costs

Equity investors, who receive a residual claim on the cash flows, tend to favor actions that increase the value of their holdings, even if that means increasing the risk that the bondholders (who have a fixed claim on the cash flows) will not receive their promised payments. Bondholders, on the other hand, want to preserve and increase the security of their claims. Because the equity investors generally control the firm's management and decision making, their interests will dominate bondholder interests unless bondholders take some protective action. By borrowing money, a firm exposes itself to this conflict and its negative consequences and it pays the price in terms of both higher interest rates and a loss of freedom in decision making.

The conflict between bondholder and stockholder interests appears in all three aspects of corporate finance: (1) deciding what projects to take (making investment decisions), (2) choosing how to finance these projects, and (3) determining how much to pay out as dividends:

- ***Risky Projects***   In the section on investment analysis, we argued that projects that earn a return that exceed the hurdle rate, adjusted to reflect the risk of the project, should be accepted and will increase firm value. The caveat, however, is that bondholders may be hurt if the firm accepts some of these projects.

Bondholders lend money to the firm with the expectation that the projects accepted will have a certain risk level, and they set the interest rate on the bonds accordingly. If the firm chooses projects that are riskier than expected (called risk shifting), however, bondholders will lose on their existing holdings because the price of the holdings will decrease to reflect the higher risk.

- *Subsequent Financing* The conflict between stockholder and bondholder interests also arises when new projects have to be financed. The equity investors in a firm may favor new debt, using the assets of the firm as security and giving the new lenders prior claims over existing lenders. Such actions will reduce the interest rate on the new debt. The existing lenders in a firm obviously do not want to give new lenders priority over their claims, because it makes the existing debt riskier (and less valuable).

- *Dividends and Stock Repurchases* Dividend payments and equity repurchases also divide stockholders and bondholders. Consider a firm that has built up a large cash reserve but has very few good projects available. The stockholders in this firm may benefit if the cash is paid out as a dividend or used to repurchase stock. The bondholders, on the other hand, will prefer that the firm retain the cash, because it can be used to make payments on the debt, reducing default risk. It should come as no surprise that stockholders, if not constrained, will pay the dividends or buy back stock, overriding bondholder concerns. In some cases, the payments are large and can increase the default risk of the firm dramatically.

The potential for disagreement between stockholders and bondholders can show up in as real costs in two ways:

a. If bondholders believe there is a significant chance that stockholder actions might make them worse off, they can build this expectation into bond prices by demanding much higher interest rates on debt.

b. If bondholders can protect themselves against such actions by writing in restrictive covenants, two costs follow:

- the direct cost of monitoring the covenants, which increases as the covenants become more detailed and restrictive
- the indirect cost of lost investments, because the firm is not able to take certain projects, use certain types of financing, or change its payout; this cost will also increase as the covenants becomes more restrictive

As firms borrow more and expose themselves to more conflicts, these agency costs will also increase.

Because agency costs can be substantial, two implications relating to optimal capital structure follow. First, the agency cost arising from **risk shifting** is likely to be greatest in firms whose investments cannot be easily observed and monitored. For example, a lender to a firm that invests in real estate is less exposed to risk shifting than is a lender to a firm that invests in people (consulting, for example) or intangible assets (as is the case with technology firms). Consequently, it is not surprising that manufacturing companies and railroads, which invest in substantial real assets, have much higher debt ratios than service companies. Second, the agency cost associated with monitoring management actions and second-guessing investment decisions is likely to be largest for firms whose projects are long term, follow unpredictable paths, and take years to come to fruition. Pharmaceutical companies in the United States, for example, which often take on research projects that take years to yield commercial products, have historically maintained low debt ratios, even though their cash flows would support more debt.

Risk Shifting: The tendency of stockholders in firms and their agents (managers) to take on much riskier projects than bondholders expect them to.

7.14   Risk Shifting and Bondholders

It is often argued that bondholders who plan to hold their bonds until maturity and collect the coupons and the face value are not affected by risk shifting that occurs after they buy the bonds because the effect is only on market value. Do you agree?

☐ Yes

☐ No

Explain.

3. Using Up Excess Debt Capacity Reduces Financial Flexibility

As noted earlier, one of the by-products of the conflict between stockholders and bondholders is the introduction of strict bond covenants that reduce the flexibility of firms to make investment, financing, or dividend decisions. It can be argued that this is part of a much greater loss of flexibility arising from taking on debt. One of the reasons firms do not use their available debt capacity is that they like to preserve it for a rainy day, when they might need the debt to meet funding needs or specific contingencies. Firms that borrow to capacity lose this flexibility and have no fallback funding if they get into trouble.

Firms value **financial flexibility** for two reasons. First, the value of the firm may be maximized by preserving some flexibility to take on future investments as they arise. Second, flexibility provides managers with more breathing room and more power, and it protects them from the monitoring that comes with debt. Thus, although the argument for maintaining flexibility in the interests of the firm is based on sound principles, it is sometimes used as camouflage by managers pursuing their own interests. There is also a trade-off between not maintaining enough flexibility (because a firm has too much debt) and having too much flexibility (by not borrowing enough).

So, how best can we value financial flexibility? If flexibility is needed to allow firms to take advantage of unforeseen investment opportunities, its value should ultimately be derived from two variables. The first is access to capital markets. After all, firms that have unlimited access to capital markets will not need to maintain excess debt capacity because they can raise funds as needed for new investments. Smaller firms and those in emerging markets, on the other hand, should value financial flexibility more. The second is the potential for excess returns on new investments. If a firm operates in a mature business where new investments, unpredictable though they might be, earn the cost of capital, there is no value to maintaining flexibility. Alternatively, a firm that operates in a volatile business with high excess returns should attach a much higher value to financial flexibility.

Financial Flexibility: The capacity of firms to meet any unforeseen contingencies that may arise (such as recessions and sales downturns) and take advantage of unanticipated opportunities (such as great projects), using the funds they have on hand and any excess debt capacity that they might have nurtured.

7.15 VALUE OF FLEXIBILITY AND FIRM CHARACTERISTICS

Both Ford and Microsoft have huge cash balances (as a percent of firm value); assume that you are a stockholder in both firms. The management of both firms claims to hold the cash because they need the flexibility. Which of the two managements are you more likely to accept this argument from?

☐ Microsoft's management

☐ Ford's management

Explain.

The Trade-Off in a Balance Sheet Format

Bringing together the benefits and the costs of debt, we can present the trade-off in a balance sheet format in Table 7.3.

Overall, if the marginal benefits of borrowing exceed the marginal costs, the firm should borrow money. Otherwise, it should use equity.

What do firms consider when they make capital structure decisions? To answer this question, Pinegar and Wilbricht surveyed financial managers at 176 firms in the

Table 7.3 TRADE-OFF ON DEBT VERSUS EQUITY	
Advantages of Borrowing	**Disadvantages of Borrowing**
1. Tax Benefit: Higher tax rates → Higher tax benefit	1. Bankruptcy Cost: Higher business risk and bankruptcy cost → Higher cost
2. Added Discipline: Greater the separation between managers and stockholders → Greater the benefit	2. Agency Cost: Greater the separation between stockholders and lenders → Higher cost
	3. Loss of Future Financing Flexibility: Greater the uncertainty about future financing needs → Higher cost

Table 7.4   FINANCIAL PRINCIPLES DETERMINING CAPITAL STRUCTURE DECISIONS

Planning Principle by Order of Importance	Percentage of Responses within Each Rank						Mean
	Unimportant	2	3	4	Important	Not Ranked	
1. Maintaining financial flexibility	0.6	0.0	4.5	33.0	61.4	0.6	4.55
2. Ensuring long-term survivability	4.0	1.7	6.8	10.8	76.7	0.0	4.55
3. Maintaining a predictable source of funds	1.7	2.8	20.5	39.2	35.8	0.0	4.05
4. Maximizing security prices	3.4	4.5	19.3	33.5	37.5	1.7	3.00
5. Maintaining financial independence	3.4	4.5	22.2	27.3	40.9	1.7	3.99
6. Maintaining a high debt rating	2.3	9.1	32.4	43.2	13.1	0.0	3.56
7. Maintaining comparability with other firms in the industry	15.9	36.9	33.0	10.8	2.8	0.6	2.47

United States.[26] They concluded that the financial principles listed in Table 7.4 determine capital structure decisions, in the order of importance in which they were given.

The foremost principles the survey participants identified were maintaining financial flexibility and ensuring long-term survivability (which can be construed as avoiding bankruptcy). Surprisingly few managers attached much importance to maintaining comparability with other firms in their industries or maintaining a high debt rating.

ILLUSTRATION 7.4   Evaluating the Debt Trade-Off: Disney, Aracruz, and Bookscape
In Table 7.5, we summarize our views on the potential benefits and costs to using debt, instead of equity, at Disney, Aracruz, and Bookscape.

Based on this analysis, qualitative though it might be, we would argue that all three firms could benefit from borrowing, as long as the borrowing does not push them below an acceptable default risk threshold.

---

[26]J. Michael Pinegar and Lisa Wilbricht, 1989, "What Managers Think of Capital Structure Theory: A Survey," *Financial Management*, 18(4), 82–91.

Table 7.5 THE DEBT EQUITY TRADE-OFF: DISNEY, ARACRUZ, AND BOOKSCAPE

Item	Disney	Aracruz	Bookscape
Tax benefits	Significant. The firm has a marginal tax rate of 37.3%. It does have large depreciation tax shields.	Significant. The firm has a marginal tax rate of 34%. It does not have very much in noninterest tax shields.	Significant. The owners of Bookscape face a 40% tax rate. By borrowing money, the income that flows through to the owner (and taxed) can be reduced.
Added discipline	Benefits will be high, because managers are not large stockholders.	Benefits are smaller, because the voting shares are closely held by insiders/managers.	Benefits are nonexistent. This is a private firm.
Bankruptcy costs	Movie and broadcasting businesses have volatile earnings. Direct costs of bankruptcy are likely to be small, but indirect costs can be significant.	Variability in paper prices makes probability of bankruptcy high. Direct and indirect costs of bankruptcy likely to be moderate.	Costs may be small, but the owner has all of his wealth invested in the firm. His liability, in the event of failure, is not limited, so the costs will viewed as very large.
Agency costs	High. Although theme park assets are tangible and fairly liquid, it is much more difficult to monitor movie and broadcasting businesses.	Low. Assets are tangible and liquid.	Low. Prime asset is lease hold, which is liquid.
Flexibility needs	Low in theme park business but high in media businesses because technological change makes future investment uncertain.	Low. Business is mature and investment needs are well established.	Low. Bookstore is established and additional investments are limited.

NO OPTIMAL CAPITAL STRUCTURE

We have just argued that debt has advantages, relative to equity, as well as disadvantages. Will trading off the costs and benefits of debt yield an optimal mix of debt and equity for a firm? In this section, we will present one argument for when it will not and the resulting conclusion that there is no such optimal mix. The seeds of this argument were sown in one of the most influential papers written in corporate finance, containing one of corporate finance's central theorems, the *Modigliani-Miller theorem*.[27]

When they first looked at the question of whether there is an optimal capital structure, Miller and Modigliani drew their conclusions in a world void of taxes, transaction costs, and the possibility of default. Based on these assumptions, they concluded that the value of a firm was unaffected by its leverage and that investment

---

[27]F. Modigliani and M. Miller, 1958, "The Cost of Capital, Corporation Finance and the Theory of Investment," *American Economic Review*, 48, 261–297.

and financing decisions could be separated. Their conclusion can be confirmed in several ways; we present two in this section. We will also present a more complex argument for why there should be no optimal capital structure even in a world with taxes, made by Miller almost two decades later.

The Irrelevance of Debt in a Tax-Free World

In their initial work, Modigliani and Miller made three significant assumptions about the markets in which their firms operated. First, they assumed there were no taxes. Second, they assumed firms could raise external financing from debt or equity, with no issuance costs. Third, they assumed there were no costs—direct or indirect—associated with bankruptcy. Finally, they operated in an environment in which there were no agency costs; managers acted to maximize stockholder wealth, and bondholders did not have to worry about stockholders expropriating wealth with investment, financing, or dividend decisions.

In such an environment, reverting back to the trade-off that we summarized in Table 7.3, it is quite clear that all the advantages and disadvantages disappear, leaving debt with no marginal benefits and no costs. In Table 7.6 we modify Table 7.3 to reflect the assumptions just listed. Debt creates neither benefits nor costs and thus has a neutral effect on value. In such an environment, the capital structure decision becomes irrelevant.

In a later study, Miller and Modigliani preserved this environment but made one change, allowing for a tax benefit for debt. In this scenario, where debt continues to have no costs, the optimal debt ratio for a firm is 100 percent debt. In fact, in such an environment the value of the firm increases by the present value of the tax savings for interest payments.

$$\text{Value of Levered Firm} = \text{Value of Unlevered Firm} + t_c B$$

where t_c is the corporate tax rate and B is the dollar borrowing. Note that the second term in this valuation is the present value of the interest tax savings from debt, treated as a perpetuity. Figure 7.8 graphs the value of a firm with just the tax benefit from debt.

Miller and Modigliani presented an alternative proof of the irrelevance of leverage, based on the idea that debt does not affect the underlying operating cash flows of the firm in the absence of taxes. Consider two firms that have the same cash flow (X) from operations. Firm A is an all-equity firm, whereas firm B has both equity and debt. The interest rate on debt is r. Assume you are an investor and you buy a fraction (α) of

Table 7.6 The Trade-Off on Debt: No Taxes, Default Risk, and Agency Costs	
Advantages of Debt	**Disadvantages of Debt**
1. Tax Benefit: Zero, because there are no taxes.	1. Bankruptcy Cost: Zero, because there are no bankruptcy costs.
2. Added Discipline: Zero, because managers already maximize stockholder wealth.	2. Agency Cost: Zero, because bondholders are fully protected from wealth transfer.
	3. Loss of Future Financing Flexibility: Not costly, because firms can raise external financing costlessly.

Figure 7.8 Value of Levered Firm: Modigliani and Miller with Taxes

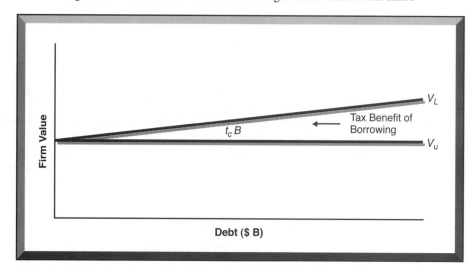

Table 7.7 CASH FLOWS TO INVESTOR FROM LEVERED AND ALL-EQUITY FIRM

	Firm A	Firm B
Type of firm	All-equity firm ($V_u = E$)	Has some equity and debt
Actions now	Investor buys a fraction α of the firm (αV_u)	Investor buys a fraction a of both equity and debt of the firm; $\alpha E_L + \alpha D_L$
Next period	Investor receives a fraction α of the cash flow (αX)	Investor receives the following: $\alpha(X - rD_L) + \alpha rD_L = \alpha X$

the equity in firm A, and the same fraction of both the equity and debt of firm B. Table 7.7 summarizes the cash flows that you will receive in the next period.

Because you receive the same total cash flow in both firms, the value you will attach for both firms has to be the same. This equivalence in values of the two firms implies that leverage does not affect the value of a firm. Note that this proof works only if the firm does not receive a tax benefit from debt; a tax benefit would give firm B a higher cash flow than firm A.

The Irrelevance of Debt with Taxes

It is clear, in the Miller-Modigliani model, that when taxes are introduced into the model, debt does affect value. In fact, introducing both taxes and bankruptcy costs into the model creates a trade-off, where the financing mix of a firm affects value, and there is an optimal mix. In an address in 1977, however, Miller argued that the debt irrelevance theorem could apply even in the presence of corporate taxes if investor taxes on the equity and interest income individuals receive from firms were included in the analysis.[28]

---

[28]M. Miller, 1977, "Debt and Taxes," *Journal of Finance,* 32, 261–275.

To demonstrate the Miller proof of irrelevance, assume that investors face a tax rate of t_d on interest income and a tax rate of t_e on equity income. Assume also that the firm pays an interest rate of r on debt and faces a corporate tax rate of t_c. The after-tax return to the investor from owning debt can then be written as:

$$\text{After-Tax Return from Owning Debt} = r(1 - t_d)$$

The after-tax return to the investor from owning equity can also be estimated. Because cash flows to equity have to be paid out of after-tax cash flows, equity income (k_e) is taxed twice—once at the corporate level and once at the equity level:

$$\text{After-Tax Return from Owning Equity} = k_e(1 - t_c)(1 - t_e)$$

The returns to equity can take two forms—dividends or capital gains; the equity tax rate is a blend of the tax rates on both. In such a scenario, Miller noted that the tax benefit of debt, relative to equity becomes smaller, because both debt and equity now get taxed, at least at the level of the individual investor.

$$\text{Tax Benefit of Debt, Relative to Equity} = \{1 - (1 - t_c)(1 - t_e)\}/(1 - t_d)$$

With this relative tax benefit, the value of the firm, with leverage, can be written as:

$$V_L = V_u + [1 - (1 - t_c)(1 - t_e)/(1 - t_d)]B$$

where V_L is the value of the firm with leverage, V_u is the value of the firm without leverage, and B is the dollar debt. With this expanded equation, which includes both personal and corporate taxes, there are several possible scenarios:

a. ***Personal tax rates on both equity and dividend income are zero***   If we ignore personal taxes, this equation compresses to the original equation for the value of a levered firm, in a world with taxes but no bankruptcy costs:

$$V_L = V_u + t_c B$$

b. ***The personal tax rate on equity is the same as the tax rate on debt***   If this were the case, the result is the same as the original one—the value of the firm increases with more debt.

$$V_L = V_u + t_c B$$

c. ***The tax rate on debt is higher than the tax rate on equity***   In such a case, the differences in the individual investor tax rates may more than compensate for the double taxation of equity cash flows. To illustrate, assume that the tax rate on ordinary income is 70 percent, the tax rate on capital gains on stock is 28 percent, and the tax rate on corporations is 35 percent. In such a case, the investor tax liabilities for debt and equity can be calculated for a firm that pays no dividend as follows:

Tax Rate on Debt Income = 70%

Tax Rate on Equity Income = $1 - (1 - 0.35)(1 - 0.28) = 0.532$ or 53.2%

This is a plausible scenario, especially considering tax law in the United States until the early 1980s. In this scenario, debt creates a tax disadvantage to investors.

d. ***The tax rate on equity income is just low enough to compensate for the double taxation*** In this case, we are back to the original debt irrelevance theorem.

$$(1 - t_d) = (1 - t_c)(1 - t_e) \dots \text{Debt is irrelevant}$$

Miller's analysis brought investor tax rates into the analysis for the first time and provided some insight into the role of investor tax preferences on a firm's capital structure. As Miller himself notes, however, this analysis does not reestablish the irrelevance of debt under all circumstances; rather, it opens up the possibility that debt could still be irrelevant despite its tax advantages.

The Consequences of Debt Irrelevance

If the financing decision is irrelevant, as proposed by Miller and Modigliani, corporate financial analysis is simplified in a number of ways. The cost of capital, which is the weighted average of the cost of debt and the cost of equity, is unaffected by changes in the proportions of debt and equity. This might seem unreasonable, especially because the cost of debt is much lower than the cost of equity. In the Miller-Modigliani world, however, any benefits incurred by substituting cheaper debt for more expensive equity are offset by increases in both their costs, as shown in Figure 7.9.

The value of the firm is also unaffected by the amount of debt it has. Thus, if the firm is valued as an all-equity entity, its value will remain unchanged if it is valued with any other debt ratio. (This actually follows from the implication that the cost of capital is unaffected by changes in leverage and from the assumption that the operating cash flows are determined by investment decisions rather than financing decisions.)

Finally, the investment decision can be made independently of the financing decision. In other words, if a project is a bad project when evaluated as an all-equity project, it will remain so using any other financing mix.

Figure 7.9 Cost of Capital in the Miller-Modigliani World

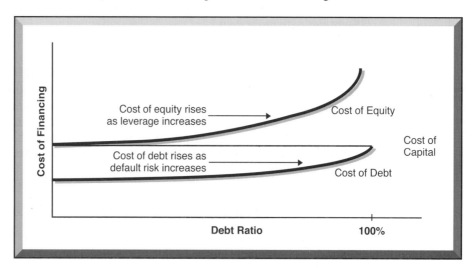

The Contribution of the Miller-Modigliani Theorem

It is unlikely that capital structure is irrelevant in the real world, given the tax preferences for debt and the existence of default risk. In spite of this, Miller and Modigliani were pioneers in moving capital structure analysis from an environment in which firms picked their debt ratios based on comparable firms and management preferences, to one that recognized the trade-off. They also drew attention to the impact of good investment decisions on firm value. To be more precise, a firm that invests in poor projects cannot hope to recoup the lost value by making better financing decisions; a firm that takes good projects will succeed in creating value, even if it uses the wrong financing mix. Finally, although the concept of a world with no taxes, default risk, or agency problems may seem a little far-fetched, there are some environments in which the description might hold. Assume, for instance, that the U.S. government decides to encourage small businesses to invest in urban areas by relieving them of their tax burden and providing a back-up guarantee on loans (default protection). Firms that respond to these initiatives might find that their capital structure decisions do not affect their value.

Finally, surveys of financial managers indicate that in practice, they do not attach as much weight to the costs and benefits of debt as we do in theory. In the survey quoted earlier by Pinegar and Wilbricht, managers were asked to cite the most important inputs governing their financial decisions. Their responses are ranked in the order of the importance managers attached to them in Table 7.8.

Table 7.8 INPUTS INTO CAPITAL STRUCTURE DECISIONS

	Percentage of Responses within Each Rank						
	Least Important			Most Important			
Inputs/assumptions by order of importance	1	2	3	4	5	Not Ranked	Mean
1. Projected cash flow from asset to be financed	1.7%	1.1%	9.7%	29.5%	58.0%	0.0%	4.41
2. Avoiding dilution of common equity's claims	2.8%	6.3%	18.2%	39.8%	33.0%	0.0%	3.94
3. Risk of asset to be financed	2.8%	6.3%	20.5%	36.9%	33.0%	0.6%	3.91
4. Restrictive covenants on senior securities	9.1%	9.7%	18.7%	35.2%	27.3%	0.0%	3.62
5. Avoiding mispricing of securities to be issued.	3.4%	10.8%	27.3%	39.8%	18.7%	0.0%	3.60
6. Corporate tax rate	4.0%	9.7%	29.5%	42.6%	13.1%	1.1%	3.52
7. Voting control	17.6%	10.8%	21.0%	31.2%	19.3%	0.0%	3.24
8. Depreciation & other tax shields	8.5%	17.6%	40.9%	24.4%	7.4%	1.1%	3.05
9. Correcting mispricing of securities	14.8%	27.8%	36.4%	14.2%	5.1%	1.7%	2.66
10. Personal tax rates of debt and equity holders	31.2%	34.1%	25.6%	8.0%	1.1%	0.0%	2.14
11. Bankruptcy costs	69.3%	13.1%	6.8%	4.0%	4.5%	2.3%	1.58

Financial managers seem to weigh financial flexibility and potential dilution much more heavily than bankruptcy costs and taxes in their capital structure decisions.

IN PRACTICE: THE DILUTION BOGEY

The dilution effect refers to the possible decrease in earnings per share from any action that might lead to an increase in the number of shares outstanding. As evidenced in Table 7.8, managers (especially in the United States) weigh these potential dilution effects heavily in decisions on what type of financing to use and how to fund projects. Consider, for instance, the choice between raising equity using a rights issue, where the stock is issued at a price below the current market price, and a public issue of stock at the market price. The latter is a much more expensive option, from the perspective of investment banking fees and other costs, but is chosen nevertheless because it results in fewer shares being issued (to raise the same amount of funds). The fear of dilution is misplaced for the following reasons:

1. Investors measure their returns in terms of total return on their investment and not just in terms of stock price. Although the stock price will go down more after a rights issue, each investor will be compensated adequately for the price drop (by either receiving more shares or by being able to sell their rights to other investors). In fact, if the transactions costs are considered, stockholders will be better off after a rights issue than after an equivalent public issue of stock.

2. Although the earnings per share will always drop in the immediate aftermath of a new stock issue, the stock price will not necessarily follow suit. In particular, if the stock issue is used to finance a good project (i.e., a project with a positive net present value), the increase in value should be greater than the increase in the number of shares, leading to a higher stock price.

Ultimately, the measure of whether a company should issue stock to finance a project should depend on the quality of the investment. Firms that dilute their stockholdings to take good investments are choosing the right course for their stockholders. ∎

THERE IS AN OPTIMAL CAPITAL STRUCTURE

The counter to the Miller-Modigliani proposition is that the trade-offs on debt may work in favor of the firm (at least initially) and that borrowing money may lower the cost of capital and increase firm value. We will examine the mechanics of putting this argument into practice in the next chapter; here, we look at the case for the existence of an optimal capital structure and look at some of the empirical evidence for and against it.

The Case for an Optimal Capital Structure

If the debt decision involves a trade-off between the benefits of debt (tax benefits and added discipline) and the costs of debt (bankruptcy costs, agency costs, and lost flexibility), it can be argued that the marginal benefits will be offset by the marginal costs *only in exceptional cases* and not always (as argued by Miller and Modigliani).

Table 7.9   DEBT RATIOS AND FUNDAMENTALS

Variable	Effect on Debt Ratios
Marginal tax rate	As marginal tax rates increase, debt ratios increase.
Separation of ownership and management	The greater the separation of ownership and management, the higher the debt ratio.
Variability in operating cash flows	As operating cash flows become more variable, the bankruptcy risk increases, resulting in lower debt ratios.
Debt holders' difficulty in monitoring firm actions, investments, and performance	The more difficult it is to monitor the actions taken by a firm, the lower the optimal debt ratio.
Need for flexibility	The greater the need for decision making flexibility in future periods, the lower the optimal debt ratio.

In fact, under most circumstances, the marginal benefits will either exceed the marginal costs (in which case debt is good and will increase firm value) or fall short of marginal costs (in which case equity is better). Accordingly, there is an optimal capital structure for most firms at which firm value is maximized.

Of course, it is always possible that managers may be operating under an illusion that capital structure decisions matter when the reality might be otherwise. Consequently, we examine some of the empirical evidence to see if it is consistent with the theory of an optimal mix of debt and equity.

Empirical Evidence

The question of whether there is an optimal capital structure can be answered in a number of ways. The first is to see if differences in debt ratios across firms can be explained systematically by differences in the variables driving the debt trade-offs. Other things remaining equal, we would expect to see relationships listed in Table 7.9.

This may seem like a relatively simple test to run, but keeping all other things equal in the real world is often close to impossible. In spite of this limitation, attempts to see if the direction of the relationship is consistent with the theory have produced mixed results.

Bradley, Jarrell, and Kim analyzed whether differences in debt ratios can be explained by proxies for the variables involved in the capital structure trade-off.[29] They noted that the debt ratio is:

- *negatively correlated with the volatility in annual operating earnings,* as predicted by the bankruptcy cost component of the optimal capital structure trade-off.

---

[29]M. Bradley, G. Jarrell, and E. H. Kim, 1984, "On the Existence of an Optimal Capital Structure: Theory and Evidence," *Journal of Finance,* 39, 857–878.

- *positively related to the level of nondebt tax shields,* which is counter to the tax hypothesis, which argues that firms with large nondebt tax shields should be less inclined to use debt.
- *negatively related to advertising and R&D expenses used as a proxy for agency costs;* this is consistent with optimal capital structure theory.

Others who have attempted to examine whether cross-sectional differences in capital structure are consistent with the theory have come to contradictory conclusions.

An alternate test of the optimal capital structure hypothesis is to examine the stock price reaction to actions taken by firms either to increase or decrease financial leverage. In evaluating the price response, we have to make some assumptions about the motivation of the firms making these changes. If we assume that firms are rational and that they make these changes to get closer to their optimal, both leverage-increasing and -decreasing actions should be accompanied by positive excess returns, at least on average. Smith (1986) noted that the evidence is *not* consistent with an optimal capital structure hypothesis, however, because leverage-increasing actions seem to be accompanied by positive excess returns whereas leverage-reducing actions seem to be followed by negative returns.[30] The only way to reconcile this finding with an optimal capital structure argument is by assuming that managerial incentives (desire for stability and flexibility) keep leverage below optimal for most firms and that actions by firms to reduce leverage are seen as serving managerial interests rather than stockholder interests.

There is a data set online that summarizes debt ratios and averages for the fundamental variables that should determine debt ratios by sector.

HOW FIRMS CHOOSE THEIR CAPITAL STRUCTURES

We have argued that firms should choose the mix of debt and equity by trading off the benefit of borrowing against the costs. There are, however, three alternative views of how firms choose a financing mix. The first is that the choice between debt and equity is determined by where a firm is in the growth life cycle. High-growth firms will tend to use debt less than more mature firms. The second is that firms choose their financing mix by looking at one financial policy of other firms in their business. The third view is that firms have strong preferences for certain types of financing, i.e., there is a financing hierarchy, and that they deviate from these preferences only when they have no choice. We will argue that in each of these approaches, firms still implicitly make the trade-off between costs and benefits, though the assumptions needed for each approach to work are different.

---

[30]C. W. Smith, 1986, "Investment Banking and the Capital Acquisition Process," *Journal of Financial Economics,* 15, 3–29.

Financing Mix and a Firm's Life Cycle

Earlier in this chapter, we looked at how a firm's financing choices might change as it makes the transition from a start-up firm to a mature firm to final decline. We can also look at how a firm's financing mix changes over the same life cycle. Typically, start-up firms and firms in rapid expansion use debt sparingly; in some cases, they use no debt at all. As the growth eases and as cash flows from existing investments become larger and more predictable, we see firms beginning to use debt. Debt ratios typically peak when firms are in mature growth.

How does this empirical observation relate to our earlier discussion of the benefits and costs of debt? We argue that the behavior of firms at each stage in the life cycle is entirely consistent with making this trade-off. In the start-up and high-growth phases, the tax benefits to firms from using debt tend to be small or nonexistent because earnings from existing investments are low or negative. The owners of these firms are usually actively involved in the management of these firms, reducing the need for debt as a disciplinary mechanism.

On the other side of the ledger, the low and volatile earnings increase the expected bankruptcy costs. The absence of significant existing investments or assets and the magnitude of new investments makes lenders much more cautious about lending to the firm, increasing the agency costs; these costs show up as more stringent covenants or in higher interest rates on borrowing. As growth eases, the trade-off shifts in favor of debt. The tax benefits increase and expected bankruptcy costs decrease as earnings from existing investments become larger and more predictable. The firm develops both an asset base and a track record on earnings, which allows lenders to feel more protected when lending to the firm. As firms get larger, the separation between owners (stockholders) and managers tends to grow, and the benefits of using debt as a disciplinary mechanism increase. We have summarized the trade-off at each stage in the life cycle in Figure 7.10.

As with our earlier discussion of financing choices, there will be variations between firms in different businesses at each stage in the life cycle. For instance, a mature steel company may use far more debt than a mature pharmaceutical company because lenders feel more comfortable lending on a steel company's assets (that are tangible and easy to liquidate) than on a pharmaceutical company's assets (which might be patents and other assets that are difficult to liquidate). Similarly, we would expect a company like IBM to have a higher debt ratio than a firm like Microsoft at the same stage in the life cycle because Microsoft has large insider holdings, making the benefit of discipline that comes from debt much smaller.

Financing Mix Based on Comparable Firms

Firms often try to use a financing mix similar to that used by other firms in their business. With this approach, Bookscape would use a low debt to capital ratio because other book retailers have low debt ratios. Bell Atlantic, on the other hand, would use a high debt to capital ratio because other phone companies have high debt to capital ratios.

The empirical evidence about the way firms choose their debt ratios strongly supports the hypothesis that they tend not to stray too far from their sector averages.

Figure 7.10 The Debt-Equity Trade-Off and Life Cycle

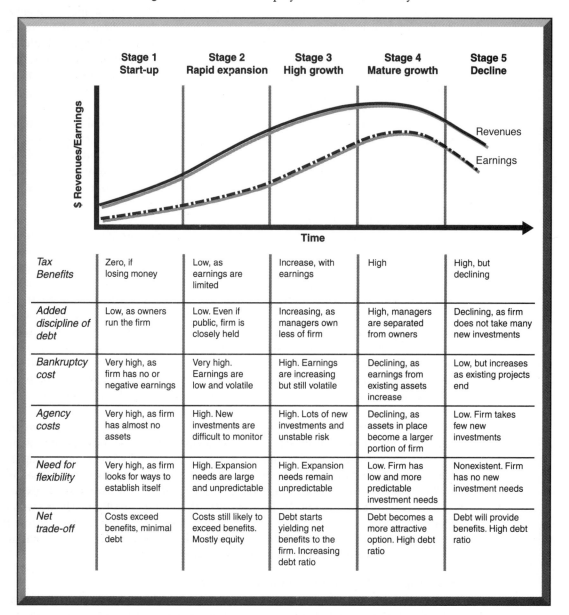

	Stage 1 Start-up	Stage 2 Rapid expansion	Stage 3 High growth	Stage 4 Mature growth	Stage 5 Decline
Tax Benefits	Zero, if losing money	Low, as earnings are limited	Increase, with earnings	High	High, but declining
Added discipline of debt	Low, as owners run the firm	Low. Even if public, firm is closely held	Increasing, as managers own less of firm	High, managers are separated from owners	Declining, as firm does not take many new investments
Bankruptcy cost	Very high, as firm has no or negative earnings	Very high. Earnings are low and volatile	High. Earnings are increasing but still volatile	Declining, as earnings from existing assets increase	Low, but increases as existing projects end
Agency costs	Very high, as firm has almost no assets	High. New investments are difficult to monitor	High. Lots of new investments and unstable risk	Declining, as assets in place become a larger portion of firm	Low. Firm takes few new investments
Need for flexibility	Very high, as firm looks for ways to establish itself	High. Expansion needs are large and unpredictable	High. Expansion needs remain unpredictable	Low. Firm has low and more predictable investment needs	Nonexistent. Firm has no new investment needs
Net trade-off	Costs exceed benefits, minimal debt	Costs still likely to exceed benefits. Mostly equity	Debt starts yielding net benefits to the firm. Increasing debt ratio	Debt becomes a more attractive option. High debt ratio	Debt will provide benefits. High debt ratio

In fact, when we look at the determinants of the debt ratios of individual firms, the strongest determinant is the average debt ratio of the industries to which these firms belong. Some would view this approach to financing as contrary to the approach where we trade off the benefits of debt against the cost of debt, but we do not view it thus. If firms within a business or sector share common characteristics, it should not be surprising if they choose similar financing mixes. For instance, software firms

Table 7.10 SURVEY RESULTS ON PLANNING PRINCIPLES

Ranking	Source	Planning Principle Cited
1	Retained earnings	None
2	Straight debt	Maximize security prices
3	Convertible debt	Cash flow and survivability
4	Common stock	Avoiding dilution
5	Straight preferred stock	Comparability
6	Convertible preferred stock	None

have volatile earnings and high growth potential and choose low debt ratios. In contrast, phone companies have significant assets in place and high and stable earnings; they tend to use more debt in their financing. Thus, choosing a debt ratio similar to that of the industry in which you operate is appropriate, when firms in the industry are at the same stage in the life cycle and, on average, choose the right financing mix for that stage.

It can be dangerous to choose a debt ratio based on comparable firms under two scenarios. The first occurs when there are wide variations in growth potential and risk across companies within a sector. Then we would expect debt ratios to be different across firms. The second occurs when firms on average have too much or too little debt given their characteristics. This can happen when an entire sector changes. For instance, phone companies have historically had stable and large earnings because they have had monopoly power. As technology and deregulation breaks down this power, it is entirely possible that earnings will become more volatile and that these firms should carry a lot less debt than they do currently.

Following a Financing Hierarchy

There is evidence that firms follow a *financing hierarchy:* retained earnings are the most preferred choice for financing, followed by debt, new equity, common, and preferred; convertible preferred is the least preferred choice. Going back again to the survey by Pinegar and Wilbricht, managers were asked to rank six different sources of financing—internal equity, external equity, external debt, preferred stock, and hybrids (convertible debt and preferred stock)—from most preferred to least preferred.[31] The results are summarized in Table 7.10.

One reason for this hierarchy is that managers value *flexibility and control.* To the extent that external financing reduces flexibility for future financing (especially if it is debt) and control (bonds have covenants; new equity attracts new stockholders into the company and may reduce insider holdings as a percentage of total holding), managers prefer retained earnings as a source of capital. Another reason is it costs nothing in terms of issuance to use retained earnings, whereas *it costs more* to use external debt and even more to use external equity.

The survey yielded some other interesting conclusions as well. External debt is strongly preferred over external equity as a way of raising funds. The values of external

---

[31]Pinegar and Wilbricht (1989); see note 26.

Figure 7.11 External Equity versus External Debt (as Percent of Extreme Funding)

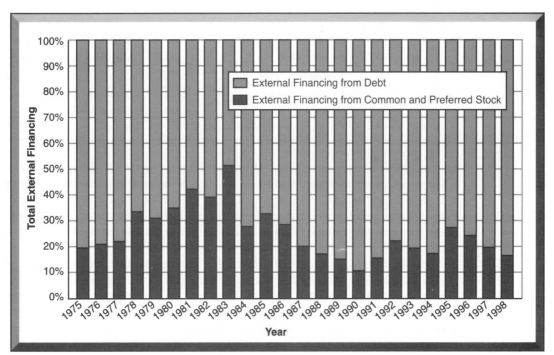

Source: Compustat.

debt and external equity issued between 1975 and 1998 by U.S. corporations are shown in Figure 7.11 and bear out this preference.

Given a choice, firms would much rather use straight debt than convertible debt, even though the interest rate on convertible debt is much lower. Managers perhaps have a much better sense of the value of the conversion option than is recognized.

A firm's choices say a great deal about its financial strength. Thus, the 1993 decisions by RJR Nabisco and GM to raise new funds through convertible preferred stock were seen by markets as an admission of their financial weakness. Not surprisingly, the financial market response to the issue of securities listed in Table 7.10 mirrors the preferences: The most negative responses are reserved for securities near the bottom of the list, the most positive (or at least the least negative) for those at the top of the list.

Why do firms have a financing hierarchy? In the discussion of financing choices so far, we have steered away from questions about how firms convey information to financial markets with their financing choices and how well the securities that the firms issue are priced. Firms know more about their future prospects than do the financial markets that they deal with; markets may under- or overprice securities issued by firms. Myers and Majluf note that in the presence of this asymmetric information, firms that believe their securities are underpriced, given their future prospects, may be inclined to reject good projects rather than raise external financing.

Alternatively, firms that believe their securities are overpriced are more likely to issue these securities, even if they have no projects available.[32] In this environment, the following implications emerge:

- Managers prefer retained earnings to external financing, because it allows them to consider projects on their merits, rather than depending on whether markets are pricing their securities correctly. It follows then that firms will be more inclined to retain earnings over and above their current investment requirements to finance future projects.

- When firms issue securities, markets will consider the issue a signal that these securities are overvalued. This signal is likely to be more negative for securities, such as stocks, where the asymmetry of information is greater, and smaller for securities, such as straight bonds, where the asymmetry is smaller. This would explain both the rankings in the financial hierarchy and the market reaction to these security issues.

7.16 VALUE OF FLEXIBILITY AND FIRM CHARACTERISTICS

You are reading the *Wall Street Journal* and notice a tombstone ad for a company offering to sell convertible preferred stock. What would you hypothesize about the health of the company issuing these securities?

☐ Nothing

☐ Healthier than the average firm

☐ In much more financial trouble than the average firm

CONCLUSION

In this chapter, we laid the groundwork for analyzing a firm's optimal mix of debt and equity by laying out the benefits and the costs of borrowing money. In particular, we made the following points:

- We differentiated between debt and equity at a generic level by pointing out that any financing that results in contractual cash flows, has prior claims in the case of default, a fixed maturity, and no voting rights is debt, whereas financing that provides for residual cash flows, has low or no priority in claims in the case of default, an infinite life, and a lion's share of the control is equity.

- Although all firms, private as well as public, use both debt and equity, the choices in financing change as a firm progresses through the life cycle, with equity dominating at the earlier stages and debt as the firm matures.

- The primary benefit of debt is a tax benefit: Interest expenses are tax-deductible and cash flows to equity (dividends) are not. This benefit increases with the tax

[32]S. C. Myers and N. S. Majluf, 1984, Corporate Financing and Investment Decisions when Firms Have Information that Investors Do Not Have," *Journal of Financial Economics,* 13, 187–221.

rate of the entity taking on the debt. A secondary benefit of debt is that it forces managers to be more disciplined in their choice of projects by increasing the costs of failure; a series of bad projects may create the possibility of defaulting on interest and principal payments.

- The primary cost of borrowing is an increase in the expected bankruptcy cost—the product of the probability of default and the cost of bankruptcy. The probability of default is greater for firms that have volatile cash flows. The cost of bankruptcy includes both the direct costs (legal and time value) of bankruptcy and the indirect costs (lost sales, tighter credit, and less access to capital). Borrowing money exposes the firm to the possibility of conflicts between stock and bondholders over investment, financing, and dividend decisions. The covenants that bondholders write into bond agreements to protect themselves against expropriation cost the firm in both monitoring costs and lost flexibility. The loss of financial flexibility that arises from borrowing money is more likely to be a problem for firms with substantial and unpredictable investment opportunities.

- In the special case where there are no tax benefits, default risk, or agency problems, the financing decision is irrelevant. In most cases, however, the trade-off between the benefits and costs of debt will result in an optimal capital structure whereby the value of the firm is maximized.

- Firms generally choose their financing mix in one of three ways—based on where they are in the life cycle, by looking at comparable firms, or by following a financing hierarchy where retained earnings is the most preferred option and convertible preferred stock the least.

LIVE CASE STUDY

ANALYZING A FIRM'S CURRENT FINANCING CHOICES

Objective: To examine a firm's current financing choices and to categorize them into debt (borrowings) and equity and to examine the trade-off between debt and equity for your firm.

Key Questions

- Where and how does the firm get its current financing?
- Would these financing choices be classified as debt, equity, or hybrid securities?
- How large, in qualitative or quantitative terms, are the advantages to this company from using debt?
- How large, in qualitative or quantitative terms, are the disadvantages to this company from using debt?
- From the qualitative trade-off, does this firm look like it has too much or too little debt?

Framework for Analysis

1. *Assessing Current Financing*

   1.1 How does the firm raise equity?
   - If it is a publicly traded firm, it can raise equity from common stock and warrants or options.
   - If it is a private firm, the equity can come from personal savings and venture capital.

   1.2 How (if at all) does the firm borrow money?
   - If it is a publicly traded firm, it can raise debt from bank debt or corporate bonds.

   1.3 Does the firm use any hybrid approaches to raising financing that combine some of the features of debt and some of equity?
   - Examples would include preferred stock, convertible bonds, and bonds with warrants attached to them.

2. *Detailed Description of Current Financing*

   2.1 If the firm raises equity from warrants or convertibles, what are the characteristics of the options (exercise price, maturity, etc.)?

   2.2 If the firm has borrowed money, what are the characteristics of the debt (maturity, coupon or stated interest rate, call features, fixed or floating rate, secured or unsecured, and currency)?

   2.3 If the firm has hybrid securities, what are the features of the hybrid securities?

3. *Breakdown into Debt and Equity*

3.1 If the firm has financing with debt and equity components (such as convertible bonds), how much of the firm's value can be attributed to debt and how much to equity?

3.2 Given the coupon or stated interest rate and maturity of the nontraded debt, what is the current estimated market value of the debt?

3.3 What is the market value of equity that the firm has outstanding?

4. *Trade-Off on Debt versus Equity*

Benefits of Debt

- What marginal tax rate does this firm face, and how does this measure up to the marginal tax rates of other firms? Are there other tax deductions that this company has (like depreciation) to reduce the tax bite?

- Does this company have high free cash flows (for example, EBITDA/firm value)? Has it taken and does it continue to have good investment projects? How responsive are managers to stockholders? (Will there be an advantage to using debt in this firm as a way of keeping managers in line or do other [cheaper] mechanisms exist?)

Costs of Debt

- How high are the current cash flows of the firm (to service the debt) and how stable are these cash flows? (Look at the variability in the operating income over time.)

- How easy is it for bondholders to observe what equity investors are doing? Are the assets tangible or intangible? If not, what are the costs in terms of monitoring stockholders or in terms of bond covenants?

- How well can this firm forecast its future investment opportunities and needs?

Getting Information about Current Financing Choices

The information about current financing choices can almost all be extracted from the financial statements. The balance sheet should provide a summary of the book values of the various financing choices made by the firm, though hybrids are usually categorized into debt and equity. The description of warrants outstanding as well as the details of the borrowing that the firm has should be available in the footnotes to the balance sheets. In particular, the maturity dates for different components of borrowing, the coupon rates and information on any other special features should be available in the notes.

Online Sources of Information
Review **www.stern.nyu.edu/~adamodar/cfin2E/project/data.htm**.

PROBLEMS AND QUESTIONS

(In the problems below, you can use a risk premium of 5.5 percent and a tax rate of 40 percent if none is specified).

1. An income bondholder receives interest payments only if the firm makes income. If the firm does not make interest payments in a year, the interest is cumulated and paid in the first year the firm makes income. Preferred stock receives preferred dividends only if the firm makes income. If a firm does not make preferred dividend payments in a year, the dividend is cumulated and paid in the first year the firm makes income. Are income bonds really preferred stock? What are the differences? For purposes of calculating debt, how would you differentiate between income bonds and regular bonds?

2. A commodity bond links interest and principal payments to the price of a commodity. Differentiate a commodity bond from a straight bond, and then from equity. How would you factor these differences into your analysis of the debt ratio of a company that has issued exclusively commodity bonds?

3. You are analyzing a new security that has been promoted as equity, with the following features:
   - The dividend on the security is fixed in dollar terms for the life of the security, which is twenty years.
   - The dividend is not tax-deductible.
   - In the case of default, the holders of this security will receive cash only after all debt holders, secured as well as unsecured, are paid.
   - The holders of this security will have no voting rights.

   Based on the description of debt and equity in the chapter, how would you classify this security? If you were asked to calculate the debt ratio for this firm, how would you categorize this security?

4. You are analyzing a convertible preferred stock with the following characteristics for the security:
   - There are 50,000 preferred shares outstanding, with a face value of $100 and a 6 percent preferred dividend rate.
   - The firm has straight preferred stock outstanding, with a preferred dividend rate of 9 percent.
   - The preferred stock is trading at $105.

   Estimate the preferred stock and equity components of this preferred stock.

5. You have been asked to calculate the debt ratio for a firm that has the following components to its financing mix:
   - The firm has 1 million shares outstanding, trading at $50 per share.
   - The firm has $25 million in straight debt, carrying a market interest rate of 8 percent.
   - The firm has 20,000 convertible bonds outstanding, with a face value of $1,000, a market value of $1,100, and a coupon rate of 5 percent.

   Estimate the debt ratio for this firm.

6. You have been asked to estimate the debt ratio for a firm with the following financing details:
   - The firm has two classes of shares outstanding: 50,000 shares of class A stock, with 2 voting rights per share, trading at $100 per share, and 100,000 shares of class B stock, with 1/2 voting right per share, trading at $90 per share.
   - The firm has $5 million in bank debt, and the debt was taken on recently.

   Estimate the debt ratio. Why does it matter when the bank debt was taken on?

7. Zycor Corporation obtains most of its funding internally. Assume that the stock has a beta of 1.2, the riskless rate is 6.5 percent, and the market risk premium is 6 percent.
   a. Estimate the cost of internal equity.
   b. Now assume that the cost of issuing new stock is 5 percent of the proceeds. Estimate the cost of external equity.

8. Office Helpers is a private firm that manufactures and sells office supplies. The firm has limited capital and is estimated to have a value of $80 million with the capital constraints. A venture capitalist is willing to contribute $20 million to the firm in exchange for 30 percent of the value of the firm. With this additional capital, the firm will be worth $120 million.
   a. Should the firm accept the venture capital?
   b. At what percentage of firm value would you (as the owner of the private firm) break even on the venture capital financing?

9. Assume now that Office Helpers decides to go public and would like to have its shares trade at a target price of $10 per share. If the IPO is likely to be underpriced by 20 percent, how many shares should the firm have?

10. You are a venture capitalist and have been approached by Cirrus Electronics, a private firm. The firm has no debt outstanding and does not have earnings now but is expected to be earning $15 million in four years, when you also expect it to go public. The average price-earnings ratio of other firms in this business is 50.
    a. Estimate the exit value of Cirrus Electronics.
    b. If your target rate of return is 35 percent, estimate the discounted terminal value of Cirrus Electronics.
    c. If you are contributing $75 million of venture capital to Cirrus Electronics, at a minimum, what percentage of the firm value would you demand in return?

11. The unlevered beta of electronics firms, on average, is 1.1. The riskless rate is 6.5 percent and the market risk premium is 6 percent.
    a. Estimate the expected return, using the CAPM.
    b. If you are a venture capitalist, why might you have a target rate of return much higher than this expected return?

12. Sunshine Media has just completed an IPO, where 50 million shares of the 125 million shares outstanding were issued to the public at an offering price of $22 per share. On the offering date, the stock price zoomed to $40 per share. Who gains from this increase in the price? Who loses, and how much?

13. IPOs are difficult to value because firms going public tend to be small and little information is available about them. Investment bankers have to underprice IPOs because they bear substantial pricing risk. Do you agree with this statement? How would you test it empirically?

14. You are the owner of a small and successful firm with an estimated market value of $50 million. You are considering going public.
    a. What are the considerations you would have in choosing an investment banker?

    b. You want to raise $20 million in new financing, which you plan to reinvest back in the firm. (The estimated market value of $50 million is based on the assumption that this $20 million is reinvested.) What proportion of the firm would you have to sell in the IPO to raise $20 million?
    c. How would your answer to **b** change if the investment banker plans to underprice your offering by 10 percent?
    d. If you wanted your stock to trade in the $20–25 range, how many shares would you have to create? How many shares would you have to issue?

15. You have been asked for advice on a rights offering by a firm with 10 million shares outstanding trading at $50 per share. The firm needs to raise $100 million in new equity. Assuming that the rights subscription price is $25, answer the following questions.
    a. How many rights would be needed to buy one share at the subscription price?
    b. Assuming that all rights are subscribed to, what will the ex-rights price be?
    c. Estimate the value per right.
    d. If the price of a right were different (higher or lower) than the value estimated in **c**, how would you exploit the difference?

16. You are stockholder in a SmallTech, a company that is planning to raise new equity. The stock is trading at $15 per share, and there are 1 million shares outstanding. The firm issues 500,000 rights to buy additional shares at $10 per share to its existing stockholders.
    a. What is the expected stock price after the rights are exercised?
    b. If the rights are traded, what is the price per right?
    c. As a stockholder, would you be concerned about the dilution effect lowering your stock price? Why or why not?

17. Assume that SmallTech has net income of $1 million and that the earnings will increase in proportion with the additional capital raised.
    a. Estimate the earning per share that SmallTech will have after the rights issue described in the last problem.

b. Assume that SmallTech could have raised the capital by issuing 333,333 shares at the prevailing market price of $15 per share (thus raising the same amount of equity as was raised in the rights issue) to the public. Estimate the earnings per share that SmallTech would have had with this alternative.

c. As a stockholder, are you concerned about the fact that the rights issue results in lower earnings per share than the general subscription offering (described in **b**)?

18. MVP, a manufacturing firm with no debt outstanding and a market value of $100 million, is considering borrowing $40 million and buying back stock. Assuming that the interest rate on the debt is 9 percent and that the firm faces a tax rate of 35 percent, answer the following questions:

a. Estimate the annual interest tax savings each year from the debt.

b. Estimate the present value of interest tax savings, assuming that the debt change is permanent.

c. Estimate the present value of interest tax savings, assuming that the debt will be taken on for ten years only.

d. What will happen to the present value of interest tax savings if interest rates drop tomorrow to 7 percent but the debt itself is fixed rate debt?

19. A business in the 45 percent tax bracket is considering borrowing money at 10 percent.

a. What is the after-tax interest rate on the debt?

b. What is the after-tax interest rate if only half of the interest expense is allowed as a tax deduction?

c. Would your answer change if the firm is losing money now and does not expect to have taxable income for three years?

20. WestingHome is a manufacturing company that has accumulated a net operating loss of $2 billion over time. It is considering borrowing $5 billion to acquire another company.

a. Based on the corporate tax rate of 36 percent, estimate the present value of the tax savings that could accrue to the company.

b. Does the existence of a net operating loss carryforward affect your analysis? (Will the tax benefits be diminished as a consequence?)

21. Answer true or false to the following questions relating to the free cash flow hypothesis (as developed by Jensen).

a. Companies with high operating earnings have high free cash flows.

b. Companies with large capital expenditures relative to earnings have low free cash flows.

c. Companies that commit to paying a large portion of their free cash flow as dividends do not need debt to add discipline.

d. The free cash flow hypothesis for borrowing money makes more sense for firms in which there is a separation of ownership and management.

e. Firms with high free cash flows are inefficiently run.

22. Assess the likelihood that the following firms will be taken over, based on your understanding of the free cash flow hypothesis. You can assume that earnings and free cash flows are highly correlated.

a. A firm with high growth, good projects, low leverage, and high earnings.

b. A firm with low growth, poor projects, low leverage, and poor earnings.

c. A firm with high growth, good projects, high leverage, and low earnings.

d. A firm with low growth, poor projects, high leverage, and good earnings.

e. A firm with low growth, poor projects, low leverage, and good earnings.

23. Nadir, an unlevered firm, has expected earnings before interest and taxes of $2 million per year. Nadir's tax rate is 40 percent, and the market value is $12 million. The stock has a beta of 1, and the risk-free rate is 9 percent. [Assume that the risk premium is 6%] Management is considering the use of debt; debt would be issued and used to buy back stock, and the size of the firm would remain constant. The default free interest rate on debt is 12 percent. Because interest expense is tax-deductible, the value of the firm would tend to increase as debt is added to the capital structure, but there would be an offset in the form of the rising cost of bankruptcy. The firm's analysts have estimated approximately that the present value of any bankruptcy cost is $8 million and the probability of bankruptcy will increase with leverage according to the following schedule:

Value of Debt	Probability of Failure
$2,500,000	0.00%
$5,000,000	8.00%
$7,500,000	20.5%
$8,000,000	30.0%
$9,000,000	45.0%
$10,000,000	52.5%
$12,500,000	70.0%

   a. What is the cost of equity and weighted average cost of capital at this time?
   b. What is the optimal capital structure when bankruptcy costs are considered?
   c. What will the value of the firm be at this optimal capital structure?

24. A firm that has no debt has a market value of $100 million and a cost of equity of 11 percent. In the Miller-Modigliani world,
   a. what happens to the value of the firm as the leverage is changed (assume no taxes)?
   b. what happens to the cost of capital as the leverage is changed (assume no taxes)?
   c. how would your answers to a and b change if there are taxes?

25. Assume that personal investors pay a 40 percent tax rate on interest income and only a 20 percent tax rate on equity income. If the corporate tax rate is 30 percent, estimate whether debt has a tax benefit, relative to equity. If a firm with no debt and $100 million in market value borrows money in this world, estimate what the value of the firm will be if the firm borrows $50 million.

26. In the illustration in Problem 25, what would the tax rate on equity income need to be for debt to not have an effect on value?

27. XYZ Pharma is a pharmaceutical company that traditionally has not used debt to finance its projects. Over the past ten years, it has also reported high returns on its projects and growth and made substantial research and development expenses over the time period. The health care business overall is growing much slower now, and the projects that the firm is considering have lower expected returns.
   a. How would you justify the firm's past policy of not using debt?
   b. Do you think the policy should be changed now? Why or why not?

28. Unitrode, which makes analog/linear integrated circuits for power management, is a firm that has not used debt in the financing of its projects. The managers of the firm contend that they do not borrow money because they want to maintain financial flexibility.
   a. How does not borrowing money increase financial flexibility?
   b. What is the trade-off you would be making if you have excess debt capacity and you choose not to use it because you want financial flexibility?

29. Consolidated Power is a regulated electric utility that has equity with a market value of $1.5 billion and debt outstanding of $3 billion. A consultant notes that this is a high debt ratio relative to the average across all firms, which is 27 percent, and suggests that the firm is overlevered.
   a. Why would you expect a electric utility to be able to maintain a higher debt ratio than the average company?
   b. Does the fact that the company is a regulated monopoly affect its capacity to carry debt?

CHAPTER 8

CAPITAL STRUCTURE: THE OPTIMAL FINANCIAL MIX

What is the optimal mix of debt and equity for a firm? In the last chapter we looked at the qualitative trade-off between debt and equity, but we did not develop the tools we need to analyze whether debt should be 0 percent, 20 percent, 40 percent, or 60 percent of capital. Debt is always cheaper than equity, but using debt increases risk in terms of default risk to lenders and higher earnings volatility for equity investors. Thus, using more debt can increase value for some firms and decrease value for others, and for the same firm, debt can be beneficial up to a point and destroy value beyond that point. We have to consider ways of going beyond the

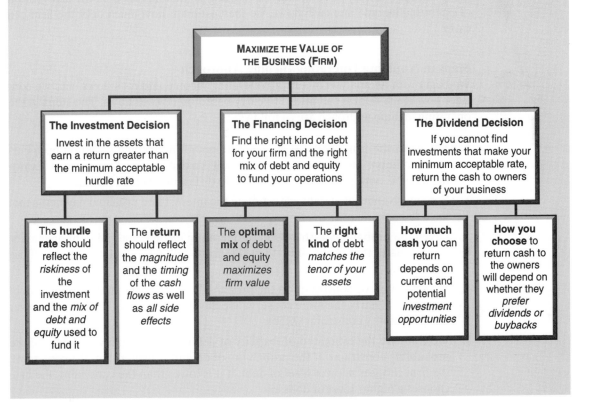

generalities in the last chapter to specific ways of identifying the right mix of debt and equity.

In this chapter, we explore four ways to find an optimal mix. The first approach begins with a distribution of future operating income; we can then decide how much debt to carry by defining the maximum possibility of default we are willing to bear. The second approach is to choose the debt ratio that minimizes the cost of capital. We review the role of cost of capital in valuation and discuss its relationship to the optimal debt ratio. The third approach, like the second, also attempts to maximize firm value, but it does so by adding the present value of tax benefits and then netting out the expected bankruptcy costs from the unlevered firm value. The final approach is to base the financing mix on the way comparable firms finance their operations.

OPERATING INCOME APPROACH

The *operating income approach* is the simplest and one of the most intuitive ways of determining how much a firm can afford to borrow. We use a firm's maximum acceptable probability of default as our starting point, and based on the distribution of operating income and cash flows, we then estimate how much debt the firm can carry.

Steps in Applying Operating Income Approach

We begin with an analysis of a firm's operating income and cash flows, and we consider how much debt it can afford to carry based on its cash flows. The steps in the operating income approach are as follows:

1. We assess the firm's capacity to generate operating income based on both current conditions and past history. The result is a distribution for expected operating income, with probabilities attached to different levels of income.

2. For any given level of debt, we estimate the interest and principal payments that have to be made over time.

3. Given the probability distribution of operating income and the debt payments, we estimate the probability that the firm will be unable to make those payments.

4. We set a limit or constraint on the probability of its being unable to meet debt payments. Clearly, the more conservative the management of the firm, the lower this probability constraint will be.

5. We compare the estimated probability of default at a given level of debt to the probability constraint. If the probability of default is higher than the constraint, the firm chooses a lower level of debt; if it is lower than the constraint, the firm chooses a higher level of debt.

Figure 8.1   Disney: Operating Income Changes 1988–2003

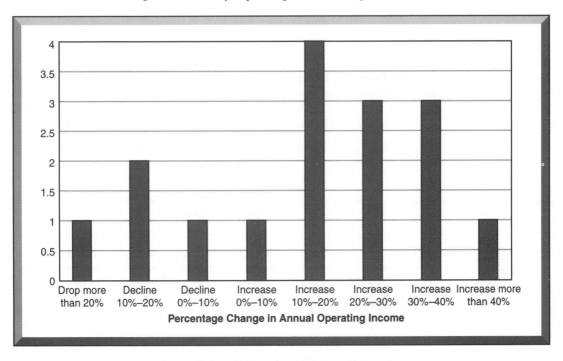

ILLUSTRATION **8.1   Estimating Debt Capacity Based on Operating Income Distribution**
In the following analysis, we apply the operating income approach to analyzing whether Disney should issue an additional $5 billion in new debt.

Step 1:   We derive a probability distribution for expected operating income from Disney's historical earnings and estimate operating income changes from 1988 to 2003 and present it in Figure 8.1.

   The average change in operating income on an annual basis over the period was 10.09 percent, and the standard deviation in the annual changes is 19.54 percent. If we assume that the changes are normally distributed, these statistics are sufficient for us to compute the approximate probability of being unable to meet the specified debt payments.[1]

Step 2:   We estimate the interest and principal payments on a proposed bond issue of $5 billion by assuming that the debt will be rated BBB, lower than Disney's current bond rating of BBB+.[2] Based on this rating, we estimated an interest rate of 5.5 percent on the debt. In addition, we assume that the sinking fund payment set aside to repay the bonds is 5 percent of the bond

---

[1]Assuming income changes are normally distributed is undoubtedly a stretch. You can try alternative distributions that better fit the actual data.

[2]The additional debt should make Disney a riskier firm, and lower its rating.

issue.[3] This results in an annual debt payment of $525 million:

$$\text{Additional Debt Payment} = \text{Interest Expense} + \text{Sinking Fund Payment}$$
$$= 0.055 \times 5,000 + 0.05 \times 5,000$$
$$= \$525 \text{ million}$$

The total debt payment then can be computed by adding the interest payment on existing debt in 2003—$666 million—as well as the operating lease expenses from 2003—$556 million—to the additional debt payment that will be created by taking on $5 billion in additional debt.

$$\text{Total Debt Payment} = \text{Interest on Existing Debt}$$
$$+ \text{Operating Lease Expense}$$
$$+ \text{Additional Debt Payment}$$
$$= \$666 \text{ million} + \$556 \text{ million} + \$525 \text{ million}$$
$$= \$1,747 \text{ million}$$

Step 3:   We can now estimate the probability of default[4] from the distribution of operating income by assuming that the percentage changes in operating income are normally distributed and by considering the operating income of $2,713 million that Disney earned in 2003 as the base year income.

t-Statistic
$$= (\text{Current EBIT} - \text{Debt Payment})/\sigma_{OI} \text{ (Current Operating Income)}$$
$$= (\$2,713 - \$1,747 \text{ million})/(0.1954 \times \$2,713) = 1.82$$

Based on the t-statistic, the probability that Disney will be unable to meet its debt payments in the next year is 3.42 percent.[5]

Step 4:   Assume that the management at Disney set a constraint that the probability of default be no greater than 5 percent.

Step 5:   Because the estimated probability of default is indeed less than 5 percent, Disney can afford to borrow more than $5 billion. If the distribution of operating income changes is normal, we can estimate the level of debt payments Disney can afford to make for a probability of default of 5 percent.

$$t\text{-Statistic for 5\% probability level} = 1.645$$

Consequently, the debt payment can be estimated as

$$(\$2,713 - X)/(0.1954 \times \$2,713) = 1.645$$

Solving for X, we estimate a break-even debt payment of

$$\text{Break-Even Debt Payment} = \$1,841 \text{ million}$$

---

[3]A sinking fund payment allows a firm to set aside money to pay off a bond when it comes due at maturity in annual installments.

[4]This is the probability of defaulting on interest payments in one period. The cumulative probability of default over time will be much higher.

[5]This is likely to be a conservative estimate because it does not allow for the fact that Disney has a cash balance of $1,583 million that can be used to service debt, if the operating income falls short.

Subtracting out the existing interest and lease payments from this amount yields the break-even additional debt payment of $619 million.

$$\text{Break-Even Additional Debt Payment} = \$1,841 - 666 - 556$$
$$= \$619 \text{ million}$$

If we assume that the interest rate remains unchanged at 5.5 percent and the sinking fund will remain at 5 percent of the outstanding debt, this yields an optimal additional debt of $5,895 million.

Optimal Additional Debt
$$= \text{Break-Even Additional Debt Payment/(Interest Rate}$$
$$+ \text{ Sinking Fund Rate)} = \$619/(0.055 + 0.05) = \$5,895 \text{ million}$$

The optimal debt level will be lower if the interest rate increases as Disney borrows more money.

Limitations of the Operating Income Approach

Although this approach may be intuitive and simple, it has some drawbacks. First, estimating a distribution for operating income is not as easy as it sounds, especially for firms in businesses that are changing and volatile. The operating income of firms can vary widely from year to year, depending on the success or failure of individual products. Second, even when we can estimate a distribution, the distribution may not fit the parameters of a normal distribution, and the annual changes in operating income may not reflect the risk of consecutive bad years. This can be remedied by calculating the statistics based on multiple years of data. For Disney, if operating income is computed over rolling two-year periods,[6] the standard deviation will increase and the optimal debt ratio will decrease.

This approach is also an extremely conservative way of setting debt policy because it assumes that debt payments have to be made out of a firm's operating income and that the firm has no access to financial markets or preexisting cash balances. Finally, the probability constraint set by management is subjective and may reflect management concerns more than stockholder interests. For instance, management may decide that it wants no chance of default and refuse to borrow money as a consequence.

Refinements on the Operating Income Approach

The operating income approach described in this section is simplistic because it is based on historical data and the assumption that operating income changes are normally distributed. We can make it more sophisticated and robust by making relatively small changes.

- You can look at simulations of different outcomes for operating income, rather than looking at historical data; the distributions of the outcomes are based both on past data and on expectations for the future.

---

[6]By rolling two-year periods, we mean 1988 and 1989, 1989 and 1990, 1991 and 1992, and so on. The resulting standard deviation is corrected for the multiple counting of the same observations.

- Instead of evaluating just the risk of defaulting on debt, you can consider the indirect bankruptcy costs that can accrue to a firm if operating income drops below a specified level.

- You can compute the present value of the tax benefits from the interest payments on the debt, across simulations, and thus compare the expected cost of bankruptcy to the expected tax benefits from borrowing.

With these changes, you can look at different financing mixes for a firm and estimate the optimal debt ratio as that mix that maximizes the firm's value.[7]

COST OF CAPITAL APPROACH

In Chapter 4, we estimated the minimum acceptable hurdle rates for equity investors (the cost of equity), and for all investors in the firm (the cost of capital). We defined the *cost of capital* to be the weighted average of the costs of the different components of financing—including debt, equity and hybrid securities—used by a firm to fund its investments. By altering the weights of the different components, firms might be able to change their cost of capital.[8] In the cost of capital approach, we estimate the costs of debt and equity at different debt ratios, use these costs to compute the costs of capital, and look for the mix of debt and equity that yields the lowest cost of capital for the firm. At this cost of capital, we will argue that firm value is maximized.

Definition of the Weighted Average Cost of Capital (WACC)

The *weighted average cost of capital (WACC)* is defined as the weighted average of the costs of the different components of financing used by a firm.

$$\text{WACC} = k_e \left(E/[D + E + PS] \right) + k_d \left(D/[D + E + PS] \right) + k_{ps} \left(PS/[D + E + PS] \right)$$

where WACC is the weighted average cost of capital; k_e, k_d, and k_{ps} are the costs of equity, debt, and preferred stock; and E, D, and PS are their respective market values.

The estimation of the costs of the individual components—equity, debt, and preferred stock—and of the weights in the cost of capital formulation is explored in detail in Chapter 4. To summarize:

- The cost of equity should reflect the riskiness of an equity investment in the company. The standard models for risk and return—the CAPM and the APM— measure risk in terms of market or nondiversifiable risk and convert the risk measure into an expected return.

---

[7]T. Opler, M. Saron and S. Titman, 1997, "Designing Capital Structure to Create Stockholder Value," *Journal of Applied Corporate Finance*, 10, 21–32.

[8]If capital structure is irrelevant, the cost of capital will be unchanged as the capital structure is altered.

- The cost of debt should reflect the default risk of the firm—the higher the default risk, the greater the cost of debt—and the tax advantage associated with debt (interest is tax-deductible).

$$\text{Cost of Debt} = \text{Pretax Interest Rate on Borrowing } (1 - \text{Tax Rate})$$

- The cost of preferred stock should reflect the preferred dividend and the absence of tax deductibility.

$$\text{Cost of Preferred Stock} = \text{Preferred Dividend/Preferred Stock Price}$$

- The weights used for the individual components should be market value weights rather than book value weights.

The Role of Cost of Capital in Investment Analysis and Valuation

To understand the relationship between the cost of capital and optimal capital structure, we first have to establish the relationship between firm value and the cost of capital. In Chapter 5, we noted that the value of a project to a firm could be computed by discounting the expected cash flows on it at a rate that reflected the riskiness of the cash flows, and that the analysis could be done either from the viewpoint of equity investors alone or from the viewpoint of the entire firm. In the latter approach, we discounted the cash flows to the firm on the project, that is, the project cash flows prior to debt payments but after taxes, at the project's cost of capital. Extending this principle, the value of the entire firm can be estimated by discounting the aggregate expected cash flows to the firm over time at the firm's cost of capital. The firm's aggregate cash flows can be estimated as cash flows after operating expenses, taxes, and any capital investments needed to create future growth in both fixed assets and working capital but before debt payments.

$$\text{Cash Flow to Firm} = \text{EBIT } (1 - t) - (\text{Capital Expenditures} - \text{Depreciation})$$
$$- \text{Change in Working Capital}$$

The value of the firm can then be written as

$$\text{Value of Firm} = \sum_{t=1}^{t=\infty} \frac{\text{CF to Firm}_t}{(1 + \text{WACC})^t}$$

The value of a firm is therefore a function of its cash flows and its cost of capital. In the specific case where the cash flows to the firm are unaffected as the debt ratio is changed, the value of the firm will increase as the cost of capital decreases. If the objective in choosing the financing mix for the firm is the maximization of firm value, this can be accomplished, in this case, by *minimizing the cost of capital.* In the more general case where the cash flows to the firm themselves change as the debt ratio changes, the optimal financing mix is the one *that maximizes firm value.*[9]

---

[9]In other words, the value of the firm might not be maximized at the point that cost of capital is minimized, if firm cash flows are much lower at that level.

Table 8.1 WACC, FIRM VALUE, AND DEBT RATIOS

D/(D + E)	Cost of Equity	Cost of Debt	WACC	Firm Value
0%	10.50%	4.80%	10.50%	$4,711
10%	11.00%	5.10%	10.41%	$4,807
20%	11.60%	5.40%	10.36%	$4,862
30%	12.30%	5.52%	10.27%	$4,970
40%	13.10%	5.70%	10.14%	$5,121
50%	14.00%	6.30%	10.15%	$5,108
60%	15.00%	7.20%	10.32%	$4,907
70%	16.10%	8.10%	10.50%	$4,711
80%	17.20%	9.00%	10.64%	$4,569
90%	18.40%	10.20%	11.02%	$4,223
100%	19.70%	11.40%	11.40%	$3,926

The optimal financing mix for a firm is simple to compute if one is provided with a schedule that relates the costs of equity and debt to the leverage of the firm. Computing the optimal debt ratio then becomes purely mechanical.

ILLUSTRATION 8.2 WACC, Firm Value, and Leverage

Assume that you are given the costs of equity and debt at different debt levels for Belfan's, a leading manufacturer of chocolates and other candies, and that the cash flow to this firm is currently $200 million. Belfan's is in a relatively stable market, and these cash flows are expected to grow at 6 percent forever, and are unaffected by the debt ratio of the firm. The WACC schedule is provided in Table 8.1, along with the value of the firm at each level of debt.

$$\text{Value of the firm} = \text{Cash flows to firm} \times (1 + g)/(\text{WACC} - g)$$
$$= \$200 \times 1.06/(\text{WACC} - 0.06)$$

The value of the firm increases (decreases) as the WACC decreases (increases), as illustrated in Figure 8.2. The optimal debt ratio, where firm value is maximized, is 40 percent.

Although this illustration makes the choice of an optimal financing mix seem trivial, it obscures some real problems that may arise in its applications. First, an analyst typically does not have the benefit of having the entire schedule of costs of financing prior to an analysis. In most cases, the only level of debt about which there is any certainty about the cost of financing is the current level. Second, the analysis assumes implicitly that the level of cash flows to the firm is unaffected by the financing mix of the firm and consequently by the default risk (or bond rating) for the firm. Although this may be reasonable in some cases, it might not in others. For instance, a firm that manufactures consumer durables (cars, televisions, etc.) might find that its sales and operating income drop if its default risk increases because investors become reluctant to buy its products.

Figure 8.2   WACC and Firm Value as a Function of Leverage

8.1 MINIMIZING COST OF CAPITAL AND MAXIMIZING FIRM VALUE

A lower cost of capital will lead to a higher firm value only if

☐ the operating income does not change as the cost of capital declines.

☐ the operating income goes down as the cost of capital goes down.

☐ any decline in operating income is offset by the lower cost of capital.

Steps in the Cost of Capital Approach

We need three basic inputs to compute the cost of capital—the cost of equity, the after-tax cost of debt, and the weights on debt and equity. The costs of equity and debt change as the debt ratio changes, and the primary challenge of this approach is in estimating each of these inputs.

Let us begin with the cost of equity. In Chapter 4, we argued that the beta of equity will change as the debt ratio changes. In fact, we estimated the levered beta as a function of the debt to equity ratio of a firm, the unlevered beta, and the firm's marginal tax rate:

$$\beta_{levered} = \beta_{unlevered} [1 + (1 - t)\text{Debt}/\text{Equity}]$$

Thus, if we can estimate the unlevered beta for a firm, we can use it to estimate the levered beta of the firm at every debt ratio. This levered beta can then be used to compute the cost of equity at each debt ratio.

$$\text{Cost of Equity} = \text{Risk-Free Rate} + \beta_{\text{levered}}(\text{Risk Premium})$$

The cost of debt for a firm is a function of the firm's default risk. As firms borrow more, their default risk will increase and so will the cost of debt. If we use bond ratings as the measure of default risk, we can estimate the cost of debt in three steps. First, we estimate a firm's dollar debt and interest expenses at each debt ratio; as firms increase their debt ratios, both dollar debt and interest expenses will rise. Second, at each debt level, we compute a financial ratio or ratios that measures default risk and use the ratio(s) to estimate a rating for the firm; again, as firms borrow more, this rating will decline. Third, a default spread, based on the estimated rating, is added on to the risk-free rate to arrive at the pretax cost of debt. Applying the marginal tax rate to this pretax cost yields an after-tax cost of debt.

Once we estimate the costs of equity and debt at each debt level, we weight them based on the proportions used of each to estimate the cost of capital. Although we have not explicitly allowed for a preferred stock component in this process, we can have preferred stock as a part of capital. However, we have to keep the preferred stock portion fixed while changing the weights on debt and equity. The debt ratio at which the cost of capital is minimized is the optimal debt ratio.

In this approach, the effect on firm value of changing the capital structure is isolated by keeping the operating income fixed and varying only the cost of capital. In practical terms, this requires us to make two assumptions. First, the debt ratio is decreased by raising new equity and retiring debt; conversely, the debt ratio is increased by borrowing money and buying back stock. This process is called *recapitalization*. Second, the pretax operating income is assumed to be unaffected by the firm's financing mix and, by extension, its bond rating. If the operating income changes with a firm's default risk, the basic analysis will not change, but minimizing the cost of capital may not be the optimal course of action, because the value of the firm is determined by both the cash flows and the cost of capital. The value of the firm will have to be computed at each debt level and the optimal debt ratio will be that which maximizes firm value.

ILLUSTRATION 8.3 Analyzing the Capital Structure for Disney: March 2004

The cost of capital approach can be used to find the optimal capital structure for a firm, as we will for Disney in March 2004. Disney had $13,100 million in debt on its books. The estimated market value of this debt ($12,915 million) was added to the present value of operating leases ($1,753 million) to arrive at a total market value for the debt of $14,668 million.[10] The market value of equity at the same time was $55,101 million; the market price per share was $26.91, and there were 2,047.6 million shares outstanding. Proportionally, 21.02 percent of the overall financing mix was debt, and the remaining 78.98 percent was equity.

---

[10]The details of this calculation are in Illustration 4.15 in Chapter 4.

The beta for Disney's stock in March 2004, as estimated in Chapter 4, was 1.2456. The Treasury bond rate at that time was 4 percent. Using an estimated market risk premium of 4.82 percent, we estimated the cost of equity for Disney to be 10.00 percent:

$$\text{Cost of Equity} = \text{Risk-Free Rate} + \text{Beta} \times (\text{Market Premium})$$
$$= 4.00\% + 1.2456\,(4.82\%) = 10.00\%$$

Disney's senior debt was rated BBB+. Based on this rating, the estimated pretax cost of debt for Disney is 5.25 percent. The tax rate used for the analysis is 37.30 percent.

$$\text{Value of Firm} = 14{,}668 + 55{,}101 = \$69{,}769 \text{ million}$$

$$\text{After-Tax Cost of Debt} = \text{Pretax Interest Rate}\,(1 - \text{Tax Rate})$$
$$= 5.25\%\,(1 - 0.373) = 3.29\%$$

The cost of capital was calculated using these costs and the weights based on market value:

$$\text{WACC} = \text{Cost of Equity}\,(\text{Equity}/[\text{Equity} + \text{Debt}])$$
$$+ \text{After-Tax Cost of Debt}\,(\text{Debt}/[\text{Debt} + \text{Equity}])$$
$$= 10.00\%\,[55{,}101/69.769] + 3.58\%\,[14{,}668/69{,}769] = 8.59\%$$

8.2 MARKET VALUE, BOOK VALUE, AND COST OF CAPITAL

Disney had a book value of equity of approximately $16.5 billion. Using the book value of debt of $13.1 billion, estimate the cost of capital for Disney using book value weights.

I. Disney's Cost of Equity and Leverage

The cost of equity for Disney at different debt ratios can be computed using the unlevered beta of the firm, and the debt equity ratio at each level of debt. We use the levered betas that emerge to estimate the cost of equity. The first step in this process is to compute the firm's current unlevered beta, using the current market debt to equity ratio and a tax rate of 37.30 percent.

$$\text{Unlevered Beta} = \text{Current Beta}/(1 + [1 - t]\text{Debt}/\text{Equity})$$
$$= 1.2456/(1 + [1 - 0.373][14{,}668/55{,}101])$$
$$= 1.0674$$

Note that this is the bottom-up unlevered beta that we estimated for Disney in Chapter 4, based on its business mix. We continued to use the Treasury bond rate of 4 percent and the market premium of 4.82 percent to compute the cost of equity at each level of debt. If we keep the tax rate constant at 37.30 percent, we obtain the levered betas for Disney in Table 8.2.

In calculating the levered beta in this table, we assumed that all market risk is borne by the equity investors; this may be unrealistic especially at higher levels of debt. We will also consider an alternative estimate of levered betas that apportions some of the market risk to the debt:

$$\beta_{\text{levered}} = \beta_u[1 + (1 - t)D/E] - \beta_{\text{debt}}(1 - t)D/E$$

The beta of debt is based on the rating of the bond and is estimated by regressing past returns on bonds in each rating class against returns on a market index. The

Table 8.2 LEVERAGE, BETAS, AND THE COST OF EQUITY

Debt Ratio	D/E Ratio	Levered Beta	Cost of Equity
0.00%	0.00%	1.0674	9.15%
10.00%	11.11%	1.1418	9.50%
20.00%	25.00%	1.2348	9.95%
30.00%	42.86%	1.3543	10.53%
40.00%	66.67%	1.5136	11.30%
50.00%	100.00%	1.7367	12.37%
60.00%	150.00%	2.0714	13.98%
70.00%	233.33%	2.6291	16.67%
80.00%	400.00%	3.7446	22.05%
90.00%	900.00%	7.0911	38.18%

levered betas estimated using this approach will generally be lower than those estimated with the conventional model.[11]

II. Disney's Cost of Debt and Leverage

Several financial ratios are correlated with bond ratings, and ideally we would build a sophisticated model to predict ratings. For purposes of this illustration, however, we use a much simpler version: We assume that bond ratings are determined solely by the interest coverage ratio, which is defined as:

Interest Coverage Ratio = Earnings Before Interest & Taxes/Interest Expense

We chose the interest coverage ratio for three reasons. First, it is a ratio used by both S&P and Moody's to determine ratings.[12] Second, there is significant correlation not only between the interest coverage ratio and bond ratings but also between the interest coverage ratio and other ratios used in analysis, such as the debt coverage ratio and the funds flow ratios. Third, the interest coverage ratio changes as a firm changes its financing mix and decreases as the debt ratio increases. The ratings agencies would argue, however, that subjective factors, such as the perceived quality of management, are part of the ratings process. One way to build these factors into the analysis would be to modify the ratings obtained from the financial ratio analysis across the board to reflect the ratings agencies' subjective concerns.[13]

---

[11]Consider, for instance, a debt ratio of 40 percent. At this level, the firm's debt will take on some of the characteristics of equity. Assume that the beta of debt at a 40 percent debt ratio is 0.40. The equity beta at that debt ratio can be computed as follows: Levered Beta = 1.0674[1 + (1 − 0.373)(40/60)] − 0.40(1 − 0.373)(40/60) = 1.335. In the unadjusted approach, the levered beta would have been 1.5136.

[12]S&P lists interest coverage ratio first among the nine ratios that it reports for different ratings classes on its Web site.

[13]For instance, assume that a firm's current rating is AA, but that its financial ratios would result in an A rating. It can then be argued that the ratings agencies are, for subjective reasons, rating the company one notch higher than the rating obtained from a purely financial analysis. The ratings obtained for each debt level can then be increased by one notch across the board to reflect these subjective considerations.

Table 8.3   BOND RATINGS AND INTEREST
COVERAGE RATIOS

Interest Coverage Ratio	Rating
> 8.5	AAA
6.50–6.50	AA
5.50–6.50	A+
4.25–5.50	A
3.00–4.25	A−
2.50–3.00	BBB
2.00–2.50	BB+
1.90–2.00	BB
1.75–1.90	B+
1.50–1.75	B
1.25–1.50	B−
0.80–1.25	CCC
0.65–0.80	CC
0.20–0.65	C
< 0.20	D

Source: Compustat.

The data in Table 8.3 were obtained based on an analysis of the interest coverage ratios of large manufacturing firms in different ratings classes. Using this table as a guideline, a firm with an interest coverage ratio of 1.65 would have a rating of B for its bonds.

The relationship between bond ratings and interest rates in March 2004 was obtained by looking at the typical default spreads for bonds in different ratings classes.[14] Table 8.4 summarizes the interest rates/rating relationship and reports the spread for these bonds over treasury bonds and the resulting interest rates, based on the treasury bond rate of 4 percent.

Because Disney's capacity to borrow is determined by its earnings power, we will begin by looking at the company's income statements in 2002 and 2003 in Table 8.5. In 2003, Disney had operating income of $2.713 billion and net income of $1,267 billion.

Based on the EBIT of $2,713 million and interest expenses of $666 million, Disney has an interest coverage ratio of 4.07 and should command a rating of A−, a notch above its actual rating of BBB+. This income statement, however, is based on treating operating leases as operating expenses. In Chapter 4, we argued that operating leases should be considered part of debt and computed the present value of Disney's lease commitments to be $1,753 million. Consequently, we have to adjust the EBIT and EBITDA for the imputed interest expense on Disney's operating leases[15]; this

---

[14]These default spreads were obtained from bondsonline.com, a service that provides, among other data on fixed income securities, updated default spreads for each ratings class.

[15]Multiplying the pretax cost of debt by the present value of operating leases yields an approximation. The full adjustment would require us to add back the entire operating lease expense and to subtract out the depreciation on the leased asset.

Table 8.4 **BOND RATINGS AND MARKET INTEREST RATES, MARCH 2004**

Rating	Typical Default Spread	Market Interest Rate on Debt
AAA	0.35%	4.35%
AA	0.50%	4.50%
A+	0.70%	4.70%
A	0.85%	4.85%
A−	1.00%	5.00%
BBB	1.50%	5.50%
BB+	2.00%	6.00%
BB	2.50%	6.50%
B+	3.25%	7.25%
B	4.00%	8.00%
B−	6.00%	10.00%
CCC	8.00%	12.00%
CC	10.00%	14.00%
C	12.00%	16.00%
D	20.00%	24.00%

Source: bondsonline.com.

Table 8.5 **DISNEY'S INCOME STATEMENT FOR 2002 AND 2003**

	2003	2002
Revenues	27,061	25,329
− Operating expenses (other than depreciation)	23,289	21,924
Earnings before interest, taxes, depreciation, and amortization (EBITDA)	3,790	3,405
− Depreciation and amortization	1,077	1,021
EBIT	2,713	2,384
− Interest expenses	666	708
+ Interest income	127	255
Taxable income	2,174	1,931
− Taxes	907	695
Net income	1,267	1,236

results in an increase of $92 million in both numbers—to $2,805 million in EBIT and $3,864 million in EBITDA.

$$\text{Adjusted EBIT} = \text{EBIT} + \text{Pretax Cost of Debt} \times \text{Present Value of Operating Leases}$$
$$= 2{,}713 + 0.0525 \times 1{,}753 = \$2{,}805 \text{ million}$$

Note that 5.25 percent is Disney's current pretax cost of debt.

Finally, to compute Disney's ratings at different debt levels, we redo the operating income statement at each level of debt, compute the interest coverage ratio at that level

Table 8.6   EFFECT OF MOVING TO HIGHER DEBT RATIOS: DISNEY

D/(D + E)	0.00%	10.00%
D/E	0.00%	11.11%
$Debt	$0	$6,977
EBITDA	$3,882	$3,882
Depreciation	$1,077	$1,077
EBIT	$2,805	$2,805
Interest	$0	$303
Pretax interest coverage	∞	9.24
Likely rating	AAA	AAA
Pretax cost of debt	4.35%	4.35%

of debt and find the rating that corresponds to that level of debt. For example, Table 8.6 estimates the interest expenses, interest coverage ratios, and bond ratings for Disney at 0 percent and 10 percent debt ratios, at the existing level of operating income.

The dollar debt is computed to be 10 percent of the current value of the firm, which we compute by adding the current market values of debt ($14,668) and equity ($55,101):

Dollar Debt at 10% Debt Ratio = 0.10($55,101 + $14,668) = $6,977 million

Note that the EBITDA and EBIT remain fixed as the debt ratio changes. We ensure this by using the proceeds from the debt to buy back stock. In a recapitalization, the assets of the firm remain unchanged but the financing mix is changed. This allows us to isolate the effect of just changing the debt ratio.

There is circular reasoning involved in estimating the interest expense. The interest rate is needed to calculate the interest coverage ratio, and the coverage ratio is necessary to compute the interest rate. To get around the problem, we began our analysis by assuming that you could borrow $6,977 million at the AAA rate of 4.35 percent; we then computed an interest expense and interest coverage ratio using that rate and estimated a rating of AAA for Disney.[16] This process is repeated for each level of debt from 10 percent to 90 percent, and the after-tax costs of debt are obtained at each level of debt in Table 8.7.

There are two points to make about this computation. We assume that at every debt level, all existing debt will be refinanced at the new interest rate that will prevail after the capital structure change. For instance, Disney's existing debt, which has a BBB+ rating, is assumed to be refinanced at the interest rate corresponding to a BBB rating when Disney moves to a 30 percent debt ratio. This is done for two reasons. The first is that existing debt holders might have protective puts that enable them to put their bonds back to the firm and receive face value.[17] The second is that the

[16]Because the interest expense rises, it is possible for the rating to drop again. Thus, a second or even third iteration might be necessary in some cases.

[17]If they do not have protective puts, it is in the best interests of the stockholders not to refinance the debt (as in the leveraged buyout of RJR Nabisco) if debt ratios are increased.

						Table 8.7 **DISNEY: COST OF DEBT AND DEBT RATIOS**	

Debt Ratio	Debt	Interest Expense	Interest Coverage Ratio	Bond Rating	Interest Rate on Debt	Tax Rate	Cost of Debt (After-Tax)
0%	$0	$0	∞	AAA	4.35%	37.30%	2.73%
10%	$6,977	$303	9.24	AAA	4.35%	37.30%	2.73%
20%	$13,954	$698	4.02	A−	5.00%	37.30%	3.14%
30%	$20,931	$1,256	2.23	BB+	6.00%	37.30%	3.76%
40%	$27,908	$3,349	0.84	CCC	12.00%	31.24%	8.25%
50%	$34,885	$5,582	0.50	C	16.00%	18.75%	13.00%
60%	$41,861	$6,698	0.42	C	16.00%	15.62%	13.50%
70%	$48,838	$7,814	0.36	C	16.00%	13.39%	13.86%
80%	$55,815	$8,930	0.31	C	16.00%	11.72%	14.13%
90%	$62,792	$10,047	0.28	C	16.00%	10.41%	14.33%

refinancing eliminates "wealth expropriation" effects—the effects of stockholders expropriating wealth from bondholders when debt is increased, and vice versa when debt is reduced. If firms can retain old debt at lower rates while borrowing more and becoming riskier, the lenders of the old debt will lose value. If we lock in current rates on existing bonds and recalculate the optimal debt ratio, we will allow for this wealth transfer.[18]

Although it is conventional to leave the marginal tax rate unchanged as the debt ratio is increased, we adjust the tax rate to reflect the potential loss of the tax benefits of debt at higher debt ratios, where the interest expenses exceed the EBIT. To illustrate this point, note that the EBIT at Disney is $2,805 million. As long as interest expenses are less than $2,805 million, interest expenses remain fully tax-deductible and earn the 37.30 percent tax benefit. For instance, at a 30 percent debt ratio, the interest expenses are $1,256 million and the tax benefit is therefore 37.30 percent of this amount. At a 40 percent debt ratio, however, the interest expenses balloon to $3,349 million, which is greater than the EBIT of $2,805 million. We consider the tax benefit on the interest expenses up to this amount:

$$\text{Maximum Tax Benefit} = \text{EBIT} \times \text{Marginal Tax Rate} = \$2,805 \text{ million} \times 0.373 = \$1,046 \text{ million}$$

As a proportion of the total interest expenses, the tax benefit is now only 31.24 percent:

$$\text{Adjusted Marginal Tax Rate} = \text{Maximum Tax Benefit/Interest Expenses} = \$1,046/\$3,349 = 31.24\%$$

This in turn raises the after-tax cost of debt. This is a conservative approach, because losses can be carried forward. Given that this is a permanent shift in leverage, it does make sense to be conservative.

---

[18]This will have the effect of reducing interest cost, when debt is increased, and thus interest coverage ratios. This will lead to higher ratings, at least in the short run, and a higher optimal debt ratio.

	Table 8.8	COST OF EQUITY, DEBT, AND CAPITAL: DISNEY	
Debt Ratio	**Cost of Equity**	**Cost of Debt (After-Tax)**	**Cost of Capital**
0%	9.15%	2.73%	9.15%
10%	9.50%	2.73%	8.83%
20%	9.95%	3.14%	8.59%
30%	10.53%	3.76%	8.50%
40%	11.50%	8.25%	10.20%
50%	13.33%	13.00%	13.16%
60%	15.66%	13.50%	14.36%
70%	19.54%	13.86%	15.56%
80%	27.31%	14.13%	16.76%
90%	50.63%	14.33%	17.96%

Note that the costs of equity in this table are higher than in Table 8.2 at debt ratios greater than 50 percent because we use the adjusted tax rates from Table 8.7.

III. Leverage and Cost of Capital

Now that we have estimated the cost of equity and the cost of debt at each debt level, we can compute Disney's cost of capital. This is done for each debt level in Table 8.8. The cost of capital, which is 9.15 percent when the firm is unlevered, decreases as the firm initially adds debt, reaches a minimum of 8.50 percent at 30 percent debt, and then starts to increase again. (See Table 8.10 for the full details of the numbers Table 8.8.) The optimal debt ratio is shown graphically in Figure 8.3.

To illustrate the robustness of this solution to alternative measures of levered betas, we reestimate the costs of debt, equity, and capital under the assumption that debt bears some market risk; the results are summarized in Table 8.9. If the debt holders bear some market risk,[19] the cost of equity is lower at higher levels of debt, and Disney's optimal debt ratio is still 30 percent, which is unchanged from the optimal calculated under the conventional calculation of the levered beta.

IV. Firm Value and Cost of Capital

The reason for minimizing the cost of capital is that it maximizes the value of the firm. To illustrate the effects of moving to the optimal on Disney's firm value, we start off with a simple valuation model, designed to value a firm in stable growth.

$$\text{Firm Value} = \text{Cash Flow to Firm} (1 + g)/(\text{Cost of Capital} - g)$$

where g = growth rate in the cash flow to the firm (in perpetuity). We begin by computing Disney's current free cash flow using its current earnings before interest and

---

[19]To estimate the beta of debt, we used the default spread at each level of debt, and assumed that 25 percent this risk is market risk. Thus, at a C rating, the default spread is 12 percent. Based on the market risk premium of 4.82 percent that we used elsewhere, we estimated the beta at a C rating to be Imputed Debt Beta at a C Rating = $(12\%/4.82\%) \times 0.25 = 0.62$. The assumption that 25 percent of the default risk is market risk is made to ensure that at a D rating, the beta of debt (1.02) is roughly equal to the unlevered beta of Disney (1.09).

Figure 8.3 Disney Cost of Capital at Different Debt Ratios

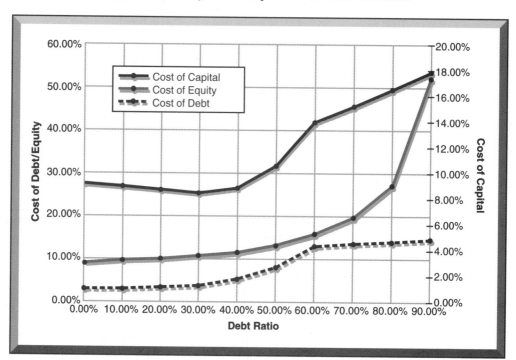

Table 8.9 COSTS OF EQUITY, DEBT, AND CAPITAL WITH DEBT CARRYING MARKET RISK: DISNEY

Debt Ratio	Beta of Equity	Cost of Equity	Interest Rate on Debt	Tax Rate	Cost of Debt (After-Tax)	Beta of Debt	WACC
0%	1.07	9.15%	4.35%	37.30%	2.73%	0.02	9.15%
10%	1.14	9.50%	4.35%	37.30%	2.73%	0.02	8.82%
20%	1.23	9.91%	5.00%	37.30%	3.14%	0.05	8.56%
30%	1.33	10.39%	6.00%	37.30%	3.76%	0.10	8.40%
40%	1.37	10.59%	12.00%	31.24%	8.25%	0.41	9.65%
50%	1.43	10.89%	16.00%	18.75%	13.00%	0.62	11.94%
60%	1.63	11.86%	16.00%	15.62%	13.50%	0.62	12.84%
70%	1.97	13.48%	16.00%	13.39%	13.86%	0.62	13.74%
80%	2.64	16.72%	16.00%	11.72%	14.13%	0.62	14.64%
90%	4.66	26.44%	16.00%	10.41%	14.33%	0.62	15.54%

taxes of $2,805 million, its tax rate of 37.30 percent, and its reinvestment in 2003 in working capital and long-term assets:

EBIT (1 − Tax Rate) = 2,805 (1 − 0.373) =	$1,759
+ Depreciation and amortization =	$1,077
− Capital expenditures =	$1,049
− Change in noncash working capital	$64
Free cash flow to the firm =	$1,722

The market value of the firm at the time of this analysis was obtained by adding up the estimated market values of debt and equity:

Market value of equity =	$55,101
+ Market value of debt =	$14,668
= Value of the firm	$69,769

Based on the current cost of capital of 8.59 percent, we solve for the implied growth rate:

Growth rate
= (Firm Value × Cost of Capital − CF to Firm)/(Firm Value + CF to Firm)
= (69,769 × 0.0859 − 1,722)/(69,769 + 1,722) = 0.0598 or 5.98%

Now assume that Disney shifts to 30 percent debt and a WACC of 8.50 percent. The firm can now be valued using the following parameters:

Cash Flow to Firm = $1,722 million
WACC = 8.50%

Growth Rate in Cash Flows to Firm = 5.98%

Firm Value = 1,722 × 1.0598/(0.0850 − 0.0598) = $72,420 million

The value of the firm will increase from $69,769 million to $72,420 million if the firm moves to the optimal debt ratio:

Increase in Firm Value = $72,420 mil − $69,769 mil = $2,651 million

With 2,047.60 million shares outstanding, assuming that stockholders can evaluate the effect of this refinancing, we can calculate the increase in the stock price:

Increase in Stock Price = Increase in Firm Value/Number of Shares Outstanding
= $2,651/2,047.60 = $1.29/share

As the current stock price is $26.91, the stock price can be expected to increase to $28.20, which translates into about a 4.8 percent increase in the price.

The limitation of this approach is that the growth rate that we have assumed in perpetuity may be too high; a good rule of thumb for stable growth is that it should not exceed the risk-free rate.[20] We can use an alternate and more conservative approach to estimate the change in firm value. Consider first the change in the cost of capital from 8.59 percent to 8.50 percent, a drop of 0.09 percent. This change in the cost of capital should result in the firm saving on its annual cost of financing its business:

Cost of Financing Disney at Existing Debt Ratio = 69,769 × 0.0859 = $5,993 million

Cost of Financing Disney at Optimal Debt Ratio = 69,769 × 0.0850 = $5,930 million

Annual Savings in Cost of Financing = $5,993 million − $5,930 million
= $63 million

Note that most of these savings are implicit rather than explicit.[21] The present value of these savings over time can now be estimated using the new cost of capital of 8.50 percent and the capped growth rate of 4 percent (set equal to the risk-free rate);

Present Value of Savings in Perpetuity
= Expected Savings Next Year/(Cost of Capital − g)
= $63/(0.085 − 0.04) = $1,400 million

Because this increase in value accrues entirely to stockholders, we can estimate the increase in value per share by dividing by the total number of shares outstanding:

Increase in Value per Share = $1,400/2,047.60 = $0.68/share

New Stock Price = $26.91 + $0.68 = $27.59

Using this approach, we estimated the firm value and cost of capital at different debt ratios in Table 8.10 and present the value change in Figure 8.4.

Because the asset side of the balance sheet is kept fixed and changes in capital structure are made by borrowing funds and repurchasing stock, this analysis implies that the stock price would increase to $27.59 on the announcement of the repurchase. Implicit in this analysis is the assumption that the increase in firm value will be spread evenly across both the stockholders who sell their stock back to the firm and those who do not. To the extent that stock can be bought back at the current price of $26.91 or some value lower than $27.59, the change in stock price will be larger. For instance, if Disney could have bought stock back at the existing price of $26.91, the increase in value per share would be $0.77.[22]

---

[20]No company can grow at a rate higher than the long-term nominal growth rate of the economy. The risk-free rate is a reasonable proxy for the long-term nominal growth rate in the economy because it is composed of two components—the expected inflation rate and the expected real rate of return. The latter has to equate to real growth in the long run.

[21]The cost of equity is an implicit cost and does not show up in the income statement of the firm. The savings in the cost of capital are therefore unlikely to show up as higher aggregate earnings. In fact, as the firm's debt ratio increases, the earnings will decrease but the per share earnings will increase.

[22]To compute this change in value per share, we first compute how many shares we would buy back with the additional debt taken on of $6,263 billion (Debt at 30% Optimal − Current Debt) and the stock price of $26.91. We then divide the increase in firm value of $3,012 million by the remaining shares outstanding: Change in Stock Price = $1,400 million/(2,047.60 − [6,263/22.26]) = $0.77 per share.

Figure 8.4   Disney Firm Value at Different Debt Ratios

8.3 RATIONALITY AND STOCK PRICE EFFECTS

Assume that Disney does make a tender offer for its shares but pays $28 per share. What will happen to the value per share for the shareholders who do not sell back?

☐ The share price will drop below the pre-announcement price of $26.91.

☐ The share price will be between $26.91 and the estimated value of $27.59.

☐ The share price will be higher than $27.59.

This spreadsheet allows you to compute the optimal debt ratio and firm value for any firm, using the same information used for Disney. It has updated interest coverage ratios and spreads built in (**capstru.xls**).

Constrained Cost of Capital Approaches

The cost of capital approach that we have described is unconstrained, because our only objective is to minimize the cost of capital. There are several reasons why a firm may choose not to view the debt ratio that emerges from this analysis as optimal. First, the firm's default risk at the point at which the cost of capital is minimized may be high enough to put the firm's survival at jeopardy. Stated in terms of bond ratings, the firm may have a below-**investment grade rating.** Second, the assumption that the operating income is unaffected by the bond rating is key. If the operating income declines as default risk increases, the value of the firm may not be maximized where the cost of capital is minimized. Third, the optimal debt ratio was computed using

Table 8.10 COST OF CAPITAL WORKSHEET FOR DISNEY

D/(D+E)	0.00%	10.00%	20.00%	30.00%	40.00%	50.00%	60.00%	70.00%	80.00%	90.00%
D/E	0.00%	11.11%	25.00%	42.86%	66.67%	100.00%	150.00%	233.33%	400.00%	900.00%
$Debt	$0	$6,977	$13,954	$20,931	$27,908	$34,885	$41,861	$48,838	$55,815	$62,792
Beta	1.07	1.14	1.23	1.35	1.56	1.93	2.42	3.22	4.84	9.67
EBITDA	$3,882	$3,882	$3,882	$3,882	$3,882	$3,882	$3,882	$3,882	$3,882	$3,882
Depreciation	$1,077	$1,077	$1,077	$1,077	$1,077	$1,077	$1,077	$1,077	$1,077	$1,077
EBIT	$2,805	$2,805	$2,805	$2,805	$2,805	$2,805	$2,805	$2,805	$2,805	$2,805
Interest	$0	$303	$698	$1,256	$3,349	$5,582	$6,698	$7,814	$8,930	$10,047
Pre-tax int. cov.	∞	9.24	4.02	2.23	0.84	0.50	0.42	0.36	0.31	0.28
Funds/debt	∞	0.38	0.17	0.10	0.03	−0.02	−0.03	−0.04	−0.05	−0.06
Likely rating	AAA	AAA	A−	BB+	CCC	C	C	C	C	C
Pre-tax cost of debt	4.35%	4.35%	5.00%	6.00%	12.00%	16.00%	16.00%	16.00%	16.00%	16.00%
Adj marginal tax rate	37.30%	37.30%	37.30%	37.30%	31.24%	18.75%	15.62%	13.39%	11.72%	10.41%
Cost of equity	9.15%	9.50%	9.95%	10.53%	11.50%	13.33%	15.66%	19.54%	27.31%	50.63%
Cost of debt	2.73%	2.73%	3.14%	3.76%	8.25%	13.00%	13.50%	13.86%	14.13%	14.33%
Cost of capital	9.15%	8.83%	8.59%	8.50%	10.20%	13.16%	14.36%	15.56%	16.76%	17.96%
Value (perpetual growth)	$62,279	$66,397	$69,837	$71,239	$51,661	$34,969	$30,920	$27,711	$25,105	$22,948

the operating income from the most recent financial year. To the extent that operating income is volatile and can decline, firms may want to curtail their borrowing. In this section, we consider ways we can bring each of these considerations into the cost of capital analysis.

Bond Rating Constraint

One way of using the cost of capital approach without putting firms into financial jeopardy, is to impose a bond rating constraint on the cost of capital analysis. Once this constraint has been imposed, the optimal debt ratio is the one that has the lowest cost of capital, subject to the constraint that the bond rating meets or exceeds the specified level.

Although this approach is simple, it is essentially subjective and is therefore open to manipulation. For instance, the management at Disney could insist on preserving a AA rating and use this constraint to justify reducing its debt ratio. One way to make managers more accountable in this regard is to measure the cost of a rating constraint.

Cost of Rating Constraint = Maximum Firm Value without Constraints
− Maximum Firm Value with Constraints

If Disney insisted on maintaining a AA rating, its constrained optimal debt ratio would be 10 percent. The cost of preserving the constraint can then be measured as the difference between firm value at the optimal of 30 percent and at 10 percent.

$$\text{Cost of Rating Constraint} = \text{Value at 30\% Debt} - \text{Value at 10\% Debt}$$
$$= \$71,239 - \$66,397$$
$$= \$4,842 \text{ million}$$

This loss in value is probably overstated because we are keeping operating income fixed. Notwithstanding this concern, the loss in value that can accrue from having an unrealistically high rating constraint can be viewed as the cost of being too conservative when it comes to debt policy.

Investment Grade Bonds: An investment grade bond has a bond rating greater than or equal to BBB. Some institutional investors, such as pension funds, are constrained from holding bonds with lower ratings.

8.4 AGENCY COSTS AND FINANCIAL FLEXIBILITY

In the last chapter, we consider agency costs and lost flexibility as potential costs of using debt. Where in the cost of capital approach do we consider these costs?

☐ These costs are not considered in the cost of capital approach.

☐ These costs are fully captured in the cost of capital through the costs of equity and debt, which increase as you borrow more money.

☐ These costs are partially captured in the cost of capital through the costs of equity and debt, which increase as you borrow more money.

Sensitivity Analysis

The optimal debt ratio we estimate for a firm is a function of all the inputs that go into the cost of capital computation—the beta of the equity, the risk-free rate, the risk premium, and the default spread. It is also indirectly a function of the firm's operating income because interest coverage ratios are based on this income, and these ratios are used to compute ratings and interest rates.

The determinants of the optimal debt ratio for a firm can be divided into variables specific to the firm, and macroeconomic variables. Among the variables specific to the firm that affect its optimal debt ratio are the tax rate, the firm's capacity to generate operating income, and its cash flows. In general, the tax benefits from debt increase as the tax rate goes up. It also follows that a firm's optimal debt ratio will increase as its tax rate increases. Firms that generate higher operating income and cash flows as a percent of firm market value also can sustain much more debt as a proportion of the market value of the firm, because debt payments can be covered much more easily by prevailing cash flows.

The macroeconomic determinants of optimal debt ratios include the level of interest rates and default spreads. As interest rates rise, the costs of debt and equity both increase. However, optimal debt ratios tend to be lower when interest rates are higher, perhaps because interest coverage ratios drop. The default spreads commanded by different ratings classes also change over time. Keeping other things constant, as the spreads increase, optimal debt ratios decrease for the simple reason that higher default spreads result in higher costs of debt.

How does sensitivity analysis allow a firm to choose an optimal debt ratio? After computing the optimal debt ratio with existing inputs, firms may put it to the test by changing both firm-specific inputs (such as operating income) and macroeconomic inputs (such as default spreads). The debt ratio the firm chooses as its optimal then reflects the volatility of the underlying variables and the risk aversion of the firm's management.

ILLUSTRATION 8.4 Sensitivity Analysis on Disney's Optimal Debt Ratio

In the base case, in Illustration 8.3, we used Disney's operating income in 2003 to find the optimal debt ratio. We could argue that Disney's operating income is subject to large swings, depending on the vagaries of the economy and the fortunes of the entertainment business, as shown in Table 8.11.

There are several ways of using the information in such historical data to modify the analysis. One approach is to look at the firm's performance during previous downturns. In Disney's case, the operating income in 2002 dropped by 15.82 percent as the firm struggled with the aftermath of the terrorist attacks of September 11,

Table 8.11 DISNEY'S OPERATING INCOME HISTORY: 1987–2003		
Year	**EBIT**	**% Change in EBIT**
1987	756	
1988	848	12.17%
1989	1,177	38.80%
1990	1,368	16.23%
1991	1,124	−17.84%
1992	1,287	14.50%
1993	1,560	21.21%
1994	1,804	15.64%
1995	2,262	25.39%
1996	3,024	33.69%
1997	3,945	30.46%
1998	3,843	−2.59%
1999	3,580	−6.84%
2000	2,525	−29.47%
2001	2,832	12.16%
2002	2,384	−15.82%
2003	2,713	13.80%

Table 8.12   EFFECTS OF OPERATING INCOME ON OPTIMAL DEBT RATIO

% Drop in EBITDA	EBIT	Optimal Debt Ratio
0%	$2,805	30%
5%	$2,665	20%
10%	$2,524	20%
15%	$2385	20%
20%	$2,245	20%

2001, and the resultant downturn in leisure travel. In 2000, Disney's self-inflicted wounds from overinvestment in the Internet business and poor movies caused operating income to plummet almost 30 percent. A second approach is to obtain a statistical measure of the volatility in operating income so that we can be more conservative in choosing debt levels for firms with more volatile earnings. In Disney's case, the standard deviation in percentage changes in operating income is 19.54 percent. Table 8.12 illustrates the impact of lowering operating from current levels on the optimal debt level.

The optimal debt ratio declines to 20 percent when the operating income decreases by 5 percent, but the optimal stays at 20 percent for larger decreases in operating income (up to 40 percent).

IN PRACTICE: EBIT VERSUS EBITDA

In recent years, analysts have increasingly turned to using EBITDA as a measure of operating cash flows for a firm. It may therefore seem surprising that we focus on operating income or EBIT far more than EBITDA when computing the optimal capital structure. The interest coverage ratios, for instance, are based on operating income and not EBITDA. Although it is true that depreciation and amortization are noncash expenses and should be added back to get to cash flows, it is dangerous for a firm with ongoing operations to depend on the cash flows generated by these items to service debt payments. After all, firms with high depreciation and amortization expenses usually have high ongoing capital expenditures. If the cash inflows from depreciation and amortization are redirected to make debt payments, the reinvestment made by firms will be insufficient to generate future growth or to maintain existing assets. ∎

Normalized Operating Income

A key input that drives the optimal capital structure is the current operating income. If this income is depressed, either because the firm is a cyclical firm or because there are firm-specific factors that are expected to be temporary, the optimal debt ratio that will emerge from the analysis will be much lower than the firm's true optimal. For example, automobile manufacturing firms would have had very low debt ratios if the optimal debt ratios had been computed based on the operating income in 2001 and 2002, which were recession years. If the drop in operating income is permanent, however, this lower optimal debt ratio is, in fact, the correct estimate.

When evaluating a firm with depressed current operating income, we must first decide whether the drop in income is temporary or permanent. If the drop is temporary, we must estimate the **normalized operating income** for the firm. Most analysts normalize earnings by taking the average earnings over a period of time (usually five years).

Normalized Income: A measure of the income that a firm can make in a normal year, where there are no unusual gains or losses either from firm-specific factors (such as write-offs and one-time sales) or macroeconomic factors (such as recessions and economic booms).

There is a data set online that summarizes operating margins and returns on capital by industry group in the United States for the most recent quarter.

Operating Income as a Function of Default Risk

In the analysis we just completed for the Disney, we assumed that operating income would remain constant while the debt ratios changed. Although this assumption simplifies the analysis substantially, it is not realistic. The operating income for many firms will drop as the default risk increases; this, in fact, is the cost we labeled as an indirect bankruptcy cost in the previous chapter. The drop is likely to become more pronounced as the default risk falls below an acceptable level; for instance, a bond rating below investment grade may trigger significant losses in revenues and increases in expenses.

A general model for optimal capital structure would allow both operating income and cost of capital to change as the debt ratio changes. We have already described how we can estimate cost of capital at different debt ratios, but we could also attempt to do the same with operating income. For instance, we could estimate how the operating income for the Aracruz would change as debt ratios and default risks change by looking at the effects of rating downgrades on the operating income of other paper and pulp companies.

If both operating income and cost of capital change, the optimal debt ratio may no longer be the point at which the cost of capital is minimized. Instead, the optimal debt ratio has to be defined as that at which the value of the firm is maximized. We will consider an example of such an analysis in a few pages, when we estimate the optimal debt ratio for Deutsche Bank.

ILLUSTRATION 8.5 Applying the Cost of Capital Approach with Normalized Operating Income to Aracruz Celulose

Aracruz Celulose, the Brazilian pulp and paper manufacturing firm, reported operating income of 887 million BR on revenues of 3,176 million BR in 2003. This was significantly higher than its operating income of 346 million BR in 2002 and 196 million

BR in 2001. We estimated the optimal debt ratio for Aracruz based on the following information:

- In 2003, Aracruz had depreciation of 553 million BR, and capital expenditures amounted to 661 million BR.
- Aracruz had debt outstanding with a market value of 4,094 million BR and a dollar cost of debt of 7.25 percent.
- The corporate tax rate in Brazil is estimated to be 34 percent.
- Aracruz had 859.59 million shares outstanding, trading at 10.69 BR per share. The beta of the stock is estimated, using comparable firms, to be 0.7040 (see Chapter 4).

In Chapter 4, we estimated Aracruz's current dollar cost of capital to be 10.33 percent, using an equity risk premium of 12.49 percent for Brazil:

$$\text{Current \$Cost of Equity} = 4\% + 0.7040\,(12.49\%) = 12.79\%$$

$$\text{Market Value of Equity} = 10.69\ \text{BR/share} \times 859.59 = 9,189\ \text{million BR}$$

Current $ Cost of Capital
$$= 12.79\%\,(9,189/[9,189 + 4,094]) + 7.25\%\,(1 - 0.34)(4,094/[9,189 + 4,094]$$
$$= 10.33\%$$

We made three significant changes in applying the cost of capital approach to Aracruz as opposed to Disney:

- The operating income at Aracruz is a function of the price of paper and pulp in global markets. Although 2003 was a very good year for the company, its income history over the past decade reflects the volatility created by shifting pulp prices. We computed Aracruz's average pretax operating margin over the past ten years to be 25.99 percent. Applying this lower average margin to 2003 revenues generates a normalized operating income of 796.71 million BR. We will compute the optimal debt ratio using this normalized value.
- In Chapter 4, we noted that Aracruz's synthetic rating of BBB, based on the interest coverage ratio, is much higher than its actual rating of B+ and attributed the difference to Aracruz being a Brazilian company, exposed to country risk. Because we compute the cost of debt at each level of debt using synthetic ratings, we run the risk of understating the cost of debt. The difference in interest rates between the synthetic and actual ratings is 1.75 percent, and we add this to the cost of debt estimated at each debt ratio from 0 percent to 90 percent. You can consider this a country-risk adjusted cost of debt for Aracruz.
- Aracruz has a market value of equity of about $3 billion (9.19 billion BR). We used the interest coverage ratio/rating relationship for smaller companies to estimate synthetic ratings at each level of debt. In practical terms, the rating that we assign to Aracruz for any given interest coverage ratio will generally be lower than the rating that Disney, a much larger company, would have had with the same ratio.

Table 8.13 **ARACRUZ CELULOSE: COST OF CAPITAL, FIRM VALUE, AND DEBT RATIOS**

Debt Ratio	Beta	Cost of Equity	Bond Rating	Interest Rate on Debt	Tax Rate	Cost of Debt (After-Tax)	WACC	Firm Value in BR
0%	0.54	10.80%	AAA	6.10%	34.00%	4.03%	10.80%	12,364
10%	0.58	11.29%	AAA	6.10%	34.00%	4.03%	10.57%	12,794
20%	0.63	11.92%	A	6.60%	34.00%	4.36%	10.40%	13,118
30%	0.70	12.72%	BBB	7.25%	34.00%	4.79%	10.34%	13,256
40%	0.78	13.78%	CCC	13.75%	34.00%	9.08%	11.90%	10,633
50%	0.93	15.57%	CCC	13.75%	29.66%	9.67%	12.62%	9,743
60%	1.20	19.04%	C	17.75%	19.15%	14.35%	16.23%	6,872
70%	1.61	24.05%	C	17.75%	16.41%	14.84%	17.60%	6,177
80%	2.41	34.07%	C	17.75%	14.36%	15.20%	18.98%	5,610
90%	4.82	64.14%	C	17.75%	12.77%	15.48%	20.35%	5,138

Using the normalized operating income, we estimated the costs of equity, debt and capital in Table 8.13 for Aracruz at different debt ratios. The optimal debt ratio for Aracruz using the normalized operating income is 30 percent, a shade below its current debt ratio of 30.82 percent, but the cost of capital at the optimal is almost identical to its current cost of capital. This indicates that Aracruz is at its optimal debt ratio. There are two qualifiers we would add to this conclusion. The first is that the volatility in paper and pulp prices will undoubtedly cause big swings in operating income over time, and with it the optimal debt ratio. The second is that as an emerging market company, Aracruz is particularly exposed to political or economic risk in Brazil in particular and Latin America in general. It is perhaps because of this fear of market crises that Aracruz has a cash balance amounting to more than 7 percent of the total firm value. In fact, the net debt ratio for Aracruz is only about 23 percent.

 IN PRACTICE: NORMALIZING OPERATING INCOME

In estimating optimal debt ratios, it is always more advisable to use normalized operating income rather than current operating income. Most analysts normalize earnings by taking the average earnings over a period of time. Because this holds the scale of the firm fixed, it may not be appropriate for firms that have changed in size over time. The right way to normalize income will vary across firms:

1. For cyclical firms, whose current operating income may be overstated (if the economy is booming) or understated (if the economy is in recession), the operating income can be estimated using the average operating margin over an entire economic cycle (usually 5 to 10 years)

$$\text{Normalized Operating Income} = \text{Average Operating Margin (across cycle)} \times \text{Current Sales}$$

2. For firms that have had a bad year in terms of operating income due to firm-specific factors (such as the loss of a contract), the operating margin for the industry in which the firm operates can be used to calculate the normalized operating income:

$$\text{Normalized Operating Income} = \text{Average Operating Margin (for industry)} \\ \times \text{Current Sales}$$

The normalized operating income can also be estimated using returns on capital across an economic cycle (for cyclical firms) or an industry (for firms with firm-specific problems), but returns on capital are much more likely to be skewed by mismeasurement and accounting factors than operating margins. ■

Extensions of the Cost of Capital Approach

The cost of capital approach, which works so well for manufacturing firms that are publicly traded, may need to be adjusted when we are called on to compute optimal debt ratios for private firms or for financial service firms, such as banks and insurance companies.

Private Firms

There are three major differences between public and private firms in terms of analyzing optimal debt ratios. One is that unlike the case for publicly traded firms, we do not have a direct estimate of the market value of a private firm. Consequently, we have to estimate firm value before we move to subsequent stages in the analysis. The second difference relates to the cost of equity and how we arrive at that cost. Although we use betas to estimate the cost of equity for a public firm, that usage might not be appropriate when we are computing the optimal debt ratio for a private firm, because the owner may not be well diversified. Finally, whereas publicly traded firms tend to think of their cost of debt in terms of bond ratings and default spreads, private firms tend to borrow from banks. Banks assess default risk and charge the appropriate interest rates.

To analyze the optimal debt ratio for a private firm, we make the following adjustments. First, we estimate the value of the private firm by looking at how publicly traded firms in the same business are priced by the market. Thus, if publicly traded firms in the business have market values that are roughly three times revenues, we would multiply the revenues of the private firm by this number to arrive at an estimated value. Second, we continue to estimate the costs of debt for a private firm using a bond rating, but the rating is synthetic, based on interest coverage ratios. We tend to require much higher interest coverage ratios to arrive at the same rating, to reflect the fact that banks are likely to be more conservative in assessing default risk at small, private firms.

ILLUSTRATION 8.6 Applying the Cost of Capital Approach to a Private Firm: Bookscape

Bookscape, a private firm, has neither a market value for its equity nor a rating for its debt. In Chapter 4, we assumed that Bookscape would have a debt to capital ratio of 16.90 percent, similar to that of publicly traded book retailers, and that the tax rate for the firm is 40 percent. We computed a cost of capital based on that assumption. We also used a total beta of 2.0606 to measure the additional risk that the owner of Bookscape is exposed to because of his lack of diversification.

$$\text{Cost of Equity} = \text{Risk-Free Rate} + \text{Total Beta} \times \text{Risk Premium}$$
$$= 4\% + 2.0606 \times 4.82\% = 13.93\%$$

$$\text{Pretax Cost of Debt} = 5.5\% \text{ (based on synthetic rating of BBB)}$$

$$\text{Cost of Capital} = 13.93\% \ (0.8310) + 5.5\% \ (1 - 0.40)(0.1690) = 12.14\%$$

To estimate the optimal capital structure for Bookscape, we made the following assumptions:

- Although Bookscape has no conventional debt outstanding, it does have one large operating lease commitment. Given that the operating lease has 25 years to run and that the lease commitment is $500,000 for each year, the present value of the operating lease commitments is computed using Bookscape's pretax cost of debt of 5.5 percent:

$$\text{Present value of Operating Lease Commitments (in '000s)}$$
$$= \$500 \text{ (PV of annuity, 5.50\%, 25 years)} = \$6,708$$

  Note that Bookscape's pretax cost of debt is based on their synthetic rating of BBB, which we estimated in Chapter 4.

- Bookscape had operating income before taxes of $2 million in the most recent financial year after depreciation charges of $400,000. Because we consider the present value of operating lease expenses to be debt, we add back the imputed interest expense on the present value of lease expenses to the EBIT to arrive at an adjusted EBIT. For the rest of the analysis, operating lease commitments are treated as debt and the interest expense estimated on the present value of operating leases:

$$\text{Adjusted EBIT (in '000s)} = \text{EBIT} + \text{Pretax Cost of Debt}$$
$$\times \text{PV of Operating Lease Expenses}$$
$$= \$2,000 + 0.055 \times \$6,708 = \$2,369$$

- To estimate the market value of equity, we looked at publicly traded book retailers and computed an average price to earnings ratio of 16.31 for these firms. Applying this multiple of earnings to Bookscape's net income of $1,320,000 in 2003 yielded an estimate of Bookscape's market value of equity.

$$\text{Estimated Market Value of Equity (in '000s)} = \text{Net Income for Bookscape}$$
$$\times \text{Average PE for Publicly Traded Book Retailers} = 1,320 \times 16.31 = \$21,525$$

- The interest rates at different levels of debt will be estimated based on a synthetic bond rating. This rating will be assessed using Table 8.14, which summarizes ratings and default spreads over the long-term bond rate as a function of interest coverage ratios for small firms that are rated by S&P as of January 2004.

  Note that smaller firms need higher coverage ratios than the larger firms to get the same rating.

Table 8.14   INTEREST COVERAGE RATIOS, RATING, AND DEFAULT SPREADS: SMALL FIRMS

Interest Coverage Ratio	Rating	Spread over Treasury Bond Rate
>12.5	AAA	0.35%
9.50–12.50	AA	0.50%
7.5–9.5	A+	0.70%
6.0–7.5	A	0.85%
4.5–6.0	A−	1.00%
4.0–4.5	BBB	1.50%
3.5–4.0	BB+	2.00%
3.0–3.5	BB	2.50%
2.5–3.0	B+	3.25%
2.0–2.5	B	4.00%
1.5–2.0	B−	6.00%
1.25–1.5	CCC	8.00%
0.8–1.25	CC	10.00%
0.5–0.8	C	12.00%
< 0.5	D	20.00%

Table 8.15   COSTS OF CAPITAL AND FIRM VALUE FOR BOOKSCAPE

Debt Ratio	Beta	Cost of Equity	Bond Rating	Interest Rate on Debt	Tax Rate	Cost of Debt (After-Tax)	WACC	Firm Value
0%	1.84	12.87%	AAA	4.35%	40.00%	2.61%	12.87%	$25,020
10%	1.96	13.46%	AAA	4.35%	40.00%	2.61%	12.38%	$26,495
20%	2.12	14.20%	A+	4.70%	40.00%	2.82%	11.92%	$28,005
30%	2.31	15.15%	A−	5.00%	40.00%	3.00%	11.51%	$29,568
40%	2.58	16.42%	BB	6.50%	40.00%	3.90%	11.41%	$29,946
50%	2.94	18.19%	B	8.00%	40.00%	4.80%	11.50%	$29,606
60%	3.50	20.86%	CC	14.00%	39.96%	8.41%	13.39%	$23,641
70%	4.66	26.48%	CC	14.00%	34.25%	9.21%	14.39%	$21,365
80%	7.27	39.05%	C	16.00%	26.22%	11.80%	17.25%	$16,745
90%	14.54	74.09%	C	16.00%	23.31%	12.27%	18.45%	$15,355

- The tax rate used in the analysis is 40 percent, and the long-term bond rate at the time of this analysis was 4 percent.

Based on this information and using the same approach used for Disney, the cost of capital and firm value are estimated for Bookscape at different debt ratios. The information is summarized in Table 8.15.

The firm value is maximized (and the cost of capital is minimized) at a debt ratio of 40 percent, though the firm value is relatively flat between 30 percent and 50 percent.

The default risk increases significantly at the optimal debt ratio, as evidenced by the synthetic bond rating of BB, and the total beta increases to 2.58.

IN PRACTICE: Optimal Debt Ratios for Private Firms

Although the trade-off between the costs and benefits of borrowing remain the same for private and publicly traded firms, there are differences between the two kinds of firms that may result in private firms borrowing less money.

- Increasing debt increases default risk and expected bankruptcy costs much more substantially for small private firms than for larger publicly traded firms. This is partly because the owners of private firms may be exposed to unlimited liability, and partly because the perception of financial trouble on the part of customers and suppliers can be much more damaging to small, private firms.

- Increasing debt yields a much smaller advantage in terms of disciplining managers in the case of privately run firms because the owners of the firm tend to be the top managers as well.

- Increasing debt generally exposes small private firms to far more restrictive bond covenants and higher agency costs than it does large publicly traded firms.

- The loss of flexibility associated with using excess debt capacity is likely to weigh much more heavily on small, private firms than on large, publicly traded firms, due to the former's lack of access to public markets.

All these factors would lead us to expect much lower debt ratios at small private firms. ■

8.5 Going Public: Effect on Optimal Debt Ratio

Assume that Bookscape is planning to make an IPO in six months. How would this information change your assessment of the optimal debt ratio?

☐ It will increase the optimal debt ratio because publicly traded firms should be able to borrow more than private businesses.

☐ It will reduce the optimal debt ratio because only market risk counts for a publicly traded firm.

☐ It may increase or decrease the optimal debt ratio, depending on which effect dominates.

Banks and Insurance Companies

There are several problems in applying the cost of capital approach to financial service firms, such as banks and insurance companies.[23] The first is that the interest coverage ratio spreads, which are critical in determining the bond ratings, have to be estimated separately for financial service firms; applying manufacturing company spreads will result in absurdly low ratings for even the safest banks and very low optimal debt ratios. Furthermore, the relationship between interest coverage ratios

---

[23]See D. Davis and K. Lee, 1997, "A Practical Approach to Capital Structure for Banks," *Journal of Applied Corporate Finance,* 10(1), 33–43. They consider some of the issues related to estimating the optimal debt ratio for a bank.

and ratings tend to be much weaker for financial service firms than it is for manufacturing firms. The second is a measurement problem that arises partly from the difficulty in estimating the debt on a financial service company's balance sheet. Given the mix of deposits, repurchase agreements, short-term financing, and other liabilities that may appear on a financial service firm's balance sheet, one solution is to focus only on long-term debt, defined tightly, and to use interest coverage ratios defined using only long-term interest expenses. The third problem is that financial service firms are regulated and have to meet capital ratios that are defined in terms of book value. If, in the process of moving to an optimal market value debt ratio, these firms violate the regulatory book capital ratios, they could put themselves in jeopardy.

ILLUSTRATION **8.7** **Applying the Cost of Capital Approach to Deutsche Bank**
We analyze the optimal capital structure for Deutsche Bank using data from 2004. To begin, we make the following assumptions:

- The earnings before long-term interest expenses and taxes amounted to 7,405 million Euros in 2003.
- Deutsche Bank was ranked AA− and paid 5.05 percent on its long-term debt in 2004. It had 82 billion in long-term debt outstanding at the end of the year.
- Deutsche Bank had 581.85 million shares outstanding, trading at 70.40 Euros per share, and the bottom-up beta of 0.98 that we estimated for the company in Chapter 4 is the current beta. The tax rate for the firm is 38 percent, and the riskless Euro rate is 4.05 percent.
- The interest coverage ratios and default spreads used to estimate the bond ratings are adjusted to reflect the ratings of financial service firms.
- The operating income for Deutsche Bank is assumed to drop if its rating drops.

Table 8.16 summarizes the interest coverage ratios and estimated operating income drops for different ratings classes. Thus, we assume that the operating income will drop 5 percent if Deutsche Bank's rating drops to AA and 20 percent if it drops to BBB. The drops in operating income were estimated by looking at the effects of ratings downgrades on banks.[24]

Based on these assumptions, the optimal long-term debt ratio for Deutsche Bank is estimated to be 40 percent, lower than its current long-term debt ratio of 67 percent. Table 8.17 summarizes the cost of capital and firm values at different debt ratios for the firm.

The optimal debt ratio is the point at which the firm value is maximized. Note that the cost of capital is actually minimized at 70 percent debt, but the firm value is highest at a 40 percent debt ratio. This is so because the operating income changes as the debt ratio changes. Although the cost of capital continues to decline as the debt ratio increases beyond 40 percent, the decline in operating income more that offsets this drop.

---

[24]We were able to find a few downgraded banks up to BBB. Below BBB, we found no banks that remained independent, because the FDIC stepped in to protect depositors. We made the drop in operating income large enough to rule out ratings below BBB.

Table 8.16 **INTEREST COVERAGE RATIOS, RATINGS, AND OPERATING INCOME DECLINES**

Long-Term Interest Coverage Ratio	Rating	Spread	Operating Income Decline
< 0.05	D	16.00%	−50.00%
0.05–0.10	C	14.00%	−40.00%
0.10–0.20	CC	12.50%	−40.00%
0.20–0.30	CCC	10.50%	−40.00%
0.30–0.40	B−	6.25%	−25.00%
0.40–0.50	B	6.00%	−20.00%
0.50–0.60	B+	5.75%	−20.00%
0.60–0.75	BB	4.75%	−20.00%
0.75–0.90	BB+	4.25%	−20.00%
0.90–1.20	BBB	2.00%	−20.00%
1.20–1.50	A−	1.50%	−17.50%
1.50–2.00	A	1.40%	−15.00%
2.00–2.50	A+	1.25%	−10.00%
2.50–3.00	AA	0.90%	−5.00%
> 3.00	AAA	0.70%	0.00%

Table 8.17 **DEBT RATIOS, COST OF CAPITAL, AND FIRM VALUE: DEUTSCHE BANK**

Debt Ratio	Beta	Cost of Equity	Bond Rating	Interest Rate on Debt	Tax Rate	Cost of Debt (After-Tax)	WACC	Firm Value (G)
0%	0.44	6.15%	AAA	4.75%	38.00%	2.95%	6.15%	$111,034
10%	0.47	6.29%	AAA	4.75%	38.00%	2.95%	5.96%	$115,498
20%	0.50	6.48%	AAA	4.75%	38.00%	2.95%	5.77%	$120,336
30%	0.55	6.71%	AAA	4.75%	38.00%	2.95%	5.58%	$125,597
40%	0.62	7.02%	AAA	4.75%	38.00%	2.95%	5.39%	$131,339
50%	0.71	7.45%	A+	5.30%	38.00%	3.29%	5.37%	$118,770
60%	0.84	8.10%	A	5.45%	38.00%	3.38%	5.27%	$114,958
70%	1.07	9.19%	A	5.45%	38.00%	3.38%	5.12%	$119,293
80%	1.61	11.83%	BB+	8.30%	32.43%	5.61%	6.85%	$77,750
90%	3.29	19.91%	BB	8.80%	27.19%	6.41%	7.76%	$66,966

IN PRACTICE: BUILDING IN REGULATORY, SELF-IMPOSED, AND LENDER CONSTRAINTS

In most analyses of optimal capital structure, an analyst will be faced with a series of constraints, some of which come from regulatory requirements, some of which are self-imposed, and some of which are imposed by existing lenders to the firm. One very common constraint imposed by all three is that the book value debt ratio not exceed a specified number. Because the analysis we have done so far has focused on market value debt ratios, there is the risk that the book value constraint may be violated. There are two solutions:

1. The first is to do the entire analysis using book value of debt and equity, looking for the optimal debt ratio. Since the approach we have described is driven by cash flows, the optimal dollar debt that is computed should not be affected significantly by doing this.

2. The second and more general approach (because it can be used to analyze any kind of constraint) is to keep track of the book value debt ratio in the traditional analysis and view the optimal capital structure as the one that minimizes the cost of capital, subject to the book value debt ratio being lesser than the specified constraint. ■

8.6 BANKRUPTCY COSTS AND DEBT RATIOS

The optimal debt ratio obtained by minimizing the cost of capital is too high because it does not consider bankruptcy costs.

☐ True

☐ False

Explain.

Determinants of Optimal Debt Ratio

The preceding analysis highlights some of the determinants of the optimal debt ratio. We can then divide these determinants into firm-specific and macroeconomic factors.

Firm-Specific Factors

Determinants specific to the firm include the firm's tax rate, pretax returns, and variance in operating income.

a. Firm's Tax Rate

In general, the tax benefits from debt increase as the tax rate goes up. In relative terms, firms with higher tax rates will have higher optimal debt ratios than will firms with lower tax rates, other things being equal. It also follows that a firm's optimal debt ratio will increase as its tax rate increases. We can illustrate this by computing the optimal debt ratio for Disney, Aracruz, and Bookscape, holding all else constant and just changing the tax rate as shown in Figure 8.5.

At a 0 percent tax rate, the optimal debt ratio is zero for all three firms. Without the benefits that accrue from taxes, the rationale for using debt disappears. As the tax rate increases, the optimal debt ratios increase for all three firms but at different rates. For Aracruz and Disney, the optimal debt ratio does not increase above 30 percent even if the tax rate increases because the operating income at both firms is not high enough to sustain much higher debt ratios; in other words, there are not enough earnings to claim additional tax benefits. For Bookscape, however, the optimal continues to increase and reaches 50 percent when the tax rate is 50 percent.

Figure 8.5   Optimal Debt Ratio and Tax Rate

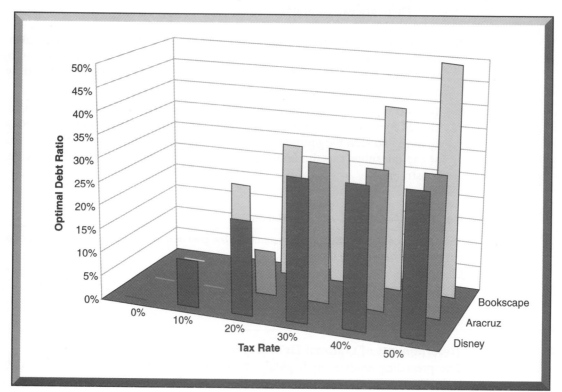

b. Pretax Returns on the Firm (in Cash Flow Terms)

The most significant determinant of the optimal debt ratio is a firm's earnings capacity. In fact, the operating income as a percentage of the market value of the firm (debt plus equity) is usually good indicator of the optimal debt ratio. When this number is high (low), the optimal debt ratio will also be high (low). A firm with higher pretax earnings can sustain much more debt as a proportion of the market value of the firm because debt payments can be met much more easily from prevailing earnings. Disney, for example, has operating income of $2,805 million, which is 4.02 percent of the market value of the firm of $69,769 million in the base case, and an optimal debt ratio of 30 percent. Doubling this to 8.04 percent will increase the optimal debt ratio to 50 percent.

c. Variance in Operating Income

The variance in operating income enters the base case analysis in two ways. First, it plays a role in determining the current beta: Firms with high (low) variance in operating income tend to have high (low) betas. Second, the volatility in operating income can be one of the factors determining bond ratings at different levels of debt: Ratings drop off much more dramatically for higher variance firms as debt levels are increased. It follows that firms with higher (lower) variance in operating income will have lower (higher) optimal debt ratios. The variance in operating income also plays a role in the constrained analysis, because higher-variance firms are much more likely to register significant drops in operating income. Consequently, the decision to increase debt should be made much more cautiously for these firms.

Macroeconomic Factors

Should macroeconomic conditions affect optimal debt ratios? In purely mechanical terms, the answer is yes. In good economic times, firms will generate higher earnings and be able to service more debt. In recessions, earnings will decline and with it the capacity to service debt. That is why prudent firms borrow based on normalized earnings rather than current earnings. Holding operating income constant, macroeconomic variables can still affect optimal debt ratios. In fact, both the level of risk-free rate and the magnitude of default spreads can affect optimal debt ratios.

a. Level of Rates

As interest rates decline, the conventional wisdom is that debt should become cheaper and more attractive for firms. Though this may seem intuitive, the effect is muted by the fact that lower interest rates also reduce the cost of equity. In fact, changing the risk-free rate has a surprisingly small effect on the optimal debt ratio as long as interest rates move within a normal range.[25] When interest rates exceed normal levels, optimal debt ratios do decline partly because we keep operating income fixed. The higher interest payments at every debt ratio reduce bond ratings and affect the capacity of firms to borrow more.

b. Default Spreads

The default spreads for different ratings classes tend to increase during recessions and decrease during economic booms. Keeping other things constant, as the spreads increase (decrease) optimal debt ratios decrease (increase), for the simple reason that higher spreads penalize firms that borrow more money and have lower ratings. In fact, the default spreads on corporate bonds declined between 1992 and 2000, leading to higher optimal debt ratios for all firms. In 2001 and 2002, as the economy slowed, default spreads widened again, leading to lower optimal debt ratios.

ADJUSTED PRESENT VALUE APPROACH

In the adjusted present value (APV) approach, we begin with the value of the firm without debt. As we add debt to the firm, we consider the net effect on value by considering both the benefits and the costs of borrowing. The value of the levered firm can then be estimated at different levels of the debt, and the debt level that maximizes firm value is the optimal debt ratio.

---

[25]The normal range for long-term interest rates in the United States for the past forty years has been between 4 and 8 percent. There was a short period between 1978 and 1982 when long-term interest rates were much higher.

Steps in the APV Approach

In the APV approach, we assume that the primary benefit of borrowing is a tax benefit and that the most significant cost of borrowing is the added risk of bankruptcy. To estimate the value of the firm with these assumptions, we proceed in three steps. We begin by estimating the value of the firm with no leverage. We then consider the present value of the interest tax savings generated by borrowing a given amount of money. Finally, we evaluate the effect of borrowing the amount on the probability that the firm will go bankrupt and the expected cost of bankruptcy.

Step 1:   *Estimate the value of the firm with no debt:* The first step in this approach is the estimation of the value of the unlevered firm. This can be accomplished by valuing the firm as if it had no debt, that is, by discounting the expected after-tax operating cash flows at the unlevered cost of equity. In the special case where cash flows grow at a constant rate in perpetuity,

$$\text{Value of Unlevered Firm} = \text{FCFF}_0(1 + g)/(\rho_u - g)$$

where $FCFF_0$ is the current after-tax operating cash flow to the firm, ρ_u is the unlevered cost of equity, and g is the expected growth rate. The inputs needed for this valuation are the expected cash flows, growth rates, and the unlevered cost of equity. To estimate the latter, we can draw on our earlier analysis and compute the unlevered beta of the firm:

$$\beta_{\text{unlevered}} = \beta_{\text{current}}/[1 + (1 - t)\text{D/E}]$$

where $\beta_{\text{unlevered}}$ = unlevered beta of the firm, β_{current} = current equity beta of the firm, t = tax rate for the firm, and D/E = current debt/equity ratio. This unlevered beta can then be used to arrive at the unlevered cost of equity. Alternatively, we can take the current market value of the firm as a given and back out the value of the unlevered firm by subtracting out the tax benefits and adding back the expected bankruptcy cost from the existing debt.

$$\text{Current Firm Value} = \text{Value of Unlevered Firm} + \text{PV of Tax Benefits} - \text{Expected Bankruptcy Costs}$$

$$\text{Value of Unlevered Firm} = \text{Current Firm Value} - \text{PV of Tax Benefits} + \text{Expected Bankruptcy Costs}$$

Step 2:   *Estimate the present value of tax benefits from debt:* The second step in this approach is the calculation of the expected tax benefit from a given level of debt. This tax benefit is a function of the tax rate of the firm and is discounted at the cost of debt to reflect the riskiness of this cash flow. If the tax savings are viewed as a perpetuity,

$$\text{Value of Tax Benefits} = [\text{Tax Rate} \times \text{Cost of Debt} \times \text{Debt}]/\text{Cost of Debt}$$
$$= \text{Tax Rate} \times \text{Debt}$$
$$= t_c D$$

The tax rate used here is the firm's marginal tax rate, and it is assumed to stay constant over time. If we anticipate the tax rate changing over time, we can still compute the present value of tax benefits over time, but we cannot use the perpetual growth equation.

Step 3: *Estimate the expected bankruptcy costs as a result of the debt:* The third step is to evaluate the effect of the given level of debt on the default risk of the firm and on expected **bankruptcy costs.** In theory, at least, this requires the estimation of the probability of default with the additional debt and the direct and indirect cost of bankruptcy. If π_a is the probability of default after the additional debt and BC is the present value of the bankruptcy cost, the present value of expected bankruptcy cost can be estimated.

$$\begin{aligned} \text{PV of Expected Bankruptcy Cost} &= \text{Probability of Bankruptcy} \\ &\quad \times \text{PV of Bankruptcy Cost} \\ &= \pi_a BC \end{aligned}$$

This step of the APV approach poses the most significant estimation problem, because neither the probability of bankruptcy nor the bankruptcy cost can be estimated directly. There are two ways the probability of bankruptcy can be estimated indirectly. One is to estimate a bond rating, as we did in the cost of capital approach, at each level of debt and use the empirical estimates of default probabilities, based on history, for each rating. For instance, Table 8.18, extracted from a study by Altman and Kishore, summarizes the probability of default over the previous ten years by bond rating class in 2000.[26]

The other is to use a statistical approach, such as a probit to estimate the probability of default, based on the firm's observable characteristics, at each level of debt.

The bankruptcy cost can be estimated, albeit with considerable error, from studies that have looked at the magnitude of this cost in actual bankruptcies. Studies that have looked at the direct cost of bankruptcy conclude that they are small relative to firm value.[27] The indirect costs of bankruptcy can be substantial, but the costs vary widely across firms. Shapiro and Titman speculate that the indirect costs could be as large as 25 to 30 percent of firm value but provide no direct evidence of the costs.[28]

The net effect of adding debt can be calculated by aggregating the costs and the benefits at each level of debt.

$$\text{Value of Levered Firm} = \text{FCFF}_0(1 + g)/(\rho_u - g) + t_c D - \pi_a BC$$

We compute the value of the levered firm at different levels of debt. The debt level that maximizes the value of the levered firm is the optimal debt ratio.

---

[26]E. I. Altman and V. Kishore, 2000, "The Default Experience of U.S. Bonds," Working Paper, Salomon Center, New York University. This study estimated default rates over ten years only for some of the ratings classes. We extrapolated the rest of the ratings.

[27]See J. N. Warner, 1977, "Bankruptcy Costs: Some Evidence," *Journal of Finance,* 32, 337–347. In this study of railroad bankruptcies, the direct cost of bankruptcy seems to be about 5 percent.

[28]See A. Shapiro, 1989, *Modern Corporate Finance,* New York: Macmillan; S. Titman, 1984, "The Effect of Capital Structure on a Firm's Liquidation Decision," *Journal of Financial Economics,* 13, 1371–75.

Table 8.18 DEFAULT RATES BY BOND RATING CLASSES

Bond Rating	Default Rate
D	100.00%
C	80.00%
CC	65.00%
CCC	46.61%
B–	32.50%
B	26.36%
B+	19.28%
BB	12.20%
BBB	2.30%
A–	1.41%
A	0.53%
A+	0.40%
AA	0.28%
AAA	0.01%

Source: Altman and Kishore (2000).

Bankruptcy Costs: The costs associated with going bankrupt. It includes both direct costs (from going bankrupt) and indirect costs (arising from the perception that a firm may go bankrupt).

IN PRACTICE: USING A PROBIT TO ESTIMATE THE PROBABILITY OF BANKRUPTCY

It is possible to estimate the probability of default using statistical techniques when sufficient data is available. For instance, if we have a database that lists all firms that went bankrupt during a period of time, as well as firms that did not go bankrupt during the same period, together with descriptive characteristics of these firms, a probit analysis can be used to estimate the likelihood of bankruptcy as a function of these characteristics. The steps involved in a probit analysis are as follows:

1. Identify the event of interest: Probits work best when the event either occurs or it does not. For bankruptcy, the event might be the filing for bankruptcy protection under the law.

2. Over a specified time period, collect information on all the firms that were exposed to the event. In the bankruptcy case, this would imply collecting information on which firms filed for bankruptcy over a certain period (say, five years).

3. Based on your knowledge of the event and other research on it, specify measurable and observable variables that are likely to be good predictors of that event. In the case of bankruptcy, these might include excessive debt ratios, declining income, poor project returns, and small market capitalization.

4. Collect information on these variables for the firms that filed for bankruptcy. Collect the same information for all other firms that were in existence at the same time and that have data available on them on these variables. (If this is too data-intensive, a random sampling of the firms that were not exposed to the event can be used.) In the bankruptcy analysis, this would imply collecting information on debt ratios, income trends, project returns, and market capitalization on the firms that filed for bankruptcy and other firms that did not across the period.

5. In a probit, the dependent variable is the occurrence of the specified event (1 if it occurs, 0 if it does not) and the independent variables are the variables specified in Step 3. The output from the probit looks very much like the output from a multiple regression, with statistical significance attached to each of the independent variables. (In the bankruptcy analysis, firms filing for bankruptcy would be tagged with a 1 and firms that survive would be categorized as 0).

Once the probit has been done, the probability of a firm defaulting can be estimated by plugging that firm's values for the independent variables into the model. The predicted value that emerges from the probit is the probability of default. ■

ILLUSTRATION 8.8   Using the APV Approach to Calculate Optimal Debt Ratio for Disney in 2004

The APV approach can be applied to estimating the optimal capital structure for Disney. The first step is to estimate the value of the unlevered firm. To do so, we start with the firm value of Disney in 2004 and net out the effect of the tax savings and bankruptcy costs arising from the existing debt.

$$\text{Current Market Value of Disney} = \text{Value of Equity} + \text{Value of Debt}$$
$$= \$55{,}101 + \$14{,}668 = \$69{,}769$$

We first compute the present value of the tax savings from the existing debt, assuming that the interest payment on the debt constitutes a perpetuity, using a marginal tax rate for Disney of 37.30 percent.

$$\text{PV of Tax Savings from Existing Debt} = \text{Existing Debt} \times \text{Tax Rate}$$
$$= \$14{,}668 \times 0.373 = \$5{,}479 \text{ million}$$

Based on Disney's current rating of BBB+, we estimate a probability of bankruptcy of 1.41 percent from Table 8.18. The bankruptcy cost is assumed to be 25 percent of the firm value, prior to the tax savings.[29] Allowing for a range of 10–40 percent for bankruptcy costs, we have put Disney's exposure to expected bankruptcy costs in the middle of the range. There are some businesses that Disney is in where the perception of distress can be damaging—theme parks, for instance—but the movie and

---

[29]This estimate is based on the Warner study, which estimates bankruptcy costs for large companies to be 10 percent of the value, and on the qualitative analysis of indirect bankruptcy costs in Shapiro and Titman.

Table 8.19   TAX SAVINGS FROM DEBT ($t_c D$): DISNEY

Debt Ratio	$Debt	Tax Rate	Tax Benefits
0%	$0	37.30%	$0
10%	$6,979	37.30%	$2,603
20%	$13,958	37.30%	$5,206
30%	$20,937	37.30%	$7,809
40%	$27,916	31.24%	$8,708
50%	$34,894	18.75%	$6,531
60%	$41,873	15.62%	$6,531
70%	$48,852	13.39%	$6,531
80%	$55,831	11.72%	$6,531
90%	$62,810	10.41%	$6,531

broadcasting businesses are less likely to be affected because projects tend to be shorter-term and on a smaller scale.

$$\text{PV of Expected Bankruptcy Cost} = \text{Probability of Default} \times \text{Bankruptcy Cost}$$
$$= 1.41\% \times (0.25 \times 69,789) = \$246 \text{ million}$$

We then compute the value of Disney as an unlevered firm.

Value of Disney as an Unlevered Firm
= Current Market Value − PV of Tax Savings
+ Expected Bankruptcy Costs = $69,789 + $5,479 − $246
= $65,556 million

The next step in the process is to estimate the tax savings in Table 8.19 at different levels of debt. Although we use the standard approach of assuming that the present value is calculated over a perpetuity, we reduce the tax rate used in the calculation, if interest expenses exceed the EBIT. The adjustment to the tax rate was described earlier in the cost of capital approach. (See Table 8.7.)

The final step in the process is to estimate the expected bankruptcy cost, based on the bond ratings, the probabilities of default, and the assumption that the bankruptcy cost is 25 percent of firm value. Table 8.20 summarizes these probabilities and the expected bankruptcy cost, computed based on the levered firm value

Expected Bankruptcy Cost at % debt
= (Unlevered Firm Value + Tax Benefits from Debt at % Debt)
× (Bankruptcy Cost as % of Firm Value) × Probability of Bankruptcy

The value of the levered firm is estimated in Table 8.21 by aggregating the effects of the tax savings and the expected bankruptcy costs.

The firm value is maximized at between 20 and 30 percent debt, which is consistent with the results of the cost of capital approach. These results are, however, very sensitive to both the estimate of bankruptcy cost as a percent of firm value and the probabilities of default.

Table 8.20   EXPECTED BANKRUPTCY COST: DISNEY

Debt Ratio	Bond Rating	Probability of Default	Expected Bankruptcy Cost
0%	AAA	0.01%	$2
10%	AAA	0.01%	$2
20%	A−	1.41%	$246
30%	BB+	7.00%	$1,266
40%	CCC	50.00%	$9,158
50%	C	80.00%	$14,218
60%	C	80.00%	$14,218
70%	C	80.00%	$14,218
80%	C	80.00%	$14,218
90%	C	80.00%	$14,218

Table 8.21   VALUE OF DISNEY WITH LEVERAGE

Debt Ratio	$Debt	Unlevered Firm Value	Tax Benefits	Expected Bankruptcy Cost	Value of Levered Firm
0%	$0	$64,556	$0	$2	$64,555
10%	$6,979	$64,556	$2,603	$2	$67,158
20%	$13,958	$64,556	$5,206	$246	$69,517
30%	$20,937	$64,556	$7,809	$1,266	$71,099
40%	$27,916	$64,556	$8,708	$9,158	$64,107
50%	$34,894	$64,556	$6,531	$14,218	$56,870
60%	$41,873	$64,556	$6,531	$14,218	$56,870
70%	$48,852	$64,556	$6,531	$14,218	$56,870
80%	$55,831	$64,556	$6,531	$14,218	$56,870
90%	$62,810	$64,556	$6,531	$14,218	$56,870

Benefits and Limitations of the APV Approach

The advantage of the APV approach is that it separates the effects of debt into different components and allows an analyst to use different discount rates for each component. In this approach, we do not assume that the debt ratio stays unchanged forever, which is an implicit assumption in the cost of capital approach. Instead, we have the flexibility to keep the dollar value of debt fixed and to calculate the benefits and costs of the fixed dollar debt.

These advantages have to be weighed against the difficulty of estimating probabilities of default and the cost of bankruptcy. In fact, many analyses that use the APV approach ignore the expected bankruptcy costs, leading them to the conclusion that firm value increases as firms borrow money. Not surprisingly, they conclude that the optimal debt ratio for a firm is 100 percent debt.

In general, with the same assumptions, the APV and the cost of capital conclusions give identical answers. However, the APV approach is more practical when firms are evaluating the feasibility of adding a dollar amount of debt, whereas the cost of capital approach is easier when firms are analyzing debt proportions.[30]

 This spreadsheet allows you to compute the value of a firm, with leverage, using the adjusted present value approach (**Apv.xls**).

COMPARATIVE ANALYSIS

The most common approach to analyzing the debt ratio of a firm is to compare its leverage to that of similar firms in the same business. A simple way to perform this analysis is to compare a firm's debt ratio to the average debt ratio for the industry in which the firm operates. A more complete analysis would consider the differences between a firm and the rest of the industry, when determining debt ratios. We will consider both ways.

Comparing to Industry Average

Firms sometimes choose their financing mixes by looking at the average debt ratio of other firms in the industry in which they operate. For instance, the table below compares the debt ratios at Disney and Aracruz to other firms in their industries.[31]

	Disney	Entertainment	Aracruz	Paper and Pulp (Emerging Market)
Market debt ratio	21.02%	19.56%	30.82%	27.71%
Book debt ratio	35.10%	28.86%	43.12%	49.00%

Source: Value Line.

Based on this comparison, Disney is operating at a debt ratio slightly higher than those of other firms in the industry in both market and book value terms, whereas Aracruz has a market debt ratio slightly higher than the average firm but a book debt ratio which is slightly lower.

The underlying assumptions in this comparison are that firms within the same industry are **comparable** and that, on average, these firms are operating at or close to their optimal. Both assumptions can be questioned, however. Firms within the same industry can have different product mixes, different amounts of operating risk, different tax rates, and different project returns. In fact, most do. For instance, Disney is considered part of the entertainment industry, but its mix of businesses is very different from that of Lion's Gate, which is primarily a movie company, or Liberty Media, which is primarily a cable broadcasting company. Furthermore, Disney's size and risk characteristics are very different from that of Pixar, which is also considered part of the same industry group. There is also anecdotal evidence that because firms

---

[30]See I. Inselbag and H. Kaufold, 1997, "Two DCF Approaches and Valuing Companies under Alternative Financing Strategies," *Journal of Applied Corporate Finance,* 10(1), 115–122.

[31]For purposes of this analysis, we looked at debt without operating leases being capitalized for the industry because of the difficulty of doing this for all of the comparable firms.

try to mimic the industry average, the average debt ratio across an industry might not be at or even close to its optimal.

Comparable (Firm): A firm similar to the firm being analyzed in terms of underlying characteristics—risk, growth, and cash flow patterns. The conventional definition of comparable firm is one that is in the same business as the one being analyzed and of similar size.

There is a data set online that summarizes market value and book value debt ratios, by industry, in addition to other relevant characteristics.

Controlling for Differences between Firms

Firms within the same industry can exhibit wide differences on tax rates, capacity to generate operating income and cash flows, and variance in operating income. Consequently, it can be dangerous to compare a firm's debt ratio to the industry and draw conclusions about the optimal financing mix. The simplest way to control for differences across firms, while using the maximum information available in the market, is to run a regression, regressing debt ratios against these variables, across the firms in a industry:

$$\text{Debt Ratio} = \alpha_0 + \alpha_1 \text{Tax Rate} + \alpha_2 \text{Pretax Returns} + \alpha_3 \text{Variance in Operating Income}$$

There are several advantages to the cross-sectional approach. Once the regression has been run and the basic relationship established (i.e., the intercept and coefficients have been estimated), the predicted debt ratio for any firm can be computed quickly using the measures of the independent variables for this firm. If a task involves calculating the optimal debt ratio for a large number of firms in a short time period, this may be the only practical way of approaching the problem because the other approaches described in this chapter are time-intensive.[32]

There are also limitations to this approach. The coefficients tend to shift over time. Besides some standard statistical problems and errors in measuring the variables, these regressions also tend to explain only a portion of the differences in debt ratios between firms.[33] However, the regressions provide significantly more information than a naive comparison of a firm's debt ratio to the industry average.

ILLUSTRATION 8.9 **Estimating Disney's Debt Ratio Using the Cross-Sectional Approach**
This approach can be applied to look at differences within a industry or across the entire market. We can illustrate looking at the Disney against firms in the entertainment sector first and then against the entire market.

---

[32]There are some who have hypothesized that underleveraged firms are much more likely to be taken over than firms that are overleveraged or correctly leveraged. If we want to find the 100 firms on the NYSE that are most underleveraged, the cross-sectional regression and the predicted debt ratios that come out of this regression can be used to find them.

[33]The independent variables are correlated with each other. This multicollinearity makes the coefficients unreliable, and they often have signs that go counter to intuition.

To look at the determinants of debt ratios within the entertainment industry, we regressed debt ratios of firms in the industry against two variables—the growth in sales over the previous five years and the EBITDA as a percent of the market value of the firm. Based on our earlier discussion of the determinants of capital structure, we would expect firms with higher operating cash flows (EBITDA) as a percent of firm value to borrow more money. We would also expect higher growth firms to weigh financial flexibility more in their debt decision and borrow less. The results of the regression are reported, with t-statistics in parentheses below the coefficients:

Debt to Capital
$$= 0.2156 - 0.1826(\text{Growth in Sales}) + 0.6797(\text{EBITDA/Firm Value})$$

$$(4.91) \quad (1.91) \quad\quad\quad\quad\quad (2.05)$$

The dependent variable is the market debt to capital ratio, and the regression has an R^2 of 14 percent. Although there is statistical significance, it is worth noting that the predicted debt ratios will have substantial standard errors associated with them. Even so, if we use the current values for these variables for Disney in this regression, we get a predicted debt ratio:

$$\text{DFR}_{\text{Disney}} = 0.2156 - 0.1826(0.0668) + 0.6797(0.0767) = 0.2555 \text{ or } 25.55\%$$

At their existing debt ratio of 21 percent, Disney is slightly underlevered. Thus, relative to the industry in which it operates and its specific characteristics, Disney could potentially borrow more.

One of the limitations of this analysis is that there are relatively few firms within each industry. This analysis can be therefore extended to all firms in the market. Although firms in different businesses differ in terms of risk and cash flows and these differences can translate into differences in debt ratios, we can control for the differences in the regression. To illustrate, we regressed debt ratios of all listed firms in the United States against four variables:

- The effective tax rate of the firm, as a proxy for the tax advantages associated with debt.
- Closely held shares as a percent of shares outstanding (CLSH) as a measure of how much separation there is between managers and stockholders (and hence as a proxy for debt as a disciplinary mechanism).
- EBITDA as a percent of enterprise value (EV) as a measure of the cash flow generating capacity of a firm
- Capital expenditures as a percent of total assets (CPXFR) as a measure of how much firms value flexibility

The results of the regression are presented next.[34]

$$\text{DFR} = 0.0488 + 0.810 \text{ Tax Rate} - 0.304 \text{ CLSH} + 0.841 \text{ EV} - 2.987 \text{ CPXFR}$$

$$(1.41^a) \quad (8.70^a) \quad\quad\quad (3.65^b) \quad\quad (7.92^b) \quad\quad (13.03^a)$$

---

[34]The numbers in parentheses below the coefficients represent t-statistics. The superscripted letters indicate statistical significance.

where DFR is debt as a percentage of the market value of the firm (debt + equity). The R^2 for this regression is 53.3 percent. If we plug in the values for Disney into this regression, we get a predicted debt ratio:

$$\text{DFR}_{\text{Disney}} = 0.0488 + 0.810(0.3476) - 0.304(0.022) + 0.841(0.0767) - 2.987(0.0209)$$
$$= 0.3257 \text{ or } 32.57\%$$

Based on the debt ratios of other firms in the market and Disney's financial characteristics, we would expect Disney to have a debt ratio of 32.57 percent. Because its actual debt ratio is 21.02 percent, Disney is underlevered.

8.7 OPTIMAL DEBT RATIOS BASED ON COMPARABLE FIRMS

The predicted debt ratio from the regression shown above will generally yield
- ☐ a debt ratio similar to the optimal debt ratio from the cost of capital approach.
- ☐ a debt ratio higher than the optimal debt ratio from the cost of capital approach.
- ☐ a debt ratio lower than the optimal debt ratio from the cost of capital approach.
- ☐ any of the above, depending on . . .

Explain.

There is a data set online that summarizes the latest debt ratio regression across the entire market.

SELECTING THE OPTIMAL DEBT RATIO

Using the different approaches for estimating optimal debt ratios, we come up with different estimates of the right financing mix for Disney and Aracruz. Table 8.22 summarizes them.

Although there are some differences in the estimates across the different approaches, a few consistent conclusions emerge: Disney, at its existing debt ratio, is

Table 8.22 **SUMMARY OF PREDICTED DEBT RATIOS**

	Disney	Aracruz
Actual debt ratio	21.02%	30.82%
Optimal		
I. Operating income	30.00%	—
II. Cost of capital		
With no constraints	30.00%	30.00%
With BBB constraint	30.00%	30.00%
III. APV	30.00%	30.00%
V. Comparable		
To industry	25.55%	28.56%
To market	32.57%	—

slightly underlevered, though the increase in value from moving to the optimal is small. Aracruz is slightly overlevered, based on normalized operating income.

Bookscape also has excess debt capacity, if we estimate the optimal debt ratio using the cost of capital approach. However, bankruptcy may carry a larger cost to the private owner of Bookscape than it would to the diversified investors of the Disney or Aracruz. We would therefore be cautious about using this excess debt capacity.

CONCLUSION

This chapter has provided background on four tools that can be used to analyze capital structure.

- The first approach is based on operating income. Using historical data or forecasts, we develop a distribution of operating income across both good and bad scenarios. We then use a predefined acceptably probability of default to specify the maximum borrowing capacity.

- The second approach is the cost of capital—the weighted average of the costs of equity, debt, and preferred stock, where the weights are market value weights and the costs of financing are current costs. The objective is to minimize the cost of capital, which also maximizes the value of the firm. A general framework is developed to use this model in real-world applications and applied to find the optimal financing mix for Disney. We find that Disney, which had almost about $14 billion in debt in 2004, would minimize its cost of capital at a debt level of 30 percent, leading to an increase in market value of the firm of about $3 billion. Even allowing for a much diminished operating income, we find that Disney has excess debt capacity.

- The third approach estimates the value of the firm at different levels of debt by adding the present value of the tax benefits from debt to the unlevered firm's value, and then subtracting out the present value of expected bankruptcy costs. The optimal debt ratio is the one that maximizes firm value.

- The final approach is to compare a firm's debt ratio to similar firms. Although comparisons of firm debt ratios to an industry average are commonly made, they are generally not very useful in the presence of large differences among firms within the same industry. A cross-sectional regression of debt ratios against underlying financial variables brings in more information from the general population of firms and can be used to predict debt ratios for a large number of firms.

The objective in all of these analyses is to come up with a mix of debt and equity that will maximize the value of the firm.

LIVE CASE STUDY

THE OPTIMAL FINANCING MIX

Objective: To estimate the optimal mix of debt and equity for your firm and to evaluate the effect on firm value of moving to that mix.

Key Questions

- Based on the cost of capital approach, what is the optimal debt ratio for your firm?
- Bringing in reasonable constraints into the decision process, what would your recommended debt ratio be for this firm?
- Does your firm have too much or too little debt
  - relative to the industry in which they operate?
  - relative to the market?

Framework for Analysis

1. *Cost of Capital Approach*
   - What is the current cost of capital for the firm?
   - What happens to the cost of capital as the debt ratio is changed?
   - At what debt ratio is the cost of capital minimized and firm value maximized? (If they are different, explain.)
   - What will happen to the firm value if the firm moves to its optimal?
   - What will happen to the stock price if the firm moves to the optimal and stockholders are rational?

2. *Building Constraints into the Process*
   - What rating does the company have at the optimal debt ratio? If you were to impose a rating constraint, what would it be? Why? What is the optimal debt ratio with this rating constraint?
   - How volatile is the operating income? What is the "normalized" operating income of this firm, and what is the optimal debt ratio of the firm at this level of income?

3. *Relative Analysis*
   - Relative to the industry to which this firm belongs, does it have too much or too little in debt? (Do a regression, if necessary.)
   - Relative to the rest of the firms in the market, does it have too much or too little in debt? (Use the market regression, if necessary.)

Getting Information about Optimal Capital Structure

To get the inputs needed to estimate the optimal capital structure, examine the 10-K report or the annual report. The ratings and interest coverage ratios can be obtained from the ratings agencies (S&P, Moody's), and default spreads can be estimated by finding traded bonds in each ratings class.

Online sources of information
www.stern.nyu.edu/~adamodar/cfin2E/project/data.htm.

PROBLEMS AND QUESTIONS

(In the problems below, you can use a risk premium of 5.5 percent and a tax rate of 40 percent if none is specified.)

1. Plastico, a manufacturer of consumer plastic products, is evaluating its capital structure. The balance sheet of the company is as follows (in millions):

Assets		Liabilities	
Fixed assets	$4,000	Debt	$2,500
Current assets	$1,000	Equity	$2,500

In addition, you are provided the following information:
*   The debt is in the form of long-term bonds, with a coupon rate of 10 percent. The bonds are currently rated AA and are selling at a yield of 12 percent (the market value of the bonds is 80 percent of the face value).
*   The firm currently has 50 million shares outstanding, and the current market price is $80 per share. The firm pays a dividend of $4 per share and has a price/earnings ratio of 10.
*   The stock currently has a beta of 1.2. The Treasury bond rate is 8 percent.
*   The tax rate for this firm is 40 percent.
    a. What is the debt/equity ratio for this firm in book value terms? In market value terms?
    b. What is the debt/(debt + equity) ratio for this firm in book value terms? In market value terms?
    c. What is the firm's after-tax cost of debt?
    d. What is the firm's cost of equity?
    e. What is the firm's current cost of capital?

2. Now assume that Plastico is considering a project that requires an initial investment of $100 million and has the following projected income statement (depreciation for the project is expected to be $5 million a year forever):

EBIT	$20 million
− Interest	$4 million
EBT	$16 million
Taxes	$6.40 million
Net income	$9.60 million

This project is going to be financed at the same debt/equity ratio as the overall firm and is expected to last forever. Assume that there are no principal repayments on the debt (it too is perpetual).
a. Evaluate this project from the equity investors' standpoint. Does it make sense?
b. Evaluate this project from the firm's standpoint. Does it make sense?
c. In general, when would you use the cost of equity as your discount rate/benchmark?
d. In general, when would you use the cost of capital as your benchmark?
e. Assume, for economies of scale, that this project is going to be financed entirely with debt. What would you use as your cost of capital for evaluating this project?

3. Plastico is considering a major change in its capital structure. It has three options:
*   **Option 1** Issue $1 billion in new stock and repurchase half of its outstanding debt. This will make it an AAA-rated firm. (AAA rated debt is yielding 11 percent in the marketplace.)
*   **Option 2** Issue $1 billion in new debt and buy back stock. This will drop its rating to A−. (A− rated debt is yielding 13 percent in the marketplace.)
*   **Option 3** Issue $3 billion in new debt and buy back stock. This will drop its rating to CCC. (CCC rated debt is yielding 18 percent in the marketplace.)
a. What is the cost of equity under each option?
b. What is the after-tax cost of debt under each option?
c. What is the cost of capital under each option?
d. What would happen to (i) the value of the firm; (ii) the value of debt and equity; and (iii) the stock price under each option if you assume rational stockholders?
e. From a cost of capital standpoint, which of the three options would you pick, or would you stay at your current capital structure?

f. What role (if any) would the variability in Plastico's income play in your decision?

g. How would your analysis change (if at all) if the money under the three options were used to take new investments (instead of repurchasing debt or equity)?

h. What other considerations (besides minimizing the cost of capital) would you bring to bear on your decision?

i. Intuitively, why doesn't the higher rating in option 1 translate into a lower cost of capital?

4. Plastico is interested in how it compares with its competitors in the same industry.

	Plastico	Competitors
Debt/equity ratio	50%	25%
Variance in EBITDA	20%	40%
EBITDA/MV of firm	25%	15%
Tax rate	40%	30%
R&D/sales	2%	5%

a. Taking each of these variables, explain at an intuitive level whether you would expect Plastico to have more or less debt than its competitors and why.

b. You have also run a regression of debt/equity ratios against these variables for all the firms on the NYSE and have come up with the following regression equation:

$$D/E = 0.10 - 0.5(\text{Variance in EBITDA})$$
$$+ 2.0(\text{EBITDA/MV})$$
$$+ 0.4(\text{Tax Rate})$$
$$+ 2.5(\text{R\&D/Sales})$$

(All inputs to the regression were in decimals, i.e., 20 percent was input as 0.20.)

Given this cross-sectional relationship, what would you expect Plastico's debt/equity ratio to be?

5. As CEO of a major corporation, you have to make a decision on how much you can afford to borrow. You currently have 10 million shares outstanding, and the market price per share is $50. You also currently have about $200 million in debt outstanding (market value). You are rated as a BBB corporation now.

- Your stock has a beta of 1.5 and the Treasure bond rate is 8 percent.
- Your marginal tax rate is 46 percent.
- You estimate that your rating will change to a B if you borrow $100 million. The BBB rate now is 11 percent. The B rate is 12.5 percent.

a. Given the marginal costs and benefits of borrowing the $100 million, should you go ahead with it?

b. What is your best estimate of the weighted average cost of capital with and without the $100 million in borrowing?

c. If you borrow the $100 million, what will the price per share be after the borrowing?

d. Assume that you have a project that requires an investment of $100 million. It has expected revenues of $50 million and costs of $30 million a year in perpetuity. Is this a desirable project by your criteria? Why or why not?

e. Does it make a difference in your decision if you are told that the cash flows from the project in **d** are certain?

6. You have been hired as a management consultant by AD Corporation to evaluate whether it has an appropriate amount of debt (the company is worried about a leveraged buyout). You have collected the following information on AD's current position:

- There are 100,000 shares outstanding at $20/share. The stock has a beta of 1.15.
- The company has $500,000 in long-term debt outstanding and is currently rated BBB. The current market interest rate is 10 percent on BBB bonds and 6 percent on T-bonds.
- The company's marginal tax rate is 40 percent.

You proceed to collect the data on what increasing debt will do to the company's ratings:

Additional Debt*	New Rating	Interest Rate
$500,000	BB	10.5
$1,000,000	B	11.5
$1,500,000	B−	13.5
$2,000,000	C	15

*In addition to the existing debt of $500,000.

a. How much additional debt should the company take on?

b. What will the price per share be after the company takes on new debt?

c. What is the WACC before and after the additional debt?

d. Assume that you are considering a project that has the following earnings in perpetuity and is of comparable risk to existing projects.

Revenues/year	$1,000,000
Cost of goods sold	$400,000 (includes depreciation of $100,000)
EBIT	$600,000
Debt payments	$100,000 (all interest payments)
Taxable income	$500,000
Tax	$200,000
After-tax profit	$300,000

If this project requires an investment of $3,000,000, what is its NPV?

7. UB is examining its capital structure with the intent of arriving at an optimal debt ratio. It currently has no debt and has a beta of 1.5. The riskless interest rate is 9 percent. Your research indicates that the debt rating will be as follows at different debt levels:

D/(D + E)	Rating	Interest Rate
0%	AAA	10%
10%	AA	10.5%
20%	A	11%
30%	BBB	12%
40%	BB	13%
50%	B	14%
60%	CCC	16%
70%	CC	18%
80%	C	20%
90%	D	25%

The firm currently has 1 million shares outstanding at $20 per share (tax rate = 40 percent).

a. What is the firm's optimal debt ratio?

b. Assuming that the firm restructures by repurchasing stock with debt, what will the value of the stock be after the restructuring?

8. GenCorp, an automotive parts manufacturer, currently has $25 million in outstanding debt and has 10 million shares outstanding. The book value per share is $10, and the market value is $25. The company is currently rated A, its bonds have a yield to maturity of 10 percent, and the current beta of the stock is 1.06. The T-bond rate is 8 percent now, and the company's tax is 40 percent.

a. What is the company's current weighted average cost of capital?

b. The company is considering a repurchase of 4 million shares at $25 per share with new debt. It is estimated that this will push the company's rating down to a B (with a yield to maturity of 13 percent). What will the company's WACC be after the stock repurchase?

9. You have been called in as a consultant for Herbert's, a sporting goods retail firm, which is examining its debt policy. The firm currently has a balance sheet as follows:

Liability		Assets	
Long-term bonds	$100	Fixed assets	$300
Equity	$300	Current assets	$100
Total	$400	Total	$400

The firm's income statement is as follows:

Revenues	$250
Cost of goods sold	$175
Depreciation	$25
EBIT	$50
Long-term interest	$10
EBT	$40
Taxes	$16
Net Income	$24

The firm currently has 100 shares outstanding, selling at a market price of $5 per share and the bonds are selling at par. The firm's current beta is 1.12, and the six-month T-bond rate is 7 percent.

a. What is the firm's current cost of equity?
b. What is the firm's current cost of debt?
c. What is the firm's current weighted average cost of capital?

Assume that management of Herbert's is considering doing a debt-equity swap (i.e., borrowing enough money to buy back seventy shares of stock at $5 per share). It is believed that this swap will lower the firm's rating to C and raise the interest rate on the company's debt to 15 percent.
d. What is the firm's new cost of equity?
e. What is the effective tax rate (for calculating the after-tax cost of debt) after the swap?
f. What is the firm's new cost of capital?

10. Terck, a leading pharmaceutical company, currently has a balance sheet that is as follows:

Liability		Assets	
Long-term bonds	$1.000	Fixed assets	$1,700
Equity	$1.000	Current assets	$300
Total	$1.000	Total	$1,000

The firm's income statement looks as follows:

Revenues	$1,000
Cost of goods sold	$400
Depreciation	$100
EBIT	$500
Long-term interest expense	$100
EBT	$400
Taxes	$200
Net income	$200

The firm's bonds are all twenty-year bonds with a coupon rate of 10 percent that are selling at 90 percent of face value (the yield to maturity on these bonds is 11 percent). The stocks are selling at a P/E ratio of 9 and have a beta of 1.25. The T-bond rate is 6 percent.
a. What is the firm's current cost of equity?
b. What is the firm's current after-tax cost of debt?
c. What is the firm's current weighted average cost of capital?

Assume that management of Terck, which is very conservative, is considering doing an equity-for-debt swap (i.e., issuing $200 more of equity to retire $200 of debt). This action is expected to lower the firm's interest rate by 1 percent.
d. What is the firm's new cost of equity?
e. What is the new WACC?
f. What will the value of the firm be after the swap?

11. You have been asked to analyze the capital structure of DASA, an environmental waste disposal firm, and make recommendations on a future course of action. DASA has 40 million shares outstanding, selling at $20 per share, and a debt/equity ratio (in market value terms) of 0.25. The beta of the stock is 1.15, and the firm currently has a AA rating, with a corresponding market interest rate of 10 percent. The firm's income statement is as follows:

EBIT	$150 million
Interest expenses	$20 million
Taxable income	$130 million
Taxes	$52 million
Net income	$78 million

The current T-bond rate is 8 percent.
a. What is the firm's current WACC?
b. The firm is proposing borrowing an additional $200 million in debt and repurchasing stock. If it does so, its rating will decline to A, with a market interest rate of 11 percent. What will the WACC be if they make this move?
c. What will the new stock price be if the firm borrows $200 million and repurchases stock (assuming rational investors)?
d. Now assume that the firm has another option to raise its debt/equity ratio (instead of borrowing money and repurchasing stock). It has considerable capital expenditures planned for the next year ($150 million). The company also currently pays $1 in dividends per share. If the company finances all its capital expenditures with debt and doubles its *dividend yield* from the current level for the next year, what would you expect the debt/equity ratio to be at the end of the next year?

12. You have been asked by JJ Corporation, a California-based firm that manufacturers and services digital satellite TV systems, to evaluate its capital structure. They currently have 70 million shares outstanding trading at $10 per share. In addition, the company has 500,000 convertible bonds, with a coupon rate of 8 percent, trading at $1000 per bond. JJ is rated BBB and the interest rate on BBB straight bonds is currently 10 percent. The beta for the company is 1.2, and the current risk-free rate is 6 percent. The tax rate is 40 percent.

    a. What is the firm's current debt/equity ratio?
    b. What is the firm's current weighted average cost of capital?

    JJ Corporation is proposing to borrow $250 million and use it for the following purposes:

    - Buy back $100 million worth of stock.
    - Pay $100 million in dividends.
    - Invest $50 million in a project with a NPV of $25 million.

    The effect of this additional borrowing will be a drop in the bond rating to B, which currently carries an interest rate of 11 percent.

    c. What will the firm's cost of equity be after this additional borrowing?
    d. What will the firm's weighted average cost of capital be after this additional borrowing?
    e. What will the value of the firm be after this additional borrowing?

13. Pfizer, one of the largest pharmaceutical companies in the United States, is considering what its debt capacity is. In March 1995, Pfizer had an outstanding market value of equity of $24.27 billion, debt of $2.8 billion, and a AAA rating. Its beta was 1.47, and it faced a marginal corporate tax rate of 40 percent. The Treasury bond rate at the time of the analysis was 6.50 percent, and AAA bonds trade at a spread of 0.30 percent over the treasury rate.

    a. Estimate the current cost of capital for Pfizer.
    b. It is estimated that Pfizer will have a BBB rating if it moves to a 30 percent debt ratio and that BBB bonds have a spread of 2 percent over the Treasury rate. Estimate the cost of capital if Pfizer moves to its optimal.
    c. Assuming a constant growth rate of 6 percent in the firm value, how much will firm value change if Pfizer moves its optimal? What will the effect be on the stock price?

    d. Pfizer has considerable R&D expenses. Will this fact affect whether Pfizer takes on the additional debt?

14. Upjohn, another major pharmaceutical company, is also considering whether it should borrow more. It has $664 million in book value of debt outstanding and 173 million shares outstanding at $30.75 per share. The company has a beta of 1.17, and faces a tax rate of 36 percent. The Treasury bond rate is 6.50 percent.

    a. If the interest expense on the debt is $55 million, the debt has an average maturity of ten years, and the company is currently rated AA– (with a market interest rate of 7.50 percent), estimate the market value of the debt.
    b. Estimate the current cost of capital.
    c. It is estimated that if Upjohn moves to its optimal debt ratio, and no growth in firm value is assumed, the value per share will increase by $1.25. Estimate the cost of capital at the optimal debt ratio.

15. Bethlehem Steel, one of the oldest and largest steel companies in the United States, is considering the question of whether it has any excess debt capacity. The firm has $527 million in market value of debt outstanding and $1.76 billion in market value of equity. The firm has earnings before interest and taxes of $131 million and faces a corporate tax rate of 36 percent. The company's bonds are rated BBB, and the cost of debt is 8 percent. At this rating, the firm has a probability of default of 2.30 percent, and the cost of bankruptcy is expected to be 30 percent of firm value.

    a. Estimate the unlevered value of the firm.
    b. Estimate the levered value of the firm, using the APV approach, at a debt ratio of 50 percent. At that debt ratio, the firm's bond rating will be CCC, and the probability of default will increase to 46.61 percent.

16. Kansas City Southern, a railroad company, had debt outstanding of $985 million and 40 million shares trading at $46.25 per share in March 1995. It earned $203 million in EBIT, and faced a marginal tax rate of 36.56 percent. The firm was interested in estimating its optimal leverage using the APV approach. The following table summarizes the estimated bond ratings and probabilities of default at each level of debt from 0 percent to 90 percent.

Debt Ratio	Bond Rating	Probability of Default
0%	AAA	0.28%
10%	AAA	0.28%
20%	A−	1.41%
30%	BB	12.20%
40%	B−	32.50%
50%	CCC	46.61%
60%	CC	65.00%
70%	C	80.00%
80%	C	80.00%
90%	D	100.00%

The direct and indirect bankruptcy costs are estimated to be 25 percent of the firm value. Estimate the optimal debt ratio of the firm, based on levered firm value.

17. In 1995, an analysis of the capital structure of Reebok provided the following results on the WACC and firm value.

	Actual	Optimal	Change
Debt ratio	4.42%	60.00%	55.58%
Beta for the stock	1.95	3.69	1.74
Cost of equity	18.61%	28.16%	9.56%
Bond rating	A−	B+	
After-tax cost of debt	5.92%	6.87%	0.95%
WACC	18.04%	15.38%	−2.66%
Firm value (with no growth)	$3,343 million	$3,921 million	$578 million
Stock price	$39.50	$46.64	$7.14

This analysis was based on the 1995 EBIT of $420 million and a tax rate of 36.90 percent.

a. Why is the optimal debt ratio for Reebok so high?

b. What might be some of your concerns in moving to this optimal?

18. You are trying to evaluate whether United Airlines (UAL) has any excess debt capacity. In 1995, UAL had 12.2 million shares outstanding at $210 per share and debt outstanding of approximately $3 billion (book as well as market value). The debt had a rating of B, and carried a market interest rate of 10.12 percent. In addition, the firm had leases outstanding, with annual lease payments anticipated to by $150 million. The beta of the stock is 1.26, and the firm faces a tax rate of 35 percent. The treasury bond rate is 6.12 percent.

a. Estimate the current debt ratio for UAL.

b. Estimate the current cost of capital.

c. Based on 1995 operating income, the optimal debt ratio is computed to be 30 percent, at which point the rating will be BBB, and the market interest rate is 8.12 percent. Estimate the change in firm value from going to the optimal.

d. Would the fact that 1995 operating income for airlines was depressed alter your analysis in any way? Explain why.

19. Intel has an EBIT of $3.4 billion and faces a marginal tax rate of 36.50 percent. It currently has $1.5 billion in debt outstanding, and a market value of equity of $51 billion. The beta for the stock is 1.35, and the pretax cost of debt is 6.80 percent. The Treasury bond rate is 6 percent. Assume that the firm is considering a massive increase in leverage to a 70 percent debt ratio, at which level the bond rating will be C (with a pretax interest rate of 16 percent).

a. Estimate the current cost of capital.

b. Assuming that all debt gets refinanced at the new market interest rate, what would your interest expenses be at 70 percent debt? Would you be able to get the entire tax benefit? Why or why not?

c. Estimate the beta of the stock at 70 percent debt, using the conventional levered beta calculation. Reestimate the beta, on the assumption that C rated debt has a beta of 0.60. Which one would you use in your cost of capital calculation?

d. Estimate the cost of capital at 70 percent debt.

e. What will happen to firm value if Intel moves to a 70 percent debt ratio?

f. What general lessons on capital structure would you draw for other growth firms?

20. NYNEX, the phone utility for the New York City area, has approached you for advice on its capital structure. In 1995, NYNEX had debt outstanding of $12.14 billion and equity outstanding of $20.55 billion. The firm had an EBIT of $1.7 billion and faced a corporate tax rate of 36 percent. The beta for the stock is 0.84, and the bonds are rated A– (with a market interest rate of 7.5 percent). The probability of default for A– rated bonds is 1.41 percent, and the bankruptcy cost is estimated to be 30 percent of firm value.

a. Estimate the unlevered value of the firm.

b. Value the firm, if it increases its debt ratio to 50 percent. At that debt ratio, its bond rating would be BBB and the probability of default would be 2.30 percent.

c. Assume now that NYNEX is considering a move into entertainment, which is likely to be both more profitable and riskier than the phone business. What changes would you expect in the optimal leverage?

21. A small, private firm has approached you for advice on its capital structure decision. It is in the specialty retailing business, and it had an EBIT last year of $500,000.

- The book value of equity is $1.5 million, but the estimated market value is $6 million.
- The firm has $1 million in debt outstanding and paid an interest expense of $80,000 on the debt last year. (Based on the interest coverage ratio, the firm would be rated AA, and would be facing an interest rate of 8.25 percent. The risk-free rate is 7 percent.)
- The equity is not traded, but the average beta for comparable traded firms is 1.05, and their average debt/equity ratio is 25 percent.

a. Estimate the current cost of capital for this firm.

b. Assume now that this firm doubles it debt from $1 million to $2 million and that the interest rate at which it can borrow increases to 9 percent. Estimate the new cost of capital and the effect on firm value.

c. You also have a regression that you have run of debt ratios of publicly traded firms against firm characteristics:

$$DBTFR = 0.15 + 1.05 \, (EBIT/Firm \; Value) - 0.10 \, (Beta)$$

Estimate the debt ratio for the private firm, based on this regression.

d. What are some of the concerns you might have in extending the approaches used by large publicly traded firms to estimate optimal leverage to smaller firms?

22. XCV Inc., which manufactures automobile parts for assembly, is considering the costs and the benefits of leverage. The CFO notes that the return on equity of the firm, which is only 12.75 percent now based on the current policy of no leverage, could be increased substantially by borrowing money. Is this true? Does it follow that the value of the firm will increase with leverage? Why or why not?

CHAPTER 9

CAPITAL STRUCTURE: THE FINANCING DETAILS

In Chapter 7, we looked at the wide range of choices available to firms to raise capital. In Chapter 8, we developed the tools needed to estimate the optimal debt ratio for a firm. Here we discuss how firms can use this information to choose the mix of debt and equity they use to finance investments and the financing instruments they can employ to reach that mix.

We begin by examining whether, having identified an optimal debt ratio, firms should move to that debt ratio from current levels. A variety of concerns may lead a firm not to use its excess debt capacity if it is underlevered, or to lower its debt if it is overlevered. A firm that decides to move from its current debt level to its optimal financing mix has two decisions to make. First, it has to consider how quickly it

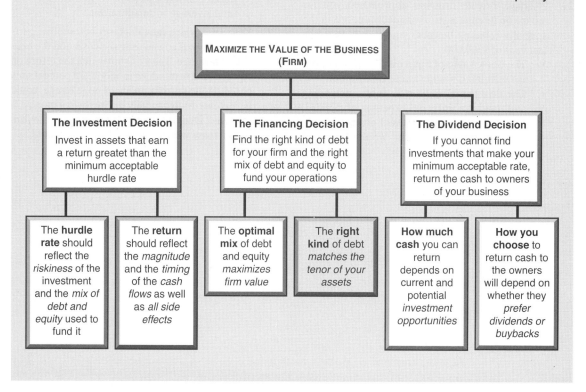

wants to move. The degree of urgency will vary widely across firms, depending on how much of a threat they perceive from being under- (or over-) levered. The second decision is whether to increase (or decrease) the debt ratio by recapitalizing investments, divesting assets and using the cash to reduce debt or equity, investing in new projects with debt or equity, or changing dividend policy.

In the second part of this chapter, we will consider how firms should choose the right financing vehicle for raising capital for their investments. We argue that a firm's choice of financing should be determined largely by the nature of the cash flows on its assets. Matching financing choices to asset characteristics decreases default risk for any given level of debt and allows the firm to borrow more. We then consider a number of real-world concerns including tax law, the views of ratings agencies, and information effects that might lead firms to modify their financing choices.

A FRAMEWORK FOR CAPITAL STRUCTURE CHANGES

A firm whose actual debt ratio is very different from its optimal has several choices to make. First, it has to decide *whether to move toward the optimal or to preserve the status quo*. Second, once it decides to move toward the optimal, the firm has to choose *between changing its leverage quickly or moving more deliberately*. This decision may also be governed by pressure from external sources, such as impatient stockholders or bond ratings agency concerns. Third, if the firm decides to move gradually to the optimal, it has to decide whether to use new financing *to invest in new projects,* or to shift its *financing mix on existing projects*.

In the previous chapter, we presented the rationale for moving toward the optimal in terms of the value that could be gained for stockholders by doing so. Conversely, the cost of preserving the status quo is that this potential value increment is lost. Although managers nominally make this decision of whether to move toward their optimal debt ratios, they will often find themselves under some pressure from stockholders if they are underlevered, or under threat of bankruptcy if they are overlevered, to move toward their optimal debt ratios.

IMMEDIATE OR GRADUAL CHANGE

In Chapter 7 we discussed the trade-off between using debt and using equity. In Chapter 8, we developed a number of approaches used to determine the optimal financing mix for a firm. The next logical step, it would seem, is for firms to move to this optimal mix. In this section, we will first consider what might lead some firms not to make this move; we follow up by looking at some of the subsequent decisions that changing the mix requires.

No Change, Gradual Change, or Immediate Change

We have implicitly assumed that firms that have debt ratios different from their optimal debt ratios, once made aware of this gap, will want to move to the optimal ratios. That does not always turn out to be the case. There are a number of firms that are underlevered, using any of the approaches described in the last section, but choose not to use their excess debt capacity. Conversely, there are a number of firms with too much debt that choose not to pay it down. At the other extreme are firms that shift their financing mix overnight to reflect the optimal mix. In this section, we look at the factors a firm might have to consider in deciding whether to leave its debt ratio unchanged, change gradually, or change immediately to the optimal mix.

To Change or Not to Change

Firms that are under- or overlevered might choose not to move to their optimal debt ratios for a number of reasons. Given our identification of the optimal debt ratio as the mix at which firm value is maximized, this inaction may seem not only irrational but value-destroying for stockholders. In some cases, it is. In some cases, however, not moving to the optimal may be consistent with value maximization.

Let's consider underlevered firms first. The first reason a firm may choose not to move to its optimal debt ratio is that it does not view its objective as maximizing firm value. If the objective of a firm is to maximize net income or maintain a high bond rating, having less debt is more desirable than having more. Stockholders should clearly take issue with managers who avoid borrowing because they have an alternative objective and force them to justify their use of the objective.

Even when firms agree on firm value maximization as the objective, there are a number of reasons why underlevered firms may choose not to use their excess debt capacity.

- When firms borrow, the debt usually comes with covenants that restrict what the firm can do in the future. Firms that value flexibility may choose not to use their excess debt capacity.

- The flexibility argument can also be extended to cover future financing requirements. Firms that are uncertain about future financing needs may want to preserve excess debt capacity to cover these needs.

- In closely held or private firms, the likelihood of bankruptcy that comes with debt may be weighted disproportionately in making the decision to borrow.[1]

These are all viable reasons for not using excess debt capacity, and they may be consistent with value maximization. We should, however, put these reasons to the financial test. For instance, we estimated in Illustration 7.3 that the value of Disney as a firm will increase almost $3 billion if it moves to its optimal debt ratio. If the reason given by the firm's management for not using excess debt capacity is the need for financing flexibility, the value of this flexibility has to be greater than $3 billion.

Firms that have too much debt, relative to their optimal level, should have a fairly strong incentive to try reducing it. Here again, there might be reasons why a firm

---

[1]We do consider the likelihood of default in all the approaches described in the last chapter. However, this consideration does not allow for the fact that cost of default may vary widely across firms. The manager of a publicly traded firm may lose his or her job in the event of default, whereas the owner of a private business may lose both wealth and reputation if he or she goes bankrupt.

may choose not to take this path. The primary fear of overlevered firms is bankruptcy. If the government makes a practice of shielding firms from the costs associated with default, by either bailing out those that default on their debt or backing up the loans made to them by banks, firms may choose to remain overlevered. This would explain why Korean firms, which looked overlevered using any financial yardstick in the 1990s, did nothing to reduce their debt ratios until the government guarantee collapsed.

IN PRACTICE: VALUING FINANCIAL FLEXIBILITY AS AN OPTION

If we assume unlimited and costless access to capital markets, a firm will always be able to fund a good project by raising new capital. If, on the other hand, we assume that there are internal or external constraints on raising new capital, financial flexibility can be valuable. To value this flexibility as an option, assume that a firm has expectations about how much it will need to reinvest in future periods based on its own past history and current conditions in the industry. Assume also that a firm has expectations about how much it can raise from internal funds and its normal access to capital markets in future periods. There is uncertainty about future reinvestment needs; for simplicity, we will assume that the capacity to generate funds is known with certainty to the firm. The advantage (and value) of having excess debt capacity or large cash balances is that the firm can meet any reinvestment needs, in excess of funds available, using its debt capacity. The payoff from these projects, however, comes from the excess returns the firm expects to make on them.

With this framework, we can specify the types of firms that will value financial flexibility the most.

a. ***Access to capital markets***   Firms with limited access to capital markets—private businesses, emerging market companies, and small market cap companies—should value financial flexibility more that those with wider access to capital.

b. ***Project quality***   The value of financial flexibility accrues not just from the fact that excess debt capacity can be used to fund projects but from the excess returns that these projects earn. Firms in mature and competitive businesses, where excess returns are close to zero, should value financial flexibility less than firms with substantial competitive advantages and high excess returns.

c. ***Uncertainty about future investment needs***   Firms that can forecast their reinvestment needs with certainty do not need to maintain excess debt capacity because they can plan to raise capital well in advance. Firms in volatile businesses where investment needs can shift dramatically from period to period will value financial flexibility more.

The bottom line is that firms that value financial flexibility more should be given more leeway to operate with debt ratios below their theoretical optimal debt ratios (where the cost of capital is minimized). ∎

Gradual versus Immediate Change

Many firms attempt to move to their optimal debt ratios, either gradually over time or immediately. The advantage of an immediate shift to the optimal debt ratio is that the firm receives the benefits of the optimal leverage concurrently, which include a lower cost of capital and a higher value. The disadvantage of a sudden change in leverage is that it abruptly changes both the way managers make decisions and the environment in which these decisions are made. If the optimal debt ratio has been incorrectly estimated, a sudden change may also increase the risk that the firm has to backtrack and reverse its financing decisions. To illustrate, assume that a firm's optimal debt ratio has been calculated to be 40 percent and the firm moves to this optimal from its current debt ratio of 10 percent. A few months later, the firm discovers that its optimal debt ratio is really 30 percent. It will then have to repay some of the debt it has taken on to get back to the optimal leverage.

Gradual versus Immediate Change for Underlevered Firms
For underlevered firms, the decision to increase the debt ratio to the optimal either quickly or gradually is determined by four factors:

1. *Degree of Confidence in the Optimal Leverage Estimate*   The greater the possible error in the estimate of optimal debt ratio, the more likely the firm will choose to move gradually to the optimal.

2. *Comparability to Industry*   When the optimal debt ratio for a firm differs markedly from that of the industry to which the firm belongs, analysts and ratings agencies might not look favorably on the change, and the firm is much less likely to shift to the optimal quickly.

3. *Likelihood of a Takeover*   Empirical studies of the characteristics of target firms in acquisitions have noted that underlevered firms are much more likely to be acquired than are overlevered firms.[2] Often, the acquisition is financed at least partially by the target firm's unused debt capacity. Consequently, firms with excess debt capacity that delay borrowing run the risk of being taken over. The greater this risk, the more likely the firm will choose to take on additional debt quickly. Several additional factors may determine the likelihood of a takeover. One is the prevalence of antitakeover laws (at the state level) and amendments to the corporate charter designed specifically to prevent hostile acquisitions. Another is the size of the firm. Because raising financing for an acquisition is far more difficult when acquiring a $100 billion firm than a $1 billion firm, larger firms may feel more protected from the threat of hostile takeovers. The third factor is the extent of holdings by insiders and managers in the company. Insiders and managers with substantial stakes may be able to prevent hostile acquisitions. The final factor is the stock price performance of the firm; stockholders in firms whose stock prices have dropped significantly over time tend to be much more receptive to the entreaties of hostile acquirers.

4. *Need for Financial Flexibility*   On occasion, firms may require excess debt capacity to meet unanticipated needs for funds, either to maintain existing projects or to invest in new ones. Firms that need and value this flexibility will be

---

[2]See K. Palepu, 1986, "Predicting Takeover Targets: A Methodological and Empirical Analysis," *Journal of Accounting and Economics,* 5, 3–35. He notes that one of the variables that seems to predict a takeover is a low debt ratio in conjunction with poor operating performance.

less likely to shift quickly to their optimal debt ratios and use up their excess debt capacity.

9.1 INSIDER HOLDINGS AND LEVERAGE

Closely held firms (where managers and insiders hold a substantial portion of the outstanding stock) are less likely to increase leverage quickly than firms with widely dispersed stockholdings.

☐ True

☐ False

Explain.

ILLUSTRATION 9.1 Debt Capacity and Takeovers

The Disney acquisition of Capital Cities in 1996, although a friendly acquisition, illustrates some of advantages to the acquiring firm of acquiring an underlevered firm. At the time of the acquisition, Capital Cities had $657 million in debt and 154.06 million shares outstanding, trading at $100 per share. Its market value debt to capital ratio was only 4.07 percent. With a beta of 0.95, a borrowing rate of 7.70 percent, and a corporate tax rate of 43.50 percent, this yielded a cost of capital of 11.90 percent. (The Treasury bond rate at the time of the analysis was 7 percent and the market risk premium was 5.50 percent.)

Cost of Capital

    = Cost of Equity[Equity/(Debt + Equity)]

      + Cost of Debt[Debt/(Debt + Equity)]

    = 12.23% [15,406/(15,406 + 657)] + 7.70% (1 − 0.435)[657/(15,406 + 657)]

    = 11.90%

Table 9.1 summarizes the costs of equity, debt, and capital, as well as the estimated firm values and stock prices at different debt ratios for Capital Cities.

Note that the firm value is maximized at a debt ratio of 30 percent, leading to an increase in the stock price of $23.69 over the market price of $100.

Table 9.1   COSTS OF FINANCING, FIRM VALUE, AND DEBT RATIOS: CAPITAL CITIES

Debt Ratio	Beta	Cost of Equity	Interest Coverage Ratio	Bond Rating	Interest Rate	Cost of Debt	Cost of Capital	Firm Value (in Millions)	Stock Price
0.00%	0.93	12.10%	∞	AAA	7.30%	4.12%	12.10%	$15,507	$96.41
10.00%	0.99	12.42%	10.73	AAA	7.30%	4.12%	11.59%	$17,007	$106.15
20.00%	1.06	12.82%	4.75	A	8.25%	4.66%	11.19%	$18,399	$115.19
30.00%	1.15	13.34%	2.90	BBB	9.00%	5.09%	10.86%	$19,708	$123.69
40.00%	1.28	14.02%	1.78	B	11.00%	6.22%	10.90%	$19,546	$122.63
50.00%	1.45	14.99%	1.21	CCC	13.00%	7.35%	11.17%	$18,496	$115.81
60.00%	1.71	16.43%	1.00	CCC	13.00%	7.35%	10.98%	$19,228	$120.57
70.00%	2.37	20.01%	0.77	CC	14.50%	9.63%	12.74%	$13,939	$86.23
80.00%	3.65	27.08%	0.61	C	16.00%	11.74%	14.81%	$10,449	$63.58
90.00%	7.30	47.16%	0.54	C	16.00%	12.21%	15.71%	$9,391	$56.71

Although debt capacity was never stated as a reason for the acquisition of Capital Cities, Disney borrowed about $10 billion for this acquisition and paid $125 per share. Capital Cities' stockholders could well have achieved the same premium if management had borrowed the money and repurchased stock. Although Capital Cities stockholders did not lose as a result of the acquisition, they would have (at least based on our numbers) if Disney had paid a smaller premium on the acquisition.

Gradual versus Immediate Change for Overlevered Firms
Firms that are overlevered also have to decide whether they should shift gradually or immediately to the optimal debt ratios. As in the case of underlevered firms, the precision of the estimate of the optimal leverage will play a role, with more precise estimates leading to quicker adjustments. So will comparability to other firms in the sector. When most or all of the firms in a sector become overlevered, as was the case with the telecommunications sector in the late 1990s, firms seem to feel little urgency to reduce their debt ratios, even though they might be struggling to make their payments. In contrast, the pressure to reduce debt is much greater when a firm has a high debt ratio in a sector where most firms have lower debt ratios.

The other factor, in the case of overlevered firms, is the possibility of default. Thus, the greater the chance of bankruptcy, the more likely the firm is to move quickly to reduce debt and move to its optimal. How can we assess the probability of default? If firms are rated, their bond ratings offer a simple measure of default risk. A firm with a below investment grade rating (below BBB) has a significant probability of default. Even if firms are not rated, we can use their synthetic ratings (based on interest coverage ratios) to come to the same conclusion.

9.2 Indirect Bankruptcy Costs and Leverage

In Chapter 7, we talked about indirect bankruptcy costs, where the perception of default risk affected sales and profits. Assume that a firm with substantial indirect bankruptcy costs has too much debt. Is the urgency to get back to an optimal debt ratio for this firm greater than or lesser than it is for a firm without such costs?

☐ Greater

☐ Lesser

Explain.

Implementing Changes in Financial Mix

A firm that decides to change its financing mix has several alternatives. In this section, we begin by considering the details of each of these alternatives to changing the financing mix, and we conclude by looking at how firms can choose the right approach for themselves.

Ways of Changing the Financing Mix

There are four basic paths available to a firm that wants to change its financing mix. One is to change the financing mix on current projects using new equity to retire debt or new debt to reduce equity; this is called *recapitalization*. The second path is to sell assets and use the proceeds to pay off debt, if the objective is to reduce the debt ratio, or to buy back stock or pay dividends to reduce equity, if the objective is to increase the debt ratio. The third is to use a disproportionately high debt or equity ratio, relative to the firm's current ratios, to finance new investments over time. The fourth option is to change the proportion of earnings that a firm returns to its stockholders in higher form of dividends or by buying back stock. As this proportion changes, the debt ratio will also change over time.

Recapitalization

The simplest and often the quickest way to change a firm's financial mix is to change the way existing investments are financed. Thus, an underlevered firm can increase its debt ratio by borrowing money and buying back stock or replacing equity with debt of equal market value.

- *Borrowing money and buying back stock (or paying a large dividend)* increases the debt ratio because the borrowing increases the debt, whereas the equity repurchase or dividend payment concurrently reduces the equity; the former accomplishes this by reducing the number of shares outstanding and the latter by lowering the stock price. Many companies have used this approach to increase leverage quickly, largely in response to takeover attempts. For example, in 1985, to stave off a hostile takeover, Atlantic Richfield borrowed $4 billion and repurchased stock to increase its debt to capital ratio from 12 percent to 34 percent.[3]

- In a **debt-for-equity swap,** a firm replaces equity with debt of equivalent market value by swapping the two securities. Here again, the simultaneous increase in debt and the decrease in equity causes the debt ratio to increase substantially. In many cases, firms offer equity investors a combination of cash and debt in lieu of equity. In 1986, for example, Owens Corning gave redeeming stockholders $52 in cash and debt with a face value of $35, for each outstanding share, thereby increasing its debt and reducing equity.

In each of these cases, the firm may be restricted by bond covenants that explicitly prohibit these actions or impose large penalties on the firm. The firm will have to weigh these restrictions against the benefits of the higher leverage and the increased value that flows from it. A recapitalization designed to increase the debt ratio substantially is called a *leveraged recapitalization,* and many of these recapitalizations are motivated by a desire to prevent a hostile takeover.[4]

Though it is far less common, firms that want to lower their debt ratios can adopt a similar strategy. An overlevered firm can attempt to *renegotiate debt agreements* and try to convince some of the lenders to take an equity stake in the firm in lieu of some or all of their debt in the firm. It can also try to get lenders to offer more generous terms, including longer maturities and lower interest rates. Finally, the firm can issue new

---

[3]The stock buyback increased the stock price and took away a significant rationale for the acquisition.

[4]An examination of twenty-eight recapitalizations between 1985 and 1988 indicates that all but five were motivated by the threat of hostile takeovers.

equity and use it pay off some of the outstanding debt. The best bargaining chip such a firm possesses is the possibility of default, because default creates substantial losses for lenders. In the late 1980s, for example, many U.S. banks were forced to trade in their Latin American debt for equity stakes or receive little or nothing on their loans.

Debt-for-Equity Swaps: A voluntary exchange of outstanding equity for debt of equal market value.

Divestiture and Use of Proceeds

Firms can also change their debt ratios by selling assets and using the cash they receive from the divestiture to reduce debt or equity. Thus an underlevered firm can sell some of its assets and use the proceeds to repurchase stock or pay a large dividend. Although this action reduces the equity outstanding at the firm, it will increase the debt ratio of the firm only if the firm already has some debt outstanding. An overlevered firm may choose to sell assets and use the proceeds to retire some of the outstanding debt and reduce its debt ratio.

If a firm chooses this path, the choice of which assets to divest is critical. Firms usually want to divest themselves of investments that are earning less than their required returns, but that cannot be the overriding consideration in this decision. The key question is whether there are potential buyers for the asset who are willing to pay fair value or more for it, where the fair value measures how much the asset is worth to the firm, based on its expected cash flows.

9.3 Asset Sales to Reduce Leverage

Assume that a firm has decided to sell assets to pay off its debt. In deciding which assets to sell, the firm should

☐ sell its worst performing assets to raise the cash.

☐ sell its best performing assets to raise the cash.

☐ sell its most liquid assets to raise the cash.

☐ none of the above (specify the alternative).

Explain.

Financing New Investments

Firms also change their debt ratios by financing new investments disproportionately with debt or equity. If they use a much higher proportion of debt in financing new investments than their current debt ratio, they will increase their debt ratios. Conversely, if they use a much higher proportion of equity in financing new investments than their existing equity ratio, they will decrease their debt ratios.

There are two key differences between this approach and the previous two. First, because new investments are spread out over time, the debt ratio will adjust gradually over the period. Second, the process of investing in new assets will increase both the firm value and the dollar debt that goes with any debt ratio. For instance, if Disney decides to increase its debt ratio to 30 percent and proposes to do so by investing in a new theme park, the value of the firm will increase from the existing level to reflect the new assets created by the investment.

Changing Dividend Payout

We will not be considering dividend policy in detail until the next chapter, but we will mention here that a firm can change its debt ratio over time by changing the proportion of its earnings that it returns to stockholders in each period. Increasing the proportion of earnings paid out in dividends (the dividend payout ratio) or buying back stock each period will increase the debt ratio for two reasons. First, the payment of the dividend or buying back stock will reduce the equity in the firm;[5] holding debt constant will increase the debt ratio. Second, paying out more of the earnings to stockholders increases the need for external financing to fund new investments; if firms fill this need with new debt, the debt ratio will be increased even further. Decreasing the proportion of earnings returned to stockholders will have the opposite effects.

Firms that choose this route have to recognize that debt ratios will change gradually over time. In fact, the value of equity in a firm can be expected to increase each period by the expected price appreciation rate. This rate can be obtained from the cost of equity, after netting out the expected portion of the return that will come from dividends. This portion is estimated with the dividend yield, which measures the expected dollar dividend as a percent of the current stock price:

$$\text{Expected Price Appreciation} = \text{Cost of Equity} - \text{Expected Dividend Yield}$$

To illustrate, in 2004 Disney had a cost of equity of 10.00 percent and an expected dollar dividend per share of $0.21. Based on the stock price of $26.91, the expected price appreciation can be computed:

$$\text{Expected Price Appreciation}_{\text{Disney}} = 10.00\% - (\$0.21/\$26.91) = 9.22\%$$

Disney's market value of equity can be expected to increase 9.22 percent next period. The dollar debt would have to increase by more than that amount for the debt ratio to increase.

9.4   Dollar Debt versus Debt Ratio

Assume that a firm worth $1 billion has no debt and needs to get to a 20 percent debt ratio. How much would the firm need to borrow if it wants to buy back stock?

☐ $200 million

☐ $250 million

☐ $260 million

☐ $160 million

How much would it need to borrow if it were planning to invest in new projects (with zero NPV)? What if the projects had an NPV of $50 million?

Choosing between the Alternatives

Given the choice between recapitalizing, divesting, financing new investments, and changing dividend payout, how can a firm choose the right way to change debt ratios?

---

[5]The payment of dividends takes cash out of the firm and puts it in the hands of stockholders. The firm has to become less valuable as a result of the action. The stock price reflects this effect.

The choice will be determined by three factors. The first is the *urgency with which the firm is trying to move to its optimal debt ratio*. Recapitalizations and divestitures can be accomplished in a few weeks and can change debt ratios significantly. Financing new investments or changing dividend payout, on the other hand, is a long-term strategy to change debt ratios. Thus, a firm that needs to change its debt ratio quickly—because it is either under threat of a hostile takeover or faces imminent default—is more likely to recapitalize or divest assets.

The second factor is the *quality of new investments*. In the earlier chapters on investment analysis, we defined a good investment as one that earns a positive NPV and a return greater than its hurdle rate. Firms with good investments will gain more by financing these new investments with new debt if the firm is underlevered, or with new equity if the firm is overlevered. Not only will the firm value increase by the value gain we computed in Chapter 8, based on the change in the cost of capital, but the positive NPV of the project will also accrue to the firm. On the other hand, using excess debt capacity or new equity to invest in poor projects is a bad strategy because the projects will destroy value.

The final consideration is the *marketability of existing investments*. Two considerations go into marketability. One is whether existing investments earn excess returns; firms are often more willing to divest themselves of assets that are earning less than the required return. The other (and in our view the more important) consideration is whether divesting these assets will generate a price high enough to compensate the firm for the cash flows lost by selling them. Ironically, firms often find that their best investments are more likely to meet the second criterion than their worst investments.

We summarize our conclusions about the right route to follow to the optimal, based on all these determinants, in Table 9.2.

We also summarize our discussion of whether a firm should shift to its financing mix quickly or gradually, as well as the question of how to make this shift, in Figure 9.1.

Table 9.2	OPTIMAL ROUTE TO FINANCING MIX			
Desired Speed of Adjustment	**Marketability of Existing Investments**	**Quality of New Investments**	**Optimal Route to Increasing Debt Ratio**	**Optimal Route to Decreasing Debt Ratio**
Urgent	Poor	Poor	Recapitalize; borrow money and buy back stock	Recapitalize; issue equity and pay off debt
Urgent	Good	Good	Divest assets and buy back stock; finance new investments with debt	Divest assets and retire debt; finance new investments with equity
Urgent	Good	Poor	Divest and buy back stock	Divest and retire debt
Gradual	Neutral or poor	Neutral or poor	Increase payout to stockholders	Retire debt each year using earnings
Gradual	Good	Neutral or poor	Divest and increase payout to stockholders	Divest and retire debt over time
Gradual	Neutral or poor	Good	Finance new investments with debt	Finance new investments with equity

Figure 9.1   A Framework for Changing Debt Ratios

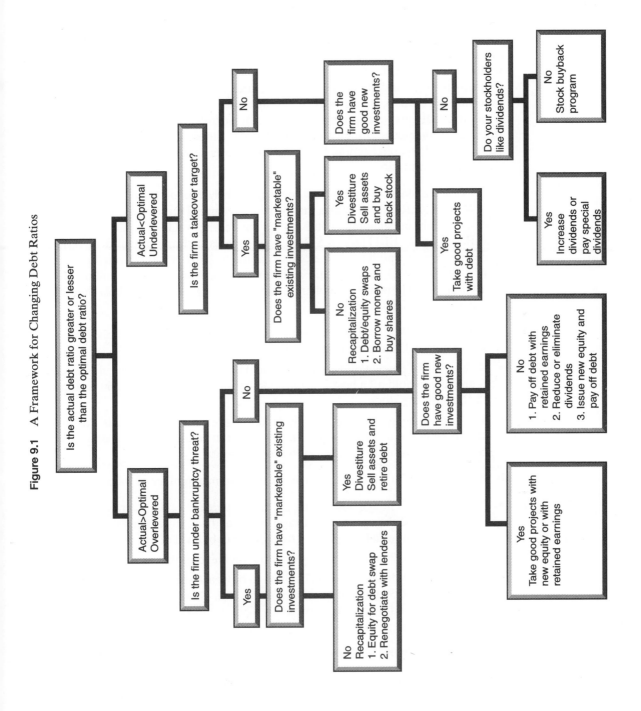

Although we have presented this choice in stark terms, where firms decide to use one or another of the four alternatives described, a combination of actions may be what is needed to get a firm to its desired debt ratio. This is especially likely when the firm is large and the change in debt ratio is significant. In the illustrations following this section, we consider three companies. The first, Nichols Research, is a small firm that gets to its optimal debt ratio by borrowing money and buying back stock. The other two, Disney and Time Warner, choose a combination of new investments and recapitalization, Disney to increase its debt ratio and Time Warner to decrease its debt ratio.

ILLUSTRATION 9.2   Increasing Financial Leverage Quickly: Nichols Research

In 1994, Nichols Research, a firm that provides technical services to the defense industry, had debt outstanding of $6.8 million and market value of equity of $120 million. Based on its EBITDA of $12 million, Nichols had an optimal debt ratio of 30 percent, which would lower the cost of capital to 12.07 percent (from the current cost of capital of 13 percent) and increase the firm value to $146 million (from $126.8 million). There are a number of reasons for arguing that Nichols should increase its leverage quickly:

- Its small size, in conjunction with its low leverage and large cash balance ($25.3 million), make it a prime target for an acquisition.

- Although 17.6 percent of the shares are held by owners and directors, this amount is unlikely to hold off a hostile acquisition because institutions own 60 percent of the outstanding stock.

- The firm has been reporting steadily decreasing returns on its projects, due to the shrinkage in the defense budget. In 1994, the return on capital was only 10 percent, which was much lower than the cost of capital.

If Nichols decides to increase leverage, it can do so in a number of ways:

- It can borrow enough money to get to 30 percent of its overall firm value ($146 million at the optimal debt ratio) and buy back stock. This would require $37 million in new debt to get to a total dollar debt level of $44 million.

- It can borrow $37 million and pay a special dividend of that amount.

- It can use the cash balance of $25 million to buy back stock or pay dividends, and increase debt to 30 percent of the remaining firm value (30 percent of $121 million).[6] This would require approximately $29.5 million in new debt, which can be used to buy back stock.[7]

ILLUSTRATION 9.3   Charting a Framework for Increasing Leverage: Disney (Before Comcast Hostile Bid)

Reviewing the capital structure analysis done for Disney in Chapter 8, we see that it had a debt ratio of approximately 21 percent in early 2004, with $14.7 billion in debt

---

[6]We assume that the optimal debt ratio will be unaffected by the paying out of the special dividend. It is entirely possible that the paying out of the cash will make the firm riskier (leading to a higher unlevered beta) and lower the optimal debt ratio.

[7]$29.5 million = $121 million $\times$ 0.30 − 6.8 million.

Debt Ratio	Cost of Capital	Firm Value (in Millions)
0%	9.15%	$62,279
10%	8.83%	$66,397
20%	8.59%	$69,837
30%	8.50%	$71,239
40%	10.20%	$51,661
50%	13.16%	$34,969
60%	14.36%	$30,920
70%	15.56%	$27,711
80%	16.76%	$25,105
90%	17.96%	$22,948

Table 9.3   DEBT RATIO, WACC, AND FIRM VALUE: DISNEY

(estimated market value) and $55.1 billion in equity. Its optimal debt ratio, based on minimizing cost of capital, was 30 percent. Table 9.3 summarizes the debt ratios, costs of capital, and firm value at debt ratios ranging from 0 percent to 90 percent. The optimal debt ratio for Disney is 30 percent, because the cost of capital is minimized and the firm value is maximized at this debt level.

In early 2004, Disney looked like it was not under any immediate pressure to increase its leverage, partly because of its size ($69 billion) and partly because its stock price had recovered from its lows of 2000.[8] However, Disney's management was under pressure to produce results quickly for its stockholders. Let us assume, therefore, that Disney decides to increase its leverage over time toward its optimal level.

The question of how to increase leverage over time can be best answered by looking at the quality of the projects that Disney had available to it in 2003. In Chapter 5, we compute the return on capital that Disney earned in 2004:

$$\text{Return on Capital} = \text{EBIT}(1 - \text{Tax Rate})/(\text{BV of Debt} + \text{BV of Equity})$$
$$= 2,713(1 - 0.373)/(14,130 + 23,879)$$
$$= 4.48\%$$

This is lower than the cost of capital of 8.59 percent that Disney faced in 2003 and the 8.40 percent it will face if it moves to the optimal.[9] If we assume that these negative excess returns are likely to continue into the future, the path to a lower optimal debt ratio is to either increase dividends or to enter into a stock buyback program for the next few years. The change in the tax treatment of dividends in 2003 makes the choice more difficult than in prior years, when stock buybacks would have been more tax-efficient.[10]

---

[8]See Jensen's alpha calculation in Chapter 4. Over the past five years, Disney has earned an excess return of 0.60 percent a year.

[9]The correct comparison should be to the cost of capital that Disney will have at its optimal debt ratio. It is, however, even better if the return on capital also exceeds the current cost of capital, because it will take time to get to the optimal.

[10]The 2003 tax law reduced the tax rate on dividends to 15 percent to match the tax rate on capital gains, thus eliminating a long-standing tax disadvantage borne by investors on dividends.

	Current Year	1	2	3	4	5
Table 9.4 **ESTIMATED DEBT RATIOS WITH EXISTING PAYOUT RATIOS: DISNEY**						
Equity	$55,101	$60,150	$65,586	$71,436	$77,730	$84,499
Debt[a]	$14,668	$13,794	$12,831	$11,769	$10,600	$9,312
Debt/(debt + equity)	21.02%	18.65%	16.36%	14.14%	12.00%	9.93%
Revenues	$27,061	$29,226	$31,564	$34,089	$36,816	$39,761
Noncash working capital	519	$561	$605	$654	$706	$763
Capital expenditures	$1,049	$1,133	$1,224	$1,321	$1,427	$1,541
+ Change in working capital	$65	$42	$45	$48	$52	$56
− Depreciation	$1,059	$1,144	$1,235	$1,334	$1,441	$1,556
− Net income[b]	$1,267	$1,368	$1,507	$1,659	$1,826	$2,011
+ Dividends	$429	$463	$510	$562	$618	$681
= New debt	($783)	($874)	($963)	($1,061)	($1,169)	($1,288)
Beta	1.25	1.22	1.20	1.18	1.16	1.14
Cost of equity	10.00%	9.88%	9.78%	9.68%	9.59%	9.50%
Growth rate		8.00%	8.00%	8.00%	8.00%	8.00%
Dividend payout ratio	33.86%	33.86%	33.86%	33.86%	33.86%	33.86%

[a]$Debt_t = Debt_{t-1} + New\ Debt_t$

[b]$Net\ Income_t = Net\ Income_{t-1}(1 + g) - Interest\ Rate(1 - t) \times (Debt_{t-1} - Debt_{t-2})$.

To make forecasts of changes in leverage over time, we made the following assumptions:

- Revenues, operating earnings, capital expenditures, and depreciation are expected to grow 8 percent a year from 2004 to 2008 (based on analyst estimates of growth). The current value for each of these items is provided in Table 9.4.

- In 2003, noncash working capital was 1.92 percent of revenues, and that ratio is expected to be unchanged over the next five years.

- The interest rate on new debt is expected to be 5.25 percent, which is Disney's pretax cost of debt. The bottom-up beta is 1.25, as estimated in Chapter 4.

- The dividend payout ratio in 2003 was 33.86 percent.

- The Treasury bond rate is 4 percent, and the risk premium is assumed to be 4.82 percent.

To estimate the expected market value of equity in future periods, we will use the cost of equity computed from the beta in conjunction with dividends. The estimated values of debt and equity, over time, are estimated as follows.

$$Equity_t = Equity_{t-1}(1 + Cost\ of\ Equity_{t-1}) - Dividends_t$$

The rationale is simple: The cost of equity measures the expected return on the stock, inclusive of price appreciation and the dividend yield, and the payment of dividends reduces the value of equity outstanding at the end of the year.[11] The value of debt is estimated by adding the new debt taken on to the debt outstanding at the end of the previous year.

We begin this analysis by looking at what would happen to the debt ratio if Disney maintains its existing payout ratio of 33.86 percent, does not buy back stock, and applies excess funds to pay off debt. Table 9.4 uses the expected capital expenditures and noncash working capital needs over the next five years, in conjunction with external financing needs, to estimate the debt ratio in each year. (Notice that cash outflows are shown as positive numbers and cash inflows as negative.)

There are two points to note in these forecasts. The first is that the net income is adjusted for the change in interest expenses that will occur as a result of the debt being paid off. The second is that the beta is adjusted to reflect the changing debt to equity ratio from year to year. Disney produces a cash surplus every year, because internal cash flows (net income + depreciation) are well in excess of capital expenditures and working capital needs. If this is applied to paying off debt, the increase in the market value of equity and the declining debt over time will cause the debt ratio to drop from 21.02 percent to 9.93 percent by the end of year five.

If Disney wants to increase its debt ratio to 30 percent, it will need to do one or a combination of the following:

1. *Increase its dividend payout ratio* The higher dividend increases the debt ratio in two ways. It increases the need for debt financing in each year, and it reduces the expected price appreciation on the equity. In Table 9.5, for instance, increasing the dividend payout ratio to 60 percent results in a debt ratio of 12.33 percent at the end of the fifth year (instead of 9.93 percent). In fact, increasing dividend payout alone is unlikely to increase the debt ratio substantially.

2. *Repurchase stock each year* This affects the debt ratio in much the same way as increasing dividends because it increases debt requirements and reduces equity. For instance, if Disney bought back 5 percent of the stock outstanding each year, the debt ratio at the end of year five would be higher as shown in Table 9.6. In this scenario, Disney will need to borrow money each year to cover its stock buybacks and the debt ratio increases to 28.30 percent by the end of year five.

3. *Increase capital expenditures each year* The first two approaches increase the debt ratio by shrinking the equity, whereas this approach increases the scale of the firm. It does so by increasing the capital expenditures, which incidentally includes acquisitions of other firms, and financing these expenditures with debt.

---

[11]The effect of dividends on the market value of equity can best be captured by noting the effect the payment on dividends has on stock prices on the ex-dividend day. Stock prices tend to drop on ex-dividend day by about the same amount as the dividend paid.

Table 9.5 ESTIMATED DEBT RATIO WITH HIGHER DIVIDEND PAYOUT RATIO

	Current Year	1	2	3	4	5
Equity	$55,101	$59,792	$64,820	$70,206	$75,975	$82,150
Debt	$14,668	$14,152	$13,587	$12,969	$12,295	$11,557
Debt/(debt + equity)	21.02%	19.14%	17.33%	15.59%	13.93%	12.33%
Capital expenditures	$1,049	$1,133	$1,224	$1,321	$1,427	$1,541
+ Change in working capital	$65	$42	$45	$48	$52	$56
− Depreciation	$1,059	$1,144	$1,235	$1,334	$1,441	$1,556
− Net income	$1,267	$1,368	$1,495	$1,633	$1,784	$1,949
+ Dividends	$429	$821	$897	$980	$1,070	$1,169
= New debt	($783)	($517)	($565)	($617)	($675)	($738)
Beta	1.25	1.23	1.21	1.19	1.18	1.16
Cost of equity	10.00%	9.91%	9.82%	9.74%	9.67%	9.60%
Growth rate		8.00%	8.00%	8.00%	8.00%	8.00%
Dividend payout ratio	33.86%	60.00%	60.00%	60.00%	60.00%	60.00%

Table 9.6 ESTIMATED DEBT RATIO WITH EQUITY BUYBACK OF 5 PERCENT A YEAR

	Current Year	1	2	3	4	5
Equity	$55,101	$57,142	$59,312	$61,617	$64,065	$66,666
Debt	$14,668	$16,801	$19,025	$21,347	$23,774	$26,316
Debt/(debt + equity)	21.02%	22.72%	24.29%	25.73%	27.07%	28.30%
Capital expenditures	$1,049	$1,133	$1,224	$1,321	$1,427	$1,541
+ Change in working capital	$65	$42	$45	$48	$52	$56
− Depreciation	$1,059	$1,144	$1,235	$1,334	$1,441	$1,556
− Net income	$1,267	$1,368	$1,408	$1,447	$1,486	$1,525
+ Dividends	$429	$463	$477	$490	$503	$516
+ Stock buybacks[a]		$3,007	$3,122	$3,243	$3,372	$3,509
= New debt	($783)	$2,133	$2,224	$2,322	$2,427	$2,542
Beta	1.25	1.26	1.28	1.30	1.32	1.33
Cost of equity	10.00%	10.09%	10.18%	10.26%	10.34%	10.42%
Growth rate		8.00%	8.00%	8.00%	8.00%	8.00%
Dividend payout ratio	33.86%	33.86%	33.86%	33.86%	33.86%	33.86%

[a]To get the stock buyback in year one: Stock Buyback = 3,007 = 0.05[(55,101 × 1.10) − 463].

Disney could increase its debt ratio fairly significantly by increasing capital expenditures. In Table 9.7, we estimate the debt ratio for Disney if it doubles its capital expenditures (relative to the estimates in the earlier tables) and meets its external financing needs with debt.

Table 9.7   ESTIMATED DEBT RATIO WITH 100 PERCENT HIGHER CAPITAL EXPENDITURES

	Current Year	1	2	3	4	5
Equity	$55,101	$60,150	$65,622	$71,553	$77,980	$84,945
Debt	$14,668	$14,927	$15,224	$15,566	$15,959	$16,408
Debt/(debt + equity)	21.02%	19.88%	18.83%	17.87%	16.99%	16.19%
Capital expenditures	$1,049	$2,266	$2,447	$2,643	$2,854	$3,083
+ Change in working capital	$65	$42	$45	$48	$52	$56
− Depreciation	$1,059	$1,144	$1,235	$1,334	$1,441	$1,556
− Net income	$1,267	$1,368	$1,469	$1,577	$1,692	$1,814
+ Dividends	$429	$463	$510	$562	$618	$681
+ Stock buybacks		$0	$0	$0	$0	$0
= New debt	($783)	$259	$298	$342	$392	$450
Beta	1.25	1.23	1.22	1.21	1.20	1.20
Cost of equity	10.00%	9.95%	9.89%	9.85%	9.81%	9.77%
Growth rate		8.00%	8.00%	8.00%	8.00%	8.00%
Dividend payout ratio	33.86%	33.86%	33.86%	33.86%	33.86%	33.86%

With the higher capital expenditures and maintaining the existing dividend payout ratio of 33.86 percent, the debt ratio is 16.19 percent by the end of year five. This is the riskiest strategy of the three because it presupposes the existence of enough good investments (or acquisitions) to cover $15 billion in new investments over the next five years. It may, however, be the strategy that is most attractive to management intent on building a global entertainment empire. In the process of expanding, though, Disney will have to figure out ways of increasing their return on capital from their existing level of 4.48 percent.

All of this analysis was based on the presumption that Disney would not be the target of a hostile acquisition. In February 2004, Comcast announced that it would try to acquire Disney. Although the bid was withdrawn three months later and excess debt capacity was never cited as a reason, the threat of an acquisition does put pressure on the timetable that Disney faces both for raising the debt ratio and improving returns on investments.

9.5   CASH BALANCES AND CHANGING LEVERAGE

Companies with excess debt capacity often also have large cash balances. Which of the following actions by a company with a large cash balance will increase its debt ratio?

☐ Using the cash to acquire another company
☐ Paying a large special dividend
☐ Paying off debt
☐ Buying back stock
Explain.

Table 9.8 ESTIMATED DEBT RATIOS: TIME WARNER

	Current Year	1	2	3	4	5
Equity	$16,689	$19,051	$21,694	$24,651	$27,960	$31,663
Debt	$9,934	$9,745	$9,527	$9,276	$8,988	$8,655
Debt/(debt + equity)	37.31%	33.84%	30.52%	27.34%	24.33%	21.47%
Capital expenditures	$300	$330	$363	$399	$439	$483
− Depreciation	$437	$481	$529	$582	$640	$704
− Net income	$35	$39	$52	$68	$88	$112
+ Dividends	$67	$0	$0	$0	$0	$0
= New debt	($105)	($189)	($218)	($251)	($289)	($332)
Beta	1.30	1.25	1.21	1.17	1.14	1.11
Cost of equity	14.15%	13.87%	13.63%	13.42%	13.24%	13.08%
Growth rate		10.00%	10.00%	10.00%	10.00%	10.00%
Payout ratio	11%	0%	0%	0%	0%	0%

ILLUSTRATION 9.4   Decreasing Leverage Gradually: Time Warner

In 1994, Time Warner had 379.3 million shares outstanding, trading at $44 per share, and $9.934 billion in outstanding debt, left over from the leveraged acquisition of Time by Warner Communications in 1989. The EBITDA in 1994 was $1.146 billion, and Time Warner had a beta of 1.30. The optimal debt ratio for Time Warner, based on its operating income, was only 10 percent. Table 9.8 examines the effect on leverage of cutting dividends to zero and using operating cash flows to invest in projects and repay debt.

Allowing for a growth rate of 10 percent in operating income, Time Warner repays $189 million of its outstanding debt in the first year. By the end of the fifth year, the growth in equity and the reduction in debt combine to lower the debt ratio to 21.47 percent.

This spreadsheet allows you to estimate the effects of changing dividend policy or capital expenditures on debt ratios over time (**chgcapstru.xls**).

9.6   INVESTING IN OTHER BUSINESS LINES

In the preceding analysis, we have argued that firms should invest in projects as long as the return on capital is greater than the cost of capital. Assume that a firm is considering acquiring another firm with its debt capacity. In analyzing the return on capital the acquiring firm can make on this investment, we should compare the return on capital to

☐   the cost of capital of the acquiring firm.

☐   the cost of capital of the target firm.

☐   a blended cost of capital of the target and acquiring firm.

☐   none of the above.

Explain.

IN PRACTICE: SECURITY INNOVATION AND CHANGING CAPITAL STRUCTURE

The changes in leverage discussed so far in this chapter have been accomplished using traditional securities, such as debt and equity, but firms that have specific objectives on leverage may find certain products that are designed to meet those objectives. Consider a few examples:

- Hybrid securities (such as convertible bonds) are combinations of debt and equity that change over time as the firm changes. To be more precise, if the firm prospers and its equity value increases, the conversion option in the convertible bond will become more valuable, thus increasing the equity component of the convertible bond and decreasing the debt component (as a percent of the value of the bond). If the firm does badly and its stock price slides, the conversion option (and the equity component) will become less valuable, and the debt ratio of the firm will increase.

- An alternative available to a firm that wants to increase leverage over time is a forward contract to buy a specified number of shares of equity in the future. These contracts lock the firms into reducing their equity over time and may carry a more positive signal to financial markets than would an announcement of plans to repurchase stock because firms are not obligated to carry through on these announcements.

- A firm with high leverage, faced with a resistance from financial markets to common stock issues, may consider more inventive ways of raising equity, such as using warrants and contingent value rights. Warrants represent call options on the firm's equity, whereas contingent value rights are put options on the firm's stock. The former have appeal to those who are optimistic about the future of the company and the latter make sense for risk averse investors who are concerned about protecting their investments. ■

CHOOSING THE RIGHT FINANCING INSTRUMENTS

In Chapter 7 we presented a variety of ways in which firms can raise debt and equity. Debt can be bank debt or corporate bonds, can vary in maturity from short to long term, can have fixed or floating rates, and can be in different currencies. In the case of equity there are fewer choices, but firms can still raise equity from common stock, warrants, or contingent value rights. Although we suggested broad guidelines that could be used to determine when firms should consider each type of financing, we did not develop a methodology by which a specific firm can pick the right kind of financing.

In this section, we lay out a sequence of steps by which a firm can choose the right financing instruments. This analysis is useful not only in determining what kind of securities should be issued to finance new investments but also in highlighting limitations in a firm's existing financing choices. The first step in the analysis is an examination of the cash flow characteristics of the assets or projects that will be financed; the objective is to try matching the cash flows on the liability stream as closely as possible to the cash flows on the asset stream. We then superimpose a series of considerations that may lead the firm to deviate from or modify these financing choices.

First, we consider the tax savings that may accrue from using different financing vehicles and weigh the tax benefits against the costs of deviating from the optimal choices. Next, we examine the influence that equity research analysts and ratings agency views have on the choice of financing vehicles; instruments that are looked on favorably by either or (better still) both groups will clearly be preferred to those that evoke strong negative responses from one or both groups. We also factor in the difficulty that some firms might have in conveying information to markets; in the presence of asymmetric information, firms may have to make financing choices that do not reflect their asset mix. Finally, we allow for the possibility that firms may want to structure their financing to reduce agency conflicts between stockholders and bondholders.

I. Matching Financing Cash Flows with Asset Cash Flows

The first and most important characteristic a firm has to consider in choosing the financing instrument it will use to raise funds is the cash flow patterns of the assets to be financed.

Why Match Asset Cash Flows to Cash Flows on Liabilities?

We begin with the premise that the cash flows of a firm's liability stream should match the cash flows of the assets that they finance. To see why, let us begin by defining firm value as the present value of the cash flows generated by the assets owned by the firm. This firm value will vary over time, not only as a function of firm-specific factors (such as project success) but also as a function of broader macroeconomic variables, such as interest rates, inflation rates, economic cycles, and exchange rates. Figure 9.2 represents the time series of firm value for a hypothetical firm, where all the changes in firm value are assumed to result from changes in macro economic variables.

Figure 9.2 Firm Value over Time

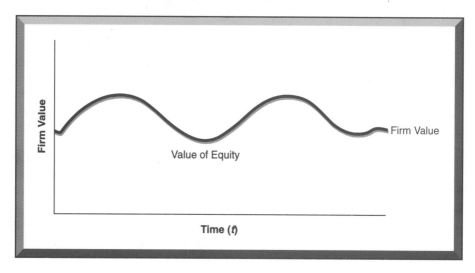

Figure 9.3   Firm Value over Time with Short-Term Debt

Firm Value

Debt Value

Firm is
bankrupt

Firm Value (y-axis)

Time (*t*)

This firm can choose to finance these assets with any financing mix and instrument it wants. The value of equity at any point in time is the difference between the value of the firm and the value of outstanding debt. Assume, for instance, that the firm chooses to finance the assets shown in Figure 9.2 using very short-term debt and that the value of this debt is unaffected by changes in macroeconomic variables. Figure 9.3 provides the firm value, debt value, and equity value over time for the firm. Note that there are periods when the firm value drops below the debt value, which would suggest that the firm is technically bankrupt in those periods. Firms that weigh this possibility into their financing decision will therefore borrow less.

Now consider a firm that finances the assets described in Figure 9.2 with debt that matches the assets exactly in terms of cash flows and also in terms of the sensitivity of debt value to changes in macroeconomic variables. Figure 9.4 provides the firm value, debt value, and equity value for this firm. Because debt value and firm value move together, the possibility of default is eliminated. This, in turn, will allow the firm to carry much more debt, and the added debt should provide tax benefits that make the firm more valuable. Thus, matching liability cash flows to asset cash flows allows firms to have higher optimal debt ratios.

9.7 THE RATIONALE FOR ASSET AND LIABILITY MATCHING

In Chapter 4, we argued that firms should focus on only market risk, because firm-specific risk can be diversified away. By the same token, it should not matter if firms use short-term debt to finance long-term assets because investors in these firms can diversify away this risk anyway.

☐   True
☐   False
Comment.

Figure 9.4 Firm Value over Time with Matched Debt

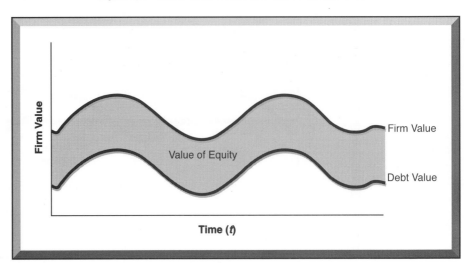

Matching Liabilities to Assets

The first step every firm should take toward making the right financing choices is to understand how cash flows on its assets vary over time. In this section, we consider five aspects of financing choices and how they are guided by the nature of the cash flows generated by assets. We begin by looking at the question of financing maturity, that is, the choice between long-term, medium-term, and short-term debt, and we argue that this choice will be determined by how long-term asset cash flows are. Next, we examine the choice between fixed and floating rate debt and how this choice will be affected by the way inflation affects the cash flows on the assets financed by the debt. Third, we look at the currency in which the debt is to be denominated and link it to the currency in which asset cash flows are generated. Fourth, we evaluate when firms should use convertible debt instead of straight rate debt and how this determination should be linked to how much growth there is in asset cash flows. Finally, we analyze other features that can be attached to debt and how these features can be used to insulate a firm against specific factors that affect cash flows on assets, either positively or negatively.

A. Financing Maturity

Firms can issue debt of varying maturities, ranging from very short-term to very long-term. In making this choice, they should first be guided by how long-term the cash flows on their assets are. For instance, firms should not finance assets that generate cash flows over the short term (say, two to three years) using twenty-year debt. In this section, we begin by examining how best to assess the life of assets and liabilities, and then we consider alternative strategies to matching financing with asset cash flows.

Measuring the Cash Flow Lives of Liabilities and Assets   When we talk about projects as having a ten-year life or a bond as having a thirty-year maturity, we are referring to the time when the project ends or the bond comes due. The cash flows on the project, however, occur over the ten-year period, and there are usually interest payments on the bond every six months until maturity. The *duration* of an asset or liability is a weighted maturity of all the cash flows on that asset or liability, where the weights are based on both the timing and the magnitude of the cash flows. In general, larger and earlier cash flows are weighted more than smaller and later cash flows. The duration of a thirty-year bond, with coupons every six months, will be lower than thirty years, and the duration of a ten-year project, with cash flows each year, will generally be lower than ten years.

A simple measure of duration for a bond, for instance, can be computed as follows:[12]

$$\text{Duration of Bond} = \frac{dP/dr}{(1+r)} = \frac{\left[\sum_{t=1}^{t=N} \frac{t \times \text{Coupon}_t}{(1+r)^t} + \frac{N \times \text{Face Value}}{(1+r)^N}\right]}{\left[\sum_{t=1}^{t=N} \frac{\text{Coupon}_t}{(1+r)^t} + \frac{\text{Face Value}}{(1+r)^N}\right]}$$

where N is the maturity of the bond, and t is when each coupon comes due. Holding other factors constant, the duration of a bond will increase with the maturity of the bond and decrease with the coupon rate on the bond. For example, the duration of a 7 percent, thirty-year coupon bond, when interest rates are 8 percent and coupons are paid each year, can be written as follows:

$$\text{Duration of 30-Year Bond} = \frac{dP/dr}{(1+r)} = \frac{\left[\sum_{t=1}^{t=30} \frac{t \times \$70}{(1.08)^t} + \frac{30 \times \$1,000}{(1.08)^{30}}\right]}{\left[\sum_{t=1}^{t=30} \frac{\$70}{(1.08)^t} + \frac{\$1,000}{(1.08)^{30}}\right]} = 12.41$$

What does the duration tell us? First, it provides a measure of when, on average, the cash flows on this bond come due, factoring in both the magnitude of the cash flows and the present value effects. This 30-year bond, for instance, has cash flows that come due in about 12.41 years, after considering the present value of both the coupons and the face value. Second, it is an approximate measure of how much the bond price will change for small changes in interest rates. For instance, this thirty-year bond will drop in value by approximately 12.41 percent for a 1 percent increase in interest rates. Note that the duration is lower than the maturity. This will generally be true for coupon-bearing bonds, though special features in the bond may sometimes increase duration.[13] For zero-coupon bonds, the duration is equal to the maturity.

---

[12]This measure of duration is called *Macaulay duration,* and it makes same strong assumptions about the yield curve; specifically, the yield curve is assumed to be flat and move in parallel shifts. Other duration measures change these assumptions. For purposes of our analysis, however, a rough measure of duration will suffice.

[13]Making the coupon rate floating, rather than fixed, will reduce the duration of a bond. Similarly, adding a call feature to a bond will decrease duration, whereas making bonds extendible will increase duration.

This measure of duration can be extended to any asset with expected cash flows. Thus, the duration of a project or asset can be estimated in terms of its predebt operating cash flows:

$$\text{Duration of Project/Asset} = \frac{dPV/dr}{(1+r)} = \frac{\left[\sum_{t=1}^{t=N} \frac{t \times CF_t}{(1+r)^t} + \frac{N \times \text{Terminal Value}}{(1+r)^N} \right]}{\left[\sum_{t=1}^{t=N} \frac{CF_t}{(1+r)^t} + \frac{\text{Terminal Value}}{(1+r)^N} \right]}$$

where CF_t is the after-tax cash flow on the project in year t and the terminal value is a measure of how much the project is worth at the end of its lifetime of N years. The duration of an asset measures both when, on average, the cash flows on that asset come due and how much the value of the asset changes for a 1 unit change in interest rates.

One limitation of this analysis of duration is that it keeps cash flows fixed while interest rates change. On real projects, however, the cash flows will be adversely affected by an increase in interest rates, and the degree of the effect will vary from business to business—more for cyclical firms (automobiles, housing) and less for noncyclical firms (food processing). Thus the actual duration of most projects will be higher than the estimates obtained by keeping cash flows constant. One way of estimating duration without depending on the traditional bond duration measures is to use historical data. If the duration is, in fact, a measure of how sensitive asset values are to interest rate changes, and a time series of data of asset values and interest rate changes is available, a regression of change in the former on the change in the latter should yield a measure of duration:

$$\Delta\text{Asset Value}_t = a + b\,\Delta\text{Interest Rate}_t$$

In this regression, the coefficient b on interest rate changes should be a measure of the duration of the assets. For firms with publicly traded stocks and bonds, the asset value is the sum of the market values of the two. For a private company or for a public company with a short history, the regression can be run, using changes in operating income as the dependent variable:

$$\Delta\text{Operating Income}_t = a + b\,\Delta\text{Interest Rate}_t$$

Here again, the coefficient b is a measure of the duration of the assets.

ILLUSTRATION 9.5   Calculating Duration for Disney Theme Park

In this application, we will calculate duration using the traditional measures for Disneyworld Bangkok, which we analyzed in Chapter 5. The cash flows for the project are summarized in Table 9.9, together with the present value estimates, calculated using the cost of capital for this project of 10.66 percent.

$$\text{Duration of the Project} = 37{,}657/749 = 50.25 \text{ years}$$

This would suggest that the cash flows on this project come due, on average, in 50.25 years. The duration is longer than the life of the project because the cash flows in the first few years are negative.

Table 9.9 CALCULATING A PROJECT'S DURATION: DISNEY THEME PARK

Year	Annual Cash Flow (in Millions)	Terminal Value (in Millions)	Present Value	Present Value × *t*
0	−$2,000		−$2,000	$0
1	−$1,000		−$904	−$904
2	−$880		−$718	−$1,437
3	−$289		−$213	−$640
4	$324		$216	$863
5	$443		$267	$1,333
6	$486		$265	$1,588
7	$517		$254	$1,781
8	$571		$254	$2,031
9	$631		$254	$2,282
10	$663	$7,810	$3,076	$30,760
			$749	$37,657

9.8 PROJECT LIFE AND DURATION

In investment analyses, analysts often cut off project lives at an arbitrary point and estimate a salvage or a terminal value. If these cash flows are used to estimate project duration, we will tend to

☐ understate duration.

☐ overstate duration.

☐ not affect the duration estimate.

Explain.

Duration Matching Strategies   We just considered ways of estimating the duration of assets and liabilities. The basic idea is to match the duration of a firm's assets to the duration of its liabilities. This can be accomplished in two ways: by matching individual assets and liabilities, or by matching the assets of the firm with its collective liabilities. In the first approach, the Disneyworld Bangkok project would be financed with bonds with duration of approximately fifty years. Although this approach provides a precise matching of each asset's characteristics to those of the financing used for it, it has several limitations. First, it is expensive to arrange separate financing for each project, given the issuance costs associated with raising funds. Second, this approach ignores interactions and correlations between projects that might make project-specific financing suboptimal for the firm. Consequently, this approach works only for companies that have a few very large, independent projects.

It is far more straightforward, and often cheaper, to match the duration of a firm's collective assets to the duration of its collective liabilities. For instance, if Disney's assets have a duration of fifteen years, and its liabilities have a duration of only five years, the firm should try to extend the duration of its liabilities. It can do so in one of three ways. First, it can finance its new investments with debt of much longer duration; thus, using 100-year bonds to finance the new theme park will increase the weighted average duration of all its debt. Second, it can repay some of its short-term debt and replace it with long-term debt. Third, it can exchange or swap short-term debt for long-term debt.

9.9 PROJECT AND FIRM DURATION

Which of the following types of firms should be most likely to use project-specific financing (as opposed to financing the portfolio of projects)?

☐ Firms with a few large homogeneous projects

☐ Firms with a large number of small homogeneous projects

☐ Firms with a few large heterogeneous projects

☐ Firms with a large number of small heterogeneous projects

Explain.

B. The Fixed/Floating Rate Choice

One of the most common choices firms face is whether to make the coupon rate on bonds (and the interest rate on bank loans) a fixed rate or a floating rate, pegged to an index rate. In making this decision, we once again examine the characteristics of the projects being financed with the debt. In particular, we argue that the use of **floating rate debt** should be more prevalent for firms that are uncertain about the duration of future projects or have cash flows that move with the inflation rate.

Uncertainty about Future Projects   The duration of assets and liabilities can be synchronized when assets and projects are well identified, interest rate sensitivity can be estimated, and the appropriate maturity for financing can be ascertained. For some firms, this estimation is difficult to do, however. The firm might be changing its business mix by divesting itself of some assets and acquiring new ones. Alternatively, the industry to which the firm belongs might be changing. In such cases, the firm may use short-term or floating rate loans[14] until it feels more certain about its future investment plans.

Cash Flows and Inflation   Floating rate loans have interest payments that increase as market interest rates rise, and fall as rates fall. If a firm has assets whose earnings increase as interest rates go up and decrease as interest rates go down, it should finance those assets with floating rate loans. The expected inflation rate is a key factor determining interest rates; higher inflation leads to higher interest rates. On floating rate loans, this rate will lead to high interest payments in periods when inflation is high and low interest payments in periods when inflation is low. Firms whose earnings increase in periods of high inflation and decrease in periods with low inflation should therefore also be more likely to use floating rate loans.

---

[14]The presence of derivatives provides an alternative for firms that are faced with this uncertainty. They can use the financing mix that is most appropriate given their current asset mix and use derivatives to manage the intermediate risk.

A number of factors determine whether a firm's earnings move with inflation. One critical ingredient is the degree of pricing power the firm possesses. Firms that have significant pricing power, either because they produce a unique product or because they are price leaders in their industries, have a much higher chance of being able to pass inflation through to their customers. Consequently, these firms should gain more by using floating rate debt. Firms that do not have pricing power are much more likely to see cash flows decline with unexpectedly high inflation, and they should be more cautious about using floating rate debt.

Floating Rate Debt: The interest rate on floating rate debt varies from period to period and is linked to a specified short-term rate; for instance, many floating rate bonds have coupon rates that are tied to the London Interbank Borrowing Rate (LIBOR).

C. The Currency Choice

Many of the points we have made about interest rate risk exposure also apply to currency risk exposure. If any of a firm's assets or projects creates cash flows denominated in a foreign currency, currency risk exists. The liabilities of a firm can be issued in these currencies to reduce the currency risk. A firm that expects 20 percent of its cash flows to be in Euros, for example, would attempt to issue Euro-denominated debt in the same proportion to mitigate the currency risk. If the Euro weakens and the assets become less valuable, the value of the debt will decline proportionately.

In recent years, firms have developed more sophisticated variations on traditional bonds to manage foreign exchange risk on investments. For instance, Philip Morris issued a dual currency bond in 1985—coupon payments were made in Swiss francs, and the principal payment was in U.S. dollars. In 1987, Westinghouse issued **principal exchange rate–linked securities (PERLS),** in which the principal payment was the U.S. dollar value of 70.13 New Zealand dollars. Finally, firms have issued bonds embedded with foreign currency options called indexed currency option notes (ICON), which combine a fixed rate bond with an option on a foreign currency. This approach is likely to work only for firms that have fairly predictable currency flows, however. For firms that do not have predictable currency flows, currency options or futures may be a cheaper way to manage currency risk, because the currency exposure may change from period to period.

PERLS: A bond, denominated in the domestic currency, where the principal payment at maturity is based on the domestic currency equivalent of a fixed foreign currency amount. For instance, this could be a dollar-denominated bond with the payment at maturity set equal to the dollar value of 900 Euros. Thus, if the dollar strengthens against the Euro during the life of the bond, the principal payment will decrease.

D. The Choice between Straight and Convertible Bonds

Firms vary in terms of how much of their value comes from projects or assets they already own and how much comes from future growth. Firms that derive the bulk of their value from future growth should use different types of financing and design their financing differently than do those that derive most of their value from assets in place. This is so because the current cash flows on high growth firms will be low relative to the market value. These cash flows can be expected to grow substantially over time as the firm invests in new projects. Accordingly, the financing approach should not create large cash outflows early; it can create substantial cash outflows later, however, reflecting the cash flow patterns of the firm. In addition, the financing should exploit the value that the perception of high growth adds to securities, and it should put relatively few constraints on investment policies.

Straight bonds do not quite fit the bill because they create large interest payments and do not gain much value from high growth perceptions. Furthermore, they are likely to include covenants designed to protect the bondholders, which restrict investment and future financing policy. Convertible bonds, by contrast, create much lower interest payments, impose fewer constraints, and gain value from higher growth perceptions. They might be converted into common stock, but only if the firm is successful. In 1999, for instance, Amazon.com, the online retailer, raised $1.25 billion from a convertible bond issue with a coupon rate of 3.5 percent.

E. Special Financing Features

Every firm is exposed to risk, coming from macroeconomic sources (such as recessions), acts of God (such as the weather), acts of competitors or technological shifts. If a firm's exposure to any or all these sources of risk is substantial, it may choose not to borrow, rather than risk default. One way firms can partially protect themselves against this default risk is to incorporate special features into bonds or debt, shielding themselves against the most serious risk or risks. Two examples of bonds provide good illustrations:

- Insurance companies have issued bonds whose payments can be drastically curtailed if there is a catastrophe that creates a substantial liability for the insurance company. By doing so, they reduce their debt payments in those periods when their overall cash flows are most negative, thereby reducing their likelihood of default.[15]

---

[15]As an example of a catastrophe bond issue, consider the bond issue made by USAA Insurance Company. The company privately placed $477 million of these bonds, backed up by reinsurance premiums, in June 1997. The company was protected in the event of any hurricane that created more that $1 billion in damage to the East Coast anytime before June 1998. The bonds came in two classes: in the first class, called principal-at-risk, the company could reduce the principal on the bond in the event of a hurricane; in the second class, which was less risky to investors, the coupon payments would be suspended in the event of a hurricane, but the principal would be protected. In return, in October 1997 the investors in these bonds were earning an extra yield of almost 1.5 percent on the principal-at-risk bonds and almost 0.5 percent on the principal-protected bonds over straight bonds.

- Companies in commodity businesses have issued bonds whose principal and interest payments are tied to the price of the commodity. Because the operating cash flows in these firms are also positively correlated with commodity prices, adding this feature to debt decreases the likelihood of default and allows the firm to use more debt. In 1980, for instance, Sunshine Mining issued fifteen-year silver-linked bond issues, which combined a debt issue with an option on silver prices. As silver prices increased, the coupon rate on the bond increased; as silver prices decreased, the coupon rate on the bond decreased as well.

IN PRACTICE: Customized Bonds

In keeping with the notion of customizing bonds to match asset cash flows, firms have come up with increasingly creative solutions in recent years. In this endeavor, they have been assisted by two developments. The first is that investors in bond markets are more open to both pricing and buying complex bonds than they were in the 1970s and even the 1980s. The second is that advancements in option pricing allow us to value complicated securities with multiple options embedded in them. Consider a few examples:

- In the early 1990s, David Bowie acquired the rights to all of his songs, bundled them, and sold bonds backed by sales of his recordings. What made the bonds unique was the fact that the interest rate on the bonds was tied to the sales of his recordings—higher (lower) rates with higher (lower) sales.
- In 2001, an Italian soccer team issued bonds to fund the construction of a stadium but tied the interest rate on the bond to the success of the team. Specifically, the interest rate on the bond would rise if the team stayed in the first division (and drew larger crowds and revenues) and drop if the team dropped to the second division. ■

9.10 Special Features and Interest Rates

Adding special features to bonds, such as linking coupon payments to commodity prices or catastrophes, will reduce their attractiveness to investors and make the interest rates paid on them higher. It follows then that

☐ companies should not add these special features to bonds.

☐ adding these special features cannot create value for the firm if the bonds are fairly priced.

☐ adding special features can still create value even if the bonds are fairly priced.

Explain.

II. Tax Implications

As firms become more creative with their financing choices and structure debt to behave more like equity, there is a danger that the tax authorities might decide to treat the financing as equity and prevent the firm from deducting interest payments. Because the primary benefit of borrowing is a tax benefit, it is important that firms preserve and, if possible, increase this tax benefit.

It is also conceivable that the favorable tax treatment of some financing choices may encourage firms to use them more than others, even if it means deviating from the choices that would be dictated by the asset characteristics. Thus, a firm that has assets that generate cash flows in Japanese yen may decide to issue dollar-denominated bonds to finance these assets if it derives a larger tax benefit from issuing dollar debt than yen debt.

The danger of structuring financing with the intention of saving on taxes is that changes in the tax law can very quickly render the benefit moot and leave the firm with a financing mix unsuited to its asset mix.

III. Views of Ratings Agencies, Equity Research Analysts, and Regulatory Authorities

Firms are rightfully concerned about the views of equity research analysts and ratings agencies on their actions, but in our view they often overestimate the influence of both groups. Analysts represent stockholders, and ratings agencies represent bondholders; consequently they take very different views of the same actions. For instance, analysts may view a stock repurchase by a company with limited project opportunities as a positive action, whereas ratings agencies may view it as negative and lower ratings in response. Analysts and ratings agencies also measure the impact of financing choices made by a firm using very different criteria. In general, analysts view a firm's actions through the prism of higher earnings per share and by looking at the firm relative to comparable firms, using multiples such as price earnings or price to book value ratios. Ratings agencies, on the other hand, measure the effect of actions on the financial ratios, such as debt ratios and coverage ratios, which they then use to assess default risk and assign ratings.

Given the weight attached to the views of both these groups, firms sometimes design securities with the intent of satisfying both. In some cases, they find ways of raising funds that seem to make both groups happy, at least on the surface. To illustrate, consider the use of leasing before generally accepted accounting principles required capitalizing of some leases. Leasing increased the real leverage of the company, and thus, the earnings per share, but it did not affect the measured leverage of the company because it was not viewed as debt. To the degree that analysts and ratings agencies rely on quantitative measures and do not properly factor in the effects of these actions, firms can exploit their limitations. In fact, they still do with operating leases. In a more recent example, a security labeled as trust preferred stock has become popular largely because of the different ways in which it is viewed by various entities. It is viewed as debt by the equity research analysts and tax authorities, with the preferred dividend being tax-deductible. Trust preferred is viewed as equity by ratings agencies, allowing the firms issuing it to retain high ratings.[16]

When securities are designed in such a way, the real question is whether the markets are fooled and, if so, for how long. A firm that substitutes leases and trust preferred for debt may fool the ratings agencies and even the debt markets for some period of time, but it cannot evade the reality that it is much more levered and hence much riskier.

---

[16]Ratings agencies initially treated trust preferred as equity. Over time, they have become more cautious. By the late 1990s, firms were being given credit for only a portion of the trust preferred (about 40 percent) as equity.

This balancing act becomes even more precarious for regulated firms such as banks and insurance companies. These firms also have to make sure that any financing actions they take are viewed favorably by regulatory authorities. For instance, financial service firms have to maintain equity capital ratios that exceed regulatory minimums. However, regulatory authorities use a different definition of equity capital than ratings agencies and equity research analysts, and firms can exploit these differences. For instance, banks are among the heaviest users of conventional preferred stock because preferred stock is treated as equity by bank regulators. In the past few years, insurance companies in the United States have issued surplus notes,[17] which are considered debt for tax purposes and equity under insurance accounting rules, enabling them to have the best of both worlds—they can issue debt, while counting it as equity.[18]

IV. The Effects of Asymmetric Information

Firms generally have more information about their future prospects than do financial markets. This asymmetry in information creates friction when firms try to raise funds. In particular, firms with good prospects try to distinguish themselves from firms without such prospects by taking actions that are costly and difficult to imitate. Firms also try to design securities to reduce the effect of uncertainty in future cash flows on bondholders. In the process, they may issue securities that are not optimal from the standpoint of matching their asset cash flows but are specifically designed to convey information to financial markets and reduce the effects of uncertain cash flows on value.

A number of researchers have used this information asymmetry argument to draw very different conclusions about the debt structure firms should use. Myers (1977) argued that firms tend to under invest as a consequence of the asymmetry of information. One proposed solution to the problem is to issue short-term debt, even if the assets being financed are long-term assets.[19] Flannery (1986) and Kale and Noe (1990) note that although both short-term and long-term debt will be mispriced in the presence of asymmetric information, long-term debt will be mispriced more.[20] Consequently, they argue that high-quality firms will issue short-term debt, and low-quality firms will issue long-term debt. Goswami, Noe, and Rebello (1995) analyze the design of securities and relate it to uncertainty about future cash flows.[21] They conclude that if the asymmetry of information concerns uncertainty about long-term cash flows, firms should issue coupon-bearing long-term debt with restrictions on

---

[17]Surplus notes are bonds where the interest payments need to be made only if the firm is profitable. If it is not, the interest payments are cumulated and paid in subsequent periods.

[18]In recent years, insurance companies have issued billions of dollars of surplus notes in the private placement market.

[19]S. C. Myers, 1977, "Determinants of Corporate Borrowing," *Journal of Financial Economics,* 5(2), 147–175.

[20]M. J. Flannery, 1986, "Asymmetric Information and Risky Debt Maturity Choice," *Journal of Finance,* 41(1), 19–38; J. R. Kale and T. H. Noe, "Risky Debt Maturity Choice in a Sequential Game Equilibrium," *Journal of Financial Research,* 8, 155–165.

[21]G. Goswami, T. Noe, and M. Rebello, 1995, "Debt Financing under Asymmetric Information," *Journal of Finance,* 50(2), 633–659.

dividends. In contrast, firms with uncertainty about near-term cash flows and significant refinancing risk should issue long-term debt, without restrictions on dividend payments. When uncertainty about information is uniformly distributed across time, firms should finance with short-term debt.

V. Implications for Agency Costs

The final consideration in designing securities is the provision of features intended to reduce the agency conflicts between stockholders and bondholders. As we noted in Chapter 7, differences between bondholders and stockholders on investment, financing, and dividend policy decisions can influence financing decisions, by increasing either the costs of borrowing or the constraints associated with borrowing. In some cases, firms design securities with the specific intent of reducing this conflict and its associated costs.

- We explained that convertible bonds are a good choice for growth companies because of their cash flow characteristics. The anxiety of bondholders about equity investors investing in riskier projects and expropriating wealth can be reduced by allowing bondholders to become stockholders if the stock price increases enough.

- More corporate bonds include embedded put options that allow bondholders to put the bonds back at face value if the firm takes a specified action (such as increasing leverage) or if its rating drops. In a variation, in 1988, Manufacturer Hanover issued rating-sensitive notes promising bondholders higher coupons if the firm's rating deteriorated over time. Thus, bond investors would be protected in the event of a downgrade.

- In the same time period, Merrill Lynch introduced liquid yield option notes (LYONs), which incorporated put and conversion features to protect against both the risk shifting and claim substitution to which bondholders are exposed.

Barclay and Smith (1996) examined debt issues by U.S. companies between 1981 and 1993 and concluded that high-growth firms are more likely to issue short-term debt with higher priority.[22] This finding is consistent with both the information asymmetry argument and the agency cost argument, because lenders are more exposed to both costs with high growth firms.

In Summary

In choosing the right financing vehicles to use, firms should begin by examining the characteristics of the assets they are financing and try to match the maturity, interest rate, currency mix, and special features of their financing to these characteristics. They can then superimpose tax considerations, the views of analysts and ratings agencies, agency costs, and the effects of asymmetric information to modify this financing mix. Figure 9.5 summarizes the discussion.

---

[22]M. J. Barclay and C. W. Smith, 1996, "On Financial Architecture: Leverage, Maturity and Priority," *Journal of Applied Corporate Finance,* 8(4), 4–17.

Figure 9.5 The Design of Debt: An Overview of the Process

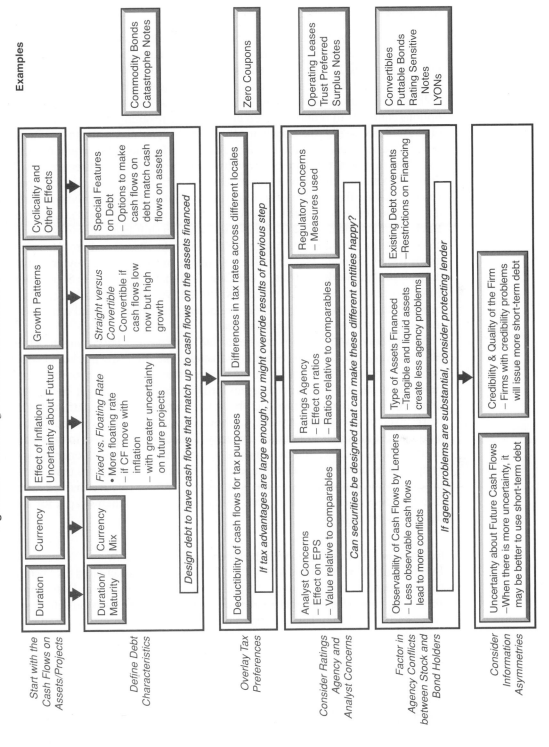

Examples

Start with the Cash Flows on Assets/Projects

| Duration | Currency | Effect of Inflation Uncertainty about Future | Growth Patterns | Cyclicality and Other Effects |

Define Debt Characteristics

| Duration/ Maturity | Currency Mix | *Fixed vs. Floating Rate* • More floating rate – if CF move with inflation – with greater uncertainty on future projects | *Straight versus Convertible* – Convertible if cash flows low now but high growth | Special Features on Debt – Options to make cash flows on debt match cash flows on assets |

Commodity Bonds
Catastrophe Notes

Design debt to have cash flows that match up to cash flows on the assets financed

Overlay Tax Preferences

Deductibility of cash flows for tax purposes

Differences in tax rates across different locales

Zero Coupons

If tax advantages are large enough, you might override results of previous step

Consider Ratings Agency and Analyst Concerns

Analyst Concerns
– Effect on EPS
– Value relative to comparables

Ratings Agency
– Effect on ratios
– Ratios relative to comparables

Regulatory Concerns
– Measures used

Operating Leases
Trust Preferred
Surplus Notes

Can securities be designed that can make these different entities happy?

Factor in Agency Conflicts between Stock and Bond Holders

Observability of Cash Flows by Lenders
– Less observable cash flows lead to more conflicts

Type of Assets Financed
– Tangible and liquid assets create less agency problems

Existing Debt covenants
–Restrictions on Financing

Convertibles
Puttable Bonds
Rating Sensitive
Notes
LYONs

If agency problems are substantial, consider protecting lender

Consider Information Asymmetries

Uncertainty about Future Cash Flows
–When there is more uncertainty, it may be better to use short-term debt

Credibility & Quality of the Firm
– Firms with credibility problems will issue more short-term debt

429

IN PRACTICE: THE ROLE OF DERIVATIVES AND SWAPS

In the past thirty years, the futures and options markets have developed to the point that firms can hedge exchange rate, interest rate, commodity price, and other risks using derivatives. In fact, firms can use derivatives to protect themselves against risk exposures generated by mismatching debt and assets. Thus, a firm that borrows in dollars to fund projects denominated in yen can use dollar/yen forward, futures, and options contracts to reduce or even eliminate the resulting risk. Given the existence of these derivatives, you may wonder why it is even necessary to go through the process we have just described to arrive at the perfect debt. We would offer two reasons. The first is that the use of derivatives can be costly, if used recurrently. Thus, a firm with a stable portion of its revenues coming from yen will find it cheaper to use yen debt rather than derivatives to correct mismatched debt. Derivatives are useful, however, to hedge against risk exposure that is transient and volatile. A company like Boeing, for instance, whose currency exposure can shift from year to year will find it cheaper to use derivatives to hedge the shifting risk. The second problem with derivatives is that although they are widely available in some cases, they are much more difficult to find in others. Thus, a Brazilian firm that borrows in U.S. dollars to fund Brazilian real–denominated projects will find it very difficult to hedge against risk beyond the short term because there are no long-term forward and futures contracts available for dollars versus Brazilian real.

What about swaps? Swaps can be useful for firms that have a much better reputation among investors in one country (usually, the domestic market in which they operate) than in other markets. In such cases, these firms may choose to raise their funds domestically even for overseas projects because they get better terms on financing. This creates a mismatch between cash inflows and outflows, which can be resolved by using currency swaps, where a firm's liabilities in one currency can be swapped for liabilities in another currency. This enables the firm to take advantage of its reputation effect and match cash flows at the same time. Generally speaking, swaps can be used to take advantage of any market imperfections that a firm might observe. Thus, if floating rate debt is attractively priced relative to fixed rate debt, a firm that does not need floating rate debt can issue it and then swap it for fixed rate debt at a later date. ■

ILLUSTRATION 9.6 **Coming Up with the Financing Details: Disney**

In this example, we describe how we would make financing choices for Disney, using two approaches, one intuitive and the other more quantitative. Both approaches should be considered in light of the analysis done in the previous chapter, which suggested that Disney had untapped debt potential that could be used for future projects.

Intuitive Approach

The intuitive approach begins with an analysis of the characteristics of a typical project and uses it to make recommendations for the firm's financing. For Disney, the analysis is complicated by the fact that as a diverse entertainment business with

	Table 9.10 DESIGNING DISNEY'S PERFECT DEBT: INTUITIVE ANALYSIS	
Business	**Project Cash Flow Characteristics**	**Type of Financing**
Studio entertainment	Movie projects are likely to 1. Be short-term 2. Have cash outflows primarily in dollars (because Disney makes most of its movies in the U.S.), but cash inflows could have a substantial foreign currency component (because of overseas revenues) 3. Have net cash flows that are heavily driven by whether the movie is a hit, which is often difficult to predict	Debt should be 1. Short-term 2. Primarily dollar debt 3. If possible, tied to the success of movies (*Lion King* or *Mulan* bonds)
Media networks	Projects are likely to be 1. Short-term 2. Primarily in dollars, though foreign component is growing 3. Driven by advertising revenues and show success (Nielsen ratings)	Debt should be 1. Short-term 2. Primarily dollar debt 3. If possible, linked to show ratings
Park resorts	Projects are likely to be 1. Very long-term 2. Primarily in dollars, but a significant proportion of revenues come from foreign tourists, who are likely to stay away if the dollar strengthens 3. Affected by success of studio entertainment and media networks divisions	Debt should be 1. Long-term 2. Mix of currencies, based on tourist makeup
Consumer products	Projects are likely to be short- to medium-term and linked to the success of the movie division; most of Disney's product offerings are derived from their movie productions	Debt should be 1. Medium-term 2. Dollar debt

theme park holdings, its typical project varies by type of business. In Chapter 4, we broke down Disney into four businesses—studio entertainment, media networks, park resorts, and consumer products. In Table 9.10 we consider the typical project in each business and the appropriate debt for each.

A Quantitative Approach
A quantitative approach estimates Disney's sensitivity to changes in a number of macro-economic variables, using two measures: Disney's firm value (the market value of debt and equity) and its operating income.

Value Sensitivity to Factors: Past Data
The value of a firm is the obvious choice when it comes to measuring sensitivity to changes in interest rates, inflation rates, or currency rates, because firm value

Table 9.11 DISNEY'S FIRM VALUE AND MACROECONOMIC VARIABLES

Period	Operating Income (in Millions)	Firm Value (in Millions)	T-Bond Rate	Change in Rate	GDP (Deflated)	Change in GDP	CPI	Change in CPI	Weighted Dollar	Change in $
2003	$2,713	$68,239	4.29%	0.40%	10,493	3.60%	2.04%	0.01%	88.82	−14.51%
2002	$2,384	$53,708	3.87%	−0.82%	10,128	2.98%	2.03%	−0.10%	103.9	−3.47%
2001	$2,832	$45,030	4.73%	−1.20%	9,835	−0.02%	2.13%	−1.27%	107.64	1.85%
2000	$2,525	$47,717	6.00%	0.30%	9,837	3.53%	3.44%	0.86%	105.68	11.51%
1999	$3,580	$88,558	5.68%	−0.21%	9,502	4.43%	2.56%	1.05%	94.77	−0.59%
1998	$3,843	$65,487	5.90%	−0.19%	9,099	3.70%	1.49%	−0.65%	95.33	0.95%
1997	$3,945	$64,236	6.10%	−0.56%	8,774	4.79%	2.15%	−0.82%	94.43	7.54%
1996	$3,024	$65,489	6.70%	0.49%	8,373	3.97%	2.99%	0.18%	87.81	4.36%
1995	$2,262	$54,972	6.18%	−1.32%	8,053	2.46%	2.81%	0.19%	84.14	−1.07%
1994	$1,804	$33,071	7.60%	2.11%	7,860	4.30%	2.61%	−0.14%	85.05	−5.38%
1993	$1,560	$22,694	5.38%	−0.91%	7,536	2.25%	2.75%	−0.44%	89.89	4.26%
1992	$1,287	$25,048	6.35%	−1.01%	7,370	3.50%	3.20%	0.27%	86.22	−2.31%
1991	$1,004	$17,122	7.44%	−1.24%	7,121	−0.14%	2.92%	−3.17%	88.26	4.55%
1990	$1,287	$14,963	8.79%	0.47%	7,131	1.68%	6.29%	1.72%	84.42	−11.23%
1989	$1,109	$16,015	8.28%	−0.60%	7,013	3.76%	4.49%	0.23%	95.10	4.17%
1988	$789	$9,195	8.93%	−0.60%	6,759	4.10%	4.25%	−0.36%	91.29	−5.34%
1987	$707	$8,371	9.59%	2.02%	6,493	3.19%	4.63%	3.11%	96.44	−8.59%
1986	$281	$5,631	7.42%	−2.58%	6,292	3.11%	1.47%	−1.70%	105.50	−15.30%
1985	$206	$3,655	10.27%	−1.11%	6,102	3.39%	3.23%	−0.64%	124.56	−10.36%
1984	$143	$2,024	11.51%	−0.26%	5,902	4.18%	3.90%	−0.05%	138.96	8.01%
1983	$134	$1,817	11.80%	1.20%	5,665	6.72%	3.95%	−0.05%	128.65	4.47%
1982	$141	$2,108	10.47%	−3.08%	5,308	−1.61%	4.00%	−4.50%	123.14	6.48%
1981	$119	$1,707	13.98%		5,395		8.90%		115.65	

Firm Value = Market Value of Equity + Book Value of Debt. CPI = Consumer Price Index.

reflects the effect of these variables on current and future cash flows as well as on discount rates. We begin by collecting past data on firm value, operating income, and the macroeconomic variables against which we want to measure its sensitivity. In the case of the Disney, we choose four broad measures (see Table 9.11):

- **Long-term Treasury bond rate,** because the sensitivity of firm value to changes in interest rates provides a measure of the duration of the projects. It also provides insight into whether the firm should use fixed or floating rate debt; a firm whose operating income increases or decreases with interest rates should consider using floating rate loans.

- **Real GDP (gross domestic product),** because the sensitivity of firm value to this variable provides a measure of the cyclicality of the firm.

- ***Exchange rates,*** because the sensitivity of firm value to currency movements provides a measure of the exposure to currency rate risk and thus helps determine what the currency mix for the debt should be.
- ***Inflation rate,*** because the sensitivity of firm value to the inflation rate helps determine whether the interest rate on the debt should be fixed or floating rate debt.

Once these data were collected, we estimated the sensitivity of firm value to changes in the macroeconomic variables by regressing changes in firm value each year against changes in each of the individual variables.

I. Sensitivity to Changes in Interest Rates

As discussed earlier, the duration of a firm's projects provides useful information for determining the duration of its debt. Although bond-based duration measures may provide some answers, they will understate the duration of assets or projects if the cash flows on these assets or projects themselves vary with interest rates. Regressing changes in firm value at Disney against changes in interest rates over this period yields the following result (with t-statistics in parentheses):[23]

$$\text{Change in Firm Value} = 0.2081 - 4.16 \, (\text{Change in Interest Rates})$$
$$(2.91) \quad (0.75)$$

Based on this regression, the duration of Disney's projects collectively is about 4.16 years. If this were a reliable estimate, Disney should try to keep the duration of its bond issues to at least 4.16 years. Unfortunately, though, there is significant error in the estimate, and the coefficient is not a reliable estimate of duration.

II. Sensitivity to Changes in the Economy

Is Disney a cyclical firm? One way to answer this question is to measure the sensitivity of firm value to changes in economic growth. Regressing changes in firm value against changes in the real GDP over this period yields the following result:

$$\text{Change in Firm Value} = 0.2165 + 0.26 \, (\text{Change in GDP})$$
$$(1.56) \quad (0.07)$$

Disney's value as a firm has not been affected significantly by economic growth. Again, to the extent that we trust the coefficients from this regression, this would suggest that Disney is not a cyclical firm.

III. Sensitivity to Changes in the Inflation Rates

We earlier made the argument, based on asset/liability matching, that firms whose values tend to move with inflation should be more likely to issue floating rate debt.

---

[23]To ensure that the coefficient on this regression is a measure of duration, we compute the change in the interest rate as follows: $(r_t - r_{t-1})/(1 + r_{t-1})$. Thus, if the long-term bond rate goes from 8 percent to 9 percent, we compute the change to be $(0.09 - 0.08)/1.08$.

To examine whether Disney fits this pattern, we regressed changes in firm value against changes in the inflation rate over this period with the following result:

$$\text{Change in Firm Value} = 0.2262 + 0.57 \text{ (Change in CPI)}$$
$$(3.22) \quad (0.13)$$

Disney's firm value is unaffected by changes in inflation because the coefficient on inflation is not statistically different from zero. Interest payments have to be made out of operating cash flows, so we will also have to look at how operating income changes with inflation before we can make a final decision on this issue.

IV. Sensitivity to Changes in the Dollar
We can answer the question of how sensitive Disney's value is to changes in currency rates by looking at how the firm's value changes as a function of changes in exchange rates. Regressing changes in firm value against changes in the dollar over this period yields the following regression:

$$\text{Change in Firm Value} = 0.2060 - 2.05 \text{ (Change in Dollar)}$$
$$(3.40) \quad (2.52)$$

Statistically, this yields the strongest relationship. Disney's firm value decreases as the dollar strengthens. Consequently, Disney should consider using nondollar debt. If it had not been very sensitive to exchange rate changes, Disney could have issued primarily dollar debt.

Cash Flow Sensitivity to Factors: Past Data
In some cases, it is more reasonable to estimate the sensitivity of operating cash flows directly against changes in interest rates, inflation, and other variables. This is particularly true when we are designing interest payments on debt, because these payments are to be made out of operating income. For instance, although our regression of firm value against inflation rates showed no relationship and led to the conclusion that Disney should not issue floating rate debt, we might reverse our view if operating income were positively correlated with inflation rates. For Disney, we repeated the analysis using operating income as the dependent variable, rather than firm value. Because the procedure for the analysis is similar, we summarize the conclusions here.

- Regressing changes in operating cash flow against changes in interest rates over this period yields the following result:

$$\text{Change in Operating Income} = 0.2189 + 6.59 \text{ (Change in Interest Rates)}$$
$$(2.74) \quad (1.06)$$

Disney's operating income, unlike its firm value, has moved with interest rates. Again, this result has to be considered with caution in light of the low *t*-statistics on the coefficients. In general, regressing operating income against interest rate changes should yield a lower estimate of duration than the firm value measure, for two reasons. One is that income tends to be smoothed out relative to value, and the other is that the current operating income does not reflect the effects of changes in interest rates on discount rates and future growth.

- Regressing changes in operating cash flow against changes in real GDP over this period yields the following regression:

$$\text{Change in Operating Income} = 0.1725 + 0.66 \, (\text{Change in GDP})$$
$$(1.10) \quad (0.15)$$

Disney's operating income, like its firm value, does not reflect any sensitivity to overall economic growth, confirming the conclusion that Disney is not a cyclical firm.

- Regressing changes in operating cash flow against changes in the dollar over this period yields the following regression:

$$\text{Change in Operating Income} = 0.1768 - 1.76 \, (\text{Change in Dollar})$$
$$(2.42) \quad (1.81)$$

Disney's operating income, like its firm value, is negatively affected by a stronger dollar.

- Regressing changes in operating cash flow against changes in inflation over this period yields the following result:

$$\text{Change in Operating Income} = 0.2192 + 9.27 \, (\text{Change in CPI})$$
$$(3.01) \quad (1.95)$$

Unlike firm value, which is unaffected by changes in inflation, Disney's operating income moves strongly with inflation, rising as inflation increases. This would suggest that Disney has substantial pricing power, allowing it to pass inflation increases into its prices and operating income. This makes a strong case for the use of floating rate debt.

The question of what to do when operating income and firm value have different results can be resolved fairly simply. For issues relating to the overall design of the debt, the firm value regression should be relied on more; for issues relating to the design of interest payments on the debt, the operating income regression should be used more. Thus, for the duration measure, the regression of firm value on interest rates should generally give a more precise estimate. For the inflation rate sensitivity, because it affects the choice of interest payments (fixed or floating), the operating income regression should be relied on more.

Bottom-Up Estimates for Debt Design

Although a regression analysis yields quantitative results (as in Illustration 9.6), those results should be taken with a grain of salt. They make sense only if the firm has been in its current business for a long time and expects to remain in it for the foreseeable future. In today's environment, in which firms find their business mixes changing dramatically from period to period as they divest some businesses and acquire new ones, it is unwise to base too many conclusions on a historical analysis.

In such cases, we might want to look at the characteristics of the industry in which a firm plans to expand, rather than using past earnings or firm value as a basis for the analysis. Furthermore, the small sample sizes used tend to yield regression estimates that are not statistically significant (as is the case with the duration estimate that we obtained for Disney from the firm value regression).

For comparison, we looked at the sector estimates for each of the sensitivity measures for the entertainment, media network, theme park and consumer product businesses:[24]

	Coefficients on Firm Value Regression				
	Interest Rates	GDP Growth	Inflation	Currency	Disney Weights
Studio entertainment	−3.70	0.56	1.41	−1.23	25.62%
Media networks	−4.50	0.70	−3.05	−1.58	49.25%
Park resorts	−6.47	0.22	−1.45	−3.21	20.09%
Consumer products	−4.88	0.13	−5.51	−3.01	5.04%
Disney	−4.71	0.54	−1.71	−1.89	100%

These bottom-up estimates, akin to bottom-up betas, suggest that Disney should be issuing long-term fixed-rate debt with a duration of 4.71 years and that firms in this sector are relatively unaffected by movements in the overall economy. Like Disney, firms in these businesses tend to be hurt by a stronger dollar, but unlike Disney, they do not have much pricing power (note the negative coefficient on inflation). The sector averages also have the advantage of being more precise than the firm-specific estimates and can be relied on more.

Overall Recommendations

Based on the analyses of firm value and operating income, as well as the sector averages, our recommendations would essentially match those of the intuitive approach, but they would have more depth because of the additional information we have acquired from the quantitative analysis:

- The debt issued should be long-term and should have duration of between four and five years.
- A significant portion of the debt should be floating rate debt, reflecting Disney's capacity to pass inflation through to its customers and the fact that operating income tends to increase as interest rates go up.
- Given Disney's sensitivity to a stronger dollar, a portion of the debt should be in foreign currencies. The specific currency used and the magnitude of the foreign currency debt should reflect where Disney generates its revenues. Based on 2003

---

[24]These sector estimates were obtained by aggregating the firm values of all firms in a sector on a quarter-by-quarter basis going back twelve years, and then regressing changes in this aggregate firm value against changes in the macroeconomic variable each quarter.

numbers, this would indicate that about 20 percent of the debt should be in Euros and about 10 percent of the debt in yen, reflecting Disney's larger exposures in Europe and Asia. As its broadcasting businesses expand into Latin America, it may want to consider using either Mexican peso or Brazilian real debt as well.

These conclusions can be used to both design the new debt issues that the firm will be making going forward, and to evaluate the existing debt on the firm's books to see if there is a mismatching of assets and financing in the current firm. Examining Disney's debt at the end of 2003, we note the following:

- Disney has $13.1 billion in debt with an average maturity of 11.53 years. Even allowing for the fact that the maturity of debt is higher than the duration, this would indicate that Disney's debt is far too long term for its existing business mix.
- Of the debt, about 12 percent is Euro debt and there is no yen-denominated debt. Based on our analysis, a larger portion of Disney's debt should be in foreign currencies.
- Disney has about $1.3 billion in convertible debt and some floating rate debt, though no information is provided on its magnitude. If floating rate debt is a relatively small portion of existing debt, our analysis would indicate that Disney should be using more of it.

If Disney accepts the recommendation that its debt should be more short-term, more foreign currency, and more floating rate debt, it can get there in two ways:

- It can swap some of its existing long-term, fixed rate, dollar debt for shorter-term, floating rate, foreign currency debt. Given Disney's standing in financial markets and its large market capitalization, this should not be difficult to do.
- If Disney is planning new debt issues, either to get to a higher debt ratio or to fund new investments, it can use primarily short-term, floating rate, foreign currency debt to fund these new investments. Although it may be mismatching the funding on these investments, its debt matching will become better at the company level.

This spreadsheet allows you to estimate the sensitivity of firm value and operating income to changes in macroeconomic variables (**macrodur.xls**).

There is a data set online that summarizes the results of regressing firm value against macroeconomic variables by sector for U.S. companies.

ILLUSTRATION 9.7 Estimating the Right Financing Mix for Bookscape, Aracruz, and Deutsche Bank

Although we will not examine the right financing type for Bookscape, Aracruz, and Deutsche Bank in the same level of detail as we did for Disney, we will summarize, based on our understanding of their businesses, what we think will be the best kind of financing for each of these firms:

- **Bookscape** Given Bookscape's dependence on revenues at its New York bookstore, we would design the debt to be
  - Long-term, because the store is a long-term investment;
  - Dollar-denominated, because all the cash flows are in dollars; and
  - Fixed rate debt, because Bookscape's lack of pricing power makes it unlikely that its cash flows can keep pace with inflation.

  It is worth noting that operating leases fulfill all of these conditions, making it the appropriate debt for Bookscape. Because that is the only debt that Bookscape carries currently, we would suggest no changes.

- **Aracruz** Aracruz operates most of its paper plants in Brazil, but gets a significant proportion of its products overseas. More than 80 percent of its revenues in 2003 were from other countries, and the bulk of these revenues were dollar-denominated. Given this structure, we would design debt to be
  - Long term, because a typical paper plant has a life in excess of twenty years;
  - Dollar-denominated, because the cash inflows are primarily in dollars; and
  - Given the volatility of paper prices, we would try to link the interest rate on debt to pulp prices, if possible.

  The existing debt at Aracruz is primarily dollar debt but it is short-term, with an average maturity of 3.20 years. Although this may reflect the difficulties that Brazilian firms have faced in borrowing long-term historically, the constraints on borrowing long-term are easing for many emerging market companies that derive the bulk of their revenues in dollars.

- **Deutsche Bank** In the case of Deutsche Bank, the recommendation is made simpler by the fact that the debt ratio we are analyzing is the long-term debt ratio. In addition to being long-term, however, the debt should reflect
  - The mix of currencies in which Deutsche Bank gets its cash flows, which should lead to significant dollar (from its U.S. holdings), Euro, and British pound (from its investment banking subsidiary) debt issues. In future years, this would expand to include more emerging market debt issues to reflect Deutsche Bank's greater dependence on cash flows from these markets.
  - It is possible that Deutsche Bank's reputation in Europe may allow it to borrow more cheaply in some markets (say, Germany) than in others. If that is the case, it can either issue its dollar-denominated or pound-denominated debt in those markets, or issued debt in Euros and then swap the debt into U.S. dollar or British pound debt.

CONCLUSION

In this chapter, we examine how firms move toward their optimal debt ratios, and how they choose the right financing vehicles to use, to finance both existing assets and new investments.

Some firms that are under- or overlevered may choose to not change their debt ratios to the optimal level. This may arise either because they do not share the objective of maximizing firm value that underlies optimal debt ratios, or because they feel that the costs of moving to the optimal outweigh the benefits. Firms that do decide to change their financing mixes can change either gradually or quickly. Firms are much more likely to change their financing mixes quickly if external pressure is brought to bear on the firm. For underlevered firms, the pressure takes the form of hostile acquisitions, whereas for overlevered firms, the threat is default and bankruptcy. Firms that are not under external pressure for change have the luxury of changing toward their optimal debt ratios gradually.

Firms can change their debt ratios in four ways. They can recapitalize existing investments, using new debt to reduce equity or new equity to retire debt. They can divest existing assets and use the cash to reduce equity or retire debt. They can invest in new projects and finance them disproportionately with debt or equity. Finally, they can increase or decrease the proportion of their earnings that are returned to stockholders in the form of dividends or stock buybacks. To decide between these alternatives, firms have to consider how quickly they need to change their debt ratios, the quality of the new investments they have, and the marketability of existing investments.

In the final section, we examined how firms choose between financing vehicles. Matching cash flows on financing to the cash flows on assets reduces default risk and increases the debt capacity of firms. Applying this principle, long-term assets should be financed with long-term debt, assets with cash flows that move with inflation should be financed with floating rate debt, assets with cash flows in a foreign currency should be financed with debt in the same currency, and assets with growing cash flows should be financed with convertible debt. This matching can be done intuitively, by looking at a typical project, or based on historical data. Changes in operating income and value can be regressed against changes in macroeconomic variables to measure the sensitivity of the firm to these variables. The results can then be used to design the optimal financing vehicle for the firm.

LIVE CASE STUDY

MECHANICS OF MOVING TO THE OPTIMAL

Objective: To determine whether your firm should move to its optimal mix (and if so, how) and to analyze the right type of debt for your firm.

Key Questions

- If your firm's actual debt ratio is different from its "recommended" debt ratio, how should they get from the actual to the optimal? In particular,
    a. should they do it gradually over time or should they do it now?
    b. should they alter their existing mix (by buying back stock or retiring debt), should they invest in new projects with debt or equity or should they change how much they pay out as dividends?
- What type of financing should this firm use? In particular,
    a. should the financing be short-term or long-term? floating rate or fixed rate?
    b. what currency should it be in?
    c. what special features should the financing have?

Framework for Analysis

1. *The Immediacy Question*
   - If the firm is underlevered, does it have the characteristics of a firm that is a likely takeover target? (Target firms in hostile takeovers tend to be smaller, have poorer project and stock price performance than their peer groups, and have lower insider holdings.)
   - If the firm is overlevered, is it in danger of bankruptcy? (Look at the bond rating if the company is rated. A junk bond rating suggests high bankruptcy risk.)

2. *Alter Financing Mix or Take Projects*
   - What kind of projects does this firm expect to have? Can it expect to make excess returns on these projects? (Past project returns is a reasonable place to start—see the section under investment returns.)
   - What type of stockholders does this firm have? If cash had to be returned to them, would they prefer dividends or stock buybacks? (Again, look at the past. If the company has paid high dividends historically, it will end up with investors who like dividends.)

3. *Financing Type*
   - How sensitive has this firm's value been to changes in macroeconomic variables such as interest rates, currency movements, inflation, and the economy?

- How sensitive has this firm's operating income been to changes in the same variables?
- How sensitive is the sector's value and operating income to the same variables?
- What do the answers to the last three questions tell you about the kind of financing that this firm should use?

Getting Information on Mechanics of Capital Structure

To get the inputs needed to estimate the capital structure mechanics, you can get the information on macroeconomic variables such as interest rates, inflation, gross national product growth and exchange rates from the Web site for the book. You can get historical information on your own firm by looking at the Value Line page for your firm, which has information for the last fifteen years on revenues and operating income.

Online Sources of Information
www.stern.nyu.edu/~adamodar/cfin2E/project/data.htm.

PROBLEMS AND QUESTIONS

(In the problems below, you can use a risk premium of 5.5 percent and a tax rate of 40 percent if none is specified.)

1. BMD is a firm with no debt on its books currently and a market value of equity of $2 billion. Based on its EBITDA of $200 million, it can afford to have a debt ratio of 50 percent, at which level the firm value should be $300 million higher.

    a. Assuming that the firm plans to increase its leverage instantaneously, what are some of the approaches it could use to get to 50 percent?

    b. Is there a difference between repurchasing stock and paying a special dividend? Why or why not?

    c. If BMD has a cash balance of $250 million at this time, will it change any of your analysis?

2. MiniSink is a manufacturing company that has $100 million in debt outstanding and 9 million shares trading at $100 per share. The current beta is 1.10, and the interest rate on the debt is 8 percent. In the latest year, MiniSink reported a net income of $7.50 per share, and analysts expect earnings growth to be 10 percent a year for the next five years. The firm faces a tax rate of 40 percent and pays out 20 percent of its earnings as dividends (the Treasury bond rate is 7 percent).

    a. Estimate the debt ratio each year for the next five years, assuming that the firm maintains it current payout ratio.

    b. Estimate the debt ratio each year for the next five years, assuming that the firm doubles its dividends and repurchases 5 percent of the outstanding stock every year.

3. IOU has $5 billion in debt outstanding (carrying an interest rate of 9 percent), and 10 million shares trading at $50 per share. Based on its current EBIT of $200 million, its optimal debt ratio is only 30 percent. The firm has a beta of 1.20, and the current Treasury bond rate is 7 percent. Assuming that the operating income will increase 10 percent a year for the next five years and that the firm's depreciation and capital expenditures both amount to $100 million annually for each of the five years, estimate the debt ratio for IOU if it

    a. maintains its existing policy of paying $50 million a year in dividends for the next five years.

    b. eliminates dividends.

4. DGF Corporation has come to you for some advice on how best to increase their leverage over time. In the most recent year, DGF had an EBITDA of $300 million, owed $1 billion in both book value and market value terms, and had a net worth of $2 billion (the market value was twice the book value). It had a beta of 1.30, and the interest rate on its debt is 8 percent (the Treasury bond rate is 7 percent). If it moves to its optimal debt ratio of 40 percent, the cost of capital is expected to drop by 1 percent.

    a. How should the firm move to its optimal? In particular, should it borrow money and take on projects or should it pay dividends/repurchase stock?

    b. Are there any other considerations that may affect your decision?

5. STL has asked you for advice on putting together the details of the new debt issues it is planning to make. What information would you need to obtain to provide this advice?

6. Assume now that you have uncovered the following facts about the types of projects STL takes:

- The projects are primarily infrastructure projects, requiring large initial investments and long gestation periods.
- Most of the new projects will be in emerging markets, and the cash flows are expected to be in the local currencies, when they do occur.
- The magnitude of the cash flows will largely depend on how quickly the economies of the emerging markets grow in the long run.

How would you use this information in the design of the projects?

7. You are attempting to structure a debt issue for Eaton Corporation, a manufacturer of automotive components. You have collected the following information on the market values of debt and equity for the past ten years:

Year	Market Value of Equity (in Millions $)	Debt (in Millions $)
1985	1,824.9	436
1986	2,260.6	632
1987	2,389.6	795
1988	1,960.8	655
1989	2,226	836
1990	1,875.9	755
1991	2,009.7	795
1992	2,589.3	833
1993	3,210	649
1994	3,962.7	1,053

In addition, you have the following information on the changes in long-term interest rates, inflation rates, gross national product (GNP), and exchange rates over the same period.

Year	Long Bond Rate	GNP Growth	Weighted Dollar	Inflation Rate
1985	11.40%	6.44%	125.95	3.50%
1986	9.00%	5.40%	112.89	1.90%
1987	9.40%	6.90%	95.88	3.70%
1988	9.70%	7.89%	95.32	4.10%
1989	9.30%	7.23%	102.26	4.80%
1990	9.30%	5.35%	96.25	5.40%
1991	8.80%	2.88%	98.82	4.20%
1992	8.10%	6.22%	104.58	3.00%
1993	7.20%	5.34%	105.22	3.00%
1994	8.00%	5.97%	98.6	2.60%

Using this information,

a. Estimate the duration of this firm's projects. How would you use this information in designing the debt issue?

b. How cyclical is this company? How would that affect your debt issue?

c. Estimate the sensitivity of firm value to exchange rates. How would you use this information in designing the debt issue?

d. How sensitive is firm value to inflation rates? How would you use this information in designing the debt issue?

e. What factors might lead you to override the results of this analysis?

8. Repeat the analysis in Problem 7 for a private firm that has provided you with the following estimates of operating income for the ten years, for which you have the macroeconomic data:

Year	Operating Income (in $ thousands)
1985	463.05
1986	411.696
1987	483.252
1988	544.633
1989	550.65
1990	454.875
1991	341.481
1992	413.983
1993	567.729
1994	810.968

9. Assuming that you do the analysis in Problem 8 with both firm value and operating income, what are the reasons for the differences you might find in the results, using each? When would you use one over the other?

10. Pfizer, a major pharmaceutical company, has a debt ratio of 10.30 percent and is considering increasing its debt ratio to 30 percent. Its cost of capital is expected to drop from 14.51 percent to 13.45 percent. Pfizer had an EBIT of $2 billion in 1995, and a book value of capital (debt + equity) of approximately $8 billion. It also faced a tax rate of 40 percent on its income. The stock in the firm is widely held, but the corporate charter includes significant antitakeover restrictions.

a. Should Pfizer move to its desired debt ratio quickly or gradually? Explain.

b. Given the choice in part **a**, explain how you would move to the optimal.

c. Pfizer is consider using the excess debt capacity for an acquisition. What are some of the concerns it should have?

11. Upjohn, also a major pharmaceutical company, is considering increasing its debt ratio from 11 percent to 40 percent, which is its optimal debt ratio. Its beta is 1.17, and the current Treasury bond rate is 6.50 percent. The return on equity was 14.5 percent in the most recent year, but it is dropping as health care matures as a business. The company has also been mentioned as a possible takeover target and is widely held.
    a. Would you suggest that Upjohn move to the optimal ratio immediately? Explain.
    b. How would you recommend that Upjohn increase its debt ratio?

12. U.S. steel companies have generally been considered mature in terms of growth and often take on high leverage to finance their plant and equipment. Steel companies in some emerging markets often have high growth rates and good growth prospects. Would you expect these companies to also have high leverage? Why or why not?

13. You are trying to decide whether the debt structure that Bethlehem Steel has currently is appropriate, given its assets. You regress changes in firm value against changes in interest rates, and arrive at the following equation

    Change in Firm Value
    $= 0.20\% - 6.33$ (Change in Interest Rates)

    a. If Bethlehem Steel has primarily short-term debt outstanding, with a maturity of one year, would you deem the debt structure appropriate?
    b. Why might Bethlehem Steel be inclined to use short-term debt to finance longer-term assets?

14. Railroad companies in the United States tend to have long-term, fixed rate, dollar-denominated debt. Explain why.

15. The following table summarizes the results of regressing changes in firm value against changes in interest rates for six major footwear companies:

Change in Firm Value
    $= a + b$ (Change in Long-Term Interest Rates)

Company	Intercept (a)	Slope Coefficient (b)
LA Gear	−0.07	−4.74
Nike	0.05	−11.03
Stride Rite	0.01	−8.08
Timberland	0.06	−22.50
Reebok	0.04	−4.79
Wolverine	0.06	−2.42

a. How would you use these results to design debt for each of these companies?
b. How would you explain the wide variation across companies? Would you use the average across the companies in any way?

16. You have run a series of regressions of firm value changes at Motorola, the semiconductor company, against changes in a number of macroeconomic variables. The results are summarized here:

Change in Firm Value
    $= 0.05 - 3.87$ (Change in Long-Term Interest Rate)

Change in Firm Value
    $= 0.02 + 5.76$ (Change in Real GNP)

Change in Firm Value
    $= 0.04 - 2.59$ (Inflation Rate)

Change in Firm Value $= 0.05 - 3.40$ ($\$/$Euro)

a. Based on these regressions, how would you design Motorola's financing?
b. Motorola, like all semiconductor companies, is sensitive to the health of high-technology companies. Is there any special feature you can add to the debt to reflect this dependence?

CHAPTER 10

DIVIDEND POLICY

At the end of each year, every publicly traded company has to decide whether to return cash to its stockholders and, if so, how much in the form of dividends. The owner of a private company has to make a similar decision about how much cash he or she plans to withdraw from the business and how much to reinvest. This is the dividend decision, and we begin this chapter by providing some background on three aspects of dividend policy. One is a purely procedural question about how dividends are set and paid out to stockholders. The second is an examination of widely used measures of how much a firm pays in the dividends. The third is an empirical examination of some patterns that firms follow in dividend policy.

Having laid this groundwork, we look at three schools of thought on dividend policy. The dividend irrelevance school believes that dividend policy does not really matter because it does not affect firm value. This argument is based on two assumptions.

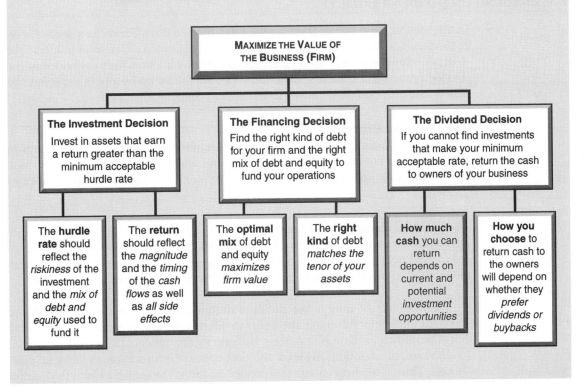

445

The first is that there is no tax disadvantage to an investor to receiving dividends, and the second is that firms can raise funds in capital markets for new investments without bearing significant issuance costs. The proponents of the second school feel that dividends are bad for the average stockholder because of the tax disadvantage they create, which results in lower value. Finally, there are those in a third group who argue that dividends are clearly good because stockholders (at least some of them) like them and react positively when dividends are increased.

Although dividends have traditionally been considered the primary approach for publicly traded firms to return cash or assets to their stockholders, they comprise only one of many ways available to the firm to accomplish this objective. In particular, firms can return cash to stockholders through equity repurchases, where the cash is used to buy back outstanding stock in the firm and reduce the number of shares outstanding. In addition, firms can return some of their assets to their stockholders in the form of spin-offs and split-offs. This chapter will focus on dividends specifically, but the next chapter will examine the other alternatives available to firms and how to choose between dividends and these alternatives.

BACKGROUND ON DIVIDEND POLICY

In this section, we consider three issues. First, how do firms decide how much to pay in dividends, and how do those dividends actually get paid to the stockholders? We then consider two widely used measures of how much a firm pays in dividends, the dividend payout ratio and the dividend yield. We follow up by looking at some empirical evidence on firm behavior in setting and changing dividends.

The Dividend Process

Firms in the United States generally pay dividends every quarter, whereas firms in other countries typically pay dividends on a semi-annual or annual basis. Let us look at the time line associated with dividend payment and define different types of dividends.

The Dividend Payment Time Line

Dividends in publicly traded firms are usually set by the board of directors and paid out to stockholders a few weeks later. There are several key dates between the time the board declares the dividend until the dividend is actually paid.

- The first date of note is the *dividend declaration date,* the date on which the board of directors declares the dollar dividend that will be paid for that quarter (or period). This date is important because by announcing its intent to increase, decrease, or maintain dividend, the firm conveys information to financial markets. Thus, if the firm changes its dividends, this is the date on which the market reaction to the change is most likely to occur.

Figure 10.1 The Dividend Time Line

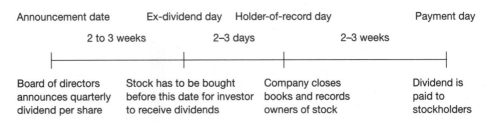

- The next date of note is the *ex-dividend date,* before which time investors must have bought the stock to receive the dividend. Because the dividend is not received by investors buying stock on or after the ex-dividend date, the stock price will generally fall on that day to reflect that loss.

- At the close of business a few days after the ex-dividend date, the company closes its stock transfer books and makes up a list of the shareholders on the *holder-of-record date.* These shareholders will receive the dividends. There should be generally be no price effect on this date.

- The final step involves mailing out the dividend checks on the *dividend payment date.* In most cases, the payment date is two to three weeks after the holder-of-record date. Although stockholders may view this as an important day, there should be no price impact on this day either.

Figure 10.1 presents these key dates on a time line.

Types of Dividends

There are several ways to classify dividends. First, dividends can be paid in cash or as additional stock. *Stock dividends* increase the number of shares outstanding and generally reduce the price per share. Second, the dividend can be a *regular dividend,* which is paid at regular intervals (quarterly, semi-annually, or annually), or a *special dividend,* which is paid in addition to the regular dividend. Most U.S. firms pay regular dividends every quarter; special dividends are paid infrequently. Finally, firms sometimes pay dividends that are in excess of the retained earnings they show on their books. These are called *liquidating dividends* and are viewed by the Internal Revenue Service as return on capital rather than ordinary income. As a result, they can have different tax consequences for investors.

Measures of Dividend Policy

We generally measure the dividends paid by a firm using one of two measures. The first is the **dividend yield,** which relates the dividend paid to the price of the stock:

Dividend Yield = Annual Dividends per Share/Price per Share

The dividend yield is significant because it provides a measure of that component of the total return that comes from dividends, with the balance coming from price appreciation.

Expected Return on Stock = Dividend Yield + Price Appreciation

Figure 10.2 Dividend Yields: Dividend-Paying Firms in the United States, January 2004

Source: Value Line, January 2004.

Some investors also use the dividend yield as a measure of risk and as an investment screen, that is, they invest in stocks with high dividend yields. Studies indicate that stocks with high dividend yields, after adjusting for market performance and risk, earn excess returns.

Figure 10.2 tracks dividend yields on the 2,700 listed stocks in the United States that paid dividends on the major exchanges in January 2004. Note, though, that 4,800 firms out of the total sample of 7,500 firms did not pay dividends. Strictly speaking, the median dividend yield for a stock in the United States is zero.

The median dividend yield among dividend paying stocks is 1.80 percent, and the average dividend yield of 2.12 percent is low by historical standards, as evidenced by Figure 10.3, which plots average dividend yields by year from 1960 to 2003.

The second widely used measure of dividend policy is the **dividend payout** ratio, which relates dividends paid to the earnings of the firm.

$$\text{Dividend Payout Ratio} = \text{Dividends}/\text{Earnings}$$

The payout ratio is used in a number of different settings. It is used in valuation as a way of estimating dividends in future periods, because most analysts estimate

Figure 10.3   Dividend Yield for U.S. Stocks, 1960–2003

Source: Bloomberg. Estimated using S&P 500 data from 1960 to 2003.

growth in earnings rather than dividends. Second, the retention ratio—the proportion of the earnings reinvested in the firm (Retention Ratio = 1 − Dividend Payout Ratio)—is useful in estimating future growth in earnings; firms with high retention ratios (low payout ratios) generally have higher growth rates in earnings than firms with lower retention ratios (higher payout ratios). Third, the dividend payout ratio tends to follow the life cycle of the firm, starting at zero when the firm is in high growth and gradually increasing as the firm matures and its growth prospects decrease. Figure 10.4 graphs the dividend payout ratios of U.S. firms that paid dividends in January 2004.

The payout ratios that are greater than 100 percent represent firms that paid out more than their earnings as dividends. The median dividend payout ratio in January 2004 among dividend-paying stocks, was about 30 percent, whereas the average payout ratio was approximately 35 percent.

Dividend Yield: The dollar dividend per share divided by the current price per share.

Dividend Payout: The dividend paid as a percent of the net income of the firm. If the earnings are negative, it is not meaningful.

Figure 10.4   Dividend Payout Ratios for Dividend-Paying U.S. Companies, January 2004

Source: Estimated using Value Line data on companies in January 2004.

10.1   DIVIDENDS THAT EXCEED EARNINGS

Companies should never pay out more than 100 percent of their earnings as dividends.

☐   True

☐   False

Explain.

There is a data set online that summarizes average dividend yields and payout ratios for U.S. companies from 1960 to the present.

Empirical Evidence on Dividend Policy

We observe several interesting patterns when we look at the dividend policies of firms in the United States in the past fifty years. First, dividends tend to lag behind earnings; that is, increases in earnings are generally followed by increases in dividends, and decreases in earnings sometimes by dividend cuts. Second, dividends are "sticky" because firms are typically reluctant to change dividends; in particular, firms avoid cutting dividends even when earnings drop. Third, dividends tend to follow a much smoother path than do earnings. Finally, there are distinct differences in dividend policy over the life cycle of a firm, resulting from changes in growth rates, cash flows, and project availability.

Figure 10.5   Dividends and Earnings on U.S. Companies, 1960–2004

Source: Estimated from Compustat annual database.

Dividends Tend to Follow Earnings

It should not come as a surprise that earnings and dividends are positively correlated over time because dividends are paid out of earnings. Figure 10.5 shows the movement in both earnings and dividends between 1960 and 2003. Take note of two trends in this graph. First, dividend changes trail earnings changes over time. Second, the dividend series is much smoother than is the earnings series.

In the 1950s, John Lintner studied the way firms set dividends and noted three consistent patterns.[1] First, firms set **target dividend payout ratios** by deciding on the fraction of earnings they are willing to pay out as dividends in the long term. Second, they change dividends to match long-term and sustainable shifts in earnings, but they increase dividends only if they feel they can maintain these higher dividends. Because firms avoid cutting dividends, dividends lag earnings. Finally, managers are much more concerned about changes in dividends than about levels of dividends.

Fama and Babiak identified a lag between earnings and dividends by regressing changes in dividends against changes in earnings in both current and prior

---

[1]J. Lintner, 1956, "Distribution of Income of Corporations among Dividends, Retained Earnings and Taxes," *American Economic Review,* 46, 97–113.

periods.[2] They confirmed Lintner's findings that dividend changes tend to follow earnings changes.

Target Dividend Payout Ratio: The desired proportion of earnings that a firm wants to pay out in dividends.

10.2 DETERMINANTS OF DIVIDEND LAG

Which of the following types of firms is likely to wait *least* after earnings go up before increasing dividends?

☐ A cyclical firm, whose earnings have surged because of an economic boom

☐ A pharmaceutical firm whose earnings have increased steadily over the past five years, due to a successful new drug

☐ A personal computer manufacturer, whose latest laptop's success has translated into a surge in earnings

Explain.

Dividends Are Sticky

Firms generally do not change their dollar dividends frequently. This reluctance to change dividends, which results in sticky dividends, is rooted in several factors. One is the firm's concern about its capability to maintain higher dividends in future periods. Another is that markets tend to take a dim view of dividend decreases, and the stock price drops to reflect that. Figure 10.6 provides a summary of the percentages of all firms that increased, decreased, or left unchanged their annual dividends per share from 1989 to 2003.

As you can see, in most years the number of firms that do not change their dollar dividends far exceeds the number that do. Among the firms that change dividends, a much higher percentage, on average, increase dividends than decrease them.

Dividends Follow a Smoother Path than Earnings

As a result of the reluctance to raise dividends until the firm feels able to maintain them and to cut dividends unless they absolutely have to, dividends follow a much smoother path than earnings. This view that dividends are not as volatile as earnings on a year-to-year basis is supported by a couple of empirical facts. First, the variability in historical dividends is significantly lower than the variability in historical earnings. Using annual data on aggregate earnings and dividends from 1960 to 2003, for instance, the standard deviation of year-to-year changes in dividends is 5 percent, whereas the standard deviation in year-to-year changes in earnings is about 14 percent. Second, the standard deviation in earnings yields across companies is significantly higher than the standard deviation in dividend yields.

A Firm's Dividend Policy Tends to Follow the Life Cycle of the Firm

In previous chapters, we introduced the link between a firm's place in the life cycle and its financing mix and choices. In particular, we noted five stages in the growth

---

[2]E. F. Fama and H. Babiak, 1968, "Dividend Policy: An Empirical Analysis," *Journal of the American Statistical Association,* 63(324), 1132–1161.

Figure 10.6   Dividend Changes: U.S. Corporations

Source: Compustat.

life cycle—start-up, rapid expansion, high growth, mature growth, and decline. In this section, we will examine the link between a firm's place in the life cycle and its dividend policy. Not surprisingly, firms adopt dividend policies that best fit where they are currently in their life cycles. For instance, high-growth firms with great investment opportunities do not usually pay dividends, whereas stable firms with larger cash flows and fewer projects tend to pay more of their earnings out as dividends. Figure 10.7 looks at the typical path that dividend payout follows over a firm's life cycle.

This intuitive relationship between dividend policy and growth is emphasized when we look at the relationship between a firm's payout ratio and its expected growth rate. For instance, we classified firms on the New York Stock Exchange in January 2004 into six groups, based on analyst estimates of expected growth rates in earnings per share for the next five years and estimated the dividend payout ratios and dividend yields for each class; these are reported in Figure 10.8. The firms with the highest expected growth rates pay the lowest dividends, both as a percent of earnings (payout ratio) and as a percent of price (dividend yield).[3]

---

[3]These are growth rates in earnings for the next five years projected by Value Line for firms in January 2004.

Figure 10.7 Life Cycle Analysis of Dividend Policy

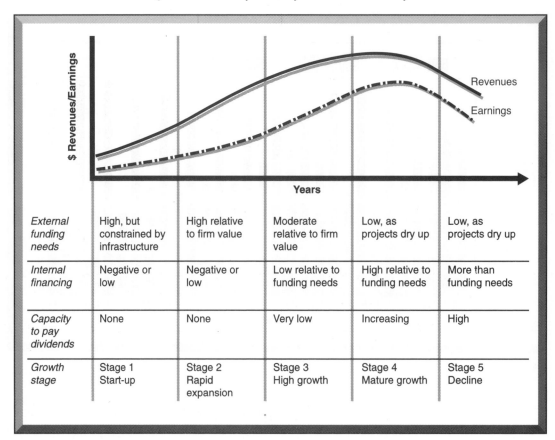

	Stage 1	Stage 2	Stage 3	Stage 4	Stage 5
External funding needs	High, but constrained by infrastructure	High relative to firm value	Moderate relative to firm value	Low, as projects dry up	Low, as projects dry up
Internal financing	Negative or low	Negative or low	Low relative to funding needs	High relative to funding needs	More than funding needs
Capacity to pay dividends	None	None	Very low	Increasing	High
Growth stage	Stage 1 Start-up	Stage 2 Rapid expansion	Stage 3 High growth	Stage 4 Mature growth	Stage 5 Decline

10.3 DIVIDEND POLICY AT GROWTH FIRMS

Assume that you are following a growth firm whose growth rate has begun easing. Which of the following would you most likely observe in terms of dividend policy at the firm?

☐ An immediate increase of dividends to reflect the lower reinvestment needs

☐ No change in dividend policy, and an increase in the cash balance

☐ No change in dividend policy, and an increase in acquisitions of other firms

Explain.

Differences in Dividend Policy across Countries

Figures 10.5 to 10.8 showed several trends and patterns in dividend policies at U.S. companies. They share some common features with firms in other countries, and there are some differences. As in the United States, dividends in other countries are sticky and follow earnings. However, there are differences in the magnitude of dividend

Figure 10.8   Dividend Yield and Payout Ratios—Growth Class

Source: Value Line Database projected for firms in January 2004.

payout ratios across countries. Figure 10.9 shows the proportion of earnings paid out in dividends in the G-7 countries in 1982–1984 and again in 1989–1991.[4]

These differences can be attributed to:

1. ***Differences in Stage of Growth***   Just as higher-growth companies tend to pay out less of their earnings in dividends (see Figure 10.8), companies in countries with higher growth pay out less in dividends. For instance, Japan had much higher expected growth in 1982–1984 than the other G-7 countries and paid out a much smaller percentage of its earnings as dividends.

2. ***Differences in Tax Treatment***   Unlike the United States, where dividends are doubly taxed, some countries provide at least partial protection against the double taxation of dividends. For instance, Germany taxes corporate retained earnings at a higher rate than corporate dividends, and the UK allows investors a dividend tax credit.

3. ***Differences in Corporate Control***   When there is a separation between ownership and management, as there is in many large publicly traded firms, and where stockholders have little control over managers, the dividends paid by firms will be lower. Managers, left to their own devices, have an incentive to accumulate cash.

---

[4]R. Rajan and L. Zingales, 1995, "What Do We Know about Capital Structure? Some Evidence from International Data," *Journal of Finance,* 50, 1421–1460.

Figure 10.9   Dividend Payout Ratios in G-7 Countries, 1982–1984 and 1989–1991

Source: Rajan and Zingales (1995).

Not surprisingly, the dividend payout ratios of companies in emerging markets are much lower than the dividend payout ratios in the G-7 countries. The higher growth and relative power of incumbent management in these countries contribute to keeping these payout ratios low.

10.4   DIVIDEND POLICIES AND STOCK BUYBACK RESTRICTIONS

Some countries do not allow firms to buy back stock from their stockholders. Which of the following would you expect of dividend policies in these countries (relative to countries that don't restrict stock buybacks)?

☐   Higher portion of earnings will be paid out in dividends; more volatile dividends

☐   Lower portion of earnings will be paid out in dividends; more volatile dividends

☐   Higher portion of earnings will be paid out in dividends; less volatile dividends

☐   Lower portion of earnings will be paid out in dividends; less volatile dividends

Explain.

ILLUSTRATION **10.1**   Dividends, Dividend Yields, and Payout Ratios

In this illustration, we will examine the dividends paid at Disney, Aracruz, and Deutsche Bank between 2001 and 2003. For each year we will also compute the dividend yield and dividend payout ratio for each firm.

	Deutsche Bank			Disney			Aracruz		
	2001	2002	2003	2001	2002	2003	2001	2002	2003
Dividend per share	€1.30	€1.30	€1.30	$0.21	$0.21	$0.21	R$0.14	R$0.18	R$0.32
Earnings per share	€2.44	€0.64	€0.27	$0.11	$0.60	$0.65	R$0.20	R$0.01	R$0.85
Stock price	€79.40	€43.90	€65.70	$20.72	$16.31	$23.33	R$3.91	R$6.76	R$10.60
Dividend yield	1.64%	2.96%	1.98%	1.01%	1.29%	0.90%	3.53%	2.69%	3.00%
Dividend payout	53.28%	203.13%	481.48%	190.91%	35.00%	32.31%	69.01%	1818.44%	37.41%

Of the three companies, Aracruz had the highest dividend yield across the three years. Disney and Deutsche Bank paid the same dividends per share each year, but the volatility in their stock prices and earnings made the payout ratios and dividend yields volatile. In fact, Deutsche maintained its dividends at 1.30 Euros per share in the face of declining earnings per share in 2002 and 2003, a testimonial to the stickiness of dividends.

As noted earlier in the book, Aracruz, like most Brazilian companies, maintains two classes of shares—voting share (called common and held by insiders) and nonvoting shares (called preferred shares, held by outside investors). The dividend policies are different for the two classes with preferred shares getting higher dividends. In fact, the failure to pay a mandated dividend to preferred stockholders (usually set at a payout ratio of 35 percent) can result in preferred stockholders getting some voting control of the firm. Effectively, this puts a floor on the dividend payout ratio.

WHEN ARE DIVIDENDS IRRELEVANT?

There is a school of thought that argues that what a firm pays in dividends is irrelevant and that stockholders are indifferent about receiving dividends. Like the capital structure irrelevance proposition, the dividend irrelevance argument has its roots in a paper crafted by Miller and Modigliani.[5]

The Underlying Assumptions

The underlying intuition for the dividend irrelevance proposition is simple. Firms that pay more dividends offer less price appreciation but must provide the same total return to stockholders, given their risk characteristics and the cash flows from

---

[5]M. Miller and F. Modigliani, 1961, "Dividend Policy, Growth and the Valuation of Shares," *Journal of Business,* 34, 411–433.

their investment decisions. Thus, if there are no taxes, or if dividends and capital gains are taxed at the same rate, investors should be indifferent to receiving their returns in dividends or price appreciation.

For this argument to work, in addition to assuming that there is no tax advantage or disadvantage associated with dividends, we also have to assume the following:

- There are no transaction costs associated with converting price appreciation into cash by selling stock. If this were *not* true, investors who need cash urgently might prefer to receive dividends.

- Firms that pay too much in dividends can issue stock, again with no issuance or transaction costs, and use the proceeds to invest in good projects. In addition, managers of firms that pay too little in dividends do not waste the cash pursuing their own interests (i.e., managers with large surplus cash flows do not use them to invest in bad projects). Consequently, the investment decisions of the firm are unaffected by its dividend decisions, and the firm's operating cash flows are the same no matter which dividend policy is adopted.

There is also an implicit assumption that this stock is fairly priced. Under these assumptions, neither the firms paying the dividends nor the stockholders receiving them will be adversely affected by firms paying either too little or too much in dividends.

10.5 DIVIDEND IRRELEVANCE

Based on the Miller-Modigliani assumptions, dividends are least likely to affect value for what types of firms?

☐ Small companies with substantial investment needs

☐ Large companies with significant insider holdings

☐ Large companies with significant holdings by pension funds (which are tax-exempt) and minimal investment needs

Explain.

A Proof of Dividend Irrelevance

To provide a formal proof of irrelevance, assume that LongLast Corporation, an unlevered furniture manufacturing firm, has operating income after taxes of $100 million, is growing at 5 percent a year, and has a cost of capital of 10 percent. Furthermore, assume that this firm has reinvestment needs of $50 million, also growing at 5 percent a year, and there are 105 million shares outstanding. Finally, assume that this firm pays out residual cash flows as dividends each year. The value of LongLast can be estimated as follows:

$$\text{Free Cash Flow to the Firm} = \text{EBIT}(1 - \text{Tax Rate}) - \text{Reinvestment Needs}$$
$$= \$100 \text{ million} - \$50 \text{ million} = \$50 \text{ million}$$

$$\text{Value of the Firm} = \text{Free Cash Flow to Firm } (1 + g)/(\text{WACC} - g)$$
$$= \$50(1.05)/(0.10 - 0.05) = \$1{,}050 \text{ million}$$

$$\text{Price per Share} = \$1{,}050 \text{ million}/105 \text{ million} = \$10.00$$

Based on its cash flows, this firm could pay out $50 million in dividends now.

$$\text{Dividend per Share} = \$50 \text{ million}/105 \text{ million} = \$0.476$$

$$\text{Total Value per Share} = \$10.00 + \$0.476 = \$10.476$$

The total value per share measures what stockholders get in price and dividends from their stock holdings.

Scenario 1: LongLast Doubles Dividends
To examine how the dividend policy affects firm value, assume that LongLast is told by an investment banker that its stockholders would gain if the firm paid out $100 million in dividends instead of $50 million. It now has to raise $50 million in new financing to cover its reinvestment needs. Assume that LongLast can issue new stock with *no issuance cost* to raise these funds. If it does so, the firm value will remain unchanged, because the value is determined not by the dividend paid but by the cash flows generated on the projects. Because the growth rate and the cost of capital are unaffected, we get:

$$\text{Value of the Firm} = \$50(1.05)/(0.10 - 0.05) = \$1,050 \text{ million}$$

The existing stockholders will receive a much larger dividend per share, because dividends have been doubled:

$$\text{Dividends per Share} = \$100 \text{ million}/105 \text{ million shares} = \$0.953$$

To estimate the price per share at which the new stock will be issued, note that after the new stock issue of $50 million, the old stockholders in the firm will own only $1,000 million of the total firm value of $1,050 million.

$$\text{Value of the Firm for Existing Stockholders after Dividend Payment} = \$1,000 \text{ million}$$

$$\text{Price per Share} = \$1,000 \text{ million}/105 \text{ million} = \$9.523$$

The price per share is now lower than it was before the dividend increase, but it is exactly offset by the increase in dividends.

$$\text{Value Accruing to Stockholder} = \$9.523 + \$0.953 = \$10.476$$

Thus, if the operating cash flows are unaffected by dividend policy, we can show that the firm value will be unaffected by dividend policy and that the average stockholder will be indifferent to dividend policy because he or she receives the same total value (price + dividends) under any dividend policy.

Scenario 2: LongLast Stops Paying Dividends
To consider an alternate scenario, assume that LongLast pays out no dividends and retains the residual $50 million as a cash balance. The value of the firm to existing stockholders can then be computed as follows:

$$\text{Value of Firm} = \text{Present Value of After-Tax Operating CF} + \text{Cash Balance}$$
$$= \$50(1.05)/(0.10 - 0.05) + \$50 \text{ million} = \$1,100 \text{ million}$$

$$\text{Value per Share} = \$1,100 \text{ million}/105 \text{ million shares} = \$10.476$$

Table 10.1 VALUE PER SHARE TO EXISTING STOCKHOLDERS FROM DIFFERENT
DIVIDEND POLICIES

Value of Firm (Operating CF)	Dividends	Value to Existing Stockholders	Price per Share	Dividends per Share	Total Value per Share
$1,050	$—	$1,100	$10.476	$—	$10.476
$1,050	$10.00	$1,090	$10.381	$0.095	$10.476
$1,050	$20.00	$1,080	$10.286	$0.190	$10.476
$1,050	$30.00	$1,070	$10.190	$0.286	$10.476
$1,050	$40.00	$1,060	$10.095	$0.381	$10.476
$1,050	$50.00	$1,050	$10.000	$0.476	$10.476
$1,050	$60.00	$1,040	$9.905	$0.571	$10.476
$1,050	$70.00	$1,030	$9.810	$0.667	$10.476
$1,050	$80.00	$1,020	$9.714	$0.762	$10.476
$1,050	$90.00	$1,010	$9.619	$0.857	$10.476
$1,050	$100.00	$1,000	$9.524	$0.952	$10.476

Note that the total value per share remains at $10.476. In fact, as shown in Table 10.1, the value per share remains $10.476 no matter how much the firm pays in dividends.

When LongLast pays less than $50 million in dividends, the cash accrues in the firm and adds to its value. The increase in the stock price again is offset by the loss of cash flows from dividends. When it pays out more, the price decreases but is exactly offset by the increase in dividends per share.

Note, however, that the value per share remains unchanged because we assume that there are no tax differences to investors between receiving dividends and capital gains, that firms can raise new capital with no issuance costs, and that firms do not change their investment policy even when they have excess cash. These assumptions eliminate the costs associated with paying either more in dividends or less.

Implications of Dividend Irrelevance

If dividends are, in fact, irrelevant, firms are spending a great deal of time pondering an issue about which their stockholders are indifferent. A number of strong implications emerge from this proposition. Among them, the value of equity in a firm should not change as its dividend policy changes. This does not imply that the price per share will be unaffected, however, because larger dividends should result in lower stock prices and more shares outstanding. In addition, in the long run, there should be no correlation between dividend policy and stock returns. Later in this chapter, we will examine some studies that have attempted to examine whether dividend policy is actually irrelevant in practice.

The assumptions needed to arrive at the dividend irrelevance proposition may seem so onerous that many reject it without testing it. That would be a mistake, however, because the argument does contain a valuable message: Namely, a firm that has invested in bad projects cannot hope to resurrect its image with stockholders by offering them higher dividends. Conversely, a firm that invests its money well will be forgiven by stockholders even if it chooses not to pay out what it can afford in dividends. This may yield some insight into why investors are much more sanguine about cash being accumulated in some companies than in others.

THE "DIVIDENDS ARE BAD" SCHOOL

In the United States, dividends have historically been taxed at much higher rates than capital gains. Based on this tax disadvantage, the second school of thought on dividends argued that dividend payments reduce the returns to stockholders after personal taxes. Stockholders, they posited, would respond by reducing the stock prices of the firms making these payments, relative to firms that do not pay dividends. Consequently, firms would be better off either retaining the money they would have paid out as dividends or repurchasing stock. In 2003, the basis for this argument was largely eliminated when the tax rate on dividends was reduced to match the tax rate on capital gains. In this section, we will consider both the history of tax-disadvantaged dividends and the potential effects of the tax law changes.[6]

The History of Dividend Taxation

The tax treatment of dividends varies widely depending on who receives the dividend. Until 2003, individual investors were taxed at ordinary tax rates, corporations are sheltered from paying taxes on at least a portion of the dividends they receive, and pension funds are not taxed at all.

Individuals

Since the inception of income taxes in the early twentieth century in the United States, dividends received on investments have been treated as ordinary income when received by individuals and taxed at ordinary tax rates. In contrast, the price appreciation on an investment has been treated as capital gains and taxed at a different and much lower rate. Figure 10.10 graphs the highest marginal tax rate on dividends in the United States and the highest marginal capital gains tax rate since 1954 (when capital gains taxes were introduced).

Barring a brief period after the 1986 tax reform act, when dividends and capital gains were both taxed at 28 percent, the capital gains tax rate has been significantly lower than the ordinary tax rate in the United States. In 2003, the tax rate on dividends was dropped to 15 percent to match the tax rate on capital gains, thus nullifying the tax disadvantage of dividends.

There are two points worth making about this chart. The first is that these are the highest marginal tax rates and that most individuals are taxed at lower rates. In fact, some older and poorer investors may pay no taxes on dividends if they fall below the threshold for income taxes. The second and related issue is that the capital gains

---

[6]Adding to the uncertainty is the fact that the tax changes of 2003 are not permanent and are designed to sunset (disappear) in 2010. It is unclear whether the tax disadvantages of dividends have disappeared for the long term or only until 2010.

Figure 10.10 Ordinary Income and Capital Gains Tax Rates

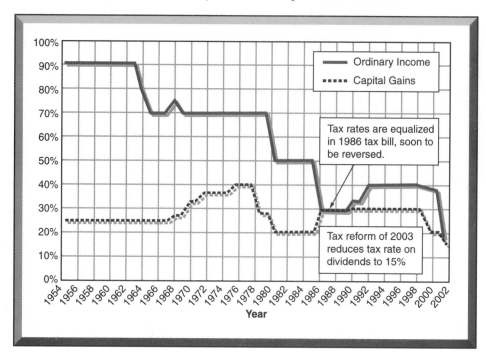

taxes can be higher for some of these individuals than the ordinary tax rate they pay on dividends. Overall, however, wealthier individuals have more invested in stocks than poorer individuals, and it seems fair to conclude that individuals have collectively paid significant taxes on the income that they have received in dividends over the past few decades.

Institutional Investors

About two-thirds of all traded equities are held by institutional investors rather than individuals. These institutions include mutual funds, pension funds, and corporations, and dividends get taxed differently in the hands of each.

- Pension funds are tax-exempt. They are allowed to accumulate both dividends and capital gains without having to pay taxes. There are two reasons for this tax treatment. One is to encourage individuals to save for their retirement and to reward savings (as opposed to consumption). The other reason for this is that individuals will be taxed on the income they receive from their pension plans and that taxing pension plans would in effect tax the same income twice.

- Mutual funds are not directly taxed, but investors in them are taxed for their share of the dividends and capital gains generated by the funds. If high-tax-rate individuals invest in a mutual fund that invests in stocks that pay high dividends, these high dividends will be allocated to the individuals based on their holdings and taxed at their individual tax rates.

- Corporations are given special protection from taxation on dividends they receive on their holdings in other companies, with 70 percent of the dividends exempt from taxes.[7] In other words, a corporation with a 40 percent tax rate that receives $100 million in dividends will pay only $12 million in taxes. Here again, the reasoning is that dividends paid by these corporations to their stockholders will ultimately be taxed.

Tax Treatment of Dividends in Other Markets

Many countries have plans in place to protect investors from the double taxation of dividends. There are two ways in which they can do this. One is to allow corporations to claim a full or partial tax deduction for dividends paid. The other is to give partial or full tax relief to individuals who receive dividends.

Corporate Tax Relief

In some countries, corporations are allowed to claim a partial or full deduction for dividends paid. This brings their treatment into parity with the treatment of the interest paid on debt, which is entitled to a full deduction in most countries. Among the Organization for Economic Co-operation and Development (OECD) countries, the Czech Republic and Iceland offer partial deductions for dividend payments made by companies, but no country allows a full deduction. In a variation, Germany until recently applied a higher tax rate to income that was retained by firms than to income that was paid out in dividends. In effect, this gives a partial tax deduction to dividends.

Why don't more countries offer tax relief to corporations? There are two factors. One is the presence of foreign investors in the stock who now also share in the tax windfall. The other is that investors in the stock may be tax-exempt or pay no taxes, which effectively reduces the overall taxes paid on dividends to the treasury to zero.

Individual Tax Relief

There are far more countries that offer tax relief to individuals than to corporations. This tax relief can take several forms:

- ***Tax credit for taxes paid by corporation***   Individuals can be allowed to claim the taxes paid by the corporation as a credit when computing their own taxes. Consider, for example, a company with a 30 percent tax rate and income of $100 million that pays its entire after-tax income as dividends to individuals with 40 percent tax rates. These individuals would be allowed to claim a tax credit of $30 million against the taxes owed. In effect, this will mean that only individuals

---

[7]The exemption increases as the proportion of the stock held increases. Thus, a corporation that owns 10 percent of another company's stock has 70 percent of dividends exempted. This rises to 80 percent if the company owns between 20 and 80 percent of the stock and to 100 percent if the company holds more than 80 percent of the outstanding stock.

with marginal tax rates that exceed the corporate tax rate will be taxed on dividends. Australia, Finland, Mexico, and New Zealand allow individuals to get a full credit for corporate taxes paid. Canada, France, the United Kingdom, and Turkey allow for partial tax credits.

- *Lower tax rate on dividends*   Dividends get taxed at a lower rate than other income to reflect the fact that it is paid out of after-tax income. In some countries, the tax rate on dividends is set equal to the capital gains tax rate. South Korea, for instance, has a flat tax rate of 16.5 percent for dividend income. This is the path the United States chose in 2003 to grant relief from double taxation to stock investors.

In summary, it is far more common for countries to provide tax relief to investors than to corporations. Part of the reason for this is political. By focusing on individuals, you can direct the tax relief only toward domestic investors and only to those investors who pay taxes in the first place.

Timing of Tax Payments

When the 1986 tax reform was signed into law, equalizing tax rates on ordinary income and capital gains, some believed that all the tax disadvantages of dividends had disappeared. Others noted that even with the same tax rates, dividends carried a tax disadvantage because the investor had no choice as to when to report the dividend as income; taxes were due when the firm paid out the dividends. In contrast, investors retained discretionary power over when to recognize and pay taxes on capital gains because such taxes were not due until the stock was sold. This timing option allowed the investor to reduce the tax liability in one of two ways. First, by taking capital gains in periods of low income or capital losses to offset against the gain, the investor could now reduce the taxes paid. Second, deferring a stock sale until an investor's death could result in tax savings, especially if the investor is not subject to estate taxes.

Assessing Investor Tax Preferences for Dividends

As you can see from the foregoing discussion, the tax rate on dividends can vary widely for different investors—individual, pension fund, mutual fund, or corporation—receiving the dividends and even for the same investor on different investments. It is difficult therefore to look at a company's investor base and determine their preferences for dividends and capital gains. A simple way to measure the tax disadvantage associated with dividends is to measure the price change on the ex-dividend date and compare it to the actual dividend paid. The stock price on the ex-dividend day should drop to reflect the loss in dividends to those buying the stock after that day. It is not clear, however, whether the price drop will be equal to the dividends if dividends and capital gains are taxed at different rates.

To see the relationship between the price drop and the tax rates of the marginal investor, assume that investors in a firm acquired stock at some point in time at a price P, and that they are approaching an ex-dividend day, in which the dividend is known to be D. Assume that each investor in this firm can either sell the stock before the ex-dividend day at a price P_B or wait and sell it after the stock goes ex-dividend at a price P_A. Finally, assume that the tax rate on dividends is t_o and that the tax rate on capital gains is t_{cg}. The cash flows the investor will receive from selling *before* the stock goes ex-dividend is

$$CF_B = P_B - (P_B - P)t_{cg}$$

In this case, by selling before the ex-dividend day, the investor receives no dividend. If the sale occurs *after* the ex-dividend day, the cash flow is

$$CF_A = P_A - (P_A - P)t_{cg} + D(1 - t_o)$$

If the cash flow from selling before the ex-dividend day were greater than the cash flow from selling after for all investors, they would all sell before, resulting in a drop in the stock price. Similarly, if the cash flows from selling after the ex-dividend day were greater than the cash flows from selling before to all investors, everyone would sell after, resulting in a price drop after the ex-dividend day. To prevent either scenario, the marginal investors in the stock have to be indifferent between selling before and after the ex-dividend day. This will occur only if the cash flows from selling before are equal to the cash flows from selling after:

$$P_B - (P_B - P)t_{cg} = P_A - (P_A - P)t_{cg} + D(1 - t_o)$$

This can be simplified to yield the following ex-dividend day equality:

$$\frac{P_B - P_A}{D} = \frac{(1 - t_o)}{(1 - t_{cg})}$$

Thus, a necessary condition for the marginal investor to be indifferent between selling before and after the ex-dividend day is that the price drop on the ex-dividend day must reflect the investor's tax differential between dividends and capital gains.

By turning this equation around, we would argue that by observing a firm's stock price behavior on the ex-dividend day and relating it to the dividends paid by the firm we can, in the long run, form some conclusions about the tax disadvantage the firm's stockholders attach to dividends. In particular:

If	Tax Treatment of Dividends and Capital Gains
$P_B - P_A = D$	Marginal investor is indifferent between dividends and capital gains
$P_B - P_A < D$	Marginal investor is taxed more heavily on dividends
$P_B - P_A > D$	Marginal investor is taxed more heavily on capital gains

Although there are obvious measurement problems associated with this measure, it does provide some interesting insight into how investors view dividends.

The first study of ex-dividend day price behavior was completed by Elton and Gruber in 1970.[8] They examined the behavior of stock prices on ex-dividend days for stocks listed on the NYSE between 1966 and 1969. Based on their finding that the price drop was only 78 percent of the dividends paid, Elton and Gruber concluded that dividends are taxed more heavily than capital gains. They also estimated the price change as a proportion of the dividend paid for firms in different dividend yield classes and reported that price drop is larger, relative to the dividend paid, for firms in the highest dividend yield classes than for firms in lower dividend yield classes. This difference in price drops, they argued, reflected the fact that investors in these firms are in lower tax brackets. Their conclusions were challenged, however, by some who argued justifiably that the investors trading on the stock on ex-dividend days are not the normal investors in the firm; rather, they are short-term, tax-exempt investors interested in capturing the difference between dividends and the price drops.

Implications

There is no argument that dividends have historically been treated less favorably than capital gains by the tax authorities. In the United States, the double taxation of dividends, at least at the level of individual investors, should have created a strong disincentive to pay or to increase dividends. Other implications of the tax disadvantage argument include the following:

- Firms with an investor base composed primarily of individuals typically should have paid lower dividends than firms with investor bases predominantly made up of tax-exempt institutions.
- The higher the income level (and hence the tax rates) of the investors holding stock in a firm, the lower should have been the dividend paid out by the firm.
- As the tax disadvantage associated with dividends increased, the aggregate amount paid in dividends should have decreased. Conversely, as the tax disadvantage associated with dividends decreased, the aggregate amount paid in dividends should have increased.

The tax law changes of 2003 have clearly changed the terms of this debate. By reducing the tax rate on dividends, they have made dividends more attractive at least to individual investors than they were prior to the change. We would expect companies to pay more dividends in response. Although it is still early to test out this hypothesis, there is some evidence that companies are changing dividend policy in response to the tax law change. Technology companies like Microsoft that had never paid dividends before have initiated dividends. In Figure 10.11, we look at the percent of S&P 500 companies that pay dividends by year both in terms of number of firms and the market cap of these firms.

There was an uptick in both the number of companies paying dividends in 2003 and the dividends paid, reversing a long decline in both statistics. It will be interesting to see whether this continues into the future.

---

[8]E. J. Elton and M. J. Gruber, 1970, "Marginal Stockholder Rates and the Clientele Effect," *Review of Economics and Statistics,* 52, 68–74.

Figure 10.11   Dividends on S&P 500 Companies

IN PRACTICE: DIVIDEND POLICY FOR THE NEXT DECADE

As firms shift toward higher dividends, they may be put at risk because of volatile earnings. There are two ways they can alleviate the problem.

- One is to shift to a policy of *residual dividends,* where dividends paid are a function of the earnings in the year rather than a function of dividends last year. Note that the sticky dividend phenomenon in the United States, where companies are reluctant to change their dollar dividends, is not universal. In countries like Brazil, companies target dividend payout ratios rather than dollar dividends and there is no reason why U.S. companies cannot adopt a similar practice. A firm that targets a constant dividend payout ratio will pay more dividends when its earnings are high and less when its earnings are low, and the signaling effect of lower dividends will be mitigated if the payout policy is clearly stated up front.

- The other option is to adopt a policy of regular dividends that will be based on sustainable and predictable earnings and to supplement these with special dividends when earnings are high. In this form, the special dividends will take the place of stock buybacks.

In summary, you can expect both more dividends from companies and more creative dividend policies, if the dividend tax law stands. In 2004, British Petroleum provided a preview of innovations to come by announcing that they would supplement their regular dividends with any extra cash flows generated if the oil price stayed above $30 a barrel, thus creating dividends that are tied more closely to their cash flows. ∎

10.6 CORPORATE TAX STATUS AND DIVIDEND POLICY

Corporations are exempt from paying taxes on 70 percent of the dividends they receive from their stock holdings in other companies, whereas they face a capital gains tax rate of 20 percent. If all the stock in your company is held by other companies, and the ordinary tax rate for companies is 36 percent,

☐ dividends have a tax advantage relative to capital gains.

☐ capital gains have a tax advantage relative to dividends.

☐ dividends and capital gains are taxed at the same rate.

Explain.

THE "DIVIDENDS ARE GOOD" SCHOOL

Notwithstanding the tax disadvantages, firms continue to pay dividends and many investors view such payments positively. A third school of thought argues dividends are good and can increase firm value. Some of the arguments used are questionable, but some have a reasonable basis in fact. We consider both in this section.

Some Reasons for Paying Dividends That Do Not Measure Up

Some firms pay and increase dividends for the wrong reasons. We will consider two of those reasons in this section.

The Bird-in-the-Hand Fallacy

One reason given for the view that investors prefer dividends to capital gains is that dividends are certain, whereas capital gains are uncertain. Proponents of this view of dividend policy feel that risk-averse investors will therefore prefer the former. This argument is flawed. The simplest response is to point out that the choice is not between certain dividends today and uncertain capital gains at some unspecified point in the future but between dividends today and an almost equivalent amount in price appreciation today. This comparison follows from our earlier discussion, where we noted that the stock price dropped by slightly less than the dividend on the ex-dividend day. By paying the dividend, the firm causes its stock price to drop today.

Another response to this argument is that a firm's value is determined by the cash flows from its projects. If a firm increases its dividends but its investment policy remains unchanged, it will have to replace the dividends with new stock issues. The investor who receives the higher dividend will therefore find him- or herself losing, in present value terms, an equivalent amount in price appreciation.

Temporary Excess Cash

In some cases, firms are tempted to pay or initiate dividends in years in which their operations generate excess cash. Although it is perfectly legitimate to return excess

Figure 10.12   Issuance Costs for Stocks and Bonds (As Percent of Proceeds)

Source: Ibbotson, Sindelar, and Ritter (1988).

cash to stockholders, firms should also consider their own long-term investment needs. If the excess cash is a temporary phenomenon, resulting from having an unusually good year or a nonrecurring action (such as the sale of an asset), and the firm expects cash shortfalls in future years, it may be better off retaining the cash to cover some or all these shortfalls. Another option is to pay the excess cash as a dividend in the current year and issue new stock when the cash shortfall occurs. The substantial expense associated with new security issues makes this a costly strategy in the long run. Figure 10.12 summarizes the cost of issuing bonds and common stock by size of issue in the United States.[9]

Because issuance costs increase as the size of the issue decreases and for common stock issues, small firms should be especially cautious about paying out temporary excess cash as dividends. This said, it is important to note that some companies do

_____

[9]R. G. Ibbotson, J. L. Sindelar, and J. R. Ritter, 1988, "Initial Public Offerings," *Journal of Applied Corporate Finance,* 1(2), 37–45.

Figure 10.13 Equity Issues by Dividend Class, United States, 1998

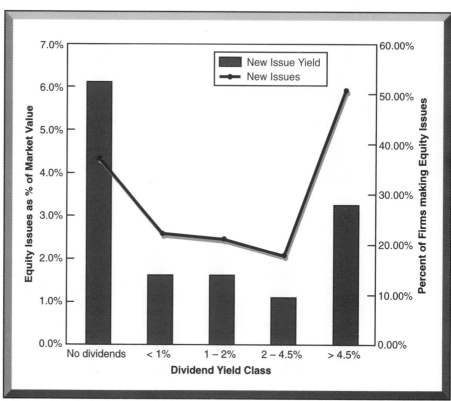

Source: Compustat database, 1998.

pay dividends and issue stock during the course of the same period, mostly out of a desire to maintain their dividends. Figure 10.13 reports new stock issues by firms as a percentage of firm value, classified by their dividend yields, in 1998.

Although it is not surprising that firms that pay no dividends are most likely to issue stock, it is surprising that firms in the highest dividend yield class also issue significant proportions of new stock (approximately half of all the firms in this class also make new stock issues). This suggests that many of these firms are paying dividends on the one hand and issuing stock on the other, creating significant issuance costs for their stockholders in the process.

Some Good Reasons for Paying Dividends

Although the tax disadvantages of dividends were clear before 2003, especially for individual investors, there were some good reasons why firms that were paying dividends then did not suspend them. First, some investors liked to receive dividends and did not care about the tax disadvantage, either because they paid no or very low taxes or because they needed the regular cash flows. Firms that had paid dividends over long periods were likely to have accumulated investors with these characteristics, and cutting or eliminating dividends would not have been viewed favorably by this group.

Second, changes in dividends allow firms to signal to financial markets how confident they feel about future cash flows. Firms that are more confident about their future are therefore more likely to raise dividends; stock prices often increase in response. Cutting dividends is viewed by markets as a negative signal about future cash flows, and stock prices often decline in response. Third, firms can use dividends as a tool for altering their financing mix and moving closer to an optimal debt ratio. Finally, the commitment to pay dividends can help reduce the conflicts between stockholders and managers by reducing the cash flows available to managers.

Some Investors Like Dividends

Prior to the tax law change in 2003, many in the "dividends are bad" school of thought argued that rational investors should have rejected dividends due to their tax disadvantage. Whatever the merits of that argument, some investors had a strong preference for dividends and viewed large dividends positively. The most striking empirical evidence for this came from studies of companies that had two classes of shares: one that paid cash dividends, and another that paid an equivalent amount of stock dividends; thus, investors are given a choice between dividends and capital gains.

In 1978, John Long studied the price differential on Class A and B shares traded on Citizens Utility.[10] Class B shares paid a cash dividend, and Class A shares paid an equivalent stock dividend. Moreover, Class A shares could be converted at little or no cost to Class B shares at the option of its stockholders. Thus, an investor could choose to buy Class B shares to get cash dividends or Class A shares to get an equivalent capital gain. During the period of this study, the tax advantage was clearly on the side of capital gains; thus, we would expect to find Class B shares selling at a discount on Class A shares. The study found, surprisingly, that the Class B shares sold at a premium over Class A shares. Figure 10.14 reports the price differential between the two share classes over the period of the analysis.

Although it may be tempting to attribute this phenomenon to the irrational behavior of investors, that may not be the case. Not all investors liked dividends—many felt its tax burden—but there were also many who viewed dividends positively. These investors may not have been paying much in taxes and consequently did not care about the tax disadvantage associated with dividends. Or they might have needed and valued the cash flow generated by the dividend payment. Why, you might ask, did they not sell stock to raise the cash flow they needed? The transaction costs and the difficulty of breaking up small holdings and selling unit shares may have made selling small amounts of stock infeasible.[11]

---

[10]John B. Long Jr., 1978, "The Market Valuation of Cash Dividends: A Case to Consider," *Journal of Financial Economics,* 6(2/3), 235–264.

[11]Consider a stockholder who owns 100 shares trading at $20 per share, on which she receives a dividend of $0.50 per share. If the firm did not pay a dividend, the stockholder would have to sell 2.5 shares of stock to raise the $50 that would have come from the dividend.

Figure 10.14   Price Differential on Citizens Utility Stock

Source: Long (1978).

Table 10.2   PRICE DIFFERENTIAL BETWEEN CASH AND STOCK DIVIDEND SHARES

Company	Premium on Cash Dividend Shares over Stock Dividend Shares
Consolidated Bathurst	19.30%
Donfasco	13.30%
Dome Petroleum	0.30%
Imperial Oil	12.10%
Newfoundland Light & Power	1.80%
Royal Trustco	17.30%
Stelco	2.70%
TransAlta	1.10%
Average	7.54%

Source: Bailey (1988).

Bailey (1998) extended Long's study to examine Canadian utility companies, which also offered dividend and capital gains shares, and had similar findings.[12] Table 10.2 summarizes the price premium at which the dividend shares sold. Note once again that on average the cash dividend shares sell at a premium of 7.5 percent over the stock dividend shares. We caution that although these findings do not

---

[12]W. Bailey, 1988, "Canada's Dual Class Shares: Further Evidence on the Market Value of Cash Dividends," *Journal of Finance,* 43(5), 1143–1160.

indicate that *all* stockholders like dividends, they do indicate that the stockholders in these specific companies liked cash dividends so much that they were willing to overlook the tax disadvantage that existed during the period and paid a premium for shares that offered them.

The Clientele Effect

Stockholders examined in the studies just described clearly like cash dividends. At the other extreme are companies that pay no dividends, whose stockholders seem perfectly content with that policy. Given the vast diversity of stockholders, it is not surprising that over time, investors tended to invest in firms whose dividend policies matched their preferences. Stockholders in high tax brackets who did not need the cash flow from dividend payments tended to invest in companies that paid low or no dividends. By contrast, those in low tax brackets who needed the cash from dividend payments, and tax-exempt institutions that needed current cash flows, invested in companies with high dividends. This clustering of stockholders in companies with dividend policies that match their preferences is called the *clientele effect*.

The existence of a clientele effect is supported by empirical evidence. One study looked at the portfolios of 914 investors to see whether their choices were affected by their tax brackets. The study found that older and poorer investors were more likely to hold high-dividend-paying stocks than were younger and wealthier investors. In another study, dividend yields were regressed against the characteristics of the investor base of a company (including age, income, and differential tax rates).[13]

$$\text{Dividend Yield}_t = a + b\beta_t + c\,\text{Age}_t + d\,\text{Income}_t + e\,\text{Differential Tax Rate}_t + \varepsilon_t$$

Variable	Coefficient	Implies
Constant	4.22%	
Beta coefficient	−2.145	Higher beta stocks pay lower dividends.
Age/100	3.131	Firms with older investors pay higher dividends.
Income/1,000	−3.726	Firms with wealthier investors pay lower dividends.
Differential tax rate	−2.849	If ordinary income is taxed at a higher rate than capital gains, the firm pays less dividends.

Source: Pettit (1977).

Not surprisingly, this study found that safer companies, with older and poorer investors, tended to pay more in dividends than companies with wealthier and younger investors. Overall, dividend yields decreased as the tax disadvantage of dividends increased.

---

[13]R. R. Pettit, 1977, "Taxes, Transactions Costs and the Clientele Effect of Dividends," *Journal of Financial Economics,* 5, 419–436.

10.7   DIVIDEND CLIENTELE AND TAX-EXEMPT INVESTORS

Pension funds are exempt from paying taxes on either ordinary income or capital gains and also have substantial ongoing cash flow needs. What types of stocks would you expect these funds to buy when dividends are taxed at higher rates (across all investors)?

☐   Stocks that pay high dividends

☐   Stocks that pay no or low dividends

Explain.

Consequences of the Clientele Effect

The existence of a clientele effect has some important implications. First, it suggests that firms get the investors they deserve because the dividend policy of a firm attracts investors who like it. Second, it means that firms will have a difficult time changing an established dividend policy, even if it makes complete sense to do so. For instance, U.S. telephone companies have traditionally paid high dividends and acquired an investor base that liked these dividends. In the 1990s, many of these firms entered new businesses (entertainment, multimedia, etc.), with much larger reinvestment needs and less stable cash flows. Although the need to cut dividends in the face of the changing business mix might seem obvious, it was nevertheless a hard sell to stockholders, who had become used to the dividends.

The clientele effect also provides an alternative argument for the irrelevance of dividend policy, at least when it comes to valuation. In summary, if investors migrate to firms that pay the dividends that most closely match their needs, no firm's value should be affected by its dividend policy. Thus, a firm that pays no or low dividends should not be penalized for doing so, because its investors *do not want* dividends. Conversely, a firm that pays high dividends should not have a lower value because its investors like dividends. This argument assumes that there are enough investors in each dividend clientele to allow firms to be fairly valued, no matter what their dividend policy.

Empirical Evidence on the Clientele Effect

If there is a strong enough clientele effect, the returns on stocks should not be affected over long periods by the dividend payouts of the underlying firms. If there is a tax disadvantage associated with dividends, the returns on stocks that pay high dividends should be higher than the returns on stocks that pay low dividends to compensate for the tax differences. Finally, if there is an overwhelming preference for dividends, these patterns should be reversed.

In their study of the clientele effect, Black and Scholes created twenty-five portfolios of NYSE stocks, classifying firms into five quintiles based on dividend yield, and then subdivided each group into five additional groups based on risk (beta) each year for thirty-five years, from 1931 to 1966.[14] When they regressed total returns on these portfolios against the dividend yields, the authors found no statistically significant relationship between them. These findings were contested in a study in 1979 by Litzenberger and Ramaswamy, who used updated dividend yields every month and examined whether the total returns in ex-dividend months were correlated with

---

[14]F. Black, and M. Scholes, 1974, "The Effects of Dividend Yield and Dividend Policy on Common Stock Prices and Returns," *Journal of Financial Economics,* 1, 1–22.

dividend yields.[15] They found a strong *positive* relationship between total returns and dividend yields, supporting the hypothesis that investors are averse to dividends. They also estimated that the implied tax differential between capital gains and dividends was approximately 23 percent. Miller and Scholes countered by arguing that this finding was contaminated by the stock price effects of dividend increases and decreases.[16] In response, Litzenberger and Ramaswamy removed from the sample all cases in which the dividends were declared and paid in the same month and concluded that the implied tax differential was only 4 percent, which was not significantly different from zero.

In the interest of fairness, we should point out that most studies of the clientele effect have concluded that total returns and dividend yields are positively correlated. Although many of them contend that this is true because the implied tax differential between dividends and capital gains is significantly different from zero, there are alternative explanations for the phenomena. In particular, although one may disagree with Miller and Scholes's conclusions, their argument—that the higher returns on stocks that pay high dividends might have nothing to do with the tax disadvantages associated with dividends but may instead be a reflection of the price increases associated with unexpected dividend increases—has both a theoretical and an empirical basis.

10.8   DIVIDEND CLIENTELE AND CHANGING DIVIDEND POLICY

Phone companies in the United States have for long had the following features: They are regulated, have stable earnings, low reinvestment needs and pay high dividends. Many of these phone companies are now considering entering the multimedia age and becoming entertainment companies, which requires more reinvestment and creates more volatility in earnings. If you were the CEO of the phone company, would you

☐ announce an immediate cut in dividends as part of a major capital investment plan?

☐ continue to pay high dividends, and use new stock issues to finance the expansion?

☐ do something else?

Explain.

Dividends Operate as an Information Signal

Financial markets examine every action a firm takes for implications for future cash flows and firm value. When firms announce changes in dividend policy, they are conveying information to markets, whether or not they intend to do so.

Financial markets tend to view announcements made by firms about their future prospects with a great deal of skepticism because firms routinely make exaggerated claims. At the same time, some firms with good investment prospects are undervalued by markets. How do such firms convey information credibly to markets? Signaling theory suggests that these firms need to take actions that cannot be easily imitated by firms without good projects. Increasing dividends is viewed as one such action. By increasing dividends, firms create a cost to themselves, because they

---

[15]R. H. Litzenberger and K. Ramaswamy, 1979, "The Effect of Personal Taxes and Dividends on Capital Asset Prices: Theory and Empirical Evidence," *Journal of Financial Economics,* 7, 163–196.

[16]M. H. Miller and M. S. Scholes, 1978, "Dividends and Taxes," *Journal of Financial Economics,* 6(4), 333–364.

Figure 10.15 Excess Returns around Announcements of Dividend Changes

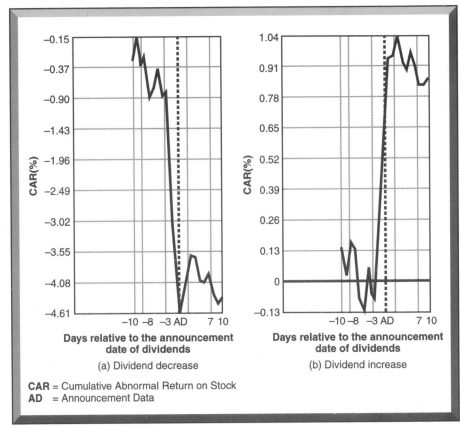

Source: Aharony and Swary (1981).

commit to paying these dividends in the long run. Their willingness to make this commitment indicates to investors that they believe they have the capacity to generate these cash flows in the long run. This positive signal should therefore lead investors to reevaluate the cash flows and firm values and increase the stock price.

Decreasing dividends is a negative signal, largely because firms are reluctant to cut dividends. Thus, when a firm take this action, markets see it as an indication that this firm is in substantial, long-term financial trouble. Consequently, such actions lead to a drop in stock prices.

The empirical evidence concerning price reactions to dividend increases and decreases is consistent, at least on average, with this signaling theory. Figure 10.15 summarizes the average excess returns around dividend changes for firms.[17]

We should view this explanation for dividend increases and decreases cautiously, however. Although it is true that firms with good projects may use dividend increases to convey information to financial markets, is it the most efficient way? For smaller

---

[17]J. Aharony and I. Swary, 1981, "Quarterly Dividends and Earnings Announcements and Stockholders' Returns: An Empirical Analysis," *Journal of Finance,* 36, 1–12.

firms, which have relatively few signals available to them, the answer might be yes. For larger firms, which have many ways of conveying information to markets, dividends might not be the least expensive or the most effective signals. For instance, information may be more effectively and economically conveyed through an analyst report on the company.

There is another reason for skepticism. An equally plausible story can be told about how an increase in dividends sends a negative signal to financial markets. Consider a firm that has never paid dividends in the past but has registered extraordinary growth and high returns on its projects. When this firm first starts paying dividends, its stockholders may consider this an indication that the firm's projects are neither as plentiful nor as lucrative as they used to be. However, Palepu and Healy found that the initiation of dividends does not signal a decline in earnings growth in a study of 151 firms from 1970 to 1979.[18]

10.9   Dividends as Signals

Silicon Electronics, a company with a history of not paying dividends, high earnings growth, and reinvestment back into the company, announces that it will be initiating dividends. You would expect the stock price to

☐   go up.
☐   go down.
☐   remain unchanged.

Explain.

Dividend Policy Is a Tool for Changing Financing Mix

Dividend policy cannot be analyzed in a vacuum. Firms can use dividend policy as a tool to change their debt ratios. We previously examined how firms that want to increase or decrease leverage can do so by changing their dividend policy: increasing dividends increases financial leverage over time, and decreasing dividends reduces leverage.

When dividends increase, stockholders sometimes get a bonus in the form of a wealth transfer from lenders to the firm. Lenders would rather have firms accumulate cash than pay it out as dividends. The payment of dividends takes cash out of the firm, and this cash could have been used to cover outstanding interest or principal payments. Not surprisingly, bond prices decline on the announcement of large increases in dividends. It is equity investors who gain from the loss in market value faced by bondholders. Bondholders, of course, try to protect themselves against this loss by restricting how much firms can pay out in dividends.

Managerial Interests and Dividend Policy

We have considered dividend policy almost entirely from the perspective of equity investors in the firm. In reality, though, managers set dividend policy, and it should come as no surprise that there may be a potential for a conflict of interests between stockholders and managers.

---

[18]K. Palepu and P. Healy, 1988, "Earnings Information Conveyed by Dividend Initiations and Omissions," *Journal of Financial Economics,* 21, 149–175.

Table 10.3 Management Beliefs about Dividend Policy			
Statement of Management Beliefs	**Agree**	**No Opinion**	**Disagree**
1. A firm's dividend payout ratio affects the price of the stock.	61%	33%	6%
2. Dividend payments provide a signaling device of future prospects.	52%	41%	7%
3. The market uses divided announcements as information for assessing firm value.	43%	51%	6%
4. Investors have different perceptions of the relative riskiness of dividends and retained earnings.	56%	42%	2%
5. Investors are basically indifferent with regard to returns from dividends and capital gains.	6%	30%	64%
6. A stockholder is attracted to firms that have dividend policies appropriate to the stockholder's tax environment.	44%	49%	7%
7. Management should be responsive to shareholders' preferences regarding dividends.	41%	49%	10%

The Source of the Conflict

When examining debt policy, we noted that one reason for taking on more debt was to induce managers to be more disciplined in their project choices. Implicit in this free cash flow argument is the assumption that accumulated cash, if left to the discretion of the managers of the firm, would be wasted on poor projects. If this is true, we can argue that forcing a firm to make a commitment to pay dividends provides an alternative way of forcing managers to be disciplined in project choice by reducing the cash that is available for discretionary uses.

If this is the reason stockholders want managers to commit to paying larger dividends, firms in which there is a clear separation between ownership and management should pay larger dividends than should firms with substantial insider ownership and involvement in managerial decisions.

What Do Managers Believe about Dividend Policy?

Given the pros and cons for paying dividends and the lack of a consensus on the effect of dividends on value, it is worth considering what managers factor in when they make dividend decisions. Baker, Farrelly, and Edelman (1985) surveyed managers on their views on dividend policy and reported the level of agreement with a series of statements.[19] Table 10.3 summarizes their findings.

It is quite clear from this survey that, rightly or wrongly, managers believe that their dividend payout ratios affect firm value and operate as signals of future prospects. They also operate under the presumption that investors choose firms with dividend policies that match their preferences and that management should be responsive to their needs.

---

[19]Baker, H. Kent, Gail E. Farrelly, and Richard B. Edelman, 1985, "A Survey of Management Views on Dividend Policy," *Financial Management,* 14(3), 78–84.

In an updated and comprehensive survey of dividend policy published in 2004,[20] Brav, Graham, Harvey, and Michaely conclude that management's focus is not on the level of dividends but on changes in these dividends. Indicating a shift from views in prior studies, many managers in this survey saw little gain from increasing dividends, even in response to higher earnings and preferred stock buybacks instead. In fact, many managers in companies that paid dividends regret the level of dividends paid by their firms, indicating that they would have set the dividend at a much lower level if they had the choice. In contrast to the survey quoted in the last paragraph, managers also rejected the idea that dividends operate as useful financial signals. From the survey, the authors conclude that the rules of the game for dividends are the following: do not cut dividends, have a dividend policy similar to your peer group, preserve a good credit rating, maintain flexibility, and do not take actions that reduce earnings per share.

10.10 CORPORATE GOVERNANCE AND DIVIDEND POLICY

In countries where stockholders have little or no control over incumbent managers, you would expect dividends paid by companies to be

☐ lower than dividends paid in other countries.

☐ higher than dividends paid in other countries.

☐ about the same as dividends paid in other countries.

CONCLUSION

There are three schools of thought on dividend policy. The first is that dividends are neutral and neither increase nor decrease value. Stockholders are therefore indifferent between receiving dividends and enjoying price appreciation. This view is based on the assumptions that there are no tax disadvantages to investors associated with receiving dividends, relative to capital gains, and that firms can raise new equity for new investments without issuance costs.

The second view is that dividends destroy value for stockholders because they are taxed at much higher rates than capital gains. Until the tax code was changed in 2003, the evidence for this tax disadvantage was strong both in the tax code and in markets, when we examine how stock prices change on ex-dividend days. On average, stock prices decline by less than the amount of the dividend, suggesting that stockholders in most firms consider dividends to be less attractive than equivalent capital gains.

The third school of thought makes the argument that dividends can be value increasing, at least for some firms. In particular, firms that have accumulated stockholders who prefer dividends to capital gains should continue to pay large, increasing dividends to keep their investor clientele happy. Furthermore, increasing dividends can operate as a positive signal to financial markets and allow a firm to change its financing mix over time. Finally, forcing firms to pay out dividends reduces the cash available to managers for new investments. If managers are not investing with the objective of maximizing stockholder wealth, this can make stockholders better off.

---

[20]A. Brav, J. R. Graham, C. R. Harvey, and R. Michaely, 2004, "Payout Policy in the 21st Century," Working Paper, Duke University, Durham, NC.

LIVE CASE STUDY

THE TRADE-OFF ON DIVIDEND POLICY

Objective: To examine how much cash your firm has returned to its stockholders and in what form (dividends or stock buybacks) and to evaluate whether the trade-off favors returning more or less.

Key Questions

- Has this firm ever paid out dividends? If yes, is there a pattern to the dividends over time?

- Given this firm's characteristics today, do you think that this firm should be paying more dividends, less dividends, or no dividends at all?

Framework for Analysis

1. *Historical Dividend Policy*

- How much has this company paid in dividends over the past few years?

- How have these dividends related to earnings in these years?

2. *Firm Characteristics*

- How easily can the firm convey information to financial markets? In other words, how necessary is it for them to use dividend policy as a signal?

- Who are the marginal stockholders in this firm? Do they like dividends or would they prefer stock buybacks?

- How well can this firm forecast its future financing needs? How valuable is preserving flexibility to this firm?

- Are there any significant bond covenants that you know of that restrict the firm's dividend policy?

- How does this firm compare with other firms in the sector in terms of dividend policy?

Getting Information on Dividend Policy

You can get information about dividends paid back over time from the financial statements of the firm. (The statement of changes in cash flows is usually the best source.) To find typical dividend payout ratios and yields for the sector in which this firm operates examine the data set on industry averages on the Web site for the book.

Online Sources of Information
www.stern.nyu.edu/~adamodar/cfin2E/roject/data.htm.

PROBLEMS AND QUESTIONS

(In the problems below, you can use a risk premium of 5.5 percent and a tax rate of 40 percent if none is specified.)

1. If Consolidated Power is priced at $50.00 with dividend, and its price falls to $46.50 when a dividend of $5.00 is paid, what is the implied marginal rate of personal taxes for its stockholders? Assume that the tax on capital gains is 40 percent of the personal income tax.

2. You are comparing the dividend policies of three dividend-paying utilities. You have collected the following information on the ex-dividend behavior of these firms.

	NE Gas	SE Bell	Western Electric
Price before	50	70	100
Price after	48	67	95
Dividends/share	4	4	5

If you were a tax-exempt investor, which company would you use to make "dividend arbitrage" profits? How would you go about doing so?

3. Southern Rail has just declared a dividend of $1. The average investor in Southern Rail faces an ordinary tax rate of 50 percent. Although the capital gains rate is also 50 percent, it is believed that the investor gets the advantage of deferring this tax until future years (the effective capital gains rate will therefore be 50 percent discounted back to the present). If the price of the stock before the ex-dividend day is $10 and it drops to $9.20 by the end of the ex-dividend day, how many years is the average investor deferring capital gains taxes? (Assume that the opportunity cost used by the investor in evaluating future cash flows is 10 percent.)

4. LMN Corporation, a real estate company, is planning to pay a dividend of $0.50 per share. Most of the investors in LMN are other corporations that pay 40 percent of their ordinary income and 28 percent of their capital gains as taxes. However, they are allowed to exempt 85 percent of the dividends they receive from taxes. If the shares are selling at $10 per share, how much would you expect the stock price to drop on the ex-dividend day?

5. UJ Gas is a utility that has followed a policy of increasing dividends every quarter by 5 percent over dividends in the prior year. The company announces that it will increase quarterly dividends from $1.00 to $1.02 next quarter. What price reaction would you expect to the announcement? Why?

6. Microsoft, which has had a history of high growth and pays no dividends, announces that it will start paying dividends next quarter. How would you expect its stock price to react to the announcement? Why?

7. JC Automobiles is a small auto parts manufacturing firm, that has paid $1.00 in annual dividends each year for the past five years. It announces that dividends will increase to $1.25 next year. What would you expect the price reaction to be? Why? If your answer is different from the previous problem, explain the reasons for the difference.

8. Would your answer be different for the previous problem if JC Automobiles were a large firm followed by thirty-five analysts? Why or why not?

9. WeeMart, a retailer of children's clothes, announces a cut in dividends following a year in which both revenues and earning dropped significantly. How would you expect its stock price to react? Explain.

10. RJR Nabisco, in response to stockholder pressure in 1996, announced a significant increase in dividends paid to stockholders financed by the sale of some of its assets. What would you expect the stock price to do? Why?

11. RJR Nabisco also had $10 billion in bonds outstanding at the time of the dividend increase in Problem 10. How would you expect the bonds to react to the announcement? Why?

12. When firms increase dividends, stock prices tend to increase. One reason given for this price reaction is that dividends operate as a positive signal. What is the increase in dividends signaling to markets? Will markets always believe the signal? Why or why not?

Chapter 11

Analyzing Cash Returned to Stockholders

Companies return cash to stockholders in the form of dividends, but they can buy back stock as an alternative. How much have companies returned to their stockholders, and how much could they have returned? As stockholders in these firms, would we want them to change their policies and return more or less than they are currently? In this chapter, we expand our definition of cash returned to stockholders to include stock buybacks. As we will document, firms in the United States have turned increasingly to buying back stock to either augment regular dividends or, in some cases, to substitute for cash dividends.

Using this expanded measure of actual cash flows returned to stockholders, we consider two ways in which firms can analyze whether they are returning too little or

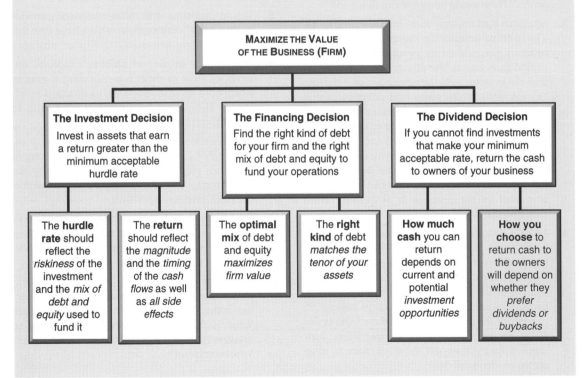

MAXIMIZE THE VALUE
OF THE BUSINESS (FIRM)

The Investment Decision
Invest in assets that earn a return greater than the minimum acceptable hurdle rate

The Financing Decision
Find the right kind of debt for your firm and the right mix of debt and equity to fund your operations

The Dividend Decision
If you cannot find investments that make your minimum acceptable rate, return the cash to owners of your business

The **hurdle rate** should reflect the *riskiness* of the investment and the *mix of debt and equity* used to fund it

The **return** should reflect the *magnitude* and the *timing* of the *cash flows* as well as *all side effects*

The **optimal mix** of debt and equity *maximizes firm value*

The **right kind** of debt *matches the tenor of your assets*

How much cash you can return depends on current and potential *investment opportunities*

How you choose to return cash to the owners will depend on whether they *prefer dividends or buybacks*

too much to stockholders. First, we examine how much cash is left over after reinvestment needs have been met and debt payments made. We consider this cash flow to be the cash available for return to stockholders and compare it to the actual amount returned. We categorize firms into those that return more to stockholders than they have available in this cash flow, firms that return what they have available, and those that return less than they have available. We then examine the firms that consistently return more or less cash than they have available and the consequences of these policies. For this part of the analysis, we bring in two factors—the quality of the firm's investments and the firm's plans to change its financing mix. We argue that stockholders are more willing to trust management with excess free cash flow if the firm has a track record of good investments. Also, firms that return more cash than they have available are on firm ground if they are trying to increase their debt ratios.

In the second approach to analyzing dividend policy, we consider how much comparable firms in the industry pay as dividends. Many firms set their dividend policies by looking at their peer groups. We discuss this practice and suggest some refinements in it to allow for the vast differences that often exist between firms in the same sector.

In the last part of this chapter, we look at how firms that decide they are paying too much or too little in dividends can change their dividend policies. Because firms tend to attract stockholders who like their existing dividend policies, and because dividends convey information to financial markets, changing dividends can have unintended and negative consequences. We suggest ways firms can manage a transition from a high dividend payout to a low dividend payout or vice versa.

CASH RETURNED TO STOCKHOLDERS

In the previous chapter, we considered the decision about how much to pay in dividends and three schools of thought about whether dividend policy affected firm value. Until the middle of the 1980s, dividends remained the primary mechanism for firms to return cash to stockholders. Starting in that period, we have seen firms increasingly turn to buying back their own stock, using either cash on hand or borrowed money, as a mechanism for returning cash to their stockholders.

The Effects of Buying Back Stock

First let's consider the effect of a stock buyback on the firm doing the buyback. The stock buyback requires cash, just as a dividend would, and thus has the same effect on the assets of the firm—a reduction in the cash balance. Just as a dividend reduces the book value of the equity in the firm, a stock buyback reduces the book value of equity. Thus, if a firm with a book value of equity of $1 billion buys back $400 million in equity,[1]

---

[1] The stock buyback is at market value. Thus, when the market value is significantly higher than the book value of equity, a buyback of stock will reduce the book value of equity disproportionately. For example, if the market value is five times the book value of equity, buying back 10 percent of the stock will reduce the book value of equity by 50 percent.

the book value of equity will drop to $600 million. Both a dividend payment and a stock buyback reduce the overall market value of equity in the firm, but the way they affect the market value is different. The dividend reduces the market price on the ex-dividend day and does not change the number of shares outstanding. A stock buyback reduces the number of shares outstanding and is often accompanied by a stock price increase. For instance, if a firm with 100 million shares outstanding trading at $10 per share buys back 10 million shares, the number of shares will decline to 90 million, but the stock price may increase to $10.50. The total market value of equity after the buyback will be $945 million, a drop in value of 5.5 percent.

Unlike a dividend, which returns cash to all stockholders in a firm, a stock buyback returns cash selectively to those stockholders who choose to sell their stock to the firm. The remaining stockholders get no cash; they gain indirectly from the stock buyback if the stock price increases. In the example above, stockholders in the firm will find the value of their holdings increasing by 5 percent after the stock buyback.

IN PRACTICE: HOW DO YOU BUY BACK STOCK?

The process of repurchasing equity will depend largely on whether the firm intends to repurchase stock in the open market at the prevailing market price or to make a more formal tender offer for its shares. There are three widely used approaches to buying back equity:

- ***Repurchase Tender Offers*** In a repurchase tender offer, a firm specifies a price at which it will buy back shares, the number of shares it intends to repurchase, and the period of time for which it will keep the offer open and invites stockholders to submit their shares for the repurchase. In many cases, firms retain the flexibility to withdraw the offer if an insufficient number of shares are submitted or to extend the offer beyond the originally specified time period. This approach is used primarily for large equity repurchases.

- ***Open Market Repurchases*** In the case of open market repurchases, firms buy shares in the market at the prevailing market price. Although firms do not have to disclose publicly their intent to buy back shares in the market, they do have to comply with SEC requirements to prevent price manipulation or insider trading. Finally, open market purchases can be spread out over much longer time periods than tender offers and are more widely used for smaller repurchases. In terms of flexibility, an open market repurchase affords the firm much more freedom in deciding when to buy back shares and how many shares to repurchase.

- ***Privately Negotiated Repurchases*** In privately negotiated repurchases, firms buy back shares from a large stockholder in the company at a negotiated price. This method is not as widely used as the first two and may be employed by managers or owners as a way of consolidating control and eliminating a troublesome stockholder. ■

The Magnitude of Stock Buybacks

In the past decade, more firms have used equity repurchases as an alternative to paying dividends. Figure 11.1 summarizes dividends paid and equity repurchases at U.S. corporations between 1989 and 2002.

Figure 11.1   Stock Buybacks and Dividends: Aggregate for U.S. Firms, 1989–2002

Source: Compustat database (2003).

It is worth noting that although aggregate dividends at all U.S. firms have grown at an annual rate of about 1.18 percent over this period, stock buybacks have grown 9.83 percent a year. In another interesting shift, the proportion of cash returned to stockholders in the form of stock buybacks has climbed from 32 percent in 1989 to about 57 percent in 2002. Stock buybacks, in the aggregate, exceeded dividends, in the aggregate, in 1999 for the first time in U.S. corporate history. Although the slowdown in the economy resulted in both dividends and stock buybacks decreasing in 2001 and 2002, buybacks still exceeded dividends in 2002.

This shift has been less dramatic outside the United States. Firms in other countries have been less likely to use stock buybacks to return cash to stockholders for a number of reasons.[2] First, until 2003, dividends in the United States faced a much higher tax burden, relative to capital gains, than dividends paid in other countries. Many European countries, for instance, allow investors to claim a tax credit on dividends to compensate for taxes paid by the firms paying dividends. Stock buybacks, therefore, provided a much greater tax benefit to investors in the United States than they did to investors outside the United States by shifting income from dividends to capital gains. Second, stock buybacks were prohibited or tightly constrained in many countries. Third, a strong reason for the increase in stock buybacks in the United States was

---

[2]This may be changing as well. In 2003, large European companies bought back more stock than their U.S. counterparts.

Table 11.1 CASH RETURNED TO STOCKHOLDERS: DISNEY, ARACRUZ, AND DEUTSCHE BANK (IN MILLIONS)

	Disney			Aracruz			Deutsche Bank		
Year	Dividends	Equity Repurchases	Cash to Equity	Dividends	Equity Repurchases	Cash to Equity	Dividends	Equity Repurchases	Cash to Equity
1994	$153	$571	$724	$80	$0	$80	€400	€0	€400
1995	$180	$349	$529	$113	$0	$113	€459	€0	€459
1996	$271	$462	$733	$27	$0	$27	€460	€0	€460
1997	$342	$633	$975	$28	$0	$28	€489	€0	€489
1998	$412	$30	$442	$24	$26	$51	€600	€0	€600
1999	$0	$19	$19	$18	$0	$18	€707	€0	€707
2000	$434	$166	$600	$58	$23	$81	€801	€0	€801
2001	$438	$1,073	$1,511	$63	$0	$63	€808	€0	€808
2002	$428	$0	$428	$74	$2	$76	€808	€0	€808
2003	$429	$0	$429	$109	$3	$112	€808	€0	€808

pressure from stockholders on managers to pay out idle cash. This pressure was far less in the weaker corporate governance systems that exist outside the United States.

For the rest of this section, we will be using the phrase "dividend policy" to mean not just what gets paid out in dividends but also the cash returned to stockholders in the form of stock buybacks.

ILLUSTRATION 11.1 Dividends and Stock Buybacks: Disney, Aracruz, and Deutsche Bank
In Table 11.1, we consider how much Disney, Aracruz, and Deutsche Bank have returned to stockholders in dividends and how much stock they have bought back each year between 1994 and 2003.

All three companies paid dividends over the ten-year period, but there are interesting differences between the companies. Deutsche Bank has the steadiest dividend payment record as the total dividend paid increased from 400 million Euros in 1994 to 808 million Euros in 2003. Dividends were never cut during the entire period and have generally grown, though the amount paid has remained unchanged from 2001 to 2003. Disney has generally also increased its dividends over the period, with one notable exception. In 1999, Disney did not pay dividends because its operating performance turned negative. Aracruz has had the most volatile history in terms of dividends paid, with dividends rising in six of the ten years examined and falling in four of the ten years.

Looking at stock buybacks, Disney has been the most active player, buying stock in eight out of the ten years, with a buyback exceeding $1 billion in 2001. Aracruz has bought back relatively small amounts of stock over the same period, mostly as treasury stock;[3] Deutsche Bank has never bought back stock. These differences

---

[3]The key difference between buybacks and treasury stock is that the number of shares in the company remains unchanged with the latter. In the United States, companies are not allowed to keep treasury stock on their books for extended periods.

reflect the markets in which these firms operate. As noted earlier, companies in the United States have generally bought back more stock than their counterparts in other markets. Stock buybacks are rare in Brazil and were not allowed in Germany for much of the period examined.

Reasons for Stock Buybacks

Firms that want to return substantial amounts of cash to their stockholders can either pay large special dividends or buy back stock. There are several advantages to both the firm and its stockholders to using stock buybacks as an alternative to dividend payments. There are four significant advantages to the firm:

- Unlike regular dividends, which typically commit the firm to continue payment in future periods, equity repurchases are one-time returns of cash. Consequently, firms with excess cash that are uncertain about their ability to continue generating these cash flows in future periods often repurchase stocks rather than pay dividends. (They could also choose to pay special dividends because these do not commit the firm to making similar payments in the future.)

- The decision to repurchase stock affords a firm much more flexibility to reverse itself and spread the repurchases over a longer period than does a decision to pay an equivalent special dividend. In fact, there is substantial evidence that many firms that announce ambitious stock repurchases do reverse themselves and do not carry the plans through to completion.

- Equity repurchases may provide a way of increasing insider control in firms, because they reduce the number of shares outstanding. If the insiders do not tender their shares back, they will end up holding a larger proportion of the firm and, consequently, having greater control.

- Finally, equity repurchases may provide firms with a way of supporting their stock prices when they are declining.[4] For instance, in the aftermath of the stock market crash of 1987, many firms initiated stock buyback plans to keep prices from falling further.

There are two potential benefits that stockholders might perceive in stock buybacks:

- Equity repurchases may offer tax advantages to stockholders. This was clearly true before 2003, because dividends were taxed at ordinary tax rates, whereas the price appreciation that results from equity repurchases was taxed at capital gains rates. Even when dividends and capital gains are taxed at the same rate, stockholders have the option not to sell their shares back to the firm and therefore do not have to realize the capital gains in the period of the equity repurchases whereas they have no choice when it comes to dividends.

---

[4]This will be true only if the price decline is not supported by a change in the fundamentals—drop in earnings, declining growth, and so on. If the price drop is justified, a stock buyback program can, at best, provide only temporary respite.

Table 11.2   **RETURNS AROUND STOCK REPURCHASE TENDER OFFERS**

	1962–1979	1980–1986	1962–1986
Number of buybacks	131	90	221
Percentage of shares purchased	15.45%	16.82%	16.41%
Abnormal return to all stockholders	16.19%	11.52%	14.29%

- Equity repurchases are much more selective in terms of paying out cash only to those stockholders who need it. This benefit flows from the voluntary nature of stock buybacks: Those who need the cash can tender their shares back to the firm, and those who do not can continue to hold on to them.

In summary, equity repurchases allow firms to return cash to stockholders and still maintain flexibility for future periods.

Intuitively, we would expect stock prices to increase when companies announce that they will be buying back stock. Studies have looked at the effect on stock price of the announcement that a firm plans to buy back stock. There is strong evidence that stock prices increase in response. Lakonishok and Vermaelen examined a sample of 221 repurchase tender offers that occurred between 1962 and 1986 and at stock price changes in the fifteen days around the announcement.[5] Table 11.2 summarizes the fraction of shares bought back in these tender offers and the change in stock price for two subperiods: 1962–1979 and 1980–1986.

The abnormal return represents the return earned by these stocks over and above what you would have expected them to earn, given their risk and the market performance over the period. On average, across the entire period, the announcement of a stock buyback increased stock value by 14.29 percent.

IN PRACTICE: EQUITY REPURCHASE AND THE DILUTION ILLUSION

Some equity repurchases are motivated by the desire to reduce the number of shares outstanding and therefore increase the earnings per share. If we assume that the firm's price earnings ratio will remain unchanged, reducing the number of shares will usually lead to a higher earnings per share and a higher price. This provides a simple rationale for many companies embarking on equity repurchases.

There is a problem with this reasoning, however. Although the reduction in the number of shares might increase earnings per share, the increase is usually caused by higher debt ratios and not by the stock buyback per se. In other words, a special dividend of the same amount would have resulted in the same returns to stockholders. Furthermore, the increase in debt ratios should increase the riskiness of the stock and lower the price earnings ratio. Whether a stock buyback will increase or decrease the price per share will depend on whether the firm is moving to its optimal

---

[5]J. Lakonishok and T. Vermaelen, 1990, "Anomalous Price Behavior around Repurchase Tender Offers," *Journal of Finance,* 45, 455–478.

debt ratio by repurchasing stock, in which case the price will increase, or moving away from it, in which case the price will drop.

To illustrate, assume that an all equity-financed firm in the specialty retailing business, with 100 shares outstanding, has $100 in earnings after taxes and a market value of $1,500. Assume that this firm borrows $300 and uses the proceeds to buy back twenty shares. As long as the after-tax interest expense on the borrowing is less than $20, this firm will report higher earnings per share after the repurchase. If the firm's tax rate is 50 percent, for instance, the effect on earnings per share is summarized in the table below for two scenarios: one where the interest expense is $30 and one where the interest expense is $55. As long as the interest expense is greater than $40 ($20 after taxes), the firm will report higher earnings per share after the repurchase.

EFFECT OF STOCK REPURCHASE ON EARNINGS PER SHARE			
	Before Repurchase	**After Repurchase**	
		Interest Expense = $30	Interest Expense = $55
EBIT	$200	$200	$200
− Interest	$0	$30	$55
= Taxable income	$200	$170	$145
− Taxes	$100	$85	$72.50
= Net income	$100	$85	$72.50
# Shares	100	80	80
Earnings per share	$1.00	$1.0625	$0.91

If we assume that the price earnings ratio remains at 15, the price per share will change in proportion to the earnings per share. Realistically, however, we should expect to see a drop in the price earnings ratio as the increase in debt makes the equity in the firm riskier. Whether the drop will be sufficient to offset or outweigh an increase in earnings per share will depend on whether the firm has excess debt capacity and whether, by going to a 20 percent debt ratio, it is moving closer to its optimal debt ratio. ■

Choosing Between Dividends and Equity Repurchases

Firms that plan to return cash to their stockholders can either pay them dividends or buy back stock. How do they choose? The choice will depend on the following factors:

- *Sustainability and Stability of Excess Cash Flow* Both equity repurchases and increased dividends are triggered by a firm's excess cash flows. If the excess cash flows are temporary or unstable, firms should repurchase stock; if they are stable and predictable, paying dividends provides a stronger signal of future project quality.

- *Stockholder Tax Preferences* If stockholders are taxed at much higher rates on dividends than capital gains, they will be better off if the firm repurchases stock.

Table 11.3 CHARACTERISTICS OF FIRMS BUYING BACK STOCK VERSUS THOSE INCREASING DIVIDENDS

	Firms Buying Back Stock	Firms Increasing Dividends	Difference Is Significant
Book/market	56.90%	51.70%	Yes
Options/shares	7.20%	6.30%	No
No. of institutional holders	219.4	180	Yes

If, on the other hand, stockholders are taxed less on dividends, they will gain if the firm pays a special dividend.

- *Predictability of Future Investment Needs* Firms that are uncertain about the magnitude of future investment opportunities should use equity repurchases as a way of returning cash to stockholders. The flexibility that is gained by avoiding what may be perceived as a fixed obligation will be useful if they need cash flows in future periods to fund attractive new investments.

- *Undervaluation of the Stock* For two reasons, an equity repurchase makes even more sense when managers believe their stock is undervalued. First, if the stock remains undervalued, the remaining stockholders will benefit if managers buy back stock at less than true value. The difference between the true value and the market price paid on the buyback will accrue to those stockholders who do not sell their stock back. Second, the stock buyback may send a signal to financial markets that the stock is undervalued, and the market may react accordingly by pushing up the price.

- *Management Compensation* Managers often receive options on the stock of the companies that they manage. The prevalence and magnitude of such option-based compensation can affect whether firms use dividends or buy back stock. The payment of dividends reduces stock prices while leaving the number of shares unchanged. The buying back of stock reduces the number of shares, and the share price usually increases on the buyback. Because options become less valuable as the stock price decreases and more valuable as the stock price increases, managers with significant option positions may be more likely to buy back stock than pay dividends.

Bartov, Krinsky, and Lee examined three of these determinants—undervaluation, management compensation, and institutional investor holdings (as a proxy for stockholder tax preferences)—of whether firms buy back stock or pay dividends.[6] They looked at 150 firms announcing stock buyback programs between 1986 and 1992 and compared these firms to others in their industries that chose to increase dividends instead. Table 11.3 reports on the characteristics of the two groups.

The option holdings of managers seemed to have no statistical impact on whether firms bought back stock or increased dividends, but firms buying back stock had higher book to market ratios than firms increasing dividends and more institutional stockholders. The higher book to price ratio can be viewed as an indication that these firms

---

[6]E. Bartov, I. Krinsky, and J. Lee, 1998, "Some Evidence on How Companies Choose between Dividends and Stock Repurchases," *Journal of Applied Corporate Finance,* 11, 89–96.

are more likely to view themselves as undervalued. The larger institutional holding might suggest a greater sensitivity to the tax advantage of stock buybacks.

11.1   STOCK BUYBACKS AND STOCK PRICE EFFECTS

For which of the following types of firms would a stock buyback be most likely to lead to a drop in the stock price?

☐ Companies with a history of poor project choice

☐ Companies that borrow money to buy back stock

☐ Companies that are perceived to have great investment opportunities

Explain.

A CASH FLOW APPROACH TO ANALYZING DIVIDEND POLICY

Given what firms are returning to their stockholders in the form of dividends or stock buybacks, how do we decide whether they are returning too much or too little? In the cash flow approach, we follow four steps. We first measure how much cash is available to be paid out to stockholders after meeting debt service and reinvestment needs and compare this amount to the amount actually returned to stockholders. We then have to consider how good existing and new investments in the firm are. Third, based on the cash payout and project quality, we consider whether firms should be accumulating more cash or less. Finally, we look at the relationship between dividend policy and debt policy.

Step 1: Measuring Cash Available to Be Returned to Stockholders

To estimate how much cash a firm can afford to return to its stockholders, we begin with the net income—the accounting measure of the stockholders' earnings during the period—and convert it to a cash flow by subtracting out a firm's reinvestment needs. First, any capital expenditures, defined broadly to include acquisitions, are subtracted from the net income because they represent cash outflows. Depreciation and amortization, on the other hand, are added back in because they are noncash charges. The difference between capital expenditures and depreciation is referred to as *net capital expenditures* and is usually a function of the growth characteristics of the firm. High-growth firms tend to have high net capital expenditures relative to earnings, whereas low-growth firms may have low (and sometimes even negative) net capital expenditures.

Second, increases in working capital drain a firm's cash flows, whereas decreases in working capital increase the cash flows available to equity investors. Firms that are growing fast, in industries with high working capital requirements (retailing, for instance), typically have large increases in working capital. Because we are interested in the cash flow effects, we consider only changes in *noncash working capital* (ΔWorking Capital) in this analysis.

Finally, equity investors also have to consider the effect of changes in the levels of debt on their cash flows. Repaying the principal on existing debt represents a cash outflow to equity investors, but the debt repayment may be fully or partially financed by the issue of new debt, which is a cash inflow. Again, netting the repayment of old debt against the new debt issues provides a measure of the cash flow effects of changes in debt.

Allowing for the cash flow effects of net capital expenditures, changes in working capital, and net changes in debt on equity investors, we can define the cash flows left over after these changes as the *free cash flow to equity* (*FCFE*):

$$
\begin{aligned}
\text{Free Cash Flow to Equity (FCFE)} = {}& \text{Net Income} \\
& - (\text{Capital Expenditures} - \text{Depreciation}) \\
& - (\Delta\text{Working Capital}) \\
& + (\text{New Debt Issued} - \text{Debt Repayments})
\end{aligned}
$$

This is the cash flow available to be paid out as dividends.

This calculation can be simplified if we assume that the net capital expenditures and working capital changes are financed using a fixed mix of debt and equity.[7] If δ is the proportion of the net capital expenditures and working capital changes raised from debt financing, the effect on cash flows to equity of these items can be represented as follows:

$$
\begin{aligned}
& \text{Equity Reinvestment Associated with Capital Expenditure Needs} \\
& \quad = (\text{Capital Expenditure} - \text{Depreciation})(1 - \delta)
\end{aligned}
$$

$$
\begin{aligned}
& \text{Equity Reinvestment Associated with Working Capital Needs} \\
& \quad = (\Delta\text{Working Capital})(1 - \delta)
\end{aligned}
$$

Accordingly, the cash flow available for equity investors after meeting capital expenditure and working capital needs is:

$$
\begin{aligned}
\text{Free Cash Flow to Equity} = {}& \text{Net Income} \\
& - (\text{Capital Expenditures} - \text{Depreciation})(1 - \delta) \\
& - (\Delta\text{Working Capital})(1 - \delta)
\end{aligned}
$$

Note that the net debt payment item is eliminated, because debt repayments are financed with new debt issues to keep the debt ratio fixed. The target or optimal debt ratio of the firm can be used to forecast the free cash flow to equity that will be available in future periods. Alternatively, in examining past periods, we can use the firm's average debt ratio over the period to arrive at approximate free cash flows to equity.

IN PRACTICE: Estimating the FCFE at a Financial Service Firm

The standard definition of FCFE is straightforward to put into practice for most manufacturing firms, because the net capital expenditures, noncash working capital needs, and debt ratio can be estimated from the financial statements. In contrast, the estimation of FCFE is difficult for financial service firms for several reasons. First, estimating net capital expenditures and noncash working capital for a bank or insurance company is difficult because all the assets and liabilities are in the form of financial claims. Second, it is difficult to define short-term debt for financial service firms, again due to the complexity of their balance sheets.

---

[7]The mix has to be fixed in book value terms. It can be varying in market value terms.

To estimate the FCFE for a bank, we begin by categorizing the income earned into three categories—*net interest income* from taking customer deposits and lending them out at a higher interest rate, *arbitrage income* from buying financial claims (at a lower price) and selling financial claims (of equivalent risk) at a higher price, and *advisory and fee income* from providing financial advice and services to firms. For each of these sources of income, we traced the equity investment that would be needed:

Type of Income	Net Investment Needed
Net Interest Income	Net Loans – Total Deposits
Arbitrage Income	Investments in Financial Assets – Corresponding Financial Liabilities
Advisory Income	Training and Recruiting Expenses

(Net Loans = Total Loans – Bad Debt Provisions)

The first two categories of net investment can usually be obtained from the balance sheet, and changes in these net figures from year to year can be treated as the equivalent of net capital expenditures. In theory, training expenses should be capitalized and treated as tax-deductible capital expenditures, but they are seldom shown in enough detail at most firms for this to be feasible. ■

ILLUSTRATION **11.2   Estimating FCFE: Disney, Aracruz, and Deutsche Bank**
In Table 11.4, we estimate the FCFE for Disney from 1994 to 2003, using historical information from their financial statements.

The depreciation numbers also include amortization and the capital expenditures include acquisitions; the acquisition of Capital Cities/ABC is reflected in the large jump in capital expenditures in 1996 and in depreciation in the years after as goodwill was amortized. Increases in noncash working capital, shown as positive numbers,

Table 11.4   ESTIMATES OF FCFE FOR DISNEY: 1994–2003 (IN MILLIONS)

Year	Net Income	Depreciation	Capital Expenditures	Change in Noncash WC	FCFE (before Debt CF)	Net CF from Debt	FCFE (after Debt CF)
1994	$1,110.40	$1,608.30	$1,026.11	$654.10	$1,038.49	$551.10	$1,589.59
1995	$1,380.10	$1,853.00	$896.50	($270.70)	$2,607.30	$14.20	$2,621.50
1996	$1,214.00	$3,944.00	$13,464.00	$617.00	($8,923.00)	$8,688.00	($235.00)
1997	$1,966.00	$4,958.00	$1,922.00	($174.00)	$5,176.00	($1,641.00)	$3,535.00
1998	$1,850.00	$3,323.00	$2,314.00	$939.00	$1,920.00	$618.00	$2,538.00
1999	$1,300.00	$3,779.00	$2,134.00	($363.00)	$3,308.00	($176.00)	$3,132.00
2000	$920.00	$2,195.00	$2,013.00	($1,184.00)	$2,286.00	($2,118.00)	$168.00
2001	($158.00)	$1,754.00	$1,795.00	$244.00	($443.00)	$77.00	($366.00)
2002	$1,236.00	$1,042.00	$1,086.00	$27.00	$1,165.00	$1,892.00	$3,057.00
2003	$1,267.00	$1,077.00	$1,049.00	($264.00)	$1,559.00	($1,145.00)	$414.00
Average	$1,208.55	$2,553.33	$2,769.96	$22.54	$969.38	$676.03	$1,645.41

represent a drain on the cash. In 1994, for example, noncash working capital increased by $654.10 million, reducing the cash available for stockholders in that year by the same amount. Finally, the net cash flow from debt is the cash generated by the issuance of new debt, netted out against the cash outflow from the repayment of old debt. Again, using 1994 as an example, Disney issued $551.10 million more in new debt than it paid off on old debt, and this represents a cash inflow in that year.

We have computed two measures of FCFE, one before the net debt cash flow and one after. Using 1994 as an illustration, we compute each as follows:

$$\text{FCFE before Net Debt CF} = \text{Net Income} + \text{Depreciation} - \text{Capital Expenditures} - \text{Change in Noncash Working Capital}$$
$$= 1,110.40 + 1,608.30 - 1,026.11 - 654.10$$
$$= \$1,038.49 \text{ million}$$

$$\text{FCFE after Net Debt CF} = \text{FCFE before Net Debt CF} + \text{Net Debt Cash Flow}$$
$$= 1,038.49 + 551.10 = \$1,589.59 \text{ million}$$

As Table 11.4 indicates, Disney had negative free cash flows to equity in two of the ten years, in 1996 because of the Capital Cities acquisition and in 2001 because they reported a loss. The average annual FCFE before net debt issues over the period was $969 million, and the average net debt issued over the period was $676 million, resulting in an annual FCFE after net debt issues of $1,645 million.

A similar estimation of FCFE was done for Aracruz from 1998 to 2003 in Table 11.5, again using historical information.

Between 1998 and 2003, Aracruz had big swings in net income and corresponding swings in FCFE, with FCFE being negative in three of the six years. The average annual FCFE before net debt cash flows was approximately $10 million. The cash flows from debt add to the volatility because Aracruz paid off large amounts of debt in 1999 and 2000 and raised large amounts of debt in 1998, 2001, and 2003. The average annual FCFE after net debt cash flows was $37.54 million.

We can compute Aracruz's FCFE each year using the approximation that we described in the last section. To do this, we first have to compute the net debt cash flows as percent of reinvestment needs over this period. Using the average values for

Table 11.5 FCFE FOR ARACRUZ IN US$ FROM 1998 TO 2003 (IN MILLIONS)

Year	Net Income	Depreciation	Capital Expenditures	Change in Noncash WC	FCFE (before Net Debt CF)	Net Debt Cash Flow	FCFE (after Net Debt CF)
1998	$3.45	$152.80	$88.31	$76.06	($8.11)	$174.27	$166.16
1999	$90.77	$158.83	$56.47	$2.18	$190.95	($604.48)	($413.53)
2000	$201.71	$167.96	$219.37	$12.30	$138.00	($292.07)	($154.07)
2001	$18.11	$162.57	$421.49	($56.76)	($184.06)	$318.24	$134.19
2002	$111.91	$171.50	$260.70	($5.63)	$28.34	$36.35	$64.69
2003	$148.09	$162.57	$421.49	($7.47)	($103.37)	$531.20	$427.83
Average	$95.67	$162.70	$244.64	$3.45	$10.29	$27.25	$37.54

Table 11.6 Approximate FCFE for Aracruz from 1998 to 2003 (in Millions)

Year	Net Income	(Capital Expenditures − Depreciation) × (1 − DR)	Change in Noncash WC (1 − DR)	FCFE
1998	$3.45	($43.91)	$51.78	($4.42)
1999	$90.77	($69.69)	$1.48	$158.98
2000	$201.71	$35.00	$8.38	$158.34
2001	$18.11	$176.28	($38.64)	($119.53)
2002	$111.91	$60.73	($3.83)	$55.02
2003	$148.09	$176.28	($5.09)	($23.11)
Average	$95.67	$55.78	$2.35	$37.54

debt cash flows, capital expenditures, depreciation, and changes in noncash working capital between 1998 and 2003:

Average Debt Ratio
= Net Debt Cash Flow/(Capital Expenditures − Depreciation
+ Change in Noncash Working Capital)
= 27.25/(244.64 − 162.70 + 3.45) = 31.92%

The FCFE each year can then be estimated using the average debt ratio (DR), instead of the actual net debt cash flows. Table 11.6 contains the estimates of FCFE each year using this approach for Aracruz.

Note that the average FCFE from 1998 and 2003 remains unchanged at $37.54 million a year when we use the approximation. The FCFE in each year is different, though, from the estimates in Table 11.5 because we are smoothing out the effects of the cash flows from debt.

To estimate the FCFE for Deutsche Bank, we used the categories developed earlier for banks—net interest income, arbitrage income, and advisory and fee income from providing financial advice and services to firms. To estimate the net investment made in 2003 for each source of income and ignoring training expenses, we used the balance sheet numbers for 2002 and 2003. Table 11.7 reports these numbers.

We then categorized these changes into the "interest income" investments, "arbitrage income" investments, and "other" investments, considering interbank investments as interest income investments.

Interest Income Investments
= (Net Loans + Interbank Investments − Deposits)$_{2003}$
− (Net Loans + Interbank Investments − Deposits)$_{2002}$

Arbitrage Investments = (ST and LT Investments + Security Purchases
− ST Borrowings − LT Borrowings − ST Liabilities − LT Liabilities)$_{2003}$
− (ST and LT Investments − ST Borrowings − LT Borrowings
− ST Liabilities − LT Liabilities)$_{2002}$

Other Investments = (Net Fixed Assets + Other Assets)$_{2003}$
− (Net Fixed Assets + Other Assets)$_{2002}$

Table 11.7 DEUTSCHE BANK: 2002 AND 2003 FINANCIALS (IN MILLIONS)			
	2002	**2003**	**Change**
Interbank assets	€25,691.00	€14,649.00	−€11,042.00
Net loans	€167,303.00	€144,946.00	−€22,357.00
Security purchases/resell	€155,258.00	€185,215.00	€29,957.00
Short-term investments	€318,681.00	€370,002.00	€51,321.00
Long-term investments	€4,729.00	€2,569.00	−€2,160.00
Net fixed assets	€8,883.00	€5,786.00	−€3,097.00
Other assets	€68,732.00	€73,751.00	€5,019.00
Total noncash assets	€749,277.00	€796,918.00	€47,641.00
Total deposits	€327,625.00	€306,154.00	−€21,471.00
Short-term borrowings	€125,842.00	€155,002.00	€29,160.00
Long-term borrowing	€92,388.00	€82,018.00	−€10,370.00
Short-term liabilities	€172,379.00	€222,838.00	€50,459.00
Long-term liabilities	€10,130.00	€9,400.00	−€730.00
Liabilities	€728,364.00	€775,412.00	€47,048.00

With these definitions, and based on Deutsche Bank's net income of 1,365 million Euros in 2003, we estimated the FCFE:

Net Income	€1,365
− Interest Income Investments	− (−€11,928.00)
− Arbitrage Investments	− €10,599.00
− Other Investments	− €1,922.00
FCFE	€772.00

This analysis would suggest that Deutsche Bank had 772 million Euros available to be returned to stockholders in 2003.

11.2 DEFINING FCFE

The reason that the net income is not the amount that a company can afford to pay out in dividends is because

☐ earnings are not cash flows.
☐ some of the earnings have to be reinvested back in the firm to create growth.
☐ there may be cash inflows or outflows associated with the use of debt.
☐ all of the above.

Explain.

Measuring the Payout Ratio

The conventional measure of dividend policy—the dividend payout ratio—gives us the value of dividends as a proportion of earnings. In contrast, our approach

Table 11.8   DISNEY: DIVIDENDS AS PERCENTAGE OF EARNINGS AND CASH RETURNED AS PERCENTAGE OF FCFE

Year	Net Income (Millions)	Dividends (Millions)	Payout Ratio	FCFE (Millions)	Cash Returned to Stockholders (Millions)	Cash Returned/ FCFE
1994	$1,110.40	$153.20	13.80%	$1,589.59	$723.90	45.54%
1995	$1,380.10	$180.00	13.04%	$2,621.50	$528.70	20.17%
1996	$1,214.00	$271.00	22.32%	($235.00)	$733.00	NA
1997	$1,966.00	$342.00	17.40%	$3,535.00	$975.00	27.58%
1998	$1,850.00	$412.00	22.27%	$2,538.00	$442.00	17.42%
1999	$1,300.00	$0.00	0.00%	$3,132.00	$19.00	0.61%
2000	$920.00	$434.00	47.17%	$168.00	$600.00	357.14%
2001	($158.00)	$438.00	NA	($366.00)	$1,511.00	NA
2002	$1,236.00	$428.00	34.63%	$3,057.00	$428.00	14.00%
2003	$1,267.00	$429.00	33.86%	$414.00	$429.00	103.62%
1994–2003 (Total)	$12,085.50	$3,087.20	25.54%	$16,454.09	$6,389.60	38.83%

measures the total cash returned to stockholders as a proportion of FCFE:

$$\text{Dividend Payout Ratio} = \text{Dividends/Earnings}$$

$$\text{Cash to Stockholders to FCFE Ratio} = (\text{Dividends} + \text{Equity Repurchases})/\text{FCFE}$$

The ratio of cash returned to stockholders to FCFE shows how much of the cash available to be paid out to stockholders is actually returned to them in the form of dividends and stock buybacks. If this ratio over time is equal or close to 100 percent, the firm is paying out all that it can to its stockholders. If it is significantly less than 100 percent, the firm is paying out less than it can afford and is using the difference to increase its cash balance or to invest in marketable securities. If it is significantly over 100 percent, the firm is paying out more than it can afford and is either drawing on an existing cash balance or issuing new stock.

ILLUSTRATION **11.3   Comparing Dividend Payout Ratios to FCFE Payout Ratios: Disney and Aracruz**

In the following analysis, we compare the dividend payout ratios to the cash to stockholders as a percent of FCFE for Disney and Aracruz. Table 11.8 shows both numbers for Disney from 1994 to 2003.

As you can see, Disney paid out 25.54 percent of its aggregate earnings as dividends over this period.[8] Over the same period, it returned 38.83 percent of its FCFE to its stockholders in the form of dividends and stock buybacks. Though the payout ratio gives us little information about the company, the cash returned as a percent of

---

[8]To compute the payout ratio over the entire period, we first aggregated earnings and dividends over the entire period and then divided the aggregate dividends by the aggregate earnings. This avoids the problems created by averaging ratios where outliers (very high ratios) are common.

Table 11.9 ARACRUZ DIVIDENDS AS PERCENTAGE OF EARNINGS AND CASH RETURNED AS PERCENT OF FCFE (IN MILLIONS)

Year	Net Income	Dividends	Payout Ratio	FCFE	Cash Returned to Stockholders	Cash Returned/ FCFE
1998	$3.45	$24.39	707.51%	$166.16	$50.79	30.57%
1999	$90.77	$18.20	20.05%	($413.53)	$18.20	NA
2000	$201.71	$57.96	28.74%	($154.07)	$80.68	NA
2001	$18.11	$63.17	348.87%	$134.19	$63.17	47.08%
2002	$111.91	$73.80	65.94%	$64.69	$75.98	117.45%
2003	$148.09	$109.31	73.81%	$427.83	$112.31	26.25%
1998–2003 (Total)	$574.04	$346.83	60.42%	$225.27	$401.12	178.07%

FCFE suggests that Disney accumulated cash during this period. Even if we ignore the cash flows generated by debt in estimating FCFE, Disney returned only 65.91 percent of its FCFE to its stockholders in the form of dividends and stock buybacks.[9]

Table 11.9 shows dividend payout ratios and cash returned to stockholders as a percent of FCFE for Aracruz from 1998 to 2003.

As with Disney, the payout ratio and the cash returned as a percent of FCFE tell different stories. Aracruz paid out 60.42 percent of its aggregate earnings over the period as dividends, but the total cash returned as a percent of aggregate FCFE was in excess of 100 percent. Some of the dividends were clearly funded using cash accumulated at the start of the period.

This spreadsheet allows you to estimate the free cash flow to equity and the cash returned to stockholders for a period of up to ten years (**dividends.xls**).

There is a data set online that summarizes dividends, cash returned to stockholders, and FCFE by sector in the United States.

Why Firms May Not Pay Out What Is Available

For several reasons, many firms pay out less to stockholders, in the form of dividends and stock buybacks, than they have available in free cash flows to equity. The reasons vary from firm to firm and we list some here.

- The managers of a firm may gain by retaining cash rather than paying it out as a dividend. The desire for empire building makes increasing the size of the firm an objective on its own. Alternatively, management may feel the need to build up a cash cushion to tide them over periods when earnings may dip; in such periods, the cash cushion may help buffer the earnings drop and may allow managers to remain in control.

- The firm may be unsure about its future financing needs and may choose to retain some cash to take on unexpected investments or meet unanticipated needs.

---

[9]This number was estimated using the FCFE prior to net debt cash flows in Table 11.4.

- The firm may have volatile earnings and may retain cash to help smooth out dividends over time.

- Bondholders may impose restrictions on cash payments to stockholders, which may prevent the firm from returning available cash flows to its stockholders.

At the other end of the spectrum, there are firms that pay out more cash than they generate in FCFE though this is a less common phenomenon. Here again, there are several possible reasons.

- When earnings are volatile and swing from period to period, firms may choose to pay more than their FCFE in down periods and hope to make up for it when earnings recover.

- Firms that have historically paid high dividends often are under pressure to maintain those dividends even when earnings drop, for fear of sending a bad signal to the market.

- Firms that are under levered can use a policy of returning more cash to their stockholders as a way of reducing equity and increasing debt ratios.

11.3   What Happens to the FCFE that Are Not Paid Out?

In 2003, Microsoft had FCFE of roughly $9 billion, paid no dividends, and bought back no stock. Where would you expect to see the difference of $9 billion show up in Microsoft's financial statements?

☐   It will be invested in new projects.

☐   It will be in retained earnings, increasing the book value of equity.

☐   It will increase the cash balance of the company.

☐   None of the above.

Explain.

Evidence on Dividends and FCFE

We can observe the tendency of firms to pay out less to stockholders than they have available in FCFE by examining cash returned to stockholders paid as a percentage of FCFE. In 2003, for instance, the median cash returned to FCFE ratio across dividend paying firms listed in the United States was 60 percent. Figure 11.2 shows the distribution of cash returned as a percent of FCFE across all dividend-paying firms.

A value less than 100 percent means that the firm is paying out less in dividends and stock buybacks than it has available in free cash flows and that it is generating surplus cash. For those firms that did not make net debt payments (debt payments in excess of new debt issues) during the period, this cash surplus appears as an increase in the cash balance. A value greater than 100 percent indicates that the firm is paying out more in dividends than it has available in cash flow. These firms have to finance these dividend payments either out of existing cash balances or by making new stock and debt issues. Note that there are almost 300 firms in this period that paid dividends even though they had negative FCFE. These firms will have to come up with enough funds, either from existing cash balances or new stock issues, to cover both the dividends and the cash deficit.

Figure 11.2   Dividends Paid as Percent of FCFE

Source: Value Line, 2003.

This spreadsheet allows you to estimate the FCFE for a firm over a period for up to ten years and compare it to dividends paid (**dividends.xls**).

Step 2: Assessing Project Quality

The alternative to returning cash to stockholders is reinvestment. Consequently, a firm's investment opportunities influence its dividend policy. Other things remaining equal, a firm with better projects typically has more flexibility in setting dividend policy and defending it against stockholder pressure for higher dividends. But how do we define a good project?

According to our analysis of investment decisions, a good project is one that earns at least the hurdle rate, which is the cost of equity if cash flows are estimated on an equity basis, or the cost of capital if cash flows are measured on a predebt basis. In theory, we could estimate the expected cash flows on every project available to the firm and calculate the internal rates of return (IRR) or net present value (NPV) of each project to evaluate project quality. There are several practical problems with this, however. First, we have to be able to obtain the detailed cash flow estimates and hurdle rates for all available projects, which can be daunting if the firm has dozens or even hundreds of projects. The second problem is that even if these cash flows are available for existing projects, they will not be available for future projects.

As an alternative approach to measuring project quality, we can use one or more of the measures we developed in Chapter 5 to evaluate a firm's current project portfolio:

- Accounting return differentials, where we compare the accounting return on equity to the cost of equity and the accounting return on capital to the cost of capital.
- Economic value added (EVA), which measures the excess return earned on capital invested in existing investments and can be computed either on an equity or capital basis. We did note the limitations of each of these approaches in Chapter 5, but they still provide a measure of the quality of a firm's existing investments.

Using past project returns as a measure of future project quality can result in errors if a firm is making a transition from one stage in its growth cycle to the next or if it is in the process of restructuring. In such situations, it is entirely possible that the expected returns on new projects will differ from past project returns. Consequently, it may be worthwhile scrutinizing past returns for trends that may carry over into the future. The average return on equity or capital for a firm will not reveal these trends very well because they are slow to reflect the effects of new projects, especially for large firms. An alternative accounting return measure, which better captures year to year shifts, is the *marginal return on equity or capital,* which is defined as follows:

$$\text{Marginal Return on Equity}_t = \frac{\text{Net Income}_t - \text{Net Income}_{t-1}}{\text{Book Value of Equity}_t - \text{Book Value of Equity}_{t-1}}$$

$$\text{Marginal Return on Capital} = \frac{\text{EBIT}(1-t)_t - \text{EBIT}(1-t)_{t-1}}{\text{Book Value of Capital}_t - \text{Book Value of Capital}_{t-1}}$$

Although the marginal return on equity (capital) and the average return on equity (capital) will move in the same direction, the marginal returns typically change much more than do the average returns, the difference being a function of the size of the firm. These marginal returns can be used to compute the quality of the new projects.

The alternative to using accounting returns to measure the quality of a firm's projects is to look at how well or badly a firm's stock has done in financial markets. In Chapter 4, we compared the returns earned by a stock to the returns earned on the market after adjusting for risk (Jensen's alpha). The risk-adjusted excess return that we estimated becomes a measure of whether a stock has under- or outperformed the market. A positive excess return would then be viewed as an indication that a firm has done better than expected, whereas a negative excess return would indicate that a firm has done worse than anticipated.

Finally, accounting income and stock returns may vary year to year, not only because of changes in project quality but also because of fluctuations in business cycles and interest rates. Consequently, the comparisons between returns and hurdle rates should be made over long enough periods, say, five to ten years, to average out these other effects.

Figure 11.3 Return on Equity, Return on Stock, and Cost of Equity: Disney

ILLUSTRATION **11.4 Evaluating Project Quality at Disney and Aracruz**

In Illustration 5.9, we examined the quality of existing investments at Disney and Aracruz, using both accounting returns and EVA. In the following analysis, we examine both accounting and market measures of return at Disney and Aracruz over the most recent time period and compare them to the appropriate hurdle rates to evaluate the quality of the projects taken at each firm during the period. We begin with an analysis of Disney's accounting return on equity, the return from holding the stock, and the required return (given the beta and market performance during each year) from 1994 to 2003 as shown in Figure 11.3.[10]

As you can see, the verdict is not favorable to Disney, especially after the acquisition of Capital Cities in 1996. The return on equity for the firm, which exceeded 20 percent in the two years prior to the acquisition, plummeted in the years after to single digits. Accounting rules can be blamed partially for the decline immediately after the acquisition because the book value of equity at Disney jumped when it bought ABC. However, the continuing decline in return on equity in 1998 and 1999 cannot be attributed to the book value, and neither can the poor stock price performance between 1998 and 2002. It is clear that any promised synergy in this merger

---

[10]For instance, to estimate the expected return in 1998, we use the following: Expected Return in 1998 = Risk-Free Rate at Beginning of 1998 + Beta (Return on Market in 1998 − Risk-Free Rate at Beginning of 1998). An average beta of 1.20 was used over the entire period for Disney.

Figure 11.4   Return on Equity, Return on Stock, and Cost of Equity: Aracruz

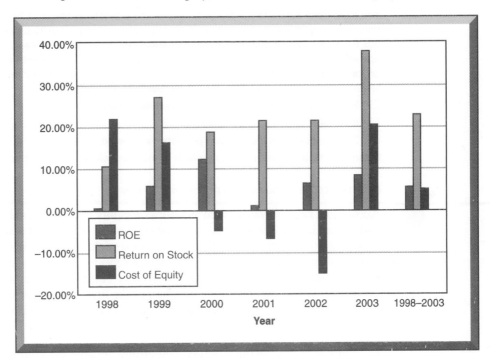

had not materialized over the following seven years. Although there are individual years in which Disney project returns and stock returns exceed the required return, the average return on equity over the entire period is 7.50 percent, which is lower than the cost of equity of 14.62 percent. The average annual return from holding Disney stock is 8.27 percent, which is also lower than the required return. Based on the company's performance over the past few years, there is little to suggest that Disney's managers can be trusted with cash.

Repeating this analysis for Aracruz for the 1998–2003 time period yields different results. Figure 11.4 summarizes returns on equity, returns on the stock, and the required return at the firm for each year between 1998 and 2003.

During this period, Aracruz earned an average return on equity of 5.68 percent, barely in excess of its cost of equity of 5.27 percent, but an investor in its stock would have seen an average annual return of 22.84 percent over the same period. Stockholders may be willing, at this stage, to accept the firm's contention that its projects are delivering sufficient returns, but a key question will be how much these returns are dependent on the price of paper/pulp holding up in future years. Looking at Aracruz's history, it is quite clear that much of the volatility in returns from year to year can be attributed to commodity price variation.

This spreadsheet allows you to estimate the average return on equity and cost of equity for a firm for a period of up to ten years (**dividends.xls**).

11.4 HISTORICAL, AVERAGE, AND PROJECTED RETURNS ON CAPITAL

You have been asked to judge the quality of the projects available at Super Meats, a meat processing company. It has earned an average return on capital of 10 percent over the previous five years, but its marginal return on capital last year was 14 percent. The industry average return on capital is 12 percent, and it is expected that Super Meats will earn this return on its projects over the next five years. If the cost of capital is 12.5 percent, which of the following conclusions would you draw about Super Meat's projects?

☐ It invested in good projects over the last five years.

☐ It invested in good projects last year.

☐ It can expect to invest in good projects over the next five years.

In terms of setting dividend policy, which of these conclusions matter the most?

IN PRACTICE: DEALING WITH ACCOUNTING RETURNS

Accounting rates of return, such as return on equity and capital, are subject to abuse and manipulation. For instance, decisions on how to account for acquisitions, choice of depreciation methods (accelerated versus straight line), and whether to expense or capitalize an item (R&D) can all affect reported income and book value. In addition, in any specific year, the return on equity and capital can be biased upward or downward depending on whether the firm had an unusually good or bad year. To estimate a fairer measure of returns on existing projects, we recommend the following:

1. Normalize the income before computing returns on equity or capital. For Aracruz, using the average income over the past three years, instead of the most recent year, provides returns on equity or capital that are much closer to the required returns.

2. Back out cosmetic earnings effects caused by accounting decisions, such as the one on pooling versus purchase. This is precisely why we should consider Disney's income prior to the amortization of the Capital Cities acquisition in computing returns on equity and capital.

3. If there are operating expenses designed to create future growth, rather than current income, capitalize those expenses and treat them as part of book value while computing operating income prior to those expenses. ∎

Step 3: Evaluating Dividend Policy

Once we have measured a firm's capacity to pay dividends and assessed its project quality, we can decide whether the firm should continue its existing policy of returning cash to stockholders, return more cash, or return less. The assessment will depend on how much of the FCFE is returned to stockholders each period and how good the firm's project opportunities are. There are four possible scenarios:

- *A firm may have good projects and may be paying out more (in dividends and stock buybacks) than its FCFE* In this case, the firm is losing value in two ways. First, by paying too much in dividends, it creates a cash shortfall that has to be met by issuing more securities. Second, the cash shortfall often creates capital rationing constraints; as a result, the firm may reject good projects it otherwise would have taken.

- ***A firm may have good projects and may be paying out less than its FCFE as a dividend***   Although it will accumulate cash as a consequence, the firm can legitimately argue that it will have good projects in the future in which it can invest the cash, though investors may wonder why it did not take the projects in the current period.

- ***A firm may have poor projects and may be paying out less than its FCFE as a dividend***   This firm will also accumulate cash, but it will find itself under pressure from stockholders to distribute the cash because of their concern that the cash will be used to finance poor projects.

- ***A firm may have poor projects and may be paying out more than its FCFE as a dividend***   This firm first has to deal with its poor project choices, possibly by cutting back on those investments that make returns below the hurdle rate. Because the reduced capital expenditure will increase the FCFE, this may take care of the dividend problem. If it does not, the firm will have to cut dividends as well.

Figure 11.5 illustrates the possible combinations of cash payout and project quality.

Figure 11.5   Analyzing Dividend Policy

In this matrix, Aracruz, with its (barely) superior project returns and its history of paying out more in dividends than it has available in FCFE falls in the quadrant where cutting dividends and redirecting the cash to projects seems to make the most sense. Disney, on the other hand, which pays less in dividends than it has available in FCFE and has a recent history of poor project returns, clearly will come under pressure to return more cash to its stockholders.

Note, however, that the pressure to pay dividends comes from the lack of trust in Disney's management rather than any greed on the part of stockholders. For a contrast, consider Microsoft, which had $11.175 billion in FCFE in 2003 and returned only $857 million in dividends. The company's high return on equity (>25 percent) and superior stock price performance earned it the flexibility to pay out far less in cash than it generated, with little protest from stockholders.

We might obtain estimates of return on equity and FCFE by looking at past data, but the entire analysis should be forward-looking. The objective is not to estimate return on equity on past projects but to forecast expected returns on future investments. Only to the degree that past information is useful in making these forecasts is it an integral part of the analysis.

Consequences of Payout Not Matching FCFE

The consequences of the cash payout to stockholders not matching the FCFE can vary depending on the quality of a firm's projects. In this section, we examine the consequences of paying out too little or too much for firms with good projects and for firms with bad projects. We also look at how managers in these firms may justify their payout policy and how stockholders are likely to react to the justification.

A. Poor Projects and Low Payout

There are firms that invest in poor projects and accumulate cash by not returning any to stockholders. We discuss stockholder reaction and management response to the dividend policy.

Consequences of Low Payout   When a firm pays out less than it can afford to in dividends, it accumulates cash. If a firm does not have good projects in which to invest this cash, it faces several possibilities. In the most benign case, the cash accumulates in the firm and is invested in financial assets. Assuming that these financial assets are fairly priced, the investments are zero NPV projects and should not negatively affect firm value. There is the possibility, however, that the firm may find itself the target of an acquisition, financed in part by its large holdings of liquid assets.

In the more damaging scenario, as the cash in the firm accumulates, the managers may be tempted to invest in projects that do not meet their hurdle rates, either to reduce the likelihood of a takeover or to earn higher returns than they would on financial assets.[11] These actions will lower the value of the firm. Another

---

[11]This is especially likely if the cash is invested in Treasury bills or other low-risk, low-return investments. On the surface, it may seem better for the firm to take on risky projects that earn, say 7 percent, than invest in Treasury bills and make 3 percent, though this clearly does not make sense after adjusting for the risk.

possibility is that the management may decide to use the cash to finance an acquisition. This hurts stockholders in the firm because some of their wealth is transferred to the stockholders of the acquired firms. The managers will claim that such acquisitions have strategic and synergistic benefits. The evidence indicates, however, that most firms that have financed takeovers with large cash balances, acquired over years of paying low dividends while generating a high FCFE, have reduced stockholder value.

Stockholder Reaction   Because of the negative consequences of building large cash balances, stockholders of firms that pay insufficient dividends and do not have "good" projects should pressure managers to return more of the cash. This is the basis for the free cash flow hypothesis, where dividends serve to reduce free cash flows available to managers and, by doing so, reduce the losses management actions can create for stockholders.

Management's Defense   Not surprisingly, managers of firms that pay out less in dividends than they can afford view this policy as being in the best long-term interests of the firm. They maintain that although the current project returns may be poor, future projects will both be more plentiful and have higher returns. Such arguments may be believable initially, but they become more difficult to sustain if the firm continues to earn poor returns on its projects. Managers may also claim that the cash accumulation is needed to meet demands arising from future contingencies. For instance, cyclical firms will often state that large cash balances are needed to tide them over the next recession. Again, although there is some truth to this view, whether the cash balance that is accumulated is reasonable has to be assessed by looking at the experience of the firm in prior recessions.

Finally, in some cases, managers will justify a firm's cash accumulation and low dividend payout based on the behavior of comparable firms. Thus, a firm may claim that it is essentially matching the dividend policy of its closest competitors and that it has to continue to do so to remain competitive. The argument that "every one else does it" cannot be used to justify a bad dividend policy, however.

Although all these justifications seem consistent with stockholder wealth maximization or the best long-term interests of the firm, they may really be smoke screens designed to hide the fact that this dividend policy serves managerial rather than stockholder interests. Maintaining large cash balances and low dividends provides managers with two advantages: It increases the funds that are directly under their control and thus increases their power to direct future investments, and it increases their margin for safety by stabilizing earnings and thus protects their jobs.

B. Good Projects and Low Payout

Although the outcomes for stockholders in firms with poor projects and low dividends range from neutral to terrible, the results may be more positive for firms that have a better selection of projects and whose management have had a history of earning high returns for stockholders.

Consequences of Low Payout The immediate consequence of paying out less in dividends than is available in FCFE is the same for firms with good projects as it is for firms with poor projects: The cash balance of the firm increases to reflect the cash surplus. The long-term effects of cash accumulation are generally much less negative for these firms, however, for the following reasons:

- These firms have projects that earn returns greater than the hurdle rate, and it is likely that the cash will be used productively in the long run.
- The high returns earned on internal projects reduces both the pressure and the incentive to invest the cash in poor projects or in acquisitions.
- Firms that earn high returns on their projects are much less likely to be targets of takeovers, reducing the threat of hostile acquisitions.

To summarize, firms that have a history of investing in good projects and expect to continue to have such projects in the future may be able to sustain a policy of retaining cash rather than paying out dividends. In fact, they can actually create value in the long run by using this cash productively.

Stockholder Reaction Stockholders are much less likely to feel a threat to their wealth in firms that have historically shown good judgment in picking projects. Consequently, they are more likely to agree when managers in those firms withhold cash rather than pay it out. Although there is a solid basis for arguing that managers cannot be trusted with large cash balances, this proposition does not apply equally across all firms. The managers of some firms earn the trust of their stockholders because of their capacity to deliver extraordinary returns on both their projects and their stock over long periods of time. These managers will be generally have much more flexibility in determining dividend policy.

The notion that greedy stockholders force firms with great investments to return too much cash too quickly is not based in fact. Rather, stockholder pressure for dividends or stock repurchases is greatest in firms whose projects yield marginal or poor returns and least in firms whose projects have high returns.

Management Responses Managers in firms that have posted stellar records in project and stock returns clearly have a much easier time convincing stockholders of the desirability of withholding cash rather than paying it out. The most convincing argument for retaining funds for reinvestment is that the cash will be used productively in the future and earn excess returns for the stockholders. Not all stockholders will agree with this view, especially if they feel that future projects will be less attractive than past projects, which might occur if the industry in which the firm operates is maturing. For example, many specialty retail firms, such as The Limited, found themselves under pressure to return more cash to stockholders in the early 1990s as margins and growth rates in the business declined.

C. Poor Projects and High Payout

In many ways, the most troublesome combination of circumstances occurs when firms pay out much more in dividends than they can afford, and at the same time earn disappointing returns on their projects. These firms have problems with both their investment and their dividend policies, and the latter cannot be solved adequately without addressing the former.

Consequences of High Payout   When a firm pays out more in dividends than it has available in FCFE, it is creating a cash deficit that has to be funded by drawing on the firm's cash balance, by issuing stock to cover the shortfall, or by borrowing money to fund its dividends. If the firm uses its cash reserves, it will reduce equity and raise its debt ratio. If it issues new equity, the drawback is the issuance cost of the stock. By borrowing money, the firm increases its debt ratio.

Because the FCFE is after capital expenditures, this firm's real problem is not that it pays out too much in dividends, but that it invests too much in bad projects. Cutting back on these projects would therefore increase the FCFE and might eliminate the cash shortfall created by paying dividends.

Stockholder Reaction   The stockholders of a firm that pays more in dividends than it has available in FCFE face a dilemma. On the one hand, they may want the firm to reduce its dividends to eliminate the need for additional borrowing or equity issues each year. On the other hand, the management's record in picking projects does not evoke much trust that the firm is using funds wisely, and it is likely that the funds saved by not paying the dividends will be used on other poor projects. Consequently, these firms will first have to solve their investment problems by cutting back on poor projects, which, in turn, will increase the FCFE. If the cash shortfall persists, the firm should then cut back on dividends.

It is therefore entirely possible, especially if the firm is underleveraged to begin with, that the stockholders will not push for lower dividends but will try to convince managers to improve project choice instead. It is also possible that they will encourage the firm to eliminate enough poor projects that the FCFE covers the expected dividend payment.

Management Responses   The managers of firms with poor projects and dividends that exceed FCFE may not think that they have investment problems rather than dividend problems. They may also disagree that the most efficient way of dealing with these problems is to eliminate some of the capital expenditures. In general, their views will be the same as managers who have a poor investment track record. They will claim the period used to analyze project returns was not representative, it was an industry-wide problem that will pass, or the projects have long gestation periods.

Overall, it is unlikely that these managers will convince the stockholders of their good intentions on future projects. Consequently, there will be a strong push toward cutbacks in capital expenditures, especially if the firm is borrowing money to finance the dividends and does not have much excess debt capacity.

11.5 Sᴛᴏᴄᴋʜᴏʟᴅᴇʀ Pʀᴇssᴜʀᴇ ᴀɴᴅ Dɪᴠɪᴅᴇɴᴅ Pᴏʟɪᴄʏ

Which of the following companies would you expect to see under greatest pressure from its stockholders to buy back stock or pay large dividends? (All of the companies have costs of capital of 12 percent.)

☐ A company with a historical return on capital of 25 percent, and a small cash balance.

☐ A company with a historical return on capital of 6 percent, and a small cash balance.

☐ A company with a historical return on capital of 25 percent, and a large cash balance.

☐ A company with a historical return on capital of 6 percent, and a large cash balance.

The managers at the company argue that they need the cash to do acquisitions. Would this make it more or less likely that stockholders will push for stock buybacks?

☐ More likely

☐ Less likely

D. Good Projects and High Payout

The costs of trying to maintain unsustainable dividends are most evident in firms that have a selection of good projects to choose from. The cash that is paid out as dividends could well have been used to invest in some of these projects, leading to a much higher return for stockholders and higher stock prices for the firm.

Consequences of High Payout　When a firm pays out more in dividends than it has available in FCFE, it creates a cash shortfall. If this firm also has good projects available but cannot invest in them because of capital rationing constraints, the firm is paying a hefty price for its dividend policy. Even if the projects are passed up for other reasons, the cash this firm is paying out as dividends would earn much better returns if left to accumulate in the firm.

Dividend payments also create a cash deficit that now has to be met by issuing new securities. Issuing new stock carries a potentially large issuance cost, which reduces firm value. But if the firm issues new debt, it might become overleveraged, and this may reduce value.

Stockholder Reaction　The best course of action for stockholders is to insist that the firm pay out less in dividends and invest in better projects. If the firm has paid high dividends for an extended period of time and has acquired stockholders who value high dividends even more than they value the firm's long-term health, reducing dividends will be difficult. Even so, stockholders may be much more amenable to cutting dividends and reinvesting in the firm if the firm has a ready supply of good projects at hand.

Management Responses　The managers of firms that have good projects while paying out too much in dividends have to figure out a way to cut dividends while differentiating themselves from those firms that are cutting dividends due to declining earnings. The initial suspicion with which markets view dividend cuts can be overcome (at least partially) by providing markets with information about project quality at the time of the dividend cut. If the dividends have been paid for a long time, however, the firm may have stockholders who like the high dividends and may not particularly be interested in the projects that the firm has available. If this is the case, the initial reaction to the dividend cut, no matter how carefully packaged, will be negative. However, as disgruntled stockholders sell their holdings, the firm will acquire new stockholders who will be more willing to accept the lower dividend and higher investment policy.

11.6 DIVIDEND POLICY AND HIGH-GROWTH FIRMS

High-growth firms are often encouraged to start paying dividends to expand their stockholder base, because there are stockholders who will not or cannot hold stock that do not pay dividends. Do you agree with this rationale?

☐ Yes

☐ No

Explain.

Step 4: Interaction Between Dividend Policy and Financing Policy

The analysis of dividend policy is further enriched—and complicated—if we bring the firm's financing mix into the decision as well. In Chapter 9 we noted that one of the ways a firm can increase leverage over time is by increasing dividends or repurchasing stock; at the same time, it can decrease leverage by cutting or not paying dividends. Thus we cannot decide how much a firm should pay in dividends without determining whether it is under- or overlevered and whether or not it intends to close this leverage gap.

An underlevered firm may be able to pay more than its FCFE as dividend and may do so intentionally to increase its debt ratio. An overlevered firm, on the other hand, may have to pay less than its FCFE as dividends because of its desire to reduce leverage. In some of the scenarios already described, leverage can be used to strengthen the suggested recommendations. For instance, an underlevered firm with poor projects and a cash flow surplus has an added incentive to raise dividends and reevaluate investment policy because it will be able to increase its leverage by doing so. In some cases, however, the imperatives of moving to an optimal debt ratio may act as a barrier to carrying out changes in dividend policy. Thus, an overlevered firm with poor projects and a cash flow surplus may find the cash better spent reducing debt rather than paying out dividends.

ILLUSTRATION 11.5 Analyzing the Dividend Policy of Disney and Aracruz

Using the cash flow approach, we are now in a position to analyze Disney's dividend policy. To do so, we will draw on three findings:

- Earlier, we compared the cash returned to stockholders by Disney between 1994 and 2003 to its FCFE. On average, Disney paid out 38.83 percent of its FCFE as

Table 11.10   FORECASTED FCFE AND CASH AVAILABLE FOR STOCK BUYBACKS: DISNEY (IN MILLIONS)

	Current	Expected Growth Rate	1	2	3	4	5
Net income	$1,267	6.00%	$1,343	$1,424	$1,509	$1,600	$1,696
– (Cap Ex – Deprec'n) (1 – DR)	($20)		$9	$41	$79	$123	$174
– Change in non-cash working capital (1 – DR)	($185)		$22	$23	$24	$26	$28
FCFE	$1,471		$1,313	$1,359	$1,405	$1,450	$1,494
Expected dividends	$429	0.00%	$429	$429	$429	$429	$429
Cash available for stock buybacks	$1,042		$884	$930	$976	$1,021	$1,065
Revenues	$27,061	6.00%	$28,685	$30,406	$32,230	$34,164	$36,214
Noncash WC	$519		$550	$583	$618	$655	$694
Capital expenditures	$1,049	10.00%	$1,154	$1,269	$1,396	$1,536	$1,689
Depreciation	$1,077	6.00%	$1,142	$1,210	$1,283	$1,360	$1,441

dividends. In recent years, though, Disney has had significant operating problems, and its depressed net income reflects these troubles (Table 11.8).

- We then compared Disney's return on equity and stock to the required rate of return and found that the company had underperformed on both measures (Figure 11.3).

- Finally, in our analysis in Chapter 8, we noted that Disney was slightly underlevered, with an actual debt ratio of 21 percent and an optimal debt ratio of 30 percent.

Given its recent operating problems, we would recommend that Disney maintain its existing dividend payments for the next year. If the higher earnings that the company has reported in recent quarters are sustained, the FCFE will be higher than the dividend payments. In Table 11.10, we forecast the FCFE for Disney over the next five years and compare it to existing dividend payments.

Note that we have assumed that revenues, net income, and depreciation will grow 6 percent a year for the next five years and that non-cash working capital remains at its existing percentage (1.92 percent) of revenues. We have also assumed that capital expenditures will grow faster (10 percent) over the next five years to compensate for reduced investment in prior years. Finally, we assumed that 30 percent of the net capital expenditures and working capital changes would be funded with debt, reflecting the optimal debt ratio we computed for Disney in Chapter 8. Based on these forecasts, and assuming that Disney maintains its

Table 11.11   EXPECTED FCFE AND CASH AVAILABLE FOR DIVIDENDS
(IN MILLIONS)

	Current	Expected Growth Rate	1	2	3	4	5
Net income	$148	5.00%	$155	$163	$171	$180	$189
– (Cap Ex – Deprec'n) (1 – DR)	$176		$120	$126	$133	$139	$146
– Change in non-cash working capital (1 – DR)	($5)		$5	$5	$6	$6	$6
FCFE	($23)		$30	$32	$33	$35	$37
Expected dividends	$109	0.00%	$109	$109	$109	$109	$109
Cash available for stock buybacks			($79)	($78)	($76)	($74)	($73)
Revenues	$1,003	5.00%	$1,053	$1,106	$1,161	$1,219	$1,280
Noncash WC	$150		$158	$166	$174	$183	$192
Capital expenditures	$331	5.00%	$347	$365	$383	$402	$422
Depreciation	$163	5.00%	$171	$179	$188	$198	$207

existing dividend, Disney should have about $4.876 million in excess cash that it can return to its stockholders either as dividends or in the form of stock buybacks over the period.

Examining Aracruz, we find that the firm is paying out more in dividends than it has available in FCFE. If you couple this finding with large investment needs, potentially good project returns, and superior stock price performance, is seems clear that Aracruz will gain by cutting its dividends. In fact, this conclusion is strengthened when we forecast the FCFE for the next five years and compare them to the dividends being paid in Table 11.11.

In making these estimates, we assumed that revenues, net income, capital expenditures and depreciation will all grow 5 percent a year for the next five years and the noncash working capital will remain at 15 percent of revenues. For capital expenditures, which have been volatile over the past few years, we used the average amount from 2000–2003 as the base year number. If Aracruz maintains its existing dividends, the firm will find itself facing cash deficits in each of the next five years, aggregating to about $381 million. Although the case for cutting dividends is strong, Aracruz has a potential problem because of its share structure, where the preferred shares held by outside investors get no voting rights but are compensated for with a larger dividend. Cutting dividends may violate the commitments given to preferred stockholders and trigger at least a partial loss of control. Although there is no easy solution, it highlights a cost of trading off dividends for control.

For a framework for analyzing dividend policy, see Figure 11.6.

Figure 11.6 A Framework for Analyzing Dividend Policy

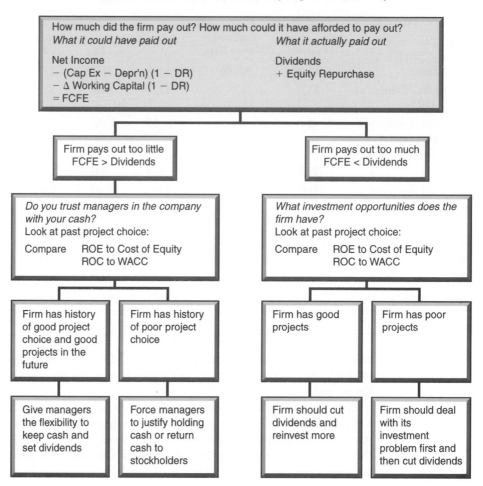

A COMPARABLE FIRM APPROACH TO ANALYZING DIVIDEND POLICY

So far, we have examined the dividend policy of a firm by looking at its cash flows and the quality of its investments. There are managers who believe that their dividend policies are judged relative to those of their competitors. This comparable-firm approach to analyzing dividend policy is often used narrowly, by looking at only firms that are in the same industry group or sector. As we will illustrate, it can be used more broadly, by looking at the determinants of dividend policy across all firms in the market.

Using Firms in the Industry

In the simplest form of this approach, a firm's dividend yield and payout are compared to those of firms in its industry and accordingly judged to be adequate, excessive, or inadequate. Thus, a utility stock with a dividend yield of 3.5 percent may be criticized for paying out an inadequate dividend if utility stocks, on average, have a much higher dividend yield. In contrast, a computer software firm that has a dividend yield of 1.0 percent may be viewed as paying too high a dividend if software firms pay a much lower dividend on average.

Although comparing a firm to comparable firms on dividend yield and payout may have some intuitive appeal, it can be misleading. First, it assumes that all firms within the same industry group have the same net capital expenditure and working capital needs. These assumptions may not be true if firms are in different stages of the life cycle. Second, even if the firms are at the same stage in their life cycles, the entire industry may have a dividend policy that is unsustainable or suboptimal. Third, it does not consider stock buybacks as an alternative to dividends. The third criticism can be mitigated when the approach is extended to compare cash returned to stockholders, rather than just dividends.

There is a data set online that summarizes the dividend yields and payout ratios by sector for U.S. companies.

ILLUSTRATION **11.6**   Analyzing Disney's Dividend Payout Using Comparable Firms

In comparing Disney's dividend policy to its peer group, we analyze the dividend yields and payout ratios of comparable firms in 2003, as shown in Table 11.12. We defined comparable firms as entertainment companies with a market capitalization in excess of $1 billion.

Of the twenty-six companies in this group, only five paid dividends. Relative to the other companies in this sector, Disney pays high dividends. The interesting question, though, is whether Disney should be setting dividend policy based on entertainment firms, most of which are smaller, riskier and much less diversified than Disney, or on large firms in other businesses that resemble it in terms of cash flows and risk.

For Deutsche Bank, we used large money-center European banks as comparable firms. Table 11.13 provides the listing of the firms, as well as their dividend yields and payout ratios.

On both dividend yield and payout ratios, Deutsche Bank pays a much higher dividend than the typical European bank. It is interesting, though, that the British banks are the highest dividend payers in the group, with Lloyds maintaining a dividend yield of 7.18%.

For Aracruz, we looked at the average dividend yield and payout ratios of four sets of comparable firms—Latin American paper and pulp companies, emerging market paper and pulp companies, U.S. paper and pulp companies, and all paper and pulp companies listed globally. Table 11.14 summarizes these statistics.

Aracruz has a dividend yield and payout ratio similar to that of other Latin American paper and pulp companies, though it is higher than dividends paid out by paper companies listed elsewhere.

With all three companies, the dangers of basing dividend policy on comparable firms are clear. The "right" amount to pay in dividends will depend heavily on what we define "comparable" to be. If managers are allowed to pick their peer group, it is easy to justify even the most irrational dividend policy.

Table 11.12 PAYOUT RATIOS AND DIVIDEND YIELDS: ENTERTAINMENT COMPANIES

Company	Dividend Yield	Dividend Payout
Astral Media	0.00%	0.00%
Belo Corp.	1.34%	34.13%
CanWest Global Communications	0.00%	0.00%
Cinram International	0.00%	0.00%
Clear Channel	0.85%	35.29%
Cox Radio	0.00%	0.00%
Cumulus Media	0.00%	0.00%
Disney	0.90%	32.31%
Emmis Communications	0.00%	0.00%
Entercom Communications	0.00%	0.00%
Fox Entmt Group	0.00%	0.00%
Hearst-Argyle Television	0.00%	0.00%
InterActiveCorp	0.00%	0.00%
Liberty Media	0.00%	0.00%
Lin TV	0.00%	0.00%
Metro Goldwyn Mayer	0.00%	0.00%
Pixar	0.00%	0.00%
Radio One	0.00%	0.00%
Regal Entertainment Group	2.70%	66.57%
Sinclair Broadcast	0.00%	0.00%
Sirius Satellite	0.00%	0.00%
Time Warner	0.00%	0.00%
Univision Communications	0.00%	0.00%
Viacom	0.56%	19.00%
Westwood One	0.00%	0.00%
XM Satellite	0.00%	0.00%
Average	0.24%	7.20%

Source: Value Line Database.

11.7 PEER GROUP ANALYSIS

Assume that you are advising a small, high-growth bank, which is concerned about the fact that its dividend payout and yield are much lower than other banks. The CEO of the bank is concerned that investors will punish the bank for its dividend policy. What do you think?

☐ I think that the bank will be punished for its errant dividend policy.

☐ I think that investors are sophisticated enough for the bank to be treated fairly.

☐ I think that the bank will not be punished for its low dividends as long as it tries to convey information to its investors about the quality of its projects and growth prospects.

Table 11.13 **PAYOUT RATIOS AND DIVIDEND YIELDS: EUROPEAN BANKS**

Company	Dividend Yield	Dividend Payout
Banca Intesa Spa	1.57%	167.50%
Banco Bilbao Vizcaya Argenta	0.00%	0.00%
Banco Santander Central Hisp	0.00%	0.00%
Barclays Plc	3.38%	35.61%
Bnp Paribas	0.00%	0.00%
Deutsche Bank Ag	1.98%	481.48%
Erste Bank Der Oester Spark	0.99%	24.31%
Hbos Plc	2.85%	27.28%
Hsbc Holdings Plc	2.51%	39.94%
Lloyds Tsb Group Plc	7.18%	72.69%
Royal Bank of Scotland Group	3.74%	38.73%
Sanpaolo Imi Spa	0.00%	0.00%
Societe Generale	0.00%	0.00%
Standard Chartered Plc	3.61%	46.35%
Unicredito Italiano Spa	0.00%	0.00%
Average	1.85%	62.26%

Source: Value Line Database.

Table 11.14 **PAYOUT RATIOS AND DIVIDEND YIELDS: PAPER AND PULP COMPANIES**

Group	Dividend Yield	Dividend Payout
Latin America	2.86%	41.34%
Emerging market	2.03%	22.16%
United States	1.14%	28.82%
All paper and pulp	1.75%	34.55%
Aracruz	3.00%	37.41%

Using the Market

The alternative to using only comparable firms in the same industry is to study the entire population of firms and try to estimate the variables that cause differences in dividend policy across firms. We outlined some of the determinants of dividend policy in the last chapter, and we could try to arrive at more specific measures of each of these determinants. For instance,

- *Growth Opportunities* Firms with greater growth opportunities should pay out less in dividends than firms without these opportunities. Consequently, dividend payout ratios (yields) and expected growth rates in earnings should be negatively correlated.

- *Investment Needs* Firms with larger investment needs (capital expenditures and working capital) should pay out less in dividends than firms without these needs. Dividend payout ratios and yields should be lower for firms with significant reinvestment needs.

- *Insider Holdings* As noted earlier in the chapter, firms where stockholders have less power are more likely to hold on to cash and not pay out dividends. Hence, dividend payout ratios and insider holdings should be negatively correlated with each other.

- *Financial Leverage* Firms with high debt ratios should pay lower dividends because they have already precommitted their cash flows to make debt payments. Therefore, dividend payout ratios and debt ratios should be negatively correlated with each other.

Because there are multiple measures that can be used for each of these variables, we chose specific proxies—analyst estimates of growth in earnings for growth opportunities, capital expenditures as a percent of total assets for investment needs, percent of stock held by insiders for insider holdings, and total debt as a percent of market capitalization as a measure of financial leverage. Using data from the end of 2003, we regressed dividend yields and payout ratios against all of these variables and arrived at the following regression equations (t-statistics are in parentheses below coefficients):

$$PYT = 0.3889 - 0.738\,CPXFR - 0.214\,INS + 0.193\,DFR - 0.747\,EGR$$
$$\quad\ (20.41)\quad (3.42)\qquad\quad (3.41)\qquad\ (4.80)\qquad\ (8.12)$$
$$R^2 = 18.30\%$$

$$YLD = 0.0205 - 0.058\,CPXFR - 0.012\,INS + 0.0200\,DFR - 0.047\,EGR$$
$$\quad\ (22.78)\quad (5.87)\qquad\quad (3.66)\qquad\ (9.45)\qquad\ (11.53)$$
$$R^2 = 28.5\%$$

where PYT = Dividend Payout Ratio = Dividends/Net Income; YLD = Dividend Yield = Dividends/Current Price; CPXFR = Capital Expenditures/Book Value of Total Assets; EGR = expected growth rate in earnings over next five years (analyst estimates); DFR = Debt/(Debt + Market Value of Equity); and INS = insider holdings as a percent of outstanding stock.

The regressions explain about 20–30 percent of the differences in dividend yields and payout across firms in the United States. The two strongest factors are earnings growth and the debt ratio, with higher-growth firms with lower debt ratios paying out less of their earnings as dividends and having lower dividend yields. Although this contradicts our hypothesis that higher leverage should lead to lower payout, it is not difficult to explain. It can be attributed to the fact that firms with more stable earnings have higher debt ratios, and these firms can also afford to pay more dividends. In addition, firms with high insider holdings tend to pay out less in dividends than do firms with low insider holdings, and firms with high capital expenditures needs pay less in dividends than firms without these needs.

Table 11.15   DATA FOR CROSS-SECTIONAL REGRESSIONS

	Disney	Aracruz
Insider holdings	2.60%	20.00%
Capital expenditures/total assets	2.10%	2.00%
Debt/capital	21.02%	31.00%
Expected growth in earnings	8.00%	23.00%

There is a data set online that summarizes the results of regressing dividend yield and payout ratio against fundamentals for U.S. companies.

ILLUSTRATION **11.7**   Analyzing Dividend Payout Using the Cross-Sectional Regression
To illustrate the applicability of the market regression in analyzing the dividend policy of Disney and Aracruz, we estimate the values of the independent variables in the regressions for the two firms, as shown in Table 11.15.

Substituting into the regression equation for the dividend payout ratio, we predicted the following payout ratios for the two firms:

$$\text{For Disney} = 0.3889 - 0.738(0.021) - 0.214(0.026) + 0.193(0.2102)$$
$$- 0.747(0.08) = 34.87\%$$

$$\text{For Aracruz ADR} = 0.3889 - 0.738(0.02) - 0.214(0.20) + 0.193(0.31)$$
$$- 0.747(0.23) = 21.94\%$$

Substituting into the regression equation for the dividend yield, we predict the following dividend yields for the two firms:

$$\text{For Disney} = 0.0205 - 0.058(0.021) - 0.012(0.026) + 0.0200(0.2102)$$
$$- 0.047(0.08) = 1.94\%$$

$$\text{For Aracruz ADR} = 0.0205 - 0.058(0.02) - 0.012(0.20) + 0.0200(0.31)$$
$$- 0.047(0.23) = 1.23\%$$

Based on this analysis, Disney with its dividend yield of 0.91 percent and a payout ratio of 32.31 percent is paying too little in dividends. Aracruz with a payout ratio of 37.41 percent and a dividend yield of 3 percent is paying too much in dividends, though the conclusion has to be tempered by the fact that the company is being compared to companies in the United States.

MANAGING CHANGES IN DIVIDEND POLICY

In Chapter 10, we noted the tendency on the part of investors to buy stocks with dividend policies that meet their specific needs. Thus, at least prior to 2003, investors who wanted high current cash flows and did not care much about the tax consequences migrated to firms that paid high dividends; those who wanted price appreciation and were concerned about the tax differential held stock in firms that paid low or no dividends. One consequence of this clientele effect is that changes in

Table 11.16 **EXCESS RETURNS AROUND DIVIDEND CUT ANNOUNCEMENTS**

Category	Periods around Announcement Date		
	Prior Quarter	Announcement Period	Quarter After
Simultaneous announcement of earnings decline/loss ($N = 176$)	−7.23%	−8.17%	+1.80%
Prior announcement of earnings decline or loss ($N = 208$)	−7.58%	−5.52%	+1.07%
Simultaneous announcement of investment or growth opportunities ($N = 16$)	−7.69%	−5.16%	+8.79%

dividends, even if entirely justified by the cash flows, may not be well received by stockholders. In particular, a firm with high dividends that cuts them drastically may find itself facing unhappy stockholders who value those dividends. At the other extreme, a firm with a history of not paying dividends that suddenly institutes a large dividend may also find that its stockholders are not pleased.

Is there a way in which firms can announce changes in dividend policy that minimizes the negative fallout that is likely to occur? In this section, we will examine dividend changes and the market reaction to them and draw broader lessons for all firms that may plan to make such changes.

Empirical Evidence

Firms may cut dividends for several reasons; some clearly have negative implications for future cash flows and the current value of the firm, whereas others have more positive implications. In particular, the value of firms that cut dividends because of poor earnings and cash flows should drop, whereas the value of firms that cut dividends because of a dramatic improvement in project choice should increase. At the same time, financial markets tend to be skeptical of the latter claims, especially if the firm making the claims reports lower earnings and has a history of poor project returns. Thus, there is value to examining closely timed earnings and dividend cut announcements, to see if the market reaction changes as a consequence.

Woolridge and Ghosh looked at 408 firms that cut dividends, and the actions taken or information provided by these firms in conjunction with the dividend cuts.[12] In particular, they examined three groups of companies: The first group announced an earnings decline or loss with the dividend cut; the second had made a prior announcement of earnings decline or loss; and the third made a simultaneous announcement of growth opportunities or higher earnings. The results are summarized in Table 11.16.

We can draw several interesting conclusions from this study. First, the vast number of firms announcing dividend cuts did so in response to earnings declines (384) rather than in conjunction with investment or growth opportunities (16). The market seems

---

[12]J. R. Woolridge and C. Ghosh, 1986, "Dividend Cuts: Do They Always Signal Bad News?" In *The Revolution in Corporate Finance*. Blackwell.

to react negatively to all of them, however, suggesting that it does not attach much credibility to the firm's statements. The negative reaction to the dividend cut seems to persist in the case of the firms with an earnings decline, whereas it is reversed in the case of the firms with an earnings increase or better investment opportunities.

Woolridge and Ghosh also found that firms that announced stock dividends or stock repurchases in conjunction with the dividend cuts fared much better than firms that did not. Finally, they noted the tendency across the entire sample for prices to correct themselves, at least partially, in the year following the dividend cut. This would suggest that markets tend to overreact to the initial dividend cut, and the price recovery can be attributed to the subsequent correction.

In an interesting case study, Soter, Brigham, and Evanson looked at Florida Power & Light's dividend cut in 1994.[13] FPL was the first healthy utility in the United States to cut dividends by a significant amount (32 percent). At the same time as it cut dividends, FPL announced that it was buying back 10 million shares over the next three years and emphasized that dividends would be linked more directly to earnings. On the day of the announcement, the stock price dropped 14 percent but recovered this amount in the month after the announcement and earned a return of 23.8 percent in the year after, significantly more than the S&P 500 over the period (11.2 percent) and other utilities (14.2 percent).

Lessons for Firms

There are several lessons for a firm that plans to change its dividend policy. First, no matter how good the rationale may be to cut dividends, it should expect markets to react negatively to the initial announcement for two reasons. The first reason is the well-founded skepticism with which markets greet any statement by the firm about dividend cuts. A second is that large dividend changes typically make the existing investor clientele unhappy. Although other stockholders may be happy with the new dividend policy, the transition will take time, during which period stock prices fall. Second, if a firm has good reasons for cutting dividends, such as an increase in project availability, it will gain at least partial protection by providing information to markets about these projects.

CONCLUSION

We began this chapter by expanding our definition of cash returned to stockholder to include stock buybacks with dividends. Firms in the United States especially have turned to buying back stock and returning cash selectively to those investors who need it.

With this expanded definition, we first used a cash flow–based approach to decide whether a firm is paying too much or too little to its stockholders. To form this judgment, we first estimate what the firm has available to pay out to its stockholders; we

---

[13]D. Soter, E. Brigham, and P. Evanson, 1996, "The Dividend Cut 'Heard 'Round the World': The Case of FPL," *Journal of Applied Corporate Finance,* 9, 4–15. This is also a Harvard Business School case study authored by Ben Esty.

measure this cash flow by looking at the cash left over after reinvestment needs have been met and debt has been serviced, and call it the free cash flow to equity. We then looked at the quality of the firm's projects; firms with better projects get more leeway from equity investors to accumulate cash than firms with poor projects. We next consider the effect of wanting to increase or decrease the debt ratio on how much cash is returned to stockholders. Finally, we consider all three factors—the cash flow available for stockholders, the returns on prospective investments, and the need to increase or decrease debt ratios—in coming up with broad conclusions about dividend policy. Firms with a good track record in investing can pay out less in dividends than is available in cash flows, and not face significant pressure from stockholders to pay out more. When the managers of firms are not trusted by their stockholders to invest wisely, firms are much more likely to face pressure to return excess cash to stockholders.

We also analyzed a firm's dividend policy by looking at the dividend policies of comparable firms in the business. In this approach, a firm paying out less in dividends than comparable firms would be viewed as paying too little and one that is paying out more would be viewed as paying too much. We used both a narrow definition of comparable firms (firms in the same line of business) and a broader definition (all firms in the market). We controlled for differences in risk and growth across firms using a multiple regression.

We closed the chapter by looking at how firms that intend to change their dividend policy can minimize the side costs of doing so. This is especially true when firms have to reduce their dividends to meet legitimate reinvestment needs. Although the initial reaction to the announcement of a dividend cut is likely to be negative, firms can buffer some of the impact by providing information to markets about the investments that they plan to accept with the funds.

Given the tax law changes, at least in the United States, in 2003, it may be time to revisit the whole basis for dividend policy. Historically, in the United States and Western Europe, firms have locked themselves into a dance with investors where they institute dividends and are then committed to maintaining these dividends, in good times and in bad. In fact, much of what we observe in dividend policy—from sticky dividends to the reluctance to increase dividends in the face of good news and to cut dividends in the face of bad news—can be traced to this commitment. This commitment has also led companies to increasingly shift to stock buybacks as an alternative to dividends. If dividends no longer have a tax disadvantage, it is time for firms to shift to a more flexible dividend payout policy, where dividends reflect what they can afford to pay rather than their historical dividends.

A FRAMEWORK FOR ANALYZING DIVIDENDS

Objective: To determine whether your firm should change its dividend policy, based on an analysis of its investment opportunities and comparable firms.

Key Questions
- How much could this firm have returned to its stockholders over the past few years? How much did it actually return?
- Given this dividend policy and the current cash balance of this firm, would you push the firm to change its dividend policy (return more or less cash to its owners)?
- How does this firm's dividend policy compare to those of its peer group and to the rest of the market?

Framework for Analysis

1. *Cash Return to Stockholders*
- How much has the firm paid out in dividends each year for the past few years?
- How much stock has it bought back each year for the past few years?
- Cumulatively, how much cash has been returned to stockholders each year for the past few years?

2. *Affordable Dividends*
- What was the FCFE that this firm had over the last few years?
- What is the current cash balance for this firm?

3. *Management Trust*
- How well have the managers of the firm picked investments, historically? (Look at the investment return section.)
- Is there any reason to believe that future investments of this firm will be different from the historical record?

4. *Changing Dividend Policy*
- Given the relationship between dividends and FCFE and the trust you have in the management of this firm, would you change this firm's dividend policy?

5. *Comparing to Sector and Market*
- Relative to the sector to which this firm belongs, does it pay too much or too little in dividends? (Do a regression, if necessary.)
- Relative to the rest of the firms in the market, does it pay too much or too little in dividends? (Use the market regression, if necessary.)

Getting Information on Analyzing Dividend Policy

You can get the information that you need to estimate FCFE and returns on equity from past financials. You will also need a beta (see risk and return section) and a debt ratio (see risk and return section) to estimate the free cash flows to equity. Finally, you will need stock returns for your stock and the returns on a market index over the period of your analysis.

Online Sources of Information
www.stern.nyu.edu/~adamodar/cfin2E/project/data.htm.

PROBLEMS AND QUESTIONS

(In the problems below, you can use a risk premium of 5.5 percent and a tax rate of 40 percent if none is specified.)

1. Stock buybacks really do not return cash to stockholders because only those who sell back stock receive the cash. Is this statement true or false? Explain.

2. In the past decade, we have seen an increase in the percent of cash returned to stockholders in the form of dividends. Why?

3. Lube Oil, a chain of automobile service stations, reports net income of $100 million after depreciation of $50 million. The firm has capital expenditures of $80 million, and the noncash working capital increased from $25 to $40 million. Estimate the firm's FCFE, assuming that the firm is all equity financed.

4. Lube Oil, in Question 3, paid a dividend of $20 million and bought back $25 million in stock. Estimate how much the cash balance of the firm changed during the year.

5. How would your answers to the last two questions change if you were told that Lube Oil started the year with $120 million in debt and ended the year with $135 million?

6. Now assume that Lube Oil has a return on equity of 5 percent and a cost of equity of 10 percent. As a stockholder in Lube Oil, would you want the firm to change its dividend policy? Why or why not?

7. Tech Products reported a net loss of $80 million for the latest financial year. In addition, the firm reported a net capital expenditure of $70 million, and a change in noncash working capital of $10 million. Finally, the firm had $10 million in debt at the start of the year that it paid off during the year. Estimate the FCFE.

8. Tech Products, from Question 7, pays a dividend of $40 million. Assuming that the firm started the period with no cash, how did it raise the funding for the dividend payment?

9. New Age Telecomm is a young, high-growth telecommunications firm. It pays no dividends, though the average dividend payout for other firms in the telecommunications sector is 40 percent. Is New Age paying too little in dividends? Why or why not?

10. The following is a regression of dividend payout ratios on the risk and ln(market capitalization: in millions) of chemical firms:

    Dividend Payout Ratio = 0.14 + 0.05
    [ln(Market Capitalization)] − 0.1(Beta)

    Harman Chemicals has a market capitalization of $1.5 billion and a beta of 1.2. It pays out 22 percent of its earnings as dividends. How does this dividend payout compare to the industry?

11. JLChem Corporation, a chemical manufacturing firm with changing investment opportunities, is considering a major change in dividend policy. It currently has 50 million shares outstanding and pays an annual dividend of $2 per share. The firm's current and projected income statements are provided below (in millions):

	Current	Projected for Next Year
EBITDA	$1,200	$1,350
− Depreciation	$200	$250
EBIT	$1,000	$1,100
− Interest expense	$200	$200
EBT	$800	$900
− Taxes	$320	$360
Net income	$480	$540

The firm's current capital expenditure is $500 million. It is considering five projects for the next year:

Project	Investment	Beta	IRR (Using Cash Flows to Equity)
A	$190 million	0.6	12.0%
B	$200 million	0.8	12.0%
C	$200 million	1.0	14.5%
D	$200 million	1.2	15.0%
E	$100 million	1.5	20.0%

The firm's current beta is 1.0, and the current Treasury bill rate is 5.5 percent. The firm expects working capital to increase $50 million both this year and next. The firm plans to finance its net capital expenditures and working capital needs with 30 percent debt.

a. What is the firm's current payout ratio?

b. What proportion of its current FCFE is it paying out as dividends?

c. What would your projected capital expenditure be for next year (i.e., which of the five projects would you accept and why)?

d. How much cash will the company have available to pay out as dividends next year? (What is the maximum amount the company can pay out as dividends?)

e. Would you pay out this maximum amount as dividends? Why or why not? What other considerations would you bring to this decision?

f. JLChem currently has a cash balance of $100 million (after paying the current year's dividends). If it pays out $125 million as dividends next year, what will its projected cash balance be at the end of the next year?

12. GL Corporation, a retail firm, is making a decision on how much it should pay out to its stockholders. It has $100 million in investible funds. The following information is provided about the firm:

- It has 100 million shares outstanding, each share selling for $15. The beta of the stock is 1.25 and the risk-free rate is 8 percent. The expected return on the market is 16 percent.
- The firm has $500 million of debt outstanding. The marginal interest rate on the debt is 12 percent.
- The corporate tax rate is 50 percent.
- The firm has the following investment projects:

Project	Investment Requirement	After-Tax Return on Capital
A	$15 million	27%
B	$10 million	20%
C	$25 million	16%
D	$20 million	14%
E	$30 million	12%

The firm plans to finance all its investment needs at its current debt ratio.

a. Should the company return money to its stockholders?

b. If so, how much should be returned to stockholders?

13. InTech, a computer software firm that has never paid dividends before, is considering whether it should start doing so. This firm has a cost of equity of 22 percent and a pre-tax cost of debt of 10 percent (the tax rate is 40 percent). The firm has $100 million in debt outstanding and 50 million shares outstanding, selling for $10 per share. The firm currently has net income of $90 million and depreciation charges of $10 million. It also has the following projects available:

Project	1	2	3
Initial Investment	$10 million	$40 million	$50 million
Annual EBIT	$1 million	$5 million	$5 million
Salvage	$2.5 million	$10 million	$10 million
Lifetime	5 years	10 years	10 years
Depreciation	$500,000	$1 million	$1 million

The firm plans to finance its future capital investment needs using 20 percent debt.

a. Which of these projects should the firm accept?

b. How much (if any) should the firm pay out as dividends?

14. LimeAde, a large soft drink manufacturing firm, is faced with the decision of how much to pay out as dividends to its stockholders. It expects to have a net income of $1,000 (after depreciation of $500), and it has the following projects:

Project	Initial Investment	Beta	IRR (to Equity Investors)
A	$500	2.0	21%
B	$600	1.5	20%
C	$500	1.0	12%

The firm's beta is 1.5 and the current risk-free rate is 6 percent. The firm plans to finance net capital expenditures (Cap Ex – Depreciation) and working capital with 20 percent debt. The firm also has current revenues of $5,000, which it expects to grow at 8 percent. Working capital will be maintained at 25 percent of revenues. How much should the firm return to its stockholders as a dividend?

15. NoLone, an all-equity manufacturing firm, has net income of $100 million currently and expects this number to grow at 10 percent a year for the next three years. The firm's working capital increased by $10 million this year and is expected to increase by the same dollar amount each of the next three years. The depreciation is $50 million and is expected to grow 8 percent a year for the next three years. Finally, the firm plans to invest $60 million in capital expenditure for each of the next three years. The firm pays 60 percent of its earnings as dividends each year. NoLone has a cash balance currently of $50 million. Assuming that the cash does not earn any interest, how much would you expect to have as a cash balance at the end of the third year?

16. Boston Turkey is a publicly traded firm, with the following income statement and balance sheet from its most recent financial year:

Income Statement

Revenues	$1,000,000
– Expenses	$400,000
– Depreciation	$100,000
EBIT	$500,000
– Interest Expense	$100,000
Taxable Income	$400,000
– Tax	$160,000
Net Income	$240,000

Balance Sheet

Assets		Liabilities	
Property, plant, and equipment	$1,500,000	Accounts payable	$500,000
Land and buildings	$500,000	Long-term debt	$1,000,000
Current assets	$1,000,000	Equity (100,000 shares)	$1,500,000
Total	$3,000,000	Total	$3,000,000

Boston Turkey expects its revenues to grow 10 percent next year and its expenses to remain at 40 percent of revenues. The depreciation and interest expenses will remain unchanged next year. The working capital, as a percentage of revenue, will also remain unchanged next year.

The managers of Boston Turkey claim to have several projects available to choose from next year, in which they plan to invest the funds from operations, and they suggest that the firm really should not be paying dividends. The projects have the following characteristics:

Project	Equity Investment	Expected Annual Cash Flow to Equity	Beta
A	$100,000	12,500	1.00
B	$100,000	14,000	1.50
C	$50,000	8,000	1.80
D	$50,000	12,000	2.00

The Treasury bill rate is 3 percent, and the Treasury bond rate is 6.25 percent. The firm plans to finance 40 percent of its future net capital expenditures (Cap Ex – Depreciation) and working capital needs with debt.

a. How much can the company afford to pay in dividends next year?

b. Now assume that the firm actually pays out $1.00 per share in dividends next year. The current cash balance of the firm is $150,000. How much will the cash balance of the firm be at the end of next year, after the payment of the dividend?

17. Z-Tec, a firm providing Internet services, reported net income of $10 million in the most recent year, while making $25 million in capital expenditures (depreciation was $5 million). The firm had no working capital needs and uses no debt.

a. Can the firm afford to pay out dividends right now? Why or why not?

b. Assuming net income grows 40 percent a year and that net capital expenditures grow 10 percent a year, when will the firm be in a position to pay dividends?

18. You are analyzing the dividend policy of Conrail, a major railroad, and you have collected the following information from the past five years.

Year	Net Income (Millions)	Capital Expenditure (Millions)	Depreciation (Millions)	Δ Noncash Working Capital (Millions)	Dividends (Millions)
1991	$240	$314	$307	$35	$70
1992	$282	$466	$295	$(110)	$80
1993	$320	$566	$284	$215	$95
1994	$375	$490	$278	$175	$110
1995	$441	$494	$293	$250	$124

The average debt ratio during this period was 40 percent, and the total noncash working capital at the end of 1990 was $10 million.
a. Estimate how much Conrail could have paid in dividends during this period.
b. If the average return on equity during the period was 13.5 percent, and Conrail had a beta of 1.25, what conclusions would you draw about their dividend policy? (The average Treasury bond rate during the period was 7 percent, and the average return on the market was 12.5 percent during the period.)

19. Assume now that you have been asked to forecast cash flows that you will have available to repurchase stock and pay dividends during the next five years for Conrail (from Problem 18). In making these forecasts, you can assume the following:
• Net income is anticipated to grow 10 percent a year from 1995 levels for the next five years.
• Capital expenditures and depreciation are expected to grow 8 percent a year from 1995 levels.
• The revenues in 1995 were $3.75 billion and are expected to grow 5 percent each year for the next five years. The working capital as a percent of revenues is expected to remain at 1995 levels.
• The proportion of net capital expenditures and depreciation that will be financed with debt will drop to 30 percent.
a. Estimate how much cash Conrail will have available to pay dividends or repurchase stocks over the next five years.
b. How will the perceived uncertainty associated with these cash flows affect your decision on dividends and equity repurchases?

20. Cracker Barrel, which operates restaurants and gift stores, is reexamining its policy of paying minimal dividends. In 1995, Cracker Barrel reported net income of $66 million; it had capital expenditures of $150 million in that year and claimed depreciation of only $50 million. The working capital in 1995 was $43 million on sales of $783 million. Looking forward, Cracker Barrel expects the following:
• Net income is expected to grow 17 percent a year for the next five years.
• During the five years, capital expenditures are expected to grow 10 percent a year, and depreciation is expected to grow 15 percent a year.
• The working capital as a percent of revenues is expected to remain at 1995 levels, and revenues are expected to grow 10 percent a year during the period.
• The company has not used debt to finance its net capital expenditures and does not plan to use any for the next five years.
a. Estimate how much cash Cracker Barrel would have available to pay out to its stockholders over the next five years.
b. How would your answer change if the firm plans to increase its leverage by borrowing 25 percent of its net capital expenditure and working capital needs?

21. Assume that Cracker Barrel, from Problem 20, wants to continue with its policy of not paying dividends. You are the CEO of Cracker Barrel and have been confronted by dissident stockholders, demanding to know why you are not paying out your FCFE (estimated in the previous problem) to your stockholders. How would you defend your decision? How receptive will stockholders be to your defense? Would it make any difference that Cracker Barrel has earned a return on equity of 25 percent

over the previous five years and that its beta is only 1.2?

22. Manpower, which provides nongovernment employment services in the United States, reported net income of $128 million in 1995. It had capital expenditures of $50 million and depreciation of $24 million in 1995, and its working capital was $500 million (on revenues of $5 billion). The firm has a debt ratio of 10 percent and plans to maintain this debt ratio.

   a. Estimate how much Manpower will have available to pay out as dividends next year if earnings and reinvestment are expected to grow by 10 percent a year.

   b. The current cash balance is $143 million. If Manpower is expected to pay $12 million in dividends next year and repurchase no stock, estimate the expected cash balance at the end of the next year.

23. How would your answers to the previous problem change if Manpower in plans to pay off its outstanding debt of $100 million next year and become a debt-free company?

24. You are an institutional investor and have the collected the following information on five maritime firms to assess their dividend policies.

Company	FCFE	Dividends Paid	ROE	Beta
Alexander & Brown	$55	$35	8%	0.80
American President	$60	$12	14.5%	1.30
OMI	–$15	$5	4.0%	1.25
Overseas Shipholding	$20	$12	1.5%	0.90
Sea Containers	–$5	$8	14%	1.05

The average risk-free rate during the period was 7 percent, and the average return on the market was 12 percent.

   a. Assess which of these firms you would pressure to pay more in dividends.

   b. Which of the firms would you encourage to pay less in dividends?

   c. How would you modify this analysis to reflect your expectations about the future of the entire sector?

25. You are analyzing the dividend policy of Black and Decker, a manufacturer of tools and appliances. The following table summarizes the dividend payout ratios, yields, and expected growth rates of other firms in the waste disposal business.

Company	Payout Ratio	Dividend Yield	Expected Growth
Fedders	11%	1.2%	11.0%
Maytag	37%	2.8%	23.0%
National Presto	67%	4.9%	13.5%
Toro	15%	1.5%	16.5%
Whirlpool	30%	2.5%	20.5%
Black & Decker	24%	1.3%	23.0%

   a. Compare Black and Decker's dividend policy to those of its peers, using the average dividend payout ratios and yields.

   b. Do the same comparison, controlling for differences in expected growth.

26. The following regression was run using all NYSE firms in 1995

$$YIELD = 0.0478 - 0.0157\ BETA$$
$$+\ 0.0000008\ MKTVAL$$
$$+\ 0.6797\ DBTRATIO$$
$$+\ 0.0002\ ROE$$
$$-\ 0.09\ NCEX/TA \quad R^2 = 12.88\%$$

where BETA = beta of the stock, MKTVAL = market value of equity + book value of debt, DBTRATIO = book value of debt/MKTVAL, ROE = return on equity in 1994, and NCEX/TA = (capital expenditures – depreciation)/total assets. The corresponding values for Black and Decker, in 1995, were as follows:

$$Beta = 1.30$$

$$MKTCAP = \$5,500\ million$$

$$DBTRATIO = 35\%$$

$$ROE = 14.5\%$$

$$NCEX/TA = 4.00\%$$

Black and Decker had a dividend yield of 1.3 percent and a dividend payout ratio of 24 percent in 1995. (Enter percent as decimal: 35 percent is 0.35.)

a. Estimate the dividend yield for Black and Decker, based on the regression.

b. Why might your answer be different using this approach than the answer to the prior question, where you used only the comparable firms?

27. Handy and Harman, a leading fabricator of precious metal alloys, pays out only 23 percent of its earnings as dividends. The average dividend payout ratio for metal fabricating firms is 45 percent. The average growth rate in earnings for the entire sector is 10 percent (Handy and Harman is expected to grow 23 percent). Should Handy and Harman pay more in dividends just to get closer to the average payout ratio? Why or why not?

CHAPTER 12

VALUATION: PRINCIPLES AND PRACTICE

In this chapter, we look at how to value a firm and its equity, given what we now know about its investment, financing, and dividend decisions. We will consider two approaches to valuation. The first and most fundamental approach to valuing a firm is *discounted cash flow valuation,* which extends the present value principles that we developed to analyze projects to value a firm. The value of any firm is determined by four factors—its capacity to generate cash flows from assets in place, the expected growth rate of these cash flows, the length of time it will take for the firm to reach stable growth, and the cost of capital. Consequently, to increase the value of a firm, we have to change one or more of these variables.

The second way of valuing a firm or its equity is to base the value on how the market is valuing similar or comparable firms; this approach is called *relative valuation*.

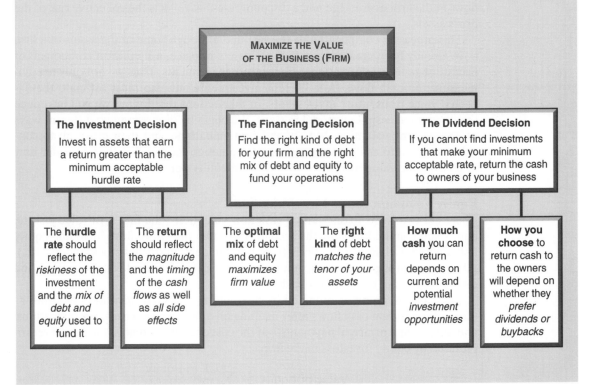

This approach can yield values that are different from a discounted cash flow valuation, and we will look at some of the reasons these differences occur.

In this chapter, we will take the perspective of investors in financial markets in estimating value. Investors assess the value of a firm's stock to decide whether to buy the stock or, if they already own it, whether to continue holding it.

DISCOUNTED CASH FLOW VALUATION

In discounted cash flow valuation, we estimate the value of any asset by discounting the expected cash flows on that asset at a rate that reflects their riskiness. In a sense, we measure the intrinsic value of an asset. The value of any asset is a function of the cash flows generated by that asset, the life of the asset, the expected growth in the cash flows, and the riskiness associated with these cash flows. In other words, it is the present value of the expected cash flows.

$$\text{Value of Asset} = \sum_{t=1}^{t=N} \frac{\text{E(Cash Flow}_t)}{(1 + r)^t}$$

where the asset has a life of N years and r is the discount rate that reflects both the riskiness of the cash flows and financing mix used to acquire the asset. If we view a firm as a portfolio of assets, this equation can be extended to value a firm, using cash flows to the firm over its life and a discount rate that reflects the collective risk of the firm's assets.

This process is complicated by the fact that although some of the assets of a firm have already been created, and thus are assets-in-place, a significant component of firm value reflects expectations about future investments. Thus we not only need to measure the cash flows from current investments but also must estimate the expected value from future investments. In the sections that follow, we will introduce the discounted cash flow model in steps. We begin by discussing two different ways of approaching valuation—equity and firm valuation—and then move on to consider how best to estimate the inputs into valuation models. We then consider how to go from the value of a firm to the value of equity per share.

Equity Valuation versus Firm Valuation

There are two paths to discounted cash flow valuation—the first is to value just the equity stake in the business; the second is to value the entire firm, including equity and any other claims in the firm (from bondholders, preferred stockholders, etc.). Although both approaches discount expected cash flows, the relevant cash flows and discount rates are different for each.

The **value of equity** is obtained by discounting expected cash flows to equity—that is, the residual cash flows after meeting all operating expenses, tax obligations, and interest and principal payments—at the cost of equity—that is, the rate of return required by equity investors in the firm.

$$\text{Value of Equity} = \sum_{t=1}^{t=n} \frac{\text{CF to Equity}_t}{(1 + k_e)^t}$$

where CF to Equity$_t$ = expected cash flow to equity in period t, and k_e = cost of equity. The dividend discount model is a special case of equity valuation, where the value of a stock is the present value of expected future dividends.

The **value of the firm** is obtained by discounting expected cash flows to the firm, that is, residual cash flows after meeting all operating expenses, taxes and reinvestment needs, but prior to debt payments—at the weighted average cost of capital (WACC)—that is, the cost of the different components of financing used by the firm, weighted by their market value proportions.

$$\text{Value of Firm} = \sum_{t=1}^{t=n} \frac{\text{CF to Firm}_t}{(1 + \text{WACC})^t}$$

where CF to Firm$_t$ = expected cash flow to firm in period t, and WACC = weighted average cost of capital. Although the two approaches use different definitions of cash flow and discount rates, they will yield consistent estimates of the value of equity as long as the same set of assumptions is applied for both. It is important to avoid mismatching cash flows and discount rates, because discounting cash flows to equity at the weighted average cost of capital will lead to an upwardly biased estimate of the value of equity, whereas discounting cash flows to the firm at the cost of equity will yield a downwardly biased estimate of the value of the firm.

Value of Equity: The value of the equity stake in a business; in the context of a publicly traded firm, the value of the common stock in the firm.

Value of Firm: The value of all investors who have claims on the firm; thus, it includes lenders and debt holders, who have fixed claims, and equity investors, who have residual claims.

12.1 Firm Valuation and Leverage

It is often argued that equity valuation requires more assumptions than firm valuation, because cash flows to equity require explicit assumptions about changes in leverage, whereas cash flows to the firm are predebt cash flows and do not require assumptions about leverage. Is this true?

☐ Yes

☐ No

Explain.

Choosing the Right Valuation Model

All discounted cash flow models ultimately boil down to estimating four inputs—current cash flows, an expected growth rate in these cash flows, a point in time when the firm will be growing at a rate it can sustain forever, and a discount rate to use in discounting these cash flows. In this section, we will examine the choices available in terms of each of these inputs.

In terms of cash flows, there are three choices—dividends or free cash flows to equity (FCFE) for equity valuation models, and free cash flows to the firm (FCFF) for firm valuation models. Discounting dividends usually provides the most conservative estimate of value for the equity in any firm, because most firms pay less in dividends than they can afford to. In the dividend policy section, we noted that the FCFE, that is, the cash flow left over after meeting all investment needs and making debt payments, is the amount that a firm can pay in dividends and stock buybacks. The value of equity, based on the FCFE, will therefore yield a more realistic estimate of value for equity, especially in the context of a takeover, since the acquirer can lay claim to the entire FCFE rather than just the dividends. Even if a firm is not the target of a takeover, it can be argued that the value of equity has to reflect the possibility of a takeover, and hence the expected FCFE. The choice between FCFE and FCFF is really a choice between equity and firm valuation. Done consistently, both approaches should yield the same values for the equity in a business. As a practical concern, however, cash flows to equity are after net debt issues or payments and become much more difficult to estimate when financial leverage is changing over time, whereas cash flows to the firm are predebt cash flows and are unaffected by changes in financial leverage. Ease of use dictates that firm valuation will be more straightforward under this scenario.

Although we can estimate cash flows from the most recent financial statements, the challenge in valuation is in estimating them in future years. In most valuations, this takes the form of an *expected growth rate in earnings* that is then used to forecast earnings and cash flows in future periods. The growth rates estimated should be consistent with our definition of cash flows. When forecasting cash flows to equity, we will generally forecast growth in net income or earnings per share that are measures of equity earnings. When forecasting cash flows to the firm, the growth rate that matters is the growth rate in operating earnings.[1]

The choice of *discount rates* will be dictated by the choice in cash flows. If the cash flow being discounted is dividends or FCFE, the appropriate discount rate is the cost of equity. If the cash flow being discounted is the cash flow to the firm, the discount rate has to be the cost of capital.

The final choice that all discounted cash flow models have to make relates to *expected growth patterns*. Because firms have infinite lives, the way we apply closure is to estimate a terminal value at a point in time and dispense with estimating cash flows beyond that point. To do this in the context of discounted cash flow valuation, we have to assume that the growth rate in cash flows beyond this point in time is constant forever, an assumption that we refer to as stable growth. If we do this, the present value of these cash flows can be estimated as the present value of a growing perpetuity. There are three questions that every valuation then has to answer:

1. How long into the future will a company be able to grow at a rate higher than the stable growth rate?

2. How high will the growth rate be during the high-growth period, and what pattern will it follow?

---

[1] We should generally become much more conservative in our growth estimates as we move up the income statements. Generally, growth in earnings per share will be lower than the growth in net income, and growth in net income will be lower than the growth in operating income.

Figure 12.1 The Ingredients in a Valuation

3. What will happen to the firm's fundamentals (risk, cash flow patterns, etc.) as the expected growth rate changes?

At the risk of being simplistic, we can broadly classify growth patterns into three categories—firms that are in stable growth already, firms that expect to maintain a constant high growth rate for a period and then drop abruptly to stable growth, and firms that will have high growth for a specified period and then grow through a transition phase to reach stable growth at some point in the future. As a practical point, it is important that as the growth rate changes, the firm's risk and cash flow characteristics change as well. In general, as expected growth declines toward stable growth, firms should see their risk approach the average and reinvestment needs decline. These choices are summarized in Figure 12.1.

We will examine each of these valuation models in more detail in the next section.

 This spreadsheet allows you to pick the right discounted cash flow valuation model for your needs, given the characteristics of the business you are valuing (**model.xls**).

IN PRACTICE: WHAT IS A STABLE GROWTH RATE?

Determining when your firm will be in stable growth is difficult to do without first defining what we mean by a *stable growth rate*. There are two insights to keep in mind when estimating a stable growth rate. First, because this growth rate in the firm's cash flows is expected to last forever, the firm's other measures of performance (including revenues, earnings, and reinvestment) can be expected to grow at the same rate. Consider the long-term consequences of a firm whose earnings grow

6 percent a year forever while its dividends grow at 8 percent. Over time, the dividends will exceed earnings. Similarly, if a firm's earnings grow at a faster rate than its dividends in the long run, the payout ratio will converge toward zero, which is also not a steady state. The second issue relates to what growth rate is reasonable as a stable growth rate. Again, the assumption that this growth rate will last forever establishes rigorous constraints on reasonableness. In the long run, a firm cannot grow at a rate significantly greater than the growth rate in the economy in which it operates. Thus, a firm that grows at 8 percent forever in an economy growing at 4 percent will eventually become larger than the economy. In practical terms, if the valuation is done in nominal (real) terms, the stable growth rate cannot be larger than the nominal (real) growth rate in the economy in which the firm operates.

Can a stable growth rate be much lower than the growth rate in the economy? There are no logical or mathematical limits on the downside. Firms that have stable growth rates much lower than the growth rate in the economy will become smaller in proportion to the economy over time. Because there is no economic basis for arguing that this cannot happen, there is no reason to prevent analysts from using a stable growth rate much lower than the nominal growth rate in the economy. In fact, the stable growth rate can be a negative number. Using a negative stable growth rate will ensure that your firm peaks in the last year of high growth and becomes smaller each year after that.

There is one rule of thumb that works well in setting a cap on the stable growth rate. The stable growth rate should generally not exceed the risk-free rate used in a valuation. Why should the two be related? The risk-free rate can be decomposed into an expected inflation rate and an expected real interest rate. If we assume that the real growth rate of an economy will be equal to the real interest rate in the long run, the risk-free rate becomes a proxy for the nominal growth rate in the economy. ∎

12.2 CYCLICAL FIRMS AND CONSTANT GROWTH RATES

Models built on the assumption of an expected constant growth rate over time cannot be used for cyclical firms, whose earnings growth is likely to be very volatile over time—high during economic booms, and very low or negative during recessions.

☐ True

☐ False

Explain.

Estimation in Discounted Cash Flow Models

Although all discounted cash flow models require the same four ingredients—cash flows, a discount rate, a period of high growth, and a growth rate during the period—there are different estimation challenges we face with each model. In this section, we will begin by estimating these inputs to the simplest of the three models, the dividend discount model, and then extend the discussion to cash flow to equity and firm valuation models.

I. Dividend Discount Models

When an investor buys stock, he or she generally expects to get two types of cash flows—dividends during the holding period and an expected price at the end of the holding period. Because this expected price is itself determined by future dividends, the value of a stock is the present value of just expected dividends. The dividend discount model is therefore the most direct and most conservative way of valuing a stock because it counts only those cash flows that are actually paid out to stockholders.

Setting Up the Model

In its most general form, the value of a stock in the dividend discount model is the present value of the expected dividends on the stock in perpetuity.

$$\text{Value per Share of Stock} = \sum_{t=1}^{t=\infty} \frac{\text{Expected Dividends in Period } t}{(1 + \text{Cost of Equity})^t}$$

Because we cannot estimate dividends in perpetuity, we generally allow for a period where dividends can grow at extraordinary rates, but we allow for closure in the model by assuming that the growth rate will decline to a stable rate that can be sustained forever at some point in the future. By assuming stable growth at some point in the future, we can stop estimating annual dividends and estimate what we think the stock will be worth at the end of the extraordinary growth period.

$$\text{Value}_0 = \sum_{t=1}^{t=n} \frac{E(\text{Dividends})_t}{(1 + r)^t} + \frac{\text{Terminal Value}_n}{(1 + r)^n}$$

where

$$\text{Terminal Value}_n = \frac{E(\text{Dividends})_{n+1}}{(r_n - g_n)}$$

where r is the cost of equity and g_n is the expected growth rate in dividends in perpetuity after year n.[2] Note that it is possible for a firm to already be in stable growth, in which case this model collapses into its simplest form:

Value of a Stock in Stable Growth Now = Expected Dividends Next Year/$(r_n - g_n)$

This model is called the Gordon growth model and is a special case of the dividend discount model. It can be used only for firms that are already in stable growth.[3]

Estimating Model Inputs

By breaking down the general version of the dividend discount model, we find four basic components. The first is the length of the high-growth period, during which the firm can sustain extraordinary growth. The second is the expected dividends each year during the high-growth period. The third is the cost of equity that stockholders will demand for holding the stock, based on their assessments of risk. The final input is the expected price at the end of the high-growth period—the **terminal value.** In this section, we will consider the challenges associated with estimating each of these components.

---

[2]The cost of equity can be different for the high-growth and stable growth periods. Hence, r_n is the cost of equity for the stable growth period.

[3]When the Gordon growth model is used to value high-growth companies, it is entirely possible that $g > r$ and the model will yield a negative value. If this occurs, the problem is not with the model but in its misapplication to a high-growth firm.

Terminal Value: The expected value of a stock (or equity) at the end of a specified holding period.

a. Length of High-Growth Period The question of how long a firm will be able to sustain high growth is perhaps the most difficult to answer in a valuation, but two points are worth keeping in mind. One is that it is not a question of whether but when; all firms will ultimately become stable-growth firms because high growth makes firms larger, and the firm's size will eventually become a barrier to further growth. The second is that high growth in valuation, at least high growth that creates value, comes from firms earning high returns on their marginal investments. Using the terminology that we have used before in investment analysis, it comes from firms having a return on equity (capital) that is well in excess of the cost of equity (capital). Thus, when we assume that a firm will experience high growth for the next five or ten years, we also implicitly assume that it will earn excess returns (over and above the cost of equity or capital) during that period. In a competitive market, these excess returns will eventually draw in new competitors, and the excess returns will disappear.

We should look at three factors when considering how long a firm will be able to maintain high growth.

1. *Size of the Firm in Relation to the Market* Smaller firms are much more likely to earn excess returns and maintain them than otherwise similar larger firms. This is so because they have more room to grow and a larger potential market. When looking at the size of the firm, we should look not only at its current market share but also the potential growth in the total market for its products or services. Thus, Microsoft may have a large market share of the computer software market, but it may be able to grow in spite of it because the entire software market is growing. On the other hand, Boeing dominates the market for commercial aircraft, but we do not expect the overall market for aircraft to increase substantially. Boeing, therefore, is far more constrained in terms of future growth.

2. *Existing Growth Rate and Excess Returns* Although the returns we would like to estimate are the marginal returns on new investments, there is a high correlation between the returns on current investments and these marginal returns. Thus, a firm earning excess returns of 20 percent on its current investments is far more likely to have large positive excess returns on its marginal investments and a long growth period than a firm currently earning excess returns of 2 percent. There are cases where this rule will not work, such as in industries going through major restructuring.

3. *Magnitude and Sustainability of Competitive Advantages* This is perhaps the most critical determinant of the length of the high-growth period. If there are significant barriers to entry and sustainable competitive advantages, firms can maintain high growth for longer periods. On the other hand, if there are no or only minor barriers to entry, or if the firm's existing competitive advantages are fading, we should be far more conservative about allowing for long growth periods. The quality of existing management also influences growth. Some top

Table 12.1	ASSESSMENT OF LENGTH OF HIGH-GROWTH PERIOD		
	Disney	**Aracruz**	**Deutsche Bank**
Firm size/ market size	Firm is one of the largest players in the entertainment and theme park business, but the businesses are being redefined and are expanding.	Firm has a small market share of the paper/pulp business, but the business is mature.	Firm has a significant market share of a mature business.
Current excess returns	Firm is earning less than its cost of capital and has done so for past few years.	Returns on capital are largely a function of paper/pulp prices, but on average have been less than the cost of capital.	Firm has a return on equity that has lagged its cost of equity in recent years.
Competitive advantages	Has some of the most recognized brand names in the world. Knows more about operating theme parks than any other firm in the world. Has skilled animation studio staff.	Cost advantages because of access to Brazilian rain forests. Has invested in newer, updated plants and has skilled workforce.	Has a name brand and edge in the commercial banking business in Germany, but this advantage is dissipating as Europe becomes one banking market.
Length of high-growth period	Ten years, entirely because of its strong competitive advantages (which have been wasted over the past few years), but the excess returns are likely to be small.	Five years, largely due to access to cheap raw material.	Five years, mostly to allow firms to recover to predownturn levels.

managers have the capacity to make the strategic choices that increase competitive advantages and create new ones.[4]

Again, the sensitivity of value to changes in the length of the **high-growth period** can always be estimated. Some analysts use growth periods greater than ten years, but the combination of high growth rates and long growth periods creates a potent mix in terms of increasing the size of the firm, in many cases well beyond the realm of what is reasonable. Looking back, there are very few firms that have been able to grow at high rates for more than ten years.

High-Growth Period: A period during which a company's earnings or cash flows are expected to grow at a rate much higher than the overall growth rate of the economy.

ILLUSTRATION 12.1   Length of High-Growth Period

To assess how long high growth will last at Disney, Aracruz, and Deutsche Bank, we assessed their standings on each of the above characteristics in Table 12.1.

---

[4]Jack Welch at GE and Robert Goizueta at Coca-Cola are good examples of CEOs who made a profound difference in the growth of their firms and the market assessment of their values.

What about Bookscape? The single biggest competitive advantage possessed by this firm is its long-term lease at favorable terms in a superb location in New York City. It is unlikely that the firm will be able to replicate this advantage elsewhere. In addition, this is a private firm, which leads us to conclude that there will be no high-growth period.

12.3 LENGTH OF HIGH-GROWTH PERIOD AND BARRIERS TO ENTRY

Assume that you are analyzing two firms, both of which are enjoying high growth. The first firm is Earthlink Network, an Internet service provider, which operates in an environment with few barriers to entry and extraordinary competition. The second firm is Biogen, a biotechnology firm that is enjoying growth from two drugs for which it owns patents for the next decade. Assuming that both firms are well managed, which of the two firms would you expect to have a longer high-growth period?

☐ Earthlink Network

☐ Biogen

☐ Both are well managed and should have the same high-growth period

b. Expected Dividends during High-Growth Period   The first step in estimating expected dividends during the high-growth period is to estimate the expected earnings for each year. This can be done in one of two ways—you can apply an expected growth rate to current earnings, or you can begin by estimating future revenues first and then estimate net profit margins in each year. The first approach is easier, but the second provides for more flexibility because margins can change over time. The resulting expected earnings are paired with estimated dividend payout ratios in each period, which may change over the high-growth period. This may seem like an awkward procedure because expected dividends could well be estimated using the current dividends and applying a dividend growth rate, but it is used for two reasons. First, most analyst projections for growth are stated in terms of revenues and earnings rather than dividends. Second, separating earnings forecasts from dividend payout provides more flexibility in terms of changing dividend payout ratios as earnings growth rates change. In particular, it allows us to raise dividend payout ratios as earnings growth rates decline.

The growth rate in earnings can be estimated using one of three approaches. The first is to look at the past and measure the **historical growth rate in earnings** over previous years. When measuring earnings growth, we have to consider how far back to go in time and whether to use arithmetic average or geometric average growth rates.[5] In general, geometric growth rates yield more meaningful values than arithmetic average growth rates. The second is to look at estimates made by others following the same stock. In fact, growth estimates made by equity research analysts following a stock are public information and are easily accessible.[6] The third is to consider the fundamentals and to estimate a growth rate based on a firm's investment policy. In

---

[5] Arithmetic average growth rates represent simple averages of growth rates over multiple years. The geometric average growth rate is a compounded growth rate.

[6] I/B/E/S, First Call, and Zacks are services that track equity research analyst forecasts continuously, and the consensus estimate across all analysts is publicly available.

particular, the growth in earnings per share of a firm can be written as the product of two variables—the percentage of the net income retained in the firm to generate future growth (retention ratio) and the return earned on equity in these new investments:

$$\text{Expected Growth Rate} = \text{Retention Ratio} \times \text{Return on Equity}$$

Thus, a firm with a return on equity of 20 percent and a retention ratio of 70 percent should have earnings growth of 14 percent a year. Reverting back to the discussion of dividend policy in Chapter 10, note that the retention ratio and the payout ratio are two sides of the same coin:

$$\text{Retention Ratio} = 1 - \text{Payout Ratio}$$

Because the retention ratio cannot exceed 100 percent, the expected growth in earnings per share in the long run for a firm cannot exceed its return on equity.

Assuming that we can obtain all three estimates of the growth rate in earnings for a firm, which one should we use in valuing a company? Past growth should be weighted least, because earnings are volatile and past growth has generally not been highly correlated with future growth.[7] Analyst estimates are useful signposts of what the investment community thinks about a company and could include information that is not in the financial statements. In particular, it could reflect changes in both the company's management and strategic plans. However, trusting analysts, no matter how well informed they may be, to come up with the most important input in a valuation is not prudent. Ultimately, the fundamental growth equation offers the most promise because it relates growth back to what the firm does and also constrains us to pay for growth (by requiring firms to reinvest) as we estimate value.

Historical Growth Rate (in Earnings): The growth rate over the past few periods in earnings; it can be calculated either by averaging the year-specific growth rates (arithmetic average) or by estimating at the compounded growth rate over the whole period.

12.4 DIFFERENCES IN GROWTH RATES

The growth rates from historical earnings, analyst projections, and fundamentals can often be very different. These differences can be best explained by which of the following statements?

☐ The past is not always a good indicator of the future.

☐ Analysts are biased toward making optimistic estimates of growth.

☐ The inputs used to estimate fundamental growth reflect what happened last year rather than what we expect will happen in the future.

☐ All of the above.

---

[7]One of the most famous studies of growth was titled *Higgledy Piggledy Growth* (I. M. D. Little, 1962, *Higgledy Piggledy Growth,* Oxford: Institute of Statistics) precisely because earnings growth was so difficult to predict based on history.

ILLUSTRATION 12.2 Growth in Earnings per Share: Deutsche Bank

In 2003, Deutsche Bank reported net income of 1,365 million Euros on a book value of equity of 29,991 million Euros at the end of 2002. The resulting return on equity for the firm is 4.55 percent:

$$\text{Return on Equity} = \text{Net Income}_{2003}/\text{Book Value of Equity}_{2002}$$
$$= 1,365/29,991 = 4.55\%$$

This is lower than the cost of equity for the firm, which is 8.76 percent, and the average return on equity for European banks, which is 11.26 percent. In the four quarters ended in March 2004, Deutsche Bank paid out dividends per share of 1.50 Euros on earnings per share of 4.33 Euros. The resulting retention ratio is 65.36 percent.

$$\text{Retention Ratio} = 1 - \text{Dividends per Share/Earnings per Share}$$
$$= 1 - 1.50/4.33 = 65.36\%$$

If Deutsche Bank maintains its existing return on equity (ROE) and retention ratio for the long run, its expected growth rate will be anemic.

$$\text{Expected Growth Rate}_{\text{Existing Fundamentals}} = \text{Retention Ratio} \times \text{ROE}$$
$$= 0.6536 \times 0.0455 = 2.97\%$$

For the next five years, we will assume that the return on equity will improve to the industry average of 11.26 percent and the retention ratio will stay unchanged at 65.36 percent. The expected growth in earnings per share is 7.36 percent.

$$\text{Expected Growth Rate}_{\text{Modified Fundamentals}} = 0.6536 \times 0.1126 = 7.36\%$$

c. Cost of Equity   The dividends and terminal price should be discounted back at a rate that reflects the risk in the investment to stockholders to arrive at the current value. In Chapter 4, we argued that the only risk that diversified investors see in a stock is market risk, and this risk can be measured with a beta (in the capital asset pricing model) or multiple betas (in the arbitrage pricing or multifactor models). The same reasoning applies here. In fact, the costs of equity that we estimated for Disney, Deutsche Bank, and Aracruz in Chapter 4 will be the costs of equity that will be used if we were valuing stock in these companies using a dividend discount model. The only point that relates specifically to valuation is that high-growth firms tend to have higher betas than low-growth firms. Building on this premise, it is important that as we change growth rates over time, we also adjust risk accordingly. Thus, when a firm goes from high growth to low growth, its beta should be moved toward one to reflect the lower growth.

d. Terminal Value   The last component of the model is the value attached to the equity at the end of a period of high growth. This value is estimated from expected dividends in the first time period following the high-growth period, the cost of equity in the stable phase, and the expected stable growth rate in dividends as follows:

$$\text{Value of Equity in Year } n = \frac{\text{Expected Dividends}_{n+1}}{r_n - g_n}$$

where r_n is the cost of equity in the stable growth period and g_n is the expected growth rate in dividends beyond year n (forever).

Figure 12.2   Two-Stage Growth Model

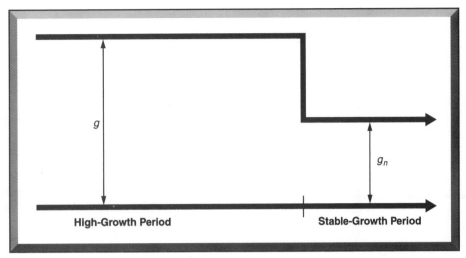

Before you estimate terminal value, you need to map out a path for the earnings growth during the high growth phase to move toward the stable growth rate. The simplest assumption to make is that your earnings growth rate is constant for the high-growth period, after which the growth rate drops to the stable level, as shown in Figure 12.2.

This is a two-stage model, and its limitation is obvious. It assumes that the growth rate is high during the initial period and is transformed overnight to a lower, stable rate at the end of the period. Although these sudden transformations in growth can happen, it is much more realistic to assume that the shift from high growth to stable growth happens gradually over time. The assumption that the growth rate drops precipitously from its level in the initial phase to a stable rate also implies that this model is more appropriate for firms with modest growth rates in the initial phase. For instance, it is more reasonable to assume that a firm growing at 8 percent in the high-growth period will see its growth rate drop to 4 percent, than it is for a firm growing at 40 percent in the high-growth period. If we assume that the growth rate and payout ratio are fixed for the high-growth period, the present value of the dividends during the high-growth period can be estimated as follows:[8]

$$\text{PV of High-Growth Dividends}_0 = \frac{\text{Dividends}_0 \times (1 + g) \times \left(1 - \dfrac{(1 + g)^n}{(1 + r)^n}\right)}{r - g}$$

---

[8]Unlike the stable growth model equation, this one can be used even if the expected growth rate exceeds the discount rate. Although this makes the denominator negative, it will also result in a negative numerator, and the net effect will be positive. The only condition when it will not work is if $g = r$, but the PV of dividends in that case will just be the product of the number of years of growth and dividends today because the growth and the discounting effects each year will cancel out.

Figure 12.3 High Growth Followed by Transition

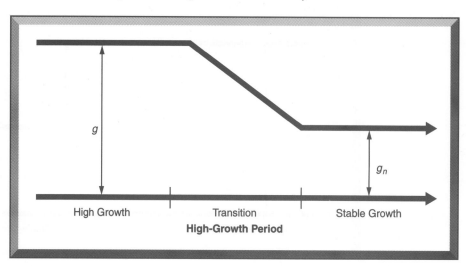

A more general formulation would allow for growth during the high-growth period, followed by a gradual reduction to stable growth over a transition period, as illustrated in Figure 12.3. This model allows growth rates and payout ratios to change gradually during the transition period.

Whatever path you devise to get your firm to stable growth, it is not just the growth rate that should change in stable growth. The other characteristics of the firm should also change to reflect the stable growth rates.

- As noted earlier, the cost of equity should be more reflective of that of a mature firm. If it is being estimated using a beta, that beta should be closer to one in stable growth even though it can take on very high or very low values in high growth.

- The dividend payout ratio, which is usually low or zero for high-growth firms, should increase as the firm becomes a stable-growth firm. In fact, drawing on the fundamental growth equation from the last section, we can estimate the payout ratio in stable growth:

$$\text{Dividend Payout Ratio} = 1 - \text{Retention Ratio}$$
$$= 1 - \text{Expected Growth Rate/ROE}$$

If we expect the stable growth rate to be 4 percent and the return on equity in stable growth to be 12 percent, the payout ratio in stable growth will be 66.67 percent $(1 - 4/12)$.

- The return on equity in stable growth, if used to estimate the payout ratio, should be also reflective of a stable-growth firm. The most conservative estimate to make in stable growth is that the return on equity will be equal to the cost of equity, thus denying the firm the possibility of excess returns in perpetuity. If this is too rigid a framework, you can assume that the return on equity will converge on an industry average in the stable-growth phase.

If there is a transition period for growth, as in Figure 12.3, the betas and payout ratios should adjust in the transition period, as the growth rate changes.

12.5 TERMINAL VALUE AND PRESENT VALUE

The bulk of the present value in most discounted cash flow valuations comes from the terminal value. Therefore it is reasonable to conclude that the assumptions about growth during the high-growth period do not affect value as much as assumptions about the terminal value.

☐ True

☐ False

Explain.

Closing Thoughts on the Dividend Discount Model

Many analysts view the dividend discount model as outmoded, but it is a useful starting point in valuing all companies and may be the only choice in valuing companies where estimating cash flows is not feasible. As noted in Chapter 11, estimating free cash flows for financial service companies is often difficult both because the line between operating and capital expenses is fuzzy and because working capital, defined broadly, could include much of what is on the balance sheet. Although we can arrive at approximations of cash flows by making assumptions about capital expenditures, we are often left in the uncomfortable position of assuming that dividends represent FCFE for these firms. Even for firms where we can estimate FCFE with reasonable precision, the dividend discount model allows us to estimate a "floor value" in most cases because firms tend to pay out less in dividends than they have available in FCFE.

It is often argued that the dividend discount model cannot be used to value high-growth companies that pay little in dividends. That is true only if we use the inflexible version of the model whereby future dividends are estimated by growing current dividends. In the more flexible version, where both payout ratios and earnings growth can change over time, the dividend discount model can be extended to cover all types of firms.

There is one final point worth making in this section. We can estimate the value of equity on a per-share basis by using dividends per share, or we can obtain the aggregate value of equity using total dividends paid. The two approaches will yield the same results if there are no management options, warrants, or convertible bonds outstanding. If there are equity options, issued by the firm, that are outstanding, it is safest to value the equity on an aggregate basis. We will consider how best to deal with equity options in arriving at a value per share later in this chapter.

12.6 PAYOUT RATIOS AND EXPECTED GROWTH

The dividend discount model cannot be used to value stock in a company with high growth that does not pay dividends.

☐ True

☐ False

Explain.

Table 12.2 **PRESENT VALUE OF EXPECTED DIVIDENDS FOR HIGH-GROWTH PERIOD**

Year	EPS	Payout Ratio	DPS	PV at 8.76%
1	€4.65	34.64%	€1.61	€1.48
2	€4.99	34.64%	€1.73	€1.46
3	€5.36	34.64%	€1.86	€1.44
4	€5.75	34.64%	€1.99	€1.42
5	€6.18	34.64%	€2.14	€1.41
	Present value of expected dividends =			€7.22

 There is a file online contains the industry averages by sector for returns on capital, retention ratios, debt equity ratios, and costs of debt.

ILLUSTRATION **12.3** **Valuing Equity Using the Dividend Discount Model: Deutsche Bank**
In Illustration 12.2, we estimated the annual growth rate for the next five years at Deutsche Bank to be 7.36 percent, based on an estimated ROE of 11.26 percent and a retention ratio of 65.36 percent. In 2003, the earnings per share at Deutsche Bank were 4.33 Euros, and the dividend per share was 1.50 Euros. Our earlier analysis of the risk at Deutsche Bank provided us with an estimate of beta of 0.98, which used in conjunction with the Euro risk-free rate of 4.05 percent and a risk premium of 4.82 percent, yielded a cost of equity of 8.76 percent (see Illustration 4.11).

Based on these inputs, we estimate the expected earnings per share and dividends per share for the next five years and the present value of these dividends in Table 12.2.

Note that we could have arrived at the same present value using the shortcut described earlier (because the payout ratio and the cost of equity remain unchanged for the high-growth period):

$$\text{PV of High-Growth Dividends}_0 = \frac{1.50 \times (1.0736) \times \left(1 - \dfrac{(1.0736)^5}{(1.0876)^5}\right)}{0.0876 - 0.0736} = 7.22$$

At the end of year five, we will assume that Deutsche Bank's earnings growth will drop to 4 percent and stay at that level in perpetuity. In keeping with the assumption of stable growth, we will also assume that

- The beta will rise marginally to 1, resulting in a slightly higher cost of equity of 8.87 percent.

$$\text{Cost of Equity} = \text{Risk-Free Rate} + \text{Beta} \times \text{Risk Premium}$$
$$= 4.05\% + 4.82\% = 8.87\%$$

- The return on equity will drop to the cost of equity of 8.87 percent, thus preventing excess returns from being earned in perpetuity.

- The payout ratio will adjust to reflect the stable period growth rate and return on equity.

Stable Period Payout Ratio = $1 - g/\text{ROE} = 1 - 0.04/0.0887 = 0.5490$ or 54.9%

The expected dividends in year six are calculated using this payout ratio:

$$\text{Expected Dividends in Year 6} = \text{Expected EPS}_6 \times \text{Stable Period Payout Ratio}$$
$$= \text{€}6.18(1.04) \times 0.549 = \text{€}3.5263$$

The value per share at the end of the fifth year can be estimated using these inputs:

$$\text{Terminal Value per Share} = \text{Expected Dividends in Year 6}/(\text{Cost of Equity} - g)$$
$$= \text{€}3.5263/(0.0887 - 0.04) = \text{€}72.41$$

The present value of the terminal value is computed using the high-growth period cost of equity:

$$\text{Present Value of Terminal Value} = \text{Terminal Value}/(1 + r)^n$$
$$= 72.41/1.0876^5 = 47.59$$

The total value per share is the sum of this value and the present value of the expected dividends in the high growth period:

$$\text{Value per Share} = \text{PV of Expected Dividends in High Growth}$$
$$+ \text{PV of Terminal Value} = \text{€}7.22 + \text{€}47.59 = \text{€}54.81$$

The market price of Deutsche Bank at the time of this valuation was 66 Euros per share. Based on our assumptions, Deutsche Bank looks overvalued.

II. FCFE Models

In Chapter 11, while developing a framework for analyzing dividend policy, we estimated the free cash flow to equity as the cash flow that the firm can afford to pay out as dividends and contrasted it with the actual dividends. We noted that many firms do not pay out their FCFE as dividends; thus, the dividend discount model may not capture their true capacity to generate cash flows for stockholders. A more appropriate model then is the *FCFE model*.

Setting Up the Model
The FCFE is the residual cash flow left over after meeting interest and principal payments and providing for reinvestment to maintain existing assets and create new assets for future growth. The FCFE is measured as follows:

$$\text{FCFE} = \text{Net Income} + \text{Depreciation} - \text{Capital Expenditures}$$
$$- \Delta\text{Working Capital} - \text{Principal Repayments} + \text{New Debt Issues}$$

where ΔWorking Capital is the change in noncash working capital.

In the special case where the capital expenditures and the working capital are financed at the target debt ratio δ and principal repayments are made from new debt issues, the FCFE is measured as follows:

$$\text{FCFE} = \text{Net Income} - (1 - \delta)(\text{Capital Expenditures} - \text{Depreciation})$$
$$- (1 - \delta)\Delta\text{Working Capital}$$

There is one more way we can present the FCFE. If we define the portion of the net income that equity investors reinvest back into the firm as the equity reinvestment rate, we can state the FCFE as a function of this rate.

Equity Reinvestment Rate

$$= \frac{(\text{Capital Expenditures} - \text{Depreciation} + \Delta\text{Working Capital})(1 - \delta)}{\text{Net Income}}$$

FCFE = Net Income (1 − Equity Reinvestment Rate)

Once we estimate the FCFE, the general version of the FCFE model resembles the dividend discount model, with FCFE replacing dividends in the equation:

Value of the Stock = PV of FCFE during High Growth + PV of Terminal Price

$$\text{Value}_0 = \sum_{t=1}^{t=n} \frac{E(\text{FCFE})_t}{(1 + r)^t} + \frac{\text{Terminal Value}_n}{(1 + r)^n}$$

where

$$\text{Terminal Value}_n = \frac{E(\text{FCFE})_{n+1}}{(r_n - g_n)}$$

where the expected FCFEs are estimated each year for the high growth period, r is the cost of equity in high growth, r_n is the cost of equity in stable growth, and g_n is the stable growth rate.

There is one key difference between the two models, though. Although the dividends can never be less than zero, the FCFE can be negative. This can occur even if earnings are positive, if the firm has substantial working capital and capital expenditure needs. In fact, the expected FCFE for many small, high-growth firms will be negative at least in the early years, when reinvestment needs are high, but will become positive as the growth rates and reinvestment needs decrease.

IN PRACTICE: Estimating Capital Expenditure and Working Capital Needs

Two components go into estimating reinvestments. The first is net capital expenditures, which is the difference between capital expenditures and depreciation. Although these numbers can easily be obtained for the current year for any firm in the United States, they should be used with the following caveats:[9]

1. Firms seldom have smooth capital expenditure streams. They can go through periods when capital expenditures are very high, followed by periods of relatively light expenditures. Consequently, when estimating the capital expenditures to use for forecasting future cash flows, we should look at capital expenditures over time and normalize them by taking an average, or we should look at industry norms.

---

[9]It is surprisingly difficult to obtain the capital expenditure numbers even for large, publicly traded firms in some markets outside the United States. Accounting standards in these markets often allow firms to lump investments together and report them in the aggregate.

2. If we define capital expenditures as expenses designed to generate benefits over many years, research and development (R&D) expenses are really capital expenditures. Consequently, R&D expenses need to be treated as capital expenditures, and the research asset that is created as a consequence needs to be amortized, with the amortization showing up as part of depreciation.[10]

3. Finally, when estimating capital expenditures, we should not distinguish between internal investments (which are usually categorized as capital expenditures in cash flow statements) and external investments (which are acquisitions). The capital expenditures of a firm therefore need to include acquisitions, whether they are funded with stock or cash. Because firms seldom make acquisitions every year, and each acquisition has a different price tag, the point about normalizing capital expenditures applies even more strongly to this item.

   The second component of reinvestment is the cash that needs to be set aside for working capital needs. As in the chapters on investment analysis, we define working capital needs as noncash working capital, and the cash flow effect is the period-to-period change in this number. Again, although we can estimate this change for any year using financial statements, it has to be used with caution. Changes in noncash working capital are volatile, with big increases in some years followed by big decreases in the following years. To ensure that the projections are not the result of an unusual base year, we tie the changes in working capital to expected changes in revenues or costs of goods sold at the firm over time. For instance, we use the noncash working capital as a percent of revenues, in conjunction with expected revenue changes each period, to estimate projected changes in noncash working capital. As a final point, noncash working capital can be negative, which can translate into positive cash flows from working capital as revenue increases. It is prudent, when this occurs, to set noncash working capital needs to zero.[11] ∎

Estimating Model Inputs
Just as in the dividend discount model, there are four basic inputs needed for this model to be usable. First, the *length of the high-growth period* is defined. Second, the *FCFE* each period during the growth period is computed; this means that net capital expenditures, working capital needs, and the debt financing mix are all estimated for the high-growth period. Third, the *rate of return* stockholders will demand for holding the stock is estimated. Finally, the *terminal value of equity at the end of the high-growth period* is calculated, based on the estimates of stable growth, the FCFE, and required return after the high-growth ends. Of the four inputs, the length of the high-growth period and the rate of return required by stockholders are the same for the dividend discount and FCFE valuation models. On the other two, the differences in the inputs are minor but still worth emphasizing.

---

[10]Capitalizing R&D is a three-step process. First, you need to specify, on average, how long it takes for research to pay off (amortizable life). Second, you have to collect data on R&D expenses from the past for an equivalent period. Third, the past R&D expenses have to be written off (straight line) over the amortizable life.

[11]Although it is entirely possible that firms can generate positive cash flows from working capital decreasing for short periods, it is dangerous to assume that this can occur forever.

a. Estimating FCFE during High-Growth Period As in the dividend discount model, we start with the earnings per share and estimate expected growth in earnings. Thus the entire discussion about earnings growth in the dividend discount model applies here as well. The only difference is in the estimation of fundamental growth. When estimating fundamental growth in the dividend discount model, we used the retention ratio and the return on equity to estimate the expected growth in earnings. When estimating fundamental growth in the FCFE valuation model, it is more consistent to use the equity reinvestment rate defined in the last section and the return on equity to estimate expected growth:

Expected Growth in Net Income = Equity Reinvestment Rate × Return on Equity

Unlike the retention ratio, which cannot be less than 0 percent, the equity reinvestment rate can be negative (if capital expenditures drop below depreciation) or greater than 100 percent. If the equity reinvestment rate is negative and is expected to remain so for the foreseeable future, the expected growth in earnings will be negative. If the equity reinvestment rate is greater than 100 percent, the net income can grow at a rate higher than the return on equity, though the firm will have to issue new stock to fund the reinvestment.[12]

Once the earnings are estimated, the net capital expenditures, working capital needs, and debt financing needs have to be specified to arrive at the FCFE. Just as the dividend payout ratio was adjusted to reflect changes in expected growth, the net capital expenditure and working capital needs should change as the growth rate changes. In particular, high growth companies will have relatively higher net capital expenditures and working capital needs. In other words, the equity reinvestment rate will generally be high in high growth and decline as the growth rate declines. A similar point can be made about leverage. High-growth, high-risk firms generally do not use much leverage to finance investment needs; as the growth tapers off, however, the firm will be much more willing to use debt, suggesting that debt ratios will increase as growth rates drop.

There is one final point worth making about equity valuations. Because the net income includes both income from operations and income from cash and marketable securities, we have two choices when it comes to equity valuations. The first and easier (albeit less precise) option is to discount the total FCFE (including the income from cash holdings) at a cost of equity that is adjusted to reflect the cash holdings.[13] The present value of equity will then incorporate the cash holdings of the company. The second and more precise way is to discount the net income, without including the interest income from cash, at a cost of equity that reflects only the operations of the firm and then to add the cash and marketable securities on to this present value at the end.

---

[12]If the equity reinvestment rate exceeds 100 percent, the net income of the firm is insufficient to cover the equity reinvestment needs of the firm. Fresh equity will have to be issued to fund the difference. This will increase the number of shares outstanding.

[13]The beta for equity will be based on a levered beta, adjusted for the cash holdings of the company. In other words, if the company is 20 percent cash and 80 percent operations, the unlevered beta will be estimated attaching a 20 percent weight to cash and a beta of zero for cash. The levered beta will then be computed using the current market debt to equity ratio.

Figure 12.4 Equity Reinvestment and Net Income at Aracruz, 1999–2003

 There is a file online that contains the industry averages by sector for net capital expenditures and working capital as a percent of revenues.

ILLUSTRATION 12.4 Estimating Growth Rate in Net Income

Like many manufacturing firms, Aracruz has volatile reinvestment outlays and the cash flows from debt swing wildly from year to year. In Figure 12.4, we report net income and equity reinvestment (capital expenditures – depreciation + change in noncash working capital – net cash flow from debt) each year from 1999 to 2003.

Rather than base the equity reinvestment rate on the most recent year's numbers, we will use the average values for each of the variables over the entire period to compute a normalized equity reinvestment rate:

Normalized Equity Reinvestment Rate
$$= \text{Average Equity Reinvestment}_{99-03}/\text{Average Net Income}_{99-03}$$
$$= 213.17/323.12 = 65.97\%$$

To estimate the return on equity, we look at only the portion of the net income that comes from operations (ignoring the income from cash and marketable securities) and divide by the book value of equity net of cash and marketable securities. This noncash ROE is a cleaner measure of the returns on equity in operating assets.

Noncash ROE
= (Net Income − After-Tax Interest Income on Cash)$_{2003}$/(BV of Equity − Cash)$_{2002}$

Aracruz had net income of $148.09 million in 2003, interest income before taxes of $43.04 million, and a tax rate of 34 percent. The book value of equity at the end of 2002 was $1,760.58 million, of which cash represented $273.93 million.

$$\text{Noncash ROE}_{\text{Aracruz}} = (148.09 - 43.04[1 - 0.34])/(1,760.58 - 273.93)$$
$$= 0.0805 \text{ or } 8.05\%$$

The expected growth in net income can be computed as the product of the noncash ROE and the equity reinvestment rate.

$$\text{Expected Growth in Net Income} = \text{Equity Reinvestment Rate} \times \text{Noncash ROE}$$
$$= 65.97\% \times 8.05\% = 5.31\%$$

Based on fundamentals, we would expect Aracruz's net income to grow 5.31 percent a year.

IN PRACTICE: PATHS TO A HIGHER ROE

The expected growth rate in earnings per share and net income are dependent on the return on equity that a firm makes on its new investments. The higher the return on equity, the higher the expected growth rate in earnings. But how do firms generate higher returns on equity? Algebraically, the return on equity can be decomposed into a return on capital and a leverage effect:

Return on Equity
= Return on Capital + (D/E)(Return on Capital − Cost of Debt[1 − Tax Rate])

where Return on Capital = EBIT(1 − Tax Rate)/(Book Value of Debt + Book Value of Equity) and D/E = Book Value of Debt/Book Value of Equity. The second term in the equation reflects the influence of debt. To the extent that a firm can earn a return on capital that exceeds the after-tax cost of debt, its return on equity will increase as it uses more debt. A firm with a return on capital of 12 percent, a debt to equity ratio of 0.5, and an after-tax cost of debt of 4 percent will have a return on equity of 16 percent. Lest firms view this as a free lunch, we hasten to point out that using more debt will also increase the firm's beta and cost of equity and the value of equity may very well decrease with higher borrowing, even though the return on equity and expected growth rate may be higher. ■

b. Estimating Terminal Value As with the dividend discount model, the terminal value in the FCFE model is determined by the stable growth rate and cost of equity. The difference between this model and the dividend discount model lies primarily in the cash flow used to calculate the terminal price: The latter uses expected dividends in the period after high growth ends, whereas the former uses the FCFE in that period:

$$\text{Terminal Value of Equity}_n = \frac{\text{FCFE}_{n+1}}{r_n - g_n}$$

In estimating that cash flow, the net capital expenditures and working capital needs should be consistent with the definition of stability. The simplest way to ensure this is to estimate an equity reinvestment rate from the stable period return on equity:

Equity Reinvestment Rate in Stable Growth
= Stable Growth Rate/Stable Period ROE

This is exactly the same equation we used to compute the retention ratio in stable growth in the dividend discount model.

Many analysts assume that stable-growth firms have capital expenditures that offset depreciation and no working capital requirements. This will yield a equity reinvestment rate of zero, which is consistent only with a stable growth rate of zero. Using a stable growth rate of 3 or 4 percent while allowing for no reinvestment essentially allows your firm to grow without paying for the growth and will yield too high a value for the firm.

Reconciling FCFE and Dividend Discount Model Valuations
The FCFE discounted cash flow model can be viewed as an alternative to the dividend discount model. Because the two approaches sometimes provide different estimates of value, however, it is worth examining why this occurs.

There are two conditions under which the value obtained from using the FCFE in discounted cash flow valuation will be the same as the value obtained from using the dividend discount model. The first is obvious: When the dividends are equal to the FCFE, the value will be the same. The second is more subtle: When the FCFE is greater than dividends, but the excess cash (FCFE − Dividends) is invested in projects with a net present value of zero, the values will also be similar. For instance, investing in financial assets that are fairly priced should yield an NPV of zero.[14]

More often, the two models will provide different estimates of value. First, when the FCFE is greater than the dividend and the excess cash either earns below-market returns or is invested in negative NPV projects, the value from the FCFE model will be greater than the value from the dividend discount model. This is not uncommon. There are numerous case studies of firms having accumulated large cash balances by paying out low dividends relative to FCFE that have chosen to use this cash to finance unwise takeovers (the price paid is greater than the value received). Second, the payment of smaller dividends than the firm can afford lowers debt-equity ratios; accordingly, the firm may become underleveraged, reducing its value.

---

[14]Mechanically, this will work out only if you keep track of the cash build-up in the dividend discount model and add it to the terminal value. If you do not do this, you will undervalue your firm with the dividend discount model.

In those cases where dividends are greater than FCFE, the firm will have to issue new shares or borrow money to pay these dividends, leading to at least one of three possible negative consequences. One is the flotation cost on these security issues, which can be substantial for equity issues. Second, if the firm borrows the money to pay the dividends, the firm may become overleveraged (relative to the optimal), leading to a loss in value. Finally, paying too much in dividends can lead to capital rationing constraints, whereby good projects are rejected, resulting in a loss of wealth.

When the two models yield different values, two questions remain: (1) What does the difference between the two models tell us? (2) Which of the two models is appropriate to use in evaluating the market price? In most cases, the value from the FCFE model will exceed the value from the dividend discount model. The difference between the value obtained from the FCFE model and that obtained from the dividend discount model can be considered one component of the value of controlling a firm—that is, it measures the value of controlling dividend policy. In a hostile takeover, the bidder can expect to control the firm and change the dividend policy (to reflect FCFE), thus capturing the higher FCFE value. In the more infrequent case—the value from the dividend discount model exceeds the value from the FCFE—the difference has less economic meaning but can be considered a warning on the sustainability of expected dividends.

As for which of the two values is more appropriate for evaluating the market price, the answer lies in the openness of the market for corporate control. If there is a significant probability that a firm can be taken over or its management changed, the market price will reflect that likelihood; in that case, the value from the FCFE model would be a more appropriate benchmark. As changes in corporate control become more difficult, either because of a firm's size and/or legal or market restrictions on takeovers, the value from the dividend discount model will provide a more appropriate benchmark for comparison.

12.7   FCFE AND DISCOUNT DIVIDEND VALUE

Most firms can be valued using FCFE and discount dividend valuation models. Which of the following statements would you most agree with on the relationship between these two values?

☐   The FCFE value will always be higher than the discount dividend value.

☐   The FCFE value will usually be higher than the discount dividend value.

☐   The discount dividend value will usually be higher than the FCFE value.

☐   The discount dividend value will generally be equal to the FCFE value.

ILLUSTRATION 12.5   FCFE Valuation: Aracruz

To value Aracruz using the FCFE model, we will use the expected growth in net income that we estimated in Illustration 12.4 and value the equity in operating assets first and then add on the value of cash and other nonoperating assets. We will also value the company in U.S. dollars, rather than Brazilian real, because the firm generates so much of its cash flows in dollars. Summarizing the basic information that we will be using:

- The net income for the firm in 2003 was $148.09 million, but $28.41 million of this income represented income from financial assets.[15] The net income from nonoperating assets is $119.68 million.

- In 2003, capital expenditures amounted to $228.82 million, depreciation was $191.51 million, and noncash working capital increased by $10.89 million. The net cash inflow from debt was $531.20 million, resulting in a large negative equity reinvestment in that year.

$$\text{Equity Reinvestment Rate}_{2003} = (228.82 - 191.51 + 10.89 - 531.20)/119.68$$
$$= -403.58 \text{ percent}$$

We will use the average equity reinvestment rate of 65.97 percent, based on the average values from 1999–2003, that we computed in Illustration 12.4 as the equity reinvestment rate for the next five years. In conjunction with the noncash return on equity of 8.05 percent that we computed in that illustration, we estimate an expected growth rate of 5.31 percent a year for the next five years.

- In Illustration 4.7, we estimated a beta for equity of 0.7576 for the paper business that Aracruz operates.[16] With a nominal U.S. dollar risk-free rate of 4 percent and an equity risk premium of 12.49 percent for Brazil (also estimated in Chapter 4), we arrive at a dollar cost of equity of 13.46 percent.

$$\text{Cost of Equity} = 4\% + 0.7576(12.49\%) = 13.46\%$$

After year five, we will assume that the beta will remain at 0.7576 and that the equity risk premium will decline to 8.66 percent.[17] The resulting cost of equity is 10.56 percent.

$$\text{Cost of Equity in Stable Growth} = 4\% + 0.7576(8.66\%) = 10.56\%$$

- After year five, we will assume that the growth in net income will drop to the inflation rate (in U.S. dollar terms) of 2 percent and that the return on equity will rise to 10.56 percent (which is also the cost of equity). The equity reinvestment rate in stable growth can then be estimated as follows:

$$\text{Equity Reinvestment Rate}_{\text{Stable Growth}}$$
$$= \text{Expected Growth Rate}/\text{Return on Equity}$$
$$= 2\%/10.56\% = 18.94\%$$

---

[15]The pretax income from financial assets was $43.04 million. We used a 34 percent tax rate to arrive at after-tax income.

[16]We used the equity beta of just the operating asssets in this valuation. If we had chosen to include the cash from financial holdings as part of net income, we would have used Aracruz's consolidated equity beta of 0.7040.

[17]We halved the country risk premium from 7.67 percent to 3.84 percent. We assume that as Brazil grows, it will become a less risky country in which to invest.

Table 12.3   EXPECTED FCFE AT ARACRUZ, YEARS 1–5

	1	2	3	4	5
Net income (noncash)	$126.04	$132.74	$139.79	$147.21	$155.03
Equity reinvestment rate	65.97%	65.97%	65.97%	65.97%	65.97%
FCFE	$42.89	$45.17	$47.57	$50.09	$52.75
Present value at 13.46%	$37.80	$35.09	$32.56	$30.23	$28.05

FCFE = Net Income (1 − Reinvestment Rate).

To value the equity in Aracruz, we begin by estimating the FCFE from operations in Table 12.3.

To estimate the terminal value of equity, we first estimate the FCFE in year six:

FCFE in Year 6

$$= \text{Net Income in Year 6 } (1 - \text{Equity Reinvestment Rate}_{\text{Stable Growth}})$$
$$= 155.03(1.02)(1 - 0.1894) = \$128.18 \text{ million}$$

The terminal value is then computed using the stable period cost of equity of 10.56 percent:

Terminal Value of Equity = $128.18/(0.1056 − 0.02) = \$1,497.98$ million

The current value of equity is the sum of the present values of the expected cash flows in Table 12.3, the present value of the terminal value of equity, and the value of cash and nonoperating assets today:

Present Value of FCFEs in High-Growth Phase = $163.73

+ Present Value of Terminal Equity Value = $1,497.98/1.1346^5 = \$796.55$

= Value of Equity in Operating Assets = $960.28

+ Value of Cash and Marketable Securities = $352.28

Value of Equity in Firm = $1,312.56

Dividing by the 859.59 million shares outstanding yields a value per share of $1.53. Converted into Brazilian real at the exchange rate of 3.15 BR/$ prevailing at the time of this valuation, we get a value per share of 4.81 BR per share, well below the market price of 7.50 BR/share.

IN PRACTICE: RECONCILING VALUE WITH THE MARKET PRICE

When you value a company and arrive at a number very different from the market price, as we have with both Aracruz and Deutsche Bank, there are three possible explanations. The first is that we are mistaken in our assumptions and that our valuations are wrong while the market is right. Without resorting to the dogma of efficient markets, this is a reasonable place to start because this is the most likely scenario. The second is that the market is wrong and we are right, in which case we have to decide whether we have enough confidence in our valuations to act on them. If we find a company to be undervalued, this would require buying and holding the stock. If the stock is overvalued, we would have to sell short. The problem, though, is that there is no guarantee that markets, even if they are wrong, will correct their mistakes in the near future. In other words, a stock that is overvalued can become even more overvalued, and a stock that is undervalued may stay that way for years, wreaking havoc on our portfolio. This also makes selling short a much riskier strategy because you generally have to cover your position in a few months.

One way to measure market expectations is to solve for a growth rate that will yield the market price. In the Aracruz valuation, for instance, we would need an expected growth rate of 19.50 percent in earnings over the next five years to justify the current market price. This is called an implied growth rate and can be compared to the estimate of growth we used in the valuation of 5.31 percent. ∎

III. FCFF Models

The dividend discount and FCFE models are models for valuing the equity in a firm directly. The alternative is to value the entire business and then to use this value to arrive at a value for the equity. That is precisely what we try and do in firm valuation models, where we focus on the operating assets of the firm and the cash flows they generate.

Setting Up the Model

The cash flow to the firm can be measured in two ways. One is to add up the cash flows to all of the different claim holders in the firm. Thus, the cash flows to equity investors (which take the form of dividends or stock buybacks) are added to the cash flows to debt holders (interest and net debt payments) to arrive at the cash flow to the firm. The other approach to estimating cash flow to the firm, which should yield equivalent results, is to estimate the cash flows to the firm prior to debt payments but after reinvestment needs have been met:

$$\text{EBIT}(1 - \text{Tax Rate}) - (\text{Capital Expenditures} - \text{Depreciation})$$
$$- \text{Change in Noncash Working Capital} = \text{Free Cash Flow to the Firm}$$

The difference between capital expenditures and depreciation (net capital expenditures) and the increase in noncash working capital represent the reinvestment made by the firm to generate future growth. Another way of presenting the same equation is to add the net capital expenditures and the change in working capital and state that value as a percentage of the after-tax operating income. This ratio of reinvestment to after-tax operating income is called the *reinvestment rate,* and the FCFF can be written as:

$$\text{Reinvestment Rate}$$
$$= \frac{(\text{Capital Expenditures} - \text{Depreciation} + \Delta \text{Working Capital})}{\text{EBIT}(1 - \text{Tax Rate})}$$

$$\text{Free Cash Flow to the Firm} = \text{EBIT}(1 - t)(1 - \text{Reinvestment Rate})$$

Note that the reinvestment rate can exceed 100 percent if the firm has substantial reinvestment needs.[18] If that occurs, the FCFF will be negative even though after-tax operating income is positive. The cash flow to the firm is often called an unlevered

---

[18]In practical terms, this firm will need external financing, either from debt or equity, to cover the excess reinvestment.

cash flow, because it is unaffected by debt payments or the tax benefits flowing from these payments.[19]

As with the dividends and the FCFE, the value of the operating assets of a firm can be written as the present value of the expected cash flows during the high-growth period and a terminal value at the end of the period:

$$\text{Value}_0 = \sum_{t=1}^{t=n} \frac{E(\text{FCFF})_t}{(1 + r)^t} + \frac{\text{Terminal Value}_n}{(1 + r)^n}$$

where

$$\text{Terminal Value}_n = \frac{E(\text{FCFF})_{n+1}}{(r_n - g_n)}$$

where r is the cost of capital in high growth, r_n is the cost of capital in stable growth, and g_n is the expected growth rate in perpetuity.

Estimating Model Inputs

As with the dividend discount and the FCFE discount models, there are four basic components that go into the value of the operating assets of the firm—a period of high growth, the FCFF during that period, the cost of capital to use as a discount rate, and the terminal value for the operating assets of the firm. We have additional steps to take to get to the value of equity per share. In particular, we have to incorporate the value of nonoperating assets, subtract out debt, and then consider the effect of options outstanding on the equity of the firm.

a. Estimating FCFF during High-Growth Period   We base our estimate of a firm's value on expected future cash flows, not current cash flows. The forecasts of earnings, net capital expenditures, and working capital will yield these expected cash flows. One of the most significant inputs into any valuation is the expected growth rate in operating income. As with the growth rates we estimated for dividends and net income, the variables that determine expected growth are simple. The expected growth in operating income is a product of a firm's reinvestment rate, that is, the proportion of the after-tax operating income that is invested in net capital expenditures and noncash working capital, and the quality of these reinvestments, measured as the after-tax return on the capital invested.

Expected Growth$_{\text{EBIT}}$ = Reinvestment Rate × Return on Capital

where the reinvestment rate is as defined in the last section and the return on capital is as follows:

Return on Capital = EBIT$(1 - t)$/(Book Value of Debt + Book Value of Equity)

Both measures should be forward-looking, and the return on capital should represent the expected return on capital on future investments.

---

[19]The tax benefits from interest payments, which are cash benefits, show up in the discount rate when we compute the after-tax cost of debt. If we add this tax benefit as a cash flow to the FCFF, we double count the tax benefit.

The reinvestment rate is often measured using a firm's past history on reinvestment. Although this is a good place to start, it is not necessarily the best estimate of the future reinvestment rate. A firm's reinvestment rate can ebb and flow, especially in firms that invest in relatively few large projects or acquisitions. For these firms, looking at an average reinvestment rate over time may be a better measure of the future. In addition, as firms grow and mature, their reinvestment needs (and rates) tend to decrease. For firms that have grown significantly over the past few years, the historical reinvestment rate is likely to be higher than the expected future reinvestment rate. For these firms, industry averages for reinvestment rates may provide a better indication of the future than using numbers from the past. Finally, it is important that we continue treating R&D expenses and operating lease expenses consistently. The R&D expenses in particular need to be categorized as part of capital expenditures for purposes of measuring the reinvestment rate.

The return on capital is often based on the firm's return on capital on existing investments, where the book value of capital is assumed to measure the capital invested in these investments. Implicitly, we assume that the current accounting return on capital is a good measure of the true returns earned on existing investments, and that this return is a good proxy for returns that will be made on future investments. This assumption, of course, is open to question if the book value of capital is not a good measure of the capital invested in existing projects or if the operating income is mismeasured or volatile. Given these concerns, we should consider not only a firm's current return on capital but also any trends in this return as well as the industry average return on capital. If the current return on capital for a firm is significantly higher than the industry average, the forecasted return on capital could be set lower than the current return to reflect the erosion that is likely to occur as competition responds.

Finally, any firm that earns a return on capital greater than its cost of capital is earning an excess return. These excess returns are the result of a firm's competitive advantages or barriers to entry into the industry. High excess returns locked in for very long periods imply that a firm has a permanent competitive advantage. It is prudent to consider decreasing these excess returns over time.

IN PRACTICE: AFTER-TAX OPERATING INCOME

The income statement for a firm provides a measure of the operating income of the firm in the form of the EBIT and a tax rate in the form of an effective tax rate. Because the operating income we would like to estimate is before capital and financing expenses, we have to make at least two adjustments to the accounting operating income:

- The first adjustment is for financing expenses that accountants treat as operating expenses. The most significant example is operating leases. Because these lease payments constitute fixed commitments into the future, are tax-deductible, and since the failure to make lease payments can result in bankruptcy, we treat these expenses as financial expenses. The adjustment, which we describe in detail in Chapter 4, results in an increase in both the operating income and the debt outstanding at the firm.

- The second adjustment is to correct for the incidence of one-time or irregular income and expenses. Any expense (or income) that is truly a one-time expense (or income) should be removed from the operating income and should not be used in forecasting future operating income. Although this would seem to indicate that all extraordinary charges should be expunged from operating income, there are some extraordinary charges that seem to occur at regular intervals—say, once every four or five years. Such expenses should be viewed as irregular rather than extraordinary expenses and should be built into forecasts. The easiest way to do this is to annualize the expense. Put simply, this would mean taking one-fifth of any expense that occurs once every five years, and computing the income based on this apportioned expense.

As for the tax rate, the effective tax rates reported by most firms are much lower than the marginal tax rates. As with the operating income, we should look at the reasons for the difference and see if these firms can maintain their lower tax rates. If they cannot, it is prudent to shift to marginal tax rates in computing future after-tax operating income. ■

ILLUSTRATION 12.6 Estimating Growth Rate in Operating Income: Disney

We begin by estimating the reinvestment rate and return on capital for Disney in 2003 using the numbers from the latest financial statements. We converted operating leases into debt and adjusted the operating income and capital expenditure accordingly.[20]

$$\text{Reinvestment Rate}_{2003}$$
$$= (\text{Cap Ex} - \text{Depreciation} + \text{Chg in Noncash WC})/\text{EBIT}(1 - t)$$
$$= (1{,}735 - 1{,}253 + 454)/(2{,}805[1 - 0.373]) = 53.18\%$$

$$\text{Return on Capital}_{2003} = \text{EBIT}(1 - t)_{2003}/(\text{BV of Debt}_{2002} + \text{BV of Equity}_{2002})$$
$$= 2{,}805(1 - 0.373)/(15{,}883 + 23{,}879) = 4.42\%$$

If Disney maintains its 2003 reinvestment rate and return on capital for the next few years, its growth rate will be only 2.35 percent.

Expected Growth Rate from Existing Fundamentals = $53.18\% \times 4.42\% = 2.35\%$

To make estimates for the future, we look at Disney's returns on capital from 1995 to 2003 in Figure 12.5.

Note the dramatic drop in the return on capital after the Capital Cities acquisition from more than 19 percent in 1997 to less than 10 percent in 1998.[21] Although this may sound optimistic, we will assume that Disney will be able to earn a return

---

[20]The book value of debt is augmented by the $1,753 million in present value of operating lease commitments. The unadjusted operating income for Disney was $2,713 million. The operating lease adjustment adds the imputed interest expense on the PV of operating leases to the operating income (5.25% of $1,753 million = $92 million) to the unadjusted operating income.

[21]Part of this drop can be explained by accounting factors; the acquisition of Capital Cities increased the book value of equity and debt substantially.

Figure 12.5   Return on Capital, Disney

on capital of 12 percent on its new investments and that the reinvestment rate will remain 53.18 percent for the immediate future.[22] The expected growth in operating income over this period will be 6.38 percent.

$$\text{Expected Growth Rate in Operating Income}$$
$$= \text{Return on Capital} \times \text{Reinvestment Rate}$$
$$= 12\% \times 0.5318 = 6.38\%$$

There is a data set online that summarizes reinvestment rates and return on capital by industry group in the United States for the most recent quarter.

b. Estimating Cost of Capital   Unlike equity valuation models, where the cost of equity is used to discount cash flows to equity, the cost of capital is used to discount cash flows to the firm. The cost of capital is a composite cost of financing that includes the costs of both debt and equity and their relative weights in the

---

[22]We are, however, leaving the return on capital on existing investments at 4.42 percent because improving those returns will be much more difficult.

financing structure:

$$\text{Cost of Capital} = k_{\text{equity}}(\text{Equity}/[\text{Debt} + \text{Equity}]) + k_{\text{debt}}(\text{Debt}/[\text{Debt} + \text{Equity}])$$

where the cost of equity represents the rate of return required by equity investors in the firm and the cost of debt measures the current cost of borrowing, adjusted for the tax benefits of borrowing. The weights on debt and equity have to be market value weights. We discussed the cost of capital estimation extensively earlier in this book, in the context of both investment analysis and capital structure. We will now consider each of the inputs in the model in the context of valuing a firm.

The cost of equity, as we have defined it through this book, is a function of the nondiversifiable risk in an investment, which in turn is measured by a beta (in the single factor model) or betas (in the multiple factor models). We argued that the beta(s) are better measured by looking at the average beta(s) of other firms in the business, that is, bottom-up estimates, and reflecting a firm's current business mix and leverage. This argument is augmented when we value companies by the fact that a firm's expected business mix and financial leverage can change over time, and its beta will change with both. As the beta changes, the cost of equity will also change from year to year.

Just as the cost of equity can change over time as a firm's exposure to market risk changes, so can the cost of debt as its exposure to default risk changes. The default risk of a firm can be expected to change for two reasons. One is that the firm's size will change as we project earnings further into the future; the volatility in these earnings is also likely to change over time. The second reason is that changes occur in a firm's debt ratio. If we expect a firm's financial leverage to change over time, it will affect its capacity to service debt and hence its cost of borrowing. The after-tax cost of debt can also change as a consequence of expected changes in the tax rate over time.

As a firm changes its leverage, the weights attached to equity and debt in the cost of capital computation will change. Should a firm's debt ratio be changed over the forecast period? The answer to this depends on two factors. The first is whether the firm is initially under- or overlevered. If it is at its appropriate leverage, there is a far smaller need to change debt ratios in the future. The second is the views of the firm's management and the degree to which they are responsive to the firm's stockholders. Thus, if the management of a firm is firmly entrenched and steadfast in its opposition to debt, an underlevered firm will stay that way over time. In an environment where stockholders have more power, there will eventually be pressure on this firm to increase its leverage toward its optimal level.

Illustration 12.7   Cost of Capital: Disney

Recapping the inputs we used to estimate the cost of capital in Disney, we will make the following assumptions:

- The beta for the first five years will be the bottom-up beta of 1.2456 that we estimated in Illustration 4.5. In conjunction with a risk-free rate of 4 percent and market risk premium of 4.82 percent, this yields a cost of equity of 10 percent.

$$\text{Cost of Equity} = \text{Risk-Free Rate} + \text{Beta} \times \text{Risk Premium}$$
$$= 4\% + 1.2456(4.82\%) = 10\%$$

- The cost of debt for Disney for the first five years, based on its rating of BBB+, is 5.25 percent. Using Disney's tax rate of 37.30 percent gives an after-tax cost of debt of 3.29 percent:

$$\text{After-Tax Cost of Debt} = 5.25\%(1 - 0.373) = 3.29\%$$

- The current market debt ratio of 21 percent debt, estimated in Illustration 4.15, will be used as the debt ratio for the first five years of the valuation. Keep in mind that this debt ratio is computed using the market value of debt (inclusive of operating leases) of $14,668 million and a market value of equity of $55,101 million.

The cost of capital for Disney, at least for the first five years of the valuation, is 8.59 percent.

Cost of Capital
$$= \text{Cost of Equity}(E/[D + E]) + \text{After-Tax Cost of Debt}(D/[D + E])$$
$$= 10\%(0.79) + 3.29\%(0.21) = 8.59\%$$

12.8 Firm Valuation and Leverage

A standard critique of the use of cost of capital in firm valuation is that it assumes that leverage stays stable over time (through the weights in the cost of capital). Is this true?

☐ Yes
☐ No

There is a data set online that summarizes the costs of capital for firms in the United States by industry group.

c. Estimating Terminal Value   The approach most consistent with a discounted cash flow model assumes that cash flows beyond the terminal year will grow at a constant rate forever, in which case the terminal value can be estimated as follows:

$$\text{Terminal Value}_n = \text{Free Cash Flow to Firm}_{n+1}/(\text{Cost of Capital}_n - g_n)$$

where the cost of capital and the growth rate in the model are sustainable forever. We can use the relationship between growth and reinvestment rates that we noted earlier to estimate the reinvestment rate in stable growth:

$$\text{Reinvestment Rate in Stable Growth} = \text{Stable Growth Rate}/\text{ROC}_n$$

where the ROC_n is the return on capital that the firm can sustain in stable growth. This reinvestment rate can then be used to generate the FCFF in the first year of stable growth:

$$\text{Terminal Value} = \frac{\text{EBIT}_{n+1}(1 - t)\left(1 - \dfrac{g_n}{\text{ROC}_n}\right)}{(\text{Cost of Capital}_n - g_n)}$$

In the special case where ROC is equal to the cost of capital, this estimate simplifies to become the following:

$$\text{Terminal Value}_{\text{ROC=WACC}} = \frac{\text{EBIT}_{n+1}(1 - t)}{\text{Cost of Capital}_n}$$

Thus, in every discounted cash flow valuation, there are two critical assumptions we need to make on stable growth. The first relates to when the firm we are valuing will become a stable-growth firm, if it is not one already. The second relates to what the characteristics of the firm will be in stable growth, in terms of return on capital and cost of capital. We examined the first question earlier in this chapter when we looked at the dividend discount model. Let us consider the second question now.

As firms move from high growth to stable growth, we need to give them the characteristics of stable-growth firms. A firm in stable growth will be different from that same firm in high growth in a number of dimensions. For instance,

- As we noted with equity valuation models, high-growth firms tend to be *more exposed to market risk* (and have higher betas) than stable-growth firms. Thus, although it might be reasonable to assume a beta of 1.8 in high growth, it is important that the beta be lowered, if not to one at least toward one in stable growth.[23]

- High-growth firms tend to have *high returns on capital and earn excess returns*. In stable growth, it becomes more difficult to sustain excess returns. There are some who believe that the only assumption sustainable in stable growth is a zero excess return assumption; the return on capital is set equal to the cost of capital. Although we agree in principle, with this view it is difficult in practice to assume that all investments, including those in existing assets, will suddenly lose the capacity to earn excess returns. Because it is possible for entire industries to earn excess returns over long periods, we believe that assuming a firm's return on capital will move toward its industry average sometimes yields more reasonable estimates of value.

- Finally, high-growth firms tend to *use less debt* than stable-growth firms. As firms mature, their debt capacity increases. The question of whether the debt ratio for a firm should be moved toward its optimal cannot be answered without looking at the incumbent managers' power relative to their stockholders and their views about debt. If managers are willing to change their debt ratios and stockholders retain some power, it is reasonable to assume that the debt ratio will move to the optimal level in stable growth; if not, it is safer to leave the debt ratio at existing levels.

12.9   NET CAPITAL EXPENDITURES, FCFE, AND STABLE GROWTH

Assume that you are valuing a high-growth firm with high risk (beta) and large reinvestment needs (high reinvestment rate). You assume the firm will be in stable growth after five years, but you leave the risk and reinvestment rate at high-growth levels. Will you undervalue or overvalue this firm?

☐   Undervalue the firm

☐   Overvalue the firm

---

[23]As a rule of thumb, betas above 1.2 or below 0.8 are inconsistent with stable-growth firms. Two-thirds of all firms have betas that fall within this range.

ILLUSTRATION **12.8**   Stable Growth Inputs and Transition Period: Disney

We will assume that Disney will be in stable growth after year ten. In its stable growth phase, we will assume the following:

- The beta for the stock will drop to one, reflecting Disney's status as a mature company. This will lower the cost of equity for the firm to 8.82 percent.

$$\text{Cost of Equity} = \text{Risk-Free Rate} + \text{Beta} \times \text{Risk Premium}$$
$$= 4\% + 1 \times 4.82\% = 8.82\%$$

- The debt ratio for Disney will rise to 30 percent. This is the optimal we computed for Disney in Chapter 8, and we are assuming that investor pressure will be the impetus for this change. Because we assume that the cost of debt remains unchanged at 5.25 percent, this will result in a cost of capital of 7.16 percent

$$\text{Cost of Capital} = 8.82\%(0.70) + 5.25\%(1 - 0.373)(0.30) = 7.16\%$$

- The return on capital for Disney will drop from its high-growth period level of 12 percent to a stable growth return of 10 percent. This is still higher than the cost of capital of 7.16 percent, but Disney's competitive advantages are unlikely to dissipate completely by the end of the tenth year.
- The expected growth rate in stable growth will be 4 percent. In conjunction with the return on capital of 10 percent, this yields a stable period reinvestment rate of 40 percent:

$$\text{Reinvestment Rate} = \text{Growth Rate/Return on Capital} = 4\%/10\% = 40\%$$

The values of all of these inputs adjust gradually during the transition period, from years six to ten, from high-growth levels to stable-growth values.

d. From Operating Asset Value to Firm Value   The operating income is the income from operating assets, and the cost of capital measures the cost of financing these assets. When the operating cash flows are discounted to the present, we value the operating assets of the firm. Firms, however, often have significant amounts of cash and marketable securities on their books. The value of these assets should be added to the value of the operating assets to arrive at firm value.

Cash and marketable securities can easily be incorporated into firm value, whereas other nonoperating assets are more difficult to value. Consider, for instance, minority holdings in other firms and subsidiaries, where income statements are not consolidated.[24] If we consider only the reported income from these holdings, we will miss a significant portion of the value of the holdings.[25] The most accurate way to incorporate these holdings into firm value is to value each subsidiary or firm in which there are holdings and assign a proportional share of this value to the firm. If a firm owns more than 50 percent of a subsidiary, accounting standards in the

---

[24]When income statements are consolidated, the entire operating income of the subsidiary is shown in the income statement of the parent firm. Firms do not have to consolidate financial statements if they hold minority stakes in firms and take a passive role in their management.

[25]When firms hold minority, passive interests in other firms, they report only the portion of the dividends they receive from these investments. With minority, active holdings, they report the portion of the net income that is attributable to them, but not as part of operating income.

United States require that the firm fully consolidate the income and assets of the subsidiary into its own. The portion of the equity that does not belong to the firm is shown as minority interest on the balance sheet and should be subtracted out to get to the value of the equity in the firm.[26]

There is one final asset to consider. Firms with defined pension liabilities sometimes accumulate pension fund assets in excess of these liabilities. Although the excess does belong to the owners of the firm, they face a tax liability if they claim it. The conservative rule would be to assume that the social and tax costs of reclaiming the excess pension funds are so large that few firms would ever even attempt to do so.

ILLUSTRATION **12.9** **Value of Nonoperating Assets at Disney**

At the end of 2003, Disney reported holding $1,583 million in cash and marketable securities. In addition, Disney reported a book value of $1.849 million for minority investments in other companies, primarily in foreign Disney theme parks.[27] In the absence of detailed financial statements for these investments, we will assume that the book value is roughly equal to the market value. Note that we consider the rest of the assets on Disney's balance sheet including the $6.2 billion it shows in capitalized TV and film costs and $19.7 billion it shows in goodwill and intangibles to be operating assets that we have already captured in the cash flows.[28]

Finally, Disney consolidates its holdings in a few subsidiaries in which it owns less than 100 percent. The portion of the equity in these subsidiaries that does not belong to Disney is shown on the balance sheet as a liability (minority interests) of $428 million. As with its holdings in other companies, we assume that this is also the estimated market value and subtract it from firm value to arrive at the value of equity in Disney.

There is a data set online that summarizes the value of cash and marketable securities by industry group in the United States for the most recent quarter.

e. From Firm Value to Equity Value   The general rule that you should use is the debt you subtract from the value of the firm should be at least equal to the debt that you use to compute the cost of capital. Thus, if you decide to convert operating leases to debt to compute the cost of capital, you should subtract out the debt value of operating leases from the value of operating assets to estimate the value of equity. If the firm you are valuing has preferred stock, you would use the market value of the stock (if it is traded) or estimate a market value (if it is not) and deduct it from firm value to get to the value of common equity.[29]

---

[26]Optimally, we would like to subtract out the market value of the minority interests rather than the book value, which is reported in the balance sheet.

[27]Disney owns 39 percent of Euro Disney and 43 percent of the proposed Thailand Disney park. It also owns 37.5 percent of the A&E network and 39.6 percent of E! Television.

[28]Adding these on to the present value of the cash flows would represent double counting.

[29]Estimating market value for preferred stock is relatively simple. Preferred stock generally is perpetual and the estimated market value of the preferred stock is therefore (Preferred Dividend)/(Cost of Preferred Stock). The cost of preferred stock should be higher than the pretax cost of debt because debt has a prior claim on the cash flows and assets of the firm.

There may be other claims on the firm that do not show up as debt for purposes of computing cost of capital but should be subtracted out from firm value to get to the value of equity.

- *Expected Liabilities on Lawsuits*   You could be analyzing a firm that is the defendant in a lawsuit, where it potentially could have to pay tens of millions of dollars in damages. You should estimate the probability that this will occur and use this probability to estimate the expected liability. Thus, if there is a 10 percent chance that the firm could lose in a lawsuit and the expected damage award is $1 billion, you would reduce the value of the equity in the firm by $100 million (Probability × Expected Damages). If the expected liability is not expected to occur until several years from now, you would compute the present value of the payment.

- *Unfunded Pension and Health Care Obligations*   If a firm has significantly underfunded a pension or a health plan, it will need to set aside cash in future years to meet these obligations. Although it would not be considered debt for cost of capital purposes, it should be subtracted from firm value to arrive at equity value.

- *Deferred Tax Liability*   The deferred tax liability that shows up on the financial statements of many firms reflects the fact that firms often use strategies that reduce their taxes in the current year while increasing their taxes in future years. Of the three items listed here, this one is the least clearly defined, because it is not clear when or even whether the obligation will come due. Ignoring it, though, may be foolhardy, because the firm could find itself making these tax payments in the future. The most sensible way of dealing with this item is to consider it an obligation, but one that will come due only when the firm's growth rate moderates. Thus, if you expect your firm to be in stable growth in ten years, you would discount the deferred tax liability back ten years and deduct this amount from the firm value to get to equity value.

f. From Equity Value to Equity Value per Share   Once the value of the firm, inclusive of nonoperating assets, has been estimated, we generally subtract the value of the outstanding debt to arrive at the value of equity and then divide the value of equity by the number of shares outstanding to estimate the value per share. This approach works only when common stock is the only equity outstanding. When there are warrants and employee options outstanding, the estimated value of these options has to be subtracted from the value of the equity before we divide by the number of shares outstanding. The same procedure applies when the firm has convertible bonds outstanding, because these conversion options represent claims on equity as well.

For those unwilling to use option pricing models, there are two shortcuts available. One is to divide the value of equity by the fully diluted number of shares outstanding rather than by the actual number.[30] This approach will underestimate the

---

[30]We assume that all options will be exercised and compute the number of shares that will be outstanding in that event.

value of the equity because it fails to consider the cash proceeds from option exercise. The other shortcut, which is called the *treasury stock approach,* adds the expected proceeds from the exercise of the options (exercise price multiplied by the number of options outstanding) to the numerator before dividing by the number of shares outstanding. Although this approach will yield a more reasonable estimate than the first one, it does not include the time premium of the options outstanding. Thus, it tends to overstate the value of the common stock.

This spreadsheet allows you to value the options outstanding in a firm, allowing for the dilution effect (**warrants.xls**).

ILLUSTRATION 12.10 Value of Equity Options

Disney has granted considerable numbers of options to its managers. At the end of 2003, there were 219 million options outstanding, with a weighted average exercise price of $26.44 and weighted average life of six years. Using the current stock price of $26.91, an estimated standard deviation of 40 percent,[31] a dividend yield of 1.21 percent, a riskfree rate of 4 percent and an option pricing model, we estimate the value of these equity options to $2.129 billion.[32] The value we have estimated for the options above is probably too high because we assume that all the options are exercisable. In fact, a significant proportion of these options (about 50 percent) are not vested yet,[33] and this fact will reduce their estimated value. We will also assume that these options, when exercised, will generate a tax benefit to the firm equal to 37.3 percent of their value:

$$\text{After-Tax Value of Equity Options} = 2{,}129(1 - 0.373) = \$1{,}334.67 \text{ million}$$

Reconciling Equity and Firm Valuations
This model, unlike the dividend discount model or the FCFE model, values the firm rather than equity. The value of equity, however, can be extracted from the value of the firm by subtracting out the market value of outstanding debt. Because this model can be viewed as an alternative way of valuing equity, two questions arise: Why value the firm rather than equity? Will the values for equity obtained from the firm valuation approach be consistent with the values obtained from the equity valuation approaches described in the previous section?

The advantage of using the firm valuation approach is that cash flows relating to debt do not have to be considered explicitly, because the FCFF is a predebt cash flow, whereas they do have to be taken into account in estimating FCFE. In cases where the leverage is expected to change significantly over time, this is a significant saving because estimating new debt issues and debt repayments when leverage is changing can become increasingly messy the further into the future you go. The firm

---

[31]We used the historical standard deviation in Disney's stock price to estimate this number.

[32]The option pricing model used is the Black-Scholes model, adjusted for potential dilution. It is explained in Appendix 4.

[33]When options are not vested, they cannot be exercised. When providing options to their employees, firms often require that they continue as employees for a set period (vesting period) before they can exercise these options.

valuation approach does, however, require information about debt ratios and interest rates to estimate the WACC. It is still easier to do firm valuation than equity valuation when debt ratios are expected to change over time.

The value for equity obtained from the firm valuation and equity valuation approaches will be the same if you make consistent assumptions about financial leverage. Getting them to converge in practice is much more difficult. Let us begin with the simplest case—a no-growth, perpetual firm. Assume that the firm has $166.67 million in EBIT and a tax rate of 40 percent. Assume that the firm has equity with a market value of $600 million, with a cost of equity of 13.87 percent, and debt of $400 million, with a pretax cost of debt of 7 percent. The firm's cost of capital can be estimated:

$$\text{Cost of Capital} = (13.87\%)\left(\frac{600}{1{,}000}\right) + (7\%)(1 - 0.4)\left(\frac{400}{1{,}000}\right) = 10\%$$

$$\text{Value of the Firm} = \frac{\text{EBIT}(1 - t)}{\text{Cost of Capital}} = \frac{166.67(1 - 0.4)}{0.10} = \$1{,}000$$

Note that the firm has no reinvestment and no growth. We can value equity in this firm by subtracting out the value of debt.

$$\begin{aligned}\text{Value of Equity} &= \text{Value of Firm} - \text{Value of Debt}\\ &= \$1{,}000 - \$400 = \$600 \text{ million}\end{aligned}$$

Now let us value the equity directly by estimating the net income:

$$\begin{aligned}\text{Net Income} &= (\text{EBIT} - \text{Pretax Cost of Debt} \times \text{Debt})(1 - t)\\ &= (166.67 - 0.07 \times 400)(1 - 0.4) = \$83.202 \text{ million}\end{aligned}$$

The value of equity can be obtained by discounting this net income at the cost of equity:

$$\text{Value of Equity} = \frac{\text{Net Income}}{\text{Cost of Equity}} = \frac{83.202}{0.1387} = \$600 \text{ million}$$

Even this simple example works because of the following assumptions that we made implicitly or explicitly during the valuation.

1. The values for debt and equity used to compute the cost of capital were equal to the values that we obtained in the valuation. Notwithstanding the circularity in reasoning—you need the cost of capital to obtain the values in the first place—it indicates that a cost of capital based on market value weights will not yield the same value for equity as an equity valuation model if the firm is not fairly priced in the first place.

2. There are no extraordinary or nonoperating items that affect net income but not operating income. Thus, to get from operating to net income, all we do is subtract out interest expenses and taxes.

3. The interest expenses are equal to the pretax cost of debt multiplied by the market value of debt. If a firm has old debt on its books, with interest expenses that are different from this value, the two approaches will diverge.

If there is expected growth, the potential for inconsistency multiplies. You have to ensure that you borrow enough money to fund new investments to keep your debt ratio at a level consistent with what you are assuming when you compute the cost of capital.

 This spreadsheet allows you to compare the equity values obtained using FCFF and FCFE models (**fcffvsfcfe.xls**).

ILLUSTRATION 12.11 FCFF Valuation: Disney

To value Disney, we will consider all of the numbers that we have estimated already in this section. Recapping those estimates:

- The operating income in 2003, before taxes and adjusted for operating leases, is $2,805 million. Although this represents a significant comeback from the doldrums of 2002, it is still lower than the operating income in the 1990s and results in an after-tax return on capital of only 4.42 percent (assuming a tax rate of 37.30 percent).

- For years one through five, we will assume that Disney will be able to raise its return on capital on new investments to 12 percent and that the reinvestment rate will be 53.18 percent (see Illustration 12.6). This will result in an expected growth rate of 6.38 percent a year.

- For years one through five, we will assume that Disney will maintain its existing debt ratio of 21 percent and its current cost of capital of 8.59 percent (see Illustration 12.7).

- The assumptions for stable growth (after year ten) and for the transition period were listed in Illustration 12.8.

In Table 12.4, we estimate the after-tax operating income, reinvestment, and free cash flow to the firm each year for the next ten years.

Table 12.4 ESTIMATED FCFF, DISNEY

Year	Expected Growth	EBIT	EBIT (1 − t)	Reinvestment Rate	Reinvestment	FCFF
Current		$2,805				
1	6.38%	$2,984	$1,871	53.18%	$994.92	$876.06
2	6.38%	$3,174	$1,990	53.18%	$1,058.41	$931.96
3	6.38%	$3,377	$2,117	53.18%	$1,125.94	$991.43
4	6.38%	$3,592	$2,252	53.18%	$1,197.79	$1,054.70
5	6.38%	$3,822	$2,396	53.18%	$1,274.23	$1,122.00
6	5.90%	$4,047	$2,538	50.54%	$1,282.59	$1,255.13
7	5.43%	$4,267	$2,675	47.91%	$1,281.71	$1,393.77
8	4.95%	$4,478	$2,808	45.27%	$1,271.19	$1,536.80
9	4.48%	$4,679	$2,934	42.64%	$1,250.78	$1,682.90
10	4.00%	$4,866	$3,051	40.00%	$1,220.41	$1,830.62

Table 12.5 PRESENT VALUE OF FREE CASH FLOWS TO FIRM, DISNEY

Year	Cost of Capital	FCFF	PV of FCFF
1	8.59%	$876.06	$806.74
2	8.59%	$931.96	$790.31
3	8.59%	$991.43	$774.21
4	8.59%	$1,054.70	$758.45
5	8.59%	$1,122.00	$743.00
6	8.31%	$1,255.13	$767.42
7	8.02%	$1,393.77	$788.91
8	7.73%	$1,536.80	$807.42
9	7.45%	$1,682.90	$822.90
10	7.16%	$1,830.62	$835.31
		PV of cash flows during high growth =	$7,894.66

In Table 12.5, we estimate the present value of the FCFF using the cost of capital. Because the beta and debt ratio change each year from year six to ten, the cost of capital also changes each year.

To compute the present value of the cash flows in years six through ten, we have to use the compounded cost of capital over the previous years. To illustrate, the present value of $1,536.80 million in cash flows in year eight is:

$$\text{Present Value of Cash Flow in Year 8} = \frac{1,536.80}{(1.0859)^5(1.0831)(1.0802)(1.0773)}$$
$$= \$807.42$$

The final piece of the valuation is the terminal value. To estimate the terminal value, at the end of year ten, we estimate the free cash flow to the firm in year eleven:

$$\text{FCFF}_{11} = \text{EBIT}_{10}(1 - t)(1 + g_n)(1 - \text{Reinvestment Rate}_{\text{Stable Growth}})$$
$$= 4,866(1 - 0.373)(1.04)(1 - 0.40) = \$1,903.84 \text{ million}$$

$$\text{Terminal Value} = \text{FCFF}_{11}/(\text{Cost of Capital}_{\text{Stable Growth}} - g)$$
$$= 1,903.84/(0.0716 - 0.04) = \$60,219.11 \text{ million}$$

The value of the firm is the sum of the present values of the cash flows during the high-growth period, the present value of the terminal value, and the value of the nonoperating assets that we estimated in Illustration 12.9.

PV of cash flows during the high growth phase   = $7,894.66

PV of Terminal Value

$$= \frac{60,219.11}{(1.0859)^5(1.0831)(1.0802)(1.0773)(1.0745)(1.0716)} = \$27,477.81$$

+ Cash and Marketable Securities   = $1,583.00

+ Nonoperating Assets (Holdings in Other Companies) = $1,849.00

Value of the Firm   = $38,804.48

Subtracting out the market value of debt (including operating leases) of $14,668.22 million and the value of the equity options (estimated to be worth $1,334.67 million in Illustration 12.10) yields the value of the common stock:

$$\begin{aligned}
&\text{Value of Equity in Common Stock} \\
&\quad = \text{Value of Firm} - \text{Debt} - \text{Equity Options} \\
&\quad = \$38,804.48 - \$14,668.22 - \$1,334.67 = \$22,801.59
\end{aligned}$$

Dividing by the number of shares outstanding (2,047.60 million), we arrive at a value per share of $11.14, well below the market price of $26.91 at the time of this valuation.

12.10 NET CAPITAL EXPENDITURES AND VALUE

In the valuation above, we assumed that the reinvestment rate would be 40 percent in perpetuity to sustain the 4 percent stable growth rate. What would the terminal value have been if instead we had assumed that the reinvestment rate was zero while continuing to use a stable growth rate of 4 percent?

☐ Higher than $60.219 billion (estimated in Illustration 21.11)

☐ Lower than $60.219 billion

IN PRACTICE: ADJUSTED PRESENT VALUE

In Chapter 8, we presented the adjusted present value (APV) approach to estimate the optimal debt ratio for a firm. In that approach, we begin with the value of the firm without debt. As we add debt to the firm, we consider the net effect on value by considering both the benefits and the costs of borrowing. To do this, we assume that the primary advantage of borrowing is a tax benefit and the most significant cost is the added risk of bankruptcy.

The first step in this approach is the estimation of the value of the unlevered firm. This can be accomplished by valuing the firm as if it had no debt, that is, by discounting the expected FCFF at the unlevered cost of equity. In the special case where cash flows grow at a constant rate in perpetuity, the value of the firm is easily computed.

$$\text{Value of Unlevered Firm} = \frac{\text{FCFF}_0(1 + g)}{\rho_u - g}$$

where FCFF_0 is the current after-tax operating cash flow to the firm, ρ_u is the unlevered cost of equity, and g is the expected growth rate. In the more general case, you can value the firm using any set of growth assumptions you believe are reasonable for the firm.

The second step is the calculation of the expected tax benefit from a given level of debt. This tax benefit is a function of the tax rate of the firm and is discounted at the cost of debt to reflect the riskiness of this cash flow. If the tax savings are viewed as a perpetuity,

$$\text{Value of Tax Benefits} = \frac{(\text{Tax Rate})(\text{Cost of Debt})(\text{Debt})}{\text{Cost of Debt}}$$

$$= (\text{Tax Rate})(\text{Debt})$$

$$= t_c D$$

The tax rate used here is the firm's marginal tax rate, and it is assumed to stay constant over time. If we anticipate the tax rate changing over time, we can still compute the present value of tax benefits over time, but we cannot use the perpetual growth equation.

The third step is to evaluate the effect of the given level of debt on the default risk of the firm and on expected bankruptcy costs. In theory at least, this requires the estimation of the probability of default with the additional debt and the direct and indirect cost of bankruptcy. If π_a is the probability of default after the additional debt and BC is the present value of the bankruptcy cost, the present value of expected bankruptcy cost can be estimated.

$$\text{PV of Expected Bankruptcy cost}$$
$$= (\text{Probability of Bankruptcy})(\text{PV of Bankruptcy Cost}) = \pi_a BC$$

This step of the APV approach poses the most significant estimation problems, because neither the probability of bankruptcy nor the bankruptcy cost can be estimated directly.

In theory, both the APV and the cost of capital approach will yield the same values for a firm if consistent assumptions are made about financial leverage. The difficulties associated with estimating the expected bankruptcy cost, though, often lead many to use an abbreviated version of the APV model, where the tax benefits are added to the unlevered firm value and bankruptcy costs are ignored. This approach will overvalue firms. ■

Valuing Private Businesses

All of the principles that we have developed for valuation apply to private companies as well. In other words, the value of a private company is the present value of the expected cash flows that you would expect that company to generate over time, discounted back at a rate that reflects the riskiness of the cash flows. The differences that exist are primarily in the estimation of the cash flows and the discount rates:

- When estimating cash flows, keep in mind that although accounting standards may not be adhered to consistently in publicly traded firms, they can diverge dramatically in private firms. In small, private businesses, we should reconstruct financial statements rather than trust the earnings numbers that are reported. There are also two common problems that arise in private firm accounting that we have to correct for. The first is the failure on the part of many owners to attach a cost to the time that they spend running their businesses. Thus the owner of a store who spends most of every day stocking the store shelves, staffing the cash register, and completing the accounting will often not show a salary associated with these activities in his or her income statement, resulting in overstated earnings. The second is the intermingling of personal and business expenses that is endemic in many private businesses. When reestimating earnings, we have to strip the personal expenses out of the analysis.

- When estimating discount rates for publicly traded firms, we hewed to two basic principles. With equity, we argued that the only risk that matters is the risk that cannot be diversified away by marginal investors, who we assumed were well diversified. With debt, the cost of debt was based on a bond rating and the default spread associated with that rating. With private firms, both these assumptions will come under assault. First, the owner of a private business is almost never diversified and often has his or her entire wealth tied up in the firm's assets. That is why we developed the concept of a total beta for private firms in Chapter 4, where we scaled the beta of the firm up to reflect all risk and not just nondiversifiable risk. Second, private businesses usually have to borrow from the local bank and do not have the luxury of accessing the bond market. Consequently, they may well find themselves facing a higher cost of debt than otherwise similar publicly traded firms.

• The final issue relates back to terminal value. With publicly traded firms, we assume that firms have infinite lives and use this assumption, in conjunction with stable growth, to estimate a terminal value. Private businesses, especially smaller ones, often have finite lives since they are much more dependent on the owner/founder for their existence.

With more conservative estimates of cash flows, higher discount rates to reflect the exposure to total risk and finite life assumptions, it should come as no surprise that the values we attach to private firms are lower than those that we would attach to otherwise similar publicly traded firms. This also suggests that private firms that have the option of becoming publicly traded will generally opt to do so even though the owners might not like the oversight and loss of control that comes with this transition.

ILLUSTRATION 12.12 Valuing a Private Business: Bookscape

To value Bookscape, we will use the operating income of $2 million that the firm had in its most recent year as a starting point. Adjusting for the operating lease commitments that the firm has, we arrive at an adjusted operating income of $2.369 million.[34] To estimate the cost of capital, we draw on the estimates of total beta and the assumption that the firm's debt to capital ratio would resemble the industry average of 16.90 percent that we made in Chapter 4 (see Illustration 4.16):

Cost of Capital
= Cost of Equity(D/[D + E]) + After-Tax Cost of Debt(D/[D + E])
= 13.93%(0.831) + 5.50%(1 − 0.4)(0.169) = 0.1214 or 12.14%

The total beta for Bookscape is 2.06, and we will continue to use the 40 percent tax rate for the firm.

In Chapter 5, we estimated a return on capital for Bookscape of 12.68 percent, and we will assume that the firm will continue to generate this return on capital for

---

[34]In Illustration 4.15, we estimated the present value of the operating lease commitments at Bookscape to be $6.7 million. To adjust the operating income, we add back the imputed interest expense on this debt, obtained by multiplying the pretax cost of borrowing by the present value of the operating leases (5.50 percent of $6.7 million).

the foreseeable future, while growing its earnings at 4 percent a year. The resulting reinvestment rate is 31.54 percent:

Reinvestment Rate = Growth Rate/Return on Capital = 4%/12.68% = 31.54%

The present value of the cash flows, assuming perpetual growth, can be computed as follows:

Value of Operating Assets = 2,368.88(1 − 0.40)(1 − 0.3154)/(0.1214 − 0.04)
= $12.483 million

+ Value of Cash Holdings = $2.500 million

= Value of the Firm = $14.939 million

− Value of Debt (Operating Leases) = $6.707 million

= Value of Equity = $8.231 million

If we wanted to be conservative and assume that the cash flows will continue for only forty years, the value of the operating assets drops marginally to $12.3 million.

IN PRACTICE: Illiquidity Discounts in Private Firm Valuation

If you buy stock in a publicly traded firm and then change your mind and decide to sell, you face modest transaction costs. If you buy a private business and change your mind, it is far more difficult to reverse your decision. As a consequence, many analysts valuing private businesses apply an illiquidity discount that ranges from 20 to 40 percent of the value to arrive at a final value. Although the size of the discount is large, there is surprisingly little analysis that goes into the magnitude of the discount. In fact, it is almost entirely based on studies of restricted stock issued by publicly traded firms. These stock are placed with investors who are restricted from trading on the stock for two years after the issue. The price on the issue can be compared to the market price of the traded shares of the company to get a sense of the discount that investors demand for the enforced illiquidity. Because there are relatively few restricted stock issues, the sample sizes tend to be small and involve companies that may have other problems raising new funds.

Although we concede the necessity of illiquidity discounts in the valuation of private businesses, the discount should be adjusted to reflect the characteristics of the firm in question. Other things remaining equal, we would expect smaller firms with less liquid assets and in poorer financial health to have much larger illiquidity discounts attached to their values. One way to make this adjustment is to take a deeper look at the restricted stock issues for which we have data and look at reasons for the differences in discounts across stocks.[35] Another way is to view the bid-ask spread as the illiquidity discount on publicly traded companies and extend an analysis of the

---

[35]Silber did this in a 1989 study, where he found that the discount tended to be larger for companies with smaller revenues and negative earnings. See W. L. Silber, 1991, "Discounts on Restricted Stock: The Impact of Illiquidity on Stock Prices," *Financial Analysts Journal,* 60–64.

determinants of these spreads to come up with a reasonable measure of illiquidity discounts for private businesses.[36] ■

Value Enhancement

In a discounted cash flow valuation, the value of a firm is the function of four key inputs—the cash flows from existing investments, the expected growth rate in these cash flows for the high-growth period, the length of time before the company becomes a stable-growth company, and the cost of capital. Put simply, to enhance the value of a firm, we have to change one or more of these inputs:

a. *Increase cash flows from existing assets* There are a number of ways we can increase cash flows from assets. First, we can use assets more efficiently, cutting costs and improving productivity. If we succeed, we should see higher operating margins and profits. Second, we can, within the bounds of the law, reduce the taxes we pay on operating income through good tax planning. Third, we can reduce maintenance capital expenditures and investments in working capital—inventory and accounts receivable—thus increasing the cash left over after these outflows.

b. *Increase the growth rate during the high-growth period* Within the structure that we used in the last section, there are only two ways of increasing growth. We can reinvest more in internal investments and acquisitions, or we can try to earn higher returns on the capital that we invest in new investments. To the extent that we can do both, we can increase the expected growth rate. One point to keep in mind, though, is that increasing the reinvestment rate will almost always increase the growth rate, but it will not increase value if the return on capital on new investments lags the cost of capital.

c. *Increase the length of the high-growth period* It is not growth per se that creates value but excess returns. Because excess returns and the capacity to continue earning them comes from the competitive advantages possessed by a firm, a firm has to either create new competitive advantages—brand name, economies of scale, and legal restrictions on competition all come to mind—or augment existing ones.

d. *Reduce the cost of capital* In Chapter 8, we considered how changing the mix of debt and equity may reduce the cost of capital, and in Chapter 9, we considered how matching your debt to your assets can reduce your default risk and reduce your overall cost of financing. Holding all else constant, reducing the cost of capital will increase firm value.

Which one of these four approaches you choose will depend on where the firm you are analyzing or advising is in its growth cycle. For large mature firms, with little or no growth potential, cash flows from existing assets and the cost of capital offer the most promise for value enhancement. For smaller, risky, high-growth firms, it is likely to be changing the growth rate and the growth period that generate the biggest increases in value.

---

[36]See *Investment Valuation,* 2nd ed. (Aswath Damodaran, 2001, New York: Wiley), for more details.

ILLUSTRATION **12.13   Value Enhancement at Disney**

In Illustration 12.11, we valued Disney at $11.14 a share. In the process, though, we assumed that there would be no significant improvement in the return on capital that Disney earns on its existing assets, which at 4.42 percent is well below the cost of capital of 8.59 percent. To examine how much the value per share could be enhanced at Disney if it were run differently, we made the following changes:

- We assumed that the current after-tax operating income would increase to $3,417 million, which would be 8.59 percent of the book value of capital. This, in effect, would ensure that existing investments do not destroy value.

- We also assumed that the return on capital on new investments would increase to 15 percent from the 12 percent used in the status quo valuation. This is closer to the return that Disney used to make prior to its acquisition of Capital Cities. We kept the reinvestment rate unchanged at 53.18 percent. The resulting growth rate in operating income (for the first five years) is 7.98 percent a year.

- We assumed that the firm would increase its debt ratio immediately to 30 percent, which is its current optimal debt ratio (from Chapter 8). As a result the cost of capital will drop to 8.40 percent.

Keeping the assumptions about stable growth unchanged, we estimate significantly higher cash flows for the firm for the high-growth period in Table 12.6.

The terminal value is also pushed up, as a result of the higher growth in the high growth period:

$$\text{Terminal Value} = \text{FCFF}_{11}/(\text{Cost of Capital} - g)$$
$$= 6,433(1.04)/(0.0716 - 0.04)$$
$$= \$126,967 \text{ million}$$

				Table 12.6 EXPECTED FCFF, DISNEY				
Year	Expected Growth	EBIT	EBIT (1 − t)	Reinvestment Rate	Reinvestment	FCFF	Cost of Capital	PV of FCFF
Current		$5,327						
1	7.98%	$5,752	$3,606	53.18%	$1,918	$1,688	8.40%	$1,558
2	7.98%	$6,211	$3,894	53.18%	$2,071	$1,823	8.40%	$1,551
3	7.98%	$6,706	$4,205	53.18%	$2,236	$1,969	8.40%	$1,545
4	7.98%	$7,241	$4,540	53.18%	$2,414	$2,126	8.40%	$1,539
5	7.98%	$7,819	$4,902	53.18%	$2,607	$2,295	8.40%	$1,533
6	7.18%	$8,380	$5,254	50.54%	$2,656	$2,599	8.16%	$1,605
7	6.39%	$8,915	$5,590	47.91%	$2,678	$2,912	7.91%	$1,667
8	5.59%	$9,414	$5,902	45.27%	$2,672	$3,230	7.66%	$1,717
9	4.80%	$9,865	$6,185	42.64%	$2,637	$3,548	7.41%	$1,756
10	4.00%	$10,260	$6,433	40.00%	$2,573	$3,860	7.16%	$1,783

The value of the firm and the value per share can now be estimated:

Present Value of FCFF in High-Growth Phase = $16,254.91

+ Present Value of Terminal Value of Firm = $58,645.39

+ Value of Cash, Marketable Securities, & Nonoperating Assets = $3,432.00

Value of Firm = $78,332.30

− Market Value of Outstanding Debt = $14,648.80

− Value of Equity in Options = $1,334.67

Value of Equity in Common Stock = $62,348.84

Market Value of Equity/Share = $30.45

Disney's value per share increases from $11.14 per share in Illustration 12.11 to $30.45 a share when we make the changes to the way it is managed.[37]

IN PRACTICE: THE VALUE OF CONTROL

The notion that control is worth 15 percent or 20 percent or some fixed percent of every firm's value is deeply embedded in valuation practice, and it is not true. The value of control is the difference between two values—the value of the firm run by its existing management (status quo) and the value of the same firm run optimally.

Value of Control = Optimal Value for Firm − Status Quo Value

Thus, a firm that takes poor investments and funds them with a suboptimal mix of debt and equity will be worth more if it takes better investments and funds them with the right mix of debt and equity. In general, the worse managed a firm is, the greater the value of control. This view of the world has wide ramifications in corporate finance and valuation:

- In a hostile acquisition, which is usually motivated by the desire to change the way that a firm is run, you should be willing to pay a premium that at best is equal to the value of control. You would prefer to pay less to preserve some of the benefits for yourself (rather than give them to target company stockholders).

- In companies with voting and nonvoting shares, the difference in value between the two classes should be a function of the value of control. If the value of control is high, and there is a high likelihood of control changing, the value of the voting shares will increase relative to nonvoting shares.

In the Disney valuation, the value of control can be estimated by comparing the value of Disney run optimally with the status quo valuation done earlier in the chapter.

Value of Control$_{\text{Disney}}$ = Optimal Value − Status Quo Value
= $30.45 − $11.14 = $19.31 per share

---

[37]You may wonder why the dollar debt does not change even though the firm is moving to a 30 percent debt ratio. In reality, it will increase, but the number of shares will decrease when Disney recapitalizes. The net effect is that the value per share will be close to our estimated value.

The fact that Disney trades at $26.91 can be an indication that the market thinks that there will be significant changes in the way the firm is run in the near future, though it is unclear whether these changes will occur voluntarily or through hostile actions. ■

RELATIVE VALUATION

In discounted cash flow valuation, the objective is to find the value of assets, given their cash flow, growth, and risk characteristics. In relative valuation, the objective is to value assets, based on how similar assets are currently priced in the market. In this section, we consider how asset prices are standardized before being compared to similar assets, and how to control for differences across comparable firms.

Standardized Values and Multiples

To compare the values of similar assets in the market, we need to standardize the values in some way. They can be standardized relative to the earnings they generate, to the book value or replacement value of the assets themselves, or to the revenues that they generate. We discuss each method next.

1. Earnings Multiples

One of the more intuitive ways to think of the value of any asset is as a multiple of the earnings it generates. When buying a stock, it is common to look at the price paid as a multiple of the earnings per share generated by the company. This *price/earnings ratio* can be estimated using earnings per share over the last four quarters, which is called a *trailing PE,* or an expected earnings per share in the next financial year, called a *forward PE*. When buying a business, as opposed to just the equity in the business, it is common to examine the value of the firm, usually net of cash (enterprise value), as a multiple of the operating income or the earnings before interest, taxes, depreciation, and amortization (EBITDA). To a buyer of the equity or the firm, a lower multiple is better than a higher one, but these multiples will be affected by the growth potential and risk of the business being acquired.

2. Book Value or Replacement Value Multiples

Although markets provide one estimate of the value of a business, accountants often provide a very different estimate. The accounting estimate of book value is determined by accounting rules and is heavily influenced by the original price paid for the asset and any accounting adjustments (such as depreciation) made since that time. Investors often look at the relationship between the market's assessment of the value of equity and the book value of equity (or net worth) as a measure of how over- or undervalued a stock is; the *price/book value* ratio that emerges can vary widely across industries, depending again on the growth potential and the quality of the investments in each. When valuing businesses, we estimate this ratio using the value of the firm and the book value of all capital (rather than just the equity). For those who believe that book value is not a good measure of the true value of the assets, an alternative is to use the replacement cost of the assets; the ratio of the value of the firm to replacement cost is called the Q ratio.

3. Revenue Multiples

Both earnings and book value are accounting measures and are determined by accounting rules and principles. An alternative, which is far less affected by these factors, is to use the ratio of the value of an asset to the revenues it generates. For equity investors, this ratio is the *price/sales ratio (PS)*, where the market value of equity is divided by the revenues generated by the firm. For firm value, this ratio can be modified as the *value/sales ratio (VS)*, where the numerator becomes the value of the firm. This ratio again varies widely across sectors, largely as a function of the profit margins in each. The advantage of using revenue multiples, however, is that it becomes far easier to compare firms in different markets, with different accounting systems at work, than it is to compare earnings or book value multiples.

Determinants of Multiples

One reason commonly given for the use of these multiples to value equity and firms is that they require far fewer assumptions than discounted cash flow valuation does. This is a misconception. The difference between discounted cash flow valuation and relative valuation is that the assumptions we make are explicit in the former and remain implicit in the latter. It is important that we know what the variables are that cause multiples to change, because these are the variables we have to control for when comparing these multiples across firms.

To look under the hood, so to speak, of equity and firm value multiples, we will go back to fairly simple discounted cash flow models for equity and firm value and use them to derive our multiples. Thus, the simplest discounted cash flow model for equity, which is a stable growth dividend discount model, would suggest that the value of equity is:

$$\text{Value of Equity} = P_0 = \frac{\text{DPS}_1}{k_e - g_n}$$

where DPS_1 is the expected dividend in the next year, k_e is the cost of equity, and g_n is the expected stable growth rate. Dividing both sides by the earnings, we obtain the discounted cash flow equation specifying the PE ratio for a stable growth firm:

$$\frac{P_0}{\text{EPS}_0} = \text{PE} = \frac{\text{Payout Ratio} \times (1 + g_n)}{k_e - g_n}$$

Dividing both sides by the book value of equity, we can estimate the price/book value ratio for a stable-growth firm:

$$\frac{P_0}{\text{BV}_0} = \text{PBV} = \frac{\text{ROE} \times \text{Payout Ratio} \times (1 + g_n)}{k_e - g_n}$$

Dividing by the sales per share, the price/sales ratio for a stable-growth firm can be estimated as a function of its profit margin, payout ratio, and expected growth.

$$\frac{P_0}{\text{Sales}_0} = \text{PS} = \frac{\text{Net Profit Margin} \times \text{Payout Ratio} \times (1 + g_n)}{k_e - g_n}$$

Table 12.7 Multiples and Companion Variables (in Italics)	
Multiple	**Determining Variables**
Price/earnings ratio	*Growth,* payout, risk
Price/book value ratio	Growth, payout, risk, *ROE*
Price/sales ratio	Growth, payout, risk, *net margin*
Value/EBIT	Growth, *reinvestment needs,* leverage, risk
Value/EBIT $(1 - t)$	
Value/EBITDA	
Value/sales	Growth, reinvestment needs, leverage, risk, *operating margin*
Value/book capital	Growth, leverage, risk, *ROC*

We can do a similar analysis from the perspective of firm valuation.[38] The value of a firm in stable growth can be written as:

$$\text{Value of Firm} = V_0 = \frac{\text{FCFF}_1}{k_c - g_n}$$

where k_c is the cost of capital. Dividing both sides by the expected FCFF yields the value/FCFF multiple for a stable growth firm:

$$\frac{V_0}{\text{FCFF}_1} = \frac{1}{k_c - g_n}$$

Because the FCFF is the after-tax operating income netted against the net capital expenditures and working capital needs of the firm, the multiples of EBIT, after-tax EBIT, and EBITDA can also be estimated similarly. The value/EBITDA multiple, for instance, can be written as follows:

$$\frac{\text{Value}}{\text{EBITDA}} = \frac{(1 - t)}{k_c - g} + \frac{\text{Depr}(t)/\text{EBITDA}}{k_c - g} - \frac{\text{Cap Exp}/\text{EBITDA}}{k_c - g}$$
$$- \frac{\Delta\text{Working Capital}/\text{EBITDA}}{k_c - g}$$

The point of this analysis is not to suggest that we go back to using discounted cash flow valuation but to understand the variables that may cause these multiples to vary across firms in the same sector. If we ignore these variables, we might conclude that a stock with a PE of 8 is cheaper than one with a PE of 12, when the true reason may be that the latter has higher expected growth or we might decide that a stock with a P/BV ratio of 0.7 is cheaper than one with a P/BV ratio of 1.5, when the true reason may be that the latter has a much higher return on equity. Table 12.7 lists the

---

[38]In practice, cash and marketable securities are subtracted from firm value to arrive at what is called enterprise value. All the multiples in the following section can be written in terms of enterprise value, and the determinants remain unchanged.

multiples that are widely used and the variables that determine each; the variable that (in our view) is the most significant determinant is italicized for each multiple. This variable is what we would call the *companion variable* for this multiple, that is, the one variable we need to know to use this multiple to find under- or overvalued assets.

This spreadsheet allows you to estimate the equity multiples for a firm, given its fundamentals (**eqmult.xls**).

This spreadsheet allows you to estimate the firm value multiples for a firm, given its fundamentals (**firmmult.xls**).

The Use of Comparable Firms

When we use multiples, we tend to use them in conjunction with comparable firms to determine the value of a firm or its equity. This analysis begins with two choices—the multiple that will be used in the analysis and the group of firms that will make up the comparable firms. The multiple is computed for each of the comparable firms, and the average is computed. To evaluate an individual firm, we then compare its multiple to the average computed; if it is significantly different, we make a subjective judgment about whether the firm's individual characteristics (growth, risk, or cash flows) may explain the difference. Thus, a firm may have a PE ratio of 22 in a sector where the average PE is only 15, but we may conclude that this difference can be justified because the firm has higher growth potential than the average firm in the industry. In our judgment, if the difference on the multiple cannot be explained by the variables listed in Table 12.7, the firm will be viewed as overvalued (if its multiple is higher than the average) or undervalued (if its multiple is lower than the average). Choosing comparable firms and adequately controlling for differences across these comparable firms, then become critical steps in this process. In this section, we consider both decisions.

1. Choosing Comparables

The first step in relative valuation is usually the selection of comparable firms. A comparable firm is one with cash flows, growth potential, and risk similar to the firm being valued. It would be ideal if we could value a firm by looking at how an exactly identical firm—in terms of risk, growth, and cash flows—is priced. In most analyses, however, analysts define comparable firms to be other firms in the same business or businesses. If there are enough firms in the industry to allow for it, this list is pruned further using other criteria; for instance, only firms of similar size may be considered. The implicit assumption being made here is that firms in the same sector have similar risk, growth, and cash flow profiles and therefore can be compared with much more legitimacy.

This approach becomes more difficult to apply when there are relatively few firms in a sector. In most markets outside the United States, the number of publicly traded firms in a particular sector is small, especially if it is defined narrowly. It is also difficult to find comparable firms if differences in risk, growth, and cash flow profiles across firms within a sector are large. Thus, there may be hundreds of computer software companies listed in the United States, but the differences across these firms are also large. The trade-off is therefore simple. Defining a industry more broadly increases the number of comparable firms, but it also results in a more diverse group.

2. Controlling for Differences across Firms

In Table 12.7, we listed the variables that determined each multiple. Because it is impossible to find firms identical to the one being valued, we have to find ways of controlling for differences across firms on these variables. The process of controlling for the variables can range from very simple approaches, which modify the multiples to take into account differences on one key variable, to more complex approaches that allow for differences on more than one variable.

a. Simple Adjustments Let's start with the simple approaches. In this case, we modify the multiple to take into account the most important variable determining it. Thus, the PE ratio is divided by the expected growth rate in earnings per share for a company to determine a growth-adjusted PE ratio or the *PEG ratio*. Similarly, the PBV ratio is divided by the ROE to find a *value ratio*. These modified ratios are then compared across companies in a sector. The implicit assumption we make is that these firms are comparable on all the other measures of value, besides the one being controlled for.

ILLUSTRATION 12.14   Comparing PE Ratios and Growth Rates across Firms: Entertainment Companies

To value Disney, we look at the PE ratios and expected growth rates in EPS over the next five years, based on consensus estimates from analysts, for all entertainment companies where data is available on PE ratios and analyst estimates of expected growth in earnings over the next five years. Table 12.8 lists the firms and PE ratios.

This simple view of multiples leads us to conclude that Disney should trade at 47.08 times earnings, because that is the average for similar publicly traded firms. The resulting value for the equity would be:

$$\text{Value of Equity} = \text{Disney Net Income in 2003} \times \text{Average PE Ratio for Sector}$$
$$= \$1,267 \text{ million} \times 47.08 = \$59,650 \text{ million}$$

In this valuation, we assume that Disney has a growth rate similar to the average for the sector. One way of bringing growth into the comparison is to compute the PEG ratio, which is reported in the last column. Based on the average PEG ratio of 2.74 for the sector and the analyst estimate of growth in earnings of 12 percent for Disney for the next five years, we obtain the following value for the equity in Disney:

$$\text{Value of Equity} = \$1,267 \text{ million} \times 2.74 \times 12 = \$41,660 \text{ million}$$

Although this may seem like an easy adjustment to resolve the problem of differences across firms, the conclusion holds only if these firms are of equivalent risk. Implicitly, this approach assumes a linear relationship between growth rates and PE.[39]

---

[39]Put another way, we are assuming that as growth doubles, the PE ratio will also double.

Table 12.8 **ENTERTAINMENT FIRM PE RATIOS AND GROWTH RATES, 2004**

Company Name	Ticker Symbol	PE	Expected Growth Rate	PEG
Point 360	PTSX	10.62	5.00%	2.12
Fox Entmt Group	FOX	22.03	14.46%	1.52
Belo Corp. A	BLC	25.65	16.00%	1.60
Hearst-Argyle Television	HTV	26.72	12.90%	2.07
Journal Communications	JRN	27.94	10.00%	2.79
Saga Communic. A	SGA	28.42	19.00%	1.50
Viacom B	VIA/B	29.38	13.50%	2.18
Pixar	PIXR	29.80	16.50%	1.81
Disney (Walt)	DIS	29.87	12.00%	2.49
Westwood One	WON	32.59	19.50%	1.67
World Wrestling Ent.	WWE	33.52	20.00%	1.68
Cox Radio A	CXR	33.76	18.70%	1.81
Beasley Broadcast Group	BBGI	34.06	15.23%	2.24
Entercom Comm.	ETM	36.11	15.43%	2.34
Liberty	LC	37.54	19.50%	1.92
Ballantyne of Omaha	BTNE	55.17	17.10%	3.23
Regent Communications	RGCI	57.84	22.67%	2.55
Emmis Communications	EMMS	74.89	16.50%	4.54
Cumulus Media	CMLS	94.35	23.30%	4.05
Univision Communications	UVN	122.76	24.50%	5.01
Salem Communications	SALM	145.67	28.75%	5.07
Average for sector		47.08	17.17%	2.74 (47.08/17.17)

Source: Value Line.

12.11 UNDERLYING ASSUMPTIONS IN COMPARABLE VALUATION

Assume that you are reading an equity research report where a buy recommendation for a company is being based on the fact that its PE ratio is lower than the average for the industry. Implicitly, what is the underlying assumption or assumptions being made by this analyst?

☐ The sector itself is, on average, fairly priced.

☐ The earnings of the firms in the group are being measured consistently.

☐ The firms in the group are all of equivalent risk.

☐ The firms in the group are all at the same stage in the growth cycle.

☐ The firms in the group have similar cash flow patterns.

☐ All of the above.

There is a data set online that summarizes PE ratios and PEG ratios by industry group in the United States for the most recent quarter.

b. Adjusting for More than One Variable   When firms differ on more than one variable, it becomes difficult to modify the multiples to account for the differences across firms. We can run regressions of the multiples against the variables and then use these regressions to find predicted values for each firm. This approach works reasonably well when the number of comparable firms is large and the relationship between the multiple and the variables is stable. When these conditions do not hold, a few outliers can cause the coefficients to change dramatically and make the predictions much less reliable.

ILLUSTRATION **12.15**   **Price to Book Value Ratios and Return on Equity: European Banks**
Table 12.9 lists price/book value ratios of European banks and reports on their returns on equity and risk levels (measured using the standard deviation in stock prices over the previous five years).

Because these firms differ on both risk and return on equity, we run a regression of PBV ratios on both variables:

$$PBV = 2.27 + 3.63\ ROE - 2.68\ Standard\ Deviation \quad R^2 = 79.48\%$$
$$(5.56)\quad (3.32)\qquad\qquad (2.32)$$

Firms with higher return on equity and lower standard deviations trade at much higher price to book ratios. The numbers in parentheses are *t*-statistics and suggest

Table 12.9   EUROPEAN BANKS: PRICE TO BOOK VALUE RATIO, 2003

Name	PBV Ratio	Return on Equity	Standard Deviation
Bayerische Hypo-Und Vereinsb	0.80	–1.66%	49.06%
Commerzbank Ag	1.09	–6.72%	36.21%
Deutsche Bank Ag Reg	1.23	1.32%	35.79%
Banca Intesa Spa	1.66	1.56%	34.14%
Bnp Paribas	1.72	12.46%	31.03%
Banco Santander Central Hisp	1.86	11.06%	28.36%
Sanpaolo Imi Spa	1.96	8.55%	26.64%
Banco Bilbao Vizcaya Argenta	1.98	11.17%	18.62%
Societe Generale	2.04	9.71%	22.55%
Royal Bank of Scotland Group	2.09	20.22%	18.35%
Hbos	2.15	22.45%	21.95%
Barclays	2.23	21.16%	20.73%
Unicredito Italiano Spa	2.30	14.86%	13.79%
Kredietbank Sa Luxembourgeoi	2.46	17.74%	12.38%
Erste Bank Der Oester Spark	2.53	10.28%	21.91%
Standard Chartered	2.59	20.18%	19.93%
Hsbc Holdings	2.94	18.50%	19.66%
Lloyds Tsb Group	3.33	32.84%	18.66%
Sector Average	2.05	12.54%	24.99%

Source: Bloomberg.

that the relationships between PBV ratios and both variables in the regression are statistically significant. The R^2 indicates the percentage of the differences in PBV ratios that is explained by the independent variables. Finally, the regression itself can be used to get predicted PBV ratios for the companies in the list.[40] Thus, the predicted PBV ratio for Deutsche Bank, based on its return on equity of 1.32 percent and its standard deviation of 35.79 percent, would be 1.36.

$$\text{Predicted PBV}_{\text{Deutsche Bank}} = 2.27 + 3.63(0.0132) - 2.68(0.3579) = 1.36$$

Because the actual PBV ratio for Deutsche Bank at the time of the analysis was 1.23, this would suggest that the stock is undervalued by roughly 10 percent.

 There is a data set online that summarizes price to book ratios and returns on equity by industry group in the United States for the most recent quarter.

 There is a data set online that summarizes price to sales ratios and margins by industry group in the United States for the most recent quarter.

3. Expanding the Range of Comparable Firms

Searching for comparable firms within the sector in which a firm operates is fairly restrictive, especially when there are relatively few firms in the sector or when a firm operates in more than one sector. Because the definition of a comparable firm is not one that is in the same business but one that has the same growth, risk, and cash flow characteristics as the firm being analyzed, we need not restrict our choice of comparable firms to those in the same industry. A software firm should be comparable to an automobile firm if we can control for differences in the fundamentals.

The regression introduced in the previous section allows us to control for differences on those variables that we believe cause multiples to vary across firms. Based on the variables listed in Table 12.7, we should be able to regress PE, PBV, and PS ratios against the variables that should affect them:

$$\text{Price Earnings} = f(\text{Growth, Payout Ratios, Risk})$$

$$\text{Price to Book Value} = f(\text{Growth, Payout Ratios, Risk, ROE})$$

$$\text{Price to Sales} = f(\text{Growth, Payout Ratios, Risk, Margin})$$

It is, however, possible that the proxies that we use for risk (beta), growth (expected growth rate), and cash flow (payout) are imperfect and that the relationship may not be linear. To deal with these limitations, we can add more variables to the regression—for example, the size of the firm may operate as a good proxy for risk—and use transformations of the variables to allow for nonlinear relationships.

We ran these regressions for PE, PBV, and PS ratios across publicly listed firms in the United States in January 2004 against analyst estimates of expected growth in

---

[40]We are assuming that the relationship between a multiple and the variables driving value are linear. Because this is not always true, we might have to run nonlinear versions of these regressions.

earnings per share and other financial indicators from the most recent year.[41] The sample, which had more than 7,000 firms in it, yielded the regressions reported next. These regressions can then be used to get predicted PE, PBV, and PS ratios for each firm, which, in turn, can be compared to the actual multiples to find under- and over-valued firms.

$$PE = 9.475 + 0.814 \text{ Expected Growth} + 0.06 \text{ Payout} + 6.283 \text{ Beta} \ (R^2 = 22.1\%)$$

$$PBV = 0.140 \text{ ROE} + 0.599 \text{ Beta} + 0.08 \text{ Expected Growth} + 0.002 \text{ Payout} \ (R^2 = 47.1\%)$$

$$PS = 0.04 \text{ Expected Growth} + 0.011 \text{ Payout} + 0.549 \text{ Beta} + 0.234 \text{ Net Margin} \ (R^2 = 71.0\%)$$

The first advantage of this approach over the "subjective" comparison across firms in the same sector is that it does quantify, based on actual market data, the degree to which higher growth or risk should affect the multiples. It is true that these estimates can have error in them, but the error is a reflection of the reality that many analysts choose not to face when they make subjective judgments. Second, by looking at all firms in the market, this approach allows us to make more meaningful comparisons of firms that operate in industries with relatively few firms. Third, it allows us to examine whether all firms in an industry are under- or overvalued by estimating their values relative to other firms in the market.

ILLUSTRATION **12.16**   Applying Market Regression to Estimate Multiples: Disney

We will use the results of the market regression just summarized to estimate the appropriate value for Disney. Consider the regression for the PE ratio:

$$PE = 9.475 + 0.814 \text{ Expected Growth} + 0.06 \text{ Payout} + 6.283 \text{ Beta}$$

The corresponding values for Disney are as follows:

Expected Growth Rate = 12.00% (analyst consensus estimate for EPS growth)

Payout Ratio = 32.31%

Beta = 1.2456

The estimated price earnings ratio for Disney is:

$$PS = 9.475 + 0.814(12) + 0.06(32.31) + 6.283(1.2456) = 29.01$$

Because Disney trades at an actual PE ratio of 29.87, it is slightly overvalued, relative to the market, by about 3 percent.

 There is a data set online that summarizes the latest regressions of multiples against fundamentals for the most recent quarter.

---

[41]We ran the regression both with intercepts and without intercepts. If the intercept is negative, we report the regression without the intercept.

RECONCILING DIFFERENT VALUATIONS

The two approaches to valuation—discounted cash flow valuation and relative valuation—yield different values for Disney.[42] In fact, Disney is significantly overvalued using a discounted cash flow model but is closer to being fairly valued using relative valuation models. Even within relative valuation, we arrive at different estimates of value, depending on which multiple we use and the firms on which we based the relative valuation.

The differences in value between discounted cash flow valuation and relative valuation come from different views of market efficiency or, put more precisely, market inefficiency. In discounted cash flow valuation, we assume that markets make mistakes, they correct these mistakes over time, and these mistakes can often occur across entire sectors or even the entire market. In relative valuation, we assume that although markets make mistakes on individual stocks, they are correct on average. In other words, when we value Disney relative to other entertainment companies, we are assuming that the market has priced these companies correctly, on average, even though it might have made mistakes in the pricing of each of them individually. Thus, a stock may be overvalued on a discounted cash flow basis but undervalued on a relative basis, if the firms used in the relative valuation are all overpriced by the market. The reverse would occur if an entire sector or market were underpriced.

To conclude, we suggest the following broad guidelines on gauging value using different approaches:

- The discounted cash flow models are built on the implicit assumption of long time horizons, giving markets time to correct their errors.

- When using relative valuation, it is dangerous to base valuations on multiples where the differences across firms cannot be explained well using financial fundamentals—growth, risk, and cash flow patterns. One of the advantages of using the regression approach described in the later part of this chapter is that the R^2 and t-statistics from the regressions yield tangible estimates of the strength (or weakness) of this relationship.

12.12 VALUING AN IPO

If you were an investment banker pricing an IPO, would you primarily use discounted cash flow valuation, relative valuation, or a combination of the two?

☐ Relative valuation, because the buyers of the IPO will look at comparables

☐ Discounted cash flow valuation, because it reflects intrinsic value

☐ The higher of the two values, because it is my job to get the highest price I can for my client

☐ None of the above

Explain.

---

[42]See S. Kaplan and R. Ruback, 1995, "The Valuation of Cash Flow Forecasts: An Empirical Analysis," *Journal of Finance*, 50, 1059–93. They examine valuations in acquisitions and find that discounted cash flow models better explain prices paid than relative valuation models.

CONCLUSION

There are two basic approaches to valuation. The first is discounted cash flow valuation, in which the value of any asset is estimated by computing the present value of the expected cash flows on it. The actual process of estimation, in either case, generally requires four inputs:

- the length of the period for which a firm or asset can be expected to generate growth greater than the stable growth rate (which is constrained to be close to the growth rate of the economy in which the firm operates),
- the cash flows during the high-growth period,
- the terminal value at the end of the high growth period, and
- a discount rate.

The expected growth potential will vary across firms, with some firms already growing at a stable growth rate and others for which the expectation, at least, is that high growth will last for some period into the future. We can value the operating assets of a firm by discounting cash flows before debt payments but after reinvestment at the cost of capital. Adding the value of cash and nonoperating assets give us firm value, and subtracting out debt yields the value of equity. We can also value equity directly by discounting cash flows after debt payments and reinvestment needs at the cost of equity.

The other approach to valuation is relative valuation, where the value of any asset is estimated by looking at how similar assets are priced in the market. The key steps in this approach are defining comparable firms or assets and choosing a standardized measure of value (usually value as a multiple of earnings; cash flows, or book value) to compare the firms. To compare multiples across companies, we have to control for differences in growth, risk, and cash flows, just as we would have in discounted cash flow valuation.

LIVE CASE STUDY

VALUATION

Objective: To value your firm, based on its existing management, and your expectations for the future.

Key Questions

- What type of cash flow (dividends, FCFE, or FCFF) would you choose to discount for this firm?
- What growth pattern would you pick for this firm? How long will high growth and excess returns last?
- When will your firm be in stable growth and what will your firm look like when it reaches stable growth?
- What is your estimate of value of equity in this firm? How does this compare to the market value?

Framework for Analysis

1. *Cash Flow Estimation*

- What is this firm's accounting operating income? Would you adjust it for your valuation?
- What is your firm's effective tax rate? What is its marginal tax rate? Which would you use in your valuation?
- How much did your firm reinvest last year in internal investments, acquisitions, R&D, and working capital?

2. *Growth Pattern Choice*

- How fast have this company's earnings grown historically?
- How quickly do analysts expect this company's earnings to grow in the future?
- What do the fundamentals suggest about earnings growth at this company? (How much is being reinvested and at what rate of return?)
- If there is anticipated high growth with excess returns, what are the barriers to entry that will allow these excess returns to continue? For how long?

3. *Valuation*

- What is the value of the operating assets of the firm, based on a discounted cash flow model?
- Does the firm have cash and nonoperating assets, and what are their values?

- Are there equity options outstanding (management options, convertible bonds) and how much are they worth?
- What is the value of equity per share?

4. *Relative Valuation*

- What multiple would you use to value the firm or its equity?
- What industry does the firm belong to, and what are the comparable firms?
- How does your firm's valuation (in multiple terms) compare to those of the other firms in the industry?
- What value would you assign your firm (or its equity), given how comparable firms are valued?

Getting Information for Valuation

Most of the information that you need for valuation comes from your current or past financial statements. You will also need a beta (see risk and return section) and a debt ratio (see risk and return section) to estimate the FCFE. You can get analyst estimates of growth in several sources including Zacks and I/B/E/S.

Online Sources of Information
www.stern.nyu.edu/~adamodar/cfin2E/project/data.htm.

PROBLEMS AND QUESTIONS

(In the problems below, you can use a risk premium of 5.5 percent and a tax rate of 40 percent if none is specified.)

1. Vernon Enterprises has current after-tax operating income of $100 million and a cost of capital of 10 percent. The firm earns a return on capital equal to its cost of capital.
   a. Assume that the firm is in stable growth, growing 5 percent a year forever; estimate the firm's reinvestment rate.
   b. Given this reinvestment rate, estimate the value of the firm.
   c. What is the value of the firm, if you assume a zero reinvestment rate and no growth?

2. Assume in the previous question with Vernon Enterprises that the firm will earn a return on capital of 15 percent in perpetuity.
   a. Assume that the firm is in stable growth, growing 5 percent a year forever; estimate the firm's reinvestment rate.
   b. Given this reinvestment rate, estimate the value of the firm.

3. Cello is a manufacturer of pianos. It earned an after-tax return on capital of 10 percent last year and expects to maintain this next year. If the current year's after-tax operating income is $100 million and the firm reinvests 50 percent of this income back, estimate the FCFF next year. [After-Tax Operating Income = EBIT $(1 - t)$].

4. Cell Phone is a cellular firm that reported net income of $50 million in the most recent financial year. The firm had $1 billion in debt, on which it reported interest expenses of $150 million in the most recent financial year. The firm had depreciation of $100 million for the year, and capital expenditures were 200 percent of depreciation. The firm has a cost of capital of 11 percent. Assuming that there is no working capital requirement, and a constant growth rate of 4 percent in perpetuity, estimate the value of the firm.

5. Netsoft is a company that manufactures networking software. In the current year, the firm reported operating earnings before interest and taxes of $200 million (operating earnings does not include interest income), and these earnings are expected to grow 4 percent a year in perpetuity. In addition, the firm has a cash balance of $250 million on which it earned interest income of

$20 million. The unlevered beta for other networking software firm is 1.20, and these firms have on average cash balances of 10 percent of firm value. If Netsoft has a debt ratio of 15 percent, a tax rate of 40 percent, a return on capital of 10 percent on operating assets, and a pre-tax cost of debt of 10 percent, estimate the value of the firm. (The risk-free rate is 6 percent, and you can assume a market risk premium of 5.5 percent.)

6. Gemco Jewelers earned $5 million in after-tax operating income in the most recent year. The firm also had capital expenditures of $4 million and depreciation of $2 million during the year, and the noncash working capital at the end of the year was $10 million.
   a. Assuming that the firm's operating income will grow 20 percent next year, and that all other items (capital expenditures, depreciation, and noncash working capital) will grow at the same rate, estimate the FCFF next year.
   b. If the firm can grow at 20 percent for the next five years, estimate the present value of the FCFF over that period. You can assume a cost of capital of 12 percent.
   c. After year five, the firm's capital expenditures will decline to 125 percent of revenues, and the growth rate will drop to 5 percent (in both operating income and noncash working capital). In addition, the cost of capital will decline to 10 percent. Estimate the terminal value of the firm at the end of year five.
   d. Estimate the current value of the operating assets of the firm.

7. Now assume that Gemco Jewelers has $10 million in cash and nonoperating assets and that the firm has $15 million in outstanding debt.
   a. Estimate the value of equity in the firm.
   b. If the firm has 5 million shares outstanding, estimate the value of equity per share.
   c. How would your answer to **b** change if you learn that the firm has 1 million options outstanding, with an exercise price of $25 and five years to maturity? (The estimated value per option is $7.)

8. Union Pacific Railroad reported net income of $770 million after interest expenses of $320 million in a recent financial year. (The corporate tax rate was 36 percent.) It reported depreciation of $960 million in that year, and capital spending was $1.2 billion. The firm also had $4 billion in debt outstanding on the books, was rated AA (carrying a yield to maturity of 8 percent), and was trading at par (up from $3.8 billion at the end of the previous year). The beta of the stock is 1.05, and there were 200 million shares outstanding (trading at $60 per share), with a book value of $5 billion. Union Pacific paid 40 percent of its earnings as dividends and working capital requirements are negligible. (The Treasury bond rate is 7 percent.)

   a. Estimate the FCFF for the most recent financial year.

   b. Estimate the value of the firm now.

   c. Estimate the value of equity and the value per share now.

9. Lockheed, one of the largest defense contractors in the United States, reported EBITDA of $1,290 million in a recent financial year, prior to interest expenses of $215 million and depreciation charges of $400 million. Capital expenditures amounted to $450 million during the year, and working capital was 7 percent of revenues (which were $13,500 million). The firm had debt outstanding of $3.068 billion (in book value terms), trading at a market value of $3.2 billion, and yielding a pretax interest rate of 8 percent. There were 62 million shares outstanding, trading at $64 per share, and the most recent beta is 1.10. The tax rate for the firm is 40 percent. (The Treasury bond rate is 7 percent.) The firm expects revenues, earnings, capital expenditures, and depreciation to grow at 9.5 percent a year for the next 5 years, after which the growth rate is expected to drop to 4 percent. (Even though this is unrealistic, you can assume that capital spending will offset depreciation in the stable-growth period.) The company also plans to lower its debt/equity ratio to 50 percent for the steady state (which will result in the pretax interest rate dropping to 7.5 percent).

   a. Estimate the value of the firm.

   b. Estimate the value of the equity in the firm and the value per share.

10. In the face of disappointing earnings results and increasingly assertive institutional stockholders, Eastman Kodak was considering the sale of its health division, which earned $560 million in EBIT in the most recent year on revenues of $5.285 billion. The expected growth in earnings was expected to moderate to 6 percent for the next 5 years, and to 4 percent after that. Capital expenditures in the health division amounted to $420 million in the most recent year, whereas depreciation was $350 million. Both are expected to grow 4 percent a year in the long run. Working capital requirements are negligible.

   The average beta of firms competing with Eastman Kodak's health division is 1.15. Although Eastman Kodak has a debt ratio (D/[D + E]) of 50 percent, the health division can sustain a debt ratio (D/[D + E]) of only 20 percent, which is similar to the average debt ratio of firms competing in the health sector. At this level of debt, the health division can expect to pay 7.5 percent on its debt, before taxes. (The tax rate is 40 percent, and the Treasury bond rate is 7 percent.)

   a. Estimate the cost of capital for the division.

   b. Estimate the value of the division.

11. You have been asked to value Alcoa and have come up with the following inputs.

   • The stock has a beta of 0.90, estimated over the last five years. During this period, the firm had an average debt/equity ratio of 20 percent and an average cash balance of 15 percent.

   • The firm's current market value of equity is 1.6 billion and its current market value of debt is $800 million. The current cash balance is $500 million.

   • The firm earned earnings before interest and taxes of $450 million, which includes the interest income on the current cash balance of $50 million. The firm's tax rate is 40 percent.

   • The firm is in stable growth, and its earnings from operations are expected to grow 5 percent a year. The net capital expenditures next year are expected to be $90 million.

   • The riskfree rate is 6 percent and the firm can borrow at 7 percent.

   Estimate the value of the noncash assets of the firm, its total value, and the value of its equity.

12. You are analyzing a valuation done on a stable firm by a well-known analyst. Based on the expected FCFF next year of $30 million, and an expected growth rate of 5 percent, the analyst has estimated a value of $750 million. However, he has made the mistake of using the book values of debt and equity in his calculation. Although you do not know the book value weights he used, you know that the firm has a cost of equity of 12 percent and an after-tax cost of debt of 6 percent. You also know that the market value of equity is three times the book value of equity, and the market value of debt is equal to the book value of debt. Estimate the correct value for the firm.

13. You have been asked to value Office Help, a private firm providing office support services in the New York area.

   • The firm reported pretax operating income of $10 million in its most recent financial year on revenues of $100 million. In the most recent financial year, you note that the owners of the business did not pay themselves a salary. You believe that a fair salary for their services would be $1.5 million a year.

   • The cost of capital for comparable firms that are publicly traded is 9 percent. (You can assume that this firm will have similar leverage and cost of capital.)

   • The firm is in stable growth and expects to grow 5 percent a year in perpetuity. The tax rate is 40 percent.

   The average illiquidity discount applied to private firms is 30 percent, but you have run a regression and arrived at the following estimate for the discount:

   Illiquidity Discount = 0.30 − 0.04
       (ln [Revenues in millions])

   Estimate the value of Office Help for sale in a private transaction (to an individual).

14. National City, a bank holding company, reported earnings per share of $2.40 and paid dividends per share of $1.06. The earnings had grown 7.5 percent a year over the prior five years, and were expected to grow 6 percent a year in the long run. The stock had a beta of 1.05 and traded for ten times earnings. The Treasury bond rate was 7 percent.
   a. Estimate the P/E ratio for National City.

b. What long-term growth rate is implied in the firm's current PE ratio?

15. The following were the P/E ratios of firms in the aerospace/defense industry with additional data on expected growth and risk:

Company	P/E Ratio	Expected Growth	Beta	Payout
Boeing	17.3	3.5%	1.10	28%
General Dynamics	15.5	11.5%	1.25	40%
General Motors—Hughes	16.5	13.0%	0.85	41%
Grumman	11.4	10.5%	0.80	37%
Lockheed	10.2	9.5%	0.85	37%
Logicon	12.4	14.0%	0.85	11%
Loral	13.3	16.5%	0.75	23%
Martin Marietta	11.0	8.0%	0.85	22%
McDonnell Douglas	22.6	13.0%	1.15	37%
Northrop	9.5	9.0%	1.05	47%
Raytheon	12.1	9.5%	0.75	28%
Rockwell	13.9	11.5%	1.00	38%
Thiokol	8.7	5.5%	0.95	15%
United Industrial	10.4	4.5%	0.70	50%

a. Estimate the average and median P/E ratios. What, if anything, would these averages tell you?

b. An analyst concludes that Thiokol is undervalued because its P/E ratio is lower than the industry average. Under what conditions is this statement true? Would you agree with it here?

c. Using the PEG ratio, assess whether Thiokol is undervalued. What are you assuming about the relationship between value and growth when you use PEG ratios?

d. Using a regression, control for differences across firms on risk, growth, and payout. Specify how you would use this regression to spot under- and overvalued stocks. What are the limitations of this approach?

16. NCH, which markets cleaning chemicals, insecticides, and other products, paid dividends of $2.00 per share on earnings of $4.00 per share. The book value of equity per share was $40.00, and earnings are expected to grow 6 percent a year in the long term. The stock has a beta of

0.85, and sells for $60 per share. The Treasury bond rate is 7 percent.

a. Based on these inputs, estimate the price/book value ratio for NCH.

b. How much would the return on equity have to increase to justify the price/book value ratio at which NCH sells for currently?

17. You are trying to estimate a price per share on an IPO of a company involved in environmental waste disposal. The company has a book value per share of $20 and earned $3.50 per share in the most recent time period. Although it does not pay dividends, the capital expenditures per share were $2.50 higher than depreciation per share in the most recent period, and the firm uses no debt financing. Analysts project that earnings for the company will grow 25 percent a year for the next five years. You have data on other companies in the environmental waste disposal business:

Company	Price	BV/ Share	EPS	DPS	Beta	Exp. Growth
Air & Water	$9.60	$8.48	$0.40	$0.00	1.65	10.5%
Allwaste	$5.40	$3.10	$0.25	$0.00	1.10	18.5%
Browning Ferris	$29.00	$11.50	$1.45	$0.68	1.25	11.0%
Chemical Waste	$9.40	$3.75	$0.45	$0.15	1.15	2.5%
Groundwater	$15.00	$14.45	$0.65	$0.00	1.00	3.0%
Intn'l Tech.	$3.30	$3.35	$0.16	$0.00	1.10	11.0%
Ionics	$48.00	$31.00	$2.20	$0.00	1.00	14.5%
Laidlaw	$6.30	$5.85	$0.40	$0.12	1.15	8.5%
OHM	$16.00	$5.65	$0.60	$0.00	1.15	9.50%
Rollins	$5.10	$3.65	$0.05	$0.00	1.30	1.0%
Safety-Kleen	$14.00	$9.25	$0.80	$0.36	1.15	6.50%

The average debt/equity ratio of these firms is 20 percent, and the tax rate is 40 percent.

a. Estimate the average price/book value ratio for these comparable firms. Would you use this average P/BV ratio to price the IPO?

b. What subjective adjustments would you make to the price/book value ratio for this firm and why?

18. Longs Drug, a large U.S. drugstore chain operating primarily in northern California, had sales per share of $122 on which it reported earnings per share of $2.45 and paid a dividend per share of $1.12. The company is expected to grow 6 percent in the long run, and has a beta of 0.90. The current Treasury bond rate is 7 percent.

a. Estimate the appropriate price/sales multiple for Longs Drug.

b. The stock is currently trading for $34 per share. Assuming the growth rate is estimated correctly, what would the profit margin need to be to justify this price per share?

19. You have been asked to assess whether Walgreen, a drugstore chain, is correctly priced relative to its competitors in the drugstore industry. The following are the price/sales ratios, profit margins, and other relative details of the firms in the drugstore industry.

Company	P/S Ratio	Profit Margin	Payout	Expected Growth	Beta
Arbor Drugs	0.42	3.40%	18%	14.0%	1.05
Big B	0.30	1.90%	14%	23.5%	0.70
Drug Emporium	0.10	0.60%	0%	27.5%	0.90
Fay's	0.15	1.30%	37%	11.5%	0.90
Genovese	0.18	1.70%	26%	10.5%	0.80
Longs Drug	0.30	2.00%	46%	6.0%	0.90
Perry Drugs	0.12	1.30%	0%	12.5%	1.10
Rite-Aid	0.33	3.20%	37%	10.5%	0.90
Walgreen	*0.60*	*2.70%*	*31%*	*13.5%*	*1.15*

Based entirely on a subjective analysis, do you think that Walgreen is overpriced because its price/sales ratio is the highest in the industry? If it is not, how would you rationalize its value?

20. Time Warner is considering a sale of its publishing division. The division had earnings EBITDA of $550 million in the most recent year (depreciation was $150 million), growing at an estimated 5 percent a year (you can assume that depreciation grows at the same rate). The return on capital in the division is 15 percent, and the corporate tax rate is 40 percent. If the cost of capital for the division is 9 percent, estimate the following:

a. Value/FCFF multiple.

b. Value/EBIT multiple.

c. Value/EBITDA multiple.

APPENDIX 1

BASIC STATISTICS

The problem that we face in financial analysis today is not having too little information but too much. Making sense of large and often contradictory information is part of what we are called on to do when analyzing companies. Basic statistics can make this job easier. In this appendix, we consider the most fundamental tools available in data analysis.

SUMMARIZING DATA

Large amounts of data are often compressed into more easily assimilated summaries, which provide the user with a sense of the content, without overwhelming him or her with too many numbers. There are a number of ways data can be presented. We will consider two here—one is to present the data in a distribution, and the other is to provide summary statistics that capture key aspects of the data.

Data Distributions

When presented with thousands of data items, you can break the numbers down into individual values (or ranges of values) and indicate the number of individual data items that take on each value or range of values. This is called a *frequency distribution*. If the data can only take on specific values, as is the case when we record the number of goals scored in a soccer game, you get a *discrete distribution*. When the data can take on any value within the range, as is the case with income or market capitalization, it is called a *continuous distribution*.

The advantages of presenting the data in a distribution are twofold. For one thing, you can summarize even the largest data sets into one distribution and get a measure of what values occur most frequently and the range of high and low values. The second is that the distribution can resemble one of the many common ones about which we know a great deal in statistics. Consider, for instance, the distribution that we tend to draw on the most in analysis: the normal distribution, illustrated in Figure A1.1.

A normal distribution is symmetric, has a peak centered around the middle of the distribution, and tails that are not fat and stretch to include infinite positive or negative values. Not all distributions are symmetric, though. Some are weighted toward extreme positive values and are called positively skewed, and some toward extreme negative values and are considered negatively skewed. Figure A1.2 illustrates positively and negatively skewed distributions.

Summary Statistics

The simplest way to measure the key characteristics of a data set is to estimate the summary statistics for the data. For a data series, $X_1, X_2, X_3, \ldots X_n$, where n is

Figure A1.1   Normal Distribution

Figure A1.2   Skewed Distributions

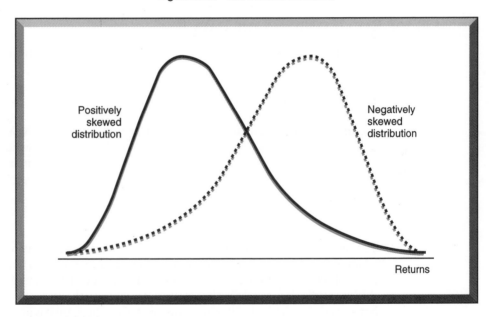

Positively
skewed
distribution

Negatively
skewed
distribution

Returns

the number of observations in the series, the most widely used summary statistics are as follows:

• The mean (μ), which is the average of all of the observations in the data series.

$$Mean = \mu_X = \frac{\sum\limits_{j=1}^{j=n} X_j}{n}$$

- The median, which is the midpoint of the series; half the data in the series is higher than the median and half is lower.
- The variance, which is a measure of the spread in the distribution around the mean and is calculated by first summing up the squared deviations from the mean, and then dividing by either the number of observations (if the data represent the entire population) or by this number, reduced by one (if the data represent a sample).

$$\text{Variance} = \sigma_X^2 = \sum_{j=1}^{j=n} \frac{(X_j - \mu)^2}{n - 1}$$

The standard deviation is the square root of the variance.

The mean and the standard deviation are called the first two moments of any data distribution. A normal distribution can be entirely described by just these two moments; in other words, the mean and the standard deviation of a normal distribution suffice to characterize it completely. If a distribution is not symmetric, the skewness is the third moment that describes both the direction and the magnitude of the asymmetry and the kurtosis (the fourth moment) measures the fatness of the tails of the distribution relative to a normal distribution.

LOOKING FOR RELATIONSHIPS IN THE DATA

When there are two series of data, there are a number of statistical measures that can be used to capture how the series move together over time.

Correlations and Covariances

The two most widely used measures of how two variables move together (or do not) are the correlation and the covariance. For two data series, $X(X_1, X_2,)$ and $Y(Y, Y \ldots)$, the covariance provides a measure of the degree to which they move together and is estimated by taking the product of the deviations from the mean for each variable in each period.

$$\text{Covariance} = \sigma_{XY} = \sum_{j=1}^{j=n} \frac{(X_j - \mu_X)(Y_j - \mu_Y)}{n - 2}$$

The sign on the covariance indicates the type of relationship the two variables have. A positive sign indicates that they move together and a negative sign that they move in opposite directions. Although the covariance increases with the strength of the relationship, it is still relatively difficult to draw judgments on the strength of the relationship between two variables by looking at the covariance because it is not standardized.

The correlation is the standardized measure of the relationship between two variables. It can be computed from the covariance:

$$\text{Correlation} = \rho_{XY} = \sigma_{XY}/\sigma_X \sigma_Y = \frac{\sum_{j=1}^{j=n} (X_j - \mu_X)(Y_j - \mu_Y)}{\sqrt{\sum_{j=1}^{j=n} (X_j - \mu_X)^2} \sqrt{\sum_{j=1}^{j=n} (Y_j - \mu_Y)^2}}$$

The correlation can never be greater than one or less than negative one. A correlation close to zero indicates that the two variables are unrelated. A positive correlation indicates that the two variables move together, and the relationship is stronger as the correlation gets closer to one. A negative correlation indicates the two variables move in opposite directions, and that relationship gets stronger as the correlation gets closer to negative one. Two variables that are perfectly positively correlated ($\rho_{XY} = 1$) essentially move in perfect proportion in the same direction, whereas two variables that are perfectly negatively correlated move in perfect proportion in opposite directions.

Regressions

A simple *regression* is an extension of the correlation/covariance concept. It attempts to explain one variable, the dependent variable, using the other variable, the independent variable.

Scatter Plots and Regression Lines

Keeping with statistical tradition, let Y be the dependent variable and X be the independent variable. If the two variables are plotted against each other with each pair of observations representing a point on the graph, you have a scatterplot, with Y on the vertical axis and X on the horizontal axis.

In a simple regression, we attempt to fit a straight line through the points that best fits the data. In its simplest form, this is accomplished by finding a line that minimizes

A Scatter Plot

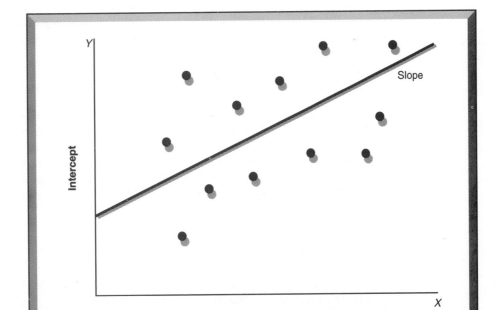

the sum of the squared deviations of the points from the line. Consequently, it is called an *ordinary least squares* (OLS) regression. When such a line is fit, two parameters emerge—one is the point at which the line cuts through the Y-axis, called the intercept of the regression, and the other is the slope of the regression line:

$$Y = a + bX$$

The slope (b) of the regression measures both the direction and the magnitude of the relationship between the dependent variable (Y) and the independent variable (X). When the two variables are positively correlated, the slope will also be positive, whereas when the two variables are negatively correlated, the slope will be negative. The magnitude of the slope of the regression can be read as follows: For every unit increase in the dependent variable (X), the independent variable will change by b (slope).

Estimating Regression Parameters
Although there are statistical packages that allow us to input data and get the regression parameters as output, it is worth looking at how they are estimated in the first place. The slope of the regression line is a logical extension of the covariance concept introduced in the last section. In fact, the slope is estimated using the covariance:

$$\text{Slope of the Regression} = b = \frac{\text{Covariance}_{XY}}{\text{Variance of } X} = \frac{\sigma_{XY}}{\sigma_X^2}$$

The intercept (a) of the regression can be read in a number of ways. One interpretation is that it is the value that Y will have when X is zero. Another is more straightforward and is based on how it is calculated. It is the difference between the average value of Y, and the slope-adjusted value of X.

$$\text{Intercept of the Regression} = a = \mu_Y - b\mu_X$$

Regression parameters are always estimated with some error or statistical noise, partly because the relationship between the variables is not perfect and partly because we estimate them from samples of data. This noise is captured in a couple of statistics. One is the R^2 of the regression, which measures the proportion of the variability in the dependent variable (Y) that is explained by the independent variable (X). It is also a direct function of the correlation between the variables:

$$R^2 \text{ of the Regression} = \text{Correlation}_{YX}^2 = \rho_{YX}^2 = \frac{b^2 \sigma_X^2}{\sigma_Y^2}$$

An R^2 value close to one indicates a strong relationship between the two variables, though the relationship may be either positive or negative. Another measure of noise in a regression is the standard error, which measures the "spread" around each of the two parameters estimated—the intercept and the slope. Each parameter has an associated standard error, which is calculated from the data:

$$\text{Standard Error of Intercept} = \text{SE}_a = \sqrt{\frac{\left(\sum_{j=1}^{j=n} X_j^2\right)\left(\sum_{j=1}^{j=n} (Y_j - bX_j)^2\right)}{(n-2)\sum_{j=1}^{j=n} (X_j - \mu_X)^2}}$$

$$\text{Standard Error of Slope} = \text{SE}_b = \sqrt{\frac{\left(\sum_{j=1}^{j=n} (Y_j - bX_j)^2\right)}{(n-2)\sum_{j=1}^{j=n} (X_j - \mu_X)^2}}$$

If we make the additional assumption that the intercept and slope estimates are normally distributed, the parameter estimate and the standard error can be combined to get a t-statistic that measures whether the relationship is statistically significant.

$$t\text{-Statistic for Intercept} = a/\text{SE}_a$$
$$t\text{-Statistic from Slope} = b/\text{SE}_b$$

For samples with more than 120 observations, a t-statistic greater than 1.95 indicates that the variable is significantly different from zero with 95% certainty, whereas a statistic greater than 2.33 indicates the same with 99% certainty. For smaller samples, the t-statistic has to be larger to have statistical significance.[1]

Using Regressions
Although regressions mirror correlation coefficients and covariances in showing the strength of the relationship between two variables, they also serve another useful purpose. The regression equation described in the last section can be used to estimate predicted values for the dependent variable, based on assumed or actual values for the independent variable. In other words, for any given Y, we can estimate what X should be:

$$X = a + b(Y)$$

How good are these predictions? That will depend entirely on the strength of the relationship measured in the regression. When the independent variable explains a high proportion of the variation in the dependent variable (R^2 is high), the predictions will be precise. When the R^2 is low, the predictions will have a much wider range.

From Simple to Multiple Regressions
The regression that measures the relationship between two variables becomes a multiple regression when it is extended to include more than one independent variable ($X1$, $X2$, $X3$, $X4$ ...) in trying to explain the dependent variable Y. Although the

---

[1]The actual values that t-statistics need to take can be found in a table for the t distribution, which can be found in any standard statistics book or software package.

graphical presentation becomes more difficult, the multiple regression yields output that is an extension of the simple regression.

$$Y = a + bX1 + cX2 + dX3 + eX4$$

The R^2 still measures the strength of the relationship, but an additional R^2 statistic called the adjusted R^2 is computed to counter the bias that will induce the R^2 to keep increasing as more independent variables are added to the regression. If there are k independent variables in the regression, the adjusted R^2 is computed as follows:

$$R^2 = \frac{\left(\sum_{j=1}^{j=n} (Y_j - bX_j)^2 \right)}{n - 1}$$

$$\text{Adjusted } R^2 = \frac{\left(\sum_{j=1}^{j=n} (Y_j - bX_j)^2 \right)}{n - k}$$

Multiple regressions are powerful tools that allow us to examine the determinants of any variable.

Regression Assumptions and Constraints

Both the simple and multiple regressions described in this section assume linear relationships between the dependent and independent variables. If the relationship is not linear, we have two choices. One is to transform the variables by taking the square, square root, or natural log (for example) of the values and hope that the relationship between the transformed variables is more linear. The other is to run nonlinear regressions that attempt to fit a curve (rather than a straight line) through the data.

There are implicit statistical assumptions behind every multiple regression that we ignore at our own peril. For the coefficients on the individual independent variables to make sense, the independent variables need to be uncorrelated with each other, a condition that is often difficult to meet. When independent variables are correlated with each other, the statistical hazard that is created is called *multicollinearity*. In its presence, the coefficients on independent variables can take on unexpected signs (positive instead of negative, for instance) and unpredictable values. There are simple diagnostic statistics that allow us to measure how far the data may be deviating from our ideal when running a multiple regression.

CONCLUSION

In the course of trying to make sense of large amounts of contradictory data, there are useful statistical tools on which we can draw. Although we have looked at the only most basic ones in this appendix, there are far more sophisticated and powerful tools available.

APPENDIX 2

FINANCIAL STATEMENTS

Financial statements provide the fundamental information that we use to analyze and answer corporate finance questions. Therefore, it is important that we understand the principles governing these statements by looking at three questions:

- How valuable are the assets of a firm? Assets can come in several forms: those with long lives, such as land and buildings; those with shorter lives, such as inventory; and intangible assets that still produce revenues for the firm, such as patents and trademarks.
- How did the firm raise the funds to finance these assets? In acquiring them, firms can use the funds of the owners (equity) or borrowed money (debt), and the mix is likely to change as the assets age.
- How profitable are these assets? A good investment, we argued, is one that makes a return greater than the hurdle rate. To evaluate whether the investments that a firm has already made are good, we need to estimate the returns being made on these investments.

We will look at the way accountants would answer these questions and why the answers might be different when doing financial analysis. Some of these differences can be traced to the differences in objectives—accountants try to measure the current standing and immediate past performance of a firm, whereas financial analysis is much more forward-looking.

THE BASIC ACCOUNTING STATEMENTS

There are three basic accounting statements that summarize information about a firm. The first is the *balance sheet,* shown in Figure A2.1, which summarizes the assets owned by a firm, the value of these assets, and the mix of debt and equity used to finance these assets at a point in time.

The next is the *income statement,* shown in Figure A2.2, which provides information on the revenues and expenses of the firm and the resulting income made during a period. The period can be a quarter (if it is a quarterly income statement) or a year (if it is an annual report).

Finally, there is the *statement of cash flows,* shown in Figure A2.3, which specifies the sources and uses of cash of the firm from operating, investing, and financing activities during a period. The statement of cash flows can be viewed as an attempt to explain how much the cash flows during a period were and why the cash balance changed during the period.

Figure A2.1   The Balance Sheet

ASSET MEASUREMENT AND VALUATION

When analyzing any firm, we would like to know the types of assets that it owns, the values of these assets and the degree of uncertainty about these values. Accounting statements do a reasonably good job of categorizing the assets owned by a firm, a partial job of assessing the values of these assets, and a poor job of reporting uncertainty about asset values. In this section, we will begin by looking at the accounting principles underlying asset categorization and measurement and the limitations of financial statements in providing relevant information about assets.

Accounting Principles Underlying Asset Measurement

The accounting view of asset value is to a great extent grounded in the notion of *historical cost,* which is the original cost of the asset, adjusted upward for improvements made to the asset since purchase and downward for loss in value associated with the aging of the asset. This historical cost is called the *book value.* Although the generally accepted accounting principles for valuing an asset vary across different kinds of assets, three principles underlie the way assets are valued in accounting statements.

- *An abiding belief in book value as the best estimate of value*   Accounting estimates of asset value begin with the book value. Unless a substantial reason is given to do otherwise, accountants view the historical cost as the best estimate of the value of an asset.

Figure A2.2 Income Statement

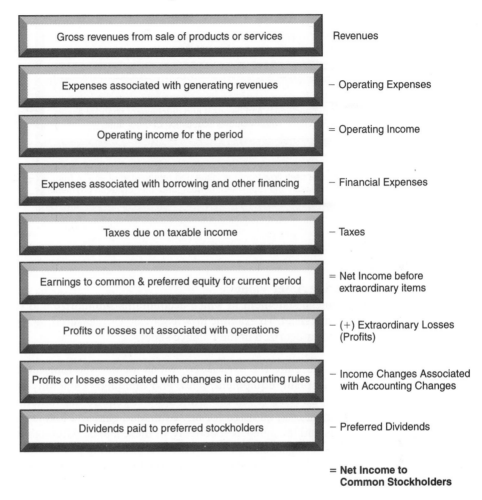

- *A distrust of market or estimated value*   When a current market value exists for an asset that is different from the book value, accounting convention seems to view it with suspicion. The market price of an asset is often viewed as both much too volatile and too easily manipulated to be used as an estimate of value for an asset. This suspicion runs even deeper when values are estimated for an asset based on expected future cash flows.

- *A preference for underestimating value rather than overestimating it*   When there is more than one approach to valuing an asset, accounting convention takes the view that the more conservative (lower) estimate of value should be used rather than the less conservative (higher) estimate of value.

Figure A2.3 Statement of Cash Flows

Measuring Asset Value

The financial statement in which accountants summarize and report asset value is the balance sheet. To examine how asset value is measured, let us begin with the way assets are categorized in the balance sheet.

- First, there are the *fixed assets,* which include the long-term assets of the firm, such as plant, equipment, land, and buildings. Generally accepted accounting principles (GAAP) in the United States require the valuation of fixed assets at historical cost, adjusted for any estimated gain and loss in value from improvements and the aging, respectively, of these assets. Although in theory the adjustments for aging should reflect the loss of earning power of the asset as it ages, in practice they are much more a product of accounting rules and convention, and these adjustments are called *depreciation*. Depreciation methods can very broadly be categorized into straight line (where the loss in asset value is assumed to be the same every year over its lifetime) and accelerated (where the asset loses more value in the earlier years and less in the later years).

- Next, we have the short-term assets of the firm, including inventory (such as raw materials, work in progress, and finished goods), receivables (summarizing moneys owed to the firm), and cash; these are categorized as *current assets*. It is in this category accountants are most amenable to the use of market value. Accounts receivable are generally recorded as the amount owed to the firm based on the billing at the time of the credit sale. The only major accounting issue is when the firm has to recognize accounts receivable that are not collectible; some firms create provisions for bad debt whereas others record them as they occur. There is some discretion allowed to firms in the valuation of inventory, with three commonly used approaches—first-in, first-out (FIFO), where the inventory is valued based on the cost of material bought latest in the year; last-in, first-out (LIFO), where inventory is valued based on the cost of material bought earliest in the year; and weighted average, which uses the average cost over the year.

- In the category of *investments and marketable securities,* accountants consider investments made by firms in the securities or assets of other firms and other marketable securities, including Treasury bills or bonds. The way these assets are valued depends on the way the investment is categorized and the motive behind the investment. In general, an investment in the securities of another firm can be categorized as a minority, passive investment; a minority, active investment; or a majority, active investment. If the securities or assets owned in another firm represent less than 20 percent of the overall ownership of that firm, an investment is treated as a minority, passive investment. These investments have an acquisition value, which represents what the firm originally paid for the securities, and often a market value. For investments held to maturity, the valuation is at acquisition value, and interest or dividends from this investment are shown in the income statement under net interest expenses. Investments that are available for sale or trading investments are shown at current market value. If the securities or assets owned in another firm represent between 20 percent and 50 percent of the overall ownership of that firm, an investment is treated as a minority, active investment. Although these investments have an initial acquisition value, a proportional share (based on ownership proportion) of the net income and losses made by the firm in which the investment was made is used to adjust the acquisition cost. In addition, the dividends received from the investment reduce the acquisition cost. This approach to valuing investments is called the equity approach. If the securities or assets owned in another firm represent more than 50 percent of the overall ownership of that firm, an investment is treated as a majority active investment.[1] In this case, the investment is no longer shown as a financial investment but is replaced by the assets and liabilities of the firm in which the investment was made. This approach leads to a consolidation of the balance sheets of the two firms, where the assets and liabilities of the two firms are merged and presented as one balance sheet. The share of the equity in the subsidiary that is owned by other investors is shown as a minority interest on the liability side of the balance sheet.

- Finally, we have what is loosely categorized as *intangible assets.* These include patents and trademarks that presumably will create future earnings and cash flows and also uniquely accounting assets, such as goodwill, that arise because of acquisitions made by the firm. Patents and trademarks are valued differently depending on whether they are generated internally or acquired. When patents and trademarks are generated from internal sources, such as research, the costs incurred in developing the asset are expensed in that period, even though the asset might have a life of several accounting periods. Thus, the intangible asset is not usually valued in the balance sheet of the firm. In contrast, when an intangible asset is acquired from an external party, it is treated as an asset. When a firm

---

[1]Firms have evaded the requirements of consolidation by keeping their share of ownership in other firms below 50 percent.

acquires another firm, the purchase price is first allocated to tangible assets and then allocated to any intangible assets, such as patents or trade names. Any residual becomes goodwill. Although accounting standards in the United States gave firms latitude in how they dealt with goodwill until recently, the current requirement is much more stringent. All firms that do acquisitions and pay more than book value have to record goodwill as assets, and this goodwill has to be written off, if the accountants deem it to be impaired.[2]

MEASURING FINANCING MIX

The second set of questions that we would like to answer (and accounting statements to shed some light on) relates to the current value and subsequently the mixture of debt and equity used by the firm. The bulk of the information about these questions is provided on the liability side of the balance sheet and the footnotes.

Accounting Principles Underlying Liability and Equity Measurement

Just as with the measurement of asset value, the accounting categorization of liabilities and equity is governed by a set of fairly rigid principles. The first is a *strict categorization of financing into either a liability or equity* based on the nature of the obligation. For an obligation to be recognized as a liability, it must meet three requirements:

- It must be expected to lead to a future cash outflow or the loss of a future cash inflow at some specified or determinable date.
- The firm cannot avoid the obligation.
- The transaction giving rise to the obligation has happened already.

In keeping with the earlier principle of conservatism in estimating asset value, accountants recognize as liabilities only cash flow obligations that cannot be avoided.

The second principle is that the value of both liabilities and equity in a firm are *better estimated using historical costs* with accounting adjustments, rather than with expected future cash flows or market value. The process by which accountants measure the value of liabilities and equities is inextricably linked to the way they value assets. Because assets are primarily valued at historical cost or at book value, both debt and equity also get measured primarily at book value. In what follows, we will examine the accounting measurement of both liabilities and equity.

Measuring the Value of Liabilities

Accountants categorize liabilities into current liabilities, long-term debt, and long-term liabilities that are neither debt nor equity; the last category includes leases, underfunded pension and health care obligations, and deferred taxes.

---

[2]To make this judgment, accountants have to value the acquired company at regular intervals and compare the value that they get to the price paid. If the value is substantially lower than the price, the company has to write off an equivalent portion of the goodwill.

- *Current liabilities* include all obligations that the firm has coming due in the next accounting period. These generally include accounts payable (representing credit received from suppliers and other vendors to the firm), short-term borrowing (representing short-term loans taken to finance the operations or current asset needs of the business), and the short-term portion of long-term borrowing (representing the portion of the long-term debt or bonds that is coming due in the next year). As with current assets, these items are usually recorded at close to their current market value.

- *Long-term debt* for firms can take one of two forms: a long-term loan from a bank or other financial institution, or a long-term bond issued to financial markets, in which case the creditors are the investors in the bond. Accountants measure the value of long-term debt by looking at the present value of payments due on the loan or bond at the time of the borrowing. For bank loans, this will be equal to the nominal value of the loan. With bonds, however, there are three possibilities. When bonds are issued at par value, for instance, the value of the long-term debt is generally measured in terms of the nominal obligation created in terms of principal (face value) due on the borrowing. When bonds are issued at a premium or a discount on par value, the bonds are recorded at the issue price, but the premium or discount to the face value is amortized over the life of the bond. In all these cases, the book value of debt is unaffected by changes in interest rates during the life of the loan or bond.

- *Lease obligations* include obligations to lessors on assets that firms have leased. There are two ways of accounting for leases. In an operating lease, the lessor (or owner) transfers only the right to use the property to the lessee. At the end of the lease period, the lessee returns the property to the lessor. Because the lessee does not assume the risk of ownership, the lease expense is treated as an operating expense in the income statement, and the lease does not affect the balance sheet. In a capital lease, the lessee assumes some of the risks of ownership and enjoys some of the benefits. Consequently, the lease, when signed, is recognized both as an asset and as a liability (for the lease payments) on the balance sheet. The firm gets to claim depreciation each year on the asset and also deducts the interest expense component of the lease payment each year.

- In a *pension plan,* the firm agrees to provide certain benefits to its employees, either by specifying a defined contribution (wherein a fixed contribution is made to the plan each year by the employer, without any promises as to the benefits to be delivered in the plan) or a defined benefit (wherein the employer promises to pay a certain benefit to the employee). In the latter case, the employer has to put sufficient money into the plan each period to meet the defined benefits. A pension fund whose assets exceed its liabilities is an overfunded plan, whereas one whose assets are less than its liabilities is an underfunded plan. Disclosures to that effect have to be included in financial statements, generally in the footnotes.

- Firms often use different methods of accounting for tax and financial reporting purposes, leading to a question of how tax liabilities should be reported. Because accelerated depreciation and favorable inventory valuation methods for tax accounting purposes lead to a deferral of taxes, the computed taxes on the income reported in the financial statements will often be much greater than the actual tax paid. In some cases, though, the reverse can be true. The same principles of matching expenses to income that underlie accrual accounting require that the *deferred income tax* be recognized in the financial statements as a liability (if the firm underpaid taxes) or as an asset (if the firm overpaid taxes).

Measuring the Value of Equity

The accounting measure of equity is a historical cost measure. The value of equity shown on the balance sheet reflects the original proceeds received by the firm when it issued the equity, augmented by any earnings made since then (or reduced by losses, if any) and reduced by any dividends paid out during the period. A sustained period of negative earnings can make the book value of equity negative. In addition, any unrealized gain or loss in marketable securities that are classified as available-for-sale is shown as an increase or decrease in the book value of equity in the balance sheet.

When companies buy back stock for short periods with the intent of reissuing the stock or using it to cover option exercises, they are allowed to show the repurchased stock as *treasury stock,* which reduces the book value of equity. Firms are not allowed to keep treasury stock on the books for extended periods and have to reduce their book value of equity and the number of shares outstanding by the value of repurchased stock in the case of actions such as stock buybacks. Because these buybacks occur at the current market price, they can result in significant reductions in the book value of equity.

Accounting rules still do not seem to have come to grips with the effect of warrants and equity options (such as those granted by many firms to management) on the book value of equity. If warrants are issued to financial markets, the proceeds from this issue will show up as part of the book value of equity. In the far more prevalent case, where options are given or granted to management, there is no effect on the book value of equity. When the options are exercised, the cash inflows do ultimately show up in the book value of equity, and there is a corresponding increase in the number of shares outstanding. The same point can be made about convertible bonds, which are treated as debt until conversion, at which point they become part of equity.

As a final point on equity, accounting rules still seem to consider preferred stock, with its fixed dividend, as equity or near equity, largely because of the fact that preferred dividends can be deferred or accumulated without the risk of default. Preferred stock is valued on the balance sheet at its original issue price, with any accumulated unpaid dividends added on. To the extent that there can still be a loss of control in the firm (as opposed to bankruptcy), we would argue that preferred stock shares almost as many characteristics with unsecured debt as it does with equity.

MEASURING EARNINGS AND PROFITABILITY

How profitable is a firm? What did it earn on the assets in which it invested? These are fundamental questions we would like financial statements to answer. Accountants use the income statement to provide information about a firm's operating activities over a specific time period. In terms of our description of the firm, the income statement is designed to measure the earnings from assets in place.

Accounting Principles Underlying Measurement of Earnings and Profitability

Two primary principles underlie the measurement of accounting earnings and profitability. The first is the principle of accrual accounting. In accrual accounting, the revenue from selling a good or service is recognized in the period in which the good is sold or the service is performed (in whole or substantially). A corresponding effort is made on the expense side to match expenses to revenues.[3] This is in contrast to cash accounting, wherein revenues are recognized when payment is received and expenses are recorded when they are paid.

The second principle is the categorization of expenses into operating, financing, and capital expenses. Operating expenses are expenses that at least in theory provide benefits only for the current period; the cost of labor and materials expended to create products that are sold in the current period is a good example. Financing expenses are expenses arising from the nonequity financing used to raise capital for the business; the most common example is interest expenses. Capital expenses are expected to generate benefits over multiple periods; for instance, the cost of buying land and buildings is treated as a capital expense.

Operating expenses are subtracted from revenues in the current period to arrive at a measure of operating earnings from the firm. Financing expenses are subtracted from operating earnings to estimate earnings to equity investors or net income. Capital expenses are written off over their useful life (in terms of generating benefits) as depreciation or amortization.

Measuring Accounting Earnings and Profitability

Because income can be generated from a number of different sources, accounting principles require that income statements be classified into four sections: income from continuing operations, income from discontinued operations, extraordinary gains or losses, and adjustments for changes in accounting principles.

Accounting principles require publicly traded companies to use accrual accounting to record earnings from continuing operations. Although accrual accounting is straightforward in firms that produce goods and sell them, there are special cases in which accrual accounting can be complicated by the nature of the product or service being offered. For instance, firms that enter into long-term contracts with their customers, for instance, are allowed to recognize revenue on the basis of the percentage of the contract that is completed. As the revenue is recognized on a percentage of completion basis, a corresponding proportion of the expense is also recognized. When there is considerable uncertainty about the capacity of the buyer of a good or service to pay for a service, the firm providing the good or service may recognize the income only when it collects portions of the selling price under the installment method.

Operating expenses should reflect only those expenses that create revenues in the current period. In practice, however, a number of expenses are classified as operating expenses that do not meet this test. The first is depreciation and amortization. Although the notion that capital expenditures should be written off over multiple

---

[3]If a cost (such as an administrative cost) cannot be easily linked with a particular revenues, it is usually recognized as an expense in the period in which it is consumed.

periods is reasonable, the accounting depreciation that is computed on the original historical cost often bears little resemblance to the actual economic depreciation. The second expense is research and development expenses, which accounting standards in the United States classify as operating expenses but which clearly provide benefits over multiple periods. The rationale used for this classification is that the benefits cannot be counted on or easily quantified. The third is operating lease expenses, which are closer to being financial than operating expenses.

Much of financial analysis is built around the expected future earnings of a firm, and many of these forecasts start with the current earnings. It is therefore important that we know how much of these earnings come from the ongoing operations of the firm and how much can be attributed to unusual or extraordinary events that are unlikely to recur on a regular basis. Nonrecurring items include the following:

1. *Unusual or infrequent items,* such as gains or losses from the divestiture of an asset or division and write-offs or restructuring costs. Companies sometimes include such items as part of operating expenses. As an example, in 1997 Boeing took a write-off of $1,400 million to adjust the value of assets it acquired in its acquisition of McDonnell Douglas, and it showed this as part of operating expenses.

2. *Extraordinary items,* which are defined as events that are unusual in nature, infrequent in occurrence, and material in impact. Examples include the accounting gain associated with refinancing high-coupon debt with lower-coupon debt and gains or losses from marketable securities that are held by the firm.

3. *Losses associated with discontinued operations,* which measure both the loss from the phase-out period and the estimated loss on the sale of the operations. To qualify, however, the operations have to be separable from the firm.

4. *Gains or losses associated with accounting changes,* which measure earnings changes created by accounting changes made voluntarily by the firm (such as a change in inventory valuation and change in reporting period) and accounting changes mandated by new accounting standards.

Measures of Profitability
Although the income statement allows us to estimate how profitable a firm is in absolute terms, it is just as important that we gauge the profitability of the firm in relative returns. The simplest and most useful gauge of profitability is relative to the capital employed to get a rate of return on investment. This can be done either from the viewpoint of just the equity investors or by looking at the entire firm.

I. Return on Assets (ROA) and Return on Capital (ROC)
The return on assets (ROA) of a firm measures its operating efficiency in generating profits from its assets, prior to the effects of financing.

$$\text{ROA} = \frac{\text{EBIT}(1 - \text{Tax Rate})}{\text{Total Assets}}$$

Earnings before interest and taxes (EBIT) is the accounting measure of operating income from the income statement, and total assets refers to the assets as measured using accounting rules, that is, using book value for most assets. Alternatively, ROA can be written as

$$\text{ROA} = \frac{\text{Net Income} + \text{Interest Expenses} (1 - \text{Tax Rate})}{\text{Total Assets}}$$

By separating the financing effects from the operating effects, the ROA provides a cleaner measure of the true return on these assets.

ROA can also be computed on a pretax basis with no loss of generality, by using the EBIT and not adjusting for taxes:

$$\text{Pretax ROA} = \frac{\text{EBIT}}{\text{Total Assets}}$$

This measure is useful if the firm or division is being evaluated for purchase by an acquirer with a different tax rate or structure.

A more useful measure of return relates the operating income to the capital invested in the firm, where capital is defined as the sum of the book value of debt and equity. This is the return on capital (ROC). When a substantial portion of the liabilities is either current (such as accounts payable) or non–interest-bearing, this approach provides a better measure of the true return earned on capital employed in the business.

$$\text{After-Tax ROC} = \frac{\text{EBIT}(1 - t)}{\text{BV of Debt} + \text{BV of Equity}}$$

$$\text{Pretax ROC} = \frac{\text{EBIT}}{\text{BV of Debt} + \text{BV of Equity}}$$

where BV = book value.

The ROC of a firm can be written as a function of its operating profit margin and its capital turnover ratio:

$$\text{After-Tax ROC} = \frac{\text{EBIT}(1 - t)}{\text{BV of Capital}} = \frac{\text{EBIT}(1 - t)}{\text{Sales}} \times \frac{\text{Sales}}{\text{BV of Capital}}$$
$$= \text{After-Tax Operating Margin} \times \text{Capital Turnover Ratio}$$

$$\text{Pretax ROC} = \text{Pretax Operating Margin} \times \text{Capital Turnover Ratio}$$

Thus, a firm can arrive at a high ROC by either increasing its profit margin or more efficiently using its capital to increase sales. There are likely to be competitive and technological constraints on increasing sales, but firms still have some freedom within these constraints to choose the mix of profit margin and capital turnover that maximizes their ROC. The return on capital varies widely across firms in different businesses, largely as a consequence of differences in profit margins and capital turnover ratios.

II. Return on Equity (ROE)

Although ROC measures the profitability of the overall firm, the return on equity (ROE) examines profitability from the perspective of the equity investor by relating profits to the equity investor (net profit after taxes and interest expenses) to the book value of the equity investment.

$$\text{ROE} = \frac{\text{Net Income}}{\text{Book Value of Common Equity}}$$

Because preferred stockholders have a different type of claim on the firm than common stockholders, the net income should be estimated after preferred dividends, and the book value of common equity should not include the book value of preferred stock.

SUMMARY

Financial statements remain the primary source of information for most investors and analysts. There are differences, however, in how accounting and financial analysis approach answering a number of key questions about the firm.

The first question that we examined related to the nature and the value of the assets owned by a firm. The focus on the original price of assets in place (book value) in accounting statements can lead to significant differences between the stated value of these assets and their market value. With growth assets, accounting rules often result in low or no values.

The second question analyzed related to the financing used by a firm to fund its assets. Accounting rules broadly categorize financing into liabilities—short term and long term—and equity. As with assets, there is a bias toward using historical costs in measuring both.

The third issue that we examined was the measurement of profitability. The two principles that govern how profits are measured are accrual accounting and the categorization of expenses into operating, financing, and capital expenses. Operating and financing expenses are shown in income statements. Capital expenditures are depreciated or amortized over several time periods. Accounting standards miscategorize operating leases and R&D expenses as operating expenses (when the former should be categorized as financing expenses and the latter as capital expenses).

APPENDIX 3

TIME VALUE OF MONEY

The simplest tools in finance are often the most powerful. *Present value* is a concept that is intuitively appealing, simple to compute, and has a wide range of applications. It is useful in decision making ranging from simple personal decisions—buying a house, saving for a child's education, and estimating income in retirement—to more complex corporate financial decisions—picking projects in which to invest as well as the right financing mix for these projects.

TIME LINES AND NOTATION

Dealing with cash flows that are at different points in time is made easier using a time line that shows both the timing and the amount of each cash flow in a stream. Thus a cash flow stream of $100 at the end of each of the next four years can be depicted on a time line like the one shown in Figure A3.1.

In the figure, 0 refers to right now. A cash flow that occurs at time 0 is therefore already in present value terms and does not need to be adjusted for time value. A distinction must be made between a *period* of time and a *point* in time. The portion of the time line between 0 and 1 refers to period 1, which in this example is the first year. The cash flow that occurs at time 1 refers to the cash flow that occurs at the end of period 1. Had the cash flows been at the beginning of each year instead of at the end of each year, the time line would have been redrawn as it appears in Figure A3.2.

Note that in present value terms, a cash flow that occurs at the beginning of year two is the equivalent of a cash flow that occurs at the end of year one.

Cash flows can be either positive or negative; positive cash flows are called cash inflows and negative cash flows are called cash outflows. For notational purposes, we

Figure A3.1 A Time Line for Cash Flows: $100 in Cash Flows Received at the End of Each of the Next Four Years

Figure A3.2 A Time Line for Cash Flows: $100 in Cash Received at the Beginning of Each of the Next Four Years

will assume the following for the chapter that follows:

Notation	Stands For
PV	Present value
FV	Future value
CF_t	Cash flow at the end of period t
A	Annuity: constant cash flows over several periods
r	Discount rate
g	Expected growth rate in cash flows
n	Number of years over which cash flows are received or paid

THE INTUITIVE BASIS FOR PRESENT VALUE

There are three reasons why a cash flow in the future is worth less than the same cash flow today.

1. *Individuals prefer present consumption to future consumption* People would have to be offered more in the future to give up present consumption. If the preference for current consumption is strong, individuals will have to be offered much more in terms of future consumption to give up current consumption, a trade-off that is captured by a high "real" rate of return or discount rate. Conversely, when the preference for current consumption is weaker, individuals will settle for much less in terms of future consumption and, by extension, a low real rate of return or discount rate.

2. *When there is monetary inflation, the value of currency decreases over time* The greater the inflation, the greater the difference in value between a nominal cash flow today and the same cash flow in the future.

3. *A promised cash flow might not be delivered for a number of reasons* The promisor might default on the payment, the promisee might not be around to receive payment, or some other contingency might intervene to prevent the promised payment or to reduce it. Any uncertainty (risk) associated with the cash flow in the future reduces the value of the cash flow.

The process by which future cash flows are adjusted to reflect these factors is called discounting, and the magnitude of these factors is reflected in the discount rate. The discount rate can be viewed as a composite of the expected real return (reflecting consumption preferences in the aggregate over the investing population), the expected inflation rate (to capture the deterioration in the purchasing power of the cash flow), and the uncertainty associated with the cash flow.

THE MECHANICS OF TIME VALUE

The process of discounting future cash flows converts them into cash flows in present value terms. Conversely, the process of compounding converts present cash flows into future cash flows. There are five types of cash flows—simple cash flows, annuities, growing annuities, perpetuities, and growing perpetuities—which we discuss next.

Simple Cash Flows

A simple cash flow is a single cash flow in a specified future time period; it can be depicted on a time line as in Figure A3.3.

Figure A3.3   Present Value of a Cash Flow

Cash inflow: CF_t

Discounting converts future cash flow into cash flow today

where CF_t = the cash flow at time t.

This cash flow can be discounted back to the present using a discount rate that reflects the uncertainty of the cash flow. Concurrently, cash flows in the present can be compounded to arrive at an expected future cash flow.

I. Discounting a Simple Cash Flow

Discounting a cash flow converts it into present value terms and enables the user to do several things. First, once cash flows are converted into present value terms, they can be aggregated and compared. Second, if present values are estimated correctly, the user should be indifferent between the future cash flow and the present value of that cash flow. The present value of a cash flow can be written as follows

$$\text{Present Value of Simple Cash Flow} = \frac{CF_t}{(1 + r)^t}$$

where r = discount rate.

Other things remaining equal, the present value of a cash flow will decrease as the discount rate increases and continue to decrease the further into the future the cash flow occurs.

Figure A3.4   Present Value of $500,000 in Ten Years

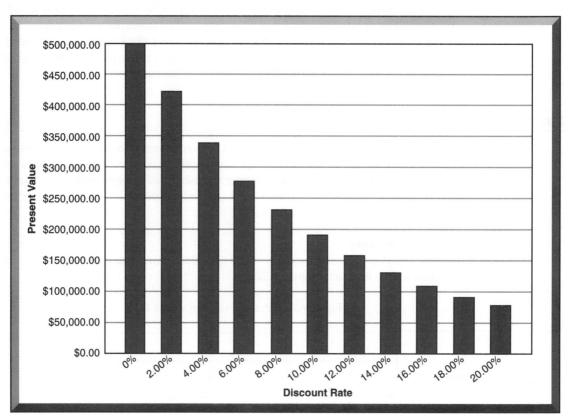

To illustrate this concept, assume that you own are currently leasing your office space and expect to make a lump-sum payment to the owner of the real estate of $500,000 ten years from now. Assume that an appropriate discount rate for this cash flow is 10 percent. The present value of this cash flow can then be estimated:

$$\text{Present Value of Payment} = \frac{\$500,000}{(1.10)^{10}} = \$192,772$$

This present value is a decreasing function of the discount rate, as illustrated in Figure A3.4.

II. Compounding a Cash Flow

Current cash flows can be moved to the future by compounding the cash flow at the appropriate discount rate.

$$\text{Future Value of Simple Cash Flow} = CF_0(1 + r)^t$$

where CF_0 = cash flow now, r = discount rate. Again, the compounding effect increases with both the discount rate and the compounding period.

Table A3.1	Future Values of Investments—Asset Classes		
Holding Period (Years)	**Stocks**	**Treasury Bonds**	**Treasury Bills**
1	$112.40	$105.20	$103.60
5	$179.40	$128.85	$119.34
10	$321.86	$166.02	$142.43
20	$1,035.92	$275.62	$202.86
30	$3,334.18	$457.59	$288.93
40	$10,731.30	$759.68	$411.52

As the length of the holding period is extended, small differences in discount rates can lead to large differences in future value. In a study of returns on stocks and bonds between 1926 and 1997, Ibbotson and Sinquefield found that stocks on the average made 12.4 percent, Treasury bonds made 5.2 percent, and Treasury bills made 3.6 percent. Assuming that these returns continue into the future, Table A3.1 provides the future values of $100 invested in each category at the end of a number of holding periods—one year, five years, ten years, twenty years, thirty years, and forty years.[1]

The differences in future value from investing at these different rates of return are small for short compounding periods (such as one year) but become larger as the compounding period is extended. For instance, with a forty-year time horizon, the future value of investing in stocks, at an average return of 12.4 percent, is more than thirteen times larger than the future value of investing in Treasury bonds at an average return of 5.2 percent and more than twenty-five times the future value of investing in Treasury bills at an average return of 3.6 percent.

III. The Frequency of Discounting and Compounding

The frequency of compounding affects both the future and present values of cash flows. In the examples just discussed, the cash flows were assumed to be discounted and compounded annually—that is, interest payments and income were computed at the end of each year, based on the balance at the beginning of the year. In some cases, however, the interest may be computed more frequently, such as on a monthly or semi-annual basis. In these cases, the present and future values may be very different from those computed on an annual basis; the stated interest rate on an annual basis can deviate significantly from the effective or true interest rate. The effective interest rate can be computed as follows:

$$\text{Effective Interest Rate} = \left(1 + \frac{\text{Stated Annual Interest Rate}}{n} \right)^n - 1$$

where n = number of compounding periods during the year (2 = semi-annual; 12 = monthly). For instance, a 10 percent annual interest rate, if there is semi-annual compounding, works out to an effective interest rate of

$$\text{Effective Interest Rate} = 1.05^2 - 1 = 0.1025 \text{ or } 10.25\%$$

---

[1]See *Stocks, Bonds, Bills and Inflation Yearbook,* 1998, Ibbotson Associates, Chicago.

Table A3.2 **EFFECT OF COMPOUNDING FREQUENCY ON EFFECTIVE INTEREST RATES**

Frequency	Rate	n (Days)	Formula	Effective Annual Rate
Annual	10%	1	0.10	10%
Semi-annual	10%	2	$(1 + 0.10/2)^2 - 1$	10.25%
Monthly	10%	12	$(1 + 0.10/12)^{12} - 1$	10.4713%
Daily	10%	365	$(1 + 0.10/365)^{365} - 1$	10.5156%
Continuous	10%		$\exp^{0.10} - 1$	10.5171%

As compounding becomes continuous, the effective interest rate can be computed as follows

$$\text{Effective Interest Rate} = \exp^r - 1$$

where exp = exponential function and r = stated annual interest rate. Table A3.2 provides the effective rates as a function of the compounding frequency.

As you can see, compounding becomes more frequent, the effective rate increases.

Annuities

An *annuity* is a constant cash flow that occurs at regular intervals for a fixed period of time. Defining A to be the annuity, the time line for an annuity may be drawn as follows:

An annuity can occur at the end of each period, as in this time line, or at the beginning of each period.

I. Present Value of an End-of-the-Period Annuity

The present value of an annuity can be calculated by taking each cash flow and discounting it back to the present and then adding up the present values. Alternatively, a formula can be used in the calculation. In the case of annuities that occur at the end of each period, this formula can be written as

$$PV \text{ of an Annuity} = PV(A, r, n) = A \left[\frac{1 - \dfrac{1}{(1 + r)^n}}{r} \right]$$

where A = annuity, r = discount rate, and n = number of years.

Accordingly, the notation we will use for the present value of an annuity will be $PV(A, r, n)$.

Figure A3.5   Payment of $3,000 at the End of Each of Next Five Years

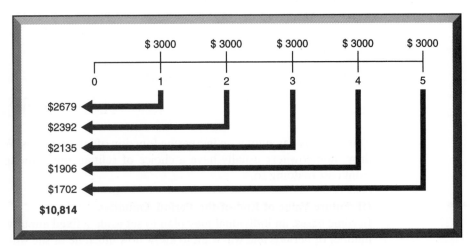

To illustrate, assume again that you are have a choice of buying a copier for $10,000 cash down or paying $3,000 a year, at the end of each year, for five years for the same copier. If the opportunity cost is 12 percent, which would you rather do?

$$PV \text{ of } \$3,000 \text{ Each Year for Next 5 Years} = \$3,000 \left[\frac{1 - \dfrac{1}{(1.12)^5}}{0.12} \right] = \$10,814$$

The present value of the installment payments exceeds the cash-down price; therefore, you would want to pay the $10,000 in cash now.

Alternatively, the present value could have been estimated by discounting each of the cash flows back to the present and aggregating the present values as illustrated in Figure A3.5.

II. Amortization Factors: Annuities Given Present Values

In some cases, the present value of the cash flows is known and the annuity needs to be estimated. This is often the case with home and automobile loans, for example, where the borrower receives the loan today and pays it back in equal monthly installments over an extended period of time. This process of finding an annuity when the present value is known is examined here:

$$\text{Annuity Given Present Value} = A(PV, r, n) = PV \left[\frac{r}{1 - \dfrac{1}{(1 + r)^n}} \right]$$

Suppose you are trying to borrow $200,000 to buy a house with a conventional thirty-year mortgage with monthly payments. The annual percentage rate (APR) on the loan is 8 percent. The monthly payments on this loan can be estimated using the annuity due formula:

$$\text{Monthly Interest Rate on Loan} = \text{APR}/12 = 0.08/12 = 0.0067$$

$$\text{Monthly Payment on Mortgage} = \$200,000 \left[\frac{0.0067}{1 - \dfrac{1}{(1.0067)^{360}}} \right] = \$1,473.11$$

This monthly payment is an increasing function of interest rates. When interest rates drop, homeowners usually have a choice of refinancing, although there is an upfront cost to doing so.

III. Future Value of End-of-the-Period Annuities

In some cases, an individual may plan to set aside a fixed annuity each period for a number of periods and will want to know how much he or she will have at the end of the period. The future value of an end-of-the-period annuity can be calculated as follows:

$$FV \text{ of an Annuity} = \text{FV}(A, r, n) = A \left[\frac{(1 + r)^n - 1}{r} \right]$$

Thus, the notation we will use for the future value of an annuity will be $\text{FV}(A, r, n)$.

Individual retirement accounts (IRAs) allow some taxpayers to set aside up to \$2,000 a year for retirement and exempts the income earned on these accounts from taxation. If an individual starts setting aside money in an IRA early in his or her working life, the value at retirement can be substantially higher than the nominal amount actually put in. For instance, assume that this individual sets aside \$2,000 at the end of every year, starting when she is twenty-five years old, for an expected retirement at the age of sixty-five, and that she expects to make 8 percent a year on her investments. The expected value of the account on her retirement date can be estimated as follows:

$$\text{Expected Value of IRA Set Aside at 65} = \$2,000 \left[\frac{(1.08)^{40} - 1}{0.08} \right] = \$518,113$$

The tax exemption adds substantially to the value because it allows the investor to keep the pretax return of 8 percent made on the IRA investment. If the income had been taxed at, say, 40 percent, the after-tax return would have dropped to 4.8 percent, resulting in a much lower expected value:

$$\text{Expected Value of IRA Set Aside at 65 if Taxed} = \$2,000 \left[\frac{(1.048)^{40} - 1}{0.048} \right]$$
$$= \$230,127$$

As you can see, the available funds at retirement drops by more than 55% as a consequence of the loss of the tax exemption.

IV. Annuity Given Future Value

Individuals or businesses who have a fixed obligation to meet or a target to meet some time in the future need to know how much they should set aside each period to reach this target. If you are given the future value and are looking for an annuity—$A(FV, r, n)$ in terms of notation:

$$\text{Annuity Given Future Value} = A(FV, r, n) = FV\left[\frac{r}{(1 + r)^n - 1}\right]$$

As an example, consider a balloon payment loan. In any *balloon payment loan,* only interest payments are made during the life of the loan, and the principal is paid at the end of the period. Companies that borrow money using balloon payment loans or conventional bonds (which share the same features) often set aside money in sinking funds during the life of the loan to ensure that they have enough at maturity to pay the principal on the loan or the face value of the bonds. Thus, a company with bonds with a face value of $100 million coming due in ten years would need to set aside the following amount each year (assuming an interest rate of 8 percent):

$$\text{Sinking Fund Provision Each Year} = \$100,000,000\left[\frac{0.08}{(1.08)^{10} - 1}\right] = \$6,902,950$$

The company would need to set aside $6.9 million at the end of each year to ensure that there are enough funds ($10 million) to retire the bonds at maturity.

V. Effect of Annuities at the Beginning of Each Year

The annuities considered thus far in this appendix are end-of-the-period cash flows. Both the present and future values will be affected if the cash flows occur at the beginning of each period instead of the end. To illustrate this effect, consider an annuity of $100 at the end of each year for the next four years, with a discount rate of 10 percent.

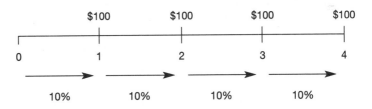

Contrast this with an annuity of $100 at the beginning of each year for the next four years, with the same discount rate.

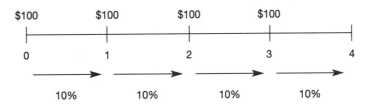

Because the first of these annuities occurs right now and the remaining cash flows take the form of an end-of-the-period annuity over three years, the present value of this annuity can be written as follows:

$$PV \text{ of \$100 at Beginning of Each of Next 4 Years} = \$100 + \$100 \left[\frac{1 - \dfrac{1}{(1.10)^3}}{0.10} \right]$$

$$= \$348.69$$

In general, the present value of a beginning-of-the-period annuity over n years can be written as follows:

$$PV \text{ of Beginning of Period Annuities over } n \text{ Years} = A + A \left[\frac{1 - \dfrac{1}{(1 + r)^{n-1}}}{r} \right]$$

This present value will be higher than the present value of an equivalent annuity at the end of each period.

The future value of a beginning-of-the-period annuity typically can be estimated by allowing for one additional period of compounding for each cash flow:

$$FV \text{ of a Beginning-of-the-Period Annuity} = A(1 + r) \left[\frac{(1 + r)^n - 1}{r} \right]$$

This future value will be higher than the future value of an equivalent annuity at the end of each period.

Consider again the example of an individual who sets aside \$2,000 at the end of each year for the next forty years in an IRA account at 8 percent. The future value of these deposits amounted to \$518,113 at the end of forty years. If the deposits had been made at the beginning of each year instead of the end, the future value would have been higher:

$$\text{Expected Value of IRA (Beginning of Year)} = \$2,000(1.08) \left[\frac{(1.08)^{40} - 1}{0.08} \right]$$

$$= \$559,562$$

As you can see, the gains from making deposits at the beginning of each period can be substantial.

Growing Annuities

A *growing annuity* is a cash flow that grows at a constant rate for a specified period of time. If A is the current cash flow, and g is the expected growth rate, the time line for a growing annuity appears as follows:

Note that to qualify as a growing annuity, the growth rate in each period has to be the same as the growth rate in the prior period.

In most cases, the present value of a growing annuity can be estimated by using the following formula:

$$PV \text{ of a Growing Annuity} = A(1 + g)\left[\frac{1 - \dfrac{(1 + g)^n}{(1 + r)^n}}{r - g} \right]$$

The present value of a growing annuity can be estimated in all cases, but one—where the growth rate is equal to the discount rate. In that case, the present value is equal to the nominal sums of the annuities over the period, without the growth effect.

$$PV \text{ of a Growing Annuity for } n \text{ Years (when } r = g) = nA$$

Note that this formulation works even when the growth rate is greater than the discount rate.[2]

To illustrate a growing annuity, suppose you have the rights to a gold mine for the next twenty years, over which time you plan to extract 5,000 ounces of gold every year. The current price per ounce is $300, but it is expected to increase 3 percent a year. The appropriate discount rate is 10 percent. The present value can be estimated as follows:

$$PV \text{ of Extracted Gold} = \$300 \times 5,000 \times (1.03)\left[\frac{1 - \dfrac{(1.03)^{20}}{(1.10)^{20}}}{0.10 - 0.03} \right] = \$16,145,980$$

The present value of the gold expected to be extracted from this mine is $16.146 million; it is an increasing function of the expected growth rate in gold prices. Figure A3.6 illustrates the present value as a function of the expected growth rate.

Perpetuities

A perpetuity is a constant cash flow at regular intervals forever. The present value of a perpetuity can be written as

$$PV \text{ of Perpetuity} = \frac{A}{r}$$

where A is the perpetuity. The most common example offered for a perpetuity is a console bond. A console bond is a bond that has no maturity and pays a fixed coupon. Assume that you have a 6 percent coupon console bond. The value of this bond, if the interest rate is 9 percent, is as follows:

$$\text{Value of Console Bond} = \$60/0.09 = \$667$$

---

[2]Both the denominator and the numerator in the formula will be negative, yielding a positive present value.

Figure A3.6 Present Value of Extracted Gold as a Function of Growth Rate

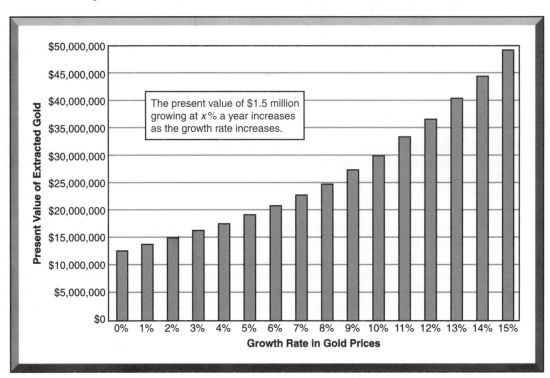

The value of a console bond will be equal to its face value (which is usually $1,000) only if the coupon rate is equal to the interest rate.

Growing Perpetuities

A growing perpetuity is a cash flow that is expected to grow at a constant rate forever. The present value of a growing perpetuity can be written as:

$$PV \text{ of Growing Perpetuity} = \frac{CF_1}{(r - g)}$$

where CF_1 is the expected cash flow next year, g is the constant growth rate, and r is the discount rate. Although a growing perpetuity and a growing annuity share several features, the fact that a growing perpetuity lasts forever puts constraints on the growth rate. It has to be less than the discount rate for this formula to work.

Growing perpetuities are especially useful when valuing equity in publicly traded firms, because they could potentially have perpetual lives. Consider a simple example. In 1992, Southwestern Bell paid dividends per share of $2.73. Its earnings and dividends had grown at 6 percent a year between 1988 and 1992 and were expected to grow at the same rate in the long run. The rate of return required by investors on stocks of equivalent risk was 12.23 percent. With these inputs, we can value the stock

Figure A3.7   Southwestern Bell: Value versus Expected Growth

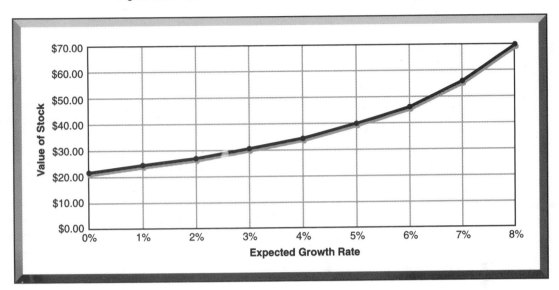

using a perpetual growth model:

$$\text{Value of Stock} = \$2.73 \times 1.06/(0.1223 - 0.06) = \$46.45$$

As an aside, the stock was actually trading at $70 per share. This price could be justified by using a higher growth rate. The value of the stock is graphed in Figure A3.7 as a function of the expected growth rate.

The growth rate would have to be approximately 8 percent to justify a price of $70. This growth rate is often referred to as an implied growth rate.

CONCLUSION

Present value remains one of the simplest and most powerful techniques in finance, providing a wide range of applications in both personal and business decisions. Cash flows can be moved back to present value terms by discounting and moved forward by compounding. The discount rate at which the discounting and compounding are done reflect three factors: (1) the preference for current consumption, (2) expected inflation, and (3) the uncertainty associated with the cash flows being discounted.

In this appendix, we explored approaches to estimating the present value of five types of cash flows: simple cash flows, annuities, growing annuities, perpetuities, and growing perpetuities.

APPENDIX 4

OPTION PRICING

In general, the value of any asset is the present value of the expected cash flows on that asset. In this appendix, we will consider an exception to that rule when we will look at assets with two specific characteristics:

- They derive their value from the values of other assets.
- The cash flows on the assets are contingent on the occurrence of specific events.

These assets are called options, and the present value of the expected cash flows on them will understate their true value. We will describe the cash flow characteristics of options, consider the factors that determine their value, and examine how best to value them.

CASH FLOWS ON OPTIONS

There are two types of options. A *call option* gives the buyer of the option the right to buy the underlying asset at a fixed price, whereas a *put option* gives the buyer the right to sell the underlying asset at a fixed price. In both cases, the fixed price at which the underlying asset can be bought or sold is called the *strike* or *exercise price*.

To look at the payoffs on an option, consider first the case of a call option. When you acquire the right to buy an asset at a fixed price, you want the price of the asset to increase above that fixed price. If it does, you make a profit, because you can buy at the fixed price and then sell at the much higher price; this profit has to be netted against the cost initially paid for the option. However, if the price of the asset decreases below the strike price, it does not make sense to exercise your right to buy it at a higher price. In this scenario, you lose what you originally paid for the option. Figure A4.1 summarizes the net cash payoff at expiration to the buyer of a call option.

With a put option, you get the right to sell at a fixed price, and you want the price of the asset to decrease below the exercise price. If it does, you buy the asset at the current price and then sell it back at the exercise price, claiming the difference as a gross profit. When the initial cost of buying the option is netted against the gross profit, you arrive at an estimate of the net profit. If the value of the asset rises above the exercise price, you will not exercise the right to sell at a lower price. Instead, the option will be allowed to expire without being exercised, resulting in a net loss of the original price paid for the put option. Figure A4.2 summarizes the net cash payoff on buying a put option.

With both call and put options, the potential for profit to the buyer is significant, but the potential for loss is limited to the price paid for the option.

Figure A4.1   Net Payoff on Call Option

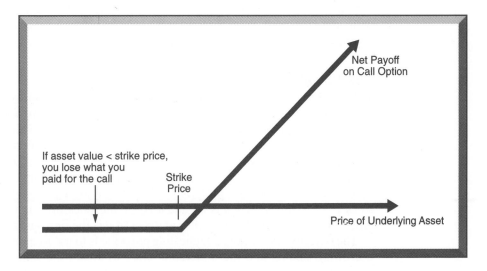

Figure A4.2   Net Payoff on Put Option

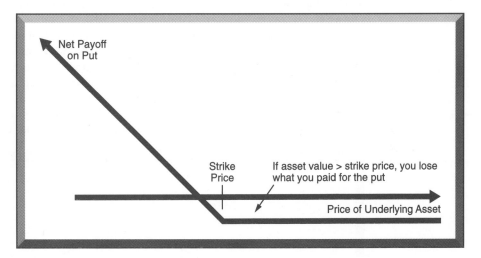

DETERMINANTS OF OPTION VALUE

What is it that determines the value of an option? At one level, options have expected cash flows just like all other assets, and may seem like good candidates for discounted cash flow valuation. The two key characteristics of options—that they derive their value from some other asset, and the fact that their cash flows are contingent on the occurrence of a specific event—does suggest an easier alternative. We can create a portfolio that has the same cash flows as the option being valued by combining a position in the underlying asset with borrowing or lending. This portfolio is called a *replicating portfolio* and should cost the same amount as the option. The principle that two assets (the option and the replicating portfolio) with identical cash flows cannot sell at different prices is called the *arbitrage principle*.

The Binomial Model

The simplest model for illustrating the replicating portfolio and arbitrage principles on which option pricing is the binomial model. The *binomial option pricing model* is based on a simple formulation for the asset price process in which the asset, in any time period, can move to one of two possible prices. The general formulation of a stock price process that follows the binomial is shown in Figure A4.3.

In this figure, S is the current stock price; the price moves up to Su with probability p and down to Sd with probability $1 - p$ in any time period. For instance, if the stock price today is \$100, u is 1.1 and d is 0.9, the stock price in the next period can either be \$110 (if u is the outcome) and \$90 (if d is the outcome).

The objective in creating a replicating portfolio is to use a combination of risk-free borrowing/lending and the underlying asset to create the same cash flows as the option being valued. In the case of the general formulation, where stock prices can either move up to Su or down to Sd in any time period, the replicating portfolio for a call with a given strike price will involve borrowing \$B and acquiring Δ of the underlying asset. Of course, this formulation is of no use if we cannot determine how much we need to borrow and what Δ is. There is a way, however, of identifying both variables. To do this, note that the value of this position has to be same as the value of the call, no matter what the stock price does. Let us assume that the value of the call is C_u if the stock price goes to Su, and C_d if the stock price goes down to Sd. If we had

Figure A4.3 General Formulation for Binomial Price Path

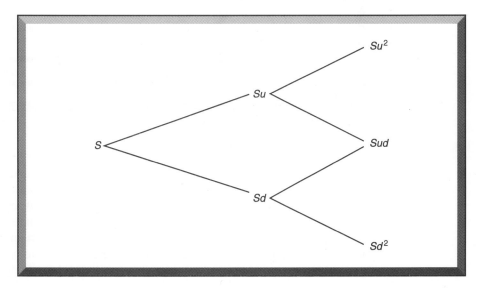

borrowed $\$B$ (with an interest rate r) and bought Δ shares of stock with the money, the value of this position under the two scenarios would have been as follows.

	Value of Position	Value of Call
If stock price goes up to Su	$\Delta Su - \$B(1 + r)$	C_u
If stock price goes down to Sd	$\Delta Sd - \$B(1 + r)$	C_d

Note that in either case, we have to pay back the borrowing with interest. Because the position has to have the same cash flows as the call, we get

$$\Delta Su - \$B(1 + r) = C_u$$

$$\Delta Sd - \$B(1 + r) = C_d$$

Solving for Δ, we get

$$\Delta = \text{Number of Units of the Underlying Asset Bought} = (C_u - C_d)/(Su - Sd)$$

where C_u = value of the call if the stock price is Su and C_d = value of the call if the stock price is Sd.

When there are multiple periods involved, we have to begin with the last period, where we know what the cash flows on the call will be, solve for the replicating portfolio, and then estimate how much it would cost us to create this portfolio. We use this value as the estimated value of the call and estimate the replicating portfolio in the previous period. We continue to do this until we get to the present. The replicating portfolio we obtain for the present can be priced to yield a current value for the call.

$$\text{Value of the Call} = \text{Current Value of Underlying Asset} \times \Delta$$
$$- \text{Borrowing Needed to Replicate the Option}$$

ILLUSTRATION A4.1   An Example of Binomial Valuation

Assume that the objective is to value a call with a strike price of $50, which is expected to expire in two time periods, on an underlying asset whose price currently is $50 and is expected to follow a binomial process. Figure A4.4 illustrates the path of underlying asset prices and the value of the call (with a strike price of 50) at the expiration.

Note that because the call has a strike price of $50, the gross cash flows at expiration are as follows:

If the stock price moves to $100: Cash Flow on Call = $100 − $50 = $50

If the stock price moves to $50: Cash Flow on Call = $50 − $50 = $0

If the stock price moves to $25: Cash Flow on Call = $0 (option is not exercised)

Now assume that the interest rate is 11%. In addition, define

$$\Delta = \text{Number of shares in the replicating portfolio}$$

$$B = \text{Dollars of borrowing in replicating portfolio}$$

Figure A4.4   Binomial Price Path

Figure A4.5   Replicating Portfolios When Price Is $70

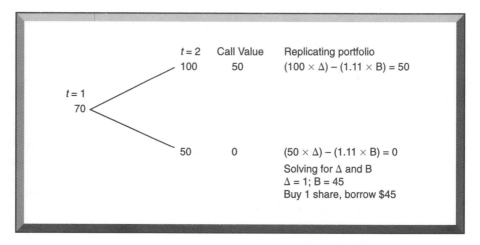

The objective in this analysis is to combine Δ shares of stock and $\$B$ of borrowing to replicate the cash flows from the call with a strike price of $50.

The first step in doing this is to start with the last period and work backward. Consider, for instance, one possible outcome at $t = 1$. The stock price has jumped to $70 and is poised to change again, either to $100 or $50. We know the cash flows on the call under either scenario, and we also have a replicating portfolio composed of Δ shares of the underlying stock and $\$B$ of borrowing. Writing out the cash flows on the replicating portfolio under both scenarios (stock price of $100 and $50), we get the replicating portfolios in Figure A4.5.

Figure A4.6   Replicating Portfolio When Price Is $35

In other words, if the stock price is $70 at $t = 1$, borrowing $45 and buying one share of the stock will give the same cash flows as buying the call. The value of the call at $t = 1$, if the stock price is $70, should therefore be the cash flow associated with creating this replicating position and it can be estimated as follows:

$$70\Delta - B = 70 - 45 = 25$$

The cost of creating this position is only $25, because $45 of the $70 is borrowed. This should also be the price of the call at $t = 1$ if the stock price is $70.

Consider now the other possible outcome at $t = 1$ where the stock price is $35 and is poised to jump to either $50 or $25. Here again, the cash flows on the call can be estimated, as can the cash flows on the replicating portfolio composed of Δ shares of stock and $$B$ of borrowing. Figure A4.6 illustrates the replicating portfolio.

Because the call is worth nothing under either scenario, the replicating portfolio also is empty. The cash flow associated with creating this position is obviously zero, which becomes the value of the call at $t = 1$ if the stock price is $35.

We now have the value of the call under both outcomes at $t = 1$; it is worth $25 if the stock price goes to $70 and $0 if it goes to $35. We now move back to today ($t = 0$), and look at the cash flows on the replicating portfolio. Figure A4.7 summarizes the replicating portfolios as viewed from today.

Using the same process as in the previous step, we find that borrowing $22.50 and buying 5/7 of a share will provide the same cash flows as a call with a strike price of $50. The cost to the investor of borrowing $22.52 and buying 5/7 of a share at the current stock price of $50 yields:

$$\text{Cost of Replicating Position} = 5/7 \times \$50 - \$22.52 = \$13.19$$

This should also be the value of the call.

Figure A4.7   Replicating Portfolios for Call Value

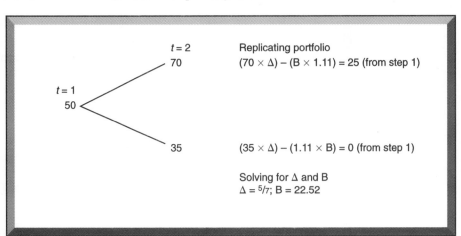

The Black-Scholes Model

Although the binomial model provides an intuitive feel for the determinants of option value, it requires a large number of inputs in terms of expected future prices at each node. As we make time periods shorter in the binomial model, we can make one of two assumptions about asset prices. We can assume that price changes become smaller as periods get shorter; this leads to price changes becoming infinitesimally small as time periods approach zero, leading to a continuous price process. Alternatively, we can assume that price changes stay large even as the period gets shorter; this leads to a jump price process, where prices can jump in any period.[1] When the price process is continuous, the binomial model for pricing options converges on the Black-Scholes model. The model, named after its co-creators, Fischer Black and Myron Scholes, allows us to estimate the value of any option using a small number of inputs and has been shown to be remarkably robust in valuing many listed options.[2]

The Model

The derivation of the Black-Scholes model is far too complicated to present here, but it is based on the idea of creating a portfolio of the underlying asset and the riskless asset with the same cash flows and hence the same cost as the option being valued. The value of a call option in the Black-Scholes model can be written as a

---

[1]Although we do not consider jump process option pricing models in this appendix, they do exist but are not widely used because of the difficulties we face in estimating their parameters.

[2]See F. Black and M. Scholes, 1972, "The Valuation of Option Contracts and a Test of Market Efficiency," *Journal of Finance,* 27, 399–417.

function of the five variables:

S = Current value of the underlying asset

K = Strike price of the option

t = Life to expiration of the option

r = Riskless interest rate corresponding to the life of the option

σ^2 = Variance in the ln(value) of the underlying asset

The value of a call is then:

$$\text{Value of Call} = SN(d_1) - Ke^{-rt}N(d_2)$$

where

$$d_1 = \frac{\ln\left(\dfrac{S}{K}\right) + \left(r + \dfrac{\sigma^2}{2}\right)t}{\sigma\sqrt{t}}$$

$$d_2 = d_1 - \sigma\sqrt{t}$$

Note that e^{-rt} is the present value factor and reflects the fact that the exercise price on the call option does not have to be paid until expiration. $N(d_1)$ and $N(d_2)$ are probabilities, estimated by using a cumulative standardized normal distribution and the values of d_1 and d_2 obtained for an option. The cumulative distribution is shown in Figure A4.8.

In approximate terms, these probabilities yield the likelihood that an option will generate positive cash flows for its owner at exercise, that is, when $S > K$ in the case of a call option and when $K > S$ in the case of a put option. The portfolio that

Figure A4.8 Cumulative Normal Distribution

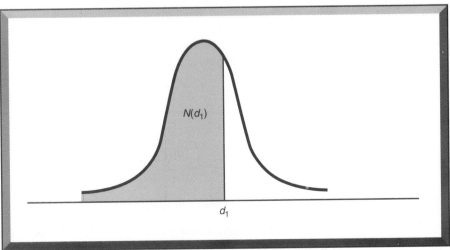

replicates the call option is created by buying $N(d_1)$ units of the underlying asset, and borrowing $Ke^{-rt}N(d_2)$. The portfolio will have the same cash flows as the call option and thus the same value as the option. $N(d_1)$, which is the number of units of the underlying asset that are needed to create the replicating portfolio, is called the option delta.

Model Limitations and Fixes

The Black-Scholes model was designed to value options that can be exercised only at maturity and on underlying assets that do not pay dividends. In addition, options are valued based on the assumption that option exercise does not affect the value of the underlying asset. In practice, assets do pay dividends, options sometimes get exercised early, and exercising an option can affect the value of the underlying asset. Although they are not perfect, adjustments provide partial corrections to the Black-Scholes model.

1. Dividends

The payment of a dividend reduces the stock price; note that on the ex-dividend day, the stock price generally declines. Consequently, call options will become less valuable, and put options more valuable for higher expected dividend payments. There are two ways of dealing with dividends in the Black-Scholes:

- **Short-Term Options** One approach to dealing with dividends is to estimate the present value of expected dividends that will be paid by the underlying asset during the option life and subtract it from the current value of the asset to use as S in the model.

  Modified Stock Price = Current Stock Price − Present Value of Expected Dividends during the Life of the Option

- **Long-Term Options** Because it becomes impractical to estimate the present value of dividends as the option life becomes longer, there is an alternate approach. If the dividend yield (y = dividends/current value of the asset) on the underlying asset is expected to remain unchanged during the life of the option, the Black-Scholes model can be modified to take dividends into account.

$$C = Se^{-yt}N(d_1) - Ke^{-rt}N(d_2)$$

where

$$d_1 = \frac{\ln\left(\frac{S}{K}\right) + \left(r - y + \frac{\sigma^2}{2}\right)t}{\sigma\sqrt{t}}$$

$$d_2 = d_1 - \sigma\sqrt{t}$$

From an intuitive standpoint, the adjustments have two effects. First, the value of the asset is discounted back to the present at the dividend yield to take into account the expected drop in asset value resulting from dividend payments.

Second, the interest rate is offset by the dividend yield to reflect the lower carrying cost from holding the replicating portfolio. The net effect will be a reduction in the value of calls estimated using this model.

2. Early Exercise

The Black-Scholes model was designed to value options that can be exercised only at expiration. Options with this characteristic are called European options. In contrast, most options that we encounter in practice can be exercised any time until expiration. These options are called American options. The possibility of early exercise makes American options more valuable than otherwise similar European options; it also makes them more difficult to value. In general, though, with traded options, it is almost always better to sell the option to someone else rather than exercise early, because options have a time premium, that is, they sell for more than their exercise value. There are two exceptions. One occurs when the underlying asset pays large dividends, thus reducing the expected value of the asset. In this case, call options may be exercised *just before an ex-dividend date,* if the time premium on the options is less than the expected decline in asset value as a consequence of the dividend payment. The other exception arises when an investor holds both the underlying asset and *deep in-the-money puts*—that is, puts with strike prices well above the current price of the underlying asset—on that asset and at a time when interest rates are high. In this case, the time premium on the put may be less than the potential gain from exercising the put early and earning interest on the exercise price.

There are two basic ways of dealing with the possibility of early exercise. One is to continue to use the unadjusted Black-Scholes model and regard the resulting value as a floor or conservative estimate of the true value. The other is to try adjusting the value of the option for the possibility of early exercise. There are two approaches for doing so. One uses the Black-Scholes to value the option to each potential exercise date. With options on stocks, this basically requires that we value options to each ex-dividend day and choose the maximum of the estimated call values. The second approach is to use a modified version of the binomial model to consider the possibility of early exercise. In this version, the up and down movements for asset prices in each period can be estimated from the variance and the length of each period.[3]

3. The Impact of Exercise on the Value of the Underlying Asset

The Black-Scholes model is based on the assumption that exercising an option does not affect the value of the underlying asset. This may be true for listed options on stocks, but it is not true for some types of options. For instance, the exercise of warrants increases the number of shares outstanding and brings fresh cash into the firm,

---

[3]To illustrate, if σ^2 is the variance in ln(stock prices), the up and down movements in the binomial can be estimated as follows: $u = e[(r - \sigma^2/2)(T/m) + \sqrt{(\sigma^2 T/m)}]$ and $d = e[(r - \sigma^2/2)(T/m) - \sqrt{(\sigma^2 T/m)}]$, where u and d are the up and down movements per unit time for the binomial, T is the life of the option, and m is the number of periods within that lifetime.

both of which will affect the stock price.[4] The expected negative impact (dilution) of exercise will decrease the value of warrants compared to otherwise similar call options. The adjustment for dilution in the Black-Scholes to the stock price is fairly simple. The stock price is adjusted for the expected dilution from the exercise of the options. In the case of warrants, for instance:

$$\text{Dilution-Adjusted } S = \frac{Sn_s + Wn_w}{n_s + n_w}$$

where S = current value per share of stock, n_w = number of warrants outstanding, W = value per warrants, and n_s = number of shares outstanding. When the warrants are exercised, the number of shares outstanding will increase, reducing the stock price. The numerator reflects the market value of equity, including both stocks and warrants outstanding. The reduction in S will reduce the value of the call option.

There is an element of circularity in this analysis, since the value of the warrant is needed to estimate the dilution-adjusted S and the dilution-adjusted S is needed to estimate the value of the warrant. This problem can be resolved by starting the process off with an assumed value for the warrant (say, the exercise value or the current market price of the warrant). This will yield a value for the warrant and this estimated value can then be used as an input to re-estimate the warrant's value until there is convergence.

CONCLUSION

An option is an asset with payoffs that are contingent on the value of an underlying asset. A call option provides its holder with the right to buy the underlying asset at a fixed price, whereas a put option provides its holder with the right to sell at a fixed price, any time before the expiration of the option. The value of an option is determined by six variables—the current value of the underlying asset, the variance in this value, the strike price, life of the option, the riskless interest rate and the expected dividends on the asset. This is illustrated in both the binomial and the Black-Scholes models, which value options by creating replicating portfolios composed of the underlying asset and riskless lending or borrowing.

---

[4]Warrants are call options issued by firms, either as part of management compensation contracts or to raise equity.

INDEX

Bold page numbers indicate definitions; "*n*" following a page number (47*n*) refers the reader to a footnote on that page.